# Personnel Management

# Personnel Management

PRINCIPLES, PRACTICES, AND POINT OF VIEW

WALTER DILL SCOTT, Ph.D.

ROBERT C. CLOTHIER, LL.D.

*President Emeritus, Rutgers University*
*Vice-president, Scott Company*

WILLIAM R. SPRIEGEL, Ph.D.

*Professor of Management, College of Business*
*Administration, The University of Texas*
*and Management Consultant*
*Formerly Dean of College of Business*
*Administration, The University of Texas*
*Chairman of Department of Management, School*
*of Commerce, Northwestern University,*
*and Industrialist*

SIXTH EDITION

McGRAW-HILL BOOK COMPANY

New York     Toronto     London

1961

# Preface

We are glad to recognize the enduring contribution of the late Dr. Walter Dill Scott and Robert C. Clothier, LL.D., whose first edition in 1923 established a basic approach to *personnel management* that has been preserved in this sixth edition of *Personnel Management*. We have striven to maintain a balance between theory and current practice. The present edition has been written in the light of a comprehensive survey of personnel practices of 852 companies that answered a 5-page questionnaire. This survey is reproduced in Appendix A.

In this edition we have added a new chapter on Human Relations and rearranged the sequence of the chapters. In order to keep from increasing the size of the book, three chapters have been eliminated by consolidation and the omission of some historical material. It is hoped that the rearrangement of the chapters may aid in a logical presentation to college students. However, the treatment of a given subject is such that a teacher may omit certain chapters and present the others in any order that seems most logical to him. While our book is written primarily for college and university students, the operating personnel man will find illustrations of modern practices and the relative use of most personnel procedures as revealed in the survey of 852 companies.

The entire book is written from the viewpoint of the employer who strives to direct the efforts of his employees in such a manner as to get efficient production with personal satisfactions to the participants. Recognition is given to conflicts of interests at times in wage determination, production standards, and other relationships. In the broad areas of business operations the business process, recognizing individual differences, interests, and capacities, provides a way of life as well as a method of earning a living. The personnel management policies and practices described in this book are designed to promote the common interest of the consumer, employer, and employee.

We are indebted to Dr. Gordon V. Anderson, professor of educational psychology and director of the Testing and Counseling Center of the University of Texas, for his contribution to the chapters on psychology. He did most of the work on these chapters. Dr. E. L. Lanham's studies in job evaluation have been used extensively in the chapter entitled Job Evaluation. We are also indebted to Prof. Joseph Towle of Washington University for his continued cooperation over the years. Our heaviest debt is to the great number of leaders in personnel who have answered queries, provided illustrations, and given freely of counsel. To list all of them would require the naming of almost every leader in the personnel division of the American Management Association. Behind every illustration in our text is a man making a contribution to better human relations in business.

*William R. Spriegel*

*Planning*

*SCS*

*Merit Rating*

*Staffing*

# Contents

# Contents

## Part V. The Labor Movement

## Part VI. Wage and Salary Administration, Employee Remuneration, and Other Incentives

## Part VII. Other Operational Problems in Personnel Administration and Management

## Part VIII. Employee Representation and Social Controls

## Part IX. Measuring Performance

## Appendixes

# Text-Films

Five 16-mm. sound motion pictures and five follow-up 35-mm. silent filmstrips correlated with Scott, Clothier, and Spriegel, *Personnel Management,* are available singly or as a complete series.

## Supervisory Conferences

The film shows the purpose of supervisory conferences and their importance in labor-management relations. Pointing out that conferences will not always give the answers to immediate problems, it shows how the informal give-and-take of a properly handled supervisory conference series can gradually improve the attitudes and understanding of the supervisors in their handling of everyday situations.

## Grievance Hearing

This film—the story of one grievance hearing—emphasizes the factors that are common to most grievance procedures. The prime purpose is to stimulate an informed discussion of grievance procedure in industry—why it is important, what it accomplishes, and how it works under the realistic give-and-take of collective bargaining.

## The Interview

Showing the importance of the employment interview, the film first gives a brief review of poor hiring methods and then illustrates a good interview step by step. The importance of a properly trained interviewer and the various tools at his disposal are discussed.

## Communications

Highlighting the need for effective, two-way communication in all phases of industry, the film illustrates the problems arising from the

ix

lack of efficient communications in a manufacturing company and how these problems were solved by the adoption of better methods. The film also shows several examples of communication tools in action.

## Job Evaluation and Merit Rating

Showing the various factors which must be taken into consideration in job evaluation, the film pictures the job analyst at work preparing the job description and discussing it with the job-evaluation committee. Emphasizing the difference between job evaluation and merit rating, the film goes on to show various methods of merit rating and the need for objectivity in making ratings.

CHAPTER 1

# Various Concepts of Labor

**The background.** The life of the worker was not a particularly happy one during the Middle Ages when viewed from the standards of the twentieth century. His ambition was to be able to live, and his efforts were devoted to earning the bare means of subsistence. As he and his children were born, so they lived and died. The concept of equal rights was undreamed of by them. In America, fresh and unfettered by traditions and class privileges, there appeared hope for better things. During the early part of the nineteenth century, there was little similarity between industrial conditions in America and in Europe. The majority of our people lived on the land and there earned their livelihood. There was work for all, and food in abundance. In the cities and towns, this was the age of the small tradesman, the household industry, the small workshop. In a degree probably never before attained, the workers were regarded as fellow citizens. Eli Whitney's cotton gin increased the demand for cheap labor and gave additional impetus to slavery. The institution of slavery, with its attendant social evils, was greatly expanded. It is difficult for us to believe that a nation conceived in liberty and dedicated to the concept of equality could sanction slavery. We must remember that the economic need was apparently great and social justice was then, as it is now, in a state of flux and growth. Eli Whitney also laid the foundation for the development of mass production by introducing the technique of interchangeable parts. This technique enabled the Industrial Revolution that had started in Europe to go forward at a pace not dreamed of at the time of its original introduction in the manufacture of rifles for the Army.

**The influence of the industrial revolution (1700–1800).** These dates are not inclusive or exclusive. They are merely illustrative of an era of great economic and social change. The steam engine and

1

the spinning jenny set in motion the great forces of the Industrial Revolution. Before the Civil War, the northeastern part of the United States had begun its great industrial development based upon the application of steam to mechanical devices. The Southeast, with its slave labor, its agricultural economy, and its social concepts, was slower to apply mechanical power to its manufacturing needs. Throughout the land, home production and the small shop gave way to the factory. Industry was learning that, by grouping workers together in large numbers and standardizing their activities, production and distribution could be tremendously increased and costs reduced.

Where the workers in a single group previously numbered a handful, they now began to number hundreds and thousands. Previously, the employer enjoyed the friendship of his associates at the bench; it now became possible for him to know them only casually, if at all—to know their faces and names perhaps, but not their weaknesses and their strengths, their interests, their ambitions, their family fortunes, their follies, and their hobbies. They became to him merely a group of workers whose labor must be bought. Without the employer's knowledge and probably against his real desires, there arose various attitudes toward labor. None of these various concepts was ever held in its pure state by any appreciable number of people. They did represent, in part, some employers' attempt to rationalize their attitudes or approaches to management-employee relationships.

**The commodity concept of labor.** The observation that wages were high when labor was scarce in relation to demand and were low when labor was substantially in excess of demand gave rise to the idea that *labor, affected by the law of supply and demand, was like a commodity, the price of which was determined by the supply and the demand for it.* Although it was believed that the law of supply and demand could not be modified, much less overcome, nevertheless it was also evident that, even though this conception of labor might be correct in part, it did not include many vital factors of production.

**The machinery concept of labor.** Some observers recognized that the employer bought and sold, not actual labor, but the products this labor produced. *The value of labor was determined by the goods it brought forth.* This observation led to the *machinery concept* of labor. *The employer regarded his employees largely as operating organisms or machines,* capable of a certain amount of output. This philosophy led to an impersonal attitude toward workers. It is little wonder that the worker's mind was diverted to protection rather than to production. The resulting inefficiency, together with the growing knowledge that neither the commodity nor the machinery conception of labor was complete, led to the beginnings of the welfare movement.

**The good-will approach to labor.** The introduction of large groups of women workers brought in special problems. *Employers finally began to realize that the welfare of their employees had a direct effect upon their productivity. Safety, first aid, lunchrooms, rest rooms, bulletin boards, visiting nurses, and a horde of ameliorating movements were introduced.* At this stage the large employer without a welfare movement was considered backward. These welfare efforts of themselves became the points of attack of labor organizations. The visiting nurse was looked upon as a spy; bulletin boards were interpreted as devices of propaganda; first-aid stations were often ridiculed as places where no "he man" would permit any fussing over a minor injury; even the costs of safety devices were sometimes objected to on the grounds of lowering wages. Labor in many instances took the attitude: "Put the money in our pay envelopes, and we will take care of ourselves."

The employer who was most active in the welfare movement often had intense labor strife. Employers obsessed with the welfare idea became increasingly paternalistic. It became evident that doing something for the welfare of employees not only failed to solve management's problems but often introduced new and especially antagonistic attitudes.

**The natural-resource idea of labor value.** At the time when a concerted movement was being made to conserve our natural resources it was but natural to look upon our workers as providing a great resource to be protected. *Out of this conception came child-labor laws, restriction of hours for women workers, workmen's compensation and health and accident legislation.* Occasionally an employer tried a new humanitarian idea. If it worked, large numbers of other employers fell in line. Finally, legislative enactment prescribed the once new practice for those who were slow to adopt the new program. Not all labor legislation has by any means evolved in this manner, since much social legislation has been initiated by and accomplished through the efforts of labor organizations.

**The humanitarian approach to labor.** From 1910 to 1917 the humanitarian conception of labor gripped the imagination of employers. It stated that arbitrary or paternalistic control by management was likely to lead to trouble. *It declared that the minds of the workers as well as their bodies must be considered by management and that the state of their minds had much to do with the value of their services.* It protested that, if men are not "on side" in interest and loyalty, they are apt to be *in absentia* on the job. It asserted that management wants in its workers, not merely their physical presence, but the full measure of service that physical presence makes possible.

The human approach stated that the workers had certain *"inalienable" rights as human beings, that these rights were as important as the rights of other persons, and that it was industry's duty to recognize these rights.* The new doctrine held that all men are equal, in the sense that they have many of the same impulses and reactions. It held that industry had a moral obligation, not only to permit its workers to enjoy their rights, but to encourage and help them to make as much of themselves as possible. In short, *this doctrine stated that business has at least four obligations—to their stockholders, to their customers, to the public, and to their employees.* It must be frankly admitted that even today the concept of profits through service is still an emerging philosophy.[1]

**The concept of individual differences.** Certain psychologists began to study labor-management relationships. They found that *men often differ one from the other in mental abilities, emotional stabilities, traditions, and sentiments far more than they differ physically.* It was recognized that one man may have special aptitudes along certain lines and that another may lack these entirely. It became apparent that, if one had the ability to learn in a degree entirely lacking in the other, to try to develop them in the same way was impracticable. It was clearly evident that if one man had distinct ambitions along one line, another along another, any stereotyped incentive would stimulate them unequally. The temperamental differences between men were recognized by progressive employers. The worker cannot be separated from his job. A reciprocal relationship exists between them. The worker influences the nature of his job, and the job in turn influences the attitudes of the worker.

**The citizenship concept of labor.** *As a citizen in a democracy has certain inalienable rights and a voice in determining and exercising these rights, so do workers, as industrial citizens, have a right to be consulted in determining the rules and regulations under which they work.* The legal recognition of this concept of labor is relatively recent[2] in origin.

*Industrial democracy,* with its shop committees, industrial councils, employee-representation plans, and the like, grew out of this approach. True industrial democracy, however, is more than that form

---

[1] See L. Urwick, *The Elements of Administration,* Harper & Brothers, New York, 1943, p. 27.

[2] See Chaps. 21 to 22 and 32 to 34 for the evolution of this concept and its legal basis.

of organization whereby employers and employees meet jointly for discussion of difficulties. It is, as Edward A. Filene puts it, "a guarantee that the management of the business shall be responsible and largely dependent for its rewards on its efficiency. It is no use to give employees a part of the control if inefficient management curtails profits so that they do not benefit." This concept recognizes that the worker's investment of his labor gives him certain rights and responsibilities. Like political democracy, *industrial democracy is self-government by the people, determining the mutual relationships of employer and employee, terms of employment, conditions of labor, rules and regulations affecting employees, and the relationships of employees to each other.*

This relationship of employees to each other has too often been overlooked. Attention has been focused largely upon the relation of the employer and the employee, neglecting the fact that no matter how close the relationship or how mutual the understanding between management and worker, if there is discord among employees, one infringing upon the rights of another, there can be no true democracy.

**The customer attitude toward workers.** With the inauguration of the one-price system, the merchant discovered that, if he treated everyone as a gentleman, a few would exploit him; conversely, if he treated everyone as a crook, many would exploit him. The losses from the exploitations of the few, however, were so greatly discounted by the increased business from the good will of the many that he could afford to discount the minor losses to secure the greater profits from the larger business. Thus evolved the sales slogan, "The customer is always right." Many enlightened employers believe that too much emphasis has been put upon obtaining the good will of the customer and not enough on obtaining the good will of labor. These employers believe that the concept that "The worker is always right" when spelled out in relations with employees will on balance be favorable. At least they reason that we should respect the integrity of our employees as much as we do our customers. Such a philosophy tends to encourage mutual trust, increased productivity, and satisfying morale. Public utilities have for a long time had a complaint desk where customers could bring their grievances, but the mere fact that complaints were received was not enough. Public utility companies came to hold that every customer must go away satisfied. Many industries with union contracts are still in the early complaint-desk stage. It must not be inferred that, even when management and the worker are in this combined state of agreement, they can in turn neglect or exploit the customer, as has been the case in several instances. The customer, when he believes he is exploited in this fashion, does exactly what the worker does when he thinks he is exploited: he turns to defensive measures—organizations, demands, and strikes. He boycotts the seller and substitutes other products to meet his necessities.

**The partnership concept of labor.** The earliest effort to translate the partnership idea into action was the fostering of stock-ownership plans. More recently, profit sharing has come into prominence. In some instances, the sliding wage scale tied to volume of business and profits has the partnership concept in part at least as its basis. The partnership relationship implies mutual responsibilities as well as the sharing of the fruits of the joint endeavors. Some persons contend that there can be no such thing as a partnership between management and labor unless labor is willing to share losses as well as profits. It is perfectly true that labor is seldom in a position to sustain any substantial loss in out-of-pocket money; yet it is also true that the workers actually do suffer during periods of slack business. Partnership between management and the workers does not have to carry with it the full responsibilities of ownership to be effective.

Some argue that the partnership concept of labor is fallacious, that there can be no mutuality of interests between owners who are seeking large profits and workers who desire high wages. Under certain circumstances in the short run, these criticisms are sound; however, in the long run, which is immeasurably more important to both management and labor, their interests are identical. In the short run, the competitive situation and general business conditions may make necessary the reduction of wages. It is natural that labor would not like this; yet, even under these conditions, in the relatively short run, it is better for labor to have a reduced wage than to continue at a high rate until the business is forced to liquidate. Management and labor are mutually interested in producing a product that will meet with public approval and that can be sold at a price that will result in volume production, high wages, and satisfactory profits.

**The eclectic approach.** The foregoing concepts of labor have been presented as representative of attitudes in general rather than of specific viewpoints tenaciously held. Each of the various conceptions of labor has a germ of truth in it and contributes something to an *eclectic conception* of labor that strives to appropriate the truth in any of the various labor concepts. This is in substance the view held by careful students of modern labor problems. Scientific management, in its attempt to formulate a rational conception of labor, has approached the problem from as many angles as gave promise of shedding light on the subject. The individual and group relationships have been analyzed from the physiological, psychological, sociological, and economic points of view. Each has contributed to a better understanding of employer-employee relationships.

There have been numerous cases in recent years where the employer's governing philosophy has closely approached either the *citizenship conception* or the *partnership conception* of labor as far as actual practice is concerned. Many attempts at works councils, management-workers' committees, multiple management, industrial democracy, company unions, international unions, profit sharing, pension programs have in them elements of both the partnership and the citizen concepts of labor. These will be discussed in later chapters.

**The worker-in-his-work unit.** In management's attempt to understand its responsibilities and relationship to labor the concept of balance and the total situation has emerged. Neither the worker nor the work situation responds to fragmentary analysis. The total situation is controlling. These facets of the total situation may be considered in terms of:

1. Capacities—referring to those abilities, to those attainments, inherited or acquired, that a worker has, is capable of, and must, to a certain degree at least, exercise in his work.

2. Interests—not only an individual's desires and ambitions, but also his instinctive, impulsive tendencies, vague yearnings, and ill-defined cravings that may or may not stir him to his fullest action in performing his duties.

3. Opportunities—not only opportunities for advancement, although that is included, but opportunities to exercise his capacities and satisfy his interests.

4. Personality—the sum total of a worker's reaction to his experiences and environment. Personality is manifest by an individual's reception by others. Management has only a minor role in influencing personality, but the worker's personality has a great influence upon his opportunities.

Figure 1.1 illustrates a perfect adjustment, one in which the worker possesses the exact *capacities* required for the work, the work similarly

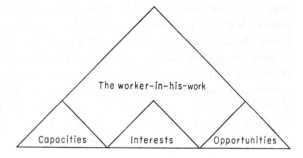

FIG. 1.1. Graph showing perfect balance between capacities, interests, and opportunities.

affords the *opportunity* for exercising these *capacities*, and the worker's *interests* are generally satisfied in the performance of his duties. When the three factors of capacities, interests, and opportunities in a given work situation are in balance as illustrated by Fig. 1.1, the personality factor is almost invariably satisfactory. The late Prof. Hamrin of Northwestern University conceives the worker-in-his-work unit to be similar to a square, with capacities, interests, opportunities, and personality each representing one of the equal sides. When any one of these four factors expands or contracts, it definitely influences the others. Such a perfect balance of the four elements of the worker-in-his-work unit is seldom achieved in actual industrial practice. A lack of balance forms one of the major causes of waste in production.

An imbalance in capacities, interests, or opportunities can result in an imbalance in the worker-in-his-work unit. Some 25 years ago a worker was discharged for neglect of duty by his foreman. Since this was a small concern, the president interviewed the worker. He asked the worker's foreman if he would consent to let the worker continue to work in another department. He was given a small space in another department and encouraged to try to develop his idea on which he was working to the neglect of his former duties. In a relatively short time he came forth with an item that is known to every person who reads this book. This worker was not suited to routine work. Neither was he qualified for a supervisory position to which he was later promoted, but he has made outstanding contributions to the success of this company through his experiments. In another case a man was being trained for a supervisory position in a new plant. After 6 weeks' trial it became evident that he did not possess the required mechanical ability for a mechanical department. He was transferred to the shipping department, where he became a successful foreman.

A Detroit regional sales manager of a large, nationally known firm was offered the Chicago office, which was the largest assignment other than the sales manager's. The Detroit man turned it down and suggested that his assistant be given the opportunity. This was done. Today the assistant is president of the company, and the vice-president is another former assistant to the Detroit regional manager. The Detroit man is still on the job. He simply did not care for the larger opportunity and had sense enough not to take it and regret it the rest of his life. Such a situation is much to be preferred to a similar situation in which the regional sales manager accepted the promotion and later asked to be returned to his old position.

**The worker's entire personality.** The industrial workplace and workers combine to form a social unit that extends over into the outside lives of the workers. Certain occupations have a higher social rating than others, and the employee's social status both within and without the organization is definitely influenced by his occupation.

As individuals mature in the social and industrial organization, they pass through various stages of personality adjustment. Some of these are very simple, and others are at times somewhat strenuous. The ordinary person (if it be possible to think of such an individual) has relatively little difficulty in making these adjustments. There are others who may be classified as problem workers. They may have little difficulty in performing the physical tasks but have serious problems in emotional and personality adjustments. Industry as a rule is not in a position to render the advice necessary to fit these problem cases into the industrial pattern since they require the services of a trained psychiatrist.[3] Nevertheless, many employees can be helped in their personal adjustments by the sympathetic leadership and guidance of their supervisors.

**Summary.** During the emergence of personnel management as it is conceived today, a number of theories of the nature of labor have held the center of the stage. None of these has ever been completely accepted or held in its pure state by any substantial majority of businessmen. The *eclectic* approach with considerable emphasis upon the citizenship and partnership concepts of labor seems to give promise of promoting long-run industrial peace. This certainly does not mean that there will be no frictions, any more than any one philosophy will stabilize the family relationship. Neither do these approaches eliminate the need for profits. Business is run for profits through service with due regard for the rights of consumers, workers, owners, and the community. The eclectic approach to labor recognizes the totality of the worker-in-his-work unit. The employee's *interests, capacities,* and *opportunities* definitely condition his reaction to his work unit. The failure of management to recognize the individual differences involving interests, capacities, and opportunities has contributed much to the unhappiness and confusion of the worker-in-his-work unit. *The employee is both a social and economic entity, possessing different characteristics in various work situations.*

---

[3] See F. J. Roethlisberger and William J. Dickson, *Management and the Worker,* Harvard University Press, Cambridge, Mass., 1940, for a most interesting discussion of the evolution of the counseling program at the Western Electric Company, Hawthorne Plant. See also W. R. Spriegel, Ed Schulz, and William B. Spriegel, *Elements of Supervision,* John Wiley & Sons, Inc., New York, 1957, Chap. 10, "The Supervisor and Mental Health."

## CHAPTER 2

# The Organization and Functions of the
# Personnel Division (or Department)

**Organization terminology and definitions.** *An organization is the structural relationship between the various factors in an enterprise.* Organizational structures are designed to overcome the limitations of people and to create an environment in which men's energies will be released to concentrate on the work at hand. Oliver Sheldon[1] defines organization as "the process of so combining the work which individuals have to perform with the faculties necessary for its execution that the duties so formed, provide the best channels for the efficient systematic, positive, and coordinated application of the available effort." Mooney and Reiley[2] give an operational slant to their definition: "Organization, therefore, refers to more than the frame of the edifice. It refers to the complicated body, with all of its correlated functions. It refers to those functions as they appear in action, the very pulse and heartbeats, the circulation, the respiration, the vital movement, so to speak of the organized unit."

Organizational terminology is not universally accepted by the practitioners. An enterprise that starts in a small way establishes departments on a functional basis. When these departments get so large that they have to be broken down into two or more smaller units, sentiment, in some instances, causes the department heads to want to hold on to the name department and to give the smaller units some other name such as sections or even divisions. Actually the larger functional unit is more appropriately designated the division, and the smaller units making up the division should be called departments. Theoretically it is preferable to speak of the personnel or industrial relations division composed of the employment, medical,

---

[1] Oliver Sheldon, *The Philosophy of Management,* Sir Isaac Pitman and Sons, Ltd., London, 1923, p. 32.

[2] James D. Mooney and Alan C. Reiley, *The Principles of Organization,* Harper & Brothers, New York, 1939, p. 3.

labor relations, training, and other departments. The interchange in the use of the words *department* and *division* is not serious since the people in the particular company soon become familiar with the given usage.

One of the basic principles of organization building is the grouping of related functions into a division or department. On this basis the manufacturing, sales, finance, engineering, accounting, personnel, and other divisions are created.

**The functions of the personnel division.** In terms of grouping activities of similar nature together the personnel division may readily be responsible for all activities that are people- or employee-centered other than those activities directly related to the primary operations of the business. In other words the personnel phases of all departments are a proper concern of the personnel division. This does not mean that the responsible operating head of a line or staff division or department would wash his hands of all personnel activities. Real personnel management is personal and a direct responsibility of the operating head of any organizational unit. The personnel division is a *staff group* specializing solely in personnel activities and assisting the operating personnel in performing their personnel duties. In terms of hiring, training, and similar activities the basic load may be given to the personnel division. The operating heads are still interested in seeing that their employees get the best possible services in these areas. If the company's policies of personnel management are to be uniformly and effectively carried out, there should be an organization within the company, a division (if the reader will not allow the word to suggest separation and detachment) that should be charged with the maintenance of personnel records, with the practices based upon them, with selection, transfer, and promotion in cooperation with departmental executives, and with the responsibility for seeing that the company's policies relating to personnel practices and procedures are carried out. The personnel division is responsible on a staff basis for concentrating on those aspects of operations which are primarily concerned with the relationship of management to employees and employees to employees and with the development of the individual and group. Stated somewhat differently, a group of personnel specialists expressed their concepts as follows:[4] "The objective of Personnel Management, Personnel Administration, or Industrial Relations in an organization is to attain maximum individual development, desirable working relationships between employers and employees, and employees and employees, and effective molding of human resources as contrasted with physical resources."

Persons not familiar with the intricate relationships in groups may think it strange to include the relationships between "employees and employees" as a concern of management. As a matter of fact, some of the most disturbing conflicts are between employees themselves. Jurisdictional disputes between craft unions, between craft unions and industrial unions, and between member unions of the AFL-CIO federation and independent unions have led to a great deal of bitterness. There is frequently friction between members of a given union and other employees who prefer not to belong to any union. It must not be inferred that the personnel division is solely interested in harmony between union or nonunion groups, for such an approach would be wholly erroneous. The personnel division has a basic interest in any activity that concerns human relations as contrasted with the purely material considerations of operations. The primary function of the personnel division is to employ qualified workers in sufficient numbers to meet the requirements of the business enterprise and to participate in all activities that will tend to keep the employee a satisfied, cooperative, and productive worker.

**Activities included in the personnel function.**[3] There are certain basic functions that naturally belong in the personnel division, such as employment, training, transfers, promotions, wage and salary administration, job evaluation, merit rating; health and safety, and recreation. There are other activities that are at times placed in the personnel department, such as security police, suggestion systems, cafeterias; company stores; legal aid for employees, mutual aid societies and other financial aids, health, medical, and hospital insurance, as well as life insurance; motion and time studies for wage settings, employee housing, profit sharing, and other activities. Actually it is not unusual for management to give almost any activity to the personnel division that needs to be carried on but that does not naturally fall into one of the established functions. The public relations department in some organizations is under the personnel division, or division of industrial relations as it is often called in manufacturing industries; yet it is frequently a separate staff functional department reporting to a major executive. Figure 2.1 portrays the personnel functions of the Carrier Corporation. The activities and functions tabulated below are frequently under the supervision of the personnel division:

[3] See National Industrial Conference Board, Inc., "Organization of Personnel Administration," *Studies in Personnel Policy* 73, New York, 1946, and "Personnel Administration in the Small Company," *Studies in Personnel Policy* 117, New York, 1951; American Management Association, "How to Establish and Maintain a Personnel Department," *Research Report* 4, New York, 1944, pp. 19–23.

## PERSONNEL ADMINISTRATION

| MEDICAL | LABOR RELATIONS | WAGE AND SALARY ADMINISTRATION | EMPLOYMENT | PERSONNEL SERVICES | TRAINING | DIRECTORS OF PERSONNEL (GS, MSD, UED) |
|---|---|---|---|---|---|---|
| 1. Administer the corporation medical program. | 1. Administer labor relations program for Syracuse plants. | 1. Maintain current hourly and salary job descriptions. | 1. Maintain adequate sources of manpower supply. | 1. Assist in administration of Carrier Employees Security Plan and Group Insurance Plan. | 1. Coordinate and assist in the administration of corporate training activities. | 1. Advise Divisional Management on all matters involving personnel policies and functions. |
| 2. Supervise work of the Medical Department and plant First Aid Stations. | 2. Supervise negotiations with Union representing Syracuse hourly employees. | 2. Administer hourly and salary job evaluation programs. | 2. Interview and test applicants; assist in selection and follow-up of new employees. | 2. Participate in community activities concerned with employees' interests. Serve as advisor to committees appointed to conduct Community Chest-Red Cross Campaign, and employees' clubs and organizations. | 2. Prepare course material for and conduct supervisory training courses. | 2. Maintain close contact with employees and supervisors and represent their interests and points of view in discussions with Divisional Management. |
| 3. Maintain medical records and statistics. | 3. Assist in negotiations with Union representing Toronto hourly employees. | 3. Maintain current wage and salary administration manuals. | 3. Maintain personnel records. | | 3. Prepare and conduct trade training programs. | 3. Advise employees on personal problems and assist in handling all phases of communications with employees. |
| 4. Establish standards of medical fitness and assist management and employment managers in the selection and placement of applicants and employees. | 4. Interpret labor agreement, Labor Relation Policies and procedures and plant rules. | 4. Conduct wage and salary surveys. | 4. Maintain employment statistics. | 3. Supervise recreation program. | 4. Supervise apprentice training programs. | 4. Maintain close relationship with Union officers and stewards. Work with supervisors and the Labor Relations Department on employee-employer relations problems. |
| 5. Give medical treatment for industrial injuries and diseases and limited medical treatment for non-industrial injuries and diseases. | 5. Assist in handling grievances and in eliminating situations causing complaints. | 5. Check compliance with announced wage and salary policy. | 5. Assist in controlling labor turnover. | 4. Advise employees on personal interests. | 5. Coordinate manufacturing engineering training program. | |
| 6. Work with insurance companies in compensation and rehabilitation matters. | 6. Maintain liaison with Sales Division and Marine Department on labor relations matters. | 6. Maintain essential wage and salary records. | 6. Check compliance with Federal and State employment laws and regulations. | 5. Assist with arrangements for company picnics, parties, dinners, etc. | 6. Assist in administration of the Carrier Institute of Business and in planning Program of Carrier Cabinet. | 5. Assist Divisional Management in administration of salaries and coordinate the following activities: performance reviews and preparation of job descriptions. |
| 7. Work in conjunction with management and Safety and Training Department in industrial safety and industrial hygiene matters. | 7. Check compliance with Federal and State labor laws and regulations. | 7. Check compliance with Federal and State wage and hour laws and regulations. | 7. Maintain employee counselling services. | 6. Supervise company bulletin boards. | 7. Supervise manufacturing training facilities. | 6. Maintain close contact with Department Heads of Personnel Division to coordinate Personnel functions with Divisional operations. |
| 8. Identify medical causes of loss of employee efficiency; e.g., absenteeism, defective vision, contact dermatitis. | 8. Administer seniority regulations. | 8. Assist in resolving employee or Union complaints arising from administration of the job evaluation plan. | 8. Process and coordinate transfers, promotions and leaves of absence. | 7. Submit deferment requests; maintain good relations with procurement agencies for armed services. | 8. Develop educational exhibits, visual aids, training manuals. | 7. Coordinate manpower requirements (salary and hourly) and participate in the selection and placement of individuals in key positions within the Division. |
| 9. Maintain good relationships with private physicians and community health and medical agencies. | 9. Administer hourly merit rating plan. | 9. Administer performance review program. | 9. Conduct exit interviews. | 8. Assist in handling complaints and grievances for employees not in bargaining unit. | 9. Administer induction programs for new employees. | 8. Serve on Salary Committee as Divisional representative. |
| | 10. Provide for Veterans Counselling Service and check compliance with Federal and State Veteran Laws and Regulations. | 10. Department Head serves as Salary Committee representative for the Personnel Division and as secretary of that Committee. | 10. Administer clerical training programs. | 9. Arrange for sale of company products to employees. | 10. Administer corporate tuition refund plan. | |
| | 11. Department Head serves as chairman of Management Wage Practices Committee and Management Grievance Committee. | | 11. Issue identification badges. | | 11. Conduct other educational and informational meetings for company personnel as requested. | |
| | | | 12. Assign lockers. | | 12. Advise employees on educational needs and opportunities. | |
| | | | 13. Check unemployment insurance claims. | | | |

FIG. 2.1. Personnel functions of the personnel division of the Carrier Corporation, Syracuse, N.Y.

1. Employment. (See Fig. A.1 in Appendix.)
   - 1.1    Source of labor supply.
   - 1.2    Information regarding prevailing community rates.
   - 1.3    Conduct surveys and studies regarding community rates, job requirements, and job specifications.
   - 1.4    Selection.
     - 1.41   The application blank.
     - 1.42   The interview.
     - 1.43   Tests. (Fig. A.2a.)
     - 1.44   Physical examination.
     - 1.45   Checking of reference, records, and approval of supervisor.
     - 1.46   Assignment to a specific job.
   - 1.5    Introduction of the worker to the company's policies and to his department supervisor.
   - 1.6    Follow-up of the new employee for initial adjustment.
   - 1.7    Maintenance of records of all employees hired, resigned, discharged, transferred, and laid off (unless there is a separate department handling this).

2. Promotions, transfers, discharges, demotions, and separations.
   - 2.1    Establishment of lines of promotion.
     - 2.11   Records to aid in the identification of eligible men for promotion.
     - 2.12   Information for the organization relative to promotion policies and lines of promotion.
     - 2.13   Establishment, in cooperation with employees, of rules and regulations regarding seniority.
   - 2.2    Establishment of policies regarding transfers.
     - 2.21   Transfers for the immediate convenience of the company.
     - 2.22   Transfers for the conveniences of the employee.
     - 2.23   Transfers to increase employee flexibility as a part of stabilization-of-employment program.
     - 2.24   Provision for necessary records to make effective a transfer program.
     - 2.25   Rules governing the pay for employees who are transferred temporarily or permanently and covering the seniority rights of transferred employees.
   - 2.3    Demotion.
     - 2.31   Because of a failure of the employee to meet job requirements.
     - 2.32   Because of a curtailment of operations.
     - 2.33   Because of employee's preference arising from personal reasons.
     - 2.34   Because another employee has greater seniority (in cases where employees may select jobs on the basis of seniority).
   - 2.4    Formulation of policies regarding discharges.
     - 2.41   Information to supervisors regarding company policies governing discharges.
     - 2.42   Information to employees regarding company discharge policies.
     - 2.43   Detailed records with supporting data of all discharges.
     - 2.44   Removal of the causes for discharges as far as possible.
   - 2.5    Separations initiated by the employees.
     - 2.51   Conduct of exit interviews of all employees leaving the company.

2.52   Determination of the cause for all employees' leaving.

2.53   Records of all separations and analysis of them to discover causes.

2.54   Removal of causes of separations as far as possible.

3. Formulation and direction of training program in keeping with company objectives. (Fig. A.6.)

3.1   Prehiring training in cooperation with local public or private vocational training enterprises.

3.2   Apprentice training.

3.3   Training of new employees.

3.4   Training of present employees in improved methods.

3.5   Training of employees for transfer, promotion, and versatility.

3.6   Training of foremen and minor supervisors.

3.7   Training program for executives.

3.8   Special training programs for college graduates and other selected employees.

3.9   Cooperation with schools and colleges.

3(10)   Cooperation with employees' clubs in their educational programs.

3(11)   Vestibule schools.

3(12)   General training of workers in company policies, company organization, and company products.

3(13)   Cooperation with safety and health departments in training for:
   3(13)1   Safety.
   3(13)2   Health practices.

3(14)   Promoting suggestions from employees.

3(15)   Library and magazine circulation.

3(16)   Americanization programs (relatively unimportant since immigration has been restricted).

3(17)   Special annual report designed especially to provide information desired by employees. (This may be a part of a broader training program in economics of business.)

4. Job analysis and evaluation. (This function may be performed by the industrial engineering department or the organization department.) (Fig. A.7.)

4.1   Analysis of all jobs of office, supervisory, and manual workers.

4.2   Writing of descriptions of each job.

4.3   Writing of specifications for each job position.

4.4   Evaluation of each job or position according to some scheme that will show the relative worth of each.

4.5   Making wage surveys to find the going rates in the community.

4.6   Establishment of job classifications in terms of wage brackets.

4.7   Making any adjustments that are necessary to keep wages and salaries in line with community or government requirements and to pay adequately for services expected.

5. Remuneration and incentives. (Fig. A.4.)

5.1   Formulation of wage plans.

5.2   Formulation of vacation programs.

5.3   Studies in cost of living and community wages with recommendations to management relative to the company's practices.

5.4   Formulation of policies for rewarding employees' suggestions.

5.5   Periodic review of each employee's earnings with a view to adjustment.

5.6 Supervisory bonuses or profit-sharing programs.

5.7 Employee profit-sharing programs.

5.8 Union negotiations (where a union exists).

6. Health and sanitation. (Fig. A.3.)

6.1 Initial physical examinations.

6.2 Periodic physical examinations.

6.3 First aid to the injured.

6.4 Medical treatment for minor illnesses.

6.5 Hospitalization programs.

6.6 Sanitation as related to health.

6.7 Health education.

6.8 Cooperation with local health authorities.

6.9 Studies of the causes and methods of eliminating:

6.91 Fatigue.

6.92 Monotony.

6.93 Mental strain.

6.94 Occupational diseases.

6(10) Studies covering:

6(10)1 Rest periods.

6(10)2 Mutual benefit society's experience in payment for absence due to accidents, illness, etc.

6(11) Dental care (not a part of most programs).

7. Safety and institutional protection.

7.1 Safety education.

7.2 Studies in the causes of accidents.

7.3 Mechanical guards.

7.4 Safety inspection and guidance of employees' safety committees.

7.5 Promotion of safety contests.

7.6 Formulation of safe-practice codes.

7.7 Fire protection.

7.8 Guards and watch service.

8. Financial aids to employees.

8.1 Advances on wages to new employees.

8.2 Employees' mutual benefit societies.

8.3 Credit unions.

8.4 Profit-sharing programs.

8.5 Mutual saving programs.

8.6 Employee stock-ownership plans.

8.7 Pension plans.

8.8 Unemployment insurance.

8.9 Workmen's compensation insurance.

8(10) Group life insurance.

8(11) Group hospitalization.

8(12) Group medical insurance.

8(13) Special discounts on company's products.

8(14) Loans to employees during layoffs.

8(15) Certain annual wage guarantees.

8(16) Aid in payment of tuition for attendance at evening classes in approved schools and colleges.

9. Employee service activities. (Fig. A.3.)
   - 9.1     Recreational activities.
   - 9.2     Housing, gardens, parks, and similar activities.
   - 9.3     Boys' clubs.
   - 9.4     Restaurants.
   - 9.5     Company stores for employees.
   - 9.6     Legal advice (usually does not include appearance in court).
   - 9.7     Counsel in personal matters.
   - 9.8     Visiting nurses.
   - 9.9     General educational activities not related to training for company jobs.
   - 9(10)   Plant magazine. (This is frequently listed under education.)
10. Research, record keeping, reports, and follow-up. (Where this department is a separate section of the personnel division, many items listed elsewhere in this outline will be brought into this grouping.) (Fig. A.8.)
   - 10.1    Central file of all major personnel records. These may be actually kept in the employment department.
   - 10.2    Periodic check of all records for such items as promotions, wage increases, transfers, special training, and counseling.
   - 10.3    Study of all statistical data to determine trends or action to be inaugurated.
   - 10.4    Special reports to executives and supervisors.
   - 10.5    Study and analysis of personnel trends and programs of others.
   - 10.6    The personnel audit.
11. Employee-employer and community cooperation.
   - 11.1    Various forms of employee-employer representation.
   - 11.2    Community cooperation.
     - 11.21   Community funds.
     - 11.22   Safety campaigns.
     - 11.23   "Cleanup" drives.
   - 11.3    Procedures for:
     - 11.31   Promoting company welfare in terms of improved product and competitive position.
     - 11.32   Layoffs, discharges, and promotions.
   - 11.4    Practically any personnel activity may be a matter of formal cooperation between management and the employees.
12. Labor union contracts and cooperation. (Chapter 32.)
   - 12.1    Negotiate contracts. (This function comes under the personnel division in many large companies; in others it is a separate department reporting to a top executive.)
   - 12.2    Settling grievances through the formal grievance procedure.
   - 12.3    Union-management collaboration in establishing standards.
   - 12.4    Union-management collaboration in reducing waste, improving processes, and increasing production.

**Types of organization.** Since one of the functions often assigned to the personnel division is the organization department, a brief discussion of organization types should help the student to evaluate the organization of the personnel division. Organization structure seeks

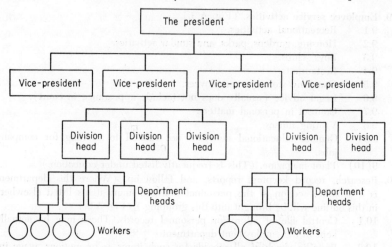

Fig. 2.2. The line type of organization.

to create an atmosphere and relationships within which organizational objectives may be accepted by the employees, responsibilities and lines of supervision are clearly defined, personal satisfactions are enhanced, and the company can move slowly but with confidence toward its goal. Sound organizational structure establishes procedures, practices, and standards and by its very nature becomes a support as well as a control. The personnel function is a staff assignment to the personnel department. In the line organization, authority flows from the president or head of the concern through his lieutenants divisionally to the department heads, group heads, foremen, and, lastly, to the rank-and-file workers.[4] Such an organization is illustrated in Fig. 2.2. This line type of organization provides for direct managerial control, it is economical, it is definite, and it fixes responsibility for each line of activity. For these reasons, it is particularly suited to smaller companies.

In a line organization a sharp line of demarcation separates department from department. It would, consequently, be impracticable to set up a personnel department as a line department, since its value to the operating executives in other departments, where the real work of personnel lies, would be impeded and rendered ineffective. The line type of organization is not flexible in the large enterprise.

[4] See Richard H. Lansburgh and W. R. Spriegel, *Industrial Management,* John Wiley & Sons, Inc., New York, 1955, pp. 5.1–5.21; see also W. R. Spriegel and Ernest C. Davies, *Principles of Business Organization,* Prentice-Hall, Inc., Englewood Cliffs, N.J., 1960, Chaps. 5 and 6 and App. A.

It forces the line officers in their individual fields to perform additional duties requiring special knowledge for which they may not be especially fitted. It leaves every executive dependent upon his own abilities and resources and fails to give him specialized staff aid in matters (such as purchasing, legal assistance, personnel, methods, inspection, and engineering) in which he needs expert counsel.

In *Taylor's functional organization,* authority flows from the president functionally to the department heads. Each department reports to one specialist with reference to production, to another with reference to finance, to another with reference to personnel, etc. This type is the extreme form of functionalized organization. Functional organization in its complete form as advocated by Taylor is never found today. In some large enterprises the top organizational structure is largely of the functional type. Figure 2.3 illustrates the functional type of organization applied only to the top management and middle management level. In Taylor's organization the functional control went all the way down to the worker. In this type of organization, the operating executives are freed from the necessity of performing work outside their special fields and are offered expert counsel and advice as needed in the performance of their duties. Such an organization, however, depends too highly upon the personal ability of individuals to cooperate. Sharp lines of authority are absent, and the effectiveness of managerial control, of coordination of effort, and of discipline is severely hampered.

The *line-and-staff organization* combines the good characteristics of both the line and the functional types of organization and enjoys most of the advantages of both. It has as a skeleton the line organization, but expert staff officers exist to give the line executives specialized

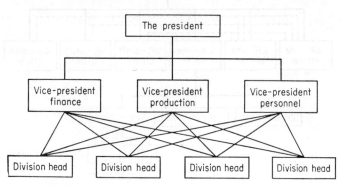

Fig. 2.3. The functional organization. (*Taylor's.*)

advice and assistance in the performance of those duties outside their own fields for which they are not especially fitted. In graphic form, this type of organization is illustrated in Fig. 2.4. Each of the staff officers may in person or through his staff assistants render staff aid to each of the division heads or even to the department heads. Naturally, this assistance does not have to be accepted. To show all these contacts on an organizational chart would make it a series of crossing dashed lines. With the exception of most smaller organizations, where it is possible for personal intimacy to exist in high degree, the line-and-staff organization is favored by most companies. Even where no conscious thought has been given to problems of organization and where no organization charts have been prepared, it is usually the line-and-staff type of organization that is used.

There are some inherent weaknesses in the line-and-staff organization peculiar to this structure itself. These can be overcome by dynamic leadership, clear definition of function, fixing of responsibilities, and establishing definite lines of supervision, plus intensive indoctrination in the principles of the objective and staff and line responsibilities. The line-and-staff weaknesses include:

1. *Staff advice* is frequently interpreted as a *line order*. This is especially true when the staff officer craves authority over people.

2. Since the line officer is responsible for results, the *psychology* of the staff officers' not being responsible for the results of his advice may *lead to carelessness*. It may also give some line officers an excuse for shortcomings.

3. Some line officers *may lean too heavily* on the staff for ideas and planning, thus *weakening their own leadership*.

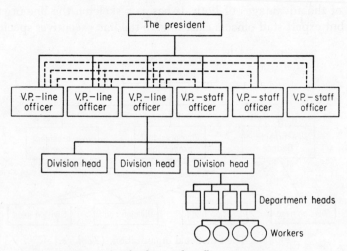

Fig. 2.4. The line-and-staff organization.

4. *Friction may develop* between the line officer and the staff unless each clearly understands the fine balance in each other's responsibilities. In the line-and-staff organization actions should follow the law of the situation.[5]

It should be clearly recognized that in the line-and-staff relationship there is a "no man's land" that can be navigated with safety and to the economic advantage of the enterprise only when both the line and the staff: (1) are thoroughly indoctrinated in the objective of the enterprise; (2) have accepted this objective as their own and are able to relate its achievement to the achievement of their own personal objectives; (3) have been thoroughly trained in organizational theory and principles and have operated under a top management that respects the importance of sound organizational structure and careful operating within the framework of this structure. To the above conditions should be added a fourth item, namely, that the personnel in the organization have the emotional security and stability to do in fact that which they know, according to accepted principles, ought to be done. Actual performance in terms of following established lines of supervision and fixed responsibility is more closely related to emotional balance and security than to a knowledge of the existing structure and a knowledge of sound organizational principles. A man may be an organizational specialist in terms of theory yet not practice what he "verbalizes" when he is personally concerned. An overambitious individual, somewhat insecure emotionally, may readily try to seek personal advantage by going over the head of his superior and by "knocking" his associates when he thinks that it will enhance his own status by so doing. An emotionally insecure man is a dangerous person to be placed in a position of authority over others. It may not be a matter of capacity in terms of intellectual potential or skills in such cases. He simply is short in terms of personal integrity.

**Personnel management or administration as a staff function.** Viewed from the standpoint of the enterprise as a whole the personnel division is a staff unit. Within the division itself, the organizational structure is usually of the line type. As a staff division, the personnel organization can be of maximum value to the entire enterprise. There is a tendency in some organizations for the personnel department to take unto itself line authority, in fact if not in name. Such a procedure

[5] See Ralph C. Davis, *The Fundamentals of Top Management,* Harper & Brothers, New York, 1951, p. 152, "Effective executive leadership depends on the executive's ability and courage to face the facts in the situation, interpret the facts properly in the light of the situation's requirements, and follow the course of action they dictate."

tends to cause the foremen and other line officers to shirk their responsibilities in industrial relations, which in turn reduces the effectiveness of the major efforts of the personnel unit.[6] There is a substantial amount of friction in many companies between the personnel division and line departments when the personnel division gets the reputation of wanting to take over line responsibilities. Much of this arises from a lack of understanding of organizational principles, but some of it arises from an emotional desire to exercise authority over others rather than a willingness to use the authority of ideas. The above discussion of the insecurity factor and emotional nonacceptance of organizational responsibilities not only is applicable to some of the frictions arising in some companies between the personnel division and some line departments but also applies to frictions between the controller's division, industrial engineering division, purchasing department, and other staff departments and line departments.[7]

The personnel division (1) is charged with the responsibility of advising management, from the chairman of the board of directors to the lowest line supervisor, on all questions affecting the employer-employee relationship; (2) is responsible for performing all the functions of employing workers for the various departments within the organization; (3) represents management in many of the relationships that affect the organization as a whole; and (4) is further charged with representing the legitimate claims of the workers to management. Real personnel relationships will always remain decentralized when the maximum *personal satisfactions* are realized. The personnel man who strives to take over, in the central personnel office, duties that rightfully belong in the respective departments is rendering a disservice to the proper administration of the personnel function. He is letting his own desire for "power over" and empire building take precedence over the service function, which is the proper area of personnel activities. Of course there are some activities that properly belong to the central personnel office. Among these functions

---

[6] See Paul Pigors, L. C. McKenney, and T. O. Armstrong, *Social Problems in Labor Relations*, McGraw-Hill Book Company, Inc., New York, 1939, pp. 10–15, 125–127; "The Functions and Scope of Personnel Administration," *Personnel*, July, 1947, pp. 5–8; "Organization of the Personnel Department," *Personnel*, May, 1952, pp. 437–441. National Industrial Conference Board, Inc., "Organization of Personnel Administration," *Studies in Personnel Policy* 73, New York, 1946.

[7] See Spriegel and Davies, *op. cit.*, App. A, "The Staff Relationships," for an extended discussion of this entire relationship and the delicate balance that needs to be maintained in order to promote the primary objectives of the enterprise. Frictions between individuals and departments create an unnecessary drag on the productive efforts of both individuals and groups. See also National Industrial Conference Board, Inc., "Improving Staff and Line Relationships," *Studies in Personnel Policy* 153, New York, 1954.

are: (1) maintaining a central file on all employees, (2) cultivating sources of labor supply, (3) initial screening of prospective employees, (4) the supervision of first-aid rooms and medical department, (5) advising all departments and divisions in personnel matters, and (6) advising management on collective bargaining and representing management in collective bargaining in companies where this function is so large that top management does not have the time to handle it. Other activities may be delegated to the central personnel office when management so elects. In all cases, *staff divisions or departments* (including personnel departments) *should keep in mind that theirs is a function subsidiary to the line officers whom they serve.* These staff divisions represent management and as such are not acting in terms of the same authority that a line officer possesses. Staff responsibility is a derived responsibility, whereas line responsibility is a direct, primary responsibility. The personnel division is the centralized clearing agency for aiding all other departments effectively to carry out their responsibilities in all personnel matters.

**Organizations for multiplant operations.** The number of companies operating multiplant units is very great. Practically any student of personnel is acquainted with the names of a number of these companies. The Western Electric Company has developed a very complete personnel program, as portrayed by Fig. 2.5. The actual relationship of the top personnel man in a branch plant to the home office is nearly always a reflection of the organizational philosophy of the company as a whole. After examining some 20 of the organization charts and explanatory letters from nationally known companies whose personnel directors are leaders in their professions, one is forced to the conclusion (if those leaders in the field may be used as indicative) that the prevailing philosophy is *decentralized control with central staff advice.* At each level the personnel function is tied to the line officer, with staff aid and counsel from the home office as manifest by the dashed lines. This relationship is shown in Figs. 2.6 and 2.7 of the Pittsburgh Plate Glass Company. On the other hand one large company has the local personnel manager of each plant report directly to the vice-president in charge of industrial relations at the home office. The local personnel manager in this company is responsible for giving aid and assistance to the local plant manager, but his reporting relationship is to the director of personnel division in the home office. Negotiating the union contract is handled by individuals appointed by the president of the company and consisting of line management and representatives of industrial relations, acting either as members of the committee or as advisors to the com-

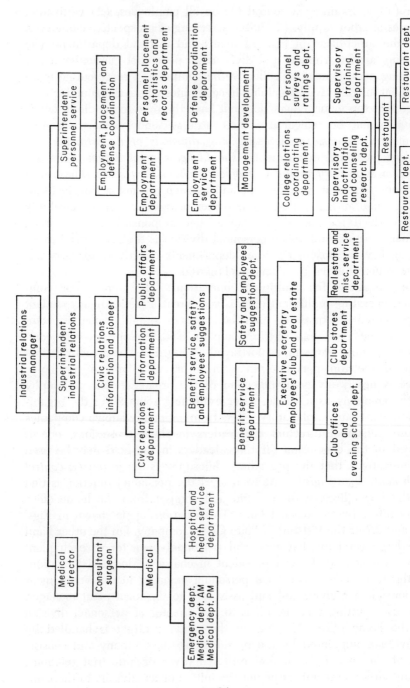

Fig. 2.5. Industrial Relations Department, Western Electric Company, Hawthorne Plant.

24

mittee. Negotiations are held in the company's main office. Negotiations that affect only local plants are conducted at the plant locations. The vice-president in charge of industrial relations of this plant said, "Our industrial relations setup is rather centralized, but we believe that there is sufficient autonomy of local action for efficient operation."

In order not to place the individual plant managers at the disadvantage of being "played one against the other" or of facing a skilled union negotiator for whom the operating plant manager is no match, management very often negotiates the basic union contract at the central office. Items that are strictly local in character are negotiated at the plant level. One director of industrial relations said, "While we wholeheartedly believe in keeping personnel relations at the plant level, our experience with the union has forced us to deal at the company level in the case of the contract with the union representing our production workers. We have wage differentials in different locations but the terms of the main contract are negotiated for all plants at once. We have many different contracts for maintenance employees that are negotiated at the plant level." Most companies give a great deal of freedom to the local plant manager and his personnel director. The home office personnel department provides staff assistance to the plant managers and their personnel departments. Figures 2.6 and 2.7 show the personnel program of the Pittsburgh Plate Glass Company.

Figure 2.8 shows the attempt to handle the personnel program by a great merchandising company, R. H. Macy and Company, Inc., of New York. A comparison of these organization charts shows some marked differences; yet the similarities are immeasurably greater than are the differences. *Personnel management is management,* and the fundamental differences between retail personnel, manufacturing personnel, public utility personnel, or banking personnel are not so great as the differences in organization structure in these different types of business. Some persons who know only personnel management in their narrow field like to think that their personnel problems are different from others. Of course, this is true, but likewise the personnel problems of two stores or factories owned by the same company are different. Nevertheless, the basic principles are the same in the various fields of personnel management.

While organization charts of large companies show functional specialization, one must be on guard against thinking of these activities as standing alone. Each is to a substantial degree dependent on and interrelated with the other. Personnel policies and practices should possess organic unity, just as all company policies should.

**The size of the personnel division.** The specific functions assigned to the personnel division influence the size of the personnel division or the ratio of the number of people in the personnel division to the number of persons in the other divisions in the company. Some companies do not have a cafeteria of their own, but one is operated by an outside firm. Some companies have no union relationship, make no morale surveys, have no organized safety program or recreation program. In a few instances the timekeeping function is performed in the personnel division, as is plant protection. It is hazardous to give any ratio that is desirable unless all the facts are available. This ratio changes as conditions change even when the functions remain the same. Tables 2.1 to 2.3 show the relationship of size to per capita personnel costs and the personnel ratios, the functional personnel ratios by type of organization, and the median personnel functional ratios by industry groups. These data are the results of Dr. Dale Yoder's extensive surveys since 1950 and are in all probability the

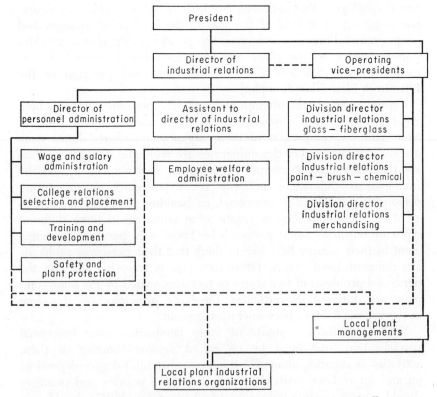

Fig. 2.6. Organization of the industrial relations department—general office, Pittsburgh Plate Glass Company, 1959.

most reliable researches in this area in the United States. These data speak for themselves. It is especially interesting to note the influence of size upon the per capita cost and the personnel ratio (Table 2.1). It is also interesting to observe that *benefits and services* are substantially lower in trade, transportation, and government than in manufacturing, finance, and utilities.

**Characteristics of the successful personnel director.** The eight functions shown in Tables 2.2 and 2.3 show the areas for which the personnel director is responsible. Pages 14 to 17 also show these functions broken down in greater detail. It is evident that the personnel director is first of all an executive requiring essentially the same executive qualities as other executives. Like other executives the personnel director needs technical competence in the areas of his division's specialties. He need not be a specialist in all the areas of the personnel division, yet he should have a high degree of skill and competence in at least one of the areas. The chief officer of the in-

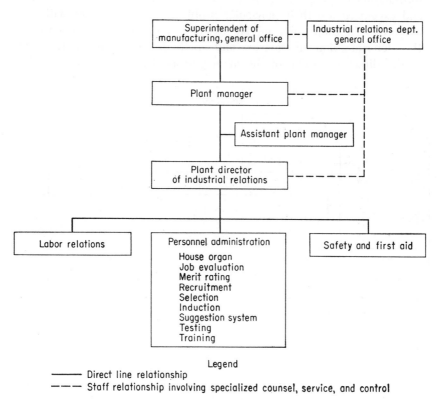

FIG. 2.7. Organization of the industrial relations department—plant, Pittsburgh Plate Glass Company, September, 1959.

dustrial relations and personnel function must have a keen sense of social justice and be fully appreciative of the rights and interests of the men and women at work, as well as of the economic necessities of management. His philosophy of social justice should include two fundamental concepts: (1) industry is a partnership between management, men, and owners whose objective is profits through service; (2) industry can profit greatly by developing and coordinating the capacities, the interests, and the opportunities of each worker and of each member of management. He must be able to couple this sense of social justice with a warm personal interest in people. This in turn must be controlled by a wealth of common sense, which will protect him from sentimentality on one side and from coldness on the other. He must be a man qualified to advise management on matters of personnel and capable of talking without fear or favor with any executive in the organization. He advises the higher command with reference to matters of personnel and collaborates with them in the formulation of personnel policies. He advises with department heads and executives on their particular problems and cooperates with the executives in their solution. He exercises an important influence in the determination of salaries and methods of payment. He acts as the direct executive of the main personnel functions, such as de-

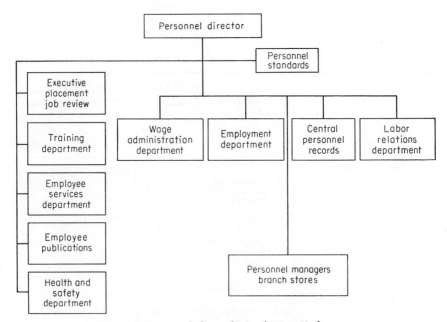

Fɪɢ. 2.8. Personnel chart of Macy's New York store.

*Table 2.1   Median Costs and Personnel Ratios by Company Size, 1959*\*

| No. of employees | No. of companies | Median per capita costs | Median over-all personnel ratio |
|---|---|---|---|
| 1–499 | 72 | $58.06 | 0.80 |
| 500–999 | 79 | 61.48 | 0.75 |
| 1,000–1,499 | 56 | 58.62 | 0.67 |
| 1,500–1,999 | 28 | 47.47 | 0.54 |
| 2,000–2,499 | 24 | 67.50 | 1.02 |
| 2,500–2,999 | 11 | 67.61 | 0.68 |
| 3,000–3,999 | 20 | 51.85 | 0.75 |
| 4,000–4,999 | 16 | 47.56 | 0.48 |
| 5,000–6,999 | 26 | 35.46 | 0.56 |
| 7,000–9,999 | 30 | 37.71 | 0.58 |
| 10,000–19,999 | 32 | 34.79 | 0.30 |
| 20,000–29,999 | 14 | 27.80 | 0.24 |
| 30,000 and over | 8 | 29.06 | 0.33 |
| All | 416 | 52.97 | 0.67 |

\* Source: Dale Yoder and Roberta J. Nelson, "Industrial Relations Budgets: Yardsticks for 1959," *Personnel*, Vol. 36, No. 4, July–August, 1959, p. 23.

*Table 2.2   Median Functional Personnel Ratios by Type of Organization, 1959*\*

| Function | Functional ratios | | | | |
|---|---|---|---|---|---|
| | All firms | Single plant | Multi-plant unit | Corporate office | All industrial relations departments within company |
| 1. Administration.......... | 0.09 | 0.11 | 0.13 | 0.04 | 0.08 |
| 2. Staffing................ | 0.11 | 0.13 | 0.12 | 0.07 | 0.10 |
| 3. Development........... | 0.04 | 0.05 | 0.06 | 0.03 | 0.06 |
| 4. Labor relations.......... | 0.06 | 0.07 | 0.09 | 0.03 | 0.06 |
| 5. Wage and salary adminis-tration................. | 0.06 | 0.07 | 0.06 | 0.04 | 0.06 |
| 6. Benefits and services...... | 0.19 | 0.20 | 0.31 | 0.09 | 0.18 |
| 7. Research............... | 0.02 | 0.03 | 0.02 | 0.01 | 0.02 |
| 8. Miscellaneous........... | 0.05 | 0.07 | 0.07 | 0.02 | 0.04 |
| Total of functional ratios.. | 0.62 | 0.73 | 0.86 | 0.33 | 0.60 |
| Median over-all ratios..... | 0.67 | 0.80 | 0.92 | 0.35 | 0.63 |

\* Source: Dale Yoder and Roberta J. Nelson, "Industrial Relations Budgets: Yardsticks for 1959," *Personnel*, Vol. 36, No. 4, July–August, 1959, p. 24.

velopment of sources of labor supply, selection and placement, maintenance of personnel records, recommendations for transfer and promotion, training, incentives, rules, and research. The titles of the chief of the division concerned with the personnel functions range from vice-president through director of industrial relations, personnel manager, to employment manager. The salaries paid these personnel men range in the same order, the vice-president's being the highest and personnel director's being the lowest.[8]

*Table* 2.3    *Median Functional Ratios by Industry Group, 1959*\*

| Function | Industry group | | | | | | | |
| | All $N = 371$ | Mfg. $N = 242$ | Trade $N = 17$ | Finance $N = 23$ | Transportation $N = 19$ | Utilities $N = 29$ | Government $N = 29$ | Miscellaneous $N = 12$ |
|---|---|---|---|---|---|---|---|---|
| 1. Administration......... | 0.09 | 0.09 | 0.05 | 0.24 | 0.08 | 0.07 | 0.12 | 0.12 |
| 2. Staffing.............. | 0.11 | 0.10 | 0.07 | 0.23 | 0.08 | 0.09 | 0.17 | 0.16 |
| 3. Development.......... | 0.04 | 0.04 | 0.04 | 0.09 | 0.04 | 0.06 | 0.04 | 0.02 |
| 4. Labor relations........ | 0.06 | 0.06 | 0.02 | 0.03 | 0.05 | 0.06 | 0.02 | 0.03 |
| 5. Wage and salary administration.......... | 0.06 | 0.06 | 0.04 | 0.17 | 0.02 | 0.06 | 0.08 | 0.07 |
| 6. Benefits and services... | 0.19 | 0.21 | 0.11 | 0.25 | 0.08 | 0.23 | 0.12 | 0.16 |
| 7. Research............. | 0.02 | 0.02 | 0.01 | 0.06 | 0.02 | 0.04 | 0.01 | 0.04 |
| 8. Miscellaneous......... | 0.05 | 0.04 | 0.02 | 0.15 | 0.07 | 0.04 | 0.07 | 0.03 |
| Total of functional ratios | 0.62 | 0.62 | 0.36 | 1.22 | 0.44 | 0.65 | 0.63 | 0.63 |

\* Source: Dale Yoder and Roberta J. Nelson, "Industrial Relations Budgets: Yardsticks for 1959," *Personnel*, Vol. 36, No. 4, July–August, 1959, p. 24.

**Summary.** The organization and staffing of the industrial relations and personnel function are designed to facilitate the effective carrying out of the relationships between the employer and his employees and between the employees themselves and to mold the entire employee group into a dynamic work force that achieves efficiency in its work efforts and derives personal satisfaction from the working environment and relationships. Note that this concept embraces "profits through service." Business is both an economic and a social institution. The chief personnel officer should be a specialist in organization theory and as such be an effective adviser to top management in organizational matters, as well as being able to organize his own division in such a manner as to minimize frictions, promote good will, and release the latent energies of his own people and associates to be expended on their primary assignments. The functions set forth

[8] See Dale Yoder and Roberta J. Nelson, "Industrial Relations Salaries and Staff Ratios—1958," *Personnel*, July–August, 1959, p. 15.

in this chapter are not always included in the personnel division. They are, however, personnel functions and deserve our consideration, regardless of the particular organizational structure in a given enterprise.[9] In the smaller organizations, many of the functions are handled by the same person. Such a situation naturally precludes a high degree of specialization. Most of the personnel functions can readily be mastered by a well-trained individual who has a basic interest in people. Psychological testing and medical or health service require a specialized type of training, which relatively few men in general personnel work have. In the smaller organizations, it is frequently more advantageous to have part-time consultants rather than to try to perform a task for which the personnel staff is not trained. On the other hand, it is not unusual to find an organization using the trained nurse, when not busy in the first-aid clinic, for clerical and interviewing duties. The trained psychologist likewise may well be used by the smaller organizations in other functions than psychological research and testing.

Regardless of the organization structure the personnel function exists in every organization. Management may have no one especially charged with the responsibility of giving particular attention to human or employee needs, other than the departmental supervisor; it may by default or intent leave most of these responsibilities to the union; but the function is still there. It is a function that must be exercised by someone in the organization. As the number of people in the enterprise increases, specialization usually is increased, not only in production, sales, finance, accounting, etc., but also in those relationships involving the employer and employee. The respective specialized department heads frequently become so absorbed in their specialties that they fail to give the necessary attention to employees who aid them in their work. This statement is unfortunately also true, at times, even in the personnel division itself. The personnel department does not take over the departmental head's responsibilities, with the possible exception of keeping centralized records and taking charge of health service and hiring, but acts in an advisory staff capacity to aid him in the proper discharge of his personnel responsibilities.

[9] See American Management Association, "How to Establish and Maintain a Personnel Department," *Research Report* 4, 1944, for an excellent study of this subject; see also "Planning and Developing the Company Organization Structure" by Ernest Dale, *Research Report* 20, 1952; National Industrial Conference Board, Inc., "Improving Line and Staff Relationships," *Studies in Personnel Policy* 153, New York, 1956; and "Organization of Staff Functions," *Studies in Personnel Policy* 163, New York, 1958.

CHAPTER 3

# *Personnel Management as a Coordinating Function*

**What is coordination?** Henri Fayol, the great French student of management, said, "To coordinate means to unite and correlate all activities." Coordination is the primary function of management, but it is accomplished through the efforts of every member of the enterprise. When the members of the group are thoroughly indoctrinated in the institutional objectives, this unity of purpose serves as a strong instrument of control. The willing cooperation arising from the unity of purpose facilitates coordination. In such a situation a great deal of the coordination is secured through the informal organization. *Coordination is the orderly arrangement of group effort, to provide unity of action in the pursuit of a common purpose.*[1] Coordination is the unifying activity of management that enables the members of the organizational team to move resolutely and with confidence toward its objective.[2] Coordination may be defined as the function of relating activities with respect to time and order of performance.[3] The prime responsibility for coordination rests with management. Top management sets up the organizational structure for carrying out the institutional objective. This structure includes both the line and the staff relationships. The line organization has the primary responsibility for the entire operation, but it is aided by staff departments and individuals that participate actively in rendering service, giving advice, exercising control, and effecting coordination.

The personnel department is one of the staff departments that

[1] James D. Mooney and Alan C. Reiley, *The Principles of Organization*, 5th ed., Harper & Brothers, New York, 1939, p. 5.
[2] W. R. Spriegel and Ernest C. Davies, *Principles of Organizations and Operations*, Prentice-Hall, Inc., Englewood Cliffs, N.J., 1960, "The Staff Relationships," App. A.
[3] Ralph C. Davis, *The Fundamentals of Top Management*, Harper & Brothers, New York, 1951, p. 19. This book presents a scholarly treatment of the entire management function.

renders all four of the staff functions, namely, advice, service, co-ordination, and control. This department is in an excellent position to do a constructive job in several phases of coordination. In fact the personnel department may well provide leadership in the entire area of organization building and structure.

**Why is coordination required?** Coordination is the process of making things happen when, where, and in the degree desired. By degree desired is meant both quantity and quality of product or service. Coordination is the process of synchronizing human effort. It is an *all-pervasive* element in any effective endeavor. Coordination requires purposeful planning, organizing, and follow-up to see that things happen according to the plan within the framework of established organization. Whenever a business group reaches a size where departments are formed, coordination is required. There will be no specialized personnel department in the small firm of 50 people, although the personnel management function will be there. Coordination, or the proper timing of the various factors of group effort, is basically a function of management. This does not mean that management must exercise authority to secure coordination. It merely means that management will take the necessary steps to create the environment in which willing cooperation takes place with a full knowledge of the requirements as to time, place, and method. All that is needed to secure coordination in a well-trained group possessed of high morale is full knowledge of what is wanted and the necessary techniques and planning to enable them to perform. The larger the enterprise, the greater the effort required to provide the full knowledge and the techniques to make this effective. When the group is small enough so that the planning and executing can be carried on by face-to-face contacts, coordination is simple and relatively easy.

With the growth of a firm, large-scale departments are established, and there is a corresponding increase in both size and number of the staff departments. The personnel department is a major staff department, and its function is to serve the various departments of the company. Likewise this is the objective of most other staff departments. For the work group of a company to move smoothly toward its objective, there must be some guiding force, some directing hand, or some authority. This does not mean the imposing of the will of some superior upon a subordinate. It may mean only the *authority of the situation*. A given thing requires attention; responsibilities are clearly defined and understood; the proper person willingly carries out his responsibilities. Such a happy state of coordination can be realized only in a company where each person has been thoroughly trained, institutional objectives are understood, traditions have been established, and procedures have been tried out and have become standardized. The people have learned to work together through long practice, and the sentiments of the group are such that there is a "will to carry on." The foregoing situation is not so idealistic as might appear on first thought. The conditioning process that precedes the acceptance by people of the need for coordination and direction begins early in life. It is manifest on the baseball and football fields, in the classroom, and in other group activities associated with play and social contacts. People get satisfaction from an orderly situation that enables them to achieve their business as well as personal goals. In contrast they dislike the continual waste and lost time of faulty planning. Most people are ready to accept some degree of fixed responsibility and to recognize the necessity for the delegation of authority.

**Rights and responsibilities.** The recognized rights and responsibilities of individuals and groups are largely the product of a basic philosophy of life arising from the total conditioning of experiences. Some people possess definite biases toward *divine rights,* others toward *natural laws,* some toward the *will of the people;* possibly most persons have a mixture of all of these and more. In the United States most business rights are derived from the will of the people as expressed in the Constitution, which recognizes the right to own and use private property. With a clarification of rights, there has developed an evolutionary concept of a parallel responsibility in relation to these rights. There are rights of the owners of the enterprise, rights of management, rights of the employees, rights of the customers, and rights of the community. Modern business has come to recognize responsibilities of ownership, responsibilities of managers, responsibilities of employees, and to a limited extent the responsibilities of the customers and the community. Authority is the counterpart of responsibility. There can be no fixing of responsibility in the absence of the authority to discharge the responsibility. From an organizational standpoint, authority is a right inherent in the source of the authority. Authority is thus conceived to be the right to act or to take action. Enlightened managers do not look upon authority as a right to take action without considering the opinions and rights of subordinates. Nevertheless at every level of management and in both minor details and broad policies, decisions must be made and action taken. Someone must assume the responsibility and therefore should possess the authority of decision and action. The wise manager or department head practices consultive supervision;[4] then he decides, takes action, and assumes full responsibility for the results.

There are at least two kinds of authority, "authority over," or organizational authority, and "authority with," or informal authority. *Authority over persons* in the firm is conferred through a process of delegation from the owners through the line or staff. This authority is not effective until it is recognized by the persons who are subject to direction. This authority may appropriately be thought of as the right to direct or guide. *Authority with people,* or informal authority, is conferred by the group. It is conferred by the group because of the group's approval of the individual's leadership arising from his personality or ability, or both. Such an informal leader usually conforms to the group's sentiments and anticipates group desires. He may or may not be the best salesman or worker in the department. He may acquire his informal position of leadership by virtue of his long service and his ability to voice the sentiments of the group to superiors. Occasionally an unusually capable person with organizational authority may also be the informal group leader. This is a relatively rare yet fortunate situation. Coordination, to be effective through either organizational or informal authority, must be based upon a full appreciation and understanding of the facts and requirements of the situation. One of the truisms of sound organizational theory is that *decisions should be made as far down in an organization as competence and the required information are available.* The giving of the information and the development of competence are primary responsibilities of the line executives, but the personnel department also serves as a strong staff aid.

**Coordination as a function of management.** Figure 3.1 portrays the various functions of management. The three sides of the triangle represent the three functions of management planning, organizing, and operating. In outline form these may be viewed as follows:

1. To plan.
2. To organize.
3. To operate.
    3.1 To initiate action and to control through coordination.
    3.2 To follow up; to measure performance against established standards and the plan.

[4] Consultive supervision is a process or technique of management whereby not only are the supervised consulted before action is taken in which they are interested but the supervised are urged to contribute constructive thoughts to the solution.

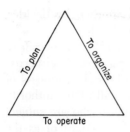

FIG. 3.1. Functions of an executive.

To operate means substantially more than mere planning and organizing. For instance, a sale in a department store requires the initiating of action to get new merchandise for the sale, pricing it, and preparing it for the big event. It also requires the planning of the advertising and actual placing of the advertisements. All these activities must be so coordinated that the public will be attracted to the store and enticed to make purchases. Not only must orders be issued to start the respective activities according to schedule, but effective control requires the continuous review of operations to see that the performance is according to plan. This checking and follow-up process may reveal certain failures that must be corrected by a transfer of employees from one department to another or a hurry-up call for stand-by employees to report for work. Most managers and supervisors are stronger on the initiating of action under the operating phase of their work than they are in the checking or follow-up phases. In outline form the functions of a store executive may be said to be:

1. To plan—to determine what is to be done and lay the broad framework of the objective.
2. To organize—to provide the structural relationships to carry out the plan. This requires clear delineation of responsibilities and the delegation of the required authority.
3. To operate within the framework of the organizational structure in the executing of the plan.
   3.1 To initiate action to start the various segments of the plan so that each function will be performed on time.
   3.2 To follow up to see that the plan has been carried out, and to measure results against the standard desired.

The factory executive would be faced with similar problems in starting a new operation or introducing a new product into his manufacturing operation. He would have:

1. To plan for financing, selling, design, production facilities, manpower, and materials.
2. To organize to take care of the new operation in case the present organization cannot absorb the new operation. It might call for a second shift.
3. To operate within the framework of the plan.
   3.1 To initiate action and to coordinate each operation.
   3.2 To follow up to see that all operations are carried out according to the plan; to measure performance.

**Securing coordination through organization.** Organization is sometimes used to refer to the persons in these various units and at other times to refer to the structural relationships between the various departments. In this paragraph we are concerned *with the structural relationships of the various departments of the enterprise as a whole and with the functions assigned the respective executive and supervisory positions.* Leadership is achieved through delegation and careful defining of functions. The delegation of functions and the clear definition of these functions establish the channels of control within which willing cooperation and coordination may take place. It must be clearly recognized that willing cooperation does not produce coordination unless there is complete understanding and knowledge of the requirements and the timing. For instance, the advertising manager and the newspapers may be eager to cooperate. If by mistake the manager should run the advertisements announcing the date of a sale 1 week in advance of the time when the event is to take place, the result would be confusion, wasted effort, and an antagonized public. The highest type of coordination takes place in an atmosphere of willing cooperation; yet at times it may be achieved in the face of reluctance. The latter situation might arise when the requirements of the company run counter to the personal desires of many of its personnel. Such a situation could arise when workers have to work on a holiday to get out critical material.

The objective of an organization is the control tower of all effort when willingly accepted by all persons in the enterprise. *A sound organizational structure in a company when conceived in the light of its objective and supported by thorough indoctrination and training of the personnel will create an atmosphere in which the company may move slowly but resolutely toward the realization of its goal.* Such an organizational structure provides all the necessary functions to facilitate coordination and willing cooperation. For instance, credit is coordinated with sales; deliveries to customers are coordinated with sales; customers' adjustments are coordinated with customers' accounts; inspection of incoming goods is coordinated with the authorization of payment of the supplier's invoice; and the mailing of statements to customers is coordinated with the available supply of clerical help to take care of the total volume of this type of work over the monthly period; increase in production of a given article is coordinated with sales and available personnel. Such coordination can be realized only when it is the specific responsibility of some person or departmental unit. In other words, operation is closely related to the organizational structure within which the operation is to take place.

Achieving coordination through properly conceived organizational structure requires the acceptance of the needed controls. When it is generally known that a given department has the specific responsibility for a given function, there is relatively little unfavorable reaction to the checking necessary for the particular control. For instance, the salesperson does not grant credit. She knows that her commission on the sale of a $500 fur coat which is to be charged is subject to the approval of the credit department. She also recognizes the need for approval of a check offered by a customer in payment for a purchase. The factory worker knows that his work is to be checked by the inspector and does not resent the maintenance of a uniform standard. It is the old story of a recognition of the need for constituted authority.

Coordination may be realized in a firm where the organization is defective, but to achieve such a goal requires unnecessary effort on the part of the personnel and supervisors. Employees should not be required to expend their efforts overcoming obstacles which arise solely from poor organization. When the company organization is developed in terms of the company's primary objective, when definite lines of supervision are established, when responsibilities are fixed, when the personnel are thoroughly trained in company policies, systems, and procedures, and when dynamic leadership is provided at every supervisory level, coordination and willing cooperation are almost certain to follow.

**Responsibility for organizational development.** The primary responsibility for organizational structure rests with top management. While top management is directly responsible for the organizational structure, it should have the assistance of a specialist who can devote his time and energy to this activity. A few large companies have set up a special *organization department* that is responsible for this function. Since the total volume of work involved is relatively small, the wage and salary administration function is sometimes placed in this department. To do this is a clear violation of the principle of functional departmentation (the grouping of similar activities together to take advantage of the principle of specialization). Wage administration is primarily related to personnel administration. It is true that the standards of performance are an industrial engineering function, but the pricing of the performance is subject to collective bargaining. In a large company the ideal situation would be one in which a vice-president had charge of all activities that pertained to the human relations functions, with specialists in the subsidiary functions reporting to him. The responsibility for organizational structure would be included as one of these functions.

Someone should constantly study the organizational relationships to keep them in balance and to strive to keep them dynamic. Vested interests tend to develop in relation to the allocation of duties and responsibilities. This tendency causes the organization to continue to operate in a given way long after requirements and conditions have changed. The organization is likely to become static rather than dynamic, as it should be to meet changing conditions. It is rare indeed for a supervisor to ask to have a particular group of his employees performing a special function transferred to someone else's supervision. The supervisor may be overworked to care for his major responsibility; yet he tends to hold on to the responsibility of supervising all his employees. There is a feeling among many department heads that the importance of their jobs is related to the number of employees they have to direct. This desire is not confined to the lowest level of supervision. The same tendency prevails among division heads. Unless there is some impartial staff unit that has time to study the organizational structure and make recommendations, this important function will be largely neglected. The personnel department is peculiarly fitted to render this service, provided that its director is himself trained in organizational theory. *It is no exaggeration to say that the personnel director in any establishment should be the No. 1 organizational specialist.* He should constantly study the various relationships in the company and the qualifications of the persons filling the respective positions.

**The personnel department's staff relationships.**[5] In an organization the staff people's responsibilities differ from the line's in that the line carries on its work in its own right as a part of the direct command of the enterprise, whereas the staff has no authority in and of itself but operates solely as a representative of the line officer or department to which it is attached. The various functions rendered by staff departments to general business may be illustrated by the following outline:

1. As a control agency in such departments as:
    1.1 Organization.
    1.2 Cost.
    1.3 Methods and systems engineering.
    1.4 Standard practice or procedure.
    1.5 Budget.

[5] The student who has not had a formal course in industrial management or business organization should read the chapters in a standard text in one of these fields that cover organization.

1.6 Personnel—selection, training, wage administration, transfers, promotions, etc.

1.7 Accounting.

1.8 Auditing.

1.9 Credit.

2. As a service agency in such departments as:
    2.1    Research and development.
    2.2    Engineering and construction.
    2.3    Purchasing.
    2.4    Statistics.
    2.5    Traffic.
    2.6    Tax.
    2.7    Real estate.
    2.8    Insurance.
    2.9    Motor vehicle or traffic.
    2(10)  Personnel—employment, restaurant, medical, etc.

3. As a coordinative agency in such departments as:
    3.1 Order and distribution.
    3.2 Planning and control.
    3.3 Merchandise.
    3.4 Personnel—transfers, wage administration, training, organization, communications with employees, and public relations.

4. Advisory agencies in such departments as:
    4.1 Legal.
    4.2 Economic.
    4.3 Public relations.
    4.4 Personnel—labor relations, training, transfer and promotion, public relations.

It will be observed that the personnel department may perform all four types of general activities that belong to staff departments. It has an important role to play in the coordination of the personnel functions and activities of the factory or store.

**The personnel department's contribution to coordination through committee representation.** Committees serve a useful purpose but are often poor excuses for proper organization. Committees are notoriously slow in getting things done; they are poor administrative agencies; they tend to compromise when the scientific facts should dictate the action. On the other hand, committees can be very effective in the organization. They provide an excellent medium for training and instruction, for disseminating information that facilitates effective coordination, and for contributing balance to policies that otherwise might readily be one-sided. The personnel manager or his representative should be a member of all committees where questions that directly concern the employees are considered. Such membership will ensure coordination and integration of all personnel policies. Whenever plant expansion or contraction is being discussed, the subject of personnel is important. The personnel director should be either chairman or secretary of the general personnel committee, which should be composed of major executives. He should also be represented on the salary administration committee, job-evaluation committee, health and safety committee, suggestion committee, public relations committee, bonus or profit-sharing committee, pension committee, inventory employee committee, executive training committee, and any other special committee where personnel relationships are important. All these committees may not exist in certain companies; yet similar committees are being created constantly. Committees usually have representatives from the line and certain other staff departments, and most committee action should include the personnel viewpoint. This keeps the consideration of human relations a vital part of all operations.

**The personnel department as a coordinating agency.** The primary responsibility for coordination rests with the top line officers. However, just as the line officer extends his ability to control through delegation to either a staff or another line executive, so does he extend his ability to coordinate by delegating a part of this responsibility to a staff executive or staff department. Management has delegated certain responsibilities to the personnel department. The authority of ideas that is the primary source of the strength of the personnel department arises from the responsibility delegated to it. The personnel department delegates only within the department itself. It provides leadership through ideas, service, and coordination. Coordination is the unifying activity of management that enables the members of the organizational team to move resolutely and with confidence toward its objective.

Figure 3.2 portrays essentially the same functions for the personnel department as Fig. 3.1 for the generalized concept of the executive. Certain activities may be delegated to the personnel department for performance or control within the scope of the policies laid down by top management or an advisory committee. A few of these functions are employment, wage and salary administration, merit rating, transfers and promotion, and training programs for college graduates. Merit rating to be effective must be done by the employee's supervisor; yet if each supervisor goes his own way, the variations in standards render the ratings worthless for the purpose of wage administration or promotions. The personnel department examines the ratings and strives to develop a high degree of uniformity in the standards used.

The personnel department contributes to the coordination of "promoting from within." Centralized records kept by the personnel department enable this department to be of great assistance to the line in making promotions. For instance, a capable salesperson or worker may be working in department *A* who is entitled to a promotion to a vacancy in department *B*. Unless there is some coordinating agency, this promotion may go to a short-service, lower-rated employee in department *B* rather than to the long-service, efficient employee in department *A*. Of course, it would be unwise to force an employee on an unwilling department head. On the other hand, the department head is not in a position to know the merits of employees in other departments in a large company. A similar need for coordination arises in the case of salary administration. One department head may be exceedingly liberal in granting raises more frequently than the company policy permits, and another one may not put through raises that the company policy requires or permits. In the first instance the personnel manager, acting as a representative of top management, restrains the executive, and in the other instance he encourages the

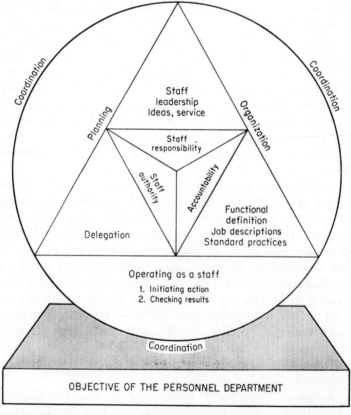

Fig. 3.2. Coordinating functions of personnel division as a staff agency. This division has no line authority but operates solely on a staff basis.

department head to follow the established company policy. In both situations the personnel department is performing an important coordinative function.

**The personnel department's role in communicating with employees.** Communications provide the basis of all coordinating. The most logical person to impart information to an employee and to transmit upward information from an employee is the supervisor. Unfortunately, some supervisors neglect this responsibility. Then there is the problem of upward communication in which the supervisor is personally involved. He screens out all that part of communication which in any way reflects on him. The problem of upward and downward communications is so difficult that top management uses every available device to accomplish the desired end. This should never lead to "bypassing" the department head. On the other hand, the same information may be made available in more than one manner, thus to ensure its reaching the person involved. The major objective of all communications with the employees by the personnel department is to develop cooperation and to coordinate company policies. The personnel department strives to integrate the various personnel practices, thus to remove the charge of discrimination, which is a cause of much discontent among employees. The personnel department may communicate with employees on matters that concern them through any of the following representative channels:

1. Employees' paper.
2. Booklets describing company policies. These employee handbooks may cover almost any item such as insurance, wages, profit sharing, suggestions, paydays, rest periods, sick leaves, vacations, recreation, safety and health, seniority rights, and union relationships.
3. Union contract.
4. Suggestion system.
5. Training classes.
6. Grievance procedures.
7. Union representatives.
8. Public address system.
9. Inserts in pay envelopes.
10. Bulletin boards.

**The personnel department role in coordinating company compliance with government regulations.** The personnel department is not the sole agency in the company that is concerned with governmental relationships. For instance, the social security and unemployment taxes are deducted by the payroll department and paid to the government by the financial officer. On the other hand, the personnel representative frequently explains to the employee the nature of these deductions and how they are figured. If the company is engaged in interstate business, the Fair Labor Standards Act covers those employees actually so engaged; the same applies to the National Labor-Management Relations Act. The company also deducts the Federal withholding tax on income. This is seldom the function performed directly by the personnel department; yet members of the personnel department often fill out the forms required. In other words, the personnel department is frequently the agency through which outside institutions make their contacts with employees. The personnel department is expected to be thoroughly informed regarding any laws that affect the employees or the company in relation to its employees. The personnel department not only informs the employees of their rights and obligations under Federal and state laws but has the responsibility of giving this same information to the department supervisors. Many employees and supervisors do not understand their rights and responsibilities. For instance, if a currently insured employee dies leaving a wife and child under eighteen, the widow and child are entitled to a pension until the child reaches eighteen. Many employees and their dependents do not know this. The personnel department can perform a socially desirable service by informing the employees and their dependents of their rights.

**The personnel department's coordinative function.** Anything that is basically a personnel function is a staff responsibility of the personnel department. The line operating executive is still the responsible head of all his men, but the personnel department is charged with the staff responsibility of assisting the line officer. Many phases of operations have a human relations counterpart. The human relations impact of changing an operation or the job content may readily be overlooked by the industrial engineer or the line supervisor. The personnel department specializes in the human element and is in a position to advise line management regarding employee reaction to change. As the company manager and his staff think their problems through in advance, organize the resources of the establishment, and control the operations, they continuously provide for changes in the social relationship within the working groups. Since the "supervisors get results through people," the company executives at all levels are constantly adjusting and motivating individual workers and groups of workers to ever-changing conditions. In the large firms some of the responsibility for these employee-employer relationships is delegated to a personnel manager and his department. For these personnel administrators, enlisting the cooperation of all supervisors and managers in the company is an opportunity as well as a challenge.

CHAPTER 4

# Personnel Policies

**The relationship of personnel policies to business policies and objectives.** Probably the most significant statement that can be made about divisional or departmental policies is that *all business policies* should *possess organic unity.* Each subsidiary policy should support the major institutional policies and objectives. Business policies may be defined as that body of principles and rules of conduct which governs an enterprise in the attainment of its objectives. Business policies are, in general, more stable than procedures and regulations; yet they are not static but are modified to meet changing conditions. Carefully defined business policies serve as a stabilizing influence to prevent the waste of energy in following programs not in harmony with the company objectives. (See Six Basic General Motors Principles, page 46.) They promote cooperation in the organization as a whole and foster initiative, particularly at the lower levels of supervision. Business policies not only establish goals; they also form the basis of controls and procedures. In substance they may be thought of as the flight plan to be followed in getting from where the business is to where it wants to go. Business policies serve as a directive in the planning, organization, and control of a business enterprise.

Policy formulation is an administrative function. There are two groups of policies, major and minor. Major personnel policies pertain to the over-all objectives, procedures, and controls that influence the organization as a whole. Minor policies cover relationships within a segment of the enterprise, with considerable emphasis on details and procedures. The board of directors formulates the major policies and establishes the framework within which the major executives establish the remaining policies necessary to carry out the major objectives of the enterprise. The major policies cover in a general way nearly every phase of the enterprise, the product, methods of financing, organizational structure, plant location, marketing, person-

45

## SIX BASIC GENERAL MOTORS PRINCIPLES

To assure the continuing success of General Motors and to maintain our competitive position, there are six principles or policies that we believe must be followed and fully developed.

### 1. *Put the Right People in the Right Places*

The careful selection and placement of employes to make sure that they are physically, mentally and temperamentally fitted to the jobs they are expected to do; to make sure that new employes can be reasonably expected to develop into desirable employes, and so that there will be a minimum number of square pegs in round holes.

### 2. *Train Everyone for the Job to Be Done*

The education and training of employes in the business, so that they will individually qualify for better jobs, so that their accomplishments will be limited only by their ambitions and abilities, and so that they will be able to do more efficiently the current work to which they are assigned.

### 3. *Make the Organization a Coordinated Team*

The effective organization of the employes of the corporation into operating units; the coordination and administration of these units, divisions and departments so that there will be a minimum amount of friction and non-productive or unnecessary work; the planning and organization of balanced facilities for the progressive manufacture of interchangeable parts; the proper control and direction of the whole enterprise without destroying the initiative of the individual employe.

### 4. *Supply the Right Tools and the Right Conditions*

The quality of tools, the facilities and the working conditions supplied for employes are highly important. The better the tools, facilities and working conditions, the more that can be produced with the same human effort and the lower the cost of the products. When this results, higher wages can be paid and more good jobs can be provided. So General Motors wants the best tools and facilities we know how to create, and is prepared to spend millions of dollars currently and in the future to acquire them.

### 5. *Give Security with Opportunity, Incentive, Recognition*

There must be individual application to the job in hand. To develop the maximum personal application to his job and his interest in it, each employe must have sound incentives to work. Such incentives include fair compensation, recognition for results achieved, reasonable security and, at the same time, opportunity and hope for advancement in the organization.

### 6. *Look Ahead, Plan Ahead . . . for More and Better Things*

Superior products to be produced and distributed. These products must be attractive and meet the demands of customers. This requires research and a policy of continuing product development and improvement.

*Following and developing these principles will help us to accomplish our objectives and enable General Motors to produce "More and Better Things for More People."*

nel, etc. Minor policies should be the outgrowth of the major policies of the organization in order to preserve unity of purpose. Minor executives, in their interpreting of the major policies, in reality create the minor policies. In some companies representatives of the employees participate in the creation of policies in which they are vitally interested.

Being a vital part of the major business policies formulated to guide the enterprise in attaining its objectives, the personnel policies naturally must conform to the broad structural relationships governing the organization as a whole. Major personnel policies comprise that body of principles and rules of conduct which governs the enterprise in its relationships with its employees. Since the major personnel policies are a part of the major company policies, the senior executives are directly responsible for the formulation of the major personnel policies. The chief executive officer of the enterprise is, in reality, the chief personnel officer, even though he may have the aid of a director of personnel who assists him in this field of specialization. The sales manager may be a line officer, but the director of personnel, to be most effective, must serve as a staff officer. Personnel policies are an integral part of the entire policy structure of an enterprise. It is not unusual to find an organization with enlightened policies in the area of sales, public relations, scientific product design, and finance, but with no concrete personnel policy other than to permit each supervisor to do as his particular fancy dictates. Such an organization may have an employment officer as a matter of convenience but otherwise may have no real personnel program. Tradition and custom have a place in any sound personnel policy; yet they are not sufficient to meet the changing personnel requirements that are constantly arising.

Minor personnel policies adhere to specific departments or other units. An employee may have plant seniority rights, the result of a major personnel policy where plant seniority is recognized, and at the same time the same employee may have departmental seniority rights, the result of a minor personnel policy. Plant seniority may give a man the right to a job in a given department, and departmental seniority may be such that he has to take the most undesirable shift. Minor personnel policies often influence departmental morale quite as much as the major personnel policies. When the two are in harmony with each other, satisfying personnel relations and a high type of morale tend to be present.

**Coverage of personnel policies.** Some companies express their personnel policies in broad terms of principles with no details. Other companies in the same industry spell out their policies in great detail. For instance, one large manufacturer who has had a bitter labor relations experience lists all specific causes for discharging employees. Another company in the same industry treats the subject of discharges more in the terms of principles, pointing out that no man will be discharged because of union affiliation but that membership in a union does not confer immunity from discharge. Another large-scale company in a different industry does not mention discharges in its published statements on labor policies; yet its booklet covers almost every other phase of employer-employee relationship. An analysis of various studies in personnel policies and practices reveal coverage of the following areas.[1]

1. History of the company's growth.
2. Employment practices and conditions of employment.
    2.1　　No age restrictions other than legal restrictions on minors.
    2.2　　Physical examinations.
    2.3　　Psychological and occupational tests.
    2.4　　Wage-payment method and pay periods.
    2.5　　Hours of work, overtime, shifts, and shift rotations.
    2.6　　Basis of promotion.
    2.7　　Layoff and rehiring.
    2.8　　Discharge and voluntary separations.
    2.9　　Seniority rights.
    2(10)　Guaranteed employment after attaining certain length of service.
    2(11)　When an employee is considered a regular employee.
3. Grievance procedure.
4. Safety rules and regulations.
5. General practices.
    5.1　　Employee identification.
    5.2　　Punching time cards and reporting in and out of the plant or department.
    5.3　　Tool checks and tool regulations.
    5.4　　Removal of tools or other personal property from the plant.
    5.5　　Purchases from the company usually at a discount.
    5.6　　Procedure for getting pay.
    5.7　　Absence.
        5.71　Leave of absence.
        5.72　Absence for jury service.
        5.73　Military leave.
        5.74　Personal reasons.
        5.75　Sick leave.
    5.8　　Change of address.

[1] See National Industrial Conference Board, Inc., "Personnel Practices in Factory and Office," New York, *Studies in Personnel Policy* 145, 1954. In fact this entire series of studies are almost exclusively studies of various personnel policies. They are very thorough. More than 175 of them have been issued. See also App. A for a summary of personnel practices in 852 companies.

5.9 Solicitation on company premises.

5(10) Automobile parking privileges.

6. Mutuality of interest between management and men.
7. Need for cooperation between management and men.
8. Employee financial aids.

 8.1 Savings and loans.

 8.2 Credit unions and mutual benefit associations.

 8.3 Group insurance.

 8.4 Profit sharing.

 8.5 Partial or entire payment of tuition for school attendance or correspondence-school courses satisfactorily completed.

 8.6 Loans during temporary layoffs.

9. Educational opportunities.

 9.1 Apprentice training.

 9.2 Factory schools, vestibule school, and training on the job.

 9.3 Training for promotion.

10. Employees' paper.
11. Suggestion system.
12. Health, hospitalization, and similar programs.
13. Vacations with pay.
14. Sickness benefits or allowances.
15. Freedom to discuss any item of interest with management.
16. Company stores.
17. Social security and other compensations.

 17.1 Unemployment compensations.

 17.2 Pensions and annuities.

 17.3 Compensation for employees injured while on duty.

18. Collective bargaining.

 18.1 Recognition of employees' rights to join any union of their choice.

 18.2 Recognition of a particular bargaining agency or agencies.

 18.3 Procedure to be followed in settling grievances or the interpretation of a bargaining contract.

 18.4 The right of an individual to be heard.

19. Procedures for disseminating information regarding company policies.
20. Discipline.
21. Garnishments.

**Factors to be considered in formulating and interpreting personnel policies.** Personnel policies should be stable yet should possess sufficient flexibility to meet changing conditions. Stable personnel policies tend to dispel uncertainty and foster a feeling of security among employees. Policies are naturally influenced by many factors: tradition in the particular industry, technological development, competition, social approval, the prevailing attitude of organized labor, the extent of unionism in the particular industry and community, government regulations, and the ideals of the management. As was indicated earlier, personnel policies must possess organic unity with other company policies. Organic unity tends to avoid unnecessary waste and promotes unity of action. A weakness in any of the major policies tends to weaken the effectiveness of the other policies. In order that personnel policies may function effectively, they should, in general, possess the following characteristics:

1. They should be specific as to principles but in general avoid minute details.
2. They should possess a high degree of permanency but should not be inflexible.
3. They should possess organic unity of purpose in keeping with the other policies of the organization.
4. They should recognize the fact that some workers prefer to deal with management on an individual basis rather than through an organized group.
5. They should recognize the desire of many workers for recognition as groups in many of their relationships.
6. They should recognize individual differences.
7. They should be formulated with due regard for the interests of all parties concerned—the employees, the public, the consumers, and the owners.
8. They should conform to government regulations.
9. They should provide for adequate means for becoming generally known to all interested parties.
10. They should be the result of careful analysis of all the facts available.

So far as the employee is concerned, the personnel policies of a company are revealed by the daily contacts with his immediate supervisors. The first step in making company personnel policies known is to inform the supervisors at each executive level. It is a sad situation when a worker learns of a personnel policy through his union steward before his immediate supervisor knows it. Supervisors may be informed of changed policies and kept aware of established policies by the following methods:

1. Written standard-practice procedures issued to cover company policies at the date of issue, with supplements to cover changes.
2. Standard bulletins or booklets that are issued to new employees.
3. Verbal instructions from immediate superiors.
4. Conference presided over by the senior executive of the particular group.
5. Conference conducted as a part of executive training program. Such a training program, regardless of the central theme for the particular series, may well include a consideration of company policies when new situations arise. This is especially true of new union contracts.

With many employees the supervisor's verbal communication is the most effective method of interpreting personnel policies. As a precaution these verbal communications should be verified by a written statement where there is substantial importance attached to the policy. The written-form method of disseminating company policies when supplemented by conferences to clarify details is highly recommended.

It provides permanency of record, may be used for later reference, and minimizes deviations that are certain to creep in unless great care is exercised. It also serves as a valuable means of instructing new employees and supervisors.

When the supervisory force is thoroughly indoctrinated with the company policies, the major part of informing the workers has been accomplished. As a matter of safety, however, it is wise to take additional steps to inform the workers directly through the medium of published booklets[2] setting forth rights, privileges, and responsibilities. This is the second step in making policies known to the workers. These booklets may well be distributed to the workers by their supervisors; however, it is appropriate for some representative of top management to make certain that they really do make the distribution. New employees may be informed regarding many angles of company policies by representatives of the personnel department in group meetings of the new employees. These group meetings of new employees may be called after regular working hours for that specific purpose. The employees, under the Fair Labor Standards Act, will usually be paid for the time thus spent. In one organization, a letter is sent from the office of the president over his signature, welcoming each new employee into the organization and calling his attention to company policies and opportunities.

The union contract (where there is one) usually covers many aspects of personnel policies. Where such a relationship exists, the representatives of the workers should be informed of all changes in personnel policies, even though they are more favorable to the workers than the contract signed as a result of collective bargaining. These worker representatives are jealous of their positions and frequently feel keenly that their positions as leaders are jeopardized when management does more than the representatives were able to wrest from management at the bargaining table. If management is committed to a union agreement, good personnel relations are frequently promoted by advising the representatives of the union regarding policies that affect their members.

The company paper or house organ is an excellent medium for informing employees of company policies. Special feature articles on safe practices may profitably be run in the factory paper. Explanations of vacation privileges, seniority regulations, savings and loan plans, health services, pension plans, partial or complete payment of tuition for school attendance, and other personnel policies find a ready audience when attractively presented in the factory paper.

[2] See Fig. A.3, item 19.

One progressive company has a keen sense of dramatizing its personnel policies. It has an attractive, folded one-page condensed statement that looks like a life insurance policy minus the fine print and qualifying exceptions. This same company also has an attractive booklet setting forth the principles that guide it in relation to its customers, employees, and stockholders. Published statements of personnel policies are in common use today. Their wide use is a development of the past 25 years. Some of these include nearly all the pertinent policies and practices in one booklet, and others have several booklets covering special subjects, such as safety, mutual-aid associations, insurance plans, profit sharing, etc. Each system has its advantages; however, the particular method is not half so important as the policies themselves and the wholehearted supervisory acceptance of the spirit behind the policies.

**Illustrations of personnel policies.** Many companies have done a fine job of formulating their personnel policies and publicizing them. For illustrative purposes sections of three of these companies' policies are reproduced.

**Eastman Kodak Company.** For many years Eastman Kodak Company has published a clear statement of its personnel policies. A section of this Employee's Guide Book in use as we go to press is reproduced below:

## CODE OF INDUSTRIAL RELATIONS

The following policies and principles governing relationships within the Company comprise the Code of Industrial Relations of the Eastman Kodak Company.

1. *Wages.* Wage rates are established on the basis of fairness to the individual for the work he is doing. It is the Company's intention:

1) To maintain uniform wage standards which will insure equitable wage payments throughout all divisions of the Company and, consistent with this,

2) To pay wages equal to or above those generally prevailing in the community for similar work performed under comparable conditions and requiring like responsibility, experience, effort, and skill. Constant attention is required, and is being given, to developing and maintaining this policy.

2. *Hours of Work and Special Payments.* The Company makes a continuous effort to maintain fair procedures covering both normal work hours and payment for overtime, shift work, and work under special conditions. The interests of Kodak people and general industrial practice are given careful consideration in establishing these procedures.

3. *Holidays.* Allowances are paid for time away from work in the observance of recognized holidays and special rates are paid for work on such holidays.

4. *Stability of Employment.* There are wide seasonal variations in the demand for many of the Company's products. In order to avoid, so far as possible, the effect of these seasonal variations upon stability of employment, the Company for

many years has given constant attention to the planning of its production schedules. As a result, a marked stability of employment has been achieved.

This planning program can not, of course, prevent lessened employment when business in general is bad and the demand for the products of the Company is greatly reduced.

5. *Vacations.* All Kodak people employed on a regular basis have an annual vacation with pay to provide a period of rest and relaxation.

6. *Wage Dividend.* For many years, Kodak people have received an annual lump-sum payment in addition to their wages, which is called the Wage Dividend. The Wage Dividend is not taken into account by the Company in establishing wage rates. It is paid in recognition of the contribution made by the loyal, steady, and effective efforts of Kodak people to the Company's success. Payment of the Wage Dividend in any year is dependent upon the cash dividends declared on the Company's common stock and upon special action by the directors.

7. *Pensions.* The Company provides for retirement annuities, payable each month for life after retirement, to all those who are qualified by their age and service.

8. *Group Life Insurance.* Group Life Insurance, equal to about two years' wages, is made available upon employment—the Company sharing the cost with the individual.

9. *Disability Benefits.* In case of total-and-permanent disability, the individual receives monthly payments for a period and in amounts determined by the individual's earnings and length of service. The Company pays the full cost of disability benefits after the individual has had 15 years of service, having shared the cost of these benefits with him up to that point.

10. *Sickness Allowance.* Under an established plan, Kodak people absent on account of illness are paid definite allowances based on their length of service and their earnings.

11. *Medical Insurance.* The Company makes available on a group basis, and shares the cost of, insurance plans which help to pay medical, surgical, and hospital expenses incurred by the individual and his or her dependents.

12. *Freedom of Discussion with Management.* The Company can not emphasize too strongly its desire that all Kodak people shall feel free to seek information or advice from members of management on any aspect of their relationships with the Company, or to call attention to any condition which may appear to them to be operating to their disadvantage. No individual need hesitate to do this, and his standing with the Company will not thereby be prejudiced in any way. He will find his foreman or supervisor or the plant industrial relations department (Personnel Department if at a Kodak Office) ready to talk over any of these matters and to give any assistance they can. The Company believes that most matters will be satisfactorily adjusted between the individual and the foreman or supervisor; but, if for any reason a person is not satisfied with such adjustment, he or she is and should feel completely at liberty to bring the matter to the attention of anyone in the management.

A definite and formal procedure for getting assistance in handling personal problems and complaints is available to anyone who may wish to use it.

13. *Improvements in Methods and Processes.* The continual development and introduction of new and improved methods and processes are necessary to the successful conduct of the business; and only by utilizing such improvements can the Company continue to provide stable employment at good wages. Nevertheless,

before such improvements are made, careful attention is given to any possible effect upon the individuals concerned. Through this policy, the Company adopts improved methods essential to its growth and at the same time endeavors to avoid any considerable hardship to the individual.

14. *Safety.* The Company has endeavored for years to lessen the accident hazards in its plants by the installation of safety devices, and by systematic safety instruction and supervision. Constant study is carried on at all Company locations to discover possible sources of accidents and to plan means of avoiding them. Protective clothing is supplied by the Company whenever it is deemed necessary for safety and health reasons. As a result of this intensive work and the co-operation of Kodak people, both the number and severity of accidents in the Company's plants have been kept at a very low rate.

15. *Working Conditions.* The Company makes every reasonable effort to provide and maintain pleasant and healthful working conditions.

16. *Hiring Ages.* The Company has not established any arbitrary age limit beyond which applicants will not be employed, provided they are physically and mentally able to perform the work.

Particular care is given to the placement of people under age 21, and no one under age 16 is employed for any job.

17. *Promotion.* The Company aims to provide channels of promotion and to advance Kodak people to more responsible work on the basis of their record of performance, integrity, and general ability. Insofar as practicable, promotions are made from within the organization.

18. *Reduction in Force and Re-employment.* In the event that business conditions require reduction in the force, consideration will be given to length of service, individual ability, workmanship, general records, and financial and family circumstances. The same factors will determine the recalling to work of those who have been laid off.

19. *Medical Service.* Adequate medical personnel and equipment are available in case of accident or illness at work. Special attention is given to the avoidance of health hazards and to the placement of Kodak men and women in work for which they are physically adapted.

20. *Savings Facilities.* Plans for saving (and in Rochester for financing the purchase of homes) are available through the Eastman Savings and Loan Association, a corporation organized independently of the Eastman Kodak Company and operated under the Banking Law of the State of New York.

21. *Training and Education.* The interests of both the individual and the organization depend largely on adequate training and the full development of the individual's abilities.

It is intended that everyone shall benefit from sound and adequate training both for his present work and for any future responsibilities which he may undertake. Thorough on-the-job training is provided in all cases. In the manufacturing establishments training in certain skilled trades is also provided. Outside studies of value to the individual in his work are encouraged.

22. *Suggestion System.* The Company welcomes constructive suggestions from Kodak people on all matters in connection with the business. All suggestions are impartially considered and cash awards are made for original ideas adopted and put into operation.

23. *Employee Co-operation.* The success of any company depends on satisfying the fair interests of customers, employees, and stockholders. The whole-

hearted co-operation needed to do this is expected of everyone in the organization.

*The foregoing statement will remain in effect unless changes are considered
necessary because of general economic conditions or because of changed circumstances within the company. No such change will be made except after due consideration of the mutual advantages, benefits, and responsibilities of the Company
and Kodak people. At times and in some cases, application of the principles may
be affected by government regulations.*

**Thompson Products, Inc.** In the attractively edited Employee
Handbook of Thompson Products, Inc., under the heading of *Human
Relations Policy,* the following *pledge* is given:

### OUR PLEDGE

We pledge, so long as the affairs of this company are in our hands, that the
following principles will govern our relations with members of the organization:

1. We will pay wages which will always compare favorably with prevailing
rates in the area for the occupation. Any employee or group of employees at any
time may request a wage survey to verify the fairness of the rate.

2. With friendliness, we will meet with employees from any group or department, or their proper representatives, to discuss any requested improvements in
conditions, hours, policies, or practices.

3. Any grievance will be fairly and promptly settled through steps provided
in our posted Grievance Procedure.

4. Practices with respect to paid vacations, paid holidays, overtime premiums,
recognition of length of service, retirement benefits, and general conditions such
as safety, cleanliness and employee accommodations will always compare favorably with good community practices.

5. We will devote our best efforts and thinking to the building of a growing
business within which will prevail an atmosphere of friendship and harmony with
steady jobs and opportunity for all.

**Western Electric Company.** The famous Hawthorne Plant of
Western Electric, where the well-known *Hawthorne Experiment* was
conducted, has for many years had its "Ten Commandments" setting
forth for its supervisors their employee relations policies as follows:[3]

It is the policy—
   I. *To pay all employees adequately for services rendered.*
   When the individual records of all employees are reviewed periodically, it
   is your duty to see that their rates of pay are adjusted fairly. Compensation should be based upon ability, responsibility, length of service and
   capacity for growth, giving due consideration to cost of living, general
   business conditions and wages paid by other concerns in the same territory for comparable work.

[3] This statement is not generally circulated to the employees. The statement was
first formulated in 1924.

II. *To maintain reasonable hours of work and safe working conditions.*

Special attention must be paid to conserving the well-being of employees in equipping and maintaining shops, warehouses, offices, restaurants and rest rooms and other facilities for comfort and convenience. Careful consideration must be given to hours of work, vacations, medical service and payment in case of absence.

III. *To provide continuous employment consistent with business conditions.*

In the management of the business a continuous effort must be made to provide steady work and permanent employment. When reduction in force is unavoidable, consideration should be given to retaining long-service employees. When additions are made to the force, preference should be given to former employees. Continuity of employees' service records should be guarded.

IV. *To place employees in the kind of work best suited to their abilities.*

Consideration must be given to placing each employee in the kind of work which offers opportunity for his maximum growth and usefulness. Great care should be used in assigning employees to work when they are first employed, and trial should be given on different types of work when necessary.

V. *To help each individual to progress in the Company's service.*

When vacancies occur, those already in the Company are entitled to first consideration. Every employee should understand the relation of his work to that of the Company as a whole, and there should be provision for training on the job, variety and progression of experience. Information and advice should be made available for those wishing to take advantage of outside educational opportunities.

VI. *To aid employees in times of need.*

It is necessary for you to understand fully the purpose and scope of the Employees' Benefit Fund for giving aid in times of disability due to sickness or accident, and for granting retiring allowances. You should keep informed regarding loan funds available for meeting other emergencies.

VII. *To encourage thrift.*

You are responsible for keeping your people informed and interested in the Stock Purchase Plan and other means available for encouraging thrift. Employees desiring information and counsel should be put in touch with those best qualified to advise on matters of home buying or building, use of banking facilities, insurance programs and other personal financial problems.

VIII. *To cooperate in social, athletic and other recreational activities.*

Encouragement may be given by supplying facilities, by sharing in the operating expenses of organized activities of this character, and by making better use of opportunities existing in the community.

IX. *To accord to each employee the right to discuss freely with executives any matters concerning his or her welfare or the Company's interest.*

It is your duty to establish the conviction among those whom you direct or with whom you come in contact that sympathetic and unprejudiced consideration will be given to any employee who wishes to discuss with you and with Company executives matters of his or her welfare or the Company's interest.

X. *To carry on the daily work in a spirit of friendliness.*

As the Company grows it must be more human—not less so. Discipline, standards and precedents become more necessary with size, but the spirit in which they are administered must be friendly as well as just. Courtesy is as important within the organization as in dealing with outsiders. Inefficiency and indifference cannot be tolerated, but the effort of supervisors must be increasingly directed at building up in every department a loyal and enthusiastic interest in the Company's work.

**Top management's attitude.** The clarity of business policies and personnel policies, whether or not they are published at all, in fact the very existence of carefully formulated policies, rests squarely on the attitudes of top management. If the basic philosophy of top management is opportunistic, there may not be any statement of policies. On the other hand, if top management has thought through its responsibilities and objectives, its policies are likely to reflect this thinking. Broadly speaking, business objectives should be to render a service or produce a product desired by the consumer in such a manner as to cover all legitimate costs and provide a reasonable return to the investors. The rendering of a service to the consumer does not exclude sound personnel relations with employees. In fact, the service is more likely to be a desirable one when personnel relations are satisfactory. Business may cover almost any economic endeavor. Whatever it is, it must meet the standard of social usefulness and so fill a social demand. Unless it does so, it will have a short life in our economic scheme.

Any program of production, manufacturing, and distribution that does not, in addition to its profits to investors and the service rendered its customers, also provide expanding opportunities for happiness in its working force is asocial in its end result. This fact must never be overlooked in any management consideration of the policies and practices of personnel.

Any failure on the part of management to observe its triple obligation—to the public, to its investors, and to its employees—must necessarily result in an ill-balanced and inherently dangerous policy of personnel administration. When management fully conceived the interdependence of these three factors, sound principles of personnel management emerged.

**Research as a basis for personnel policies.** In so far as practical considerations permit, personnel policies should emerge from a careful consideration of the facts. Of course such an item as union recognition might be dictated by the strength of the union to impose economic reprisals if recognition is refused. In such a case the fact, even though an estimate, is the prospect of loss through a strike. Of course the loss from a strike has to be offset by the constant upward demands of unions. Also the strength of unions in the community may influence the decision. If other employers are forced to pay higher rates because of union pressures, a given employer cannot hope for long to pay substantially lower wages. Of course a given employer might honestly believe that a union would assist in solving employee discontent. A research into this area would not be an easy matter, just as all research in human relationships is difficult. For instance, the nonunion employer might readily find employers in his industry who felt strongly in favor of his union relationships and another equally successful employer who accepted the union but honestly felt that its negative factors outweighed its positive advantages. Researching the results of union relationships is not a simple matter. Trial under controlled conditions is almost impossible.

Another area in which research is needed is the exit interview. Just what advantage is secured from the exit interview? Is the information received reliable and usable? How many employees have stayed with the company as the result of the exit interview? Have the results justified the cost incurred? It is immeasurably easier to ask questions of this nature than to design researches that give reasonably accurate answers to these questions. Research in human relations is difficult because controlled conditions are almost impossible to establish. This does not mean that causal relationships should not be sought. Scientific personnel management seeks to establish causal relationships and to evaluate personnel procedures in so far as they can be evaluated.

It is impossible to determine and carry out policies of health and safety without a knowledge of the facts with reference to the prevalence of accidents and illness and the causes. It is impossible to establish and practice policies designed to stabilize the work force without having the facts of labor turnover, both the amount and the causes. It is impossible to formulate and carry out policies having to do with absenteeism and tardiness without having the facts as to extent and reasons. The industrial concern intent upon establishing an effective personnel situation must know where its present policies or lack of policies is leading it with respect to developing sources of labor supply, selection and placement, transfer and promotion, methods of pay, methods of wage determination, training, creating incentive, health of mind and body, the release of employees, individual records and their use, and research and the application of its findings. It is natural that research should become more and more a factor in personnel administration. It is impossible to determine labor policies with fairness or to carry them into effect without having at hand, so far as possible, the facts of the situation.

Unfortunately, research in the field of personnel management is in its infancy in most business enterprises. Much is said about it, but relatively little is done in comparison with the need. Even the largest corporations fall far short of the possibilities in this important field. Relatively few personnel directors are trained in the techniques of personnel research. It is but natural that they would not make extensive use of a tool with which they have little familiarity. It is to be hoped that the next 10 years will witness a great development in this field.

**Summary.** Business policies are that body of principles and rules of conduct which chart the course of the enterprise in attaining its objective. They set forth the objective in usable terms. Business policies provide for controls, and the wholehearted acceptance of these policies becomes a control itself. Personnel policies comprise that body of principles and rules of conduct which governs the enterprise in its relationship with its employees. Effective personnel policies often are established in consultation with the employees themselves. Personnel policies should be in writing to ensure substantial uniformity and to give the employees the security of knowing what to expect. The success of personnel policies is determined largely by three areas of activity:

1. The success of the top management in determining labor policies wisely.

2. The success of the personnel manager in interpreting these personnel policies properly, in achieving their proper execution through the line executives, and in making the personnel division render as nearly perfect service as possible to the line executives.

3. The success of the line executives themselves, particularly the first line supervisors, in fulfilling their obligations to management and to the workers by interpreting policies wisely and interestedly and in promoting the effectiveness of their workers by dynamic leadership.

In the succeeding chapters, the procedure followed in building up a wholesome personnel situation in an industrial or commercial organization will be considered in greater detail.

CHAPTER 5

*Developing Sources of Labor Supply*

**Necessity for securing new employees.** Employees are constantly
needing to be replaced. The labor force in a medium-sized or large
organization is in a constant state of flux. The mere passage of time
causes some employees to grow older, retire, die, or become incapacitated. Replacements, additions, and reductions in a given department
take place from time to time regardless of the status of another
department. One department may be a source of labor for another one
in the plant that is expanding. Seasonal and cyclical fluctuations in
business cause a constant ebb and flow in the work force of many
companies. Certain kinds of labor turnover are unavoidable and even
beneficial, first, because they arise from reasons that are socially and
economically sound (such as marriage and promotion) and, second,
because they prevent stagnation of the work force. Business in the
United States tends to grow at least to keep pace with the growth of
the population being served. Growing businesses add employees to
their payrolls over a period of time (even though within the same
period there may be temporary seasonal or cyclical reductions). These
expansions require new men. These are not replacements; yet growth
of this kind contributes to the company's demand upon the community.
This constant flow of people into the organization creates a real need
for a reliable supply of personnel—a source of labor supply.

Expansion programs arise from several factors: (1) the normal
population growth, which requires increased goods and services to
meet the needs of the people, provided that the present standard of
living is maintained; (2) a rising standard of living, which requires
more of the same goods and services as well as the creation of new
wants to be satisfied; (3) an increase in the competitive advantage of
certain concerns, enabling them to get more of the available business
than formerly; (4) an increase in business arising from an upswing

during the recovery period of a business cycle. The number of replacements will depend largely upon the success of the employer in reducing labor turnover. During prosperous periods labor turnover is likely to be considerably higher than during slack periods. Over a period of years a labor turnover of at least 10 per cent per year is to be expected regardless of the best personnel relations. To be as low as 10 per cent would mean that each employee hired would work on an average of 10 years. As a matter of fact relatively few of them will work that long. The normal requirements for replacements necessitate the maintenance of an adequate source of labor supply.

**Securing replacements and filling new positions from present employees.** The policy of promoting from within is a policy usually preached by management and somewhat less frequently practiced. The successful promoting from within requires techniques and procedures that are somewhat complicated. The inside source of supply is the best one any company has—at least for those positions which are above the rank and file. Reliance upon this source of supply through a conscious practice of developing understudies for all executive and supervisory persons frequently causes one vacancy to result in a series of promotions. These are called "chain promotions." A certain position becomes vacant and is filled by an appointee from within the company whose former position in turn becomes vacant. This is filled in the same way, and a third position becomes vacant, ready to be filled by someone further down the line. Frequently five or six promotions are thus made possible by one vacancy (see Fig. 5.1). When such a chain has been completed, frequently it is not necessary to hire a person to fill the lowest position vacated. A readjustment or reassignment of duties will provide for the proper performance of those tasks which formerly were done by the last-promoted employee. It is well known that a condition of inflation usually exists in the lowest ranks of employees. Added employees are taken on at a time of peak load. When the peak passes, they are not laid off. When a vacancy occurs in the organization and a chain of promotions creates a vacancy in the lowest rank, the opportunity is provided for drawing in the slack, not by dismissing one of the workers, but by not hiring a new worker to fill the vacancy.

Railroads advertise a vacancy in order to give anyone within the organization the chance of obtaining the job. If two men bid for the same job, one is selected on the basis of seniority. This practice of "bidding" for vacancies is followed in individual cases of other industries. One UAW-CIO contract provides that within the department a man with the greatest seniority may have the job. The man is allowed 7 days on the job to demonstrate his ability to hold down the job. Promotion from within is the important factor in this practice, not selection by seniority. The successful application of a promotion-from-within policy requires an accurate knowledge of the capacities and interests of the individual employees throughout the organization. This knowledge cannot be gained or retained by rule-of-thumb methods. An adequate personnel procedure and proper personnel records are required. An organization obviously cannot live by feeding on itself alone. It is necessary to produce workers from outside, of course, but except in unusual cases it should not be necessary to engage workers from outside for positions above the work level.

Figure 5.1 illustrates the possibilities of a chain promotion in an office situation. The same might readily be true in a factory job, but there would be less likelihood of so many interdepartmental transfers. They would tend to be within the same department.

**Recommendations from present employees.** Present employees tend to like to recommend their friends for jobs in their company. Employees who are doing a good job tend to recommend friends who

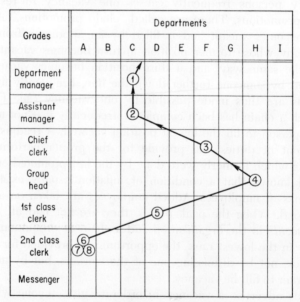

Fig. 5.1. Graph showing the possibilities of chain promotions in an office. *Department manager* (1) is promoted to official duties. *Assistant manager* (2) is promoted to the vacancy. The *assistant managership* is filled by promoting the *chief clerk* (3), whose position is filled by promoting the *group head* (4), whose position is filled by promoting the *first-class clerk* (5), whose position is filled by promoting the *second-class clerk* (6). It is found unnecessary to hire anyone to replace worker (6); her duties are absorbed by (7) and (8).

---

EMPLOYMENT DEPARTMENT:

THIS WILL INTRODUCE

_____

WHO IS INTERESTED IN OBTAINING EMPLOYMENT WITH OUR COMPANY.

RECOMMENDED BY_____

DEPT._____

---

FIG. 5.2. A sample card given to employees to give to friends as an introduction to the employment department.

will also be satisfactory workers. Some companies give their employees cards to be given to their friends to introduce them to the employment manager. The employees themselves frequently bring their friends to the employment department. This method of developing the labor supply is so obvious that it seems to require no discussion; yet many employers give little thought to it. It must be recognized that ill will may be developed during periods of unemployment when an employee recommends a friend who is not hired. Sound practice requires that the employee be told that his friend will be required to meet the rigid standards established by the firm. In some cases on the back of the card introducing the applicant some such statement as the following is printed: "It is clearly understood that this card is merely an introduction. All new employees are required to meet the standards established for each job." (See Fig. 5.2.) During periods of extreme labor shortage some companies have paid a bonus of some such amount as $5 to an employee for each new employee hired through his efforts, provided that the new employee remained for a period of 4 weeks or some other specified time.

In some companies and government institutions it is a policy not to hire relatives of present employees. Other companies advertise the fact that entire families work for them. There might be some logic in not having a relative supervise another, but it seems rather absurd to discriminate against an individual merely because he has a brother or other relative working for the company. In small communities where the company may offer the main opportunity for employment, the so-called nepotism rule may be highly undesirable, almost against the social and economic interest of the family.

**Applicants who call of their own accord at the employment office.** A company having a reputation in the community as a good place to work often has enough callers at the employment office to meet most of its needs. This is especially true in areas where the total job opportunities are not great. A careful screening of these applicants and filing of the applications of qualified applicants provide an excellent backlog of desirable employees. When vacancies are to be filled, the personnel department should consult the applications that are on file of persons generally qualified. It is highly important that these applications be properly classified, filed, and kept current.

**Former employees.** Former employees who left in good standing provide an excellent source of needed employees when the cause for their leaving has been removed. The home situation created by death or illness often is a temporary one. Department stores, offices, and factories where women are employed have found that a large proportion of former employees who left for personal reasons subsequently become available for reemployment, for rush periods even if not permanently. The employment department is in an excellent position, in the case of these former employees, to use judgment in selection. It has a record of their individual capacities and interests, not vicariously through references and outside sources of information, but directly through observation of the persons themselves on their jobs. They should be in a position to judge with considerable success the probable effectiveness of such a person in a position to be filled.

**Public schools.** High schools provide an excellent source for young people who have better than average training. Generally these young people come from middle-class and working families that form the backbone of our economy. High school graduates are especially desirable for retail establishments and office employees. Many of these young men are also willing to enter apprentice training for some of the skilled occupations. Private business schools and technical schools also provide an excellent source of labor. To be sure, such persons are usually inexperienced as far as actual business practice is concerned, but they possess the advantage of specific training that is often lacking in the casual applicant. Furthermore, the principals of such schools are more than glad to meet the employer halfway. They are coming more and more to take an active interest in placing their graduates with concerns that are advanced in their personnel outlook and desirous of employing young people capable of advancing and assuming more and more responsibility.

**Colleges and universities.** Colleges and universities are increasingly providing the potential leaders for business (see Fig. A.1, item 13)

Most of the well-known business firms have representatives who call regularly on a number of universities and colleges to interview prospective employees. They call on the placement officers even though they may not be hiring at a given time so that they can keep their contacts alive. Universities and colleges make a serious effort to provide facilities for interviewing students and to publicize these interviews. They also collect data on their students seeking employment, thus to assist the interviewers in their appraisals. Many college professors actively strive to maintain contacts with business firms who hire their students. This is especially true in the professional schools of business, engineering, pharmacy, and law. Although these business institutions frequently have certain specifications, such as a degree from an engineering college or from a school of business, it is true that the students are often hired more on the basis of personality than on the qualities necessary to meet the specifications. For example, a certain college upperclassman with a pleasing personality was presented to a number of employers seeking exclusively for technically trained men. Although this student had not taken a single technical course, he was invariably selected for employment in the various engineering industries.

**Contacts with other companies in the area.** Employment managers frequently develop a close relationship with certain other employment managers. Frequently these men have a professional outlook upon their work and are seriously interested in aiding worthy applicants or their own employees in finding jobs in case they cannot place them in their own companies. When one company has an individual worker of merit who desires promotion but for whom they have no opening, they will first notify the other companies, in order that one of the companies may, if it needs such a worker, have first call. This has become common practice in some associations of personnel management. This practice is capable of development in a way that benefits all concerned. The companies doing so win the enviable reputation of taking care of their good employees, they relieve themselves of carrying an employee on the rolls at a higher rate of pay than the occupation warrants, and they earn the confidence and good will of both their neighbor employers and the individual employees in whom they display such personal interest. In large cities there are often small subgroups of employment managers who practice the reciprocal referring of employees.

**Employment agencies.** Public employment agencies are supported by taxation and maintained by the Federal, state, or municipal governments. Private agencies, as the name indicates, are maintained by individuals for private gain. Restricted agencies are maintained by a special group and serve only the members of that group. Federal and state government agencies serve two purposes: placing applicants and shifting surplus labor from one place to another when it becomes necessary. During national emergencies public employment agencies have rendered excellent service. They have tried to continue this service in peacetime with considerable success. (See Fig. A.1, item 12.) These agencies have striven to develop professional competence. Private agencies, owing to certain practices bordering on exploitation, have not been looked upon in a favorable light by many social scientists. Private employment agencies that provide unskilled or semi-skilled workers probably have in many instances left much to be desired. On the other hand, private agencies that specialize in clerical, technical, and supervisory personnel have frequently developed a professional attitude and rendered real service. It is dangerous to generalize by classifying all private employment agencies in any one category. Restricted agencies are less common than government or privately owned ones. In several cities, for example, there are manufacturers' associations that maintain employment agencies that take applications for employment from anybody but supply the applicants only to those concerns belonging to the associations.

One basic criticism is made of large numbers of employment agencies, namely, that they are more interested in getting a good job for an applicant than in finding a good employee for an employer. From the employer's standpoint this is a severe criticism. From an ideal standpoint the employment agencies should strive to match job abilities with employers' requirements. In all too many cases the first readily available applicant is sent out for the interview, the agency being frequently more concerned with the mechanical sending of the applicants for consideration than with the selection of applicants to fit the needs of the employer. Employment agencies have an unusual opportunity for doing constructive work, but in the past this opportunity has not always been fulfilled.

**Labor unions.** Relatively speaking unions are not used extensively by employers as a source of new employees. (See Fig. A.3, item 15.) They are used in some cases where the union has a monopoly of the labor force in a given trade or business. The chief supply of workers may be through the union agent or the union employment office. Management may call upon the union to supply the needed employees and seek them elsewhere only where the union cannot provide them. The union, of course, wishes to keep the shop unionized; so every effort is made by the business agent to provide help when needed. It has been claimed that by promising a man a job if he will join the union the business agent is usually able to supply a worker for every vacancy. While the union "hiring hall," as it has been called in some places, has not found wide acceptance in business in general, it has been deeply entrenched in some places. Where it has been used, some employers have not seriously objected to it and others have accepted it only through the pressure of the union. Some employers may prefer to get their new employees through the union, thus to be relieved of most of the expense connected with recruiting. One rather large plant has no organized personnel program other than the direct relations between the line supervisors and the workers. This company relies upon the union to provide all new employees.

**Professional and trade associations.** Some of the professional groups and trade associations in cities participate in placing their members. A few of such groups maintain a roster of available personnel. In many other groups the officers of the association are in a position to make recommendations. Also in most of these groups there are outstanding members, who may or may not be officers, to whom an inquiry may be directed. Frequently college professors in the applied fields such as engineering, chemistry, and business are members of their respective groups and are valuable sources for recommendations for available personnel both from the professional groups and from present and former students. These professors are not to be confused with the regular employment offices of the colleges and universities. In addition to the foregoing groups, there are the professional management consultants, who serve their clients for a fee. Usually the management consultants do not charge the applicant (which is the custom of the employment agencies) but bill the employer for professional services when they aid in securing technical or supervisory employees.

**Advertising.** Where the employer runs a blind advertisement for technical people and supervisors, it is not unusual for his own employees to answer it. These employees may only be looking for better jobs or the large number of advertisements may cause them to think that the demand for workers is greater than it actually is. While it is recognized that advertising may tap sources not otherwise open to a given employer, generally speaking advertising is the method of securing help that should be resorted to last. The concern that has established prestige among the working population as dealing fairly with its workers in terms of compensation and opportunity for advancement and that has earned the reputation for being a good place to work should have no need, except in times of extreme labor shortages, to resort to advertising as a means of getting workers. Advertising is resorted to on an extensive scale usually during periods of tight labor supply. In large cities relatively small companies that are not well known may use advertising even during relatively slow periods of business. It is undoubtedly true that employees of good quality are secured through this channel. It is equally true that large numbers of floaters, malingerers, and others who are unfit are attracted by the advertisement in the degree to which it is made to sound attractive.

**Planning and follow-up.** Adequate records provide the basis of developing adequate sources of labor. Records are kept of former employees who may wish to return. Records are kept of promising prospects who have filed applications. Records are kept of schools and colleges that are good sources for new employees. Applications from persons who look as if they would make good employees are kept in a "prospects file." This file soon becomes worthless unless it is followed up regularly. A common practice is to send a card or a letter at stated intervals to these applicants to find out whether or not they are still desirous of being kept in mind for possible openings. These applications may be filed alphabetically or according to the job group for which the applicant has been classified. Frequently the same applicant is qualified for more than one job, which necessitates cross indexing when the file is kept on a job basis. Applications may be filed on some ready reference basis, such as the Findex system, to facilitate locating persons of special qualifications or cards of a certain age. Such a program adds materially to the effectiveness of the follow-up. Some scheme should be followed to ensure that all the applications for a given class of work are examined before selecting the desired one. If this is impractical, then it would be better to examine the oldest ones in the file first. Merely to arrange them in alphabetical sequence and start with A, proceeding until a satisfactory applicant is found, works a serious injustice to applicants whose names begin with letters near the end of the alphabet. The following example will show how absurd such a practice may become: Mr. Smithers was the friend of Mr. Watson. Watson had an application on file with a Chicago company for 6 months and had not been called when Smithers was called, and his application had been on file only 3 weeks. Needless to say, such a program bred ill will.

**Summary.** New employees are required for replacements and to meet the requirements for expansion. Replacements are required by the mere passage of time. Health problems of the workers or members of their families cause employees to move. Some employees leave for better jobs. Contractions that require layoffs may cause employees to move or get other jobs, thus not to be available when they are called back. Applicants at the employment office, schools and colleges, public and private employment agencies, friends of employees, and persons within the company at lower jobs than the vacancy are a few of the common sources used for recruiting. It is important for an employer to keep his sources of labor supply informed of his needs. This requires personal contacts and continued follow-up by correspondence. A company that acquires a reputation for being a good place to work makes the recruiting problem much easier. This phase of public relations is a continuing interest of the personnel department.

## CHAPTER 6

# The Employment Procedure

In the previous chapter the various sources of labor supply were examined. People already on the payroll were listed as a source for positions higher than the ones they currently were filling. A portion of the employment procedure may apply to them, such as another physical examination or additional tests for certain positions. Former employees were also considered as valuable sources for filling vacancies. These prospective employees often are given the full employment procedure, but their previous work records are available in addition to the new application blank. As is pointed out later in Chap. 18, Introducing the Employee to His Job, the employment procedure really starts the induction of the selected employee. The employment procedure lays the foundation for a substantial part of the entire personnel program.[1]

**The employment office.** Appropriateness is the key to the physical environment of the employment office. Elaborate furnishings are out of place in the employment office of a manufacturing enterprise. A bank or a department store may have somewhat more complete furnishings than the employment office of a manufacturing institution. In all cases, the waiting room should be clean and well ventilated, with adequate lighting facilities, drinking fountain, and comfortable places to sit down. It is frequently desirable to have a special waiting room or at least a special section in the main waiting room for women. Where large numbers are hired and a preliminary application blank is filled out prior to the interview, a table or a counter along the wall may be provided for this purpose. The interview room or rooms should be located adjacent to the main waiting room. It is highly desirable

---

[1] See National Industrial Conference Board, Inc., "Recruiting and Selecting Employees," *Studies in Personnel Policy* 144, New York, 1954, for an excellent discussion and research covering employment policies, employment interviewing, employment forms, and employment research.

that personnel records be filed in a room readily accessible to the interviewer.[2]

The applicant should be handled in a progressive manner duplicating in principle the flow of production in the shop. This program need not be impersonal. It merely facilitates a satisfactory interview, avoids confusion, and minimizes the time necessary to give each applicant a personal hearing. Where possible all backtracking is avoided. Where tests are used after a preliminary interview, the testing room may well be located in a room behind the interviewing room, accessible to the applicant without his going back to the waiting room. The medical department where the physical examination is given should be in line with the interviewing room and also accessible without going back to the waiting room. The location of the room where final records are typed, in case the interviewer does not fill these out, should be convenient to the interviewing room. A little care in locating the various sections of the employment office will save a great deal of time both for the employment staff and for the applicants and will produce a favorable impression on persons seeking employment. It is often desirable to have glass partitions in the interviewing room facing the waiting room so that persons waiting to be interviewed may see that progress is being made by others and any unnecessary mystery in connection with the interview may be avoided. The employment office should be easily reached by applicants coming in from the street. The office should also be so located, if possible, that employees may reach it without going outside the company premises. It is usually advantageous to have the employment office on the first floor; however, it may be located on the second floor when it can be easily reached from the street by a stairway.

**Personnel in the employment office.** The foregoing description of the layout of the employment office was for the relatively large company of 500 or more employees. The same functions have to be performed in the smaller employment office, but they may all be handled by one person save the physical examination. In the small company the employee may be sent to a doctor's office for the physical examination, or the doctor may come to the business establishment once or twice a week. In the very small organization, the man who does the hiring may devote a large part of his time to other duties such as production. The following functions have to be cared for in some manner: (1) establishing employment standards; (2) making initial contact with prospective employees; (3) initial interviewing; (4) testing; (5) giving physical examinations; (6) final interviewing; (7)

---

[2] See *ibid.*, "Organization of Facilities and Personnel," p. 10.

filling out necessary records and record keeping; (8) introducing the employee to his supervisor and his job; (9) following up the employee. Where the amount of work justifies the expenditure, each of these functions, with the possible exception of the last one, will be performed by one or more persons specializing in his work. It is often advantageous to have the man who hired the worker follow up his choice to see that his original judgment was sound. This keeps him in touch with shop conditions and has certain other advantages from the standpoint of the new employee. The fact that a member of the staff of the employment office may follow up a new employee does not in any manner imply that the regular supervisor is relieved of his supervisory responsibility to follow up from an operating standpoint. While the supervisor for whom the new employee is to work is not a part of the personnel of the employment office, both the supervisor and the department "sponsor" (when one is used) are tied into the employment procedure.

**Requisitions for new employees.**[3] Regardless of the size of the business the employing officer seldom hires new employees unless he has a specific request from the department needing the new employees. Of course in the very small company where the employing officer is also the department head needing the employee, no request need be made. The actual request for new employees may be made over the telephone in the case of a hurry-up emergency case. These instances should not occur very often. Even in the case of telephone requests for new employees it is good practice for the employment officer to fill out the accustomed requisition blank (see Fig. 6.1). This facilitates record keeping and serves as a reminder to hire persons meeting certain specifications. Closely related to the description of the qualifications sought in the new employee is the job specification, which should be available to the interviewer. Actually the requisition might well carry the job-specification number (where one is used), or at least it should carry the exact job-specification title. The requisition for personnel is the authority for the employment officer to provide an employee either by hiring from the outside or by transfer from within the plant. It provides considerable information and also serves as a method of control. The department needing the employee usually initiates the requisition for the employee. It should be approved by someone in authority, who checks it against the personnel budget. The requisition for help indicates the number of employees wanted, the name of the position to be filled, the grade to which the job belongs, the date needed, the rate of pay, and any other desired

[3] See *ibid.*, pp. 15–20.

## —REQUISITION FOR SALARIED EMPLOYEE—

### Separate Requisition for Each Employee

New Employee
Required by_____
Date

Position to be Filled_____ Code_____

Female ☐  Inexperienced ☐  Temporary ☐
Male ☐  Experienced ☐  Permanent ☐

Reason for Requisition—
If Replacement show name employee being replaced_____
If Addition to staff—indicate below why required—

Brief statement of duties—

List Special Qualifications

Is position non-exempt ☐
or exempt ☐

Approximate Starting Rate
based on Experience $_____

IMPORTANT—Originator must complete in detail all information requested above this line.

Department_____
Requested by_____ Approval Management_____
Date                                                            Date
Approval Dep't Head_____
Date

3 Copies Complete in Triplicate

Both ⎰Original—Employ-
require ⎱ment Dept._____
Manage-   Date Received    Name of Person Employed    Date Started
ment ⎰Duplicate—Salary
App'l ⎱Analyst_____
             Date Received    Employment Dept.    Date
Triplicate—Originating Dept.

—Use Reverse Side for Any Additional Comments—

E M D-654                    Original

Fig. 6.1. Requisition for salaried employees. (*Electromotive Division, General Motors Corporation.*)

73

### REQUISITION FOR HOURLY RATE HELP

Male ☐   Female ☐

Dept.                              Job                              Date_____

| Date needed | Starting time | Rate | Job code number | Reg. no. | Rate classification |
|---|---|---|---|---|---|
|  |  |  |  |  |  |

Replacing_____ New work ☐   Increased work ☐
Remarks_____

Approvals

Foreman_____
Supervisor_____
Superintendent_____

To be completed by the employment department

Rate progression

1 month_____   3 month_____   6 month_____

Form No. 778090   (11-55)                              (Printed in U.S.A.)

Fig. 6.2. Requisition for hourly rated workers. (*Courtesy, Frigidaire Division of General Motors.*)

data. This request should be in the hands of the employment officer when possible well in advance of the date when the employees are needed.[4] With such adequate information on the request for personnel, the employment officer can consult his files to see whether or not there are men in a lower grade for whom the vacancy would be a promotion. If there are none, he can take the necessary steps to get one from the outside. Figure 6.2 illustrates a simple form that is often used for requisitioning new employees. It may be modified to meet the requirements of the individual situation. Some requisitions have a place to indicate the number of employees of a given grade that are needed. For instance, 10 metal finishers might well be called for on one requisition. It is easily possible to construct a form where more than one class of worker is called for on one requisition. In the main, however, such a combined form is not desirable. The day-to-day requisitions for labor are ordinarily prepared in pad form with carbon so that the department head can express his needs concisely in terms acceptable to the employment manager and retain a copy for his own records.

Job specifications setting forth in considerable detail the characteristics desired of the employee aid the interviewer in hiring new men

[4] When an employee quits without notice, is discharged, etc., the request for personnel may require immediate action; otherwise, advance notice to the employment office may reasonably be expected.

from the outside and are also valuable in selecting men for transfer or promotion. Of equal importance to job specifications is some plan for grading the different jobs according to relative importance, difficulty, and skills required. A proper grading of all occupations is a valuable aid in promoting and transferring employees. The construction of the job specification is discussed later in Chap. 9.

**Matching job requisitions with persons available.** If the promotion-from-within policy is to be a reality, the first place to look for persons available for a vacancy is the current work force. Qualification cards for current employees should tell the complete story of persons being considered to fill vacancies in higher job classifications. The procedure for matching the qualifications of persons being considered for promotion from within or being hired from the outside requires a careful evaluation of (1) the application blank for the new employee or the qualification card of a present employee, (2) the interview either of current employee or of new applicant, (3) checking references of new employee or the current supervisor of present employee, (4) psychological test results, and (5) results of physical examination. The physical examination may readily be given to present employees if the new position makes demands not required of the job on which the employee is working. Of course the final step requires the new supervisor to give his approval (when this is the practice) and the release by the old supervisor in the case of promotion from within.

In case there are no available persons on the payroll, the next contact to be made is former employees whose names have been removed from the payroll because of a protracted shortage in production. If there are no such persons available, the current file of applicants is consulted. The next step is to consult the many sources of supply that have been cultivated in case additional employees are required. The details of the various outside sources of supply were treated in the previous chapter.

**The employment interview.** Figure A.1, item 2, shows that the employment interview is practically in universal use. Only in most exceptional cases are workers hired without an interview. In some instances, the interview is the most cursory of contacts. This kind of interview usually goes with the "hunch" method of selection. In its extreme form, it consists merely of a few questions and their obvious answers. Such an interview is a crude affair and does not yield those facts of character, temperament, disposition, aptitude, inclination, and interest which are best ascertained indirectly, rather than as a result of direct interrogations. Interviewing that yields the desired facts is an art. It is quite impossible to codify it or to subject it to regulations.

The nature of the conversation must be adapted to the individual being interviewed and must be so directed as to bring out the desired information. The word "conversation" is used advisedly. The conference between the interviewer and the applicant is a give-and-take of information. The interviewer is only in part a judge of the merits and qualifications of the applicant. He exercises his judgment as to the degree in which the applicant possesses those capacities and interests required in the work, but he must also regard himself as an agent of the company whose responsibility is to give the applicant all the information he is entitled to with reference to the proposed work. The interviewer furthermore must be a salesman, because the company too is on trial, with the applicant as the judge. The interview is a conference between two parties. One has something to sell; the other has something to buy. The treatment the applicant receives in the employment office has much to do with his subsequent attitude toward the company. The fact that the transaction is usually a matter of vital consequence to him places upon the employing executive the responsibility for appraising the applicant with judicial thoroughness, tact, and sympathetic understanding.

The interview for transfer or promotion is similar to that for initial hiring, but the interviewer has available more information regarding the capacities and performance of the employee under consideration than in the case of a new employee.

The multiple interview and the committee interview are sometimes used to supplement the primary employment interview. The multiple interview merely means that more than one person interviews the candidate. The individual appraisals may be turned over to one person for consolidation and decision, or the interviewers may meet as a group to find a common group appraisal. They may even call the candidate before the group or committee for further questioning. In this case it becomes a committee interview. Either the multiple interview or the committee appraisal gives more than one person's view. If the persons participating in multiple or committee interviewing work for a common judgment, it may be superior to one man's judgment.

When a large number of applicants are available in the employment office, the preliminary interview is desirable both from the company standpoint and from that of the applicants seeking employment. The preliminary interview is essentially a sorting process in which prospective applicants who give promise of meeting the requirements of the institution are selected for further conference. Those whose services may not reasonably be expected to be desired are courteously so informed. The preliminary interview is all too often delegated to a beginner or even to a watchman. This is unfortunate. To perform this task adequately requires the services of a man who has keen analytical ability and the capacity to meet people easily and one whose decisions are accompanied by prestige and authority.

**Use of the application blank in the employment procedure.** In some companies a preliminary application blank is filled out by all persons whom the preliminary interviewer thinks worthy of further interviewing. This preliminary blank does not go into so much detail as the regular application blank but does provide information that aids the interviewer in determining whether or not he desires to have the applicant fill out the more comprehensive form. Frequently, the preliminary application blank is the only one filled out until after the applicant has taken the employment tests, in which event the results of the tests are indicated in code on the preliminary interview blank. It is highly advantageous for the interviewer to have in front of him as much pertinent information as possible while conducting the hiring or placement interview. Information revealed by the application blank serves as an excellent basis for opening the interview as well as for giving the applicant a chance to talk freely. Most people can speak fluently about their own experiences.

Some companies have analyzed their application blanks and developed predictive scores from certain data called for on the blanks. Application blanks provide much of the desired information needed for appraising the applicant's suitability for the vacancy. It also provides leads to the interviewer to pursue certain lines of questioning that may reveal desired information. The application blank with proper notations by the interviewer serves as an excellent basis for later reference in case there is no vacancy at the time of the initial interview. An appropriate vacancy may arise the day following the interview or months later. At that time, the interviewer must be able to summon before him for study all the facts brought out in the interview in order to consider the applicant intelligently for the position. Were the interviewer to attempt to rely upon memory for these facts, mistakes and unfair decisions would inevitably result. It is the part of the well-balanced personnel procedure to supply the ways and means for preserving these facts intelligibly. These records become that effective source of labor which we have been previously discussing.

**Checking references.** Figure A.1, item 6, reveals the popularity of written references. Written references were found not to be so commonly used in the 1957 survey[5] as they were in the 1930 survey. Al-

[5] See App. A.

though a frank, precise statement of a former employer is of value, there are many factors that tend to cancel the value of such an expression of opinion. Perhaps the former employer, for example, formed a misconception of the qualities of the individual and even dismissed him for unsound reasons, or perhaps the employer's recollections are faulty. Even with adequate personnel records at hand he may make a faulty interpretation of the entries some time later. Still another factor, perhaps the most important, is that, no matter what is the form of the letter of inquiry, it is likely to receive little careful attention. A less obvious, but equally important, contributary factor is the human desire of the former employer not to give the applicant a "black eye," no matter how unsatisfactory his previous service may have been. An employer with the most honest intentions may purposely withhold the exact facts through a natural desire not to stand in the applicant's way in his proper desire to secure another job. A cooperative relationship between employment managers frequently is more effective than any amount of formal filling out of inquiries regarding a particular applicant. Often information will be revealed in personal conversation that will not be placed in writing. Some companies have found the telephone reference check more valuable than the written request (see Fig. 6.3).

In spite of the limited value of written references they do have merit in establishing work experience. The form used by the Staley Manufacturing Company is an illustration of the type of inquiry often sent to former employers (see Fig. 6.4). Some forms used for this purpose provide a place for the applicant's signature before which he states his willingness to have the employer reveal any information that he possesses. Often forms have a series of items after which the former employer may indicate his appraisal of the applicant by checking in appropriate places.

**Psychological tests.** Figure A.2 shows the increasing popularity of psychological tests from 1930 to 1957, together with the use of various kinds of tests. Tests designed to measure mental alertness, special aptitude, achievement, physical dexterity, etc., are used by an increasing number of employment officers as an aid in the selection of prospective employees.[6] These tests are by no means the sole method of selection. They supplement the other devices rather than replace them. They serve as a means of sorting and are more valuable in re-

---

[6] See National Industrial Conference Board, Inc., "The Use of Tests in Employment and Promotion," "Personnel Activities in American Business," and "Experience with Psychological Tests," *Studies in Personnel Policy* 14, 86, 92, **145**, New York, for other studies of the use of psychological tests.

jecting those who may not reasonably be expected to succeed than in predicting the degree of success if the applicant passes the minimum requirements of the particular test. During periods of labor shortage, tests are valuable in placing the available employees in the most suitable jobs even though the extreme shortage may necessitate the hiring of practically everyone who will work. A high score does not necessarily mean that the applicant will be superior in performance. There are too many other influences that have a bearing upon ultimate success. On the other hand, the failure to meet the minimum,

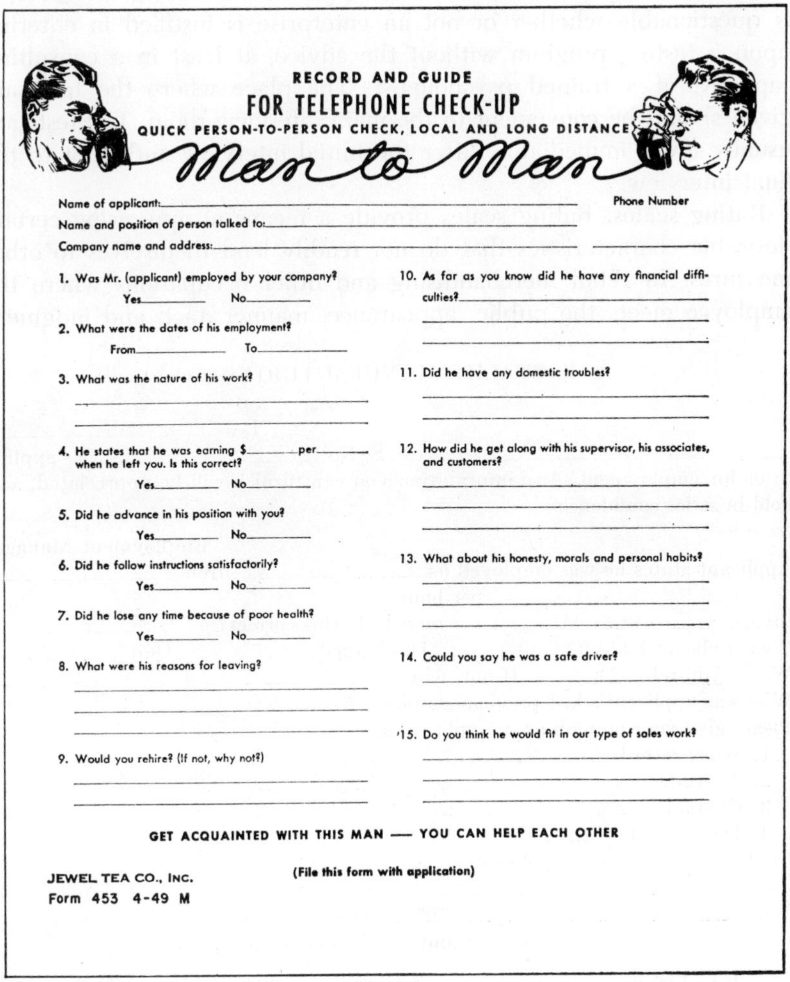

RECORD AND GUIDE
FOR TELEPHONE CHECK-UP
QUICK PERSON-TO-PERSON CHECK, LOCAL AND LONG DISTANCE
Man to Man

Name of applicant:__________ Phone Number
Name and position of person talked to:__________
Company name and address:__________

1. Was Mr. (applicant) employed by your company? Yes____ No____
2. What were the dates of his employment? From____ To____
3. What was the nature of his work?
4. He states that he was earning $____ per____ when he left you. Is this correct? Yes____ No____
5. Did he advance in his position with you? Yes____ No____
6. Did he follow instructions satisfactorily? Yes____ No____
7. Did he lose any time because of poor health? Yes____ No____
8. What were his reasons for leaving?
9. Would you rehire? (If not, why not?)
10. As far as you know did he have any financial difficulties?
11. Did he have any domestic troubles?
12. How did he get along with his supervisor, his associates, and customers?
13. What about his honesty, morals and personal habits?
14. Could you say he was a safe driver?
15. Do you think he would fit in our type of sales work?

GET ACQUAINTED WITH THIS MAN — YOU CAN HELP EACH OTHER

(File this form with application)

JEWEL TEA CO., INC.
Form 453 4-49 M

FIG. 6.3. Form used by the Jewel Tea Company in telephone checkup on applicant.

or "critical," score is fairly indicative that the applicant will not be able to measure up to the minimum requirements. Because of the time factor involved in giving achievement tests under competitive conditions, this type of test has not been widely used other than for office positions.

Considerable work has been done in an effort to measure aptitudes. This has met with a fair measure of success, and such tests have been designed so that they can be administered without too complicated equipment. Some tests have been standardized to the extent that they can be given by persons other than specialists in testing; however, it is questionable whether or not an enterprise is justified in entering upon a testing program without the advice, at least in a consulting capacity, of a trained psychologist. The place where the tests are given should be convenient to the main interview room. The tests are usually given immediately after the initial interview and prior to the final interview.

**Rating scales.** Rating scales provide a means of appraising certain desirable characteristics that do not readily lend themselves to other measures. In retail merchandising and other occupations where the employee meets the public, appearance, manner, tact, and judgment

A. E. STALEY MANUFACTURING CO.

Date_____

_____S. S. No._____has applied to us for employment. Any information you can furnish will be appreciated, and held in strict confidence.

Employment Manager
Applicant states he was employed as_____from_____
                                     per hour
to_____at_____per month. Is this correct?_____
Was applicant laid-off?_____Discharged?_____Quit?_____
Would you rehire?_____If not, why?_____
Who was applicant's last previous employer?_____
Please give your opinion as to applicant's:
  1. Work record_____
  2. Attitude_____
  3. Character_____
  4. Dependability_____
Could you recommend applicant for_____
Comments_____
Signed_____Title_____Date_____
                     Tear off and insert in envelope

Fig. 6.4. Request for information concerning former employee. This form is attached to a self-addressed envelope to be mailed to A. E. Staley Manufacturing Company. (*Courtesy, A. E. Staley Manufacturing Company.*)

proper performance. The modern practice is to require the applicant to acquire actual positive information about his job and thus prevent any "kickback" afterward to the effect that the job had been misrepresented. Some companies ask the foreman, department sponsor, or department clerk to come to the employment office to escort the new employee to his workplace. These mature individuals strive to remove any fears the new employee may have by engaging him in conversation on the way from the employment office to the department in which he is to work.

**The employment follow-up.** Especially to workers for whom the current job is their first work experience, a follow-up interview by the

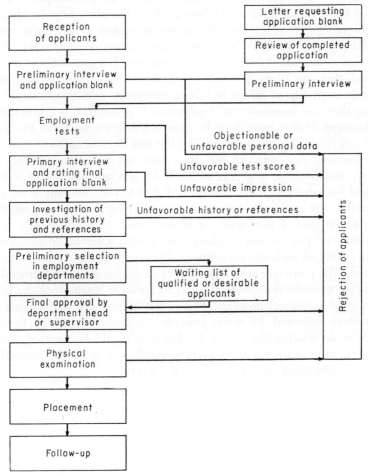

FIG. 6.6. Employment procedure. (*Adapted from Uhrbrock.*)

person who hired them is a welcome experience. It is also encouraging to persons with a wide industrial background. This plan provides for a personal interview, informal rather than formal, by a representative of the personnel department. Bewildered by his new surroundings, the new employee thinks of the personnel department as his sponsor. He recalls the interested and sympathetic attitude shown by the personnel manager, an attitude of understanding and sympathy which may be equally that of the department head or foreman, but which that executive has less opportunity to demonstrate, owing to the fact that he is faced every day with the disturbing and pressing problems of production. The informal follow-up of the new employee usually takes the form of a casual chat for a minute or two at his workplace. He is asked how he is getting along, how he likes the work, how he likes his surroundings. He is led tactfully to give utterance to any questionings or doubts that he may have entertained since starting work. Such grievances are usually imaginary or fictitious, but unless they are dispelled, they are likely to cause as much trouble as if they were real. Management cannot afford to ignore imaginary grievances merely because they are imaginary. If a grievance is justified, it is corrected by adjustment. If it is imaginary, it is corrected by explanation. Frequent contacts are highly desirable during the first days of employment.

**Summary.** The employment procedure has a lasting influence on many employees. It is a part of the induction procedure and as such should be carefully planned and carried out. The company is on trial as well as the applicant. A mutual and satisfying employment relationship is the goal of the employment procedure. It is also highly desirable to send persons not employed away with a favorable reaction to their efforts of seeking employment. Personnel work cannot be mechanized. The employer who attempts to make his personnel procedure a matter of techniques, records, and formulas is leaving out the heart of a good personnel program. Figure 6.6 graphically summarizes the procedure followed by some concerns in employing men. In case there is no waiting list, naturally this step would be omitted. When there is immediate need for factory employees, it is not unusual to omit the investigation of previous work history.

## CHAPTER 7

# The Interview as a Tool of Personnel Management

**The interview's extensive use in business.** *An interview is the purposeful exchange of ideas, the answering of questions, and communicating between two or more persons.* It is *not conversation* for the sake of conversing, a social relationship. Neither is it the exchange of ideas among a large number of people. The interview may include more than 1 person, but any attempt at exchanging ideas between 30 or 40 persons would take on the characteristics of a conference rather than an interview. The interview is used in practically every phase of business and in the professions. Certain activities require a high degree of proficiency in interviewing. Among those in areas requiring skill in interviewing are doctors, especially the psychiatrist, clinical psychologists, trial lawyers, social workers, employment managers, industrial relations managers, market analysts, salesmen, and any supervisor investigating a grievance. The interview is widely used in securing credit information, making loans, selling, adjusting complaints, diagnosing physical and mental ills, as well as in personnel administration and management. There are good interviews, mediocre interviews, and poor ones.

Interviewing is an art with some of the characteristics of a science. A careful study of satisfactory interviews discloses the factors that are common to various types. A satisfactory interview cannot be hurried by either party. On the other hand, an interview may be prolonged to the point of boredom or monotony. A capable interviewer may begin his task in the morning with a determination to do his work painstakingly and thoroughly. As noon approaches and he sees a large number of applicants still waiting for him, he becomes tempted to shorten his interview and to pass hurriedly over many salient points. For years, the interview was largely the only device used in determining whether or not to hire a prospective employee. The application blank was one of the first aids to the interview. More recently, the physical examination, psychological and trade tests, and the diagnostic interview rating chart have been added to the interview as a means of determining the fitness of an applicant for a given position. It should be noted that these are merely aids and do not supplant the employment interview. Figure A.1, item 2, shows that the employment interview is almost universally used.

**Pitfalls in interviewing.** The almost universal tendency of people to type all persons is one of the most common faults among interviewers. Interviewers tend to forget that the mere fact that an individual fits into a pattern in one characteristic is no assurance that his other interests follow a given pattern. For instance, a man may have short, stubby hands of great strength, yet be a great musician or psychologist. His hands might readily be those of a ditchdigger. As a matter of fact he might have been a successful ditchdigger had he not had an opportunity to develop his other abilities. In considering employees or prospective employees the following items should be kept in mind:

1. One individual differs from another in the personal aptitudes and special abilities that he is able to contribute to the work of his company in exchange for his salary.

2. Individuals differ in interest and motive and respond best to varying stimuli.

3. Different kinds of work require different kinds of personal abilities in the persons who are to perform them.

4. Granting equal ability, different kinds of work are done best by persons who, temperamentally, are particularly interested in them.

5. The work in each position in a company changes as time goes on; duties are added and taken away. Sometimes the change is negligible; sometimes it is great. In the measure in which it takes place, a similar change is apt to take place in the abilities and interests the work requires of the worker.

6. Environment—working conditions, supervision, relations with the employer and with fellow employees, opportunity, etc.—exercises a tremendous influence on personal efficiency and, consequently, on group production.

7. The same individual changes from day to day and from year to year in ability (both in degree and kind) and in interest.

In addition to the above considerations many persons tend to dominate the interview and do not give the interviewee a chance to reveal his feelings. Some interviewers suggest the answer by the way the question is formulated.[1]

**Types of interviews.** Most students of the interview recognize at least seven classifications of the interview in personnel administration or personnel management: (1) the preliminary employment inter-

[1] See Walter Van Dyke Bingham, Bruce Victor Moore, and John W. Gustad, *How to Interview*, 4th rev. ed., Harper & Brothers, New York, 1959, p. 16, for a penetrating discussion of this subject. This book is a classic in its field.

view; (2) the final hiring, or placement, interview; (3) the follow-up placement interview; (4) the counseling interview; (5) the routine administrative interview regarding transfer, promotion, layoff, rating, etc.; (6) the final separation interview, or the exit interview and (7) the interview concerned with fact finding and grievance adjusting. Each of these interviews has specific objectives, and the techniques are modified somewhat to attain these objectives.

*The Preliminary Employment Interview.* The preliminary interview has the distinct advantage of saving time for both the applicants and the final interviewer. It serves to sort the applicants into two groups, those concerning whom the company desires more detailed information and those in whom, for the time being at least, the company has no further interest. The preliminary interview tends to minimize unnecessary waiting by the rejected applicant and thus promotes the feeling of having been properly treated even though there was no opening available. When it is properly handled, good will is promoted in that the rejected applicants may look elsewhere the same day for employment. Where there is no preliminary application blank, the preliminary interview usually precedes the filling out of the regular application blank. Time is saved by having a preliminary application blank filled out by the applicant before the preliminary interview. This blank contains such information as the kind of position sought, experience, whether or not the applicant has worked for the firm previously, etc. The preliminary interview should be conducted by someone who inspires confidence, who is genuinely interested in people, and whose judgment is reliable in the general "sizing up" of applicants. It is no job for an ordinary watchman or clerk. Care must be exercised lest the "weeding-out" process of the preliminary interview be too hasty and desirable workers be lost. If during the preliminary interview it appears that the company may be able to use the applicant, he is referred to the testing department (when tests are used). If the applicant is a former employee, his record is looked up so that his previous history and test record may be available to the final interviewer.

In a survey of personnel practices in department stores it was found that 77 per cent of the stores used a preliminary employment interview.[2]

*The Employment Interview.* The employment interview is by all odds the most common device used in hiring new employees (see

---

[2] See William R. Spriegel, "Personnel Practices in Department Stores, 1958," *Personnel Study* 12, Bureau of Business Research, University of Texas, Austin, Texas, 1959.

Fig. A.1, item 2). "The functions of the employment interview are: to get information, to give information, and to make a friend."[3] The tendency has been to emphasize unduly the getting of information and to neglect or to forget entirely the giving of information and the favorable relationship that should be established. An interview is not completely satisfactory that fails to give due consideration to all three functions. The long-run effect of the failure "to make a friend" may be even more costly to the company than a failure to get all the information desired. The company's reputation in the community as a good place to work is closely related to the contacts made by the employment interviewer. The employment interview should provide adequate information upon which to formulate a sound decision to hire or not to hire the applicant or to file the application for later consideration in case there is not an opening at the time. A common error in interviewing, particularly when there is a shortage of desirable applicants, is to oversell the job to the applicant. A true picture of the job and working conditions should be given the applicant. An actual visit to the department to see the job and the work environment may be a part of the employment interview. In the absence of a visit to the workplace, an actual picture of the job may be included as a part of the job description which is shown the applicant (see Fig. 7.1). When the new worker finds that the job does not correspond to the picture painted for him by the employment interviewer, he is prone to be resentful and may leave when he otherwise would not have objected to the conditions. The interview provides the first step in the training program of the new employee. Personnel policies and rights and privileges are explained for the first time. The task is not finished at the time of the hiring interview, but it should be well begun.

*The Hiring Interview.*[4] The actual hiring of the employee is merely a continuation of the employment interview just discussed, with the possible addition of another interview with the supervisor in whose department the employee is to work. In a recent survey of department store personnel practices 90 per cent of the stores had the department supervisor interview the applicant before final hiring.[5] Of course in

---

[3] W. V. Bingham, "The Three Functions of the Interview in Employment," *Management Review*, Vol. 15, No. 1, January, 1926, p. 36; see also Bingham, Moore, and Gustad, *op. cit.*, p. 97.

[4] See John Munro Fraser, "The Place of the Interview in a Selection Procedure," *Personnel*, Vol. 26, No. 6; see also Bingham, Moore, and Gustad, *op. cit.*, Chap. 5, "Interviewing Applicants for Employment," p. 97, and Newel C. Kephart, *The Employment Interview in Industry*, McGraw-Hill Book Company, Inc., New York, 1952, Chaps. 1 and 10.

[5] Spriegel, *op. cit.*

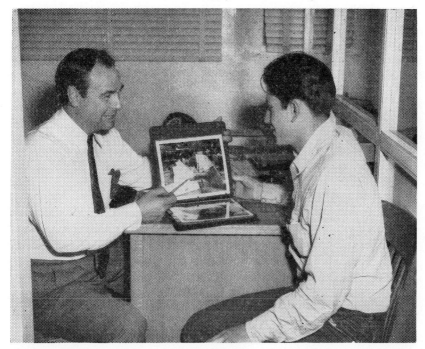

Fig. 7.1. Showing an actual picture of the job to an applicant. (*Courtesy, Ryan Aeronautical Company.*)

some cases the actual hiring may be the result of committee evaluation or multiple interviewing. This practice is seldom followed in hiring hourly rated employees, but it is often practiced in hiring executives and executive trainees from colleges. The first requirement of a satisfactory final interview is an atmosphere of friendliness. The applicant desires to sell his services, and the company is interested in securing these services either in the immediate present or at some future date. It is a dual selling relationship. The interviewer desires to sell the company's policies to the applicant. The fundamental desire should be to establish a continuing relationship that will be mutually advantageous. This can be attained only if both parties are honest with each other. The placement interviewer should have in front of him the regular application blank together with the results of all tests (where used), with the possible exception of the physical examination.[6] If the applicant has been previously employed by the company,

[6] Final placement, of course, is subject to the applicant's meeting the physical requirements of the job. The reason for giving the physical examination last is the cost involved in examining persons before there is reasonable certainty of hiring.

the record of the applicant's history will reveal items of interest in determining his fitness for reemployment. It is desirable that the final placement interview be held in private, where the applicant may feel free to answer questions and talk frankly. It is well to have men interview male applicants and women interview female applicants.

The friendly interview is designed to bring out attitudes, experiences, interests, capacities, and other personal facts that are not easily made a matter of record. The interviewer appraises the applicant in the light not only of the tests but also of other data on the application

JEWEL TEA CO., INC.
HOME SHOPPING SERVICE

*Interviewer's Evaluation of Applicant*

Date _____

_____ Applicant's Name

### Education

Does applicant's education meet our general requirements?_____
If no, explain why this should be disregarded._____

Does applicant's education suggest that he might develop with us?_____
How?_____

### Work History

How could this background be useful to us?_____

What evidences do you see which indicate how successful he has been in selling or other public contact experiences?_____

What is your impression of his reasons for leaving other employment?_____

Do you feel employment with us will satisfy him or will he be prone to leave?_____
Why?_____

### Test Results

| | Q | L | Tot. | Scale |
|---|---|---|---|---|
| Clerical_____ Thurstone Mental Alertness | | | | _____ |

Wonderlic "D"_____ Thurstone Temperament

Fig. 7.2. Front page of interviewer's appraisal form used by the Jewel Tea Company.

blank. It is not unusual for the interviewer to make use of a diagnostic interview rating chart or check list to aid him in summarizing the result of the interview. Figure 7.2 shows one page of a two-page interviewer's appraisal form for applicants, used by the Jewel Tea Company. Whether or not a formal rating chart is used, the interviewer must rate the applicant in comparison with the mental ideal of the man with whom he desires to fill a given vacancy. Provision is often made graphically or in code for recording a summarized rating on the front of the application blank. If, during the final interview, it is desired to employ the applicant, it is highly important to give him full information regarding the job. If full information is given the applicant and he accepts employment, it is reasonable to assume that he will be a friend. As a matter of fact, good will is a by-product of agreeable association rather than a thing to be secured as a direct end in itself. In case the applicant is rejected, he will usually bear no ill will, provided that he has been given due consideration and has not been hastily dismissed.

*The follow-up interview.* The follow-up interview may be conducted by the line supervisor as well as by a representative of the personnel department. In fact it should be conducted by both parties, each from his own point of view and responsibility. In this chapter our primary interest is with the personnel representative's follow-up interview. It may be well, for instance, for a representative of the personnel department to have a chat with the employee during the afternoon of his first day at work. This may send him home after his first day's work in a satisfied frame of mind; otherwise he might have a doubtful report to make to his family. No matter how effective the employment process has been, there is much information regarding the *capacities* and *interests* of the new worker that is not yet recorded. This information will be revealed as there is increased opportunity to observe the worker in his work. Such observation must be conscious and well planned. The representative of the personnel department must have it in mind as he interviews the new employee on his follow-up rounds. The new employee often talks more freely in the follow-up interview than he did before he was hired. Furthermore, the worker will have had an opportunity to observe his work and his working environment, and he may express certain distinct reactions to them that will throw further light on his *capacities* and *interests*. The follow-up technique may also yield important information concerning the *capacities* and *interests* of workers with considerable service by virtue of the fact that they have had opportunity to change and develop in capacities and interests since their initial

interviews in the employment department. Management will fall woefully short of its objectives if it thinks of the employee in terms of the
*capacities* and *interests* that he demonstrated upon being hired. In
earlier days, the intimate relationship between the employer and
employee permitted the employer to know the employee's progress
and self-development. Today management must obtain this information through conscious effort. The information as to the changed and
developed capacities and interests of the workers is recorded in the
personnel department.

The job specification may also be checked during the follow-up
interview with the new employee on the job. The job specification
that is correct today may be far from correct later on. It is essential
for the personnel department to recognize the necessity of checking
the job specification periodically to ensure its continued accuracy.
This can be done through a detailed plan that has nothing to do with
the interview follow-up. But such a procedure can be supplemented
and even replaced by a plan of interview that, in addition to serving
the purposes outlined above, will reveal changes that have taken place
in the duties and responsibilities of the various positions. It is advisable, consequently, for the interviewer to have during such interviews not only the qualification card of the individual showing his
ratings and his other *capacities* and *interests* but the job specification
as well. He is then in a position to ask the employee to read the job
specification and to tell whether or not at this time it offers a correct
picture of what he has to do. While the early follow-up contacts with
new employees can be made best on the job, it is undoubtedly good
practice in the case of employees older in service to invite them to a
regular "sit-down chat" in the employment manager's office or in
one of the interviewing rooms. This relieves the individual from the
possible embarrassment arising from the presence of his fellow
employees. It creates an atmosphere of friendliness and confidence.
The employee should be encouraged to speak freely and should be
protected by the assurance that what he says will be regarded as
confidential. The follow-up interview often furnishes information as
to working conditions and as to the mental attitude of the workers that
may have escaped the vigilance of the foremen. Unfortunately the
average employee refrains from coming to his chief with complaints
and suggestions. Many executives unconsciously assume a manner
that does not invite this kind of comment. The employees, sensing
this, hesitate to come forward with facts and fancies that might
be of great value to the executive in improving certain conditions within his department. A skilled employment interviewer

usually can inspire confidence and get the employee to unburden himself of any fancied or real grievances that he may be harboring. The personnel manager is often aware of unwholesome facts and conditions prevailing in certain departments that are not apparent to the department heads themselves.[7]

*The counseling interview.*[8] The Western Electric Company, Hawthorne Plant, Chicago, pioneered the nondirected interview. It was the outgrowth of several years of painstaking research. As originally conceived, an interviewer was assigned to a given department or area within the plant. He was not in any way responsible for production, hiring, layoffs, discipline, or any other administrative or managerial function of a routine nature. His sole function was to acquaint himself with the employees with whom he was to work, to keep the necessary records of his interviews to aid him in his work, and to enable him to pursue researches in the effectiveness of the program. He could interview an employee on his own initiative, at the suggestion of the supervisor or on the initiative of the worker. The technique underwent changes as the program progressed. This plan has been copied, with modifications to suit the needs of an individual company, by a number of companies. It was especially a popular technique during the pressures of the war efforts in World War II and the Korean conflict. The average employment interviewer is not equipped either by training or by experience to serve effectively in the capacity of an industrial counselor. By its very nature this program is somewhat expensive; yet its results, if they even partly equal the expectations of its advocates, are well worth the expenditure. Such a program does not take the place of other well-organized personnel procedures. In fact, this program should not be undertaken

---

[7] For fear this discussion may appear too idealistic and not capable of practical application, a word of warning should be given. It is not always easy for some employment interviewers to distinguish between legitimate complaints of workers and the prattlings of the chronic "kicker." Almost every organization has its problem workers who may perform their tasks satisfactorily but are constantly complaining about something. It is seldom that the ordinary employment interviewer is equipped by training and temperament to handle these personality problems. These will be discussed again under the heading of The Counseling Interview.

[8] See Carl R. Rogers, *Counseling and Psychotherapy*, Houghton Mifflin Company, Boston, 1942, Chap. 5; William J. Dickson, "Understanding and Training Employees," American Management Association, *Personnel Series* 35, pp. 4–18; Elton Mayo, *The Human Problems in American Industry*, The Macmillan Company, New York, 1933, pp. 55–98; F. J. Roethlisberger, William J. Dickson, and Harold A. Wright, *Management and the Worker*, Harvard University Press, Cambridge, Mass., 1939, pp. 185–376; see also a more recent publication, *Hawthorne Revisited* by Henry A. Landsburger, Cornell University, Ithaca, N.Y., 1958; and Bingham, Moore, and Gustad, *op. cit.*, Chaps. 11–13, on the counseling interview.

until other sound procedures have been adopted and are functioning effectively. In summary, it may be described as follows:[9]

1. Interviewer's attitude.
   1.1 One of interest and sympathetic curiosity.
   1.2 Quite as much interested in interviewing satisfied employees as those who are dissatisfied.
   1.3 An employee's interpretation of his own personal situation can be changed only by an internal or psychological change within the employee.
   1.4 An employee will take the necessary steps to correct a situation when he has clarified his thinking by talking over his problem in detail with the interviewer. This employee will initiate his own action and assume the responsibility for his acts.
   1.5 Any action initiated by the employee will tend to relate him to other people in the situation in question.
   1.6 The supervisor's relationship with his employees will be strengthened rather than weakened by the interviewing process.
2. Methods used.
   2.1 The employee is put at ease by the general surroundings and attitude of the interviewer.
   2.2 Strict confidence is guaranteed the employee in reference to anything he may say.
   2.3 The employee is encouraged to talk freely and to continue to talk until he is talked out.
   2.4 The employee is never interrupted while he is talking.
   2.5 The interviewer never argues with the employee or gives him advice.
   2.6 The interviewer strives to discover how the employee thinks and feels and why.

A few unions have developed an extensive counseling program for their members. By rendering a service to its employees, the company expects to avoid many of the pitfalls of discontented workmen, to improve plant morale, and to have a lower unit cost of production in the long run. It is a long-run program and not one the immediate returns of which are always demonstrable.

*Routine personnel interviews.*[10] The performance of the various personnel functions calls for innumerable interviews. Wage advances, transfers, promotions, special vacations without pay, and other situations that arise require a mutual agreement that can often be handled best by a personal conference. The plant supervisor conducts many of these interviews. Others are handled by the representative of the personnel department. The same fundamentals apply to this type of interview as to interviews in general. They must not be rushed.

[9] Dickson, *op. cit.*

[10] See Anne F. Fenlason, *Essentials of Interviewing*, Harper & Brothers, New York, 1952, Chap. 3, "Essentials of the Interviewing Method," for an interesting discussion of the interviewing process; Bingham, Moore, and Gustad, *op. cit.*, Chap. 1; Kephart, *op. cit.*, Chaps. 2, 6–9; Richard A. Fear, *The Evaluation Interview*, McGraw-Hill Book Company, Inc., New York, 1958.

The employee likes to feel that his problems are given adequate consideration even though his request may be rejected. Adequate records should be made of the agreement reached to avoid later misunderstanding. Facts should be available upon which to formulate an agreement. As a rule it is best that these facts, as far as they concern the individual employee, be made available to the employee. These interviews should be conducted by persons in authority and not by some clerk who merely keeps the records. This gives the employee a feeling that he is being considered as an individual who merits personal attention. Such interviews provide an excellent opportunity for constructive morale building within the organization.

*The merit rating, or appraisal, interview.* These interviews cannot be rushed. It takes careful preparation for each interview to get the best results. Each individual has a different situation that demands the personal attention of his supervisor. Full advantage of the merit rating program can be taken only when the results are examined carefully with the employee and he is told exactly what he has to do to raise his rating. This interview provides the supervisor an excellent opportunity to commend the employee for the good work he has done and to counsel him in constructive methods for self-improvement. The emphasis in the appraisal interview is on those items where constructive effort and improvements can be made. There may legitimately be a division of opinion as to whether or not the details of an appraisal should be made available to the employee. When this is done, supervisors tend to rate higher than the facts justify so as not to have to defend a lower rating in consultation with the employee. Such ratings are not very valuable for management's use in selecting employees or supervisors for promotion. Theoretically the supervisor should not hesitate to appraise his subordinates impersonally and show these ratings to his subordinate. In practice, even in the armed services where officer personnel are rating other officers, it simply does not work out according to theory. In spite of clear-cut definitions of the rating for the average individual the total ratings are substantially skewed to the high scores (the average being above the established average norm).

*The exit interview.*[11] Figure A.7, item 11, shows that the exit interview is used by 81 per cent of the firms participating in the 1957 survey. The popular opinion has prevailed that the exit interview will often reveal the causes of labor turnover and provide records

[11] See National Industrial Conference Board, Inc., "The Exit Interview," *Management Record*, Vol. 14, No. 9, September, 1952, pp. 337–338; see also Charles A. Drake, "The Exit Interview as a Tool of Management," *Personnel*, Vol. 18, No. 6, pp. 346–350, and "Mechanics of Exit Interview," *Personnel*, Vol. 20, No. 4, pp. 231–239.

that may be valuable later. Often an employee who is leaving of his own accord may be saved for the company. Frequently a transfer can be arranged if the employee does not like the work he is leaving. In the hands of a skilled interviewer the exit interview may yield valuable information. Careful analyses of reasons given by persons at the time of the exit interview, with the answers given by these same persons to an independent investigator some weeks later, cast some doubt on the reliability of the answers given originally. Some employees who have decided to quit will give almost any reasonable explanation for the decision to quit. They are not interested in the interview and want to get it over with as soon as possible.[12]

Figure 7.3 shows a form used by the American Mutual Liability Insurance Company. Such records should become a permanent part of the employee's file for future reference in case of rehiring. In the case of persons discharged, it is desirable to make a record of the reason for the discharge and to inform the employee concerning the exact reason for the action taken. The National Labor-Management Relations Act made it imperative that this cause be one that can in no way be construed as being related to the discharged employee's union membership. It is very important to give the employee a written statement of the reason for the discharge and to have him sign this statement, the carbon copy of which is made a matter of permanent record. Management, by making such a record, is in a better position to justify its action should it later be required to do so by the National Labor Relations Board.[13]

**Improving the interview.** Since the initial hiring of new employees sets the tone of the personnel of the future, the burden on the employment interviewer is a great one. The interviewer should possess a pleasing personality, tact, and the capacity to give and secure information. An employee, once selected, soon acquires certain rights that become extremely embarrassing to the company in case a mistake has been made. Seniority rights make careful selection doubly important. An employee hired during the early period of an expanding program may not at the time be so marginal as to be discharged before he attains a permanent status, but his nearness to the marginal state may saddle the company with an employee who in the long

[12] This survey was made the basis of an unpublished doctoral thesis by James Estes. Three different companies were studied. In each case the answers given at the time of the exit interview were checked against the answers given later to the investigator. In two of the companies the exit interviews checked reasonably closely with the later responses, while in the third company the exit interviews differed substantially from the reasons given later.

[13] See William Girdner, "Procedures in Discharges," *Personnel*, Vol. 14, No. 3, pp. 118–121.

run is not desired. One of the functions of the final employment interview is to avoid the selection of applicants on whom initial training expenses will be expended, only to discover that an error was made at the time of hiring. Possibly the best method of improving the interview technique is to have a series of records made of the actual interviews and analyze the defects. A stenographer in an adjacent room with a window open or by use of telephones can take

---

American Mutual Liability Insurance Company

| FOR PROMPT PROCESSING OF CHANGES IN PAYROLL RECORDS, SUBMIT SALARY ACTIONS PRIOR TO THE APPLICABLE CUT-OFF DATE. | **PERSONNEL RECOMMENDATION**<br>Form 0433 | DISPOSITION OF COPIES<br>ORIGINAL—PERSONNEL OFFICE<br>1st COPY—APPROVING SUPERVISOR<br>2nd COPY—INITIATING SUPERVISOR |

*To assure correct entries and prompt handling, reference to the accompanying instructions and to the salary administration provisions should be made, prior to executing this form.*

| FOR H. O. PERSONNEL USE ONLY | | |
|---|---|---|
| RECEIVED | | |
| REGISTERED | | |
| ENTERED | | |
| | AUDIT | |
| FILE | | |

INDIVIDUAL IDENTIFICATION:

Mr. ☐
Mrs. ☐
(1) Miss ☒ ....Christine Lee............................    (2) Company ........American Mutual..............

(3) Department ...Administration....................    (4) Division ...........Home...........................

(5) Sub-Division ......Service..........................    (6) Location ............Wakefield, Mass................

(7) Position — Title and Grade ...Control Clerk - Grade 5..............................

A. NATURE OF ACTION:

............1. Acceptance of resignation...........................

Effective ..1. 5-15-60 | Close of business | Start of business
(Date)

B. REASON FOR REQUEST:

............1. Change of personal status: Miss Lee is being married and is moving to............

............Denver, Colorado..............

C. REMARKS: (See reverse side for safe driving confirmation — new technical employments)

............Employed May 1, 1950. Recommend payment of 10 basic vacation days and 5 service days.

............All Company property accounted for. Would re-employ. - Very capable and conscientious............

............person. Exceptional ability in working with figures. Produces high quantity of work with

............accuracy. Well liked, attendance - excellent............

| | Signature | Position | Date |
|---|---|---|---|
| Recommended By | | | |
| 1st Approval | | | |
| 2nd Approval | | | |

form 0433 rev. 310F 6-58

FIG. 7.3. Form used by the American Mutual Liability Insurance Company in the exit interview. In this record Miss Lee is leaving the city.

a verbatim report of the interview. A recognition of the defects sug, gests the cure.[14]

There are many defects in interviewing that are self-evident even to the interviewer when they are called to his attention. Unless an interviewer purposely strives to avoid slipping into errors by constantly evaluating his work, he may by imperceptible degrees gradually fall into bad habits. As indicated earlier, typing people is one of the common errors. Common defects in employment interviews that have been recorded and studied are found to be:[15]

1. Interviewers have difficulty in establishing rapport with the applicants.
2. Interviewers do not have a clearly defined technique developed but tend to flounder, looking for a clue or opening.
3. Questions are not carefully formulated to elicit from the applicant freely and fully the desired information.
4. Many interviewers do too much of the talking in an attempt to put the applicant at ease.
5. Many interviewers lack skill in bringing the interview to a close.

With purposeful effort under guidance most normal persons can learn to interview effectively. Successful interviewing is both an art and a science.[16] The beginner should learn this pattern so thoroughly that he follows it without any appearance of formalism. By knowing it thoroughly he can deviate as the occasion requires without overlooking some important item. By no means should the pattern be followed in a stereotyped fashion. There is ample room for the exertion of the interviewer's personality and the recognition of individual differences of applicants while following a general pattern. The advantages claimed for the standardized interview are:[17]

[14] The applicant might hesitate to speak freely if he knew that his interview was being recorded. Since it is not the applicant but the interviewer whose performance is the primary object of the recording, the method of making the recording need not be made known to the applicant. An open window that is as high as the applicant's head and that of the stenographer in an adjacent room makes possible the recording by a secretary without disturbing the applicant.

[15] See Richard S. Uhrbrock, "Analysis of Employment Interviews," *Personnel Journal*, Vol. 12, No. 2, pp. 98–101.

[16] See Marvin J. D'Arcangelo, "General Semantics: A Tool for Improving the Employment Interview," *Personnel*, Vol. 29, No. 1; E. F. Wonderlic, "Improving Interview Techniques," *Personnel*, Vol. 18, No. 4; see also Robert N. McMurry, "Validating the Patterned Interview," *Personnel*, Vol. 23, No. 4, pp. 263–272; see also Robert L. Kahn and C. F. Connel, *The Dynamics of Interviewing*, John Wiley & Sons, Inc., New York, 1957, Chap. 9, "Learning to Interview"; Fear, *op. cit.*, Chap. 3, "How to Become a Good Interviewer"; and Bingham, Moore, and Gustad, *op. cit.*, Chap. 4, "Selection and Training of Interviewers."

[17] See American Management Association, "Manual of Employment Interviewing," *Research Report* 9, 1946, p. 52.

1. The forms cover all significant aspects of the applicant's background, leading the interviewer to consider the whole individual.

2. Information secured during the interview is recorded, providing a permanent record. The interviewer is encouraged to exercise greater care in collecting and recording his data, in formulating his conclusions, and in furnishing objective support for his judgments.

3. Economy of time is effected by their use.

4. Since the forms can be used to advantage only when written job specifications are available, companies are led to compile such specifications as a part of the personnel program.

5. Descriptive information accompanying the forms contains suggestive questions to guide the inexperienced interviewer and material to assist him in interpreting responses.

6. The standardized interviews promote greater uniformity in the performance of the interviewing staff and thereby provide a basis for comparing the performance of individual interviewers.

The native capacities of the interviewer in training are important. The interviewer should possess ability, experience, a balanced emotional life, and genuine interest in people. The interview is a social situation.[18] Naturally, he should possess the ability to adjust readily to social situations. Having mastered the pattern, the beginner should observe a successful interview, after which he and his instructor should engage in practice interviews, the instructor playing the part of the applicant. The next step would be for the interviewer to interview applicants under the supervision of the instructor. During the early days of the interviewer's experience, it is well for the instructor to counsel with him frequently on things of an unusual nature that may develop. Naturally, if the new interviewer is not familiar with the actual jobs for which he is hiring, he will study the job specifications and spend as much time as possible observing actual operations of the employees on jobs for which he hires. Regardless of particular techniques used in employment interviewing, there is no substitute for a complete understanding of the requirement of the jobs.

**Use of the patterned interview.** Some persons abhor any attempt to standardize any phase of human relationships. Others recognize that a certain amount of standardization will actually contribute to the recognition of individual differences and promote better human relations. This latter group does not follow the patterned interview blindly but uses it as an effective aid. Dr. Robert N. McMurry of Chicago has developed a patterned interview form (see pages 100 and 101) which he recommends that the interviewer fill out as he talks to

[18] See National Industrial Conference Board, Inc., "Recruiting and Selecting Employees," *Studies in Personnel Policy* 144, New York, 1954, pp. 47–70, "The Employment Interview and Final Evaluation."

# PATTERNED INTERVIEW FORM

<table>
<tr><td rowspan="7">S<br>U<br>M<br>M<br>A<br>R<br>Y</td><td>Rating:   ☐ 1   ☐ 2   ☐ 3   ☐ 4   Interviewer_____Date_____</td></tr>
<tr><td>Comments (List both favorable and unfavorable points)_____<br> In making final rating, be sure to consider </td></tr>
<tr><td>not only the man's ability and experience but also his stability, industry, perseverance, ability to get along with</td></tr>
<tr><td>others, loyalty, self-reliance, and leadership. Is he mature and realistic? Is he well motivated for this work? Are</td></tr>
<tr><td>his living standards, finances, his domestic situation, and the family influence favorable to this work? Does he</td></tr>
<tr><td>_____Position Considered for_____</td></tr>
<tr><td>have sufficient health and physical reserve?</td></tr>
</table>

Name_____Telephone Number_____Is it your phone____?_____
Present Address_____City_____State_____
  Will this location affect his attendance? Is this a desirable neighborhood? Does it appear consistent with income?
Date of your birth_____Age_____
Have you served in the Armed Services of the United States?   ☐ Yes,   ☐ No
(If yes) What were the dates?_____19__to_____19__
If rejected or exempted, what were the reasons?_____
Discuss military service as a job in chronological order with other jobs. Will this affect his performance on our job?
Why are you applying for this position?_____
                          Are his underlying reasons practical? Does he have a definite goal?
Are you employed now?   ☐ Yes,   ☐ No;   (If yes) how soon available?_____
                          What are relationships with present employer?
*Work History:* Last or Present Position       Dates from_____19__to_____19__
                                  If out of work—how long?
Company_____Division_____Address_____
                    Does this check with application?
How did you get this job?_____
                    Did he show self-reliance in getting this job? Stability of interests? Perseverance?
Nature of work at start_____Earnings at start_____
                    Did this work require energy and industry? Close attention? Cooperation?
How did the job change?_____Earnings at leaving_____
            Was progress made? Any indications of strong motivation?    Is this in line with what he can earn here?
What were your duties and responsibilities at time of leaving?_____
              Did he accept them? Indications of industry? Self-reliance? Perseverance? Leadership?
Superior_____Title_____How was he to work with?_____
           Was this close supervision?              Are there indications of loyalty? Hostility?
What did you especially like about the position?_____
            Has he been happy and content in his work? Indications of loyalty, ability to get along with others?
What did you especially dislike?_____
            Did he get along well with people? Is he inclined to be critical? Were his dislikes justified?
How much time have you lost from work?_____Reasons____
                Is he regular in attendance on the job? Are there other interests?
Reasons for leaving_____Why right then?_____
      Are his reasons for leaving reasonable and consistent?         Do they check with records?
Part-time jobs during this employment_____
            Does this indicate industry? Ambition? Lack of loyalty? Lack of interest in duties of position?
Of all the work which you have done, where have you been most successful?_____
            Was he interested in creative work? In work requiring activity? In work requiring detail?
Which have you enjoyed most?_____Least?_____Why?_____
            Does he enjoy doing the things he will have to do in this position?
What has your wife (family) thought of your jobs?_____
            Any indications of interference, of incompatibility? How influential are they in his progress?
How many weeks have you been unemployed in the past five years?_____
                Did conditions justify this time?
What did you do during that time?_____
            Did he use his time profitably?
_____How did you support yourself?_____
            Does he depend upon himself?
What unemployment compensation have you drawn?_____How long?_____
            Has he been inclined to depend on others? Does he actually want to be employed steadily?
In what legal actions have you been involved?_____
            Has he been sued? Has he sued others? Do the details indicate that he is hard to get along with?
Have you ever been arrested?   ☐ Yes,   ☐ No;
(If yes) what was the charge?_____What fines did you pay?_____
            Does he use good judgment? Is he responsible? Careful?
What accidents have you had?_____Dates_____

Fig. 7.4a. Selections from a four-page patterned interview form. (*Copyright* 1956 by *The Cartnell Corporation. Courtesy, Robert N. McMurry.*)

*Domestic and Social Situation*

☐ Married, ☐ Single, ☐ Widowed, ☐ Divorced;

Date of marriage_____Living with wife? ☐ Yes, ☐ No
Are he and his wife compatible?

(If no) Specify_____Dependents: Number_____Ages_____
Do dependents provide adequate motivation?

What plans do you have for your children?_____

How did you meet your wife?_____When?_____Her education?_____Her age?_____

What do you and your wife disagree about?_____How seriously?_____
Financial? Children? Social? Work? Personal?

Have you been married previously? ☐ No, ☐ Yes;

(If yes) How many times?_____Dates_____
Any indications of impulsiveness? Incompatibility?

What happened? Death? (If other than death) What were the reasons?_____
Do his domestic difficulties indicate immaturity?

(If other than married) What are your intentions regarding marriage?_____
Is he interested in settling down?

Are you engaged?_____To what extent are you dating?_____
Any indications of lack of maturity? Pleasure-mindedness?

What group meetings do you attend?_____Officer?_____
Are his interests stable? Does he like to associate with people?     Is he a leader?

What do you do for recreation?_____
Stability of interests? Does his recreation show maturity? Will his hobbies help his work? Are they group or solitary
activities?

What hobbies?_____To what extent do you and your wife entertain?_____
Does he seem socially well adjusted?

What else do you do evenings, Saturdays, and holidays?_____

When did you last have a drink?_____What was the occasion?_____

To what extent do you drink?_____
Is it part of his social life? Habitual? Excessive? Is he intolerant of others who drink?

What does your wife think about this job?_____
Will this affect his motivation?

What do you think about working evenings, Saturdays, and Sundays?_____

What types of people rub you the wrong way?_____
Is he biased? Opinionated? Sensitive?

*Family Background*

Are your father and mother living?  Father: ☐ Yes, ☐ No;  Mother: ☐ Yes, ☐ No;
Living together?_____
If living, what is age?     If deceased, what year?

Who brought you up?_____Who did the disciplining?_____
Any indication of overprotection?          Was he too restricted? Too neglected?

Occupation of your father when you were a boy?_____Income level of the family?_____
What was economic and social status of the family?

Number of brothers_____sisters_____; number older_____number younger_____Age differences_____
Was he the "baby" of the family?

What are present occupations of brothers?_____sisters?_____
Any indication of rivalry? Has he surpassed achievement of the rest of the family?

As a boy, what were your recreational activities?_____What jobs did you have?_____
Was he a normally active boy?                    Did he accept duties?

_____What did you do with your earnings?_____
Are there indications that he tried to get out of work? If he received pay did he accept financial responsibility?

What music lessons or other special training did you take as a boy?_____Hobbies?_____
Did he keep busy? Did he persevere in these activities? Did he put effort into them?

How did you spend your summer vacations while a boy?_____
Did he keep busy? Did he associate with others?

What part did you take in church activities? (Do NOT ask what church)_____
Did he take part in activities with people? Any indication of leadership?

To what other groups (sand lot, YMCA, Boy Scouts, 4-H clubs) did you belong?_____
Did he mix with others? Did he take part? Did he enjoy it?

How far did you advance in these groups?_____What offices held?_____
Did he make progress? Did he accept responsibility? Did he show leadership?

How old were you when you became fully self-supporting?_____Age at leaving home?_____
Has he wanted to support himself or has he been willing to continue as a dependent?

FIG. 7.4*b*. Selections from the patterned interview form by Robert N. McMurry. Pages 1 and 2 cover the work history. The second last position and the third last position are covered in the same detail as shown on page 100. The other positions are not so detailed. Other parts of the patterned interview not shown are concerned with the details of education, financial situation, and the health situation of the applicant and his family. (*Courtesy, Robert N. McMurry.*)

*Table 7.1    Order of Merit Ranking*\*

| Applicants | | Judges | | | | | | | Rank |
|---|---|---|---|---|---|---|---|---|---|
| Code | OSU test score | I | II | III | IV | V | VI | VII | |
| Jn | 224 | 3 | 8 | 4 | 3 | 1 | 5 | 5 | 3 |
| Wy | 219 | 10 | 9 | 9 | 7 | 6 | 11 | 9 | 10 |
| De | 208 | 9 | 7 | 5 | 4 | 8 | 8 | 4 | 8 |
| Sn | 207 | 8 | 10 | 10 | 9 | 7 | 7 | 8 | 9 |
| Pt | 205 | 1 | 2 | 1 | 1 | 5 | 1 | 2 | 1 |
| Mc | 195 | 6 | 1 | 2 | 2 | 4 | 10 | 1 | 2 |
| Le | 190 | 4 | 5 | 3 | 6 | 10 | 2 | 6 | 5 |
| Bw | 179 | 7 | 3 | 8 | 8 | 3 | 4 | 10 | 6.5 |
| Bn | 176 | 11 | 11 | 11 | 11 | 9 | 9 | 11 | 11 |
| Dy | 174 | 2 | 4 | 6 | 5 | 11 | 3 | 3 | 4 |
| Ls | 156 | 5 | 6 | 7 | 10 | 2 | 6 | 7 | 6.5 |

\* Source: *Personnel Psychology*, Vol. 1, No. 3, Autumn, 1948, p. 288.

the applicant.[19] In general his procedure is to have the applicant take any tests that may be used for applicants after he has filled out his application blank. While these tests are being taken and scored, the interviewer checks by telephone some of the data given on the application blank. With the application blank, test scores, and reference checks before him the interviewer fills out the patterned interview form while talking with the applicant. Every item on the form is not used for each applicant, particularly in the case of manual workers. It is believed that such a form when properly used and evaluated will add materially to the effectiveness of the interview. Doctors Lawshe and Satter of Purdue University have had success with their Interviewer's Rating Scale, the greater part of which is shown in Fig. 7.5 on page 104. It is evident that there should be more than one scale to cover the needs of the wide range of jobs likely to be present in a large company.

**Successful interviewing requires skill and objective data.** A number of experiments have been performed using experienced interviewers with results not too complimentary to the skills of the experienced interviewers. A more recent experiment is reported by Dr. Richard S. Uhrbrock as shown in Table 7.1. In this experiment 11 college graduates who had been preselected at three different colleges by psychological tests and preliminary interviews were each individually interviewed at the home office of the company by a vice-president,

[19] See McMurry, *op. cit.;* see also "Development of Instruments for Selecting and Placing Factory Employees," *Advanced Management,* September, 1945.

general superintendent, three division superintendents, a factory superintendent, and the director of industrial relations.[20] The student should note in particular the ranking given Dy and Mc. Similar "tryouts" have been carried on with different types of employers. In all these group tryouts, similar results have been secured:

1. There is not likely to be close agreement among judges as to who is the best applicant.

2. There is frequently fairly close agreement as to the bottom two or three candidates.

3. No judge who depends merely upon the traditional "once-over" and the interview is a good "picker."

4. Inexperienced judges are frequently not much worse than experienced judges.

These test interviews certainly point to the need for some form of objective test to supplement the interview. Psychological tests to be described in Chaps. 14 and 15 are valuable aids that cannot well be ignored by the informed personnel manager. Perhaps many personnel men are expecting too much from the interview. Instead of relying on the interview for most of the data used in deciding to hire or not hire an applicant, the interview should be the time and place where all the supporting test data, physical examination data, and previous work history (as checked by the interviewers) are summarized and evaluated and additional light brought to bear through further discussion. This kind of employment interview will long remain a supporting procedure for a most important decision. The interview will continue to be used and relied upon in spite of some of its weaknesses. In connection with the need for additional aids for the interview it might be well to consider the following:

1. Historically the interview was almost the exclusive procedure for hiring new employees. It will continue to play an important role. A brief interview will remain essential.

2. Under pressure of time the interview tends to be slighted.

3. The interview as usually handled is frequently inadequate to reveal pertinent information.

4. Individual interviewing is time-consuming when large numbers of people are being hired.

5. Individual interviewing is very expensive. It should be supported by all of the available aids and test data to get the maximum value from this expense.

6. The interview may be shortened by using certain newer procedures as aids in judging men.[21]

**The oral test and the interview.** It can scarcely be expected that an interviewer will have intimate knowledge of every occupation.

---

[20] This entire article should be read by anyone seriously interested in the personnel interview.

[21] See *Journal of Consulting Psychology*, Vol. 10, No. 2, p. 88.

## LAWSHE AND SATTER INTERVIEWER'S RATING SCALE

How does his appearance impress you?

☐ | ☐ | ☐ | ☐ | ☐

| Makes a very poor impression; slovenly, unkempt, or flashy. | Somewhat careless about clothes and appearance. | Clothes and appearance are ordinary; neither shabby nor exceptional. | Creates a better than average appearance. | Creates an excellent appearance; clothes are neat and appropriate. |

How well does he talk? Does he express himself clearly and adequately?

☐ | ☐ | ☐ | ☐ | ☐

| Very good expression and speech; forceful and effective. | Good expression; talks deliberately and fairly fluently. | Average expression; talks fairly well but not with great fluency. | Poor expression; tries to express himself but does not succeed very well. | Very poor expression; talks little and doesn't express self well. |

How sociable and friendly is he? Does he seem to be a good mixer?

☐ | ☐ | ☐ | ☐ | ☐

| Unfriendly, unsociable, or bashful. | Somewhat reserved or retiring. | Friendly but not overly expressive. | Friendly and quite expressive. | Extremely social; treats new acquaintances as if they were old friends. |

How good is his work record?

☐ | ☐ | ☐ | ☐ | ☐

| Excellent; never changed jobs unless there was a clear and good reason for the move. | Good; usually did not change jobs without good reason. | Average. Some change without reason and some with good reason. | Poor; several moves without apparent reason. | Very poor; frequent shifting of jobs. |

How much initiative is indicated by his past jobs and work experience? Has he been a "self-starter"?

☐ | ☐ | ☐ | ☐ | ☐

| Practically no initiative; has done little or nothing "on his own." | Lacking in initiative but once or twice has shown some. | About as apt to go ahead as not; performance variable. | Has considerable initiative but only when certain interests are involved. | Has a great deal of initiative; has done many things that show real desire to get ahead. |

How anxious does he seem to be to work for this company?

☐ | ☐ | ☐ | ☐ | ☐

| Extremely interested in the company; is completely "sold" on the organization. | Expresses an interest in the company and probably prefers it to some other companies. | Not excited about the company but might develop a feeling for the organization. | Somewhat indifferent; interested mostly in pay. | Very indifferent; just another job; might leave without notice. |

FIG. 7.5. Section of interviewer's rating scale by Lawshe and Satter.

Interview aids consisting of a series of well-chosen questions and desired answers covering the particular occupation for which an applicant is being interviewed have been developed as helps to the interviewer.[22] The personnel division of the Army has developed a

[22] See E. J. McCormick and N. B. Winstaly, "A Fifteen-minute Oral Trade Test," *Personnel*, Vol. 27, No. 2; also see American Management Association, "Manual of Employment Interviewing," *Research Report* 9, 1946, pp. 64–67, for an interesting discussion of oral tests. This study is an excellent treatise of the entire interviewing program.

series of questions covering practically every occupation in the Army. These questions enable an interviewer who is not an expert in many trades to select within reasonable limits men who are specialists. The job specification is another aid for the interviewer in asking pertinent questions and in informing the applicant regarding details of the particular job. Oral tests may take the form of showing the applicant pictures of a given machine and having him identify certain parts and describe their uses. Another method of testing is the use of questions pertaining to the particular trade or occupation.

**Summary.** In spite of weaknesses that have been discovered in researches involving the employment interview they are in almost universal use. It should be the objective of personnel administrators to improve the interview by making more use of objective information and data. The following items should be kept in mind by the interviewer to improve his effectiveness:

1. The interview should not be hurried.

2. In so far as possible, the interviewer should strive to conduct the interview from the viewpoint of the person being interviewed.

3. The interview is a discussion between equals.

4. Usually the interview should provide the necessary privacy.

5. The interviewer should ask only pertinent questions in such a manner that they will not be misunderstood and should avoid leading questions.

6. The interviewer should avoid asking personal questions until he has reached the stage where the applicant has met all other requirements, and then the reason for these questions should be explained.

7. The interview should be closed when the necessary information has been given and secured. The skilled interviewer keeps control of the interview even though he avoids all appearance of haste.

# CHAPTER 8

# *The Application Blank and the Qualification Card*

**Personnel records.** The larger the enterprise, the greater the need for records to assist in appraising the performance of employees and to aid in selecting the best-qualified person for transfer and promotion. Of course this statement of the need for adequate records applies to many operational phases of the company as it grows in size. The larger the company, the more management has to rely on abstractions for decision making. The source of the data for these abstractions is the records that are available. The most valuable two records of the personnel department are the application blank and the qualification card. The preliminary and regular interview application blanks are tools for assisting in selecting the best-qualified applicant for hiring. The regular interview application blank may become a part of the personnel folder and be a substantial part of the personnel record of an employee in companies that do not use the qualification card.[1]

The qualification card is the working record most frequently consulted by the supervisor and personnel director in companies that use this record. The qualification card may be complete, practically eliminating the need for preserving the application blank, or it may be largely a record of the work experience of the employee in the company. In some companies the essential data provided by the qualification card are printed on the jacket of the personnel folder in which the original documents covering changes of rates, transfers, and similar information are kept. A complete qualification card gives the important facts as to the employee's schooling and education; his previous business history; his physical qualities with respect to appearance, health, strength, etc.; his special abilities; his special interests, in so far as they can be discovered; his personal qualities (judgment, enterprise, initiative, cooperativeness, etc.); and his capacity for development

---

[1] See Fig. A.1, items 1 and 5, showing the use of the application blank and the qualification card.

and growth. The information for the qualification card is secured through various sources: the application blank, the interview, the physical examination, performance tests, the rating scale, mental-alertness tests, etc., each of which will be discussed separately in its own chapter. Instead of the qualification card some employers provide space on the application blank for the personnel record.

## THE APPLICATION BLANK

**The application blank.** The application blank seeks to reveal the more obvious information about the *capacities* and *interests* of the applicant. The application blank seldom can provide the more elusive information about shades of capacity or shades of interest which is necessary to effective placement. This more refined information can be brought forth in the carefully conducted interview. The application blank furnishes the means of starting the process of securing the needed information about the applicant. This statement applies to most application blanks; yet there are application blanks that have been so constructed that they possess real predictive value. Such application blanks have been carefully checked by statistical techniques for specific jobs and are thought to be predictive when properly interpreted and scored.[2] Some psychologists claim that they can interpret properly constructed application blanks by a "projective technique" in such a manner as to be extremely helpful in selecting certain types of employees such as salesmen.[3] Such interpretation can be achieved only by highly trained persons with a broad experience. It is not feasible for laymen.

**The preliminary application blank.** The preliminary application blank (Fig. 8.1) saves the applicant and the employing interviewer time, especially when it becomes apparent from this blank that the applicant is not suited to current vacancies or vacancies that are likely to become available in the reasonably near future. The company that uses the preliminary application blank when hiring is heavy may not use it when the intensive hiring program is over. It will be observed that many of the items appearing on the preliminary application blank also appear on regular employment blanks. This is particularly

[2] See Eileen Ahern, "Handbook of Personnel Forms and Records," American Management Association, *Research Report* 16, New York, 1950; also Marvin D. Dunnette and James Maetzold, "Use of Weighted Application Blanks in Hiring Seasonal Employees," *Journal of Applied Psychology*, Vol. 39, No. 5, 1955, pp. 308–310.

[3] See Gilmore J. Spences and Richard Worthington, "Validity of a Projective Technique in Predicting Sales Effectiveness," *Personnel Psychology*, Vol. 5, No. 2, Summer, 1952, for an interesting article describing this technique.

true of such items as identification, address, and the kind of work desired. Frequently during periods of heavy hiring a watchman gives each applicant a preliminary application blank as he enters the waiting room, or the blanks are on a table near where the applicant enters. These preliminary blanks may be filled out at tables, on chairs having writing arms, or on stands around the wall. They are then presented to the preliminary application interviewer, who appraises the applicant and refers him to the interviewer hiring for the particular class of work in which the applicant is interested or for which he seems a likely prospect. If there is no opening at the time, the preliminary application may be placed on file for further call instead of the permanent application blank. In some cases where the preliminary interviewer thinks that the applicant is a particularly likely prospect, he may refer him to the regular interviewer even though there is no

THE DAYTON POWER AND LIGHT COMPANY

PRELIMINARY EMPLOYMENT APPLICATION
(College)

Name_____Date_____

College Address_____Phone_____

Home Address_____Phone_____

Age_____Sex_____Single_____Married_____No. of Dependents_____

Health_____Physical Impairments_____

Course Taken_____Option_____

Most Interesting Subjects_____

Least Interesting Subjects_____

Most Difficult Subjects_____

Thesis Subject_____

Extra-curricular Activities_____

_____

Off-campus Activities_____

College Expenses:   Earned____%   Financed by Scholarship____%   G. I. Bill____%

Hobbies_____

List Kinds of Work Performed, Including Part-time and Temporary:_____

Military Service:   Branch_____From_____To_____

Degree Expected_____Graduation Date_____Scholastic Average_____

(Signature of Applicant)

(Complete this form if your school does not provide employers with an information sheet)

Fig. 8.1. Preliminary employment application blank of the Dayton Power and Light Company.

requisition for this particular work at the time. In such cases the interviewer may or may not have the regular application blank filled out.

**The employment interview application blank.** The applicant is usually requested to fill out the *regular application blank.* The entries in his own hand without advice or suggestion give information as to his penmanship at least, as to his clarity of understanding, and as to the degree of education he has attained. More specific information regarding the applicant's capacities and interests cannot be obtained by a blank filled out by the applicant. This calls for the services of a capable interviewer, as was pointed out more fully in our previous chapter. The fact that it is desirable to have the applicant fill out at least a part of the application blank, coupled with the inability of many persons to write legibly, is a strong argument for the qualification card, which will be discussed later.

The regular application blank may have a place for the coded score of the psychological tests that may be given before the final interview. In some cases the employment interviewer may talk with the applicant and appraise his general potential before sending him to take the psychological tests. In this event the interviewer will usually check by telephone with some of the applicant's previous employers to verify certain facts listed on the application blank. The information revealed by the application blank provides an excellent opening basis for the employment interview. If the applicant's work experience has been reasonably successful, he usually can talk freely about it. In case he has never worked before, the application blank will reveal this and the interviewer may open the interview by a reference to the applicant's interest in certain school subjects or activities.     ,

**Constructing the application blank.** Either the preliminary or the regular application blank serves two purposes, namely, (1) to provide a series of questions for the applicant to answer, and (2) to provide the interviewer with a check list as a basis for his conversation. For this reason the regular application blank should be as clear and simple typographically as possible. This is especially true of that part which the applicant fills out. It must be complete and provide for all the information needed in the proper placement of the new employee and must provide spaces for the entry of this information. The exact form of the blank will vary according to the business and the concern. There are two factors to be considered in the typography of the application blank: (1) keeping all the portion of the blank that is to be filled out by the applicant at the beginning, with a clear line of demarcation between his part and the remainder of the blank; and (2) arranging the data on the application blank in the same sequence

GN 1510 (EXP.)

**Western Electric Company**
INCORPORATED

**APPLICATION FOR EMPLOYMENT**

DATE_____19____

E. NUMBER

ARE YOU A CITIZEN OF UNITED STATES   YES ☐   NO ☐

PRINT NAME   (LAST)   (FIRST)   (MIDDLE OR MAIDEN)   MAN ☐   WOMAN ☐   SOCIAL SECURITY NUMBER

ADDRESS   (NUMBER)   (STREET)   (CITY)   (ZONE)   (STATE)   TELEPHONE NUMBER

DATE OF BIRTH   AGE   HEIGHT ___FT.___IN.   WEIGHT ___LBS.   RIGHT HANDED ☐   LEFT HANDED ☐   PHYSICAL DEFECTS

MARITAL STATUS   SINGLE ☐ MARRIED ☐ SEPARATED ☐   WIDOWED ☐ DIVORCED ☐   NUMBER OF CHILDREN   NUMBER AND RELATIONSHIP OF PERSONS SUPPORTED BY YOU   WIFE____ HUSBAND____ CHILDREN____ PARENTS____ OTHER____

KIND OF WORK DESIRED   WHAT OTHER WORK CAN YOU DO   SALARY OR WAGES EXPECTED

WERE YOU EVER AN EMPLOYEE OF:   WESTERN ELECTRIC   YES ☐ NO ☐   OTHER BELL SYSTEM   YES ☐ NO ☐   DIVISION_____ LOCATION_____ DATE_____

REASON FOR LEAVING

**SCHOOL RECORD**

| KIND | NAME OF SCHOOL AND LOCATION (CITY AND STATE) | SCHOOL YEARS COMPLETED | YEAR GRADUATED OR LEFT SCH. | COURSE TAKEN | DEGREE |
|---|---|---|---|---|---|
| GRADE | | | | XXXX | XXX |
| HIGH | | | | | XXX |
| VOCATIONAL OR BUSINESS | | | | | XXX |
| COLLEGE OR UNIVERSITY | | | | | |
| POST GRADUATE WORK | | | | | |
| ARMED FORCES SCHOOL | | | | | |
| OTHER | | | | | XXX |

SUBJECT OF SPECIALIZATION

HAVE YOU EVER BEEN ARRESTED? (OTHER THAN MINOR TRAFFIC VIOLATIONS)   YES ☐ NO ☐   GIVE DATE, PLACE, REASON

WERE YOU EVER DISCHARGED OR ASKED TO RESIGN BY A FORMER EMPLOYER?   YES ☐ NO ☐   EXPLAIN

ARE YOU RELATED TO ANY PRESENT OR FORMER EMPLOYEE OF THIS COMPANY?   YES ☐ NO ☐   NAME AND RELATIONSHIP

HAVE YOU RECEIVED A NOTICE OF INDUCTION OR ORDERS TO REPORT FOR ACTIVE DUTY IN THE ARMED FORCES?   YES ☐ NO ☐   DRAFT CLASSIFICATION_____

**APPLICANT'S BUSINESS EXPERIENCE**

| | NAME AND ADDRESS OF COMPANY | STARTING DATE | LEAVING DATE | OCCUPATION | REASON FOR LEAVING | RATE OF PAY |
|---|---|---|---|---|---|---|
| PRESENT OR LAST EMPLOYER 1. | | | | | | |
| | | | | | INQUIRY ☐ | |
| NEXT PREVIOUS EMPLOYER 2. | | | | | | |
| | | | | | INQUIRY ☐ | |
| NEXT PREVIOUS EMPLOYER 3. | | | | | | |
| | | | | | INQUIRY ☐ | |
| NEXT PREVIOUS EMPLOYER 4. | | | | | | |
| | | | | | INQUIRY ☐ | |

FIG. 8.2a. Page 1 of application blank. (*Courtesy, Western Electric Company.*)

as that on the qualification card, in order to facilitate the typing of the qualification card. At times it is impossible to reconcile these two requirements. Where there is conflict, the arrangement for convenience of the applicant should be controlling.

The American Management Association in its *Research Report* 16 suggests the following criteria in considering the appropriateness of any given item:

APPLICANT'S MILITARY EXPERIENCE

| SERVED IN ARMED FORCES OR MERCHANT MARINE | FROM | TO | MONTHS OF ACTIVE MILITARY SERVICE TOTAL _____ OVERSEAS _____ | | ARE YOU NOW A MEMBER OF: |
|---|---|---|---|---|---|

| MOST RECENT BRANCH | | | | ARMED FORCES RESERVE  YES ☐  NO ☐ |
|---|---|---|---|---|
| ARMY ☐ | NAVY ☐ | MOST RECENT GRADE _____ | | |
| MARINES ☐ | | DUTY ARM OR SERVICE _____ | | NATIONAL GUARD  ☐  ☐ |
| COAST GUARD ☐ | AIR FORCE ☐ | TYPE OF DISCHARGE _____ | | |

| HIGHEST RANK OR GRADE | PRINCIPAL DUTY | M.O.S. NUMBER |
|---|---|---|
| | | |
| | | |
| | | |

PERSONAL REFERENCES (DO NOT REFER TO RELATIVES OR FORMER EMPLOYERS)

| | NAME | BUSINESS | ADDRESS |
|---|---|---|---|
| 1. | | | |
| 2. | | | |
| 3. | | | |

I AGREE TO CONFORM TO THE COMPANY'S RULES, REGULATIONS AND INSTRUCTIONS AS MADE KNOWN TO ME AT THE TIME OF EMPLOYMENT OR ANY SUBSEQUENT TIME. I ALSO AGREE TO CONFORM TO THE COMPANY'S REQUIREMENTS CONCERNING PHYSICAL FITNESS AND TO PERMIT MEDICAL EXAMINATIONS BY THE COMPANY'S PHYSICIAN UPON REQUEST.

AS A CONDITION OF EMPLOYMENT IN CERTAIN CLASSES OF WORK, I AGREE TO EXECUTE AN AGREEMENT ASSIGNING INVENTIONS TO THE COMPANY.

I HEREBY AUTHORIZE INVESTIGATION OF ALL STATEMENTS CONTAINED IN THIS APPLICATION AND CERTIFY THAT SUCH STATEMENTS ARE TRUE AND UNDERSTAND THAT MISREPRESENTATION MAY BE CAUSE FOR SEPARATION.

I DECLARE THAT {I AM / I AM NOT} A CITIZEN OF THE UNITED STATES.
(CROSS OUT ONE)

SIGNATURE OF APPLICANT _____

DO NOT WRITE BELOW THIS LINE

CITIZEN STATUS

| BIRTH CERTIFICATE ☐ | | DERIVATIVE CITIZENSHIP CERTIFICATE ☐ | |
|---|---|---|---|
| BAPTISMAL CERTIFICATE ☐ | DATE BAPTIZED _____ | OTHER (EXPLAIN) ☐ | CHURCH OR AGENCY ISSUING _____ |
| AFFIDAVIT ☐ | | | |

NATURALIZATION CERTIFICATE ☐

| CERTIFICATE NUMBER _____ | WHERE ISSUED _____ | DATE ISSUED _____ | BIRTH DATE _____ | PLACE OF BIRTH _____ |
|---|---|---|---|---|

ALIEN REGISTRATION NUMBER _____ DATE _____ CITIZEN OF _____

LATEST ENTRY INTO U.S.A.: DATE _____ PLACE _____

VISA _____ ACTION TAKEN TO OBTAIN CITIZENSHIP: FIRST PAPERS _____ DATE _____

OTHER ACTION (EXPLAIN) _____

DOCUMENT CHECKED BY _____

TO BE FILLED IN BY DEPARTMENT ACCEPTING APPLICANT

IF APPLICANT IS TO BE EMPLOYED ENTER INFORMATION REQUIRED BELOW AND RETURN WITH APPLICANT.
IF APPLICANT IS NOT TO BE EMPLOYED RETURN APPLICATION WITH APPLICANT INDICATING REASON FOR REJECTION ON A SEPARATE SHEET.

| LOCAL DEPT. NO. | STARTING DATE | STARTING TIME | OCCUPATION DESCRIPTION | GRADE NO. _____ | RATE OF PAY _____ |
|---|---|---|---|---|---|
| OCCUP. CODE NO. | JOB SUB-TITLE NO. _____ | EXPENSE ☐ DIRECT ☐ | PATENT AGREEMENT FORMS SHOULD BE EXECUTED ☐ SHOULD NOT BE EXECUTED ☐ | IF REQUIRED SHOW DATE EXECUTED _____ | |
| TEMPORARY EMPLOYMENT ☐ REGULAR EMPLOYMENT ☐ | IF TEMPORARY GIVE EXPIRATION DATE | | TO REPORT TO _____ | SUPERVISOR _____ | LOCATION _____ |
| GATE NO. _____ | BLDG. _____ | FLOOR _____ | APPROVED BY EMPLOYMENT INTERVIEWER _____ | APPROVED BY AUTHORIZED SUPERVISOR _____ | |

TO BE FILLED IN BY EMPLOYMENT ORGANIZATION

| CHECK LIST: PHOTOGRAPHED ☐ | INQUIRIES | NEW PASS | NOTIFICATION |
|---|---|---|---|
| RATE | PERSONNEL CARD | TAB. CARD | FINAL CHECK |
| ) | | | |

FIG. 8.2*b*. Page 2 of application blank. (*Courtesy, Western Electric Company.*)

1. Is the item necessary for identifying the applicant?

2. Is it necessary for screening out those who are ineligible under the company's basic hiring policies? Specifically, what policy does it pertain to?

3. Does it help to decide whether the candidate is qualified? How?

4. Is it based on analysis of the job or jobs for which applicants will be selected?

5. Has it been pretested on the company's employees and found to correlate with success?

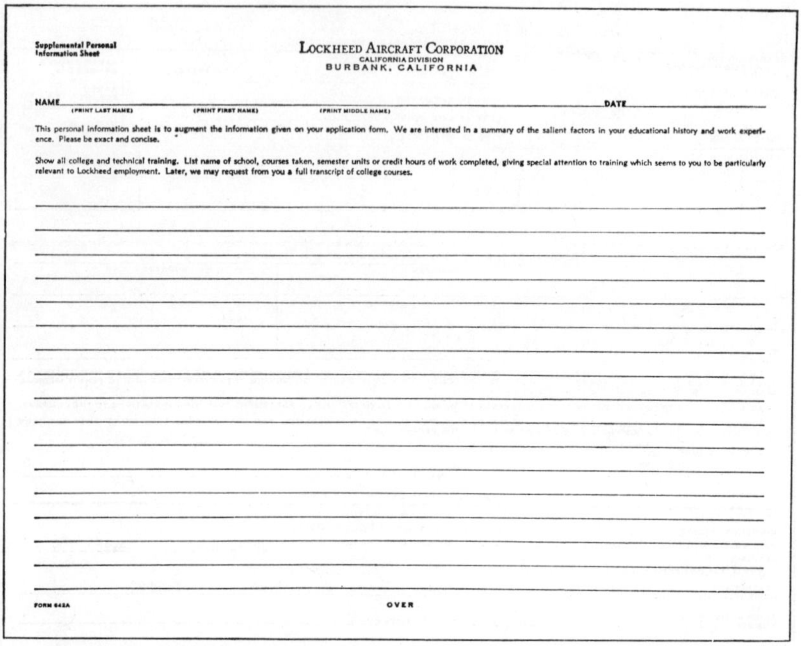

Supplemental Personal Information Sheet

LOCKHEED AIRCRAFT CORPORATION
CALIFORNIA DIVISION
BURBANK, CALIFORNIA

NAME ______ (PRINT LAST NAME) ______ (PRINT FIRST NAME) ______ (PRINT MIDDLE NAME) ______ DATE ______

This personal information sheet is to augment the information given on your application form. We are interested in a summary of the salient factors in your educational history and work experience. Please be exact and concise.

Show all college and technical training. List name of school, courses taken, semester units or credit hours of work completed, giving special attention to training which seems to you to be particularly relevant to Lockheed employment. Later, we may request from you a full transcript of college courses.

FORM 642A OVER

FIG. 8.3*a*. Supplementary personnel information sheet to accompany Lockheed's application sheet in some cases.

6. Will the information be used? How?
7. Is the application form the proper place to ask for it?
8. To what extent will answers duplicate information to be obtained at another step in the selection procedure—for example, through interviews, tests, or medical examinations?
9. Is the information needed for selection at all, or should it be obtained at induction or even later?
10. Is it probable that applicants' replies will be reliable?
11. Does the question violate any applicable Federal or state legislation?

**Use of one or more special application blanks.** The single application blank for all applicants, manual workers, technical, sales, and office simplifies the number of forms required but handicaps the interviewer in getting the specific information needed. An occasional company uses a standardized application blank for all employees but an additional sheet for technical personnel, salespersons, and office employees. This practice is to be preferred to the use of one blank for all employees. Still other companies have separate application blanks for special groups such as engineers and other professional people, salesmen, office workers, and supervisors. Such a procedure is

DO YOU HAVE ANY RELATIVES OR ACQUAINTANCES EMPLOYED BY LOCKHEED? YES ☐ NO ☐

LIST BELOW WHERE YOU HAVE LIVED FOR AT LEAST THE PAST FIVE YEARS

| FROM | | | TO | | TIME IN MONTHS | NUMBER AND STREET | CITY | STATE |
|---|---|---|---|---|---|---|---|---|
| MONTH | YEAR | | MONTH | YEAR | | | | |

FILL IN THE FOLLOWING REGARDING YOUR FAMILY

| | NAME | BIRTHPLACE (STATE OR FOREIGN COUNTRY) | CITIZEN OF WHAT (IF FOREIGN COUNTRY) | PRESENT ADDRESS (IF DECEASED, SO STATE) | EMPLOYER AND OCCUPATION |
|---|---|---|---|---|---|
| RELATIVE | | | | | |
| FATHER | | | | | |
| MOTHER | | | | | |
| HUSBAND OR MAIDEN NAME OF WIFE | | | | | |
| BROTHERS AND SISTERS | | | | | |

HAVE YOU EVER RECEIVED A SECURITY CLEARANCE? YES ☐ NO ☐ IF "YES," INDICATE WHEN GRANTED, WHERE, BY WHOM AND LEVEL OF CLEARANCE.

HAVE YOU EVER BEEN ARRESTED FOR ANY OFFENSE OTHER THAN MINOR TRAFFIC VIOLATIONS? YES ☐ NO ☐. IF YES, EXPLAIN ON A SEPARATE SHEET

PERSON TO NOTIFY IN CASE OF EMERGENCY: NAME: _____ ADDRESS: _____ TELEPHONE NO.:

DO YOU BELONG TO ANY ORGANIZATIONS YES ☐ OTHER THAN TRADE UNIONS? NO ☐ IF YES, GIVE NAME AND ADDRESS

INDICATE SHIFTS YOU ARE WILLING TO WORK ANY ☐ DAY ☐ SWING ☐ GRAVEYARD ☐

GIVE ANY OTHER NAME (INCLUDING MAIDEN NAME) BY WHICH YOU HAVE BEEN KNOWN:

HAVE YOU ANY RELATIVES OR FRIENDS YES ☐ HAVE YOU EVER BEEN OUTSIDE THE UNITED STATES, EXCEPT YES ☐ HAS IT EVER BEEN NECESSARY FOR YOU TO MAKE YES ☐ IF THE ANSWER TO ANY OF THESE QUESTIONS
LIVING IN A FOREIGN COUNTRY? NO ☐ FOR U.S. MILITARY SERVICE FOR OVER 30 DAYS? NO ☐ FREQUENT TRIPS OUTSIDE THE UNITED STATES? NO ☐ IS YES, EXPLAIN ON SEPARATE SHEET.

GIVE THREE REFERENCES NOT RELATIVES OR FORMER EMPLOYERS WHOM YOU HAVE KNOWN FOR AT LEAST THREE YEARS

| NAME | ADDRESS | TELEPHONE | OCCUPATION |
|---|---|---|---|
| | | | |

ARE YOU, OR HAVE YOU EVER BEEN A MEMBER OF ANY COMMUNIST ORGANIZATION OR POLITICAL PARTY OR ORGANIZATION WHICH ADVOCATES OR ADVOCATED THE OVERTHROW OF OUR CONSTITUTIONAL FORM OF GOVERNMENT IN THE UNITED STATES, OR DO YOU HAVE OR HAVE YOU HAD MEMBERSHIP IN OR AFFILIATION WITH ANY GROUP, ASSOCIATION OR ORGANIZATION WHICH ADVOCATES OR ADVOCATES OR ADVOCATED OR IS LENT OR LENDS SUPPORT TO ANY ORGANIZATION OR MOVEMENT ADVOCATING THE OVERTHROW OF OUR CONSTITUTIONAL FORM OF GOVERNMENT IN THE UNITED STATES.

ANSWER YES OR NO _____ IF ANSWER IS YES, NAME THE ORGANIZATION AND GIVE COMPLETE DETAILS ON SEPARATE SHEET.

I HEREBY CERTIFY THAT THE ANSWERS GIVEN BY ME TO THE FOREGOING QUESTIONS AND STATEMENTS MADE ARE TRUE AND CORRECT WITHOUT CONSEQUENTIAL OMISSIONS OF ANY KIND WHATSOEVER. I AGREE THAT THE COMPANIES SHALL NOT BE LIABLE IN ANY RESPECT IF MY EMPLOYMENT IS TERMINATED BECAUSE OF THE FALSITY OF STATEMENTS, ANSWERS OR OMISSIONS MADE BY ME IN THIS QUESTIONNAIRE. I AGREE TO SUBMIT TO PHYSICAL EXAMINATION. I ALSO AUTHORIZE THE COMPANIES, SCHOOLS OR PERSONS NAMED ABOVE TO GIVE ANY INFORMATION REGARDING MY EMPLOYMENT, TOGETHER WITH ANY INFORMATION REGARDING ME WHETHER OR NOT IT IS ON THEIR RECORDS. I HEREBY RELEASE SAID COMPANIES, SCHOOLS OR PERSONS FROM ALL LIABILITY FOR ANY DAMAGE WHATSOEVER FOR ISSUING THIS INFORMATION.

READ THE ABOVE STATEMENT AND SIGN APPLICATION HERE: _____

Fig. 8.3b. Back page of Lockheed's application blank. (Courtesy, Lockheed Aircraft Corporation.)

113

especially desirable for large companies that have a large number of people in these groups. This practice is particularly helpful where the application blank is used to take the place of the qualification card.

**Sample application blanks.**[4] Space will not permit the reproduction of samples of the various kinds of application blanks. Each company should include data that are considered pertinent to its requirements. It would be an excellent thing if all companies would carefully evaluate their application blanks and eliminate all items that are not used in appraising the applicant. This would remove many items, particularly in those cases where a qualification card is used as the permanent record. For instance, many companies have an item asking for the name of the person to be notified in case of emergency. This is wholly unnecessary on the application blank when it appears on the qualification card.

Figure 8.2 shows the application blank of Western Electric Company. This is a condensed form that seeks specific information that will assist in appraising the applicant for the job. Note the statement authorizing the company to investigate all statements made in the application blank, also the statement regarding the assigning of patents (see Fig. 8.2b). In addition to the application blank Western Electric uses a qualification card. Page 2 of Lockheed Aircraft Corporation's application blank is shown in Fig. 8.3b. Page 1 of this blank contains the traditional identification, address, personal, family, physical, and place-of-birth information, as well as education, previous work experience, military experience and status, and any special job skill or information. Page 2 (Fig. 8.3b) is especially interesting since it specifically strives to get any information that might have a bearing on the applicant's loyalty or security risk. This information is not for the purpose of identifying a minority status but solely for the protection of our national interests. Page 3 of Lockheed's application blank (Fig. 8.3a) is a supplementary sheet designed to enable the applicant to give any pertinent information that does not fit logically into the standardized form. The back of this supplementary sheet asks three questions and provides ample room for the answers, namely: (1) "Describe any work experience you have had

---

[4] For illustrative application blanks, see National Industrial Conference Board, Inc., "Employment of the College Graduate," *Studies in Personnel Policy* 152, "Recruiting and Selecting Employees," *Studies in Personnel Policy* 144, and "Personnel Forms and Records," *Research Report* 27, 87; see also American Management Association, "Handbook of Personnel Forms," *Research Report* 16, and "Recruiting and Selecting Office Employees," *Studies in Personnel Policy.*

## PERSONAL INVENTORY

1. What type of position and salary do you want to build for yourself in the future? _____

   _____ $ _____ Per Yr. _____

2. What do you feel are your strong points? _____

   _____

   Your weak points? _____

   _____

3. How do you spend your leisure time? _____

   _____

4. To what organizations do you belong? (Exclude those which are religious or may indicate race, creed or nationality.) _____

   Offices held: _____

5. What did you like best about your last job? _____

   What did you dislike? _____

6. What is (was) your father's occupation? _____

7. Do you have brothers or sisters?  ☐ Yes  ☐ No

   How often do you see them? _____

8. At what age did you become self-supporting? _____

9. Did you work part time while in school? Explain: _____

10. Do you own home? _____ Car? _____ Furniture? _____ Insurance? _____

11. Do you have any outstanding indebtedness excluding mortgage on home? Explain: _____

12. What does your wife think of sales work? _____

13. Are any of your neighbors in sales work? _____ Yes _____ No

14. What is there about yourself which you feel will contribute to success in route work with Jewel? _____

    _____

    _____

15. What salary do you feel you require? $ _____ /Wk.  Date Available _____

16. Do you have any relatives working for Jewel?

    _____ (Name) _____ (Location)

    _____ (Name) _____ (Location)

Fig. 8.4. Page 2 of the Jewel Tea Company four-page application blank. The other three pages are of the traditional type. This page is especially suited to Jewel Tea. (*Courtesy, Jewel Tea Company, Inc.*)

which relates to your field. Outline your primary duties and responsibilities, length of service in months, salary and reason for leaving. (2) Which of your previous jobs did you like best? Why? (3) What type of work do you eventually want to do? Why?"

Figure 8.4 shows the second page of the four-page application blank used by the Jewel Tea Company, Inc. Page 1 asks for personal data, marital status, name and address, and educational history. Page 3 asks for work experience according to dates and a special listing of sales experience and its nature. Page 4 asks for driving experience, supervisory experience, and leaves about 40 per cent of the page for the interviewer's checking of clerical tests, the Wonderlic Test, Thurstone Mental Ability test, Thurstone Temperament Test, physical examination, and other pertinent employment data. Page 2 (Fig. 8.4) is definitely designed to give information that will indicate success on the job and the likelihood of staying on the job if employed. Figure 7.2 shows the interviewer's evaluation of the applicant. Figure 6.3 shows the form used by Jewel Tea in checking the applicant's work history over the telephone.

Marshall Field and Company along with some other companies such as the Scott Paper Company uses a part of its application blank for publicizing the company. Page 1 of Marshall Field's application blank shows a picture of the store, while page 4 portrays employee activities, fringe benefits, employee discounts, and similar items that might cause the employee to want to work at Field's. Figure 8.5 shows pages 2 and 3 of an outstanding department store's application blank. Page 3 of this application blank asks for educational experience and personal references.

**Research needed on the predictive value of items on the application blank.** The life insurance industry has done some effective research on the predictive value of items on the application blank. The application blank suggested by the insurance industry's research calls for no information except such as (1) is essential for identification, i.e., name, date, address, telephone, or (2) possesses known predictive value. There are only seven possible answers to the inquiry concerning the number of full dependents. Each of the possible answers is here listed with its weighted value to the right:

> No dependents—3
> 1 dependent—4
> 2 dependents—6
> 3 dependents—8
> 4 dependents—8
> 5 dependents—7
> 6 or more dependents—4

Students of the application blank's predictive value are enthusiastic about the value of research by the individual company. This research should be directed to specific situations. Care must be exercised not to transfer the findings of one situation to another one without checking to verify the results. It is believed that intensive research on the predictive value of the various items on an application blank will enable an individual company to increase its effectiveness in hiring new employees. Add to the increased potential of a scientifically constructed application blank the insight that can be gained from psychological tests and physical examinations and the employment manager will be more than an artist. There will probably always be some art in conducting an employment interview. To the extent that employment may become objective, this phase of personnel administration will take on the characteristics of a profession. A few of the findings by companies that have carefully analyzed the predictive value of their application blanks are as follows:

1. A telephone company found that future success was indicated by good scholarship in school, campus activities, and graduation at an early age as compared with classmates.

2. A company selling shoes discovered that, for its sales personnel, height and weight are not diagnostic of either success or failure.

3. A company employing cab drivers found that the items that differentiated the most are age, nationality, marital status, number of children, number of dependents, trade followed, and weight.

4. An electrical company employing substation operators found differential values in age, marital status, number of children, number of dependents, nationality, and height.

5. A company manufacturing and distributing soap found four items to be indicative of success—9 years of schooling, ability to read blueprints, age twenty-five to thirty-nine, and military service and rank. All other items lacked predictive value.

6. A company conducting house-to-house selling found that, of the items on their application blank, married and age thirty-five to forty were the two items most predictive of success.

7. A canning company found that seasonal laborers could be selected in terms of place of residence, telephone, married with no children, age (under twenty-five or over fifty-five), weight, more than 125 lb. but less than 175, education—10 years or more—former employee of the company, available for work until the end of the summer, and prefers field work to inside work.[5]

## THE QUALIFICATION CARD

The much-talked-about program of promoting from within can be realized only when a systematic procedure is used to make it a reality. The personnel record, or qualification card,[6] in some form is a necessary part of any organized procedure to promote on merit

[5] Item 7 was reported by Dunnette and Maetzold, *op. cit.*

[6] Sometimes known as the "employee's record," "personal qualification record," "personal record," "progress card," or "service record."

**application for employment**      Date_____
                                                    (Month) (Day) (Year)

Name (print in full)_____ Maiden Name_____
                (Last)          (First)         (Middle)

Address_____Telephone_____
            (Number)       (Street)       (City)

Position applied for:_____Date of your birth_____
                                                       (Month) (Day) (Year)

Do you want: Full time work all year? Yes ☐   Part time work all year? Yes ☐   Working hours desired_____

Were you ever employed by M. F. & Co.? Yes ☐ Year_____      No ☐   Social Security No._____

**record of work experience**
**list last employer first**

| | DATES MO. YEAR | Name and Present Address of Company | Position you held | Salary | Reason for leaving |
|---|---|---|---|---|---|
| 1. | From_____ To_____ | | | | |
| 2. | From_____ To_____ | | | | |
| 3. | From_____ To_____ | | | | |
| 4. | From_____ To_____ | | | | |
| 5. | From_____ To_____ | | | | |
| 6. | From_____ To_____ | | | | |
| 7. | From_____ To_____ | | | | |
| 8. | From_____ To_____ | | | | |
| 9. | From_____ To_____ | | | | |
| 10. | From_____ To_____ | | | | |
| 11. | From_____ To_____ | | | | |

TO THE BEST OF MY KNOWLEDGE, THE ABOVE REPRESENTS A TRUE AND CORRECT ACCOUNT OF
MY TIME SINCE LEAVING SCHOOL

FIG. 8.5. Application blank of

in a large enterprise. Of course a simple record of work experience
plus the application blank will give the needed information. However,
it is usually advantageous to have a condensed record that is
specifically designed to reveal the worker's qualifications. *The qualification card is a condensation of the important facts pertaining to the
capacities, experiences, and interests of each worker.* The file of

**remember:** Supplying incorrect information is a violation of store rules, and is considered cause for discharge. Please read carefully. Use ink, print legibly.

**personal data**

Height_____Weight_____Where were you born?_____Religious preference_____

Single_____Married_____Separated_____Divorced_____Widowed_____No. of children_____

In case of emergency with whom shall we communicate? Name_____

Address_____Telephone_____Relationship_____

Have you any relatives now employed by Marshall Field & Company? No ☐ Yes ☐ Relationship_____

Name of relative_____Section employed in_____

Have you had military service? Yes ☐ No ☐ When_____How many months?_____

What is your Draft Classification?_____Branch of Service_____

Grade or rank at time of discharge_____What is your Military Reserve status?_____

**education**     (Please give name and location of high school and college)

Grade School_____High School_____ ☐yes ☐no Grad?

no. of years _____ Name & City _____ no. of years _____ year

College_____ Grad? ☐yes ☐no _____

Degrees:_____Major_____Minors_____

**special interests and hobbies**

_____

_____

**personal references**

Give the names and addresses of three persons, not relatives or former employers, whom you have known over three years.

| NAME | ADDRESS: | STREET | CITY | STATE | OCCUPATION |
|------|----------|--------|------|-------|------------|
|      |          |        |      |       |            |
|      |          |        |      |       |            |
|      |          |        |      |       |            |

In applying for work with Marshall Field & Company, I realize that my job will carry with it a responsibility for showing the utmost courtesy in all my relations with customers and with other employes, both in my own and other departments. I thoroughly believe in this basic policy, and will be proud to participate in the high courtesy standards of Marshall Field & Company.

**signature**

**do not write in space below**

Payroll     Job Title_____

Section_____ Classification_____ Job Grade_____Date to Begin_____

Hours Scheduled_____Total Hours per week_____

Weekly Rate_____Plus_____%     Hourly Rate_____     Testing Bureau_____

Sect. Comm. ☐ Sect. Sh. Hr. Comm. ☐ Personal Minimum_____     Fingerprints_____

Rate Justification_____     Insurance Office_____

Sales Training_____Policy Training_____     Employment Desk_____

Section Manager_____     S.S.B. File_____

Divisional Personnel Manager_____     References_____

APPROVED_____DISAPPROVED_____CONDITIONED_____To Work in Section_____Only

Reason for Disapproval_____Type of Work_____Only

Is clearance through Medical Bureau necessary before transferring to another section? Yes_____No_____

Date_____Examining Physician_____

Date Re-examined_____Remarks_____Examining Physician_____

CW
MW
PK
CD
UFO
S
EC

L
TO
SOS
PO
M
B
CS
CT

GC
SC
MO
PSS
TS
SA
A
TC
CF

an outstanding department store.

qualification cards, properly constructed and utilized, reveals the labor status of the organization and provides most of the data for a labor audit or personnel inventory. The file of qualification cards is the organization's index of manpower, an indication of its qualifications for effective service. Naturally the mere existence of qualification cards does not guarantee their use. In a well-known Chicago firm there is a well-managed personnel division that serves the entire institution. Occasionally a strong individualist talks personally with an employee in another department, offering him a certain job before clearing it either with the personnel division or with the employee's own supervisor. Usually under such circumstances there are other employees who are more entitled to the promotion than the one approached by the supervisor who is technically competent but a poor organization man. Needless to say such action engenders friction, and the employees tend to have little faith in the published statements of personnel policies.

**Contents of the qualification card.** The qualification card should contain all the essential data concerning almost anything that may arise of interest to the employee or the employer in relation to the employee and his work. The qualification card should possess the following characteristics:

1. *Up to date.* Men and women are not static, rigid units of power. On the contrary, they are plastic, changing, developing—sometimes even retrogressing. Their interests vary; their capacities change. The qualification card should, so far as possible, show the capacities and interests of the worker as he is, not as he was at some former date.

2. *Completeness.* It should record all the information about the individual that has a bearing upon his effectiveness and success in his present work or in any other work in the organization to which he may be assigned.

3. *Brevity.* This information should be recorded concisely, and irrelevant information should not be recorded at all.

4. *Availability.* The qualification card should be so constructed and filed that this information is readily available when it is wanted.

With the exception of unusual conditions there are certain basic principles that should prevail in the form of the qualification card, and there are certain types of information that are essential. Generally speaking, the following information should be provided:

1. *Personal information.* Individual's name, date of birth, social security number, address, telephone number, photograph, clock number, department and occupation; his marital status, number and kind of dependents, housing status (whether he owns his own home, rents or boards, etc.), nationality, race, citizenship, etc.[7]

2. *Physical qualifications.* Health, height, weight, physique, strength, endurance, sensory acuteness; physical limitations or disabilities.

3. *Educational qualifications.* Scholastic attainments, both in years of schooling and in nature of courses studied: common school, high school, college or university, special training such as that procured in business college, trade

---

[7] Some companies omit nationality and race for fear of being criticized by the Fair Employment Committee or some similar group. A few states have fair-employment-practices laws.

school, correspondence school, night school, or other institutions of technical training.

4. *Technical ability and aptitude.* Degree of skill and knowledge in special kinds of work as revealed by trade-test ratings, skill ratings, dexterity ratings, and other less direct sources of information such as revealed by special inquiry.

5. *Mental qualifications.* Mental alertness as revealed through objective measurements, by the use of mental-alertness tests as well as any other test scores.

6. *Merit rating.* Capacity for leadership, cooperativeness, tact, diplomacy, initiative, appearance and manner, planning ability in developing men, industriousness, sales ability, etc., as determined by rating scales based on observation.

7. *Social data.* Hobbies, civic activities and interests, athletic proclivities, etc., affecting the social relationships between the worker and his associates.

8. *Experience.* History of positions held prior to employment: names of employers, length of service in each place, nature of work, earnings, and reasons for leaving.

9. *His progress in the company work history.*

    9.1 Source of supply from which the worker was drawn and date of employment.

    9.2 Positions held: dates, earnings, reasons for transfers and promotions.

10. *Regularity and promptness*—recorded periodically.

11. *Record of accidents.* Number and kind of accidents and reasons.

12. *Suggestions and complaints.*

13. *Plant activities.* Membership on employees' committees, athletic teams, social organizations, etc.

14. *Desires:*

    14.1 *Educational.* Desire for further educational courses, either within the plant or outside.

    14.2 *Training.* Desire for such training in his work and in work to which he is ambitious for promotion.

    14.3 *Nature of work.* Statement of the work in which the individual feels he will prove most effective and in which he will find greatest satisfaction.

    14.4 *Transfer.* Reasons he desires transfer.

Obviously, a great deal of this information is a matter of history. Historical data can best be obtained by the interview. In the case of new employees, of course, these historical data are secured from the application blank. Where a standardized interview form is used, this form is usually a more valuable source of information than the blank filled out by the employee.

**Keeping the qualification card up to date.** When it is decided to use a qualification card, there are three problems to be solved, namely, (1) the initial filling out of the qualification cards for the entire enterprise when they are first inaugurated, (2) the filling out of the cards for new employees, and (3) the keeping of qualification cards up to date when employees acquire new job experiences. It is probably best to start at once filling out the initial qualification card for all new employees as they are hired, by means of the same procedure that is to be followed when all employees have a qualification card. Keeping qualification cards up to date after they are properly filled out is no small task. It is easy to overlook entering new information unless it is a part of a planned program. All transfers of importance should be entered as a matter of routine. When employees are rated as a part of a merit rating program, they should be asked whether or not they have added to their experience any item that should be made a part of their qualification cards. Such items as evening courses, correspondence courses, or any other acquired item of value should be recorded. When the supervisor reviews the employee's rating with him, he has an excellent opportunity to get this additional information.

In compiling the information for regular employees for their qualification cards when it is first inaugurated, it is unwise to attempt to obtain this information by a series of questions either in printed form or by word of mouth. Personnel work ceases to be personal when an attempt is made to apply mechanical methods to such an endeavor. Qualification cards should be filled out during a personal interview. The qualification card is the employee's spokesman in the councils of management. It is constantly rising in meetings to present his experience and special qualifications. When properly used, it pleads the employee's case when positions of greater importance and opportunity are to be filled. Obviously, where qualification cards are in use, it is a handicap to the individual if through error no card is prepared for him or if, through misunderstanding on his part as to its personal value to him, the information recorded on it is not so complete as it should be. The personal interview is the most effective manner of explaining to employees the use to be made of the qualification card and to get the desired information that is not already a matter of record in the personnel office.

**A record of physical qualification.** The medical history and record of physical strengths and weaknesses should be provided by the medical department. Where there are periodic physical examinations, a more complete physical history is available. It might seem to the uninitiated that a worker's ability to do the required work is the best measure of physical fitness, but this is not necessarily true. A man may perform heavy duties by wearing a truss in spite of suffering from a double hernia. The medical record may be abstracted and entered on the qualification card. It is not necessary, of course, to make the entries so complete as is customary in the physician's own records. There is no need for great detail in this respect, since an itemization of facts that might be significant to a trained physician might have no significance whatever for the personnel manager. Usually such data include a mention of height and weight, quality of eyesight and hearing, and a statement of special disability, such as pulmonary tendencies, inclination to nervousness, heart weaknesses, etc. It is usually advisable to specify the kind of work for which any physical limitations of the employee may render him unfit. Unless there is a periodic physical examination, the physical qualifications of an employee are not very reliable, since an individual may change markedly in the short space of 1 year. At the time of reviewing the merit rating of an employee he might well be questioned as to whether or not he has had any change in his physical condition.

**Mental capacities and personality traits.** When mental-alertness tests are given as a part of the hiring procedure, it is desirable to enter these scores on the qualification card. It is known in certain companies that, for specific kinds of work, a person who scores high in a mental-alertness test, other things being equal, will succeed in the work, whereas others who make a low score in the mental-alertness test will succeed in a far less degree. In other kinds of work a high score on mental alertness may be a liability; in such situations persons ordinarily continue to perform the work more consistently if their score in the mental-alertness test is low. The mental-alertness score on the qualification card must be interpreted with great discretion on the part of the personnel manager and his assistants. Similarly, the individual's score in other tests, such as stenographic tests, file clerk's tests, dexterity tests, and trade tests (such as those for electricians, cabinetmaker, plumber, and lathe hand), is entered in the space provided for the purpose.

Any personality factors of an unusual nature should be a matter of record on the qualification card. Both strong and weak factors should be recorded as a part of the employee periodic merit rating. Likewise personal qualities such as initiative, judgment, appearance and manner, industriousness, and cooperativeness are not always ascertainable by the interviewer. These facts are obtainable through the use of merit ratings and the interviewer's rating scale.[8] These entries are made in the spaces on the qualification card provided for them. The attendance and promptness records are available on independent records in the employee's departments, in the personnel

[8] See Chap. 11, Merit Rating, for a discussion of this technique.

department, or in the paymaster's department. The transferring of these data in condensed form to the qualification card is a simple clerical procedure.

**Illustrative qualification cards.** Each company should include in its qualification card the information it will use. It is important to be able to locate persons with needed qualifications. Figure 8.6 shows the qualification card of the Royal McBee Corporation. This company sells these cards, which may be printed to contain production control and inventory information as well as personnel data. This system of locating cards is especially valuable when particular items are keyed through punching of a V in the round holes in the margin. It is an inexpensive system that lends itself to use in companies of any size. The particular data on the card can be whatever is desired. This system has had wide use in industry and the armed services. Figure 8.6 illustrates an excellent office and factory personnel card used by the Royal McBee Corporation. The back of this particular card is used to record the work history of the employee with the company.

**Mechanical aids in locating employees of specific qualifications.** The visible index facilitates locating certain coded skills or qualifications by a rapid inspection of the trays holding the records. On the bottom of the qualification card is a work classification index, showing any desired number of small squares numbered serially. These squares and the name of the employee form the visible part of the record. Special meanings are given to these numbered squares, and, by filling in the squares with various colors, the qualifications, needs, and desires of individual employees are visibly brought to the attention of management. For example, a desirable applicant asks for a certain job. There being no vacancy at the time, he is placed in some other occupation. On the visible index of his qualification card, square 29 is filled in in blue, which indicates the job he is on; square 58 is then *crossed* in blue, indicating that the applicant wants that job and that an adjustment is necessary. When the man is placed on the desired job, square 29 is filled with black and square 58 with blue, indicating that the adjustment has been made. By various methods of this sort, it is possible to establish a definite numerical color code which, if used in a visible index file, makes it a simple matter to locate cards of employees possessing the necessary qualifications for filling vacancies as they occur and to discover employees needing special attention. The visible index qualification cards may be filed on any desired basis such as departmentally by check number, or alphabetically, or on a plant-wide basis. The small

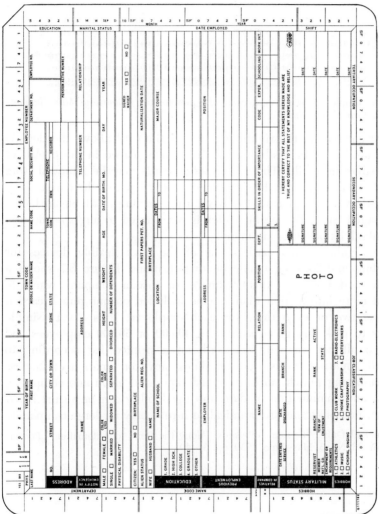

Fig. 8.6. Qualification card of the Royal McBee Corporation. (*Courtesy, Royal McBee Corporation, Athens, Ohio.*)

125

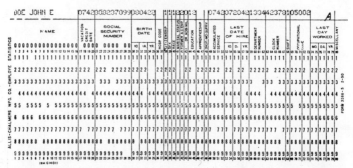

FIG. 8.7. Employee record card using the punch card. (*Courtesy, Allis-Chalmers Manufacturing Company.*)

square cut out on the right-hand side of the card allows the department number to be visible when the card is placed in the pocket of the visible index file. The visible index cards may be removed from their holders and have data recorded on the back of the cards. They are also available in a folded basis, thus making available in fact a four-paged card. The visible index is not limited to any specific use. In general, its purposes are many.

The regular punch card is one of the most flexible devices for recording and locating employee qualifications. Figure 8.7 shows a punch card used by Allis-Chalmers. In case a company wants to record more information than can be included on one punch card it can use two or even three for each employee. It is a very simple matter to pick any given skill from 40,000 or 50,000 employees and arrange all persons with this skill on a printed list according to seniority, marital status, age, or almost any combination of factors. By combining punch cards, punched tape, and electronic computers almost any combination of data and availability can be secured.[9] Of course such programs are practical, as a rule, only for large companies.

[9] See Pall Duke, "Personnel Records: Along the Road to Automation," *Personnel*, Vol. 36, No. 3, May–June, 1959, pp. 31–40.

## CHAPTER 9

# The Job Description

**The occupation, job, or position description.** *A specific occupation or position is a continuing assignment sufficiently unlike all other assignments so that the transfer of an experienced worker to that assignment from another assignment would involve special training rather than simply casual instruction or sufficiently unlike other assignments so that the conditions surrounding the performance of its duties involve unusual mental or physical strain, unusual difficulty, or unusual unpleasantness in performance.* Standardization of terminology is lacking in the area of job or occupational descriptions. Some companies use the term *position* interchangeably with *occupation* and the word *job* to refer to a particular assignment of one person within the occupation. In clerical work and retailing the term *position* is frequently used to refer to the particular assignment of one person. In manufacturing the word "job" is more frequently used to refer to the assignment on which an individual is working. Unless one assignment differs from another in the amount and kind of training involved or in strain, difficulty, or degree of unpleasantness, those two assignments may be regarded as the same occupation. The occupational description is used in establishing a mutual understanding between the department head and the personnel manager with respect to the duties of the occupation and the kind of person needed to perform those duties effectively, in acquainting the new employee with the nature of the work to which he is to be assigned, in setting the salary limits for the occupation and in evaluating its importance to the organization in dollars and cents.

The occupational description is not primarily to be used in setting up a training program in teaching a new employee the details of the specific assignment, nor in determining the one best method to perform a task, such as is done in motion- and time-study analysis. The job or position description in personnel management is designed to discover those characteristics of the job which are to be considered in hiring the worker or in transferring or promoting to the particular job. The detailed job description of the motion- and time-study engineer could be used by the personnel department as a source of many of the data needed for the personnel job description if the personnel analyst were acquainted with the industrial engineer's technical language.

**The content of the job description.** The so-called functional analysis has gained favor in recent years for jobs that are well known to most people.[1] The functional description is considerably shorter than the traditional, more detailed description, The traditional job description that may cover practically any position may well include the following:

### DESCRIPTION OF THE WORK

1. *Name and location of occupation or position.* Its symbol in the occupational code, or indexed list of occupations in the organization. Alternative names in use. Names of allied occupations from which a worker could be transferred with little additional training. Names of the divisions, departments, and units where it exists. These entries might be regarded as the *identifying* entries.

2. *Statement of duties.* A brief description of the *functions* performed by the employee rather than the details of how he performs those functions. His responsibilities are described, such as those for the custody of funds for supervision of other workers, for training subordinates, etc. A statement is made of the machines, tools, and materials used that involve some special ability or skill on the part of the worker, for instance, a drill press or a typewriter, but not a broom or time stamp.

3. *Conditions of work:*
   3.1  Location—factory, office, inside, outside, overhead, underground, solitary, gang, etc.
   3.2  Time—day, night, hours of labor, probability of overtime, peak loads, uniformity of work, etc.
   3.3  Posture—standing, sitting, stooping, walking, climbing, reaching, lifting, etc.
   3.4  Speed—quick, moderate, slow.
   3.5  Accuracy—coarse, fine, exacting.
   3.6  Degree of automaticity—varied, routine, repetitive.
   3.7  Health hazards—ventilation, illumination, nerve strain, eyestrain, physical strain (heavy, medium, light), moisture, heat, dust, humidity, fumes, acids, exposure to weather.
   3.8  Accident hazards.
   3.9  Disagreeable features—dirt, noise, oil, etc.

4. *Pay:*
   4.1  Method—monthly, weekly, biweekly, daily, hourly, piece rates.

[1] See John W. Thompson, "Functional Job Descriptions," *Personnel Journal*, Vol. 30, No. 10.

4.2   Rate—range of pay from minimum to maximum.

4.3   Bonuses, premiums—attendance, Christmas, wage, etc.

5. *Training and promotion.* Length of apprenticeship or of training period; training on the job or in separate department; basis and line of promotion— understudy jobs, related jobs, or advanced jobs.

6. *Sources of supply.*

## REQUIRED QUALIFICATIONS OF THE WORKER

7. *Sex:* preferred or restricted.

8. *Race* (when considered).

9. *Age:* minimum, maximum.

10. *Physical qualities:* height, weight, strength, eyesight. Physical impairments permitted.

11. *Education:* common school, number of years required and desired. College, number of years required, degree; business school training; technical training.

12. *Experience:* kinds and durations of employment required.

13. *Language ability:*
    13.1   English—read, write, speak.
    13.2   Other languages.

14. *Special rating:*
    14.1   Appearance and manner.
    14.2   Leadership.
    14.3   Cooperativeness.
    14.4   Initiative.
    14.5   Ability in developing men.
    14.6   Accuracy.

15. *Test rating* (*critical score*):
    15.1   Mental alertness.
    15.2   Extravert-introvert.
    15.3   Aggressive-submissive.
    15.4   Interests.
    15.5   Emotional stability.
    15.6   Mechanical aptitudes.
    15.7   Trade skills.

The foregoing outline for the job description may give the impression of considerable rigidity. While it is rather complete, it should allow all the flexibility required to cover jobs in all kinds of businesses. This outline is especially designed for a manufacturing company. In a bank the items of health hazard, accident hazard, and disagreeable features of dirt, noise, oil, etc., would be omitted. For retail sales personnel the technical items will be replaced by terms that describe knowledge and abilities used in selling responsibilities on the sales floor and personal and social characteristics.

**Collecting the data for the job description.** Various devices have been used for securing the information needed to write the job description. Each of the following methods has been used by successful companies:

A. DUTIES PERFORMED:

| No. | DESCRIPTION OF DUTIES | Time Per Period |
|-----|------------------------|-----------------|
| | DAILY: | |
| | | |
| | | |
| | | |
| | | |
| | | |
| | | |
| | | |
| | | |
| | | |
| | | |
| | WEEKLY: | |
| | | |
| | | |
| | | |
| | MONTHLY: | |
| | | |
| | | |
| | | |
| | OCCASIONAL, INFREQUENT: | |
| | | |
| | | |
| | | |
| | | |

(Add extra sheets if necessary)

2

Fig. 9.1. Position description questionnaire. (*Courtesy, National Metal Trades Association. Copyright* 1953, *National Metal Trades Association, Chicago, Ill.*)

1. Have the job analyst write the description after consultation with the worker and the supervisor. After this the analyst writes the description and submits it to the worker and supervisor for further comments and criticisms before constructing the final draft.

2. Have the immediate supervisor of the employee fill out the questionnaire.

3. Have the job analyst observe the actual work being done by the employee and fill out the job-description form.

4. Have the worker answer a questionnaire that gives all the pertinent information.

5. A combination of two or more of the above methods, such as having the employee fill out a questionnaire; having an analyst write a first draft from the

**B. OFFICE MACHINES AND EQUIPMENT USED:** (1) Check below the type of machine or equipment used. (2) Write in the name or make, and (3) indicate average percentage of time used daily (D), or weekly (W), or monthly (M):

| TYPE OF MACHINE | (1) Check | (2) VARIETY OR MODEL | (3) D% | (3) W% | (3) M% | TYPE OF MACHINE | (1) Check | (2) VARIETY OR MODEL | (3) D% | (3) W% | (3) M% |
|---|---|---|---|---|---|---|---|---|---|---|---|
| Bookkeeping | | | | | | Dictating | | | | | |
| Calculating | | | | | | Other | | | | | |
| Tabulating | | | | | | Other | | | | | |
| Typewriter | | | | | | Other | | | | | |

**C. EDUCATION REQUIRED:** (1) Check the minimum basic educational knowledge which this position requires, whether acquired in school or elsewhere; and (2) write in specific subject courses or equivalent required, if any:

| SCHOOL OR EQUIVALENT | (1) Check One | (2) LIST SUBJECT COURSES OR EQUIVALENT REQUIRED |
|---|---|---|
| Four-year high school | | |
| Plus specialized training, (up to one year) OR | | |
| Plus extensive, specialized training, (2 to 2½ years) OR | | |
| Plus broad technical training equivalent to 3-4 year apprenticeship. | | |

**D. EXPERIENCE REQUIRED:** Check below the time it will take the usual person to learn to perform the duties of the position satisfactorily under normal supervision, assuming a person has the education prescribed above. This period will include any formal training within the company:

☐ Up to 3 months     ☐ Over 3 months up to 1 year     ☐ Over 1 year up to 3 years     ☐ Over 3 years up to 5 years

**E. JUDGMENT REQUIRED:** List the number of the duty or task from Section A opposite the statement below which most nearly describes the decisions you must make on procedure or method.

| A few methods and procedures are definitely prescribed and followed: | |
|---|---|
| Apply clearly prescribed standard practice, using several procedures, with some decisions required. | |
| Must analyze facts and determine action using a wide range of procedures but within limits of standard practice. | |

**F. SUPERVISION OF YOUR WORK:** List the number of the duty or task from Section A opposite the statement below which most nearly describes the extent it is supervised:

| Short assignments, regularly checked by Supervisor. | |
|---|---|
| Proceed alone, under standard practice, refer questionable cases to Supervisor. | |
| Plan own work after definite objective set by Supervisor, unusual cases referred to Supervisor. | |

3

FIG. 9.1. (*Continued*)

questionnaire after observing the job; submitting the written description to the employee and his supervisor; rewriting the description, incorporating the suggestions of the worker and his supervisor.

Generally the first item listed above will minimize the time required for writing job descriptions and secure the following additional advantages:

1. Mutual confidence and understanding will be promoted.
2. Acceptance of the final result will be made easier.
3. Cooperation of both the workers and supervisors will be enlisted.
4. Oversights will be relatively few.

**G. ERRORS WHICH ARE NORMAL IN YOUR WORK:** List the number of the duty or task from Section A opposite the statement which most nearly describes what happens when normal errors occur in it.

| | |
|---|---|
| Errors are quickly detected because of systematic check or cross-check. | |
| Errors usually caught in succeeding operations, involve several people in a clerical correction. | |

For duties whose numbers are listed opposite second statement above, explain the nature of the usual error; how far it goes before correction; what are its consequences in lost time or money.

**H. CONTACTS WITH OTHERS:** List (1) who you must contact on your position; (2) why you must do so; and, (3) how frequently.

| POSITIONS OR PERSONS CONTACTED (1) | SUBJECT OF CONTACT (2) | FREQUENCY IN NORMAL DUTIES (3) |
|---|---|---|
| | | |
| | | |
| | | |

**I. IF YOU WORK WITH OR HAVE ACCESS TO ANY CONFIDENTIAL DATA, CHECK TYPE OF INFORMATION BELOW:**

☐ Wages and Salaries

☐ Costs

☐ Financial Statements

☐ Confidential Customer Relations on Prices, Delivery, Etc.

☐ Company Records, Minutes, Etc.

☐ Company Plans, Designs, Development Programs, Etc.

☐ (Other)_____

☐ (Other)_____

**J. WORKING CONDITIONS:** Check one of squares and list any unusual conditions in your working environment.

☐ Usual Office Conditions  Unusual Conditions:_____

☐ Shop Conditions

☐ Part Shop and Part Office Conditions

APPROVED BY:_____  POSITION RATED BY:_____

DATE:_____  DATE:_____

FIG. 9.1. (*Continued*)

The questionnaire has a strong appeal to many job analysts. It usually yields data that are misleading and that require such careful reanalysis and study that the expense saved in procuring them is more than lost in interpreting them. If job descriptions are to be used effectively, they must be accurate and kept up to date when the job changes. The construction of an adequate occupational description for a given position necessitates a personal interview with the workers who are engaged in that work by an interviewer possessing intelligence and tact and one who is trained in the technique of securing the essential facts. The interview should be supplemented by a careful observation of the actual performance of the job, during which time the description is checked as to the details.

**Training the job analyst.** It is presumed that the trainee has the necessary mental acuity and personal characteristics required for writing job descriptions. The analyst trainee should be able to grasp the principles underlying personnel work and to understand the specific objective of the occupational description. He should be able to sift the facts of each occupation, setting aside those which are unimportant and unessential and retaining those which are pertinent to the description of the occupation and of the desired worker. He must possess confidence in himself, and he must have the personality and the tact which will enable him to enlist the worker's interest. The actual training may be done on an understudy basis, the learner working with an experienced analyst, or it may be done on a group basis where there are several persons being trained. There are many excellent books that give the complete story of job evaluation. Should the work be done in a retail establishment, naturally a book covering this field should be used. If it is being done in a factory, one specializing in factory work would be preferred. Having carefully studied the literature in the field, the learner is ready to make some trial descriptions. These should naturally be checked by someone skilled in the work before going ahead. When trained by an efficient instructor, an analyst seldom requires more than 6 weeks to become skilled in writing job descriptions.

**Writing the occupational, or job, description.** Broadly speaking there are two general types of work sheets on which data for the job descriptions are collected, namely, (1) one that provides spaces for checking as many characteristics as possible, and (2) one that calls for a description of each characteristic. There can also be a combination of these two extremes. Figure 9.1 illustrates a work sheet used for compiling data for office occupations. Check blocks are freely used. The job description shown in Fig 9.2 is a work sheet used by a large bank. It is tailored to fit its particular needs. Figure 9.3 gives a job description of a factory operation. With the work sheet the analyst should go to the supervisor of the department in which he is to write job descriptions. The supervisor should introduce him to the worker. The analyst should explain to the worker just what he is trying to do. Before finishing his task the analyst should show the worker the record he has made and get suggestions from him for improvements. The data then should be talked over with the supervisor for additional corrections. With these raw data the analyst is in a position to return

| RATING | THE FIRST PENNSYLVANIA | JOB NO. | 855 |
|---|---|---|---|
| | BANKING AND TRUST COMPANY | | |
| | JOB DESCRIPTION | DATE | 4/28/58 |

| JOB NAME | Keypunch Operator | | APPVD. BY | *Geirge L Bell* |
|---|---|---|---|---|
| DEPT. Trust | | DIVISION Tabulating | APPVD. BY | |
| SECTION Clerical-Keypunch | | UNIT Cash Records | ANALYST | M.E.Cornish |

FUNCTION: Under supervision of Supervisor Clerical-Keypunch Section (871) and work supervision of Cash Records Unit Head (866), KEYPUNCHES tabulating cards for posting debit and credit items to various Trust Department ledgers, OPERATES sorter, interpreter and reproducer as required.

(Since operator sets up entries as they appear on ledgers and statements, it is important that entries be properly spaced, accurate as to detail, and worded in the approved manner.)

DUTIES - REGULAR

APPROX. % OF TIME

1. KEYPUNCHES tabulating cards from various Trust Department debit, credit, journal entry vouchers, as received in batches from Cash Records Unit Head. (Work includes remittances, security transactions, real estate and mortgage transactions commission charges, fees, interest payments, royalties, taxes, etc., each type of transaction requiring special consideration and handling. Each day's work must be completed before leaving.)

    a. OBTAINS bundles of vouchers from Unit Head, with adding machine tape attached SIGNS work control sheet and RECORDS total from tape.

    b. SELECTS type of tabulating card to be used, in accordance with type of work in batch, PLACES supply in Keypunch machine. INSERTS correct program card to control spacing, etc.

    c. PULLS master card from proper master file (24 separate files) when voucher or nature of work indicates that master cards are on file. REPRODUCES master card, REFILES original, KEYPUNCHES current information in duplicate card - date, amount, etc.

    d. KEYPUNCHES complete cards when masters are not to be used - REFERS to set-up sheet when necessary for spacing, codes, etc. CONDENSES information where necessary, USES approved wording and abbreviations. DETERMINES when two or more cards are required to complete long entries, REPEATS necessary identifying information on each card.

    e. PUNCHES name card to identify bundle of work, PLACES with bundle of punched cards in basket for delivery to Machine Room for preparation of check run. PLACES bundle of vouchers on First Checker's desk for verification of check run when received from Machine Room.

    f. MAKES corrections in bundles of work returned by First Checker after verification of check run - LOCATES card containing error (if work is not interpreted, must read punching), MAKES correction on keypunch, PLACES cards in work bin for delivery to Machine Room for second check run, PLACES bundle of vouchers in bin on Final Checker's desk for verification of second check run.

    g. PUNCHES new master cards where necessary, PLACES in drawer for verification by Unit Head before they are filed in master file.

95%

2. SORTS, REPRODUCES, INTERPRETS punched cards as required in performing certain phases of keypunch work. INSERTS wired and marked panel boards in reproducer to achieve desired results. Occasionally ADJUSTS wires in accordance with detailed instructions or diagrams.

5%

3. PREPARES program cards for new applications, in accordance with instructions. REPLACES worn program cards.

B 626

FIG. 9.2. Job description of keypunch operator.

to write the condensed occupational description. If his work has been thorough in collecting the data, he will seldom have to return to the workplace for additional information before completing the description.

After having completed the job description, the analyst should show it to the supervisor and the worker for final approval. This procedure requires time, but the favorable reactions are well worth the effort. The occupational descriptions become an integral part of the job rat-

4. FILES tabulating cards in ledger file by account number, then chronologically within account, as time permits, to assist Statement Clerks (894, 815).    Nom.

**SKILL**

MINIMUM TRAINING AND PAST EXPERIENCE, WHAT AND WHERE ACQUIRED

None.

MINIMUM NEW EXPERIENCE AND WORKING KNOWLEDGE TO BE ACQUIRED ON THIS JOB

Operation of Keypunch, Reproducer, Sorter, Interpreter. Knowledge of various tabulating cards and their use; familiarity with voucher forms, information to be punched, controls, codes, wording of entries, abbreviations, etc.

EQUIPMENT USED %

| IBM Keypunch (024-026) | . | - 90% |
| IBM Sorter (082) | ) | |
| IBM Reproducer (519-528) | ) - 5% |
| IBM Interpreter (552) | ) | |

**PHYSICAL**

POSITION: SITTING  85 % STANDING  5 % MOVING ABOUT  10 %
KINDS OF WORK %

90% - Keypunch Machine
5% - Reproducer, Sorter, Interpreter
5% - Pulling and filing cards

**WORKING CONDITIONS**

Tabulating Department, 5th Floor, Packard Building.
Noise from Keypunch Machines.
5% of time spent in Machine Room.          APPROVED BY:

_____
(EMPLOYEE)

FIG. 9.2. (*Continued*)

ing program. Job rating vitally affects rates of pay; hence it is important to have the worker's cooperation in the construction of job descriptions. In beginning the construction of the job description some rough classification of the occupations in the organization must be made, assigning to each occupation the workers who are engaged in it. This information is usually in the possession of the payroll department. There is some tentative classification in effect that is used as the basis for wage rates. Where a conscious attempt at classification has previously been made, more reliable information will be available. Whether the accuracy in these existing classifications is great or small, it is a sound policy to assume that they are correct until investigation indicates the ways in which they are wrong.

Before starting the analyzing of the jobs for the job descriptions a list should be prepared of all the jobs in the plant, store, bank, or any other type of business. An identifying number should be assigned each job or position. In many cases the accepted occupational titles are inadequate and, in some cases, misleading. In the construction of the occupational descriptions, these titles will change, as well as the knowledge of the job content. Great difficulty will be encountered in

### JOB DESCRIPTION

Job Title     Trucker—Industrial          Job No. 1     Code No. 092-04
Tool No.                                                 Dept.

1. Receives instructions from the truck dispatch office and proceeds to point at which load is to be found. (Unless working regularly in one department.)
2. Inspects move order and secures sender's signature if it is not present.
3. Loads material on skid or truck platform if necessary, picks up skid, transports it to specified point. Trucker must sign move order to indicate movement of material.
4. Obtains receiving foreman's signature on move orders, phones truck dispatch office for instructions (obtains instructions from foreman when working regularly in one department).
5. Makes out report on mechanical condition of truck and any damage caused at the end of each day.

*Remarks:*
1. Some time is spent by driver in loading and unloading his truck by hand. This time is small in proportion to time spent in other phases of the job.
2. At the end of the day, driver turns in all move orders for the day with proper signatures.
3. Driver obeys rules and instructions in the "Trucking Manual—Allis-Chalmers Manufacturing Company, Inc."
4. Until driver learns to ride truck properly, he is likely to become stiff because of the bouncing.
5. Drivers usually are not out-of-doors for periods longer than two hours.
6. One trucker works between Oil House and Shops, one works less than half the day between #1 Yard and Shops, others occasionally go to Main Office building from Shops.

DATE WRITTEN     4–30–60     COMPANY ACTIVE DATE

This description contains only the facts necessary to properly identify the job or work station.

Form 5918–2–9

FIG. 9.3. Job description of an industrial trucker. (*Courtesy, Allis-Chalmers Manufacturing Company.*)

maintaining the identity of the occupation throughout its analysis and redefinition unless the identifying number is employed to mark it. The code numbers themselves, once assigned, never change. But the code itself must be capable of expansion and revision. As an interviewer proceeds to analyze the work of a number of employees who apparently are classified alike, he may find that part of them are doing one kind of work, part another. In this case, the necessity for creating new classifications arises. These new classifications must in their turn receive identifying symbols in the numerical code. If a relatively simple code numbering system has been used in setting up the system, an entirely new system may be used after the entire program has been completed. The new system may be a combination of one of the decimal systems which is capable of indefinite expansion to include new jobs when they are created.

Some analysts have found it useful to take a photograph of the machine and the worker at work. This photograph becomes an integral part of the job description. Such photographs are very helpful in explaining a job to a job applicant in the employment office.

In writing the position descriptions the job titles or names already in use should be retained if possible. The members of the organization have naturally become familiar with these titles, and their continuance involves no change in habit of thought. If, in a given case, however, the title in use is not descriptive, the interviewer selects from the *Dictionary of Occupational Titles* a new title that is truly descriptive of the position, making sure that it does not conflict with any title already in use and that it is uniform and harmonious with other occupational titles. A standardized use of descriptive words is highly desirable. For instance, in discussing the supervision required, the following terms in italics might well have the meanings indicated:

*Immediate supervision.* The degree of supervision that an apprentice, a clerk learning office routine, or a copyist draftsman receives. It is not expected that the employee will use much initiative. Immediate supervision involves close watch over all the specific details in the work—what duties are performed, how they are performed, step by step.

*Supervision.* The degree of supervision that a new clerk would receive after the first uncertainty is over and the supervisor feels that the clerk is "catching on." Supervision does not involve so close a watch over specific details, but general phases of the work are controlled by constant reference to the supervisor for advice and decision.

*General supervision.* The degree of supervision flowing from foreman to journeyman. The worker here begins to assume his share of responsibility. He is supposed to know the mechanics of his job and use that knowledge without advice or spur. The detailed method of performing a given task is usually left entirely to the worker so long as he operates within established general practice.

*Direction.* The degree of supervision exercised over a trained worker by his administrative chief or section head. A definite objective is set, and the worker is left to go ahead, in conformity with policies with which he has no recommendatory connection. It is expected that there will be need for frequent conferences as to both the general phases of the work and the specific details.

*General direction.* The degree of supervision exercised over a section head by his administrative chief. The latter expects a finished product without appreciable reference even as to general plans of the work and with practically no reference as to the specific details of how the work is to be accomplished.

*General administrative direction.* The degree of supervision exercised over a trained technical man by his administrative head. In general administrative direction the technical features of the work are practically all in the hands of the worker. An example is the direction the president of a manufacturing corporation might exercise over the chief engineer.

**Writing position descriptions for executives.** Exactly the same principles are involved in writing position descriptions for executives and supervisors as for workers. It is more difficult to observe an executive's work as a basis of writing the description. It is a good idea to start at either the top or the bottom of the executive hierarchy and work in sequence. This is particularly an advantage when each position in the series is directly related to the others. Naturally, the description may have to be in somewhat more general terms at the policy level than in the lower ranks.[2] There is a tendency to shorten job descriptions to make them really describe the functions performed rather than to itemize everything that the employee does.[3] For instance, instead of itemizing all the various things a file clerk or typist does in an insurance company, illustrative items are listed. The functional type of description saves about half the space used in the older job descriptions that tried to spell out all the details.

**Keeping the job descriptions current.** Changes in the job requirements are constantly taking place. It is no simple problem to record all changes that modify the job description. The people who are responsible for operational and process changes are primarily interested in getting things done and not in making records or telling other departments about it. Frequently the first time a change is reported to the analyst is when a grievance is filed claiming that a given job should be reclassified into a higher bracket carrying a higher rate of pay. In spite of the fact that the supervisor is a busy man and may forget to notify the job analyst of position changes, it is his responsibility and should be so specified. Several copies of each occupational

[2] See National Industrial Conference Board, Inc., "Job Descriptions," *Studies in Personnel Policy,* 72, New York, 1946, p. 26, for a description of the foreman's job. This is an excellent source of valuable information on job descriptions.

[3] See Thompson, *op. cit.*

description should be prepared. The personnel department requires at least one complete set. In addition each department head should have a copy of the occupational description for every position in his department. There is nothing arbitrary in the suggestions that have just been outlined. The size, nature, and complexity of each organization will determine the exact procedure to be followed in preparing occupational descriptions. The foregoing procedure has proved effective. It undoubtedly contains the elements that exist in every program for the construction of occupational descriptions.

## CHAPTER 10

# *Job Evaluation*

**Terminology.** *Job rating is the operation of evaluating a particular job in relation to other jobs either within or without the organization.* In its simplest form, it may be merely a ranking of the various jobs, placing the particular job having the greatest sum total requirements at one end of the scale and the one with the least requirements at the other end of the scale, with the other jobs arranged between these two extremes according to their relative requirements. Job evaluation, or job rating, is concerned with the requirements of the job itself and not the degree to which an individual meets these requirements. Job rating is undertaken to discover the relative requirements of the respective jobs within the company, to enable management to evaluate its wages paid for the respective jobs, and to aid management in correcting any inequalities that may be discovered. In their recent surveys of the practices of various industries in relation to job evaluation, the authors found that operating people frequently use the terms *job evaluation* and *occupation evaluation* largely in the same sense. These studies included insurance companies, retail establishments, banks, automotive and automotive accessory companies, aircraft manufacturers, universities and colleges, and municipalities.[1] Industry has taken the lead in developing both job evaluation and merit rating (Fig. 10.1).

Occasionally there is confusion in the use of or the meanings assigned to the terms *job analysis, job description,* and *job specification. Job analysis is the process of critically evaluating the operations, duties, and relationships of the jobs. Job analysis precedes the writing of job descriptions and job specifications. Job description is a written record of the duties, responsibilities, and requirements of a particular*

[1] These studies are published by the Bureau of Business Research of the University of Texas as a series of personnel studies. They were made by Dr. E. Lanham and the author.

*job.* The job description is concerned with the job itself and not with the worker. *The job specification is a written record of the requirements sought in the individual worker for a given job.* The job analysis should be made before a job description is made. The job description frequently is not so detailed as the job analysis.

**Advantages of job evaluation.** In the studies of the various industries and business institutions the authors found the same general advantages being claimed for job evaluation, but frequently not in the same ratio. For instance, in banking, department stores, and municipalities very little mention was made of unions. Figure A.7, item 4, shows that 72 per cent of the companies participating in the survey had job evaluation. Tables 10.1 and 10.2 show the frequency of various advantages claimed in the automobile industry and the automobile accessory industry.

It is possible to have a crude form of job rating without job analysis; however, sound practice in/job rating is based upon a carefully drawn job description that has been compiled from accurate job analysis. Not every phase of a job analysis is used in the job description; however, a job description that is not based upon a job analysis may easily be superficial. A sound wage policy necessitates a program

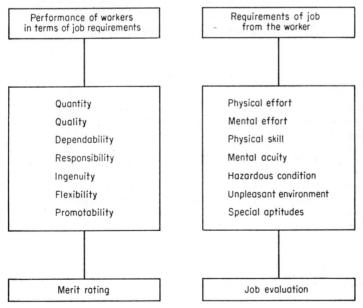

Fɪɢ. 10.1. Relationship between merit rating and job evaluation in establishing an equitable rate for a job and wage for the employee.

*Table* 10.1    *Advantages Secured from the Installation of*
*Job-evaluation Programs*°
(*Automobile Manufacturing*)

| Advantages | Number of companies |
|---|---|
| Salary equity......................................... | 10 |
| Better morale......................................... | 7 |
| Better promotion, transfer, and placement policies......... | 9 |
| Consistency, uniformity............................... | 10 |
| Factual basis for determining the worth of jobs........... | 8 |
| Better control over salary costs....................... | 7 |
| Standardization of salaries............................ | 9 |
| Reduced employee turnover........................... | 3 |
| Improved organization................................ | 6 |
| Standardized wage-payment policies.................... | 1 |
| Curtailed employee grievances......................... | 1 |
| Elimination of additional employee union organization..... | 1 |
| | 72† |

* Source: W. R. Spriegel and E. Lanham, "Job Evaluation in Automobile and Automobile Parts Manufacturing Industries," *Personnel Study* 5, Bureau of Business Research, University of Texas, Austin, Texas, 1953.

† Most companies gave more than one advantage received from the plan.

*Table* 10.2    *Advantages Secured from the Installation of*
*Job-evaluation Programs*\*
(*Automotive-parts Manufacturing*)

| Advantages | Number of companies |
|---|---|
| Factual basis for determining the worth of jobs...................... | 48 |
| Salary equity......................................... | 46 |
| Consistency, uniformity............................... | 46 |
| Better promotion, transfer, and placement policies.................... | 42 |
| Standardization of salaries............................ | 35 |
| Better morale......................................... | 33 |
| Improved organization................................ | 28 |
| Better control over salary costs....................... | 25 |
| Reduced employee turnover........................... | 14 |
| Government-agency acceptance of salary administration policies........ | 1 |
| Control of labor costs................................. | 1 |
| Greater union cooperation............................. | 1 |
| A more comprehensive basis for bargaining discussions of job classifications and pay rates......................................... | 1 |
| | 321† |

* Source: W. R. Spriegel and E. Lanham, "Job Evaluation in Automobile and Automobile Parts Manufacturing Industries," *Personnel Studies* 5, Bureau of Business Research, University of Texas, Austin, Texas, 1953.

† Most companies gave more than one advantage received from the plan.

of paying employees on the basis of output and the requirements of the job. It is not at all unusual to find that two similar jobs within the same plant pay wages differing by as much as 25 per cent.

The author's own studies and previous studies of others have shown the following advantages of job evaluation:

1. Shows the relative value of all jobs within the company.
2. Tends to eliminate inequalities of wages for similar work in the same department or different departments.
3. Serves as a basis of settling controversies over wages.
4. Aids in determining the relative value of new jobs.
5. Aids in establishing a satisfactory wage level for all jobs within the company.
6. A by-product of job rating is standardization of jobs and accurate job descriptions that are valuable in pointing out lines of promotion and employee selection and training.
7. In companies having more than one plant, job rating aids in maintaining a high degree of relative standardization even though the wage levels may vary between plants.

**Job analysis.** Job analysis includes a careful enumeration of the requirements of the job itself, also an accurate naming of the job. Standardization in job nomenclature is helpful in job rating. There are at least two types of job analysis: (1) the carefully constructed engineering analysis that is a part of methods study, and (2) the analysis that is designed primarily for the use of the personnel department. A skilled personnel man may use the more detailed methods analysis. However, the personnel man does not require so much detail for his purpose as does the methods man. The job analysis used by the personnel man in preparing his job specification must include those items which are pertinent to proper job rating. It emphasizes the factors that are required of the employee who satisfactorily fills the job.

**Types of job evaluation.** Job-evaluation systems may readily be classified into three major groups. These groups are (1) the ranking, or grading, method, (2) the Factor Comparison Plan, or the weighted-in-money method, and (3) the various point methods.[2] All types of job evaluation strive to eliminate personal bias and to introduce scientific procedures. Any type of approach when carefully used will give satisfactory results. The point system when properly validated by actual use is more likely to be capable of general use than the ranking system. In many aspects the Factor Comparison Plan is a

---

[2] See Charles W. Lytle, *Job Evaluation Methods,* The Ronald Press Company, New York, 1946, p. 32, for five classifications; see also Richard C. Smyth and Matthew J. Murphy, *Job Evaluation and Employee Rating,* McGraw-Hill Book Company, Inc., New York, 1946, Chaps. II, III, IV, for three types. When only two types are considered, the Factor Comparison Method is classed as a point system.

*Table* 10.3 *Use of Job-evaluation Systems**

| Plan | Sole plan used | Point also used | Ranking also used | Classification† also used | Factor comparison also used |
|------|------|------|------|------|------|
| Point................. | 111 | . . . | 15 | 15 | 32 |
| Ranking............... | 14 | 15 | . . . | 5 | 5 |
| Classification.......... | 13 | 15 | 5 | . . . | 6 |
| Factor comparison..... | 29 | 32 | 5 | 6 | . . . |

* Source: W. R. Spriegel, John Robert Beishline, and Alfred G. Dale, "Personnel Practices in Industry," *Personnel Study* 8 (rev.), Bureau of Business Research, University of Texas, Austin, Texas, 1958, p. 48.

† See p. 144 for a discussion of classification.

Figures indicate the number of companies using the plans listed. Thus, 111 firms use the point system and no other; 15 firms use both point and ranking systems, etc.

point system that combines the ranking system with the point system, especially during the initial stages of the development of the program. After the program has been in use for some time, the tendency is to drop off the ranking phase and continue the use of the point system.

The popularity of the various systems is portrayed by Table 10.3.

**The ranking, or grading, system of job evaluation.** The ranking system of job evaluation consists primarily in arranging the various jobs in the enterprise in an order from the simplest to the highest or the reverse, each successive job being either higher or lower than the previous one in the sequence. This system should be preceded by careful job analysis and the writing of accurate job descriptions before the rating process is undertaken. It is possible, of course, to take the jobs as they are found in the business enterprise and use the names as they are, without any attempt at standardization, and merely rank them according to the general over-all impression of the raters. Such a procedure will fall short of what may reasonably be expected of job rating. Another procedure, which is in reality merely a modification of the simple rating described above, is to establish a series of grades, or zones, and arrange all the jobs in the plant into groups within these classifications, or zones. A more common practice is to arrange all the jobs in the plant according to their requirements by rating them and then to establish the classifications, or groups. In some cases the system is originally established by a point system, after which the various jobs are arranged into groups, or classifications. In time, new jobs may be placed in one of the classifications by direct comparison without the use of points. One large company has gone through this evolutionary process largely because of union opposition to the point system as such. This company does not seem to have any special difficulty with the classification system.

In the organization and procedure for evaluating jobs under the ranking system the work may be done by an individual, several individuals, or a committee. If several individuals are working independently on the task, it will be found that in general they agree but that their rankings vary in certain details. A conference between these individuals, with each person giving his reasons why he rated one job higher than another, usually produces agreement. The detailed job description is particularly helpful when there is disagreement among raters as to the ranking of certain jobs. It is not only possible, but frequently desirable, to have workers participate in the construction of the job description and in rating the job. Usually a series of key jobs that are well known throughout the plant are first rated and the other jobs roughly compared with these key jobs to establish a rough rating, after which each job is compared in greater detail to establish its exact rank in the scale. There is a tendency to consider the current wage being paid in establishing the relative rank of a given job. So far as possible, present wages should be ignored at the time of rating jobs by the ranking method, or the ranking will not be so serviceable in wage adjustments as it should be. Rating the jobs—by the ranking method—should also ignore the qualifications of the person filling the jobs at the time, since the ranking is of the jobs and not of the workers. The particular worker may have qualifications that are higher than those required for the job. Ranking of jobs is essentially a cut-and-try process requiring infinite patience and attention to details. It usually results in a compromise or pooled judgment of the relative worth of a job. This statement also holds in some degree for the rating of jobs by the point system.

One of the most carefully worked out ranking programs was that of a well-known company in the paper industry. This company measured each job in comparison with other jobs in terms of the relative importance of the following six factors:

1. *Supervision and leadership of subordinates.*
2. *Cooperation with associates outside the line of authority:* exchange of opinion on controversial matters involving tact, diplomacy, appreciation of the other person's point of view; necessity for and degree of teamwork, exchange of information, etc.
3. *Probability and consequences of errors:* assuming that the occupation is filled by an experienced, conscientious employee, consider typical errors that are apt to be made and the consequences of each in terms of waste, damage to equipment, delays, complaints, confusion, spoilage of product, discrepancies, etc.

4. *Initiative and resourcefulness:* requirements concerning originality, creativeness, judgment, analysis of conditions and reaching independent decisions, planning, estimating, dealing with variables, etc.; extent to which supervision is received.

5. *Minimum experience requirements,* including both preliminary experience and experience in the occupations; estimated time required for inexperienced but otherwise qualified persons to reach a satisfactory degree of proficiency.

6. *Minimum education requirements:* amount of schooling or study absolutely necessary to fill successfully the occupation.

The company referred to above experimented with weighting these factors but finally settled on the plan of weighing the merits of each comparison on the basis of free discussions in the committee doing the ranking, without the use of a point system. This company rated some 700 hourly paid occupations spread over seven different plants by this system. It will be noted that *working conditions* were not listed as one of the factors of comparison. Working conditions were considered only in the case of two jobs that were considered equal in regard to the other six factors.

*Advantages Claimed for the Ranking System.* The advantages claimed for the ranking or classification system briefly are:

1. Simplicity. It is relatively easily understood by workers and supervisors. It is less mechanistic and theoretical than the point system.

2. The time element. Unless carried to the detailed point used by companies such as the paper company referred to above, it requires less time.

3. Frankness. It avoids the criticism of claiming to be scientific.

### Disadvantages of the Ranking System

1. Unless the same detailed analysis is pursued as that used in the various point systems, the analyst or committee cannot possibly be familiar with all the jobs. If the same detail is followed, most of the advantages of this system, other than simplicity, do not exist.

2. The ranking system will tell whether one job is higher than another, but not how much higher. For broad operating purposes when classifications are used this criticism is not serious.

3. There is a tendency for the analyst to assume that a job belongs to a given class merely because of the current wage. This may also influence the points given to a job, but usually not to the same degree as in the ranking system.

**The factor comparison system of job evaluation.** The late Edward N. Hay and Samuel L. H. Burk and Eugene J. Benge have championed the *Factor Comparison Method of job evaluation.* They select several (15 to 20) key jobs for which the money rates are considered satisfactory. Each of these jobs is analyzed in terms of the following factors, and that portion of the money rate which is considered appropriate is assigned to the factor:

1. Mental requirements.
2. Skill requirements.
3. Physical requirements.
4. Responsibility.
5. Working conditions.[3]

Table 10.4 illustrates the foregoing procedure. It represents the pooled judgment of the analyst and key supervisors involved. When the key jobs have been rated, all the other jobs in the company are compared with these ratings. When the ratings for all the jobs have been established, these may then be grouped into classifications. When the entire salary level is raised or lowered, adjustments may be made to compensate for the change or the original ratings may be

[3] See Eugene J. Benge, Samuel L. H. Burk, and Edward N. Hay, *Manual of Job Evaluation*, Harper & Brothers, New York, 1941, p. 42. This book describes in detail the Benge plan.

*Table* 10.4   *Key Job-evaluation Data Sheet\**

| | Requirements | | | Resp. | Work-ing cond. | Present pts. per hr. |
| | Men-tal | Skill | Physi-cal | | | |
|---|---|---|---|---|---|---|
| Automobile painter, finisher (day).. | 16 | 24 | 25 | 12 | 9 | 86 |
| Asst. engr., elect. powerhse. (shift).. | 14 | 19 | 19 | 17 | 9 | 78 |
| Boilermaker's helper (outside) (day) | 6 | 7 | 33 | 5 | 10 | 61 |
| Bricklayer, 1st class (day)......... | 17 | 28 | 30 | 14 | 11 | 100 |
| Common (heavy) laborer (day).... | 3 | 3 | 37 | 3 | 9 | 65 |
| Ethyl blending operator (day)..... | 19 | 21 | 21 | 22 | 21 | 104 |
| First oper.—pipe stills (shift)...... | 24 | 24 | 16 | 24 | 14 | 102 |
| Gyro. and marine instr. repairs (day) | 28 | 34 | 17 | 19 | 7 | 105 |
| Engine tender, boilerhouse (day)... | 6 | 8 | 23 | 12 | 7 | 56 |
| Janitor, pipe stills (day)........... | 4 | 3 | 30 | 4 | 9 | 50 |
| Operator, stabil. plant (shift)...... | 22 | 19 | 16 | 19 | 15 | 91 |
| Operator, sod. plumb. plant (shift).. | 17 | 16 | 20 | 16 | 17 | 86 |
| Pipefitter, 1st class (day)......... | 17 | 22 | 27 | 15 | 10 | 91 |
| Shop machinist, all-around (day)... | 21 | 29 | 24 | 15 | 5 | 94 |
| Sample room attendant (day)...... | 14 | 10 | 23 | 9 | 6 | 62 |
| Ship loader (shift)............... | 4 | 8 | 33 | 10 | 16 | 71 |
| Stencil cutter and tank gauger (day) | 8 | 6 | 19 | 8 | 6 | 47 |
| Tester (viscosity) (day).......... | 18 | 20 | 15 | 11 | 6 | 70 |
| Tool checker and tester (day)...... | 28 | 11 | 19 | 15 | 6 | 79 |
| Toolmaker (machine shop) (day)... | 24 | 34 | 19 | 17 | 5 | 99 |
| | | | | Rater | E. Z. Thomas | |
| | | | | Date | 3/10/ | |

\* Eugene J. Benge, Samuel L. H. Burk, and Edward N. Hay, *Manual of Job Evaluation*, 1941, Fig. 11, p. 111. Reprinted by courtesy of Harper & Brothers, publishers.

considered points from which to make adjustments when needed. Many well-known companies have used the Benge plan with success. Table 10.3 shows this system to be the second most commonly used plan today.

### Advantages of the Factor Comparison Plan

1. Flexibility. There are no limits to the value that may be assigned to each factor. Of course, by comparison a factor in a given job should not be out of line for the same factor in another job.
2. Simplicity. This plan does not require a translation from points to money.
3. The system lends itself admirably to the establishing of classification.

### Disadvantages of the Factor Comparison Plan. Some of the critics of this plan claim the following disadvantages:

1. Wages levels change from time to time, and thus adjustments are required.
2. Money rates, when used as a basis for rating, tend to influence the actual rate more than abstract points.

**The point system of evaluating jobs.** There are many different systems of job evaluation using points as a basis of establishing relative job worth. These systems differ in many details; they are predicated upon the assumption that it is possible to assign points to the respective factors considered pertinent in evaluating the individual jobs and that the sum of these points will give an index of the relative significance of the jobs being rated. In the opinion of persons accustomed to thinking in mathematical terms, these systems seem to be more precise and exact than the ranking systems of job evaluation. Whether or not they are more reliable than the ranking system will depend to a considerable extent on the validity of the points assigned to the respective characteristics evaluated and to the individual characteristics selected as being indicative of the relative requirements of the jobs. The ranking system may consider various characteristics of a job as well as the point system. However, the ranking system does not necessarily have to break the job down into its various factors, whereas the point systems always attempt to do this. The factors considered may be the same in the case of both the ranking and the point systems. It would be possible to use the point system without careful analysis and job descriptions, but the authors are not familiar with any company that has tried to do so. The assigning of points to the various job characteristics encourages job analysis even though it may not be formalized.

**Characteristics evaluated in the point systems.** The various systems differ substantially in the number of characteristics used in establishing the relative requirements of the various jobs. The Industrial Management Society uses three major divisions under which it classifies the various job characteristics, namely, (1) job conditions, (2) physical ability required, and (3) characteristics that are chiefly of a mental nature.[4] Under each of these three main headings are listed the various factors, with each factor clearly defined and under each factor a description of the degrees required, the number of points allotted to each degree, and examples of the various degrees required for the respective points allotted.[5] The factors used in the job rating plan sponsored by the National Metal Trades Association are grouped under four general headings, namely, (1) skill, (2) effort, (3) responsibility, and (4) job conditions. Under each of these four general headings are subheadings or factors bringing the total individual factors rated for each job up to 11.[6] Most of the point systems include the following five items in evaluating jobs:

1. Mental requirements.
2. Physical requirements.
3. Skill.
4. Responsibility.
5. Job or working conditions.

One large company made an elaborate statistical analysis of the factor of responsibility and concluded that it could be eliminated in evaluating jobs because the skill factor took care of responsibility. This factor was not actually eliminated because of the feeling on the part of workers and supervisors that it should be included. One large electrical manufacturer uses six factors, and another large manufacturer in the same field uses nine factors in job evaluation. The exact number of factors used is not of major importance just so long as enough are used to give a fair picture of the requirements of the job and not so many that the task becomes excessively burdensome. It is conceivable that finer shades of differences may be shown when the factors are broken down into more basic elements; however, it is not the number of factors considered but the care exercised in the use of these factors that largely determines the relative efficiency of any particular system.

**Assigning points to the various factors.** Uniformity is lacking in the point values assigned a given characteristic by various companies.

[4] Industrial Management Society, *Occupational Rating Plan for Hourly and Salaried Occupations*, Chicago, 1937, p. 2.
[5] See pp. 153–154 for a detailed listing of the various factors and the relative weighting of each factor.
[6] See National Metal Trades Association, *Job Rating*, Chicago, n.d., p. 1.

This fact is not important. The important thing is that the various factors are properly related to each other when a point value is once given. One company rated the highest-paid job at 85 points, and another company used 2,500 points for the highest-paid job. In a few cases, the companies have definitely tied in their points assigned to a given job to the hourly rate paid for this job. One company used a base of 400 points for all jobs. These 400 points are added to all jobs, the total rating for an individual job being 400 plus the sum of the points assigned for the various characteristics evaluated. This company discontinued using this plan many years ago. Today it uses a master hierarchy of common jobs. Determining a rate for any job is done on an over-all appraisal basis by taking into account the required qualities of skill, responsibility, and working conditions relative to these same qualities as required in the key, or master, job list, and in accordance with the local plant wage structure.

The number of points assigned as the maximum for the highest-paid job is of no particular significance, provided that this total is not fixed in case a new job is developed that has a total requirement higher than the maximum in use. Some systems do have a maximum number of points that can be assigned to any one characteristic. This limits the application of these systems to jobs that come within the limits set and may work an injustice should the system be applied to a job in which a certain characteristic is more important relatively than the points assigned as a maximum limit. Efforts of trade associations at standardization within a given industry would be a distinct contribution to that particular industry. The National Metal Trades Association, the National Electrical Manufacturers Association, and the Southern California Aircraft Industry have made notable contributions to this work.

The National Metal Trades Association and the Industrial Management Society each has developed a complete job-evaluation plan that has had wide use. These two plans are excellent for illustrating the point systems. Each of these systems uses detailed descriptions of each characteristic with illustrations to aid in assigning point values to any new job being rated. Space will not permit the giving of these details.

1. **National Metal Trades Association.** The National Metal Trades Association divides each factor into five degrees and assigns point values to each degree. This plan also establishes grades for various total point scores. This system has been widely used in the metal trades. This wide usage has added to its value in these trades for comparative purposes. The points assigned to the various factors and the key to the grades are given in Table 10.5.

Table 10.5   *Points Assigned to Various Factors in Job Rating**

| Factors | First degree | Second degree | Third degree | Fourth degree | Fifth degree |
|---|---|---|---|---|---|
| **Skill:** | | | | | |
| 1. Education | 14 | 28 | 42 | 56 | 70 |
| 2. Experience | 22 | 44 | 66 | 88 | 110 |
| 3. Initiative and ingenuity | 14 | 28 | 42 | 56 | 70 |
| **Effort:** | | | | | |
| 4. Physical demand | 10 | 20 | 30 | 40 | 50 |
| 5. Mental or visual demand | 5 | 10 | 15 | 20 | 25 |
| **Responsibility:** | | | | | |
| 6. Equipment or process | 5 | 10 | 15 | 20 | 25 |
| 7. Material or product | 5 | 10 | 15 | 20 | 25 |
| 8. Safety of others | 5 | 10 | 15 | 20 | 25 |
| 9. Work of others | 5 | ... | 15 | ... | 25 |
| **Job conditions:** | | | | | |
| 10. Working conditions | 10 | 20 | 30 | 40 | 50 |
| 11. Unavoidable hazards | 5 | 10 | 15 | 20 | 25 |

| Score range | Grades | Score range | Grades |
|---|---|---|---|
| Up to 139 | ... | 250–271 | 6 |
| 140–161 | ... | 272–293 | 5 |
| 162–183 | 10 | 294–315 | 4 |
| 184–205 | 9 | 316–337 | 3 |
| 206–227 | 8 | 338–359 | 2 |
| 228–249 | 7 | 360–381 | 1 |

* Reproduced by permission of the National Metal Trades Association.

**2. Industrial Management Society.** The rating plan of the Industrial Management Society represents the collective effort of a special committee of industrial engineers of this association. Like that of the National Metal Trades Association, this plan has been widely used in America and to a lesser degree in foreign countries.

A. Job conditions.
   A1  Responsibility.
      A1.1  Equipment.
      A1.2  Materials.
      A1.3  Safety of others.
   A2  Supervision.
      A2.1  Supervision received.
      A2.2  Supervision given.

  A3  Working conditions.
      A3.1  Comfort.
      A3.2  Health hazards.
      A3.3  Accident hazards.
      A3.4  Clothing spoilage.
  A4  Adaptation period required for an average experienced workman to adapt himself to new conditions of employment when changing companies.

B. Physical requirements.
  B1  Bodily requirements.
      B1.1  Acuteness of senses.
      B1.2  Strength.
      B1.3  Endurance.
  B2  Skill.
      B2.1  Dexterity.
      B2.2  Precision.
      B2.3  Versatility.

C. Mental characteristics.
  C1  Schooling.
  C2  Knowledge.
      C2.1  Equipment and tools.
      C2.2  Methods.
      C2.3  Materials.
  C3  Judgment.
  C4  Ingenuity.
  C5  Initiative.[7]

To illustrate the details of the Industrial Management Society system, the point values for a portion of the subheadings of one factor are given below. This factor is *responsibility*.

*Responsibility* is the dependence placed upon human characteristics that cannot be replaced by mechanical contrivance but must be assumed by the individual. The degree of dependability required by the job is best expressed in terms of possible monetary loss or effect on others.

A1.1 *Equipment* consists of the tools and machinery with which work is performed. The weight given for responsibility of equipment does not depend entirely upon the cost of the equipment, but also on the probability of its being damaged.

[7] Industrial Management Society, *op. cit.*, pp. 8–31.

| Description | Points | Example |
|---|---|---|
| 1. $0 up to $100 | 0 | Bench coremaker, crater, painter, crane follower |
|  | 1 | Wood patternmaker, arc welder, hand milling |
| 2. Over $100 up to $500 | 2 | Toolroom milling, job-shop heat-treater, jig and fixture toolmaker |
|  | 3 | Punch-press operator, boring mill operator, drop-forger |
|  | 4 |  |
| 3. Over $500 up to $5,000 | 5 | Electrician, jig borer, die setter |
|  | 6 | Stationary fireman, chauffeur |
|  | 7 | Mixers of inflammables and explosives |
| 4. Over $5,000 up to $20,000 | 8 | Passenger-train engineer |
|  | 9 |  |
|  | 10 | Power-plant engineer |
| 5. Over $20,000 | 11 |  |
|  | 12 |  |
|  | 13 | Airplane pilot |

A1.2 *Materials* consist of the objects on which work is being performed. Responsibility for materials covers unnecessary losses from waste, damage, or misplacement over a period of 1 week. Here also, the probability of monetary loss should govern the weight allowed.

| Description | Points | Example |
|---|---|---|
| 1. $0 to $50 | 0 | Coremaker, counter, painter, dipper, repetitive machine operator |
| 2. Over $50 to $100 | 1 | Arc welder, bench molder, glazier |
| 3. Over $100 up to $1,000 | 2 | Grinder operator, engine-lathe operator, structural-steel layer-out, electrician |
|  | 3 | Metal-planer operator, millwright |
| 4. Over $1,000 up to $5,000 | 4 |  |
|  | 5 |  |
| 5. Over $5,000 up to $10,000 | 6 |  |
|  | 7 | Maintenance electrician—high voltage |
|  | 8 | Turbine repairman |

A1.3 *Safety of others.* The value of this factor should be selected according to the probability of accident and degree of injury caused by some direct act or negligence.

| Description | Points | Example |
|---|---|---|
| 1. No possibility of causing injury | 0 | Cellophane wrapper, material inspector, bench hand, coremaker |
| | 1 | Dipper, milling machine, toolmaker |
| | 2 | Shaft grinder, engine-lathe operator, punch-press operator |
| | 3 | Crane follower, die-cast operator |
| 2. Considerable care required to prevent injury | 4 | Maintenance electrician |
| | 5 | Pipe fitter—high pressure Drop-forger |
| | 6 | Elevator operator |
| | 7 | Chauffeur |
| 3. Great care required to prevent injury | 8 | Crane operator (bridge) |
| | 9 | |
| 4. Responsible for equipment, methods, or personnel involving severe health or accident hazards | 10 | Railroad towerman |
| | 11 | |
| | 12 | |
| | 13 | |
| | 14 | |
| | 15 | |
| | 16 | Airplane pilot |

A2.1 *Supervision received* determines to a large degree the responsibility placed on the individual—the less supervision involving the greater responsibility.

| Description | Points | Example |
|---|---|---|
| 1. Always available | 0 | Screw-machine operator, bench assembler |
| | 1 | Repetitive heat-treater, job-shop machine operator |
| 2. Usually available | 2 | Layer-out, structural-steel shop assembler, floor molder |
| | 3 | Maintenance electrician, millwright, construction pipe fitter |
| | 4 | Job-shop heat-treater, chauffeur |
| 3. Self-supervisory | 5 | Stationary engineer |
| | 6 | Inspector at supplier* |

* Reproduced from *Occupational Rating Plan for Hourly and Salaried Occupations,* by permission of the Industrial Management Society.

**Rating sales, office, and supervisory jobs.** Rapid strides have been made in the development of job-evaluation plans in sales and office jobs. This is to be expected. Job evaluation has also been used in a

Table 10.6  *Job Evaluation in Department Stores**

| Questions | Yes, per cent | No, per cent | No reply, per cent |
|---|---|---|---|
| Do you have a job-evaluation or job-classification plan: | | | |
| For nonselling employees?.................. | 52 | 31 | 17 |
| For selling employees?.................... | 52 | 28 | 20 |
| For supervisors......................... | 41 | 33 | 26 |
| Is it a point system?........................ | 16 | 40 | 44 |
| Is it a ranking system?...................... | 15 | 30 | 55 |
| Is it a Factor Comparison System?............. | 18 | 27 | 55 |
| Is it a classification system?................. ... | 23 | 20 | 57 |

* Source: "1958 Survey of Personnel Practices in Department Stores," *Personnel Study* 12, Bureau of Business Research, University of Texas, Austin, Texas, 1959.

limited way with supervisory jobs. Table 10.6 illustrates the use of job evaluation in department stores.

The various factors rated by Revere Copper and Brass, Inc., for clerical jobs, together with their point ranges, follow:

| *Factor* | *Point value* |

1. Elemental factors common to all positions. Constant value assigned   45
2. Educational requirements (grammar school rates 0 and 4 years above high school rates 14–16)..................................... 0–16
3. Practical experience required.................................. 0–15
4. Analytical requirement and complexity of work.................. 0–15
5. Accuracy.................................................... 1– 8
6. Memory..................................................... 0– 8
7. Manual dexterity............................................ 0– 5
8. Supervisional requirement.................................... 0–15
9. Conditions of work.......................................... 0– 5
10. Continuity of work.......................................... 0– 5
11. Physical strain on senses..................................... 0– 5
12. Relations or contacts........................................ 0– 8

In the Revere Copper and Brass manual for evaluating clerical positions, sample descriptions for the assigning of values to each characteristic are given. For instance, under Practical Experience Required, 7 to 9 points are given "where the necessary experience would require approximately three years' employment with the company in related positions." In the sample job evaluation on page 156 the superintendent's clerk has 6 points allocated for *experience required*. The blank on page 157 shows the form used for an operating supervisory position.

## Clerical Position Evaluation Plan

Division:  #5                          Evaluated by:  John Doe
                                                      Industrial Engineer

Department:  Casting Shop
Position:  Superintendent's Clerk        Date of Evaluation:  3/1/

| Factor No. | Description | Selected Value |
|---|---|---|
| 1. | Elemental Factor Value | 45 |
| 2. | Education Requirements | 6 |
| 3. | Practical Experience Required | 6 |
| 4. | Analytical Requirements and Complexity of Work | 4 |
| 5. | Accuracy | 5 |
| 6. | Memory | 4 |
| 7. | Manual Dexterity | 1 |
| 8. | Supervisional Requirements | 0 |
| 9. | Conditions of Work | 2 |
| 10. | Continuity of Work | 1 |
| 11. | Physical Strain on Senses | 4 |
| 12. | Relations or Contacts | 2 |

Total Selected Value:  80
Converted Value:
Maximum Base Rate Indicated:
Range:

Approved By:  John Jones
                  Work Manager
Date Approved:  3/4/

Description of Position

The duties of this position are sharply defined between two groups. The first involves the weighing (1) of Casting Shop individual metal production; (2) of virgin metal loads in passage to Metals Storage and the Casting Shop; (3) of scrap metal purchases taken from trucks and railway cars to be stored in Metals Storage; (4) of plant production scrap in transit from other departments to Metal Storage Department. The second group embraces the clerical duties incident to the Casting Shop and includes: (1) the preparation of daily Casting Shop production reports and the verification of similar reports prepared by others; (2) the preparation of bonus slips for individual Casters; (3) preparation of reports on production in fulfillment of specified orders; (4) recording the amounts of production of Ajax, Detroit Electric and Reverberatory Furnaces and the Cabbaging Machine; and (5) the performance of a number of miscellaneous duties including the answering and making of telephone inquiries, running errands for supervisory officials, issuing receipts and tally sheets, and filling out employees' passes.

FIG. 10.2. Sample job evaluation of a superintendent's clerk, used by Revere Copper and Brass, Inc.

*Table* 10.7  *Point Values in Job Evaluation for Selected Executives in a
Well-known Middle Western Company*

| Factor | Auditor | Traffic manager | Industrial engineer | Purchasing manager | Range of points |
|---|---|---|---|---|---|
| Policy.................... | 6 | 6 | 6 | 10 | 2–30 |
| Planning................. | 4 | 18 | 19 | 18 | 1–30 |
| Methods................. | 20 | 15 | 29 | 5 | 2–30 |
| Administration........... | 2 | 4 | 5 | 3 | 1–30 |
| Personnel relations........ | 14 | 10 | 11 | 5 | 1–30 |
| Executive contacts........ | 17 | 7 | 11 | 22 | 1–30 |
| Outside contacts.......... | 6 | 15 | 6 | 24 | 3–30 |
| Original thinking.......... | 15 | 8 | 23 | 8 | 8–30 |
| Analysis................. | 23 | 17 | 23 | 20 | 3–30 |
| Profit................... | 8 | 15 | 23 | 30 | 8–30 |
| Total evaluation points... | 115 | 115 | 156 | 145 | |

Operating Supervision Position Evaluation Form

Division:_____Evaluated by:_____

                                                     Industrial Engineer

Department:_____

Position:_____Date of evaluation:_____

*Factor No.*               *Description*                         *Selected Values*

  1. Elemental factor value                                 _____

  2. Technical knowledge required                 _____

  3. Practical knowledge required                 _____

  4. Exercise of judgment                        _____

  5. Demand for leadership                      _____

  6. Planning                                       _____

  7. Number of employees                        _____

  8. Conditions of work                          _____

  9. Liability of damage to product               _____

                                     Total selected value:_____

                                       Converted Value:_____

                   Maximum Base Salary Indicated:_____

                                             Range:

Approved by:_____

                Works Manager

Date approved:_____

        (See reverse side for description of position.)

Fig. 10.3. Form for evaluating operating supervisory positions, used by Revere Copper and Brass, Inc.

Table 10.7 gives the point values and ranges of the characteristics of the system of rating supervisory jobs by one well-known manufacturer in the Middle West. An inspection of this table shows that the purchasing agent plays an important role in influencing profits. It should not be inferred that the relative ranking of these functions would be the same in another industry. It is interesting to note the factors that this company rates in establishing its rating of supervisory positions.

**Relating job values to wages.** Job evaluation has value even though the general average of the wages paid for the jobs may be somewhat lower than the community level. It removes inequalities in such wage scales and thus promotes contentment within the group even though the entire wage level, owing to an unfortunate competitive situation, may be lower than is desired. Job evaluation is particularly helpful in establishing rates for new jobs. Job rating also is a valuable tool in guiding the personnel department in establishing lines of promotion and in the selection and training programs. When the jobs have all been evaluated, the problem of relating the relative values of the

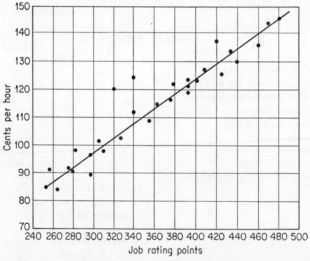

Fig. 10.4. Scatter diagram of hourly rates and job-rating points, indicating the relationship between two variables, rate per hour and job-rating points. The independent variable (job-rating points) is plotted on the X axis, and the dependent variable (cents per hour) is plotted on the Y axis. The regression line (line of average relationship) is drawn by inspection. This line may be computed, if a straight-line relationship is assumed from the formula, by $Y = a + bx$ and by the normal equations $\Sigma Y = Na + b\Sigma X$ and $\Sigma XY = a\Sigma X + b\Sigma X^2$. For a more detailed discussion of this technique see John R. Stockton, *Business Statistics*, South-Western Publishing Company, Cincinnati, 1958, Chaps. 17–18, pp. 411–450.

jobs to money wages arises. It is common practice to plot present rates on a graph having the base, or X axis, job grades or points and the vertical, or Y axis, money. This gives a scatter diagram (Fig. 10.4). From this chart it will be observed that many jobs are higher than the line of average relationship and that others of the same point value are decidedly below. Naturally, it is to be expected that there will be a range above and below the mean, but the illustrative diagram shows jobs two or three grades lower than a given grade with a scale as high as the higher-rated job.

In adjusting rates throughout the business to conform to the job requirements no problem is encountered when rates are raised. The problem arises in getting the overrated jobs down to the place where they belong. Radical cuts usually result in strikes. Better success has usually followed the training of the overpaid employees for the job grades that pay what these employees are getting and the hiring of replacements at the proper rates, thus making the adjustments in time. Occasionally a particular group, by virtue of strong union pressures, may demand and get a rate out of all proportion to their worth in terms of job evaluation. This creates a serious problem of keeping wages in line with the job-evaluation program. Teamsters frequently raise a problem of this nature. If all wages are out of line with respect to community rates, naturally they should be raised to be in line with the new scale secured by union pressure (*i.e.*, if the company is in a financial position to do so). If the other rates are in line with community rates and the one group is too high, the usual practice is merely to circle the one that is too high, an abnormal situation thus being recognized.

# CHAPTER 11

# *Merit Rating*

**Origin of merit rating.** The rating of individuals to determine their relative worth is as old as the payment of persons according to their contribution to the company. The early efforts at such rating were informal. *Merit rating of an employee is the process of evaluating the employee's performance on the job in terms of the requirements of the job.* In some instances the factor of promotability is included as an item to be considered in estimating the man's total worth to the firm. This is a sound practice in certain situations; yet a man's promotability in reality is not a part of his value in performing his present job. The term *merit rating* is not used universally in referring to the evaluation of an employee's performance. Such synonyms as service rating, personnel review, personality rating, employee appraisal, behavior rating, progress report, executive evaluation, and estimates upon nonmeasurable abilities, qualities, traits, habits, or achievements are often used. It should be clearly recognized that an employer rates an employee any time he pays one person more than another doing the same job. This may be solely on seniority, but it is a crude form of rating. Actually seniority is not an important factor in merit rating, but it is occasionally used, particularly in wage determination. Out of the work done by the Bureau of Salesmanship Research in 1916 evolved in 1917 a practical method both for selecting salesmen and for measuring the degree to which desirable traits are possessed by the salesmen in service—*i.e.*, both for selection and for merit rating. A special staff from the Bureau of Salesmanship Research after prolonged experimentation and deliberation succeeded in getting the War Department to adopt the rating scale as the official instrument:

1. For selecting candidates who might attend the military schools conducted for prospective officers.

2. For selecting from among the graduates of these schools those who were to receive commissions.

3. For periodic merit ratings for every commissioned officer. No officer was eligible for promotion unless his merit rating on the scale was as high as 60. Any officer whose rating was below 45 was subject to transfer or demotion.

Some form of merit rating has been used by the various branches of the present Defense Department ever since World War I. These systems of rating are not uniform in the different branches of the service even today. They have done a great deal of experimenting to try to refine their rating during the past 30 years.

**Use of merit rating.** As indicated above, an informal rating of employees for wage determination has been used for a long time. Management strives to improve its tools of appraisal from time to time. Unions and many employees do not like merit rating as a rule and prefer some kind of automatic raises based on seniority. Seniority alone seldom satisfies management as a basis of wage payment or for promotions. Merit ratings are used in business as a record of progress for apprentices and regular employees; as a guide in making promotions, transfers, or demotions; as a guide in making lists for bonus distribution, for seniority consideration, and for rates of pay; as an instrument for discovering hidden genius; and as a source of information that makes conferences with employees helpful. One large company in the Chicago area has a wage plan approximating that of measured day rate. This company rates only on one characteristic: How well does he perform his job? All employees meeting standard are paid a fixed hourly rate. Those going above standard are paid rates above the fixed expected rate. When an employee falls below standard for a pay period, his rate is automatically lowered 5 cents for the ensuing pay period. Should he not return to standard during the period in which his rate was 5 cents below the standard rate, his rate is lowered another 5 cents. He will continue to earn 10 cents less than standard until he has a pay period in which his average is up to standard. When this happens, he is automatically returned to the standard rate for the next pay period and all succeeding periods during which he meets standard. In other words, his rate is lowered in two steps when he is falling below standard, but he returns to the expected normal rate in one step. The primary uses made of employees' performance rating are as follows:

1. To determine the relative rate within a given range of a particular job classification.

2. To aid in selecting persons for promotion, demotion, or layoff.

3. To aid the supervisor in his conferences with an employee when trying to get him to overcome weaknesses.

*Automatic Raises*

**Merit ratings and promotions.** Some companies ask for a special rating of an employee who is being considered for promotion. This company does not ask for a rating of every person whose record is examined as a part of a sorting process to eliminate all but a few persons from whom the final selection is made. Of course in these special ratings it is important to check against previous ratings. This is especially true when the most recent rating is substantially higher than the rating immediately preceding it. Occasionally a supervisor will adjust his rating of the employee to suit his recommendation for promotion or demotion. One very large company has a union contract that states in substance that seniority gives preference when ability, merit, and capacity are equal. A referee in this company handed down a ruling several years ago that seniority would govern unless the employee for whom superior ability was claimed was head and shoulders above the one having greater seniority. In many other companies the higher merit does not have to be so pronounced. It must be remembered that where employees are promoted on the basis of due consideration to seniority and merit the supervisor must give constant care in rating his employees. For instance, if employee *A* with greater seniority than employee *B* has regularly been rated on a par with *B*, the supervisor will have a grievance on his hands if he rates *A* lower than *B* at the time of appraisal for promotion.

**Discussing the rating with the employee.** Most persons advocate the showing of an employee the rating that his supervisor gives him. There is much to commend this procedure. Many supervisors do not like to show employees their ratings when they have been marked below average. Supervisors are not anxious to have to defend their ratings, particularly with an aggressive worker who may be below average. If the supervisor can show that he has carefully rated a worker on each characteristic against his fellow workers and can point out wherein the given worker has fallen down, the supervisor can use this conference as an instructional medium. The other side of the picture presents itself when management is trying to get an appraisal of the relative value of several persons for possible promotion. In such cases a more impartial picture is likely to be presented if the supervisor does not have to defend the rating with his employees. It may even be better to have a collective rating of the persons being considered. This collective rating could readily be made by the immediate supervisor and by the supervisor above the immediate supervisor such as the general foreman and the division superintendent or in the case of there being no general foreman or division superintendent the personnel director might be the third person.

**Items considered in rating employees.** Some companies rate only one item, namely, "How well does he do his job?" Others break the rating down into great detail, listing various shades of the characteristics, totaling more than 100 shades of the various items. Those characteristics which are pertinent to success on the job are included. Various companies have rating forms for manual workers, supervisors, office workers, salespeople, middle management, and higher executives. It is seldom that any one company would have separate rating scales for each of the foregoing groups. Three scales are about all any one particular company uses. Table 11.1 illustrates the wide variety of characteristics rated by different types of companies. These illustrations are not presented as being typical. They merely show the wide diversity of items considered by some well-known companies. The sound approach is for the responsible executives and supervisors in each company to consider the factors that are to them important to success on the job and use these as a basis for rating their employees. A factor analysis could readily be made of the characteristics rated. Such an analysis would show that many of the characteristics *overlap* when a large number of characteristics are used.

**Types of employee performance ratings.** Employees are rated by various companies on the (1) numerical, (2) graphic, and (3) forced basis. A numerical system gives point or percentage values to the various characteristics. It is usually presumed that the sum of the values gives the relative value of the employee rated. Broadly speaking this may be correct; yet a person may have a fairly high total score and be rejected or released because of great deficiency in respect to one item, as when a salesperson is untrustworthy in handling money. This criticism may be obviated by having a critical score for any given characteristic below which an employee is not acceptable. Graphic rating scales use graphs for each characteristic evaluated, the rater merely checking on the scale where he thinks the employee belongs. This type of rating is easier for most people than the use of numerical values. Graphic scales may be converted into numerical values when desired by having numerical values assigned to the relative positions on the scale.

Forced rating of employees encounters some resistance from raters because they like to rate all persons above average or high. Forced rating refers to the custom of setting a distribution that is expected for a given group of employees doing similar work.[1] It is assumed

[1] See Joseph Tiffin, "Merit Rating: Its Validity and Techniques," American Management Association, *Personnel Series* 100, New York, 1946, pp. 14–23, for an interesting discussion of this type of rating.

## Table 11.1  Characteristics Used by Selected Companies in Merit Rating

| A large bank | Manufacturing | Metal manufacturing | Department store | Manufacturing plant |
|---|---|---|---|---|
| 1. Production<br>2. Accuracy<br>3. Promptness<br>4. Neatness<br>5. Thoroughness<br>6. Industriousness<br>7. Supervision required<br>8. Ease of learning<br>9. Knowledge of own work<br>10. Memory<br>11. Cooperation<br>12. Self-control<br>13. Persistence<br>14. Attitude toward job<br>15. Personal appearance<br>16. Health<br>17. Punctuality | Machine operator<br>1. Job knowledge<br>2. Quantity of work<br>3. Quality of work<br>4. Acceptance of responsibility<br>5. Cooperation<br>6. Initiative<br>Setup man<br>1. Accuracy<br>2. Job knowledge<br>3. Ability to instruct<br>4. Speed<br>5. Safety | 1. Quality of work<br>2. Quantity of work<br>3. Adaptability<br>4. Job knowledge<br>5. Dependability<br>6. Attitude | Salespeople<br>1. Appearance<br>2. Job knowledge<br>3. Knowledge of merchandise<br>4. Customer contact<br>5. Speed in selling | Supervisor<br>1. Employee relations<br>2. Meeting quality requirements<br>3. Meeting cost requirements<br>4. Meeting schedules<br>5. Maintenance<br>6. Leadership<br>7. Job knowledge<br>8. Dependability and judgment<br>9. Initiative and creative ability<br>10. Health |

164

that a normal group of workers doing the same job would fall into some such grouping as superior, above average, average, below average, and poor and that the relative percentages would be approximately 10-20-40-20-10. One company used only four groups, with percentages of 10-40-40-10. Some foremen have difficulty in distributing their men on such a basis; so they are asked to rank the men from the best to the poorest and then allot the appropriate percentage on the basis of this ranking. In case there are only 1 or 2 employees foremen are asked to rate these persons as if they were in a group of 25 or 30. These groups may be assigned code identifications or letters such as A, B, C, D, and E. In forced rating the employees are usually rated on how well they perform their jobs. Figures 11.1 and 11.2 are used by one company in forced rating. It will be noted that this form has two distinct parts, neither of which is dependent on the other. To this form for the promotability section the following could easily be added:

Recommended action to be taken:_____

---

Forced rating overcomes many of the objections raised to more complicated systems and seems to be as reliable as the more complex ones.

A second form of forced rating has encountered even more resistance than forcing supervisors to distribute their ratings on some percentage basis as described above. In this system of rating the in-

---

Name_____Dept._____
      (Last)         (First)

I. *Job Performance:*

How satisfactory is this employee in the performance of his (or her) *present* job?

NOTE: Consider such items as general productivity, including quality and quantity of work, specific job knowledge, safety, industry, dependability, cooperation, and perseverance.

Number of employees ranked_____ (_____)

This employee's rank (#1 is high)_____ (_____)

Leave blank_____ (_____)

Date_____Ranked by_____

FIG. 11.1. Form used by a large company in forced rating.

dividuals the rater does not know the rating that he gives the employee. This type of rating is developed by the use of a complicated statistical process. A series of statements in groups of four are provided. The rater is requested to check the statement in each group that is most like the person being rated and one that is least applicable to him. These ratings are then scored by a key that has been worked out in great detail. The rater does not know what kind of score he is giving a person. He merely marks him as indicated above. This system has merit when properly worked out, but some raters do not like to use a form unless they know the results of their efforts. The three groups of statements given below are illustrative of the types of statements that are used:

### FORCED-CHOICE QUADRUPLETS*

☐Makes little effort at individual instruction.
☐Organizes work well.
☐Lacks the ability to make people feel at ease.
☐Has a cool, even temperament.

☐Possesses good health and vitality.
☐Late for staff meetings.
☐Cooperates with top management.
☐Somewhat timid and retiring.

☐Always gets the job done.
☐Contradicts the words of other supervisors.
☐Consistent in expectations of the workers.
☐Refuses to admit a mistake.

* The rater is sometimes requested to mark a + for the statement that is most applicable, and a − for the statement which is least applicable.

An effective employee rating system *should rate the employee in terms of his actual performance on the present job.* A given employee might be rated C or even D on performance, yet under the promotability side be marked promotable to a higher job because of special qualifications for the higher job when he is average or even below average on his present job. Such a situation might easily arise in the case of a toolmaker by trade who is currently working on a production machine because there is no vacancy in toolmaking. A similar situation might arise in a department store or office or even among supervisors. It could readily arise in the case of a college teacher who was teaching statistics but who was primarily trained in management or marketing.

**Employee participating in rating.** As was indicated earlier, employees tend not to want to be rated but to be paid on an automatic basis of raises or to be paid, in the case of an incentive basis, solely

Name_____Dept._____
       (Last)             (First)

II. *Promotability:*

    To what extent does this employee possess abilities and aptitudes over and above those demanded by the present job?

       NOTE: Consider such items as versatility, adaptability, initiative, resourcefulness, broad job knowledge, willingness and ability to accept responsibility.

Number of employees ranked_____ (_____)

This employee's rank (#1 is high)_____ (_____)

                     Leave blank_____ (_____)

Date_____Ranked by_____

FIG. 11.2. Back of form shown in Fig. 11.1.

on objective data. This statement does not apply only to manual workers. Public school and college teachers also as groups tend to object to being rated. Any real rating of employees should consider objective data in so far as they are available. On the other hand there are some desirable phases of employment that are by their very nature subjective. This does not mean that they are unimportant. For instance, cooperation with fellow workers and supervisors may be very important. The average employee neither profits nor loses by automatic raises that conform to costs-of-living or across-the-board increases. The below-average employee, under such a system, gets more than he is worth. The above-average employee is penalized by such a system.

Where management has emphasized payment according to productivity over a period of years and has conscientiously rewarded its employees on merit, opposition to merit rating is reduced or it may even be participated in by the employees themselves. The Woodward Governor Company has had a long and successful experience in securing cooperation of employees in production and other relationships. Each member of each department rates each other member. The supervisor also rates each employee. Then the results of the worker evaluation and supervisor's evaluation are computed into a departmental evaluation list by the supervisor in consultation with the plant rating committee. The plant rating committee then establishes a master evaluation list for the entire factory. This is a list wherein all hourly wage earners, as well as supervisory and executive personnel, are

**EMPLOYEE MERIT RATING**
**SUMMARY SHEET**

_____
(Summary Date)

_____    _____    _____    _____
(Name)                 (Badge No.)              (Department)              (Occupation)

This rating chart should assist in improving the organization by analyzing the employees for improvement on their present jobs and for the possibility of advancement. The descriptive phrases over each box for each of the six questions are for guidance in making this rating. Place an "X" in the box which indicates the most accurate answer (transcribe information from Work Sheets). Be fair; do not be too strict or too lenient. Remember the employee may possess both outstanding qualities and deficiencies which may result in a high rating on one trait and a low rating on another.

| 1. IS THE EMPLOYEE SAFETY CONSCIOUS? | Often violates safety instructions. A hazard to himself and others. | Careless in work habits. Takes some chances | Generally works safely. Makes occasional safety suggestions. | Complies with safety instructions and suggests improvements for safety. | Is extremely safety conscious and is very active in promoting safety. |
|---|---|---|---|---|---|
| | ☐ | ☐ | ☐ | ☐ | ☐ |

| 2. HOW DOES THE EMPLOYEE PERFORM JOB OPERATIONS? (A. Select degree of performance.) (B. In that column only check traits needing improvement.) | Performance unsatisfactory<br>Quality ____<br>Quantity ____<br>Skill ____ | Performance fair<br>Quality ____<br>Quantity ____<br>Skill ____ | Performance meets normal requirements.<br>Quality ____<br>Quantity ____<br>Skill ____ | Does more than the job requires.<br>Quality ____<br>Quantity ____<br>Skill ____ | Far exceeds job requirements.<br>Quality ____<br>Quantity ____<br>Skill ____ |
|---|---|---|---|---|---|

| 3. IS THE EMPLOYEE DEPENDABLE? (this does not refer to absenteeism and tardiness.) | Lazy, a loafer. Wastes time. | Takes it easy. Requires close supervision. | Usually a good worker; stays on his job with normal supervision. | Steady worker; on his job under most conditions with a minimum of supervision. | Very hard worker. Can be depended on to complete all job assignments. |
|---|---|---|---|---|---|
| | ☐ | ☐ | ☐ | ☐ | ☐ |

| 4. DOES THE EMPLOYEE HAVE INITIATIVE? | Must be told more than once. Apparently does no thinking for himself. | Does only what he is told. Relies on others to help him. | Does what is required. Makes an occasional suggestion. | Resourceful Usually alert to opportunities for improvement of work. | A self starter. Sees things to be done and does them. |
|---|---|---|---|---|---|
| | ☐ | ☐ | ☐ | ☐ | ☐ |

| 5. HOW DOES THE EMPLOYEE WORK WITH OTHERS? | Does not work well with others. Antagonistic. | Occasionally in difficulty with others. Objects to some job assignments. | Gets along with others. Responds to job assignments. | Will go out of his way to help others when needed. | Very good spirit in working with others. Voluntarily steps in to help others. |
|---|---|---|---|---|---|
| | ☐ | ☐ | ☐ | ☐ | ☐ |

| 6. WHAT DOES THE EMPLOYEE KNOW ABOUT HIS JOB? | Insufficient knowledge to perform work satisfactorily. | Has some knowledge of his job; inadequate for normal performance. | Has sufficient knowledge to do his job. | Has a good working knowledge of his own and related jobs. | Exceptionally well informed about his and related jobs. |
|---|---|---|---|---|---|
| | ☐ | ☐ | ☐ | ☐ | ☐ |

COMMENTS ON OUTSTANDING QUALITIES OR DEFICIENCIES: _____

_____

_____

THIS WORKER WAS INTERVIEWED ON THIS MERIT RATING
AND WAYS OF IMPROVING WERE DISCUSSED. _____
(Date)                          Interviewing Supervisor's Signature

RATED BY: 1. _____    2. _____    3. _____

COMMENTS BY EMPLOYEE: (Optional) _____

NOTE: See reverse side for additional comments
on outstanding qualities and deficiencies.

Fig. 11.3. Employee rating form used by a large corporation.

placed in a single master list in numerical order according to their value to the company.

**Some sample rating forms.** As indicated earlier, merit rating is opposed by many employees. A part of this opposition arises from a basic distrust of anyone in authority,[2] and a part of it arises from

[2] See Chap. 13, Human Relations, p. 196.

a sincere questioning of the ability of the supervisor to judge accurately the abilities and performance of the employees. There is enough truth in this questioning of employees to justify management's going to great lengths to secure uniformity among the various raters as well as objectivity in so far as possible. It is not at all unusual for one rater to rate all persons above average. This is grossly unfair to another supervisor, and his group, when he honestly strives to follow the established and published norm. Certain forms and certain procedures aid in securing uniformity in evaluation. A graphic rating form is easier for most supervisors to fill out than one calling for a numerical value. A rating blank using a check list similar to the graphic form (Fig. 11.3) simplifies rating the employee. Actually Fig. 11.3 can be checked as if it were a graph even though it is constructed to be checked in the squares. This same form is sometimes arranged so that the high score on the first line will be to the right; on the second line the high score would be to the left. This alternating would be continued for the other lines or characteristics, thus reducing the tendency to be influenced by the "halo effect."

Some companies try to rate all employees on one form, and others use as many as three forms, one for manual workers, one for clerical and white-collar employees, and a third for supervisory and executive personnel. Three separate forms are more likely to facilitate merit rating than to try to adjust one form to encompass all employees.

Figures 11.3 and 11.4 illustrate, respectively, the summary sheet of an employee and a work sheet for one characteristic. This work sheet is an excellent device when the rater is required to arrange his employees from highest to lowest for each characteristic. Some companies ask the foreman to turn in to the personnel department only the work sheet, and clerks in the employment department fill out the summary sheets for the individual workers from the work sheets. Figure 11.5 is a section of the employee rating chart constructed by E. F. Wonderlic, president of General Finance Corporation. In addition to the two characteristics shown, this form covers in a similar manner, cooperation and conduct, adaptability and initiative, and ability to communicate ideas. On the back of the sheet, space is provided to answer the following questions.

1. Is this employee performing the task for which he is best fitted? If not, what should he do?
2. What particularly desirable good traits does he possess?
3. How, specifically, does he need to improve himself?
4. What additional comments should be made which have not been previously covered?

The items to be included in the rating of employees should be definitely related to his productivity and his desirability as an employee. It must be admitted that these two considerations do not necessarily go together. An occasional employee may be a high producer of excellent quality when he is on the job, but for various reasons his attendance is poor so that he cannot be counted on. His absenteeism may arise from many sources, such as not caring whether or not he works, poor health, family situation, emotional instabilities manifesting itself in drunkenness, the use of drugs, etc. On the other hand he may be regular in attendance, do good work, and produce above average; yet he may be a disturbing influence in the group. Still another employee may be thoroughly acceptable as an individual and group member but be low in both quality and quantity of production. The productivity of an employee for merit rating purposes is (as a rule) more important than many other items, yet the entire man is employed, and the rating should show the total picture. In rating manual workers one well-managed company includes: quantity of work, quality of work, follows instructions, acceptance of responsibility, attendance, initiative, judgment, cooperative attitude, personal qualities. This same company asks the rater to check and make comments on any unusual item that resulted in the rating as well as to

**EMPLOYEE MERIT RATING**
**WORK SHEET**

Date ______ Department ______

This rating sheet should assist you in determining how employees in the same occupation stand in relationship to each other on the question below. Place an "X" after each employee's name in the column under the descriptive phrase which best describes your answer concerning him on this question. Be fair; do not be too strict or too lenient.

**6. WHAT DOES THE EMPLOYEE KNOW ABOUT HIS JOB?**

| Name (Grouped by Occupation) | Badge Number | Insufficient knowledge to perform work satisfactorily. | Has some knowledge of his job; inadequate for normal performance. | Has sufficient knowledge to do his job. | Has a good working knowledge of his own and related jobs. | Exceptionally well informed about his and related jobs. |
|---|---|---|---|---|---|---|
| | | | | | | |
| | | | | | | |
| | | | | | | |
| | | | | | | |
| | | | | | | |
| | | | | | | |

NOTE: Comment on outstanding qualities and deficiencies on reverse side of this sheet.

Rater's Signature ______

FIG. 11.4. Work sheet for one characteristic used in merit rating.

# EMPLOYEE RATING CHART

Office.............................. Date.............. Total Points................

Name...................................................... Rated by................

Position.................................................. Approved................

**1. QUANTITY OF WORK:** Some employees are capable of unusually high, sustained output. They know their jobs thoroughly and consistently produce more than is expected of the average employee.

Others produce what is expected of them and have a good general knowledge of their jobs. They may produce at a relatively steady pace or they may work rapidly at times with corresponding periods of below-average output.

Still others produce very little more than is required as a minimum necessary to hold their jobs.

Somewhere between the extremes will be found varying degrees of work output. Consider this employee carefully on the basis of what you have observed since the date you last rated him. Write in specific examples of behavior on which your judgment is based.

| 1 | 2 | 3 | 4 | 5 |
|---|---|---|---|---|
| Unusually High | | Average | | Minimum |

**2. QUALITY OF WORK:** Some employees consistently turn out work of high quality. They rarely make mistakes. When they finish an assignment it is complete, with no loose ends.

Others usually turn out acceptable work with an average number of errors. Still others make frequent mistakes. Their work lacks neatness and is usually not well organized. They rarely finish an assignment without assistance.

Somewhere between these extremes will be found varying degrees of accuracy, neatness, completeness—the factors that make for quality workmanship.

Rate this employee carefully on the basis of what you have observed since the last time you rated him. Write in examples:

| 1 | 2 | 3 | 4 | 5 |
|---|---|---|---|---|
| Consistently High | | Average | | Frequent Mistakes |

Fig. 11.5. Two of the six items used by General Finance in rating its employees. The other characteristics are cooperation and conduct, adaptability and initiative, ability to communicate ideas, and ability to develop. On the back of this form the rater is requested to answer six pertinent questions about the rating and the employee.

171

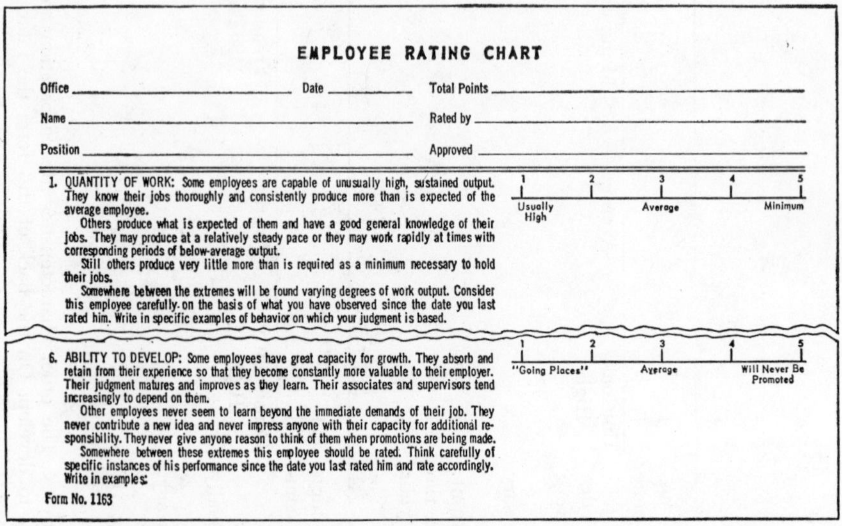

**EMPLOYEE RATING CHART**

Office _____  Date _____  Total Points _____

Name _____  Rated by _____

Position _____  Approved _____

1. QUANTITY OF WORK: Some employees are capable of unusually high, sustained output. They know their jobs thoroughly and consistently produce more than is expected of the average employee.

   Others produce what is expected of them and have a good general knowledge of their jobs. They may produce at a relatively steady pace or they may work rapidly at times with corresponding periods of below-average output.

   Still others produce very little more than is required as a minimum necessary to hold their jobs.

   Somewhere between the extremes will be found varying degrees of work output. Consider this employee carefully. on the basis of what you have observed since the date you last rated him. Write in specific examples of behavior on which your judgment is based.

   1 — 2 — 3 — 4 — 5
   Usually High     Average     Minimum

6. ABILITY TO DEVELOP: Some employees have great capacity for growth. They absorb and retain from their experience so that they become constantly more valuable to their employer. Their judgment matures and improves as they learn. Their associates and supervisors tend increasingly to depend on them.

   Other employees never seem to learn beyond the immediate demands of their job. They never contribute a new idea and never impress anyone with their capacity for additional responsibility. They never give anyone reason to think of them when promotions are being made.

   Somewhere between these extremes this employee should be rated. Think carefully of specific instances of his performance since the date you last rated him and rate accordingly. Write in examples:

   1 — 2 — 3 — 4 — 5
   "Going Places"     Average     Will Never Be Promoted

Form No. 1163

Fig. 11.6. Section of an employee rating chart. (*General Finance Corporation.*)

check one of the three following recommendations: (1) dismiss, (2) defer action until _____, (3) satisfactory—retain. Room on this form is provided for the writing in of any specific thing that is suggested that the employee do, such as "Attend night school to learn or improve his ability to read blueprints."

This same company has built its rating form for supervisors or persons directing the efforts of others in terms of the job requirements for the particular position. Each of the following requirements is rated in terms of five degrees of performance for which there are provided appropriate descriptive phrases.

1. Consider employee's interest in his job and company.

2. Consider his ability on job relations; his handling of personnel problems and grievances.

3. Consider employee's ability and interest in instructing those under him on job knowledge and good safety habits.

4. Consider employee's knowledge of his job.

5. Consider his success in going ahead with jobs assigned without being given every detail; his ability to make job improvements and to get jobs lined up and in good shape.

6. Consider employee's judgment in scheduling his work and meeting his deadlines.

7. Consider employee's industry on job.

8. Consider his reliability in meeting his responsibilities.

9. Consider employee's ability for leadership.

10. Consider his ability to cooperate with other departments and other supervision.

The descriptive phrases for item 5 above are: (1) Very resourceful. Has initiative and creativity in improving standards, processes, product, organization and in leadership in human relations. (2) Resourceful and efficient; plans work. (3) Usually meets standards. (4) Needs urging. (5) Unsatisfactory. Should the list of items given above be used in rating middle management or top management, it might be well to add another item, Contribution to profits.

Some companies strive to get the rater to plan corrective measures to help the employee improve his performance. One company known for its leadership in business practices asks the rater to answer questions like the following in connection with the rating of supervisors:

1. Have you personally contacted this foreman or supervisor in connection with this merit rating?_____
Date_____

2. Have you outlined a program of personal development with him?_____

3. What were his reactions to your suggestions?_____ _____

4. What improvement have you observed since your last contact?_____

5. What is the personal goal of this foreman or supervisor?_____

6. What steps is he taking to reach his goal?_____

7. What advanced position, if any, is this foreman or supervisor now ready to assume? _____

8. What lack of leadership qualities, if any, will likely prevent this supervisor or foreman from advancing or will make it difficult for him to work efficiently in his present position?_____

9. Do you recommend retaining this supervisor or foreman in his present position?_____

10. Do you believe that this foreman or supervisor is better adapted to, and would be more efficient in, some other capacity and why?_____

The following quotations are taken from the back of a rating sheet for supervisors used by a well-known company.

Objectives of Supervisory Merit Rating:

1. To determine the special abilities of foremen and supervisors; which information should be helpful in determining qualifications for further development and advancement.

2. To determine the specific weakness of individual foremen and supervisors as a basis for a program of improvement and education.

Foremen and supervisors shall be rated semi-annually by their two immediate supervisors acting jointly.

When rating supervisors and foremen, the department heads should base their ratings on objective evidence as much as possible. Reports, production schedules.

handling of grievances, maintaining discipline, etc., are a matter of record. Personal opinions or prejudices should be eliminated entirely from the evaluations. Judgments should be based on personal contact, experience and the written record.

Definite recommendations should be made to the plant manager for the further development of each foreman and supervisor for the correction of any shortcomings.

Subsequent ratings shall indicate to what extent the program has been carried out and the result.

**Training raters.** As indicated earlier, some raters rate too high or too low. In order to secure reasonable uniformity, raters should be trained when a program of rating is initiated, and a refresher should be given just prior to a rating period. It has at times been helpful to have each supervisor in a group that is being trained rate every other member in the group on the characteristics desired in supervisors. If this is done before the training has progressed beyond the stage of giving them the standards, it will usually be found that they rate each other so that the average is B, even though the standard clearly specifies that the average is supposed to be C. If they are then required to rank each man from the highest to the lowest and then apply their norms, the result usually corresponds to the established norm. Raters tend to rate their employees above average and to give too much weight to recent happenings, particularly when the employee may have incurred the supervisor's wrath. It is highly desirable to strive to get raters to keep simple records as a basis for rating. In order to get some semblance of uniformity, it is necessary to train the raters by group discussions of the principles involved in rating and the meaning of the standards and actual practice in rating under supervision. It has to be emphasized that the employees are being rated not against the average man in the street but against men doing similar work in the department; toolmakers are to be compared not with machine operators but with toolmakers. When raters can be induced to rate each employee on one characteristic at a time before going to the next characteristic, especially to list all employees on the same sheet from the highest to the lowest, they usually come close to the desired norm. To rate each employee completely before going to the next employee tends to increase the "halo effect." This means simply that the rating of one characteristic influences the ratings given to the other characteristics of the same employee. Some forms try to avoid this by alternating the graphic scales, having the highest score to the right on one characteristic and to the left on the next.

**Rating employees.** Bitter experience with errors in rating, discarding a valuable management aid and later reviving it under changed and improved conditions, purposeful experimentation, and the combined

## EMPLOYEE RATING REPORT

NAME_____NO_____ TOTAL POINTS_____ GROUP_____

DEPT_____OCCUPATION_____CLASS_____

RATED BY_____DATE_____APPROVED BY_____DATE_____

### INSTRUCTIONS—Read Carefully

Each employee's ability and fitness in his PRESENT occupation or for promotion may be appraised with a reasonable degree of accuracy and uniformity, through this rating report. The rating requires the appraisal of an employee in terms of his ACTUAL PERFORMANCE. It is essential, therefore, that snap judgment be replaced by careful analysis. Please follow these instructions carefully:

1. Use your own independent judgment.
2. Disregard your general impression of the employee and concentrate on one factor at a time.
3. Study carefully the definitions given for each factor and the specifications for each degree.
4. When rating an employee, call to mind instances that are typical of his work and way of acting. Do not be influenced by UNUSUAL CASES which are not typical.
5. Make your rating with the utmost care and thought; be sure that it represents a fair and square opinion. DO NOT ALLOW PERSONAL FEELINGS TO GOVERN YOUR RATING.

6. After you have rated the employee on all six factors, write under the heading "General Comments" on the back, any additional information about the employee which you feel has not been covered by the rating report, but which is essential to a fair appraisal.
7. Read all four specifications for Factor No. 1. After you have determined which specifications most nearly fits the employee, place an X in the small square over it. If the specification adequately fits the employee, place an X in the left square. If he does not quite measure up to the specification but is definitely better than the specification for the next lower degree, place an X in the right square. Repeat for each factor.

| FACTOR | R-1 | R-2 | R-3 | R-4 | R-5 | R-6 | R-7 | R-8 |
|---|---|---|---|---|---|---|---|---|

| | | | | | | | | |
|---|---|---|---|---|---|---|---|---|
| **Can You Rely on Him?** | | | | | | | | |
| **5** DEPENDABILITY — THIS FACTOR APPRAISES YOUR CONFIDENCE IN THE EMPLOYEE TO CARRY OUT ALL INSTRUCTIONS CONSCIENTIOUSLY. | ☐ ☐ WHEN YOU GIVE HIM A JOB TO DO, HAVE YOU THE UTMOST CONFIDENCE THAT YOU WILL GET WHAT YOU WANT WHEN YOU WANT IT? | | ☐ ☐ DOES HE FOLLOW INSTRUCTIONS AND DO WHAT YOU EXPECT HIM TO DO WITH LITTLE FOLLOW UP? | | ☐ ☐ DOES HE GENERALLY FOLLOW INSTRUCTIONS BUT OCCASIONALLY NEED FOLLOWING UP? | | ☐ ☐ DOES HE REQUIRE FREQUENT FOLLOW UP, EVEN ON ROUTINE DUTIES? | |
| **6** ATTITUDE — THIS FACTOR APPRAISES THE EMPLOYEE'S OPEN-MINDEDNESS, AND HIS WILLINGNESS TO COOPERATE IN CARRYING OUT SAFETY AND OTHER COMPANY POLICIES. | ☐ ☐ IS HE AN EXCEPTIONALLY GOOD TEAM WORKER? DOES HE INVARIABLY GO OUT OF HIS WAY TO COOPERATE? IS HE ALWAYS READY TO TRY OUT NEW IDEAS? | | ☐ ☐ DOES HE MEET OTHERS HALF WAY AND GO OUT OF HIS WAY TO COOPERATE? IS HE USUALLY READY TO TRY OUT NEW IDEAS? | | ☐ ☐ DOES HE USUALLY COOPERATE, BUT WITH SOME RELUCTANCE TO ACCEPT SUGGESTIONS AND TRY OUT NEW IDEAS? | | ☐ ☐ DOES HE COOPERATE ONLY WHEN HE HAS TO? IS HE UNWILLING TO TRY OUT NEW IDEAS? DOES HE HAVE LITTLE INTEREST IN HIS JOB? | |

COPYRIGHT 1938—NATIONAL METAL TRADES ASSOCIATION
NMTA FORM 30    25M    **(OVER)**

Fig. 11.7. Section of rating report used by the National Metal Trades Association. Sections 1 to 4, showing quality and quantity of work, adaptability, and job knowledge, are omitted. (*Reprinted by special permission of the National Metal Trades Association.*)

experiences of many thoughtful practitioners have evolved some rules that may serve as guides to others seeking to do a good job of merit rating. These are:

1. The rater should be challenged to illustrate the type of action that he regards as characteristic of the ratee.

2. The rater should rate all his subordinates on a single quality or trait before rating any of the subordinates on any other traits.

A part of one sheet of the graphic rating scale devised by a large steel company is reproduced as Fig. 11.4. Each sheet contains the names (typewritten) of all the subordinates who are to be rated, with the instructions and space for rating on only one trait. The raters are not only asked to rate on one trait at a time, but the sheets are so arranged that it is easier to rate at one time all the ratees on a single trait than it is to rate at one time a single ratee on all the traits.

3. Ratings should be made in response to a pertinent question. The rating scale devised for the National Metal Trades Association expresses all the specific descriptive phrases in the form of questions. The instruction and the scale for dependability and for attitude are shown in Fig. 11.7.

4. If many persons are rated on a single trait, there would ordinarily be a few

low ratings and a few high ratings but most of the ratings would be near the average or median. The distribution of the ratings would be approximately that of the normal distribution. The distribution of ratings in the respective fifths might take this form: 7-24-38-24-7 or 10-20-40-20-10.

5. Careful consideration of the descriptive phrases below the line is essential to the accurate use of the rating scale. To assure attention to these phrases, the rater should not find it easy to rate by attending exclusively to the distances on the line.

6. The trait should be defined and illustrated in terms of work performed on the job.

7. The trait upon which the employee is to be rated must be a simple trait and not a compound one. The name of the trait should suggest one type of activity or one type of result achieved by those to be rated. The trait should not include unrelated factors (e.g., neatness and endurance, physique and voice), nor should the results achieved by the trait be ambiguously expressed.

8. The trait should be defined or expressed objectively and not subjectively. Filer and O'Rourke[3] provide the following illustrations:

## LEADERSHIP

Subjective definition: rate this executive's force, self-reliance, decisiveness, tact, ability to inspire men and to command their confidence, loyalty, and cooperation.

Objective definition: rate this executive according to the success he has shown in developing a loyal and effective organization by administering justice, inspiring confidence, and winning the cooperation of his subordinates.

9. In using a rating scale, all judgments should be based on observations of concrete actions. Mere guessing should be discouraged. Several rating scale forms supply a place for checking "No opportunity to observe" or some similar expression.

10. Only those traits should be subjectively evaluated on a rating scale that cannot be measured by an objective test. Even though these following traits are on one or more rating scales, each of the traits is capable of objective measurements: accuracy, speed, volume of production, attendance, health, intelligence, and physical condition. It is apparent that all these traits, in so far as they can be measured by objective tests, should be stricken from that part of the rating scale which is subjectively determined.

11. Any trait that manifests itself in industry manifests itself also in activities away from the workbench. In order that the mind of the rater should be restricted to industry, it may be desirable to omit the title of the trait but to decide it in terms of pertinent acts in industry.

12. The rater frequently finds that the rating scale fails to include certain traits or certain considerations that are important assets or are serious liabilities in the performance of the ratee. To encourage the giving of such information, a space on the right side, on the bottom, or on the reverse side of the scale calls for such additional information.

13. The executives who are asked to rate their subordinates need to be "sold" by a brief statement issued by the president of the company.

14. Each supervisor or other employee who is to be rated needs to be "sold" also. The following statement has been so used. The subordinate executive or

[3] *Journal of Personnel Research,* Vol. 1, p. 519.

supervisor who is being rated is assured a careful analysis of his special abilities. He does not have to push himself forward to obtain recognition.

When merit ratings are properly sold, investigators report that over 90 per cent of salespeople like to be rated and will give complete cooperation to any rating plan that they consider to be fair.

15. Every employee should have the protection and the advantage that comes from being rated periodically by three of his superiors who are in most intimate contact with his work.

16. Only those traits should be rated on a rating scale that are of the greatest importance in the progress of the individual. Usually from 5 to 15 are enough. The 5 most important are usually adequate.

17. Users of the rating scale have more and more come to recognize it as a convenient instrument for improving morale. Specifically it is being used to encourage the rater to recognize the talents and to promote the interests of the ratee. One company calls its form Personal Progress Appraisal and emphasizes the steps to be taken for improvement. This company instructs the raters to answer the following question:

### HOW I CAN HELP HIM TO BE MORE EFFECTIVE ON HIS PRESENT JOB

He should be given additional instruction on_____
He should be given additional experience on such jobs as_____
He should study such subjects as_____
He should change his attitude as follows_____
There is nothing more that I can do for him because_____
Remarks: _____

18. The rater should take the ratee into his confidence, show him his ratings, and discuss them with him. One purpose of employee ratings is to discover where further training is needed. When the employee knows that his ratings are low, he may regard further training as an opportunity and not as a burden. Another purpose of employee ratings is to secure a basis for salary adjustments. If the employee knows that his ratings are low, he will realize that his pay check can be increased only by self-improvement. When he sees that his immediate superiors agree in their judgments upon his qualifications, he may realize that advancement in the company is based on merit.

**Summary.** The foregoing 18 statements might well be considered a summary. Each has been developed out of practical experience, and each one would probably increase the reliability of the rating scale that embodied it. Where good graphic rating scales have been used and where the ratings have been made by three or more trained raters, high reliability has been reported. It is very difficult to get raters to follow the established norms when they have to show the rating to the employee and discuss it with him. This is true even when a committee of three persons including the supervisor does the rating. To overcome this, management sometimes asks for a special rating of an employee being considered for promotion, assuring the raters that the rating will be kept in strict confidence.

# CHAPTER 12

# *Promotion, Demotion, Transfer, and Discharge*

**Promotion.** Ambitious new employees are anxious for promotional opportunities. A *promotion is the transfer of an employee to a job that pays more money or one that enjoys some preferred status.* To be transferred from an hourly rate to a salary may be considered a promotion in some cases even though there is no actual money raise in pay. Salaried workers frequently enjoy certain privileges not generally accorded the hourly paid workers. In order that the worker-in-his-work unit may develop systematically his capacities, interests, and opportunities, it is recommended that transfers be administered on a planned basis. Transfers are important but not sufficient to meet the needs for harmonious development of the worker. Because of the effect on employees, promotions are more important than transfers.

Not only are promotions striven for by manual workers, they likewise are important to supervisors, executives, technical workers, and office employees. To train an adequate supply of qualified executives and supervisors requires a planned program rather than relying on the strongest man's forcing his way to the top. One such plan has been explained clearly as follows:

. . . When a few years later Cleo Craig became president, we immediately began to hear about the need for moving the decision-making power farther and farther down the line. This decentralization of authority was needed, he said, to meet the coming demand for trained top leadership in management.

The day is long since past when the Bell System hired a likely-looking college graduate, preferably with an engineering degree, assigned him to a specific department, and turned him loose, hoping he would emerge twenty years later as another Vail or Gifford. Now we indulge in schemes of cross-pollenization between departments, in special college courses for the younger executives, in week-long training sessions in which the higher levels are exposed to the best thinking in such fields as sociology, economics, finance, marketing. All this has as its aim the improvement of individual leadership, but perhaps its greatest value is the influence it has on the entire working force. It clearly says that those who supplement their telephone skill and knowledge with the attributes of the fully-rounded

178

life have a better chance of moving rapidly upwards in our highly competitive hierarchy.[1]

When carefully planned and carried out, *transfers and promotions promote morale, increase efficiency, and provide opportunity for loyal employees.* The following reasons for promoting employees have been mentioned by many business executives:

1. Promotion is the stepping up of an employee to a position in which he can render greater service to the company and derive increased personal satisfaction and income from his work.

2. The knowledge that deserved promotions are being made increases the interest of other employees in the company.

3. Such knowledge causes other employees to believe that their turns will come next, and so they remain with the company and reduce the labor turnover.

4. It creates a feeling of content with the present conditions and encourages ambition to succeed within the company.

5. It increases interest in training and in self-development as necessary preparation for promotion.

6. Promotions from within the company are not so apt to be mistakes as are selections from without.

**Promotion on merit.** A philosophy of promoting on merit is subscribed to by most people, but large numbers of people *distrust management's integrity to promote on merit.* Unions frequently distrust the good faith of management when it claims the right to promote solely on merit. There is also the question of the ability of some supervisors to recognize merit. It would be a grievous error to think that unions are the only ones who distrust management to promote on merit. Many nonunion workers have exactly the same sentiments. Public school teachers tend to oppose salary increases on merit and to support automatic increases. When management claims to promote on merit, it places a real burden on itself to establish controls that will recognize merit while minimizing the charges of favoritism. This is by no means an easy task. Merit rating based as far as possible on operating facts is the soundest method. Even though employees are carefully rated periodically, there is no assurance that promotion will be on merit unless these records are consulted before making a promotion.

**Seniority as a basis for promotions.** *Seniority refers to the relative length of service of employees. Usually length of service is computed solely on the basis of the current continuous employment. This would bar the counting of previous service with the possible exception of a break due to military service.* In the case of military service the

[1] *Bell Telephone Magazine,* Vol. XXVIII, No. 2, Summer, 1959, John M. Shaw, "Thirty Years of Change," p. 46.

employee is usually removed from the payroll in the same manner that he would be if he quit. However, his absence would not be counted against him in computing the length of service for seniority purposes. One ticklish item has often caused bitterness in connection with seniority and military service. A man with 3 years' service might be drafted and kept in the Army for the duration of the conflict, such as 4 years. His replacement on his company job would build up 4 years' seniority while he was serving in the armed services. When the drafted man returned, he would nearly always be given his old job back and the 3 years of seniority he had before he left, but the seniority frequently would not include the 4 years he was away.

Seniority may refer to total company-wide or plant-wide employment, departmental, occupational, shift, or almost any combination of these. An occasional company has two seniority groups—men and women. The seniority promotion plan is as old as civilization itself. The oldest son succeeded his father as chief, king, emperor, lord of the estate, as inheritor of the wealth and the power of his father. Seniority provided certainty and dependability. It reduced rivalry and struggle. Historically, the seniority method of promotion must be regarded as a success. It is still regarded highly in America by the armed services, labor unions, Civil Service, and commercial and industrial institutions. In modern business, however, seniority is quite inadequate as a universal promotional system. It survives merely because no better system has been developed that has won public confidence. For promotional purposes it is seldom that straight seniority applies between the factory workers, office workers, and sales group. Many union contracts specify that seniority for promotional opportunity is controlling when ability is equal. Often the workers are presumed to be equal in the sight of the union and some referees or arbitrators, save in the case where one of the employees is head and shoulders above the other in ability. There are various methods of using seniority as a factor in promotion. A few of these are as follows:

1. Straight plant-wide seniority on all jobs, promotion going to the oldest employee provided that he can do the work. Frequently he is given 1 week or 10 days in which to qualify for the job.
    1.1 Straight seniority may not belong to an employee unless he has attained some specified length of service, such as 5 years, or it may apply as soon as he attains permanent status.
2. Occupational seniority.
    2.1 Within the department.
    2.2 Within the division.
    2.3 Within the entire plant.

**The Gilbreth three-positional promotion plan.** Frank and Lillian Gilbreth, two pioneers in scientific management and founders of motion and time study, were interested in every phase of management including promotions. As early as 1916 they described their promotional plan as follows:

The Three Position Plan of Promotion considers each man as occupying three positions in the organization, and considers these three positions as constantly changing in an upward spiral. . . . The three positions are as follows: First, and lowest, the position that the man has last occupied in the organization; second, the position that the man is occupying at present in the organization; third, the highest, the position that the man will next occupy. In the third position the worker occupies the place of the teacher, this position being at the same time occupied by two other men, that is, by the worker doing the work, who receives little or no instruction in the duties of that position except in an emergency, and by the worker below who is learning the work. In the second position the worker is actually in charge of the work, and is constantly also the teacher of the man next below him, who will next occupy the position. He is also, in emergencies, a learner of the duties of his present position from the man above him. In the first position the worker occupies the place of the learner, and is being constantly instructed by the man in the duties of the position immediately above.

**Preparation for promotion by use of the understudy system.** *An understudy is one who works under the direction and guidance or supervision of another,* with the specific understanding that *he (the understudy) will be given the opportunity to learn the work of the man to whom he is the understudy.* In a manual job a helper may or may not be considered an understudy. An alert helper will learn his master's skills even though he may not be a formal understudy. The understudy strives to learn all the things that his mentor does. This system is particularly effective in filling vacancies that occur in executive and supervisory positions. However, it may be extended to include practically every position—high or low. This system places on each person the responsibility (with or without the cooperation of others) for selecting and training the best available employee for his successor. When the understudy system is applied to executives, each executive selects an assistant who becomes his understudy. This understudy acts for his superior on assigned tasks. He may substitute for him in case of absence or sickness. He has reason to hope that he will succeed his superior as soon as he is qualified and there is a vacancy.

It is not always wise to permit each executive to select his subordinate without the approval of at least one or possibly more executives above him. A representative of top management should participate in the selection of all supervisors. Otherwise, more capable men in other departments may be denied promotional opportunities

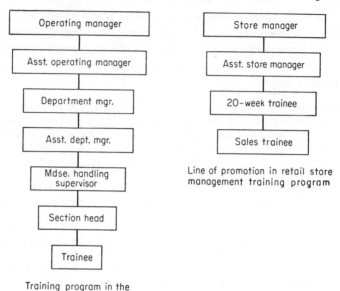

FIG. 12.1. Promotional charts in Montgomery Ward's mail-order house and retail store. (*Courtesy, Montgomery Ward and Company.*)

merely because they happen to be in a department that is not expanding rapidly or in some instances merely because their own supervisor did not leave, retire, die, or get promoted. Although others should be consulted in selecting understudies, it is not good practice to force an understudy on an unwilling executive. In the case of executives the understudy system has merit when some responsible representative of top management sees to it that the understudy is given opportunity to grow and broaden his experience.

**Promotional plans to be effective must be followed up.** Unless someone who has the interest and time to follow up the established plan is designated to see that promotions do in fact conform to the policy, the entire system will fail. When jobs have been properly analyzed, described, and evaluated, a good beginning has been made. From the job requirements it is relatively easy to construct promotional charts showing the logical line of promotion for most jobs (see Figs. 12.1 and 12.2). It must be recognized that there may be some blind-alley jobs. When persons with capacities for higher jobs get blocked on blind-alley jobs, the only solution is a transfer to other jobs that are logical steppingstones unless the employee does not desire promotion.[2] Any company that has job descriptions can readily

[2] It may seem absurd to persons not familiar with groups to assert that anyone

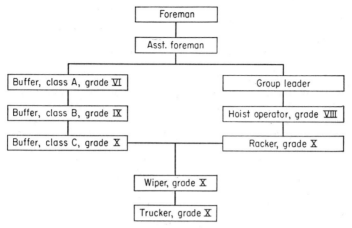

Fɪɢ. 12.2. Promotion chart in the buffing department of the Howell Company, St. Charles, Ill. The grades indicate the job classifications.

construct promotional charts for departments or divisions. Each employee has a right to know the expected line of promotion provided that he qualifies.

**An illustrative union contract covering promotions based on seniority.** There are many shades of contract requirements on promotions. In one case it may be a short statement such as "Promotions will be made on the basis of merit and seniority with seniority controlling where merit is equal." On the other hand it may be spelled out in great detail. Even though a simple statement like the foregoing is used, a body of precedent soon grows up illustrating some of the details omitted in the statement. For instance, two men may have approximately equal merit for the vacancy, but only one has the capacity to go on to higher positions. Naturally management would want to promote the man who could go on to higher positions. Should the man with less promotability get the job if he has greater seniority? If not, there should be an interpretation that management reserves the right to consider a man's potential for promotion up a promotional ladder in addition to the ability to fill the specific vacancy.

The following contract provision of the Cleveland Graphite Bronze Company is not given as an illustration of contracts in general but as an illustration of the details included in some contracts.

---

does not desire promotion; yet such is the case. Some people make enough money to care for their needs and do not wish to exert the effort to qualify for higher jobs. Others are unwilling to surrender their seniority on a lower-rated job to get the higher one. Others do not like the responsibilities that go with supervisory jobs and so refuse promotion.

## ARTICLE VI

1. *Seniority.* The Company will operate in accordance with the principles of seniority, it being understood, however, that seniority is only one factor involved in the promotion, demotion, assignment or transfer of employees. For the purpose of securing and maintaining efficient operation, the Company reserves and has the right, in its sound discretion, to promote, demote, transfer and assign employees, taking into consideration not only seniority and skill and ability, but other pertinent factors.

For employees presently on the payroll and hereafter, should it become necessary to reduce the operating force, layoffs will be made according to plant-wide occupational seniority, as hereinafter more fully explained. In recalling these employees back to work, the reverse order will be followed.

2. *Forced Layoff, Transfer or Demotion*

A. Wherever practical work schedules within a department will be reduced to forty (40) hours before a major layoff is effected in that department.

B. The Company agrees, wherever practical, to inform the Shop Committee one (1) week in advance of all layoffs.

C. In the case of temporary curtailment, three (3) days or less, the employees affected will not be considered for transfer to other jobs unless openings are available which will not displace other workers.

D. Where it appears that the curtailment will be more than temporary, adjustments in personnel (layoffs, transfers, demotions, etc.) will be made according to the principles of seniority, as stated in paragraph No. 1 above, and defined as follows:

(1) Probationary employees will be considered as having no seniority.

(2) The seniority of employees who have been with the Company less than eighteen (18) months will be figured on an occupational basis within their own departments.

Where business conditions require still further reductions, employees with seniority of less than eighteen (18) months will be laid off on a departmental and occupational basis. If, for unusual or exceptional reasons, the Company retains any such employees, the same shall be negotiated with the Union.

(3) The seniority of employees who have been with the Company more than eighteen (18) months will be figured on an occupational basis throughout the entire plant.

E. Employees who are transferred may be granted a maximum period of thirty (30) days to demonstrate their ability to perform with standard efficiency. An employee must have prior or similar experience on the job he wishes to bump.

F. Where an employee is transferred to a job of different classification, he shall, at the time of transfer, receive the prevailing rate for the job to which he is assigned.

G. Employees who have been promoted to classification not within the bargaining unit may be returned to their former status within the bargaining unit with full accumulative seniority. Any salaried employee, who was formerly a member of the bargaining unit, permanently transferred to any plant not covered by this agreement, shall lose all hourly seniority rights for the purposes of this agreement.

3. *Choice of Shift*

A. New and transferred employees shall break in on the shift where openings occur. However, such transferred employees shall have a choice of shift upon the expiration of sixty (60) days after transfer in keeping with the efficient operation of the department.

B. Older employees in seniority may take their preference of shifts in keeping with the efficient operation of the department once each year only.

### 4. Rehiring after Layoff

A. Employees laid off will be recalled on the basis of plant-wide occupational seniority, provided they have had previous experience with the Company on the available job to be performed and are able to perform the job with standard efficiency.

B. Employees laid off by the Company through no fault or cause of their own, shall be credited with their full accumulated amount of seniority provided: (1) If they have less than two (2) years seniority at the time of layoff and they are called back to work within one (1) year or, (2) If they have two (2) years or more seniority at the time of layoff and they are called back to work within two (2) years.

### 5. Job Promotion under Normal Conditions

A. Promotions and transfers to other jobs will be filled by the best qualified people available only when job openings occur.

B. Employees' seniority will be considered for these promotions.

C. Employees within the departments involved will be considered before employees from other departments.

D. When an employee continues to operate at a level below standard efficiency appropriate action may be taken.

### 6. Probationary Employees

A. All new employees shall be considered as on probation for a period of ninety (90) days after the starting date, and during such period shall not be entitled to any seniority rights under the provisions of this agreement. After probationary period, seniority shall be determined as of the date employees start to work.

B. Probationary employees will be eligible for Union membership during their probationary period, however, the Company reserves and has the right to remove such probationary employees from the payroll at any time during this period at its own discretion.

### 7. Leaves of Absence

A. Employees granted leaves of absence for medical reasons (other than maternity) or due to industrial injuries will accumulate seniority during such leaves.

B. All leaves of absence for maternity or personal reasons in excess of thirty (30) days shall be deducted from length of service. No leaves of absence may be authorized for more than two (2) years except that total disability leaves of absence may be granted for periods up to, but not exceeding, five (5) years.

C. Any employee who voluntarily enlists or who is inducted into the Armed Forces of the United States shall be given a Military Leave of Absence and will accumulate seniority for the length of the leave. Federal Legislation will govern all benefits and rights to which he is entitled.

### 8. Seniority Preference for Union Officials

A. Members of the Shop Committee, local president, vice president and secretary will be assigned to the first shift and shall have top plant-wide seniority, except that this preferential seniority shall apply to the shift and permanent lay-offs only, and will not include job preference.

B. Group Stewards, while they are in office, shall have top seniority in their respective groups. This does not include shift or job preference, except for the job held at the time of election.

### 9. *Seniority Lists*

A. The Company agrees to maintain in the Personnel Department a complete seniority listing of all its employees. This information will be made available to the Shop Committee whenever requested.

B. The Company will provide the Union with a listing of all separations, transfers and rehires.

### 10. *Loss of Seniority*

A. Employees shall forfeit seniority for any of the following reasons:

(1) If they quit.

(2) Are discharged for cause.

(3) If they are absent without leave (AWOL): (a) Absent for three (3) working days without notifying the Company. (b) Absent due to illness (unexcused) and do not substantiate the illness with a note from the attending physician before five (5) working days have elapsed.

(4) If they fail to return at the expiration of leaves of absence.

(5) If they have less than two (2) years' seniority when a period of one (1) year has elapsed since the day of layoff.

If they have two (2) years or more seniority when a period of two (2) years has elapsed since the day of layoff.

(6) Employees laid off who do not report within five (5) days of notice to return to work. It will be the responsibility of all laid-off employees to furnish the Company with their correct address and telephone number. In case of change during layoff, the employee shall notify the Company of the new address. The Company will notify all employees laid off who are called back to work, by registered letter to the last known address.

### 11. *Application of Rules*

The Company and the Union from time to time may agree upon the application of seniority rules in any particular department. Such application will be by separate agreement and be incorporated in separate documents.

### 12. *Apprenticeship Agreement*

The Company and the Union have agreed upon apprenticeship agreements, the terms of which are included in a separate document.

**Transfers.** *A transfer is the moving of an employee from one job to another.* It may involve a promotion, demotion, or no change in job status other than moving from one job to another. The wise handling of transfers is so important that some companies have placed all transfers under the control of one executive or office with power to prescribe the conditions under which requests for transfers will be approved. Under such auspices, transfers may become an important part of the total training program of the company. It is of course true that no company can comply with all requests for transfer.

The need for transfers arises from many conditions, a few of which are:

1. The employee has progressed as far as he can in his present job and is capable of handling a better job.

2. Reduction of work in the department makes necessary the reduction of workers. Another department is employing help. One of the workers who faces a layoff could fill the vacancy.

3. The worker has little interest in his present job and seeks a change. (He may or may not have previously had an interest in his job. With the passage of time a worker's interest frequently changes.)

4. Some workers lack the experience that would prepare them for better positions. Transfers to various other jobs of the company might provide that experience.

Transfers frequently involve a wage adjustment. Problems of wage adjustments arise under any of the foregoing situations. When a man is temporarily transferred for the convenience of the company, various customs are followed in relation to his wage. In some cases he is paid immediately the going rate on the new job, whether it be higher or lower. In other cases the old rate prevails for some period, such as 3 days. Often the wage policy is spelled out in the union contract. Figure 12.3 is a simple form frequently used in making transfers. Copies of this form are sent to the personnel department, to the payroll department, and at times to other departments.

Frequently there is no vacancy when an employee first requests the

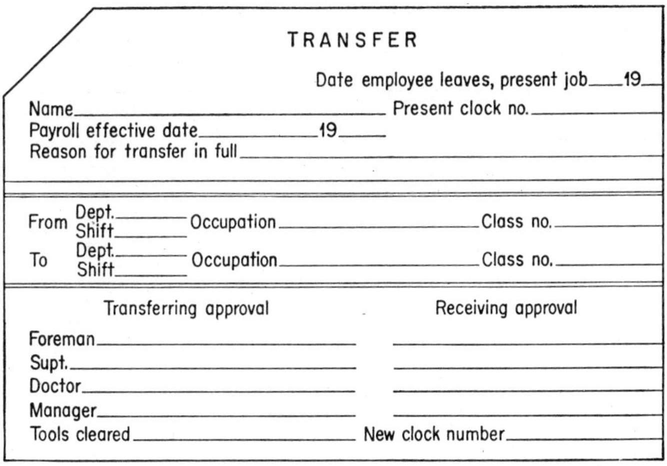

TRANSFER

Date employee leaves, present job_____19_

Name_____ Present clock no._____

Payroll effective date_____19_____

Reason for transfer in full_____

From  Dept._____ Occupation_____ Class no._____
      Shift._____

To    Dept._____ Occupation_____ Class no._____
      Shift._____

Transferring approval          Receiving approval

Foreman_____        _____
Supt._____        _____
Doctor_____        _____
Manager_____        _____
Tools cleared_____ New clock number_____

FIG. 12.3. Simple transfer form.

## Voluntary Questionnaire for Possible Transfer or Promotion

Name _____ Date _____

Date Employed _____
Date of Birth _____
Present Wages _____

Married _____  Weight _____  No. of Dependents _____
Widowed _____  Height _____  Children _____
Single _____  Age _____  Others _____

Division _____  Department _____

### EDUCATIONAL RECORD

| | NO. OF YEARS ATTENDED | NAME OF SCHOOL OR COLLEGE | YEAR GRADUATED | COURSE TAKEN, DEGREE OR CERTIFICATE OBTAINED |
|---|---|---|---|---|
| Grammar School | | | | |
| High or Prep School | | | | |
| College | | | | |
| Any other night, business, correspondence or trade school course taken | | | | |
| | | | | |

Are you now studying?  Name of School _____  Course _____

Do you hold any occupational license or certificate? Check ones listed or write in any others you hold

Plumber { Journeyman / Master  Electrician { Journeyman / Master  Gas Fitter { Journeyman / Master  _____
C.P.A. _____ Engineer _____ Class. Fireman _____ Class. Chauffeur _____

What position do you hold with the Company?

If you could be transferred to another kind of work with the Company, what work would you prefer? Give reasons and state your qualifications for this work:

Choice 1 _____

Give Reasons _____

Qualifications _____

Choice 2 _____

Give Reasons _____

Qualifications _____

Choice 3 _____

Give Reasons _____

Qualifications _____

Fig. 12.4. Form used by employee seeking a transfer. (*Courtesy, Boston Consolidated Gas Company.*)

transfer. Should the desired transfer be within the department in which he is currently working, the foreman usually notes his request and takes care of it as soon as he can if there are no questions involved requiring clearance in the personnel department. Should it involve other departments or some personnel department record, he is usually interviewed by the person in the personnel department handling transfers, who makes a record of his request (Fig. 12.4) and files it according to some organized plan. When there are vacancies in the job to which the worker wishes to be transferred, the transfer file is consulted and arrangements made for the transfer. In order to carry out a proclaimed policy of promoting from within and the policy of filling vacancies to the greatest advantage of the company, it is necessary to maintain adequate records of the capacities and skills of employees. Some companies code the various jobs and punch into a punch card the coded jobs for which an employee is qualified. In such cases all that need be done in looking for an employee possessing a given training is to run these punch cards through a sorting machine and sort them according to the code number for the vacancy. In case it is a possible promotion where seniority is to be considered the cards can be re-sorted according to seniority and a list run off with the highest-seniority man on top and a declining seniority below the top man. Frequently the qualification cards would be consulted in addition to the seniority factor. Other cards or filing systems may be used. The McBee key sort equipment has found wide acceptance. Some visible index cards may have coded skills that are recognized at a glance. Regardless of the system used, some device is required to make readily available the names of persons with certain abilities and skills when management is seeking persons to fill vacancies.

In analyzing transfer requests and actual transfers, some systematic classification is desirable. The following classification has been found useful.

1. Transfers for the convenience of the company.
    1.1 Temporary.
        1.11 Arising from temporary absenteeism.
        1.12 Shifts in the work load.
        1.13 Vacations.
    1.2 Permanent.
        1.21 Shifts in the work load.
        1.22 Vacancies requiring the special skill or ability of the transferred employee.
2. Transfers for the convenience of the employee.
    2.1 Temporary.
        2.11 Arising from the ill health of or an accident to the employee.

2.12 For family situations.

2.13 To take care of some private affairs, such as harvesting a small crop (asking to be placed on the second shift).

2.2 Permanent.

2.21 Arising from ill health or accident. (A man may have to be transferred from a plating department because of fumes to which he is allergic.)

2.22 Outside interests—to attend school or similar activities.

2.23 For family considerations. (A man whose wife has died may need to be with his children and thus be unable to work the second or third shift.)

2.24 Because of transportation. (A man may ride with another employee from a neighboring city and need to work on the same shift as the person providing the transportation.)

2.25 To learn a particular skill. (A worker occasionally will give up a higher-paying production job to learn to be a machinist.)

**Demotions.** There is no unanimity of opinion in relation to demoting an employee. Some managers hesitate to demote a man on the theory that he will not be satisfied to take the lower job and it is therefore better to discharge him than to have a disgruntled employee. This is especially their attitude toward executives. There is some merit to their argument; yet many an executive would be only too happy to be removed from a job that he recognizes he is unable to fill as it should be filled, provided that this can be done without too much shock to his personal pride. Often such men would ask to be transferred if given the opportunity. The man is not always solely responsible for his failures. His superiors have erred in judgment as well as he. Assume that Henry Nelson has been promoted to the position of superintendent after having successfully filled the various positions below him (Fig. 12.5). His service may easily be 20 years. He only

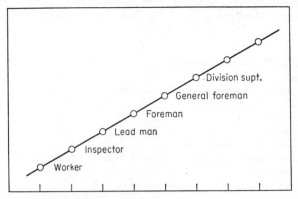

Fig. 12.5. Positions filled successfully by an executive before he reached his limit.

partially succeeds in the new job. Both management and he erred in his going on the job. It is conceivable that the general foreman under him is qualified for the division superintendency. If this situation is properly handled, Nelson will ask to be permitted to return to his old job. Such adjustments require a high type of personnel administration. Discharge is the easy way but not necessarily the sound one. This subject is entirely too complex to be treated properly in this chapter; it is one to which in business the easy method rather than the ethical one has been applied all too often. When a demotion arises from contracting operations, the problem is more easily met than when it is required because of a failure in performance. Even in these situations management should prepare the men for stepping down and not merely handle the occurrence as a matter of course. Demoted workers or supervisors have a psychological adjustment to make. Attention to this matter is a mark of real leadership and pays dividends in helping people when they really need it.

As yet there has never been devised a technique that will take all the sting out of demoting a man who is almost making good but not quite measuring up to expectations. There is no way of avoiding some heartaches in demoting an employee. All that can be hoped for is to minimize them in so far as is possible.

**Discharges.** Discharges become necessary (1) when the volume of business will not justify carrying the persons involved; (2) when a person fails to produce according to the requirements of the job, either from incapacity or from deliberately restricting production, and there is no suitable place to which he can be transferred; (3) when the individual forfeits his right to a job by violating a basic policy often involving the safety of others, the morale and discipline of the group, and possibly the quality of service expected. Contrary to popular opinion, management usually hesitates to discharge employees unless they are what is commonly called "troublemakers." This hesitancy frequently causes management to keep men who should be released. In response to the demand of labor for security of employment, Federal and state laws have been passed that restrict the right of employers to discharge employees in certain instances. Labor unions take group action against certain types of dismissals. Civil Service regulations greatly increase the security of all Civil Service employees. As a matter of fact the rigidities surrounding Civil Service employees definitely reduce efficiency according to many supervisors in government service. Many employers have formulated rules and regulations for satisfying the demands of employees for increased security of employment. Statistics dealing with labor turnover indicate that discharges are becoming infrequent and are administered primarily in the interests of the general welfare. Various surveys of the causes of discharges for cause indicate that personality or character traits are the primary reason. Discharges seldom arise from a single impulsive act that might not have been anticipated by associates. A U.S. Department of Labor survey of labor turnover among bakers reports that most discharges were administered for inefficiency, dishonesty, drunkenness, carelessness, or indifference. Infrequent causes of discharges reported were for accidents, insubordination, personal conduct, uncleanliness, infraction of rules, fomenting of discord, destructive negligence, wastefulness, and physical unfitness. A survey of the causes of discharge of office and clerical workers reports that most of the discharges were due to character traits. A few were reported as due to each of the following: carelessness, lack of cooperation, laziness, absences (not caused by illness), dishonesty, lack of specific skills, preventing promotion.

In order to avoid unnecessary grievances over discharges many companies have established rigid rules regarding the discharge. The right of the foreman to discharge has been considerably modified. In most companies, the supervisor has the right to discharge a new worker during his probationary period and to exclude a regular worker from the department but not to discharge him from the company. The supervisor may recommend a transfer of an employee out of his department. A common procedure today is for the department head to recommend a discharge, but the execution of the order is

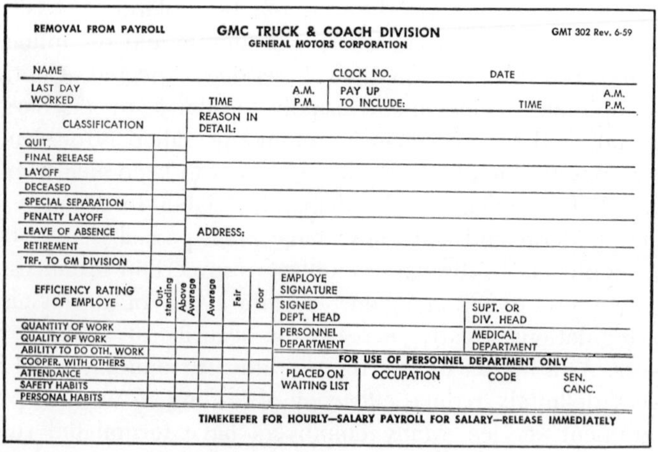

REMOVAL FROM PAYROLL — GMC TRUCK & COACH DIVISION — GENERAL MOTORS CORPORATION — GMT 302 Rev. 6-59

NAME — CLOCK NO. — DATE

LAST DAY WORKED — TIME — A.M. P.M. — PAY UP TO INCLUDE: — TIME — A.M. P.M.

| CLASSIFICATION | | REASON IN DETAIL: |
|---|---|---|
| QUIT | | |
| FINAL RELEASE | | |
| LAYOFF | | |
| DECEASED | | |
| SPECIAL SEPARATION | | |
| PENALTY LAYOFF | | |
| LEAVE OF ABSENCE | | ADDRESS: |
| RETIREMENT | | |
| TRF. TO GM DIVISION | | |

| EFFICIENCY RATING OF EMPLOYE | Out-standing | Above Average | Average | Fair | Poor |
|---|---|---|---|---|---|
| QUANTITY OF WORK | | | | | |
| QUALITY OF WORK | | | | | |
| ABILITY TO DO OTH. WORK | | | | | |
| COOPER. WITH OTHERS | | | | | |
| ATTENDANCE | | | | | |
| SAFETY HABITS | | | | | |
| PERSONAL HABITS | | | | | |

EMPLOYE SIGNATURE

| SIGNED DEPT. HEAD | SUPT. OR DIV. HEAD |
|---|---|
| PERSONNEL DEPARTMENT | MEDICAL DEPARTMENT |

FOR USE OF PERSONNEL DEPARTMENT ONLY

| PLACED ON WAITING LIST | OCCUPATION | CODE | SEN. CANC. |
|---|---|---|---|

TIMEKEEPER FOR HOURLY—SALARY PAYROLL FOR SALARY—RELEASE IMMEDIATELY

FIG. 12.6. Form for recording removal from payroll. (*G. M. C. Truck and Coach Division, General Motors Corporation.*)

```
┌─────────────────────────────────────────────────────────┐
│              AVOID VERBAL ORDERS                          │
│                                                           │
│  Mr. Richard Roe – #79802          Date  July 16,  19 53  │
│                                                           │
│  ─────────────────────────────────────────────────────   │
│  You have been absent twelve (12) working days without    │
│  satisfactory reason since May 1st, the last two days     │
│  being July 14 and 15. Unless your attendance improves,   │
│  you will be given a penalty layoff.                      │
│  ─────────────────────────────────────────────────────   │
│  ─────────────────────────────────────────────────────   │
│  ─────────────────────────────────────────────────────   │
│  ─────────────────────────────────────────────────────   │
│  ─────────────────────────────────────────────────────   │
│                                                           │
│                Signed, John Doe                           │
│                        Foreman, Department 79             │
└─────────────────────────────────────────────────────────┘
```

FIG. 12.7. Permanent record of verbal conference on any important personnel matter. (*G. M. C. Truck and Coach Division, General Motors Corporation.*)

transferred to the personnel director or to some other official or to two or more of the officials of the company. A representative of the workers may call for a review of the case, and unless the discharge is unmistakably just, the worker may be reinstated. Careful records of the cause for the removal from the payroll should be made (see Fig. 12.6). Not only should the final record be complete, but a record of events leading up to the final separation should be carefully kept. Of course, it is important that similar records be kept for all employees, or the foreman may be accused of building up a case against this particular employee merely for the purpose of "getting him." To demonstrate that the discharge was justified and was not due to unfair discrimination or to the personal prejudice of the supervisor, the availability for presentation of such evidence as the following is most convincing.

1. Permanent records of all merit ratings made by the foreman. Such records are especially valuable if there are ratings of the trait that resulted in the discharge.

2. Permanent records of ratings of the defendant's traits made by others than the foreman.

3. A memorandum of the attempts made by the foreman to help the defendant to overcome this weakness.

4. A copy of any warning that had been sent him, or a memorandum of any conference in which he had been warned (Fig. 12.7).

5. The letter of discharge, especially if the letter states the cause of the discharge.

CHAPTER 13

## Human Relations

**What is meant by "human relations"?** The term *human relations*[1]
is used by many writers as if everyone understood what it meant,
so that a clear-cut definition is avoided. In reviewing some 10 leading
books and articles not one took the time to define the term. After
reading dozens of pages in each of the books it is clear that they
are all talking about the influence of sentiments, attitudes, urges,
drives, customs, emotions, personality, conscience, the subconscious,
and similar forces upon the actions of people. By this statement it is
not meant that each of the terms mentioned is independent of the
others. Some include the others. Many of the authors talk about the
effects of good or satisfying human relations. Of course this is a
desirable goal in all group effort, but human relations is also a factor
in situations that are not considered satisfying.

*Human relations refers to the interaction of people, with special
emphasis upon the fundamental causes of individual and group
reaction.* It is primarily concerned with the causal forces that make
man and groups "tick." Human relations is especially centered on
informal organization of groups, but it also includes individual and
group reactions to formal organization. In a few rare situations the
formal and informal groups may be the same. The term human
relations is also used to refer *to the body of knowledge that has been
accumulated and established through carefully observed experience
and controlled experimentation on the reactions of man and groups
and the causes thereof.* Others look upon human relations as *a process
of motivating individuals and groups to accept a given objective, to*

---

[1] "Human relations" may be thought of as a body of knowledge, skills, and
the interaction of individuals and groups. When viewed as a subject for analysis,
a discipline, or a skill, it may be thought of as singular. If the emphasis is upon
the actual interrelationships, it would be a plural concept.

*produce effectively, and to derive reasonable satisfaction from the productive effort.* Many people use the term morale as expressing the "tone" of the satisfaction derived from desired human relations. Thus it can be seen that human relations can be thought of as a "body of knowledge," a "process of achieving a desired end and morale," as well as the "fundamental interaction of individuals and groups." In each instance causal relationships are sought.

The pure social scientist seeks to describe phenomena as he finds them and to discover what produces the factual relationships he discovers. There is a real need for this fundamental research without any particular reference to its use. Actually the pure research provides the *insight* that enables the practitioner more effectively to do his work. There has been effective research carried on for a number of years by a dedicated group of anthropologists, psychologists, sociologists, and industrial relations and personnel men. Some of it has been interdisciplinary. This chapter will examine the use of these efforts.

**The relationship of "human relations" to "industrial relations," "personnel administration," "employee relations," and "labor relations."** Using the terms "industrial relations" and "personnel administration" as both meaning the same or being interchangeable, the "objective of industrial relations is to attain the maximum individual development, desirable working relationships between employers and employees, and employees to employees, and effective molding of human resources as contrasted with physical resources." In this sense either industrial relations or personnel administration may be conceived to be the term used to embrace the bigger, all-inclusive function of relating man effectively to his work environment. Some persons prefer to limit the term industrial relations to the narrower, union-management relationships and to think of personnel administration as being the more all-inclusive term. There is no fault to be found with this usage. In this discussion we prefer to use the term labor relations to refer to union-management relationships and to use employee relations to include all other management-employee relations not included in the formal union-management contractual activities. Actually a given item may be included in a union contract and come under the employee relations function unless it becomes a point of conflict in a grievance procedure. For instance, employment, first-aid, counseling, transfers, and promotions in their normal day-to-day operations are employee relations activities. Thus they remain for most practical operating situations. They may become a subject for labor relations action or consideration in negotiating a contract or in their administration when challenged by the union through the grievance procedure.

Human relations is included in both industrial relations and labor relations. The reactions of individuals or groups in union relations are by no means always at the economic level. Many of their economic demands arise out of a demand for status or are a striking back at management because of a resentment at management's actions. At times some union demands arise out of a deep-seated class consciousness on the part of a given leader. They may even be a striking back at a class because of his not being accepted or because of his wife's or daughter's not having been accepted socially by the group represented by management. Then there is the other side of the coin: management and its representatives also have sentiments, attitudes, customs and traditions. Not only is there a human relations response by management to labor's demands as a group but to contacts between managers themselves. In other words human relations is a phase of human reaction not confined to the functional limits of employee relations or labor relations. Human relations as a "body of knowledge," as a "basic human reaction to others" or as a "skill" practiced by an effective operator in successfully motivating groups is an all-pervasive element to be found wherever man associates with man in a purposeful relationship. It may also be manifest even in casual relationships.

**Motivating forces.** Probably the strongest single urge is the *urge for survival* or for *security*. Until this particular requirement is met to a reasonable degree, other motivating forces are not particularly effective. Of course there is the minimum requirement for survival which is relatively low from the standpoint of the standards in the United States, Canada, Australia, and other countries with great natural resources and a favorable economic environment. In these countries with a high level of economic competence the strong desire to possess the comforts and physical privileges enjoyed by large numbers raises the motivating force of the desire for security far above the bare subsistence requirements. Of course, as the desire for the security moves above the subsistence level, it becomes mixed with other urges such as the desire for status and recognition. It is not always possible clearly to separate these desires when they are manifest in situations substantially above the subsistence level.

Somewhat higher than the physiological needs required for survival is the need for security or safety against physical danger, deprivation, and threats.[2] These safety needs of employees for protection against arbitrary discharge or other action by higher authority are not confined to workers at the bench. They also influence middle management

---

[2] See Douglas M. McGregor, "Adventure in Thought and Action," in *Proceedings of the Fifth Anniversary Convocation of the School of Industrial Management, Massachusetts Institute of Technology*, Cambridge, Apr. 9, 1957, p. 26.

and even top management in some cases. The intense struggle of college professors for *tenure* stems from the fear of arbitrary dismissal. While there have been relatively few actual cases of these discriminations, there have been enough of them to leave a strong desire for assurances against them. This may be known as the desire for a "fair break."

After the basic physical needs for survival are taken care of, other forces become recognizable. These forces are psychological and social. In the child before he has learned to adjust to the social responses very effectively, the psychological and emotional needs are paramount. The child's physical needs and his emotional needs are closely associated. He must have nourishment for his body and shelter against the elements, but he also needs the emotional security that comes from being tenderly held and loved by a human being, preferably his mother. As the child matures and learns to make his way into and around the many mores, customs, and traditions, the emotional security demanded in youth gives way (but is not lost) to higher psychological and social adjustments and needs. The established customs, traditions, and mores become *carriers of social values*. The desire to be accepted causes them to be powerful motivaters for conformance. This particular phase of man's existence is capable of indefinite expansion and is never fully satisfied. The indefinite expandability of this force enables it to be used as a motivater as long as the individual remains a purposeful member of any enterprise. When the physical needs of man are satisfied, they become very weak motivaters. On the other hand, to the individual or group that has endured hunger for long periods and is facing starvation, the desire to meet these needs becomes paramount, and the other forces fade into the background.

**Social needs.** When the physical requirements for subsistence and even a substantial plus factor have been added, when reasonable assurance that fair treatment will prevail in man's efforts to meet economic demands, these cease to be powerful motivaters and the social needs become more effective. Thus it can be seen that there exists a hierarchy of levels of effective desires and needs. These may be listed as subsistence, safety, psychological, and social. *Man is a social creature.* He enjoys the association and acceptance of other people. He *wants* to be *wanted*. In prehistoric times the driving of an individual out of the group was practically to condemn him to death. Within the framework of accepted social custom there are many phases that may serve to motivate man. For instance, the status factor is symbolized by a man's possessions. In antiquity it was symbolized by the size of his herds, the number of his wives, and the number of his servants. Today status may be revealed in a number of ways: the acceptance into a group, club, profession, or trade; by special privileges enjoyed, not having to punch a time card, being privileged to park one's car in a particular lot or garage, being permitted to eat in a particular lunchroom, having a private secretary, having a carpet on the floor of one's office, or having one's name on the hourly rated or salary payroll. The foregoing factors that separate or differentiate people from each other are carriers of social value and status indicators within the economic enterprise or other employment group.

The motivating forces within an enterprise formerly were well known to the community at large. The socially ordered hierarchy of job titles was generally known. If a wife at her church circle said that her husband was a toolmaker or a railroad conductor, her friends knew what he did. His wife and children had standing somewhat in keeping with the father's occupation. Today many jobs are known only to a limited few within the work group. These jobs may have high requirements for performance, but they no longer are carriers of status in the community. In such cases the status factor is transferred from the job to the wage which enables the worker to have the symbols of status, such as the clothing he and his family wear, the kind of house and community in which they live, and the kind of automobile he drives as well as the number and kinds the family owns. The wage in modern business takes the place of occupational prestige in many cases. This of course is not solely true, or it may work in reverse. For instance, banking is a prestige business, so much so that banks frequently are not compelled to be competitive with other businesses salarywise. It is not unusual for the mechanic in a manufacturing enterprise to earn as much as a bank teller.

Thus it can be seen that man is motivated by status factors. These are functions of job titles in some instances and of the salary or wage in others. Incentive wage plans are effective only within limits and with certain people. When the group sets limits on output, the incentive pull of a wage-payment plan based on output is effective only in so far as the group standard permits. Of course in those few cases where the individual's efforts are not dependent on others he may ignore the group standard and produce all he can. In such a case the motivating pull of the wage plan is the resultant of the two forces: (1) economic self-interest and (2) desire to have acceptance by the group. In most cases group acceptance is more powerful than the economic pull of an additional 5 or 10 per cent in wages.

**Self-fulfillment needs.** Most workers' efforts are directed to trying to satisfy the physical, social, and psychological needs. They seldom have much energy left to devote to those needs designated by Douglas McGregor[3] as the self-fulfillment needs. These needs are for realizing man's potentialities, self-development, and creativity. It can be readily recognized that most persons are not strongly motivated by these desires, but they do exist very strongly in some persons.

**Controlling forces.** The real motivating forces in modern industry from a human relations standpoint remain the desire for security and the social desires for recognition. Persons who have high seniority status and confidence in the continued economic success of an employer whose wages meet their economic needs are not strongly motivated by incentive systems. This is especially true if the group has set production standards above which social pressures are brought to bear. In such situations the social approval of fellow workers is usually more influential than the desire for the additional goods that could be bought by exceeding the established group norms. In situations of this nature the worker bypasses the "logics of efficiency" to conform to the "logics of sentiment," a human relations response. In this manner some of the carefully laid plans of the industrial engineer are ineffective.

**What does all this mean to the personnel director, industrial engineer, and other leaders?** It means simply that the logics of efficiency are not so strong in motivating workers to produce as it was once believed. The further man gets away from the survival and bodily requirements, the greater becomes the influence of the social, psychological, and emotional needs. Native ability is no criterion for measuring actual performance. The will to produce largely determines the level of output, assuming of course that the worker has the needed abilities and skills. When workers become involved in a change of process or increased production, their emotional strengths and physical energies can be counted on to produce. The problem of course is to contrive a situation that will enlist this involvement rather than its opposite fear of loss of wages, status, jobs, having to work harder to earn the same or even less money, resulting in restriction of production. Actually worker sentiment is not so much opposed to management as it is oriented to protecting its own group interests from harm from any source, including management.

**Status of the human relations approach.** It would be no exaggeration to say that the Hawthorne Experiment provided the great impetus to a widened interest in man's reactions to man and his group. This was followed by the publication of *Management and the Worker* by

[3] *Ibid.*

Roethlisberger and Dickson in 1940 by the Harvard University Press. The book was favorably received by most people; however, it was criticized by some as claiming too much in the light of the small number of people involved in the experiment. Actually the book made no claim that its findings were universally true. It faithfully described the classic experiment in group relationships. Later researches by the Survey Research Center of the University of Michigan, the researches at Harvard, Yale, Chicago, and in industry have added to the findings of the Hawthorne Experiment and provided clearer insight into what makes man "tick."

The Graduate School of Business Administration of Harvard University inaugurated its course in administrative practices around the cases that have been so widely studied in *The Administrator* by Glover and Hower, published by Richard D. Irwin, Inc. These same cases have been extensively used in executive development programs that are conducted by universities and colleges. Similar programs have been conducted by professional societies and by individual employers. Many universities and colleges have similar courses even though they may not be known by the name of human relations. There still remains a critical minority that accuses the persons advocating the human relations approach of being unscientific, of trying to manipulate people

|  | 1st level supervision | Department heads | Staff personnel | Staff dept. heads | Superintendents | Technical and professional | Top management |
|---|---|---|---|---|---|---|---|
| Human relations | 1 | 2 | 1 | 1 | 4 | 2 | 3 |
| Effective speaking | 2 | 5 | 2 | 5 |  | 3 | 2 |
| Creative thinking | 5 | 4 | 3 |  | 1 | 1 | 1 |
| Supervisory responsibilities | 3 | 3 | 5 | 4 |  |  |  |
| Management controls |  | 1 | 4 | 2 | 5 | 4 | 4 |
| Communications |  |  |  | 3 |  |  | 5 |

FIG. 13.1. A new look at top training interests. (*The above chart came from Factory Management and Maintenance, September,* 1958, *p.* 154.)

against their wills and without their knowledge, and of trying to become lay psychiatrists. An occasional labor leader lends his voice in condemnation. Of course, an occasional personnel man may be guilty of these charges, but a recognition of man's real nature certainly should add to the tools used by the leader in the line and the personnel administrator. It causes one to avoid the pitfalls of relying solely upon the logics of efficiency only to be defeated by the logics of sentiment of the work group. Such an equipped leader still recognizes his personal responsibility to produce a product or service at a profit within the framework of the community customs and mores. He does not turn away from his primary responsibility to become a lay psychologist or psychiatrist. On the other hand he may use the professional skills and insights of these people in solving some of his personnel problems or in directing his advertising and public relations.

In three extensive surveys made during the last few years covering the requirements of leaders or what leaders thought should be taught in leadership or executive training programs, human relations stood very high on the list.

In one of these surveys, human relations was mentioned twice as often as any other item, indicating the respondent's opinion of the "personal characteristics thought to be most needed by an executive."[4] In a second survey by the same association by Joseph M. Trickett, under *Top management attributes desired,* human relations was listed as third from the top and as first for the first line supervisor.[5] This study listed leadership and character-integrity ahead of human relations for top management men but placed human relations at the head of the list for first line supervisors. *Factory Management and Maintenance* in reporting a summary of a survey made by the National Management Association used the chart in Fig. 13.1 to show the training interests of various leadership groups. Other studies place human relations skills high on the list of desirable leadership requirements.

**The pedestrian approach.** Elton Mayo in his challenging book, *The Social Problems of an Industrial Civilization*[6] pleads for a careful study of man as he is in his actual daily life. Careful observation is the beginning of any science. There are two kinds of knowledge, *knowledge-about* secured through reflection and abstract thinking and

---

[4] See Lydia Strong, *Management Review,* American Management Association, October, 1956, pp. 871–887.

[5] Joseph M. Trickett, *A Survey of Management Development,* American Management Association, New York, 1954, pp. 42–43.

[6] See Elton Mayo, *The Social Problems of an Industrial Civilization,* Harvard University Graduate School of Business Administration, Cambridge, 1945, pp. 3–33. This book is well worth reading by all students of personnel.

*knowledge-of-acquaintance* derived from actual *experience.*[7] *Knowledge-about* may be secured from books and reflective thinking. *Knowledge-of-acquaintance* about man's actions requires considerable living and observing man as he reacts to his various situations. Every person in modern society has ample opportunity for observation if he will only use it and if he has an adequate frame of reference for interpreting what he sees. Social, religious, educational, and business groups provide the laboratory for studying human relations. Business case studies and role playing give an opportunity for the student to get the "feel" of what is meant by human relations. It is not solely the result of logical thinking in terms of economic self-interest. Many human relations acts do not conform to the *logics of efficiency,* or *costs,* but rather to the *logics of sentiment.* Careful observation shows this on all sides. Men respect the picket line even when they want to work and need the money. Likewise they restrict production to conform to the group's standards.

**Conclusion.** One chapter in a book on personnel management can call attention only to a phase of the relationships of man at work. The human relations approach seeks causal relationships—what motivating forces cause men to act as they do. *Human relations refers to the interaction of people, with special emphasis upon the fundamental causes of individual and group reaction.* It is primarily concerned with the causal forces that make man and groups "tick." The term human relations is also used to refer *to the body of knowledge that has been accumulated and established through carefully observed experience and controlled experimentation on the reactions of man and groups and the causes thereof.* Others look upon human relations as *a process of motivating individuals and groups to accept a given objective, to produce effectively, and to derive reasonable satisfaction from the productive effort.* Thus it can be seen that human relations can be thought of as a "process of achieving a desired end and morale," a "body of knowledge," and the "fundamental interaction of individuals and groups."

Man has urges or driving forces that substantially influence his reactions to given situations. These are: (1) the desire for survival, safety, and the satisfaction of bodily requirements; (2) social and psychological needs, including recognition, wanting to be wanted, status, and the appurtenances that are symbols of status; (3) the need for realizing the potentialities of the individual. This is a relatively weak motivater for most people. Their strong motivations emerge from the social and psychological forces.

[7] *Ibid.,* pp. 16-17.

The personnel manager and all other leaders of men are constantly faced with human relations problems. In the remaining chapters of this book it will be well to ask the question, "What are the human relations implications of this subject?" In trying to motivate men to meet production requirements, the supervisor does not overlook his primary responsibility for producing a product or service merely because he is aware of the influence of human relations among his men. He strives to turn these forces to the advantage both of his company and of his men.

CHAPTER 14

# Psychological Tests: Mental Ability and Clerical Aptitude and Ability

Many thousands of psychological tests have been devised. Annually many new standardized tests are constructed for national distribution. Many of them have been used extensively with success. The most widely used psychological tests for personnel work are variously called general ability or intelligence tests, mental-alertness tests, or mental-ability tests.

**Classification of tests.** Most of the general ability tests which have been constructed have included a rather wide range of problems on the basis of the view that intelligence is a rather broad, general function. Thorndike once suggested that we might think of three kinds of intelligence: abstract intelligence, concrete intelligence, and social intelligence. This is still a useful way of grouping psychological tests, especially if we consider measures of personality and adjustment as social-intelligence tests. This is a logical approach, since in personnel work we are most concerned with personality in terms of its effect on others.

*Abstract intelligence* refers to the ability to understand and to use ideas and symbols of ideas. These ideas and symbols include the material of all abstract and general thinking: chemical formulas, legal decisions, and scientific principles; all the higher forms of thinking that differentiate man from the animal; plans, programs, principles, and logical and categorical thinking, such as similar and dissimilar, profit and loss, cause and effect, right and wrong. This ability to understand and to manage ideas and their symbols is spoken of as mental alertness, general intelligence, common sense, verbal intelligence, ingenuity, and educability. Tests to measure this sort of ability will be described in the present chapter.

*Concrete intelligence* refers to the ability to understand and to operate things and mechanisms. It includes the motor control essential for skilled handwork; the mechanical imagination needed for creating or for using complicated blueprints; the coordination of hand and eye necessary for running a machine, whether it be a typewriter, a printing press, a bicycle, or an airplane. Mechanical aptitude is a term commonly used to refer to this ability, and tests for measuring it will be discussed in the next chapter.

*Social intelligence* is defined as the ability to understand and to manage men. It includes much that is ordinarily called tact and diplomacy: a winning and inspiring personality, balance and adjustment, interest in people and eagerness to serve them; and the ability to appeal to the sympathies and dominating motives in others. Measures for this kind of ability and the attitudes on which it is based will be dealt with in the next chapter.

This grouping of human abilities into three kinds of intelligence has been useful as a basis for constructing and using psychological tests. Since 1935, moreover, psychologists have been giving careful study to the nature of intelligence, abilities, and personality as they are revealed by tests. From these studies they have concluded that mental ability can be described in terms of a number of "factors." Although the exact nature of all of them is not completely understood, some of the commonly identified mental-ability factors include the following: verbal ability, number ability, memory, perceptual speed, deductive reasoning, inductive reasoning, spatial visualization, spatial orientation, and word fluency. Mechanical-aptitude factors are believed to include eye-hand coordination, finger dexterity, mechanical information, and tapping speed, as well as space-relations factors. Personality factors are not so well established, but some of the generally accepted ones are dominance or ascendance, social insight, freedom from nervous tendencies, general drive, social introversion-extraversion, and cooperativeness. It has been the hope of psychologists that tests could be built which would measure the various factors separately. This effort has been only partially successful, as yet. It is hard to develop tests which are "pure" and which do not give results with different meanings for different groups of persons. These studies of the factors of intelligence influence our ways of building tests, but the broader divisions according to aptitudes or kinds of intelligence appear to be more useful in choosing and applying tests for personnel selection and placement purposes at present.

The human mind is not something which can be measured directly. It is not something that can be laid on a scale and weighed, nor can we lay a foot rule alongside it and determine its length. The quality of the mind can be known only through its influence on behavior.

When a person answers the questions on a test, following carefully the rules provided for the administration of the test, certain characteristics of the mind are revealed indirectly and comparisons among persons are possible. Mental-alertness tests are tests which measure the speed and accuracy with which an individual understands and reacts to ideas, their symbols, and their relationships.

Thousands of mental-ability tests have been devised. Since 1896, a very large number of psychologists have directed their efforts toward discovering and improving methods to measure the speed and accuracy with which different individuals and groups of individuals understand and react to ideas and to symbols and relationships among ideas. Many that are tried out prove to be impractical. But all these efforts have resulted in the production of better tests, in improvement in the procedures of administering and grading tests, and in an increase in the reliability and validity of the tests that have survived. As the terms are here used, a *reliable* mental test is one that secures approximately the same results in the hands of two different examiners or in the hands of the same examiner on different occasions. A *valid* mental test is one that secures results which correspond closely with other criteria of intelligence, such as school grades and the degree of success in other occupations.

**Mental-ability tests.** The kinds of test problems on which most of the best mental-ability tests are based fall into six general classes:

1. Word relations (including similarities, opposites, and analogies).
2. Information (including vocabulary, word fluency, and word meaning).
3. Arithmetic problems.
4. Number series.
5. Spatial visualization items (including block counting, spatial reasoning, and other space-perception tests).
6. Nonverbal reasoning problems.

Tests built along these lines have been found to meet the needs of business organizations for purposes of selection of personnel, as well as the selection and classification needs of the armed services and of educational institutions. When it is desirable to make a special assignment or placement, the mental-alertness tests are usually supplemented by others which measure some of the special aptitudes or personality characteristics required.

Methods of presenting test materials are usually quite similar. The subject is asked to respond to a question by underlining the correct response, by writing the answer or the number of the answer in a space provided, or both of these. Sometimes the space for marking the answers are on a different sheet from the questions. Use of separate answer sheets makes scoring easier and is less expensive; however, some groups of subjects might be confused by separate answer sheets, and so they should be used with caution. To ensure understanding by all subjects, each test has definite directions and preliminary sample items and is usually graded in difficulty from the easiest to the hardest questions.

To avoid possible error in judging whether or not an answer is correct when it is not presented in the usual form, most tests present a problem and suggest a series of answers. The subject marks or underlines the answer which he believes is correct.

**Word relations.** An important aspect of general mental ability has been found to be the possession of a large number of accurate verbal concepts, together with the ability to use these concepts and the relationships among them in solving everyday problems. This kind of mental ability appears to be fundamental to much of our reasoning and to reaching logical and valid solutions to problems.

The most common methods of measuring ability to use words are the use of items requiring identification of same-opposite relationships and those set up in the form of verbal analogies. Each of these methods is illustrated below:

1. In each row select the word at the right which means the *same* or *opposite* of the first word in the row.[1]
   1.1 many     (1) ill     (2) few     (3) down     (4) sour
   1.2 deep     (1) blue     (2) shallow     (3) tense     (4) watery
   1.3 awkward     (1) clumsy     (2) loyal     (3) passive     (4) young

2. For each item below, select the word that makes the best answer.
   2.1 *Candy* is to *sweet* as *vinegar* is to—
       (1) pickle     (2) cold     (3) sour     (4) clear     (5) food

   2.2 *War* is to *hatred* as *peace* is to—
       (1) friendship     (2) victory     (3) armistice     (4) treaty     (5) freedom

   2.3 *Tent* is to *house* as *camp* is to—
       (1) army     (2) city     (3) field     (4) building     (5) meeting

**Information (including vocabulary, word fluency, and word meaning).** Investigation has demonstrated that for most purposes any information test is influenced also by the subject's ability to learn, ability to comprehend, meaningful memory, and mental alertness in general. Results on an information test have been shown to be least affected by advance in age.

[1] L. L. Thurstone and T. G. Thurstone, *American Council on Education Psychological Examination for College Freshmen,* 1938 ed., American Council on Education, Washington, D.C. Reproduced by special permission. Educational Testing Service, Cooperative Test Division, Princeton, N.J.

The following mixed relationship test illustrates the use of multiple choices in each of three forms of measuring information:

1. Underline the correct answer.
   1.1 Of what country is Rome the capital?
       Europe, France, United States, Italy, Spain
   1.2 Where does a purser work?
       store, club, ship, depot, hotel
   1.3 How many legs has a Guernsey?
       3    4    6    20
2. Underline the correct answer.
   2.1 People hear with the          eyes, ears, nose, mouth.
   2.2 The apple grows on a          shrub, vine, bush, tree.
   2.3 Bridge is played with         rackets, pins, cards, dice.
3. Underline the words that belong to objects of a particular class.
   3.1 Underline the words that are colors:
       motor, paper, green, class, poetry, dwell, purple, etc.
   3.2 Underline the words that are fruits:
       coast, pear, column, apple, planet, author, etc.
   3.3 Underline the words that are foods:
       tower, bread, cover, thread, search, nimble, potato, etc.

**Arithmetic problems.** The ability to handle numbers and number relationships as shown by success in solving arithmetic problems is closely related to abilities required for success in other general mental-ability tests, but such items have the advantage of making less demand on language ability. There are quite a few persons who will do much better or much more poorly on arithmetic items than on items based on word meanings or relationships. Arithmetic items are the best measures of the number factor in intelligence.

1. If 2 pounds of candy cost $1.20, what would ½ pound cost at the same rate?
   (*a*) 15¢ (*b*) 20¢ (*c*) 30¢ (*d*) 60¢ (*e*) 90¢
2. In making concrete, 2 parts of cement and 5 parts of gravel are used. How many cubic feet of gravel should be used for 21 cubic feet of concrete?
   (*a*) 3 (*b*) 6 (*c*) 10 (*d*) 14 (*e*) 15
3. I bought a number of books one day, four times as many the next day, and 8 books the third day. In all I bought 38 books. How many did I buy the second day?
   (*a*) 6 (*b*) 8 (*c*) 12 (*d*) 16 (*e*) 24

**Number series.** Items which test for the ability to see the relationships among a series of numbers are good measures of inductive reasoning, an important factor of intelligence. Language barriers are crossed by this type of item, after the instructions are understood, since number relationships are independent of any national language.

Number-series items may be set up either in completion form, in which the missing numbers of a series are written in by the subject, or in choice form, in which the next number of a series is selected from several possible alternatives. Several forms of this type of material may be used. Some examples are given below:

1. Fill in the blank lines with the two numbers which should come next in each row of figures.
    1.1  15 20 25 30 35 40 ___ ___
    1.2  2 3 5 8 12 17 ___ ___
    1.3  20 17 15 14 11 9 ___ ___
2. The numbers in each series below proceed according to some rule. For each series find the next number from the five answers at the right.
    2.1  2 4 6 8 10 12 (*a*) 10 (*b*) 11 (*c*) 12 (*d*) 13 (*e*) 14
    2.2  10 8 11 9 12 10 (*a*) 9 (*b*) 10 (*c*) 11 (*d*) 12 (*e*) 13
    2.3  27 27 23 23 19 19 (*a*) 15 (*b*) 16 (*c*) 17 (*d*) 18 (*e*) 19
3. Fill in the missing numbers.
    3.1  26 22 ___ 14 10 ___ 2
    3.2  4 8 6 ___ 10 ___ 18 36
    3.3  2 4 ___ ___ 18 36 54 ___
4. Cross out the number that does not belong in the series.
    4.1  2 4 8 10 16 32
    4.2  72 36 18 9 6
    4.3  50 42 35 32 29 24 20 17

**Spatial-visualization items (including block counting, spatial reasoning, and other space-perception tests).** Most of the examples of mental-ability test materials already discussed are very much like material studied in the public schools. There is some danger that test materials of this sort would give an advantage to persons who have attended school recently. To correct for this weakness, it is wise to include test items also which are unrelated to school subjects, particularly when the tests are being used in business and industry or for military classification. The factor studies of intelligence have shown *space-relations* ability to be important.

Although they are discussed here in relation to *abstract* intelligence, *space-relations* ability has been shown to be highest for those persons who excel at understanding the assembly and operation of machines and who show good practical ability in handling objects and materials. For this reason, *space-relations* ability tests are wisely included with other measures of mechanical aptitude. *Spatial visualization* has been defined as the ability to imagine how a pattern or object would look when moved into different positions or to recognize or imagine the appearance of a pattern or object when moved into different positions or to recognize or imagine the appearance of a pattern or object whose parts have been rearranged.

A very large number of different kinds of test items have been suggested for measuring space ability. Three types will be illustrated here: block counting, which has been widely used for tests in military classification; formboard-type items; and rotated figures.

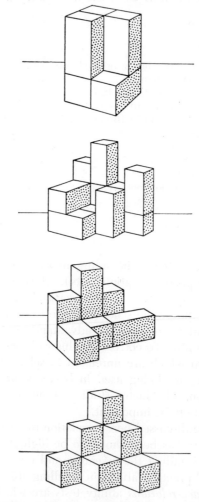

1. *Block Counting.* "There are piles of boxes, and you are to count the boxes in each pile. In each pile, all the boxes have the same size and shape. But from one problem to another, the size and shape of the boxes may change. "How many boxes?"

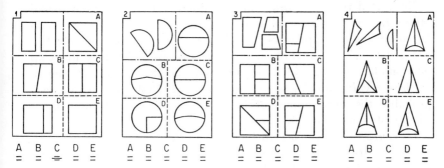

2. *Formboard-type Items.* For each of these problems, some parts are shown in the upper left-hand corner. "You are to decide which of the five figures, A, B, C, D, or E, shows how these parts can fit together. Sometimes the parts have to be turned around and sometimes they have to be turned over in order to make them fit." Underline the letter corresponding to the correct answer. Problem 1 has been marked to show the correct answer. (*R. Likert and W. G. Quasha, Revised Minnesota Paper Formboard Test, The Psychological Corporation, New York, 1939. Reproduced with permission.*)

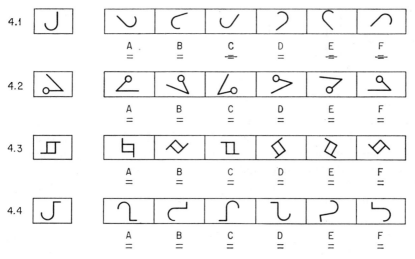

3. *Rotated Figures.* A figure is shown in a box at the left of each problem. Some of the figures lettered A, B, C, D, E, and F are like the first one, but they have been turned in different directions; some of the figures are made backward. Underline the letter of *every* figure which is *like* the first figure. Do *not* mark the figures which are made backward. Problem 1 has been marked to show the correct answers. (*L. L. Thurstone and T. G. Thurstone, SPRA Primary Mental Abilities, Research Associates, Chicago, 1947. Space-factor test items reproduced by permission.*)

**Nonverbal reasoning problems.** In order to test further for mental-ability factors which do not depend upon the use of language, reasoning problems using patterns and diagrams have been developed and are widely used in tests of mental alertness. Although these items appear similar to those which measure space ability, they do not depend on imagery for quickness in their solution. Deductive reasoning is probably the most important factor of intelligence in these items. They will be illustrated by three types:

1. *Nonverbal Analogies.* In these items, the familiar analogies form is used with designs or pictures. The task is to select a fourth design which has the same kind of relationship to the third as the second one has to the first design or picture presented.

2. *Maze Tracing.* Foresight and planning are believed to be aspects of mental ability measured by maze tracing, as well as reasoning ability. The subject draws a path through the maze which is the shortest, and which does not cross any lines. An example is given below:

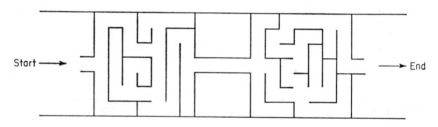

3. *Progressive Matrices.* In items of this sort, a series of designs is presented. Each successive design in the series results from a systematic change made in the preceding design. The task is to recognize the rule for these changes and apply it in selecting a final design for the series. The example at top of page 213 will illustrate this problem.[2]

Tests using some or all of these six kinds of problems have been tried out on many individuals. Each kind has been improved by eliminating items which are unreliable and by demanding a minimum of skill and of time in administering and grading.

Sometimes several or all of these kinds of problems are given singly, sometimes as a combined battery of tests, and sometimes different kinds of materials are combined into a single test. Most tests are arranged so that the easiest items are at the beginning and the hardest

[2] G. K. Bennett, H. G. Seashore, and A. G. Wesman, *Differential Aptitude Tests, Abstract Reasoning,* The Psychological Corporation, New York, 1947. Reproduced by permission.

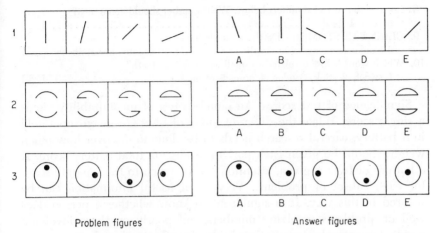

Problem figures                    Answer figures

"In this test you will see rows of designs or figures. Each row consists of four figures called Problem Figures and five called Answer Figures. The four Problem Figures make a series; you are to find out which one of the Answer Figures would be the next, or fifth one in the series."

ones at the end. When this is done, it is more likely that all persons taking the test will have an opportunity to work on all items which they can easily pass. When a test is scaled in this way and different kinds of problems are used more or less alternately, it is called a scaled spiral-omnibus test. The Wonderlic Personnel Test, Form A, is a good example of this kind. The first few items are reproduced below:

Form A

1. The last month of the year is
    1 January, 2 March, 2 July, 4 December, 5 October............. [___]
2. CAPTURE is the opposite of
    1 place, 2 release, 3 risk, 4 venture, 5 degrade................... [___]
3. Most of the items below resemble each other. Which one is least like the others?
    1 January, 2 August, 3 Wednesday, 4 October, 5 December........ [___]
4. Answer by printing YES or NO—Does R.S.V.P. mean "reply not necessary"? .................................................... [___]
5. In the following set of words which word is different from the others?
    1 troop, 2 league, 3 participate, 4 pack, 5 gang ................ [___]
6. USUAL is the opposite of
    1 rare, 2 habitual, 3 regular, 4 staunch, 5 always.................. [___]
7. Which figure can be made from these two parts?.................. [___]

        1         2         3         4         5

8. Look at the row of numbers below. What number should come next?
    8  4  2  1  ½  ¼  ? ............................................. [___]
9. CLIENT CUSTOMER—Do these words have
    1 similar meanings, 2 contradictory, 3 mean neither same nor opposite? [___]
10. Which word below is related to smell as chew is to teeth?
    1 sweet, 2 stink, 3 odor, 4 nose, 5 clean. ...................... [___]

**Significance of test scores.** An omnibus test of mental ability yields a single score. When the different kinds of tests are given separately in a battery, careful research needs to be done to discover how much weight should be given each part to produce a total battery score. If a battery of tests is given, attention can be given to the separate score for each subset of problems. Very often useful information can be secured in this way. It is significant to know whether a person does well on problems involving numbers and poorly on those involving words, for example. In vocational selection, the total, or battery, score is emphasized; in vocational guidance or in dealing with problems of placement or transfer after selection, the separate subtest scores are emphasized.

To persons unfamiliar with testing, it may seem strange that the scores obtained on such simple tests would have any practical significance. The validity of the General Classification Test used in World War II can be used as an example. The test is a scaled spiral-omnibus test using three kinds of problems: word meaning, arithmetic, and block counting. If a group of 100 men each secured a grade of 60 on this test, only 5 of them would succeed on a job requiring mechanical aptitude. If of 100 men each secured a grade of 140 on the General Classification Test, then 88 of them would succeed on a job requiring mechanical ability. This may be presented in table form as follows:

| Scores secured on General Classification Test | 60 | 80 | 100 | 120 | 140 |
|---|---|---|---|---|---|
| Number out of 100 who succeeded | 5 | 17 | 40 | 67 | 88 |

It is not always wise to choose the person for a job who has the highest score on the test. Certain types of jobs are filled most successfully by individuals who attain high mental-alertness ratings, *e.g.*, engineers and managers. Certain other types of jobs are filled most successfully by individuals who attain low mental-alertness ratings, *e.g.*, common laborers and fishermen. Still other jobs are filled most successfully by individuals who attain medium mental-alertness ratings, *e.g.*, mechanics and salespeople. The mental-alertness score is more prophetic of the future wage or salary of any large group of applicants who are worthy of employment than is any other single measure or employment procedure.

*The prophetic value of test scores increases with time.* The test scores may correlate low with the income of employees at the end of the first year of employment. If the tests were wisely selected, the correlation will be very significant after 5 years of employment but still higher after 10 years.

Mental-alertness test scores on applicants for employment can be secured with a delay of only about 1 hr. and at a cost of only about $1 per individual tested (including all overhead expense). Yet these test scores have a prophetic value greater than any other known selection procedure. However, great care needs to be taken in using psychological tests. The X ray is demonstrated as a successful diagnostic instrument only when it is supported by other modern diagnostic procedures. Chemical soil analysis is a demonstrated success in measuring the value of land only when the proper seed has been selected, the growing grain adequately cultivated, and profitable markets are obtainable.

Mental-alertness tests are highly diagnostic only under very special conditions, to which very careful attention must be given, namely:

1. The values of mental-alertness tests are demonstrated only when they are a part—a modest part—in a good employment program. (Here no mention is made concerning the value of mental-alertness tests in transfers and promotion.) Many chapters in this book refer to the development of an employment program equipped to secure, to select, and to place the right man in the right place.

2. The values of mental-alertness tests are demonstrated only when they are but a part—and a minor part—in a good personnel program. Unless after employment there are throughout the organization conditions that result in the survival of the fittest, then good employment procedures are of little or no consequence. Most of the chapters in this volume have to do with the development of a type of personnel management that creates conditions under which morale is increased, labor turnover is reduced, and the survival of the fittest in all jobs is attained.

3. The value of mental-alertness tests is demonstrated only when they are:

3.1 Properly constructed to meet the needs of a particular organization. So many mental-ability tests have been constructed that the present need is merely a wise choice from the hundreds of offerings.

3.2 Tactfully administered so that every candidate will put forth his best efforts in solving the assigned problems.

3.3 Scientifically interpreted. The grading of the papers has been reduced to a mechanical use of stencils or other tools. No dependence is placed on the personal judgment or estimate of the grader. Accordingly, the grading may be accurately accomplished by a clerk. However, interpretation of the results should be left to a psychologist who has had statistical training, who has had experience with tests, and who has had some experience with working conditions within the organization.

In order that as much value from tests be obtained as possible, through clear understanding of the tests themselves and the procedures for determining their validity, and also to increase the probability that the conditions outlined above all be met, it is recommended that large business concerns employ one or more full-time psychologists. Smaller business organizations should employ the part-time services of a psychologist. Just as many business organizations employ full-time attorneys, physicians, and engineers, it may be expected that most of the larger companies will find it profitable to employ psychologists as regular staff officers.

Small companies at the present time can secure the part-time services of competent psychologists from local colleges and universities, from state employment offices, or from professional consulting firms. Not all persons who label themselves psychologists are qualified; the American Psychological Association has set up an examining board for industrial psychologists. Those who have passed the examinations of this board and are certified as qualified are listed as *Diplomates in Industrial Psychology of the American Board of Examiners in Professional Psychology.* Inquiry should be made of those who represent themselves as industrial psychologists as to whether or not they hold this diploma. Names of diplomates in industrial psychology may be secured from the American Psychological Association.

Tests of general mental ability are by official regulation made an important factor in the personnel program of every unit of the Army, the Navy, and the Air Force. Almost all institutions of higher learning use them with their students. Twenty-five years ago such tests were used in few business organizations. However, the number of business firms using them has become very large during the past few years (see Fig. A.2).

**Clerical-aptitude and -ability tests.** Clerical occupations include those filled by persons who are usually referred to as office workers. It is obvious that there are many different kinds of jobs in this group. No single test or group of tests would be appropriate for all clerical jobs. Most of the work done is with pencil and paper. The activities include shorthand, typing, indexing, coding, filing, record and account keeping, inventory and stock work, checking, tabulating, etc. Sometimes machines are used to aid in this work. When this is done, some degree of dexterity or mechanical ability may be desired. The importance of dexterity is also related to the fact that various papers, cards, pencils, typewriters, comptometers, and other office equipment are more adroitly manipulated with agile fingers and hands.

Psychological tests can help in the selection of clerical personnel by giving information of five different kinds:

1. General mental ability: the capacity to use verbal and nonverbal concepts; to grasp the meaning of words and other symbols; to solve problems, to see relationships, and to make correct decisions.

2. Basic educational skills: ability to add and multiply, spell correctly, alphabetize, and to use the language correctly.

3. Clerical aptitude, strictly defined: the ability to observe words and numbers accurately, to see quickly and correctly what is on the paper and make the appropriate discriminative response.

4. Motor ability, particularly dexterity of the hands and fingers.

5. Occupational proficiency: the ability to do the required work as a result of training. This may be assessed by a trial on the job but is also effectively measured by a work-sample test to appraise the ability of an applicant who claims skill in any one of several types of clerical work.

The advantages of measuring the abilities of the individual for each of these kinds of information separately, rather than through application of a composite test, are fairly obvious. The employment officer is able to make use of the information about the various abilities separately for more effective placement after employment and to solve problems of transfer more wisely. A more effective program of supervision and training is also possible.

**Mental-ability tests.** Differences in mental alertness among clerical workers is probably the most important factor in determining the level at which an employee may be expected to succeed or the likelihood of advancement. A test of this sort should be given first consideration in employing clerical workers. Descriptions of tests of general mental ability have been given in the first part of this chapter.

**Tests of educational skills.** Good computational ability and correct language usage are the educational skills most pertinent to clerical work. In recognition of this, most general clerical ability tests have sections which measure these skills. Illustrations of such tests are the Psychological Corporation General Clerical Test[3] and the National Institute of Industrial Psychology (NIIP) Clerical Test (American Revision).[4] The former test has nine parts, yielding three types of scores. An over-all score is indicative of general clerical ability. The nine part scores are available as a guide in the selection or assignment of personnel for highly specialized tasks. The three section scores are obtained by combining parts 1 and 2 for a measure of routine clerical aptitude, parts 3, 4, and 5 for a measure of proficiency in computation, and parts 6 through 9 for a measure of language ability. The nine parts are as follows:

[3] *General Clerical Test,* The Psychological Corporation, New York, 1947.
[4] *The N.I.I.P. Clerical Test (American Revision),* The Psychological Corporation, New York, 1947.

1. Name and number checking.
2. Alphabetizing and filing.
3. Arithmetic computation.
4. Finding errors in addition.
5. Arithmetic reasoning.
6. Spelling.
7. Reading comprehension.
8. Vocabulary.
9. Grammar.

The NIIP Clerical Test is similar, with seven parts: oral instructions, classification, arithmetic, copying, checking, filing, and problems. This test would be most useful for routine clerical positions. Consideration of verbal facility or language ability is desirable for secretarial positions and for those which require the preparation of summaries or reports.

**Clerical aptitude.** Apart from general mental ability and the possession of pertinent educational skills, *clerical aptitude is primarily a factor of speed of perception and reaction.* It is revealed by differences in performance on psychological tests of checking, comparing, etc. Research has shown that clerical aptitude, thus defined, undergoes little change as a result of clerical experience or training. The most widely used test of clerical aptitude is the Minnesota Clerical Test. This test has items of two principal types, each developed according to a careful plan. Its use is supported by numerous research investigations. The instructions with some sample items from this test are reproduced below.[5]

## INSTRUCTIONS

On the inside pages there are two tests. One of the tests consists of pairs of names and the other of pairs of numbers. If the two names or the two numbers of a pair are *exactly the same* make a check mark ( ✓ ) on the line between them; if they are *different*, make no mark on that line. When the examiner says "Stop!" draw a line under the last pair at which you have looked.

*Samples* done correctly of pairs of *Numbers*

| 79542 | | 79524 |
|---|---|---|

| 5794367 | ✓ | 5794367 |
|---|---|---|

*Samples* done correctly of pairs of *Names*

| John C. Linder | | John C. Lender |
|---|---|---|

| Investors Syndicate | ✓ | Investors Syndicate |
|---|---|---|

[5] Dorothy M. Andrew, Donald G. Paterson, and Howard P. Longstaff, *Minnesota Clerical Test,* The Psychological Corporation, New York, 1933.

*Now try the samples below.*

| | |
|---|---|
| 66273894 | 66273984 |
| 527384578 | 527384578 |
| New York World | New York World |
| Cargill Grain Co. | Cargil Grain Co. |

This is a test for Speed and Accuracy. Work as fast as you can without making mistakes.

Do not turn this page until you are told to begin.

**Motor ability.** It is not likely that differences in motor ability will be related to differences in clerical skill to any noticeable degree. A certain minimum dexterity is clearly desirable, however, and there are certain specific clerical assignments in which it may be quite a significant factor. Tests of manual or finger dexterity, which will be discussed in the next chapter, would be appropriate for use with clerical personnel also, when desired.

**Proficiency tests.** *Work-sample tests* have been constructed to measure the ability of applicants who claim skill in any one of several types of clerical jobs. When conducted under controlled conditions and the results carefully checked as to speed and accuracy, these tests meet scientific standards.

This kind of test will give a measure of the present ability of a typist or stenographer. Work-sample tests measure fairly accurately the present clerical ability of the applicant to perform a specific task. Since it is not in and of itself an adequate clerical-aptitude test, it should be supplemented by other tests as indicated above. The proficiency test gives an indication of the present status of the prospective employee; other measures will indicate how he may be expected to perform in a wider variety of situations and what might be expected in the way of future development.

An applicant typist may be given the following work-sample test, which can be performed accurately and quickly only by an expert typist.

### INSTRUCTIONS AND COPY FOR TEST FOR TYPIST
### INSTRUCTIONS TO THE EXAMINER

1. Make sure that the typewriter is in good condition. The only form of supplies needed is typewriter paper, 8½ × 11.

2. Say to the candidate, "Be seated at this typewriter. Insert paper and adjust the typewriter for single space."

3. When these instructions have been complied with, give to the candidate the loose sheet of test copy and say, "Copy this as rapidly as possible, making no erasures, and as few mistakes as possible; and report to me as soon as you are through."

4. Record the starting time in minutes and seconds. This represents the time at which the copy is handed to the candidate, not necessarily the time that he begins to write.

5. Record the time when the candidate gives to the examiner the finished type-written copy.

6. Record on the candidate's individual score card his name and the total time in minutes. Ignore the fractional part of a minute.

7. Determine the number of errors. An error is any error in a word or the space or punctuation immediately following a word. A word which has several errors is counted as one error. Record the number of errors on the score card.

## RATING THE CANDIDATE

1. Multiply the number of minutes by 10. Ignore the fractional part of a minute.

2. Add the number of errors.

3. This sum is the candidate's score. Rate the candidate according to the following table:

Expert......................... 0 to 86 inclusive with fewer than 6 errors
Journeyman.................... 0 to 86 inclusive with more than 5 errors
Apprentice..................... 87 to 150 inclusive
Novice........................ 151 and above

## TEST COPY

This is the kind of ambition which creates things and which pushes the world along; an ambition to do or to be, to produce or to master something, and which never for an instant loses sight of the point first aimed at unless it be to aim at some point which is still higher and still harder to hit. That sort of ambition consists of only two elements, work and purpose; all men have had it who have striven with a definite end in view, even though some of them might not be willing to call it by that name. The dictionary gives several meanings of the word, but it matters very little which you accept, for the end is always the same; if you work with a desire to make a name for yourself, or if you try to establish an idea which you know to be right, you follow the same lines, and the method you adopt has for its basis ambition; there is no other word which can take its place and no other which has even a similar meaning.

Ambition may be counted as one of the best qualities of the human race; to be sure, it has led to evil a great many times, or to what has seemed at first to be such, but I doubt if there has ever been a case where a great ambition did not in the end result in great good to all mankind. Napoleon has been called the most ambitious man who ever lived and crimes without number have been laid at the door of that ambition, all of which may be true, but today the world is better in many ways because he lived in it and because he was ambitious. An ambition to make money, to have a large pay envelope, has been sneered at as unworthy the thought of any young person; that is entirely wrong, for say what you will, there are a thousand and one things which make for the best good of everybody which can be had only through the medium of hard cash; we should dress well and read good books; we should surround ourselves with a certain number of things which have been termed luxuries but which are fast becoming necessities; all these things cost money, and to get money we must earn it; therefore the ambition for a large pay envelope is simply an ambition for better conditions in life, than which there can be no more worthy ambition.

If the candidate claims skill in stenography as well as in typing, the same copy may be used but the conditions for examining are changed. If the candidate claims skill in transcribing records from a dictating machine, he is given the copy from the dictating machine, but not on the printed page as described in the instructions for the typing test. If he claims skill in taking dictation, the examiner dictates the copy at the fastest rate at which the applicant is able to make his shorthand notes.

## CHAPTER 15

# *Psychological Tests: Mechanical Aptitude, Vocational Interests, and Personality*

**Appraising personnel for manual and mechanical jobs.** In dealing with personnel who are employed in manual and mechanical positions, important aptitudes and abilities include such things as knowledge of shop mathematics, tool recognition, mechanical information, and mechanical comprehension, the ability to manipulate concrete objects, and the ability to deal visually with mechanical movements. The characteristics of a prospective employee should be assessed so as to obtain information about two aspects of his qualifications:

1. Present level of ability to perform the job for which he is being considered.
2. The trainability: the level of achievement that may be expected of him in the future.

A pressing need, but a need easily met, is to develop and administer tests to measure the job proficiency already attained by prospective employees. This is accomplished quickly, inexpensively, and accurately by means of *work-sample tests* and *analogous work tests*, which will be discussed below. A more difficult task for psychological testing in business and industry is to measure, in prospective employees and in regular employees, not the abilities already attained, but the aptitude for future development, not the skill to perform today, but a prediction of the skill that may be anticipated after years of experience.

Progress is being made continuously in job analysis and in worker analysis. We are learniing what activities are involved in each particular job. We are learning "what it takes" physiologically and psychologically to be able to develop into an expert in each of these jobs. No two jobs are exactly alike, and success in no two jobs depends on the same abilities or on the development of identical latent capacities.

222

However, certain similarities exist among mechanical occupations, so that it is possible to secure useful information through the administration of appropriate tests. But a careful check should be made in each situation to determine whether or not the tests used are distinguishing between good and inferior workers.

Studies seem to indicate that three relatively independent components account for the principal differences observed in mechanical aptitude and ability. These are *space ability, mechanical knowledge* and *comprehension,* and *manual dexterity,* including speed and steadiness of movement. Attention should also be given to the general mental ability of personnel in mechanical and manual jobs and to job proficiency. Thus information about employees in these positions which can be provided by psychological tests may be grouped into five kinds:

1. General mental ability.
2. Space ability.
3. Dexterity and motor skills.
4. Mechanical comprehension and information.
5. Occupational proficiency.

It is well to note that the usefulness of one or more of these five kinds of information may be qualified by certain collateral abilities or aptitudes required for a particular assignment. Physiological factors, such as visual or hearing acuity, educational skills, such as computational ability, reading comprehension, or language usage, or personality and temperament characteristics of various sorts may often enter in as significant determinants of success or failure in certain manual and mechanical jobs.

**General mental ability.** There is a desirable level of intelligence for each group of workers in manual and mechanical occupations. A high level of mental ability is required among workers who are concerned with complex operations and who have supervisory and other responsibilities. Among routine workers, better work adjustment is likely if the mental-alertness score is not too high. The best level for the various occupations in any company can be determined by making local studies.

Within reasonable limits, differences in mental ability and success in a particular mechanical occupation have no significant relationship.

**Space ability.** A factor which is always found to be important in mechanical success is the ability to perceive and deal with spatial relationships. Early space tests were classified as mechanical aptitude tests. Space ability is now dealt with more broadly as a factor of general mental ability; so it has been discussed under that topic in the preceding chapter.

**Dexterity and motor skills.** High-level dexterity of fingers, hands, and arms is required for many jobs. Packing, sorting, assembling, and disassembling must be done quickly and accurately. *Dexterity appears to be quite specific.* If a person does well on one dexterity test, this does not ensure that he will do well on another dexterity test or will succeed on a given job requiring dexterity. The relation between the test and the job needs to be studied and established. Speed of reaction can be measured by a simple tapping test. Measures of strength or of steadiness are rarely needed. Devices for measuring these physiological characteristics are readily available if desired. Three tests will be described below to illustrate measures of dexterity and motor skills.

1. The *O'Connor Finger Dexterity* and the *O'Connor Tweezer Dexterity* tests are widely used measures for fine motor skills. For each test, the subject is required to pick up metal pins and insert them into holes drilled in a metal plate. One test requires the pins to be handled by the fingers; for the other tweezers are used. Finger dexterity and tweezer dexterity have been found to be quite independent of each other.

2. The *Bennett Hand-Tool Dexterity Test*,[1] pictured below re-

[1] George K. Bennett, *Bennett Hand-Tool Dexterity Test,* The Psychological Corporation, New York, 1946.

FIG. 15.1. Bennett Hand-Tool Dexterity Test.

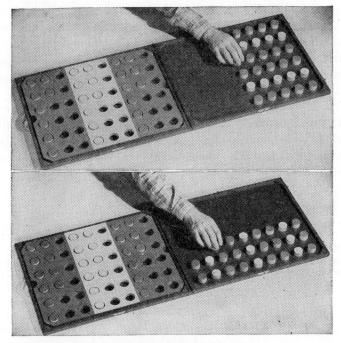

Fɪɢ. 15.2. Stromberg Dexterity Test.

quires the subject to take apart 12 fastenings from the left-hand upright, according to a prescribed sequence, then to reassemble the nuts, washers and bolts in the right-hand upright. The score is in time required. This type of manipulative test is readily accepted by applicants for mechanical work, and it has a high reliability. It has been found to have a good validity for many jobs.

3. The *Stromberg Dexterity Test*[2] is a rate of manipulation measure for assessing gross arm and hand dexterity. The task is to discriminate and sort the blocks, moving and placing them as rapidly as possible. The score is in time required. The test is pictured above. It has been found useful in selecting laundry workers, foundry molders, general factory workers, punch-press operators, assemblers, welders, and others.

**Mechanical comprehension and information.** Mechanical comprehension is a form of intelligence. Together with space ability, it constitutes essentially what was referred to in the preceding chapter as *concrete intelligence.* It has been defined by Bennett as "the capacity for learning the principles of operation of machines and devices."

[2] Eleroy L. Stromberg, *Stromberg Dexterity Test,* The Psychological Corporation, New York, 1951.

Studies made by the Air Force, during and since World War II, have shown also that an important component of mechanical aptitude is information about tools and mechanical devices and principles. The best tests of mechanical aptitude include problems relating to mechanical principles and their application and to mechanical information. Two examples are described below:

1. The *Mechanical Comprehension Tests*,[3] devised by George K. Bennett, are available in three forms for men, each form at a different level of difficulty, and in one form for women. The test consists of drawings with questions about them. The following sample items illustrate the test:

### DIRECTIONS

Look at Sample X on this page. It shows pictures of two rooms and asks, "Which room has more of an echo?" Room A has more of an echo because it has no rug or curtains; so a circle is drawn around A. Now look at Sample Y, and answer it yourself. Draw a circle around the right answer.

On the following pages there are more pictures and questions. Read each question carefully, look at the picture, and draw a circle around the best answer.

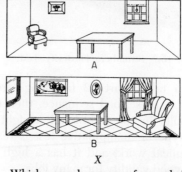

A

B

X

Which room has more of an echo?

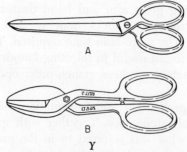

A

B

Y

Which would be the better shears for cutting metal?

[3] George K. Bennett *et al.*, *Test of Mechanical Comprehension*, The Psychological Corporation, New York, 1949.

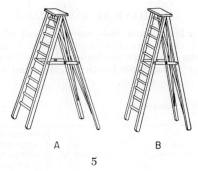

A                    B

5

Which stepladder is safer to climb on?

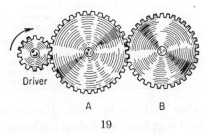

A          B

19

Which gear will turn the same way as the driver?

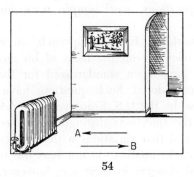

54

Which arrow shows the way the air will move along the floor when the radiator is turned on?

2. The *SRA Mechanical Aptitudes test,*[4] Form AH, illustrates the usual approach in the measurement of mechanical knowledge. A picture of some tool or mechanical device is presented, and the task is to indicate what it is or what it is used for.

[4] *SRA Mechanical Aptitudes,* Science Research Associates, Inc., Chicago, 1947.

## MECHANICAL KNOWLEDGE

How much do you know about tools, machines, and other equipment used by carpenters, plumbers, electricians, gardeners, machinists, auto mechanics, housewives, and others who work with mechanical devices? *Mechanical knowledge* is important for success in mechanical activities. This first test measures your information about *mechanical devices*.

Look at the problem below:

| P-1 | | This is used to: | A. chop wood....................... <br> B. scrape paint...................... <br> C. remove nails..................... <br> D. shape metal...................... <br> E. break rocks....................... |
| P-2 | | This is used in: | A. cranking gasoline engines........... <br> B. bending wood strips............... <br> C. opening cans.................... <br> D. removing spark plugs.............. <br> E. boring holes in wood.............. |
| P-3 | | This is: | A. a machine bolt................... <br> B. a carriage bolt................... <br> C. a window bolt.................... <br> D. a stove bolt..................... <br> E. an eye bolt...................... |

There are two other parts to this test. The second part measures space ability; the third part is a test of shop arithmetic.

**Occupational proficiency.** The most commonly used tests for proficiency in a manual or mechanical occupation are of three general types: *oral trade questions, work-sample tests,* and *analogous,* or *miniature, work tests.*

1. *Oral Trade Questions.* In this approach, an estimate is made of an applicant's proficiency on the basis of his answers to a series of questions which have been standardized for the occupation for which he is being considered. Such questions have been developed by the Army and also by the U.S. Employment Service. Care is taken to make sure that the questions distinguish between qualified and unqualified workers and that variations within an occupation or from one geographical area to another do not bias the results. There are many difficulties and dangers in their use, however; so they should be depended upon only when no other proficiency measure is available.

2. *Work-sample Tests.* The results of a work-sample test are in the form of concrete facts. They are regarded simply as a measure of the present ability of the candidate or worker, not as a prognostication of future ability. A work-sample test should not be confused with an informal "tryout" on the job, whether the tryout continues 30 sec. or 30 days. Such a tryout is, of course, a rough-and-ready test.

In many organizations, it is the only approximation to a test that is applied. Most informal tryouts on the job are unscientific and expensive; they ordinarily should be displaced as soon as possible by an actual work-sample test or by some other test in which conditions are standardized and the results are measured.

Work-sample tests, however, are not sufficient. Two applicants might take the same work-sample test at the same time and make identical scores. One may have acquired his present ability by long training and experience. He may have attained his maximum capacity and have no aptitudes requisite for promotion or transfer. The other may have attained his present status of accomplishment with less training and experience but may have aptitudes which indicate further development on the job or his fitness for transfer or promotion to positions of greater importance. Accordingly, work-sample tests should be part of a battery of tests in which special-aptitude tests are included.

2.1 A *work-sample test* for truck drivers is given to a candidate claiming ability to understand and manage a truck.

The candidate is provided with a standard truck and is permitted to make a short practice run and to try out all the gadgets. After this preliminary practice is completed, the test begins. The candidate is required to drive the truck over a prepared route that contains a hill, a short turn, a narrow passage, etc. The examiner sits to the right of the driver during the practice run and the test run and gives standardized instructions and records all errors. A candidate who makes 1 error or less is classed as an expert; 2 to 9 inclusive as a journeyman; and 11 to 15 as an apprentice.

2.2 *Work-sample tests* for wiremen have been used for many years. The Illinois Bell Telephone Company uses identical sets of a work-sample test so that several candidates may be tested at the same time without mutual interference.

The test is a complex wiring job. The examiner provides the materials and the tools, demonstrates some of the first steps in the procedure, and gives complete verbal instructions as to what the task is. These instructions are then repeated. The examiner records the time consumed in completing the job and the mistakes made. Each candidate is classified on the basis of the time he consumed and the errors he made. The score is based 50 per cent on the time consumed and 50 per cent on the quality of the work.

3. *Analogous, or Miniature, Work Tests.* An analogous, or miniature, work test is one in which an artificial situation is created that calls forth reactions from the testee nearly identical to his reactions in an actual work situation. An analogous work test has several desirable features.

1. It substitutes inexpensive equipment for the expensive equipment used in industry.

2. To the total situation it adds devices for recording automatically the responses made by the subject.

3. It reduces the complex working situation to recordable units.

Such tests are especially desirable in selecting operators for equipment which is not only expensive but in connection with which emergencies are likely to arise in which ineptitude on the part of the operator could result in personal injury or death and also in property damage.

For measuring the ability of candidates to handle various kinds of motor vehicles, many analogous work tests have been devised and have been used successfully.

3.1 To measure the reactions of a streetcar motorman under ordinary and under emergency conditions, an analogous work test has been used successfully:

A large number of motion pictures were taken from the front platform of a moving streetcar. The scenes included sharp bends of the track, people crossing in front, taxicabs approaching from side streets, children playing on or near the track, pedestrians crossing the track, etc. A front platform of a streetcar was set up in a research laboratory. The platform was provided with all the instruments common to streetcars for starting, stopping, changing the speed, and signaling. However, the "instruments" were not connected with the electric current, the brakes, and the bell. They were connected with an apparatus for recording exactly how and when they were used by the subject. Some distance in front of this fixed platform and also on all sides of the platform was a large screen on which the motion pictures were shown. These pictures, previously photographed from the platform of a moving streetcar, create an illusion of movement in the mind of the subject as he stands on the stationary platform and looks at the motion pictures.

The subject being tested stands on the "platform" and is directed to "control the car" according to the situations depicted, just as he would on an actual run. All his responses are recorded automatically.

3.2 In an attempt to measure the reactions of taxi drivers in traffic emergencies, the following is a sample of "emergencies" that were created:

A small boy (a rubber dummy) on roller skates is catapulted out from behind a parked car and directly into the path of the moving taxicab.

By means of photoelectric relays, a record is made of exactly what the taxi driver does to the fraction of a second. Every hesitation and false movement made by the subject being tested are automatically recorded.

3.3 The *roadscope* is a device for measuring ability to steer an automobile under diverse road conditions.

In a laboratory are set up a driver's seat and the equipment used in steering an automobile. What corresponds to the windshield is a device called the "roadscope." The roadscope is in reality a motion picture of a road, and the subject is told to steer his automobile according to the changing conditions indicated. The degree of his success is measured and recorded automatically.

3.4 *Analogous, or miniature, work tests* are not restricted to the measurement of ability for candidates for transportation services. The Wisconsin Miniature Test for Engine Lathe Aptitude is of special interest.

A reproduction of the testing apparatus is shown in the illustration (Fig. 15.3). It duplicates that part of an engine lathe that controls the movement of the cutting tool. To this end, the arm *A* supporting the point *P* is mounted in such a way that the latter may be moved anywhere around the bakelite plate *X* by the joint action of the two screws placed at right angles to each other and turned by the cranks *H* and *H'*. These cranks are duplicates of those actually used on an engine lathe. The task of the subject is to move the point *P* around the series of six electric contacts shown in plate *X* as rapidly as possible while going as directly as possible from one to the next. When the point touches a contact, an electric bell *B* rings to notify the subject that he has succeeded in touching it and that he may proceed to the next contact. In order to secure a graphic record of all the movements of the subject in passing around the contacts, arm *A* is extended over area *Y*, upon which is placed a piece of paper. On this extension is a point *P'* that contains a small lead pencil that traces a duplicate of the path made by point *P*. A typical record is shown as *Y* in Fig. 15.3.

The four analogous, or miniature, work tests described above are alike in that the results are measurable by the degree of their conformity to the patterns of skilled, semiskilled, unskilled, or unsuccessful workers. The standardization of each of these tests was accomplished by giving each test to a large number of skilled and semiskilled operators and also to novices and workers who had failed. The record of a worker may show that he applies a steady, even pressure to his controls or that he grasps his controls convulsively and applies his brake too suddenly. An analogous, or miniature, work test would be entirely worthless unless the record of a skilled worker followed a pattern unlike the pattern followed by a semiskilled, an unskilled, or an unsuccessful worker.

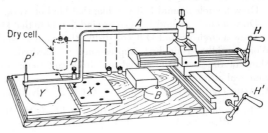

Fig. 15.3. Wisconsin Miniature Test for Engine Lathe Aptitude.

The validity of an analogous, or miniature, work test is measured in terms of the accuracy with which it ranks operators of known abilities.

**Vocational-interest tests.** Measurement of interest in an occupation often provides information which is a very useful addition to that obtained by aptitude and ability measures. It is not enough to know that a person *can* do the job; we also wish to know if he *will* do the job. A measure of interest may usually be considered as an index of motivation. This does not mean that we find out how much drive the person has, but we do find out his relative preference for the type of work under consideration, and this is usually quite closely related to the degree of satisfaction he will get from it and the likelihood that he will stick to it over a period of time.

Measures of vocational interest are not often helpful in personnel selection. When an applicant wants a particular job, he is likely to respond to such a measure according to how he believes he should answer in order to get the job rather than in terms of how he actually feels. Interest measures are useful, however, in supervision and control of personnel. Problems of adjustment and motivation of the worker on the job can be understood better when information about vocational interests is also available.

The Vocational Interest Blank by E. K. Strong, Jr.,[5] consists of 400 items. Most of these require the subject to indicate whether he "Likes," "Dislikes," or is "Indifferent to" a wide variety of activities, occupations, school subjects, and peculiarities of people. Other items require the subject to rank activities in order of preference. The instructions and some sample items are given below to illustrate the test:

*Part I. Occupations.* Indicate after each occupation listed below whether you would like that kind of work or not. Disregard considerations of salary, social standing, future advancement, etc. Consider only whether or not you would like to do what is involved in the occupation. You are not asked if you would take up the occupation permanently, but merely whether or not you would enjoy that kind of work, regardless of any necessary skills, abilities, or training which you may or may not possess.

Draw a circle around L if you like that kind of work.

Draw a circle around I if you are indifferent to that kind of work.

Draw a circle around D if you dislike that kind of work.

Work rapidly. Your first impressions are desired here. Answer all the items. Many of the seemingly trivial and irrelevant items are very useful in diagnosing your real attitude.

1. Actor (not movie)............L I D  2. Advertiser............L I D  (etc.)

[5] E. K. Strong, Jr., *Vocational Interest Blank for Men, Revised,* and *Vocational Interest Blank for Women,* Stanford University Press, Stanford, Calif., 1938, 1946.

*Part III. Amusements.* Indicate in the same manner as in Part I whether you like the following or not. If in doubt, consider your most frequent attitude. Work rapidly. Do not think over various possibilities. Record your first impression.

137. Golf................L I D 138. Fishing................L I D (etc.)

*Part VI. Order of Preference of Activities.* Indicate which three of the following ten activities you would most enjoy by checking ( ✓ ) opposite them in column 1; also indicate which three you would least enjoy by checking opposite them in column 3. Check the remaining four activities in column 2.

     1     2     3

281. (  ) (  ) (  ) Develop the theory of operation of a new machine, *e.g.* auto.

282. (  ) (  ) (  ) Operate (manipulate) the new machine (etc.).

The Strong Vocational Interest Blank is unique and entirely adequate from the point of view of reliability and validity. Several studies have shown that differences in ratings on the test are related to differences in degree of success in the occupation. This test answers the question, "Does this person tend to like the same things the successful people following a particular occupation like?" When the 400 items have been checked, it is possible to compare the responses to more than 50 different occupations for men and to more than 25 for women.

Scores obtained on the blank are converted to ratings of A, which indicates close similarity of interest pattern; B, indicating moderate similarity; or C, which indicates that one does not have the interests characteristic of those successfully engaged in the occupation.

The reported reliability of the Strong Vocational Interest Blank is high—frequently above .80. Research also indicates that there are only very slight changes of interest between successive 10-year intervals from twenty-five to fifty-five years of age; but there are marked changes in measured interests from the age of fifteen to twenty-five years.

This test is not particularly valuable for people planning to enter manual occupations or the more routine clerical fields. It is particularly valuable for the person who has attained high scores in other psychological tests, because it helps to determine what occupation will provide him with the personal values that come only to the man who likes his job. A man who possesses the talents for success in several possible occupations should probably select the one which brings him into contact with the most agreeable companions. This test helps him to select the occupation that would bring him into contact with fellow workers who have similar interests and are therefore agreeable companions.

Although each profession or occupation has a special interest pattern that is ordinarily indicated for each successful member, it is possible to reduce most professions and occupations into about seven groups according to similarity of interest pattern. Thus the interest patterns for chemist, physicist, engineer, and mathematician are quite similar, but quite unlike those of another group including the lawyer, journalist, and advertiser. The results seem to indicate that there are only a few basic or general interest areas.

Most other interest inventories measure the relative strengths among the areas of interest for the person taking the test. Among the best developed and most widely used inventories are the Kuder Preference Record[6] and the Occupational Interest Inventory.[7] Interest areas which are most generally accepted as being valid include the following: scientific, artistic, clerical or business, literary, mechanical, and social or people.

**Personality tests.** Many attempts have been made to discover the potential troublemaker before he is hired. Numerous examples could be given of persons who are quite competent to do their work but who fail to perform as steady, productive workers or who cause so much difficulty from their poor relations with other workers that they are a liability rather than an asset to the company.

Difficulties of this sort are usually associated with personality rather than ability factors. Efforts made to measure these characteristics in order to predict future behavior on the job have not been so successful as efforts to measure ability factors. The most widely used method of assessing personality for personnel purposes has been the questionnaire. The *Minnesota Multiphasic Personality Inventory*[8] is an illustration of one of the better tests of this sort. This inventory consists of 550 statements printed on cards which the subject sorts into three piles, indicating whether they are true or untrue for himself or if he "cannot say." All the statements are of a somewhat personal nature, reflecting attitudes, interests, family relations, subjective feelings and experiences, etc. Three illustrative items are given below:

> I like collecting flowers or growing house plants.
> I have periods of such great restlessness that I cannot sit long in a chair.
> One or more members of my family is very nervous.

[6] G. Frederic Kuder, *Kuder Preference Record,* Science Research Associates, Inc., Chicago, 1956.
[7] Edwin A. Lee and Louis P. Thorpe, *Occupational Interest Inventory,* California Test Bureau, Los Angeles, Calif., 1943.
[8] S. R. Hathaway and J. C. McKinley, *Minnesota Multiphasic Inventory,* The Psychological Corporation, New York, 1943.

Eight personality trends are measured. These are given designations in terms of the kinds of emotional difficulties they reflect, if severe: hypochondriasis, depression, hysteria, paranoia, psychasthenia, schizophrenia, and mania. There are also checks on the scores for accuracy, honesty, and cooperation on the part of the subject. The care with which the scales were developed and the existence of these checks give this inventory an advantage over most other personality questionnaires. Careful precautions must always be taken if information about personality is sought in this way.

Other criticisms which have been made of personality questionnaires are that generally the desirable responses can be perceived and that the score is influenced by the "response set"; *i.e.*, some persons will agree with or accept as true a statement if it applies at all, others only if they have no reservations about it. These two weaknesses are pretty well offset by the special checks used in scoring the *Minnesota Multiphasic Personality Inventory.* Another criticism of personality questionnaires is that they are not brought into relation with job demands or requirements. What kinds of personality patterns, as shown by tests, work out best on particular jobs can be discovered only by experience and research. Personality inventories should be validated against jobs just as are ability tests.

Items of the *Minnesota Multiphasic Personality Inventory* have also been published in a booklet form. The answers can be checked on a separate answer sheet. This method of testing is satisfactory for clerical personnel and those with a good educational background, but the individual card form is superior for use with persons not accustomed to handling paper-and-pencil test materials.

Another carefully developed personality questionnaire is the *Guilford-Zimmerman Temperament Survey.*[9] Its items and the scoring are based on research studies of personality factors. Ten traits are measured: general activity, restraint, ascendance, sociability, emotional stability, objectivity, friendliness, thoughtfulness, personal relations (agreeableness and cooperativeness), and masculinity. It has been found useful in business and industry when the willing cooperation of those taking it is assured.

**The forced-choice technique.** To appraise personality by some sort of self-description on the part of the subject seems to be the most accurate and direct method. In the usual personality questionnaire, however, it is hard to avoid "faking." Persons seeking employment or

[9] J. P. Guilford and W. S. Zimmerman, *Guilford-Zimmerman Temperament Survey,* Sheridan Supply Company, Beverly Hills, Calif., 1949.

advancement will often try to represent themselves as having the kind of personality which is believed desirable. To overcome this difficulty, the forced-choice technique of personality measurement was invented by R. J. Wherry. This method prevents detection of "right" answers by pairing self-descriptions which are equally desirable or undesirable from a social point of view and forcing the subject to choose between them. He selects the one which is most descriptive or least descriptive of himself. Such scales have to be built with a great deal of care to be sure the alternatives are equally balanced.

The advantages of the forced-choice technique, in addition to the elimination of "faking," are that a wider range of personality descriptions is possible than has been true with adjustment inventories, the method of answering avoids the usual difficulties arising from response set, it forces a real discrimination on the part of the subject, and it can be adapted readily to the problem of relating personality characteristics to specific job requirements by using items whose pairs differentiate between successful and unsuccessful workers.

Since it is basically a self-report, there does exist the possibility that a subject would make his responses in terms other than those of his own personality. A stereotype, or "role," may be selected, and all the responses made in terms that are believed to correspond to it. Careful attention needs to be given to the conditions under which the test is used to avoid this danger.

An example of a forced-choice item is given below:

(A) Attractive
(B) Avoids Advice
(C) Avoids Fatigue
(D) Demands Perfection
(E) Puts on Airs

The subject is asked to check the description which is "most like" and that which is "least like" himself. In this item, it was found that (A) and (D) were about equally attractive and (B) and (E) about equally unattractive. Alternative (C) is neutral. This type of item makes possible discriminations on undesirable as well as on desirable characteristics. An alternate method of response would be to have the subject rank the items, giving a more descriptive result. Rundquist has reported the use of the ranking method with Owens-Illinois Glass Company factory girls.[10] They readily understood how to respond.

A recently developed measure of personality using the forced-choice

[10] Rundquist, Edward A. "Personality Tests and Prediction," in Douglas H. Fryer and Edwin R. Henry (eds.), *Handbook of Applied Psychology*, Rinehart & Company, Inc., New York, 1950, Vol. I, p. 187.

technique is the *Gordon Personal Inventory*,[11] which gives measures of four aspects of personality: cautiousness, original thinking, personal relations, and vigor. It is a companion instrument to the *Gordon Personal Profile*,[12] which measures for ascendancy, responsibility, emotional stability and sociability.

**Supervisory ability.** The importance of careful selection of supervisory personnel is recognized by everyone. There may not be such good agreement about how this selection is to be made. Principal attention is usually given to job proficiency. The importance also of knowledge and insight into human relations and the ability to use that knowledge to increase the productivity of those under supervision has also received acceptance, but methods of appraising this kind of ability are not so well agreed upon. *How Supervise?*[13] is a psychological device which illustrates an attempt at measuring this knowledge and insight into human relations. This test consists of a series of statements describing "Supervisory Practices," to be checked as desirable (D), uncertain (?), or undesirable (U); statements describing "Company Policies," to be marked in the same way; and a series of statements covering "Supervisor Opinion," to be checked as agree (A), uncertain (?), or disagree (DA). A sample item from each of these sections is presented below:

14. Prohibiting conversation between workers on routine jobs    D ? U
35. Providing music for routine and nontechnical workers    D ? U
45. The worker's opinion of his supervisor is not very important    A ? DA

The test is available in three forms and appears to have satisfactory reliability. The scoring is done on the basis of expert opinion: the "right answer" for each item is the one which was agreed upon by the majority of a panel of judges consisting of 37 members of the government's Training within Industry program and eight persons who had written recognized books or articles in the field of industrial relations or mental hygiene.

It might be argued that the majority opinion of this group may not at all times be correct. Certainly, it is possible that a supervisory practice or policy which is desirable in one situation may be quite undesirable in another. For this reason, *How Supervise?* needs to be carefully studied for its suitability in any company. This, of course,

[11] Leonard V. Gordon, *Gordon Personal Inventory*, World Book Company, Yonkers, N.Y., 1956.
[12] Leonard V. Gordon, *Gordon Personal Profile*, World Book Company, Yonkers, N.Y., 1953.
[13] Quentin W. File, *How Supervise?*, H. H. Remmers (ed.), The Psychological Corporation, New York, 1948.

is an axiom for any psychological technique suggested for personnel use.

Some of the limitations of personality questionnaires may also apply to this test. Statements in the test may be given widely different interpretations by different subjects. Although this reduces its usefulness for selection purposes, material is provided for supervisory training, for which *How Supervise?* may be useful.

Supervisors may express belief in a particular practice or policy but behave quite differently on the job. However, it is not necessary to be concerned about this. The important question is whether or not the test separates good supervisors from poor ones. There is considerable evidence that it does. The force of these findings is tempered, however, by the likelihood that differences in scores on *How Supervise?* are sometimes due to differences in reading ability or general intelligence rather than to differences in supervisory ability. At least this seems to be true when it is used with supervisory personnel whose educational level is below that of high school graduation.

Possible applications of this test which have been suggested by its authors are: (1) to select and classify candidates for supervisory training; (2) to evaluate the outcomes of supervisory training; (3) for upgrading; (4) to check on the quality of present supervisory personnel; (5) as a basis for interviewing and counseling supervisors; (6) as material for group discussion at supervisory meetings.

**Critical-requirements technique.** The purpose of any test or other instrument used for selecting personnel is to distinguish between those who will do well on the job and those who will not. The test makes distinctions among those who do well or poorly on the test itself in very specific terms. The characteristics which distinguish between good and poor workers are not usually so clear. Much stress has been placed on the reliability and the validity of psychological tests or other selection and appraisal instruments. Attention needs to be given also to the reliability and validity of the measure against which the test is used. That measure is the criterion: a term used to refer to observable differences in job success. These observations may take the form of ratings, of production records, of salary, or of whatever else is considered a satisfactory indication of success.

Criterion measures which have been commonly used tend to be low in both reliability and validity. The critical-requirements technique has been suggested by Flanagan[14] as a way of providing a better criterion measure. According to its originator:

[14] John C. Flanagan, "Critical Requirements: A New Approach to Employee Evaluation," *Personnel Psychology*, Vol. 2, Winter, 1949, pp. 419–425.

. . . the essence of this new procedure is to establish the critical requirements of a job or activity through direct observations by participants in or supervisors of the job or activity. *A critical requirement is defined as a requirement which is crucial in the sense that it has been responsible for outstandingly effective or definitely unsatisfactory performance of an important part of the job or activity in question.* Thus a critical requirement differs from the requirements which appear important but in practice have no important effect on performance with respect to the specified activity. Observation of personnel engaged in a specific activity leads directly to critical requirements in terms of what workers actually do on the job.

Although activities on the job are the basis for *critical requirements*, these requirements may also be stated in terms of aptitudes, training, information, attitudes, habits, skills, and abilities. When stated in these terms, the inferences need to be made carefully and properly verified.

Since the determination of critical requirements is one way of defining a job, the procedure reduces the processes of making a job definition, a statement of job requirements, and a definition of job success to the same problem.

Five conditions must be met if satisfactory data are to be obtained for establishing critical requirements:

1. Actual observations must be made of the on-the-job activity and the products of such activity.

2. The aims and objectives of the activity must be known to the observer. It must be clearly specified what the worker is supposed to accomplish.

3. The basis for the specific judgments to be made by the observer must be clearly defined. It is essential that a performance or product be rated as acceptable or not by all observers.

4. The observer must be qualified to make judgments regarding the activity observed.

5. The situation must be such that reporting is accurate; and the methods of communication used must preserve this accuracy.

CHAPTER 16

# Measuring Morale

**Morale defined.** Professor Ralph C. Davis says, "Good organizational morale is a condition in which individuals and groups voluntarily make a reasonable subordination of their personal objectives to the service objectives of their organization."[1] The group morale in general may be of a high type; yet certain segments of the group may manifest a low level of morale. For instance, the entire enterprise may have a high morale index, whereas a few departments have a low ratio. A given department composed of long-service employees may have intense loyalty to the organization as a whole yet be definitely antagonistic to the current departmental supervision. Such a situation, however, would be unusual, for the group ordinarily identifies the immediate supervisor with the company and relates satisfaction and dissatisfactions alike to the "boss." Individuals may have a general attitude or morale, and they also may have specific attitudes toward different aspects of their relationships. To illustrate, a group may be well satisfied with the wages paid yet be thoroughly dissatisfied with the opportunities for promotion.

**Morale and productivity.** The productivity of a group is a composite of many factors, at least one of which is the general state of mind or the "will to do" of the group. Formerly it was thought that a high morale resulted in high productivity. The more we study the causal relationships in business, the less prone we are to oversimplify these relationships. Some researches[2] have shown the group having the highest morale not always to be the highest in productivity. From this statement it does not follow that a low morale contributes to high

[1] Ralph C. Davis, *The Fundamentals of Top Management,* Harper & Brothers, New York, 1951, p. 802.

[2] See Daniel Katz, Nathan Maccoby, and Nancy C. Morse, *Productivity, Supervision and Morale in an Office Situation,* Survey Research Center, University of Michigan, Ann Arbor, Mich., 1950. Other studies have resulted in similar findings.

productivity. Just as morale is itself made up of a number of factors, so is productivity the result of a series of complex factors. When a group is convinced that high productivity will result in its getting the things it wants most, it is reasonable to believe that productivity will be high. This will be most likely to be true in spite of the presence of other conditions that may not be so satisfying as one would desire. It is likewise reasonable to believe that if the group's satisfactions in the work situation are high and high productivity will enable it to get the things it wants most, the productivity will be at least as high as, if not higher than, it would be where satisfactions leave considerable to be desired.

Even though the high morale may not be the cause of the high productivity, a high-producing group nearly always has a reasonably high morale, in terms of the company as a whole. Morale development is almost certain to accompany successful operations where the individuals can relate their respective endeavors and objectives to the success of the enterprise as a whole. The corollary to this is that a group possessing a high type of morale will utilize the skill, initiative, and training of its members to further the success of the enterprise. Required supervision will be minimized, and collective ingenuity, thought, and effort will replace the necessity for force. Such a situation naturally minimizes waste, increases efficiency, reduces costs, and increases quality—secondary goals of every enterprise. There is probably no phase of the industrial program in which there is more wishful thinking indulged in by managers than that concerning the attitudes of their employees toward the company. From the standpoint of scientific management, techniques have been developed during the past decade to enable the manager who strives to create positive morale conditions to evaluate the effectiveness of his efforts. "A morale-building organization tends to utilize fully the skill, initiative, judgment, and training of its members, and through such utilization succeeds in building up these and other qualities in everyone, so that the abilities of all constantly expand, and the organization thus is able to succeed and grow."[3]

**Objectives of the morale survey.** Management may want to know the attitude of its employees on current practices as well as proposed actions. E. F. Wonderlic, president of General Finance, said:[4]

[3] William R. Spriegel, *Industrial Management,* John Wiley & Sons, Inc., New York, 1955, p. 6.1. Reprinted by permission of John Wiley & Sons, Inc.

[4] It is interesting to note that this statement was made several years ago, but General Finance is as enthusiastic about morale surveys as we go to press as it was when it was considering profit sharing and its pension plan.

General Finance Corporation considered adopting a profit sharing and retirement plan for its employees. Curious as to whether the people would favor the plan, questions were incorporated into the regular annual attitude survey, asking:

1. Would some type of pension savings plan be of interest to you? and

2. Would you be willing to set aside a portion of your earnings for a pension savings plan? The majority said the plan would be a great incentive to them, in answer to the first question; and nearly 75% of those who answered the questionnaire said they would gladly contribute a percentage of their monthly salaries if such a plan were adopted. This definitely played a part in forming the company's profit sharing retirement plan. The attitude survey is an annual event at General Finance Corporation. The goals are to find out what the employee thinks toward his company in relation to other industries, toward his company as such, toward his division in the company, and toward his branch or department in the division. He is also asked his reaction to the supervision he is given and his feelings toward his own job. He is asked how he regards the company's wage policies, and what he thinks of company benefits.

**How may morale be measured?** Methods of measuring morale range all the way from the "hunch," or general "feeling," appraisal to reasonably scientific efforts. In summary, the generally recognized methods of appraising morale include:

1. The supervisor's or executive's impressions.
2. The guided interview.
3. The unguided interview.
4. A combination of the guided and unguided interview.
5. An analysis of production and other records.
6. The "listening-in" process.
7. The questionnaire:
    7.1 That asks specific questions and leaves room for the interviewer to write answers.
    7.2 That asks questions and gives a series of suggested answers for each question, one of which is to be checked (multiple-choice type).
    7.3 That can be answered "yes" or "no" by checking in an appropriate square.
    7.4 That uses various combinations of 1, 2, and 3.
8. A combination of any of the foregoing methods.

**General impression of the supervisor.** Some supervisors may not be able to tell you *how they know* the morale of their men, but they enjoy such an intimate relationship with them that they *do know* what their attitudes are. Relatively few supervisors or executives are trained observers of morale. They usually know how to get things done according to the methods they have been taught, but few of them have had any special training in evaluating morale as such. Some executives are inspirational leaders and capable of developing a high morale, but few of these are trained in observing and evaluating morale standards. Executives should be encouraged to strive to sense the morale situation and should be aided by more accurate tools that are available.

## QUESTIONS USED IN A GUIDED INTERVIEW*

Name_____Date_____
Dept._____M F† U-25_____26–35_____35–up_____
What is your position?‡_____How long have you been on this job?_____
How long have you been with General Finance?_____.
What other job have you had with General Finance?_____

What did you do before you came to General Finance?_____

Who is your immediate supervisor?_____
Whom does he report to?_____
Is there anyone else in your group who you feel is better qualified to be your
   leader than the one you have now?_____
Who trained you on your work?_____Are your instructions clear?_____
Do you have the proper equipment and space to do the job assigned to you?_____
Are there any troublemakers in your department?_____

Do all people in your group respect their leader's ability, clarity of instruction,
   etc?_____
Is the work load distributed equally between various people in the department?

Are promises made to you always kept?_____Are your suggestions
   well received?_____
Have you turned in suggestions?_____
Do some people go beyond their authority in issuing orders or delaying orders?

Is your department organized in such a way as to obtain most efficient
   production?_____
Are there any other departments or individuals that in their work or comments
   justly or unjustly accuse your group of being inefficient?_____
Comparing your department with other departments here in the home office, is
   it more or less efficient than others?_____

Do you feel that other departments have a good understanding and appreciation
   of the importance of your department?_____
Compared to other places you have worked, is your department most efficient,
   least efficient, or average in efficiency?_____

How would you rate your boss in his ability (a) to handle personnel (b) to
   handle his job?_____
Compared to other places you have worked, are you (a) well satisfied with your
   job, (b) moderately satisfied with your job, or (c) not particularly happy in
   what you are doing?_____

* Courtesy of E. F. Wonderlic, General Finance Corporation.
† M and F indicate sex. The numbers signify age group.
‡ In actual use, more space is provided for answers than is shown here.

FIG. 16.1.

**The guided interview.** The guided interview was one of the earliest methods used in striving to find out what employees were thinking and "feeling." The guided interview is based on the hypothesis that employees' answers to certain questions will reveal their attitudes. Naturally the questions selected are presumed to be the ones that will call forth a true picture of how the employees feel. This series of questions is usually rather large. The interviewer seeks to direct the interview in such a manner as to secure the answers that will reveal the desired information. This list of questions may be written, and the interviewer may make notations on the list as the interview proceeds, or the questions may merely be kept in mind by the interviewer to be asked more or less spontaneously as the interview proceeds. The written list of questions is somewhat more formal, but it has the advantage of being more uniform (see Fig. 16.1). The strictly informal procedure is more natural but introduces more variables in recording the result of the interview. The success of this method is largely dependent upon the skill of the interviewer in soliciting answers and his objectivity in evaluating the results of the interview. The cost and time elements for the guided interview are likely to be somewhat less than for the unguided interview; yet they are immeasurably greater than for the collectively answered questionnaire. On the other hand, the interview is more personal than the questionnaire and may be able to reveal conditions that would not be brought out by a questionnaire. The guided interview is an excellent tool to use in certain departments or with certain groups where a questionnaire has shown that things are not as they might be desired. It is also an excellent method of investigating the morale of supervisors or other groups that are small in comparison with the employees as a whole.

**The unguided interview.** In the minds of many persons the unguided interview is associated with the Hawthorne experiments as portrayed by William J. Dickson and F. J. Roethlisberger in *Management and the Worker.*[5] The unguided interview, as a technique for measuring morale, is predicated upon the theory that, if employees are placed in a position to talk freely, they will reveal a true situation not so much by the exact thing complained of or discussed as by the interviewer's ability to relate what is said to basic causes. It is further assumed that, if the employee himself is permitted to talk through a given problem or work situation without special prompting or questioning by the

---

[5] See F. J. Roethlisberger and William J. Dickson, *Management and the Worker,* Harvard University Press, Cambridge, Mass., 1940, pp. 270–291, for an excellent discussion of the principles and techniques of the unguided interview. This entire book records one of the most interesting experiments ever conducted in the United States.

interviewer, he usually will become aware of the logic or lack of logic in the situation and choose for himself the appropriate line of action. Once he has chosen his own line of conduct, the employee is more likely to accept the results. This method of employee-attitude analysis is designed both to correct an unfavorable situation and to secure information regarding the status of morale within the group. Although by its very nature it is a more expensive method of measurement than the questionnaire method, it not only provides a means of interpreting morale but at the same time is used to build morale. Its effectiveness is dependent upon the effectiveness of the interviewers and support of the line officers. Special training and objectivity are essentials of successful interviewing of this type.

**A combination of the guided and unguided interview.** Unless the interviewer is skilled in the use of the unguided interview, he is not likely to succeed in combining the guided interview with the unguided one. It requires more training to be proficient in the unguided interview than in the guided interview. This statement does not imply that the guided interview can be conducted without training and insight. To combine the two systems, the interviewer may start with the guided interview, which should be not too long or cover too much territory. The interviewee is then invited to discuss any subject that he may like to talk about. During the guided interview some persons tend to bring in material that has no special significance in relation to the information sought. The interviewer should observe such instances and encourage the interviewee to follow up these leads during the unguided portions of the interview. As a matter of fact, few guided interviews are strictly kept on the detailed subjects laid out in the formal program. On the other hand, a conscious effort has to be put forth to get the most out of the unguided phases of the interview.

**The analysis of records as a basis of evaluating morale.** Grievances and complaints tend to reveal the state of morale of a group unless these are being artificially stimulated.[6] Excessive absenteeism or tardiness may also serve as an index of general or specific morale conditions, particularly where certain departments have an especially unfavorable record. Labor turnover is a fair index of labor unrest or morale, particularly during a period of labor shortage. It may be a fair means of comparing group attitudes as between similar groups even during normal periods of business activity; however, labor turnover may not reveal anything but intolerable conditions during severe depressions, for workers will hold onto their jobs under such conditions even though they may be greatly dissatisfied. Other objective data such as waste, seconds, lost time waiting for materials,

---

[6] See Chap. 30 for a discussion of the analysis of labor turnover.

etc., may be analyzed and interpreted in terms of causal relationships, a part of which may reflect morale conditions. This type of analysis at best is difficult and is not always reliable as an index of morale. It may show managerial deficiencies that are not directly interpretable in terms of morale unless employees are penalized because of them.

**Listening in by a trained observer.** The listening-in technique of measuring morale must not be confused with the employment of detectives to spy on workers. In the hands of an inept observer the listening-in device might be dubbed the "spy system." This could be unfortunate. Whiting Williams of Cleveland, Ohio, has developed the "listening-in" technique to the extent that it would be appropriate to call it the "Whiting Williams method." He associates with the workers at work and during recreational periods. He personally possesses the ability to make his observations largely objective, something that is unusual in men who might be available for such work. There is no place in this type of attitude measurement for persons with pronounced biases. Herein lies one of its major defects: it is difficult to secure individuals who possess the required scientific approach to do this work. Such observers are prone to report what they think their employers want them to find rather than the true situation; or they may be prompted to report very unsatisfactory situations that in fact do not exist in the hope that their services may be continued in the capacity of working observers. As a whole, this type of investigation of the morale status of employees is not satisfactory.

**The questionnaire method of measuring morale.** There are at least two kinds of questionnaire surveys, (1) the individual questioning of an employee following a patterned set of questions (see page 243) and (2) the attempt to get a number of people to answer or check off questionnaires sent them through the mail or given them in a group meeting. These questions (page 243) were used in a guided interview in which only two persons participated. A similar questionnaire, with more adequate space for answers, may be used with large groups in the same general manner as the multiple-choice questions that are merely checked. It takes considerably longer to fill out questions requiring written answers than to check a given answer in a checking type of questionnaire. The technique of asking a question and having the employee answer it has the advantage of not suggesting any particular answer to the employee, but it is difficult to evaluate, and many employees have difficulty in expressing themselves on paper. Research workers, engineers, and other employees possessing a high degree of education may reveal finer shades of meaning on this type of questionnaire than in the case of the multiple choice. Another disadvantage of asking the employee to do much writing is the fear of some employees of having their identities revealed by their handwriting peculiarities even though they do not sign the questionnaire.

The multiple-choice type of questionnaire is a second type of questionnaire (Fig. 16.2). From the standpoint of wide usage and speed in administering, the multiple-choice type of questionnaire is preferred to other types of questions. The multiple-choice questions permit considerable shading of meaning when carefully constructed, are much quicker to answer, and are readily measurable by statistical methods. The multiple-choice method supplemented by a few "yes" or "no" questions has found wide use in mass investigation of employee morale.

**Constructing the questionnaire.** A morale survey should provide (1) for a measure of over-all general job morale, (2) for the opportunity on the part of the employee to express his attitude on a large number of specific points concerning his job, working conditions, relationship to his fellow employees, relationship to his superiors, understanding of managerial policies, and so on, (3) for employee opinions on the desirability of a program that management may be contemplating, and (4) for an evaluation of the specific attitudes and beliefs in terms of their correlation with general morale. Successful use of the multiple-choice type of questionnaire depends largely upon three things: (1) the completeness with which the questionnaire is constructed; (2) the distributing and collecting of the questionnaires; (3) the analysis of the data revealed by the questionnaires as answered. Great care needs to be exercised in formulating the question in such a manner as not to color the response.

The individual questions should be objective in form, permitting the employee to indicate his preference merely by checking any one of several possible answers. Some questionnaires provide space for the employee to qualify his answer. An illustration of this provision of space for an answer is as follows:

Do you feel that you receive fair treatment here?
  Yes ☐    No ☐
If not, tell why_____

_____

The foregoing question may also be set up as follows:

Do you feel that you receive fair treatment here?
☐ Most of the time
☐ Some of the time
☐ Very seldom
Comments:_____

_____

# EMPLOYEE OPINION SURVEY

Write in the number of the group you are in:

Length of Service:
( ) Less than 1 Year
( ) 1 to 3 Years
( ) 3 to 5 Years
( ) 5 to 10 Years
( ) Over 10 Years

## QUESTIONNAIRE

1. Does the home office management have a sincere interest in State Farm employees? ( ) Yes

2. Does local top management have a sincere interest in the employees of this office? ( ) No

3. Do you get enough information about company policies to do your work well? ( ) Yes ( ) No

4. Where do you get most information about the company? (Check one)
( ) Annual Report to Employees
( ) West Central Endorsement
( ) My Supervisor
( ) Meetings
( ) Grapevine

5. How do working conditions in this office compare with the offices in which your friends work?
( ) Better
( ) Same
( ) Worse
( ) Don't know

6. How do State Farm wages compare with those paid in this area for the same type of work?
( ) Better
( ) Same
( ) Lower
( ) Don't know

7. Do you think the pay for your job is fair compared to other jobs in this office? ( ) No ( ) Yes

8. How do you think State Farm employee benefits compare with those of other companies in this area?
( ) Better
( ) Same
( ) Poorer
( ) Don't know

9. When you ask your immediate supervisor a question does he—
( ) Give you a satisfactory answer
( ) Get you a satisfactory answer
( ) Forget about it
( ) Ignore you

10. How well does your immediate supervisor get along with people?
( ) Very well
( ) All right
( ) Has trouble at times
( ) Can't get along

11. Is your immediate supervisor a good listener, or does he do all the talking? ( ) Good listener ( ) Does most of talking

12. Is your immediate supervisor a good instructor? ( ) Yes ( ) No

13. If you had a gripe or complaint about your job, whom would you tell about it? (Put in order 1, 2, 3, 4)
( ) Immediate Supervisor
( ) His Boss
( ) Personnel Department
( ) Fellow Employee

14. Do you think a union is needed in an office which pays well and treats people fairly? ( ) No ( ) Yes

15. If you gave a good idea to your boss, would you get credit for it? ( ) Yes ( ) No

16. Do you think the company is too tough or too easy in disciplining employees?
( ) Too tough
( ) Too easy
( ) About right

PLEASE COMPLETE OTHER SIDE OF QUESTIONNAIRE

Fig. 16.2. One-page sample of employee opinion survey. (*Courtesy, State Farm Insurance Companies, Bloomington, Ill., and Guy Arthur & Associates, Inc., Toccoa, Ga.*)

248

17. Do you think the best
    qualified people in this
    office are promoted?

    ( ) No

    ( ) Yes

18. Do you know how you
    stand with your imme-
    diate supervisor?

    ( ) Yes

    ( ) No

19. Does your immediate
    supervisor show an
    interest in you as an
    individual?

    ( ) No

    ( ) Yes

20. Do you feel that the
    work you do is im-
    portant?

    ( ) Yes

    ( ) No

21. Do you feel free to say
    what is on your mind
    when talking to your
    boss?

    ( ) No

    ( ) Yes

22. Do you feel the people
    in your immediate group
    work well together?

    ( ) Yes

    ( ) No

23. Does everyone in your
    immediate group do his
    share of the work?

    ( ) No

    ( ) Yes

24. Are there any trouble-
    makers in your imme-
    diate group?

    ( ) Yes

    ( ) No

25. Do you think discipline
    is maintained uniformly
    throughout the office?

    ( ) No

    ( ) Yes

26. If you were manager of your
    regional office, what would you do
    to improve it as a place to work?

---

DO NOT SIGN THIS CARD

THANKS

Guy Arthur & Associates, Inc.,—Toccoa, Georgia

Fig. 16.2. (*Continued*)

The same question may be used as indicated above, omitting any space for comments.

Some employees will check such a question "no" yet fail to give a reason, possibly from a fear that the handwriting may be identified; others print their answers; and still others write out their answers, accepting the company's statement that no attempt will be made to identify any person's answer. Only one idea should be included in one question. This will necessitate a large number of questions, but this is to be preferred to brevity at the expense of clarity. The various shades of meaning can be indicated by the exercise of care in the construction of the questionnaire. E. F. Wonderlic of General Finance has used the following:

Comparing G.F.C. with other companies what do you think of G.F.C. as a place to work?
1. About average.........._____
2. Never worked before...._____
3. One of the best........._____
4. Poorer than most........_____
5. Better than most........_____
6. One of the worst........_____

It will be observed that this arrangement forces the employee to read all the answers before checking his choice. The same choices could be arranged in an ascending or descending order, in which event the employee would tend to stop at the level that he favored rather than to read them all. This of course would tend to be true only after he discovered the pattern that was being followed.

In case specific information is being sought that is not necessarily a morale factor, the employee may check more than one item as follows, using the General Finance illustration again:

Are you kept informed of changes in company policy and personnel through the medium of:
(Check more than one if applicable)
1. Bulletins and memorandums..........._____
2. My branch manager.................._____
3. My supervisor or department head......_____
4. The "grapevine" ...................._____
5. General letters....................._____
6. Other ............................_____

Figure 16.3 shows a punch-card arrangement used by Jack Staehle of Aldens, Inc. This type of card lends itself to rapid tabulation. It would be easily possible to have two or more cards if a larger number of questions were used.

**Interpreting the questionnaire results.** Within reason the questionnaire can be so constructed as to give answers in many areas. The results may be compiled on a departmental basis. The questionnaire may provide for the indication of sex; married or single; age groups such as under twenty-one, twenty-two to twenty-five, twenty-six to thirty; length of service, under 3 months, 4 to 6 months, 7 to 12 months, 2 to 3 years, 4 to 5 years, etc.; earnings group; and other factors of interest. With breakdowns similar to these, it is possible to study the influence of any of these factors on morale. On comparing departments, it is frequently detected that a particular department has low morale, whereas the morale of the enterprise as a whole is high. An analysis of the specific questions will ordinarily indicate the source of discontent, and remedial action may be taken; or if it is not

| | | |
|---|---|---|
| YES · NO | 12. If you have been dissatisfied with your job, was it the fault of Aldens? | YES · NO | 1. Does your supervisor care about your welfare? |
| YES · NO | 13. Does Aldens have a good vacation policy? | YES · NO | 2. Is your supervisor fair with you? |
| YES · NO | 14. Does Aldens have a good holiday policy? | YES · NO | 3. Do you know what your supervisor considers a good day's work? |
| YES · NO | 15. Does Aldens have a good promotion policy? | YES · NO | 4. Does your supervisor tell you if your work is good? |
| YES · NO | 16. Does Aldens have a good sick pay policy? | YES · NO | 5. Are you reasonably sure of keeping your job as long as you do good work? |
| YES · NO | 17. Does Aldens have a good life insurance policy? | YES · NO | 6. When a better job is open, is the best qualified person promoted? |
| YES · NO | 18. Does Aldens have a good hospital insurance policy? | YES · NO | 7. When you have a problem, do you feel free to ask your supervisor for advice? |
| YES · NO | 19. Does Aldens have a good employee discount plan? | YES · NO | 8. Is your section the best to work in? |
| YES · NO | 20. Does Aldens have a good training plan? | YES · NO | 9. Is Aldens fair with you? |
| | 21. IF YOU HAVE A COMPLAINT, PLEASE LIST ON OTHER SIDE OF CARD | YES · NO | 10. When you have a complaint, are you able to get a fair hearing and a square deal? |
| | | YES · NO | 11. Is your pay fair in proportion to the amount of work you do? |

FIG. 16.3. Punch card used by Aldens in making a morale survey. (*Courtesy, Aldens, Inc., Chicago.*)

possible to remove the source of friction, a frank explanation of the reason for the inability to make the desired improvement will often have a salutary effect. At times a special guided-interview program may be required to get at the real cause in a given department.

It is possible to develop a morale index for the entire company or department. Such an index may have value, but it is more important to discover points of weakness that can be attacked specifically than to have an abstract number. By assigning numerical values to various statements, the questionnaires may be analyzed statistically. If the same attitude scale is applied to a number of companies, it is possible to make comparisons between companies. The average personnel manager is not trained in the use of statistical devices, nor does he usually have access to the morale scores of other companies. This situation lends support to the advisability of securing the advice or help of trained consultants, particularly in making the first morale survey by the questionnaire method.

**Actually conducting the survey.** Management may employ an outside consultant to conduct the entire survey. In this event the consultant must be introduced to the employees, and they should be assured that he will not reveal to anyone an individual's answer. From this point on, the consultant may operate in the same manner as described below for a company representative.

If a representative of the company conducts the survey, he should take special care to assure the employees that they cannot be identified. If there is some form of employee representation, the representatives may do the distributing and collecting of all questionnaires and may also participate in tabulating the results. In some cases the company's representatives may give the employees the questionnaires in a stamped envelope, placing them on a table and permitting the employees to get them if they wish to, or having a fellow employee distribute them. The stamped envelopes are frequently addressed to some management consultant or college professor who tabulates the results. In some cases the company representative distributes the questionnaires in a meeting of the employees from a department in a cafeteria or some other convenient place. After assuring them that management wants their honest answers and that no one's identity will be sought, he may then ask for aid in distributing the questionnaires among the employees, pointing out the fact that under such circumstances it would be impossible to identify any questionnaire by any secret code, since no one knows to whom any particular questionnaire is given. It may be well to ask some employee to collect the completed questionnaires or to have them deposited in a box.

At General Finance each employee receives a letter from the division head, who points out the importance of the attitude survey. The letter stresses the desire to obtain *frank, honest* replies. The division head in this letter points out strongly that the employee need not sign the questionnaire and that no one will be "tracked down" for his answers. And yet encouragement is given to those who desire to sign their names. Over a period of years, General Finance Corporation has built up the confidence of its employees to such a point that when the most recent attitude survey was distributed to the 267 home office employees, 166 were returned within 3 days. This is a return of 66 per cent.

**Relative importance of various factors in the minds of employees.** The particular situation in a given company and the relationship to outside forces tend to influence the ranking of various items in morale surveys. Wages will be high on the list if they are substandard or if a current fight is on over wages in negotiating a union contract. There have been a number of published rankings of various items in morale surveys. In these studies wages rank all the way from sixth to twenty-fourth. Of course, as indicated above, they could be first if this were the item currently pressing down on the thoughts of the group.

**Morale among supervisors and executives.** In personnel management the tendency is to concentrate on the worker at the point of operations and to overlook the supervisors of these workers. Students of the relationship of employee morale to that of their supervisors are keenly sensitive to the importance of supervisory morale. Guy B. Arthur, Jr., president of Guy Arthur & Associates, Inc., a national management consulting firm, who has specialized in making employee opinion surveys for many years, has said:[7]

A quarter of a million employees cannot be wrong. They have told us some very interesting things. For example, they respect a boss who insists that standards of conduct, production and quality be maintained. They like to work for a man who is a good instructor; who keeps them informed; who tells them how they stand; who is a good listener; who helps them to develop; and who follows the Golden Rule in his dealings with all people. They indicate that pay is their primary concern unless they know they are being paid competitively with others in their area and industry. Our studies definitely point out that employee opinions are a direct reflection of the way their supervisors think. Because of this, supervisory opinions must be changed before a company can expect to improve the thinking of their employees.

Similar statements have been made in various forms by many executives, but relatively few of them take the trouble to find out the exact status of supervisory and executive morale. Very often, indeed, the morale of executives in a particular division or department leaves

[7] From a letter to the author, Feb. 10, 1959.

much to be desired. The questionnaire technique followed by a combination of the guided and unguided interview is an excellent device for measuring morale. The interview provides not only information regarding morale but an opportunity for building morale. The results of executive-morale studies provide excellent material for supervisory conferences.

**Using the results of morale studies.** Studies in employees' attitudes provide the necessary data upon which to formulate personnel practices. These studies require specially trained analysts to be effective. Many of the personnel activities have been discredited, not so much because the idea behind the practice was wrong as because the persons charged with their execution were unable to carry them out effectively.[8] Certain phases of personnel relations require specialized training in every sense equivalent to that of the chemist, engineer, or plant physician. Small organizations may not be able to support a full-time physician, psychologist, or attitude analyst, but these smaller institutions may profitably use the professional services of specialists in these fields on a part-time basis. Personnel management is increasingly appropriating the services of the scientific specialist; yet the great bulk of the work is performed by the general practitioner, who is thoroughly familiar with the plant operating processes and has a genuine interest in human relations.

The personnel department may conduct researches into every phase of personnel relations to discover the effectiveness of current practices and points of irritations needing remedial action and may formulate programs based upon these findings. Employee-attitude studies provide one of the most valuable methods of determining the current status of personnel relations. These studies may reveal that supervision is satisfactory but working conditions are not in keeping with the employees' desires, that wages are satisfactory but supervision is entirely inadequate, that the training program is not meeting the requirements of the employees, that promotions in the eyes of the employees are not being made on merit, or that many other aspects of personnel management that are vital to effective operation of the enterprise are not up to expectations. The morale or attitude survey of employees supplements the labor audit in very much the same sense as the physical inventory aids in the financial audit. Although the morale survey will not take the place of a thorough personnel audit, it will provide a valuable check in its absence.

[8] See National Industrial Conference Board, Inc., "Experience with Employee Attitude Surveys," *Studies in Personnel Policy* 115, New York, 1951, for a detailed research in this important management tool.

CHAPTER 17

# Communicating with Employees and the Public

**Communicating—the basis of motivating and control.** To move people to action in a desired direction requires making known the expected action. This is achieved through some form of communication. Control is exercised through the giving of information that is understood and willingly appropriated, through coordination effected through procedures, plans, or direct orders, and through indoctrination. Control is not completed until a report is rendered concerning performance. When this is achieved, all three directions of communication ordinarily are used. There is probably no single phase of large-scale operating that is more poorly conceived than the communications system. To be truly effective, communications must be at least a three-directional affair, (1) downward from top management, (2) upward from the workers, and (3) horizontally and diagonally in both directions.

Responsibility and authority rest primarily at the top of the organization. To become effective in operations, this responsibility and authority must be delegated to individuals lower in the organization. The process of delegating requires communicating. Standing orders, operational procedures, standard practices, and any type of instruction require communicating. All leaders recognize the need for conveying to subordinates the necessary information to do their jobs, but few of them appreciate the necessity of having the technical facts fall upon receptive and willing ears. They act as if all that was necessary was to know the bare facts of the situation, not to understand their relationships. It is not enough to let subordinates know what they are expected to do. A communication is not complete unless it carries with it understanding on the part of the recipient. This understanding may not be the result of a specific communication but rather may arise out of the entire situational atmosphere.

**Vertical as well as horizontal communications.** Most persons think of vertical communications when the word is read or heard. The passing of information to persons lower in the organizational structure is vertical and downward.[1] An answer coming back through similar channels is vertical and upward. These two types of communications are by no means the only ones that make for smooth operations. When department *A* needs something from department *B*, it is common practice for the foreman of department *A* to telephone the foreman of department *B* to ask him when it will be delivered. A formal order will probably already have been issued covering the item. This type of informal communicating horizontally smooths the path of production. One of the stumbling blocks of new enterprises is the fact that it takes time to build the informal organizational customs that contribute so much to the effectiveness of an enterprise.

**Channels of communication.** The formal organizational structure gives substantial direction to the formal avenues of communicating. This by no means rules out horizontal communicating with the responsible persons with whom a supervisor must have dealings. Neither do the formal channels rule out the communications that go in all directions through informal channels. While informal channels may be very effective in certain situations, particularly when certain personality problems are involved, management should studiously avoid bypassing the responsible executives or more problems will be created than obstacles overcome. The channels most frequently used in communicating with present and prospective employees are:

1. With prospective and new employees.
    1.1    Applicants for employment.
          1.11    Advertising, both printed and radio.
          1.12    Present employees.
          1.13    Personnel bulletins or booklets.
          1.14    Interviews.
          1.15    Lectures and group discussions.
          1.16    Radio.
    1.2    With new employees.
          1.21    Formal induction procedure.
          1.22    Personnel bulletins or booklets.
          1.23    Job specifications.
          1.24    Sightseeing through the business.
          1.25    Immediate supervisor.
          1.26    Staff officers, such as production control representative, the job

---

[1] See National Industrial Conference Board, Inc., "Letters to Nonsupervisory Employees," *Studies in Personnel Policy* 123, New York, 1951.

instructor, inspection representative, counselors, and personnel representatives.

1.27    The departmental sponsor and other fellow employees.
1.28    Bulletin boards.
1.29    Union representatives (where there is a union).
1.2(10) Letters from the general manager or president.
2. With regular employees.
   2.1    Regular supervisor. When he does his job thoroughly, sympathetically, and well, this is the best channel.
   2.2    Production control representatives.
   2.3    Inspectors.
   2.4    Personnel representatives.
   2.5    Bulletin boards.
   2.6    Procedure standards.
   2.7    Plant paper for employees.
   2.8    Annual report, either the same as that given to stockholders or a special one for employees.
   2.9    Letters sent to employees.
   2(10)  Payroll inserts.
   2(11)  Published statements of company policies.
   2(12)  Union paper.
   2(13)  Management reports (to supervisors and executives only).
   2(14)  Motion pictures and sound slides.
   2(15)  Public-address system.
   2(16)  Employee assemblies, conferences, and classes.
   2(17)  Special interviews and direct contacts during the routine operations.
   2(18)  The grievance procedure.
   2(19)  Suggestion system.
   2(20)  Special committees as in various representation schemes and multiple management.

**The public relations function.** Some managers take the attitude that the normal business contact with the customers and people in the community is all that is necessary to develop a favorable community acceptance. If one were to judge business by the organization of its public relations functions, he would be forced to conclude that this is the most common attitude. If all the employees were conscious of the influence of their public contacts and if all of them were thoroughly indoctrinated in the company policies and objectives, such a program would be an ideal one. The public relations officer should be someone near the top of the organization structure who participates actively in policy determination and operations. Relatively few such men have the time, talents, or inclination for the necessary contacts to give the public a true picture of their companies' activities. Many of them try to take time when a bitter strike is being waged against them, but under such conditions the public is not keenly interested, believing that what they have to say is mere propaganda. If a company wishes to enjoy the public's confidence during periods of stress, it must build up its contacts during peaceful operations.

When formalized, the public relations functions may be attached to some top executive such as the president or general manager, to the personnel department, to the advertising department, or to the organization department. At times an outside advertising agency handles the public relations. Regardless of his location, the public relations officer must be in a position to get authoritative information quickly if he is to function effectively.

The background of many public relations officers is advertising or newspaper work. These men have skill in writing a story that the public will read, but few of them are very well informed on the business process as such. For them to function most effectively, they should be consulted before a policy is formulated, not handed a policy and told to sell it to the public. Men who have little background in business are not regarded too highly by operating heads in the matter of formulating business policies. Thus, a difficult situation arises within the business itself. The solution to this problem should be twofold: (1) top management should recognize the importance of its policy decisions from a public relations standpoint and seek all possible assistance in so wording them as to invite public acceptance; (2) public relations men should have a broader training that includes a detailed study of personnel management and labor relations, as well as sales management and advertising.

The media of communicating with the public include newspapers, billboards, radio, shows displaying the products, and open houses when the community may walk through the business house and see it in actual operation.

**Communicating with prospective employees and new employees.** In an effort to tell the company's story some firms have some information about the company on their application blanks. Methods used to communicate with prospective employees have been covered thoroughly in Chap. 5, Developing Sources of Labor Supply. It would be well for the reader to review this chapter, concentrating on the most effective methods of making contacts with prospective employees. Chapter 7, The Interview as a Tool of Personnel Management, sheds light on communicating with applicants.

Chapter 18, Introducing the Employee to His Job, treats several phases of communication with the new employee. It includes such media as the employees' handbook, induction procedure in the employment office, bulletin boards, the departmental sponsor, job specifications, trip through the plant or store, the job instructor, and the supervisor. It is highly important to keep the avenues of communication open to the new employee. He is undergoing a transition that is eased when he gets adequate information, sympathetically given in a friendly atmosphere. It is important to remember that printed matter and bulletin boards do not take the place of personal conversations and contacts with the new employee. The direct supervisor is the most logical person to convey most of the information, not only to the new employee, but to all employees.

**Communications between top management and middle management.** Some companies make a special effort to communicate effectively with their middle managers. Some large companies publish special bulletins for their supervisors and executives. General Electric has its *News Letter*, General Motors publishes its *Executive Bulletin*, Armstrong Cork Company has its *Management Notes*, Western Electric has its *News Briefs for Western Electric Management*, and other companies make similar efforts to reach middle managers and the first-line supervisors. These companies recognize the necessity for keeping all levels of management fully informed and use many avenues to achieve this goal. Middle managers serve on operating committees and meet regularly with their immediate heads to discuss operating problems. These meetings provide needed information, serve to coordinate effort, and provide personal contacts with top management as well as between other middle managers on the same organizational level. As is pointed out in Chap. 20, Training Executives and Supervisors, personal contact and training on the job are the most common and almost the sole method of training middle managers. The importance of this personal contact with top management cannot be overemphasized. There is no better method of developing mutual understanding. This is especially true when the superior in the organization practices consultive supervision or observes the ordinary rules of dynamic leadership. These rules are observed more commonly between top management and middle management than between the first-line supervisors and middle management. Personal contacts and operational procedures provide the most commonly used and most effective means of communicating between top management. About the only point at which these personal contacts fail to get the desired information to the middle managers as soon as desired is in informing them about union agreements. It is a sad commentary on management when the union has better lines of communications with the workers and stewards than has top management. This need not be so. Management can have a mimeographed statement of the essence of a contract lying on the desk of each middle manager and supervisor when he comes to work in the morning. Of course, it requires effort and some nightwork by certain people, but it is worth it.

**Communicating with the foreman and first-line supervisor.** Communications up or down from top management to the first-line supervisors through the line of control usually go through at least two levels of organization. The first-line supervisors are better served by conference training than by middle managers when viewed from the standpoint of their needs. The supervisory training program serves as an excellent medium of communicating either upward or downward between top management and the first-line supervisors. Personal contacts between the first-line supervisors and top management in large enterprises are perfunctory to the extent of being almost nonexistent. They may gather in a large group at an annual dinner, but the top management representatives would be fortunate indeed if they could call half of the foremen by name. This condition arises from the factor of size and the number of first-line supervisors. The first-line supervisors' contacts are with their general foremen or divisional superintendents.

Most of the devices of communicating with middle managers are open to use by top management in communicating with the first-line supervisor, other than personal contact in the large enterprise. The sheer fact of numbers precludes any appreciable amount of personal contact.

The personnel director may serve as a spokesman for top management in dealing with both middle management and first-line supervisors on matters of personnel relations. He is of special help to the first-line supervisor when he has a personal grievance and his regular lines of communication have been clogged. In all situations where possible, the first-line supervisor should strive to clarify a grievance with his own immediate supervisor. Failing in this, he should go up through channels when the personalities are such that he can receive a sympathetic hearing. This should always be the case, but in practice it frequently is not. In this event the first-line supervisor should have access to a representative of top management who will give a hearing on the merits of the case. It must be remembered that a supervisory grievance may be even more detrimental to smooth operations than that of an individual worker. The worker has access to a union to represent him. A failure to provide a hearing for first-line supervisors was one of the strong forces behind their unionization movement of a few years back.

**The suggestion system.** Most people look upon the suggestion system as being primarily designed to enlist the cooperation of sub-

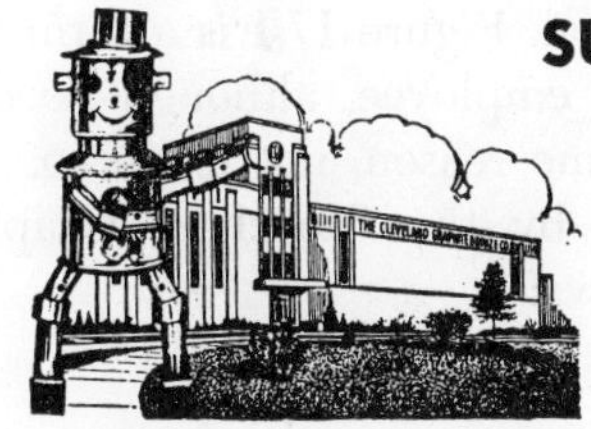

**SUGGESTIONS for PROGRESS**

**CLEVELAND GRAPHITE BRONZE**

DIVISION OF CLEVITE CORPORATION

PLEASE FILL IN THE BOXES BELOW

MY SUGGESTION APPLIES IN

| PLANT NO. | DEPT. NO. | MACHINE |
|---|---|---|
| | | |

**Nº 952 B**

DATE ________ 19____

I BELIEVE WE CAN ACCOMPLISH THE FOLLOWING:

I SUGGEST THAT:

Where necessary, attach Sketches on vellum tracing paper found in the Suggestion Boxes. Additional information may be submitted on blank paper and should be attached. Place Suggestion Number on each attached sheet. When routing of part is involved, part numbers, customer's name, operation numbers and operation descriptions must be included. "I hereby agree that the rules and regulations of the Suggestion System and the decision of the Suggestion Committee will be final as to the disposition of this suggestion or the payment of an award."

(Please Print Your Name Here) ________

PLANT NUMBER ________ DEPARTMENT NUMBER ________ BADGE NUMBER ________ ☐ HOURLY ☐ SALARY

NUMBER OF SKETCHES ATTACHED ________ NUMBER OF ADDITIONAL SHEETS ATTACHED ________ SHIFT WORKED ________

**Nº 952 B**

SUBJECT COVERED BY THIS SUGGESTION

FIG. 17.1. Suggestions form used by Cleveland Graphite Bronze. (*Courtesy, Cleveland Graphite Bronze.*)

ordinates in making improvements and in eliminating waste. This is its primary purpose, but it also provides an avenue for the worker communicating with management. Frequently, when suggestion systems are first installed, more suggestions are filed pertaining to working conditions and personnel matters than those pertaining to methods or procedures. The prevalence of such suggestions at the start of the operation of suggestion systems points to the fact that the regular lines of communications have not been used or have failed to give satisfactory answers. Suggestions may be filed by using a form that provides for the signature of the employee; or the signature may be required, or the signature may be optional. Figure 17.1 is a form that provides space for the signature of the employee, although he does not have to sign it if he prefers, for some reason, not to do so. The awards that are given for suggestions by the Cleveland Graphite Bronze Company are determined as follows:

AWARDS:

*Class* A. In general where savings can be computed, an award equal to 25 per cent of the first year's savings (gross savings less expenditures for development, labor, material, depreciation and experimentation, etc.) shall be paid.

50 per cent of such award (based on estimated savings) shall be paid as soon as reasonably convenient after the installation of the suggestion if the estimated award is $100.00 or more.

Balance (based on actual savings) shall be paid one year after the date of the installation of the suggestion.

Where the estimated award is less than $100.00 the entire amount of the award will be paid as soon as reasonably convenient after installation of the suggestion.

*Class* B. In general where there are savings which cannot be definitely computed, for example, Safety Suggestions—awards from $10.00 to $50.00 will be made. When exceptional circumstances are involved, an award, not to exceed $100.00, may be made by the suggestion committee.

OFFICIAL RULES:

1. *Title to Suggestions.* All Suggestions, upon submission, become the sole property of The Cleveland Graphite Bronze Company.

2. *Date of Suggestion.* We will endeavor to collect suggestions daily and the date they are collected will be stamped on the suggestion and will be regarded as the official date of the suggestion.

3. *Active Suggestions.* A suggestion will be considered active until such time as a decision is made and the Suggester has been notified in writing. If the Suggester cannot be notified through regular channels, a notice will be posted for 30 days on the Suggestion Boxes.

4. *Suggester's Year.* The suggester's year will be determined as follows:
   (a) When a Suggestion is adopted, his year will end one year from the date of installation of the Suggestion.
   (b) When a Suggestion is rejected, his year of protection will end one year from the official date of the rejection notice.

5. *Joint Suggestions.* When Suggestions are made jointly by more than one person, any award made will be divided equally among those whose names appear on the blank as Suggesters. If any of these are ineligible for award, the total amount to be divided will be decreased proportionally, and the award made to any one person will be the same as though all had been eligible.

6. *Unsigned Suggestions.* If a Suggester fails to sign his suggestion it will be investigated and processed in the regular manner. When a decision has been reached, the Suggestion Office will post a notice on each of the Suggestion Boxes requesting the Suggester (of Suggestion No._____) to call at the Suggestion Office for information regarding his suggestion.

This notice shall remain for a period of 30 days, and, if during this 30-day period, the Suggester does not make his identity known to the Suggestion Office by presenting the stub of the Suggestion Blank, the Company may reject or use the Suggestion in any manner, and the Suggester shall have lost his right to any award.

7. *Unacceptable Suggestions.* The following are not acceptable as suggestions:
  (a) Suggestions that deal with company policy such as negotiated labor contracts.
  (b) A suggestion that duplicates the application of an idea contained in a previously submitted suggestion.

8. *Submitting a Suggestion after Experimentation or Installation.* The Company will not assume any responsibility for the protection of the Suggester or his idea unless the Suggester submits his Suggestion in writing on a standard Suggestion Form, prior to either experimentation or installation.

9. *Protection of Suggestions.* When a suggestion is submitted and not adopted, the Suggester shall be protected (eligible for award) if it is adopted within one year from the date of rejection. If at the end of the Suggester's year it has not been adopted, it will be considered void unless the Suggester re-submits his Suggestion.
  (This may be done by the Suggester completely restating his Suggestion on a new Suggestion Blank, giving the original Suggestion number, and writing on the face of the blank the word "Re-submitted.")

Neither the Suggestion Office nor the Company will assume any responsibility for notifying Suggesters that their suggestion year is ended.

10. *Appeal for Reconsideration.* If the Suggester wishes to have a rejected Suggestion reconsidered, he must submit a letter within his Suggestion year, (not on a Suggestion Blank), to the Suggestion Office, stating the original Suggestion number, file number assigned by the Suggestion Office, and the reasons why it should be reconsidered. The appeal will be submitted to the Suggestion Committee and the Suggester will be notified in writing of the Suggestion Committee's decision.

11. *Decisions.* Decisions of the Suggestion Committee as to the disposition of any Suggestion or the amount of the award paid for it shall be final.

12. *Temporarily Ineligible Suggestions.* When a Suggestion is received pertaining to an incomplete installation of plant, equipment, machinery, procedures or processes of any type, said Suggestion will be held confidential by the Suggestion Office. It will not be shown or released for investigation or any other reason, until said installation has been declared complete and eligible for suggestions. At that time any Suggestion so held will be released and become eligible for investigation. If the idea has not already been applied, the Suggestion will, if adopted, be eligible for an award.

13. *Patentable Suggestions.* If a Suggestion is deemed to be patentable the procedure will be as follows:
  (a) If the Company desires to apply for the patent the Suggester will, in

accordance with the terms of his employment, assign all rights, title and interest to the Company and it thereby becomes Company property.

(b) If the Company is not interested in obtaining the patent, but feels that the idea has merit, the Suggester will be advised that he may himself apply for his own patent and the Company will thereupon relinquish all its rights, with the exception of a shop right.

14. *Situations Not Covered Elsewhere.* It is recognized that specific rules cannot be made to cover all possible situations.

When a situation arises which is not covered by these published rules, it will be the responsibility of the Suggestion Committee to render a decision. All such decisions shall be final, and shall be binding on both the Company and the Suggester.

15. *Changes in Policy or Rules.* The Company reserves the right to make changes in Suggestion Policies and Rules and any changes made will be considered effective as of the date changes are formally announced. Announcement of these changes will be made through notices on the Bulletin Boards, announcements in "True Bearings" or revisions in the Suggestion Manual, etc. Under no circumstances will any change affect a Suggestion submitted before the change was announced.

ELIGIBILITY RULES:

Only those on the hourly or regular salary payroll are eligible to submit suggestions and win awards. Cash awards will not be paid to employees for suggestions which are part of their regular job. The Suggestion Committee (made up of the heads of operating divisions, and others appointed by the President of Cleveland Graphite Bronze Company, who heads the committee) will determine the eligibility of each suggester. When the suggestion of an ineligible suggester is adopted, the Suggester will be notified of his ineligibility and the fact that his suggestion has been adopted. A copy of such notification will be sent to Personnel Records, to be included in the Suggester's personal file.

Even when the suggestion system is used only for economic benefits or improvements, it tends (when properly operated) to encourage an atmosphere of trust and confidence. This general attitude is as important as any particular phase of communicating. The suggestion system as a means of communicating with employees will succeed only if it is kept up to date. The suggestion system provides a means for the humblest workman to get his ideas before top management. The suggestion system should not take the place of an organized grievance procedure, but it sometimes acts as an imperfect substitute when there is no such procedure. Figure 17.2 shows the publicity given to a $10,229 suggestion award. The Cleveland Graphite Bronze Company has operated a successful suggestion system for years.

**The grievance procedure.** The grievance procedure established by agreement with a union provides a medium for the worker to transmit

Fɪɢ. 17.2. Publicizing the highest suggestion award ($10,299) for a recent year won by the man on the right. This company has made one award for $28,006. The man on the left is the manager of the suggestion system. (*Courtesy, Cleveland Graphite Bronze.*)

his grievance to management in an orderly manner and to get his answer in writing. The resolving of grievances between the primary parties concerned is the ideal. Unfortunately this is not always accomplished. There is no single procedure for handling grievances. The size of the company and the multiplicity of plants may influence the specific procedure. It is common practice for the grievance procedure to follow this pattern:

1. The worker talks over his problem informally with his supervisor. In the absence of an agreement he places his grievance in writing and files it with his union steward. (Many persons consider the grievance procedure to begin when the grievance is placed in writing and filed with the foreman.)

2. The union steward files the written grievance with the foreman. It may be discussed by the steward, the worker, and the foreman. The foreman files his answer within a limited period, such as 3 days. In the absence of an agreement the steward appeals the case to the division superintendent, general foreman, or some other line officer.

3. The same general procedure is followed by the second level of supervision as described in (2). In case of failure to agree, the next step may be to some representative of top management such as the personnel director or labor relations director.

4. Before the representative of top management, the same general procedure is followed as above. By this time the record is becoming rather complete, since reports have been made by the various interested parties. In case of failure to agree, an appeal may be made to top management.

5. In some contracts provision is made for an appeal to an impartial arbitrator in case of a failure to reach an agreement with top management.

In the absence of a union agreement, it is more difficult to have a workable grievance procedure, since there is no one to press the case for the worker.[2] Relatively few workers are capable of representing themselves before an executive substantially above the level of their immediate supervisor. One way to overcome this is to designate someone in the personnel department to aid the worker in writing up his case for appeal. This person should not be one who passes on the case in any step of the procedure. He could readily be an employment interviewer. The so-called open-door policy to the president's office is likely to be an idle gesture unless some effective means is provided to handle grievances. The steps in the procedure in the absence of an employees' organization could readily be exactly the same as if there were a union, save for the fact that the steward or other union representative is replaced by a representative of the personnel department.

**The employees' paper.** A well-edited employees' paper provides an excellent medium for communicating with employees. For the publication to provide a two-way channel, its pages must be open to employees. This may be achieved by running a column such as "The Voice of the Employees," in which letters from employees are published. All such letters should be signed when sent to the editor. A certain letter might be published with the name of the writer omitted if so requested, but it should be ignored if it comes to the editor unsigned. Certain rules are in order for such a column. For instance, violent name calling or language unbecoming a gentleman would naturally be banned. A second medium for employees to express themselves is a "union" column. Such a column is seldom used unless friendly relations exist between management and the union. Some companies where union-management relations are at sword's point make it a practice never to mention the union in the company paper. One large employer runs a column entitled "Weekly Review of Labor Relations," which discusses factual situations and studiously avoids

[2] See National Industrial Conference Board, Inc., "Grievance Procedure in Non-unionized Company," *Studies in Personnel Policy* 109, New York, 1950.

propaganda. To make such a column a success, the editor must have access to the inner councils of top management dealing with problems of labor relations.

Editing a successful employees' paper requires time and effort plus skill. Industrial editing is a profession. Some persons with special abilities may succeed in this work without formal training, but it is not a task that can be handled by any person merely because he has completed high school and needs a job. The make-up of the factory paper and its news coverage have much to do with the employees' acceptance. It is useless to attempt to reach the employees through the company paper unless they read the paper. Attractive pictures add much to any paper. The paper should feature the employees, not top executives. There is room in the company paper for safety news, suggestions, transfers and promotions of general interest, sports and recreation, personals, descriptions of processes that help the employee to see where his job fits into the total plant operation, important items concerning increased or decreased production, plant expansion, new plants, the annual report to employees, and economic discussions of interest to workers when they are well presented. A few companies have published their employees' paper as a paid advertisement in the local newspaper. This practice has much to commend it in relatively small communities. It acquaints the community with the activities of the company and its employees. It is also somewhat less expensive than publishing the same material as a separate publication. This method of publishing a house organ would not be suitable in communities larger than 150,000.

**Reporting to employees on financial matters.** Some companies have modified their regular annual reports to make them understandable to workers, thus making the one report meet the needs both of stockholders and employees. This has merit since there can be no charge by employees that management tells them one thing and the owners another. Even when special reports are issued to employees or the regular report is modified to aid their understanding, it is a good idea to reproduce the section that pertains to a *distribution of total income* in the employees' paper. More people are likely to read it in the house organ than as a special report. The pie chart or graph showing the distribution of the sales dollar is a dramatic method of presenting these facts. It is surprising how few workers understand the profit percentage. These reports may readily show the amount spent per worker on the maintenance of health and safety, the average cost per worker of accidents, the invested capital per worker, and other data of interest. The Woodward Governor Company keeps a monthly state-

FIG. 17.3. Bulletin board showing the financial condition of the company. (*Courtesy, Woodward Governor.*)

ment of the condition of the company posted at the entrance to their restaurant (Fig. 17.3).

**Using the grapevine[3] to communicate.** Most people are skeptical about the use of the grapevine for any constructive purpose. A few companies deliberately use the grapevine as a medium of getting across information to its employees. There is little question that this historic instrument will spread the news around. The great difficulty is to use it in such a manner as not to give more misinformation than information. Government agents have at times sent up trial balloons to try to get the public reaction to a particular item. If the reaction were favorable, it might be followed up. If it were unfavorable, a higher official would reject it. A skilled person may use the grapevine to advantage, but most persons will be well advised to use more conventional channels.

[3] See National Industrial Conference Board, Inc., *Studies in Personnel Policy* 129, New York, 1952, pp. 18–19. This is an excellent study that should be read by all persons seriously interested in employee communication.

Fɪɢ. 17.4. Information rack. (*Courtesy, Frigidaire Division, General Motors Corporation.*)

**The information rack.**[4] The information rack has come into use by a number of companies since 1945 or 1950 (Fig. 17.4). These companies have placed in the racks various bulletins and other desirable reading matter which the company would like to have the employees read. The racks are placed at strategic places. The contents of the racks are changed from time to time. The material is not necessarily confined to material published by the company. The objective behind the distribution of literature not specifically related to the company or the employee's work is to foster wider understanding of economic and social life. It is believed that a well-informed employee tends to be a reliable employee.

**Published statements covering personnel policies.**[5] Figure A.6, item 14, portrays the popularity of published personnel policies. About

[4] See National Industrial Conference Board, Inc., "Information Racks—A New Communication Medium," *Studies in Personnel Policy* 125, New York, 1952.

[5] See National Industrial Conference Board, Inc., "Written Statements of Personnel Policies," *Studies in Personnel Policy* 79, New York, 1947.

two out of three companies have them. These employee handbooks provide an excellent means of getting across to the employee company policies covering employee relations. This is particularly true when the supervisor points out specific items in the handbook and asks the employee questions regarding its contents. These booklets should be clearly written and contain only those things which are established personnel policies. Some companies introduce cartoons to liven up their bulletins. When these are well done, they may have merit but nothing is flatter than a cartoon for the sake of a cartoon. Instead of including all personnel policies in one booklet, some companies issue separate booklets on safety and other subjects, such as pension plans and profit sharing.

## CHAPTER 18

# Introducing the Employee to His Job

**Why a formal program for introducing the employee to his job?**
The first few days on the job, in fact the first day, may readily determine whether or not a new employee stays. Industry has found that many new employees do not return on the second day or even after the lunch period on the first day. When a new employee only stays one day, a poor job of hiring may have been done. On the other hand the experience of the worker during the first day, particularly the employee who is taking his first job, may cause him to question his ability to make good or may even raise questions in his mind as to his desire to make good in such an environment. One employee-oriented company has stated that the "Objective of this induction program is to provide the information and opportunity needed by all new employees to help them become satisfactorily adjusted to their work and assist them to develop an enthusiasm for the company, its ideals, and responsibilities." In its effort to produce a satisfied, productive employee, the company takes at least three steps, namely:

1. To define the terms of employment.
2. To acquaint the employee in detail with the requirements of the job.
3. To strive to engender, in the employee, confidence in the company and a confidence in his ability to do the job.

Any company might well have objectives similar to the foregoing; however, the details involved in carrying them out may vary greatly, not only with the central philosophy and organizational structure of the enterprise, but also with different classes of persons within the enterprise. The emphasis in a highly centralized organization may differ materially from one with decentralized responsibility. The apprentice, production engineer, stenographer, tool- and diemaker, and seasonal laborer will require somewhat different handling. In fact, there are many different procedures within a given enterprise even though they may follow a general pattern. For instance, the procedure followed in introducing an employee of the personnel division, sales

271

division, and manufacturing division in the same company may have certain common elements (may even be jointly performed); yet the details will vary considerably in the respective divisions. The differing personalities of the various foremen may readily produce a marked variation in the induction procedure. In the company quoted above, they give new sales and executive trainees just entering the company a very formal week's introduction to the company, during which time representatives of most of the major divisions talk to them.

**The induction procedure and initial hiring.** The initial hiring interview lays the groundwork for the details that follow. Some application blanks give considerable information about the company. Some blanks have a signed statement in which the employee agrees to assign all patents to the company. During the process of selection, the interviewer will naturally impart much information concerning the company, its history, traditions, and product that will serve to establish confidence and interest on the part of the worker. But the process of introducing the worker to his work, of integrating him with his position in order to create a *well-balanced worker* naturally continues after the actual selection of the worker has been completed. Someone must impart to the worker that information and that point of view which will transform him from an accepted applicant into a capable, confident and interested worker.

Since 1930 the popularity of a formal induction procedure has increased nearly 50 per cent (see Fig. A.1). The elaborateness of an induction procedure usually depends, in part, upon the level of business activity and the number of new employees. If there are only a few new employees, the program usually is less comprehensive and formal and largely on a personal basis. Informal procedures tend to fail to pay sufficient attention to those influences for and against personal morale which have so much to do with the worker's attitude during the early days and weeks of his employment. Regardless of their reliability, first impressions tend to be lasting. A failure properly to introduce an employee to his work situation and to the company's policies may readily turn a worker with high ambitions and creative impulses into a questioning worker with thwarted ambitions. Modern procedures for introducing a worker are designed to acquaint him not only with his particular task and plant regulations but also with the organization and its purposes and policies.[1] The adjustment begins

---

[1] National Industrial Conference Board, Inc., *Studies in Personnel Policy* 131, New York, 1953: "Induction Procedures for New Employees," *Conference Board Management Record,* Vol. 1, No. 12; also Fred G. Schmidt, "Introducing the New Employee," *Personnel,* July, 1952, pp. 62–67.

with the hiring interview and continues as long as the employee faces new situations, even though he may be an "old-timer."

**Explaining the conditions of employment.** In those companies giving the personnel department full authority to hire (Fig. A.1, item 7) the terms of employment should have been fully covered by the employment interviewer. Of course the same statement is true in the personnel departments that only do a screening job, the final hiring resting with the supervisor. The responsibility rests squarely upon the personnel manager to establish a definite understanding with the new employee whereby he accepts his position with complete knowledge of the terms under which he is to serve. He should have definite information as to the hours of work, as to the probability of overtime, as to the allowance made for sickness, and as to time off. He should have definite information concerning the wages he is to receive, when he is to receive them, and in what form. Likewise he should be informed as to the rules of conduct governing employees, specifically those in his occupation. He should know in advance of the penalties attached to infractions of these rules. If smoking on the job is a capital offense or if intoxication off the job or persistent tardiness is regarded as a reason for dismissal, he should be so informed at the outset. In spite of these items having been covered at the time of formal employment, the supervisor should go over them again, not only when he assigns the employee to his job, but sometime later during the week to make sure that he knows.

**Inspiring confidence in the new employee.** The new employee usually has a general idea about the reputation and integrity of the company before he is an applicant. If the company has a good reputation in the community, some of the work of inspiring confidence has already been done. Care needs to be exercised not to destroy this confidence. Although the applicant must sell his services to the organization, in no less degree must the organization through its contacts sell itself to the applicant. The applicant desires evidence as to the personnel policies of the company. He wants to know what the probabilities are of steady employment, what the company's policies are with reference to promotion and salary increase. He wants to know whether the company entertains the commodity conception of labor or whether its personnel policies are governed by a more advanced and more humane viewpoint and what its attitude is toward organized labor (if he is a union man). The applicant desires information about the working conditions within the company. It is entirely proper that he should have confidence in the company's ability to provide him the right kind of working conditions. It is perfectly proper, for instance, to make reference to the importance of the work itself in the whole scheme of company production, to the social relationships that are opened up, to the qualities of manliness and leadership that the department chief may possess. It is no infrequent occurrence for an employee to find happiness and satisfaction in a given position through the presence of factors such as these, when he might have been prevented in the first instance from entering the work at all by a consideration merely of duties and initial salary. The new employee is often more concerned with his future than with his present, and a fair statement of the opportunities for promotion and for salary increase may do much to create an intelligent willingness on his part to accept the position when a consideration of the immediate duties and reward might lead him to reject it.

**Informing the new employee about the job requirements.** While the employee is interested in working conditions and fringe benefits, he is most of all interested in the exact requirements of his job. No amount of "atmosphere" and "friendliness" changes the fact that the employee knows that *there is work to be done.* His acceptance of the job is an indication of his desire to *do the work required.* Both the employment interviewer and the first-line supervisor should tell him the nature of his job. The fact that the interviewer is working under pressure does not justify neglect; rather it provides an added reason for special care. Some employers require the new employee to read carefully the occupational description for the position to which he is about to be assigned. The wise interviewer will see that the new employee has ample time and opportunity to study the occupational description and to assimilate its contents. This practice prevents occasional individuals from claiming afterward that the job "was misrepresented to them." It is sometimes desirable to arrange for the employee to see the work itself, the desk or machine, the room or shop in which it is performed, especially where such working conditions must, by the nature of the job, rank low on the scale of desirability. Some employers have claimed that taking the employee to see the job tends to reduce the labor turnover among new employees.

The new employee sooner or later meets the department supervisor or his representative. This meeting may be a part of the actual employment process. This interview with the department head should be more than a conference in which the department head decides favorably or unfavorably upon the qualifications of the applicant. A real responsibility rests upon the department head or his assistant to supplement the efforts of the personnel manager by giving the individual as complete and as faithful a conception of his work as possible, without overemphasizing either its favorable or its unfavorable features. It is especially difficult for the busy operating chief to devote much time to this procedure, which he naturally feels should be the responsibility of the personnel department. Nevertheless, true personnel work is not a departmentalized function but a leaven permeating the entire organization. When the worker actually starts to work, the details of the job requirements are gone over again and again until he can do the work according to standard. Of course in the case of men who have never worked on the job the training period may take months. When an employee actually starts to work, he is learning the requirements of the job.

**Things covered in an induction procedure.** Each company has its own responsibility for properly getting its new employees off to a good start. Naturally procedures differ in relation to the induction procedures even among well-run personnel programs. In its *standard practice manual,* a well-known company doing an excellent job of inducting new employees lists the following items to be covered by a representative of the *plant personnel department:*

Group insurance (booklet).
Hospitalization plan (booklet).
Pension plan (booklet).
Safety and health.
Building and loan association (where in operation).
Vacation program.
Income-tax deductions and pay checks.
History of company.
Plant rules.
Suggestion system.
Plant organization and products.
Union relationship.
Periodic personnel review (merit rating).
Plant paper.

This same standard practice manual lists the following items for the immediate supervisor of the new employee to cover:

Working hours and pay provisions.
Departmental objectives.
Plant facilities, parking, lockers, transportation, cafeteria, rest rooms, etc.
Probationary period.
Union relationship.

An excellent summary of the contents of various induction programs is found in the National Industrial Conference Board, Inc., study, as follows:[2]

1. History of the company—a brief description of the early history and growth of the organization. A history built around personalities is always more interesting than one built around events.

2. The product—a story of the original product and its evolution to meet competition and consumer needs.

3. Present company organization—a brief description of the present over-all company organizational structure with special emphasis on the organization to which the new employee belongs.

4. Industrial relations policies—a statement regarding compensation, promotion, retirement plans, insurance, collective efforts, etc.

5. Employee activities—a statement of the various programs and activities carried on by the employees, such as recreation programs, mutual benefit society, credit unions, etc.

6. Company, plant, and departmental regulations—a brief discussion of the rules and regulations covering attendance, working hours, advances in pay, sick leaves, patent assignments, and other items that are of importance.

7. Safety—special emphasis upon the responsibility of the individual for himself and others.

8. Job routine—requirements of the particular job of the new employee and the job to which this one may lead in the chain of promotion.

**Whose responsibility?** One of the clearest statements of the responsibility for properly inducting new employees is found in the standard practice manual of the company quoted earlier.

The final responsibility for the induction of the new employee rests with his immediate supervisor. It is his duty to see that the employee is not only given the necessary information but also is accorded the respect and attention necessary to make him want to be, and feel that he is a real member of the organization. The Plant Personnel Department is responsible for the group phases of the program which are intended to supplement the procedure followed by the supervisor.

The responsibility belongs to the worker's supervisor, and, regardless of any assistance that he may receive, it still remains the supervisor's responsibility. The exact allocating of certain phases of the introductory process depends largely upon the size of the enterprise and the organizational philosophy in relation to centralization or decentralization of personnel functions. In a company that has delegated a substantial part of its activities to central agencies, such as production control, inspection, and personnel, it is common practice to have the employment officer or the training department take an

[2] *Conference Board Management Record*, Vol. 1, No. 12, pp. 2–3: see also National Industrial Conference Board, Inc., *Studies in Personnel Policy* 131, New York, 1953, pp. 37–48.

active part in introducing the worker to his job. In companies having relatively little centralization of functions the introductory process is frequently handled largely by the foreman. As the programs of introducing the worker become more complete, there is a tendency to increase the number of people participating in carrying out the procedure. In one large firm having some 1,600 salesmen on the road, the president of the firm writes a personal letter to each new salesman, setting forth in a friendly manner some of the policies and objectives of the firm. Other companies have a similar program. In many firms, the foreman, superintendent, and safety director participate in the induction program. Where more than one man participates, it is highly desirable that a detailed program be worked out so that the efforts of each man will supplement rather than duplicate the others.

**The role of the personnel department in the induction program.** It is practically a universal practice for the personnel department to perform certain phases of the induction procedure. During the hiring interview certain items are supposed to be carefully explained. The medical department may readily point out certain health factors. This is especially true in cases where the applicant is certified for restricted employment because of some physical impairment. During the write-up the clerk may explain the terms of the group insurance and hospitalization insurance programs. The hiring interviewer should carefully explain the wages to be expected, method of computing, and when payday comes. In some companies where a high degree of centralization prevails, representatives of the personnel department may give several employees at a time a so-called indoctrination talk. Several persons may be used in this talk. The safety director may cover safety, a nurse or a counselor with special groups of women may cover problems in which women are primarily concerned, and the personnel manager may cover most of the other company policies. In some cases a trip through the plant or store may be conducted by a representative of the personnel department. Where there is a vestibule school, many of these items are worked into the school training period. During World War II one large company hired women to be trained in the vestibule school. They were given a 3-day period of training, testing, and orientation, after which they were assigned to specific vacancies in the plant. Such a program can of course be justified only when there are substantial numbers of people being hired and trained at one time. Another method is to have an employment interviewer, apparently bent on other business, stop for a moment's chat with the new employee at his desk or machine to ask him how things are going, to answer any perplexing questions that may have arisen in his mind, to offer a word of general encouragement. A contact of this kind is usually made almost daily for the first few days until it becomes evident that the employee's uneasiness has disappeared and he is really happy and satisfied in his work.

**The supervisor's responsibility for inducting the new employees.** In a previous paragraph, Whose Responsibility? it was clearly pointed out that the supervisor has a primary responsibility for getting his new employee started off properly. It is natural that the part of the introductory procedure handled by the supervisor be given more attention by the new employee than that given by any other person. The same courtesy and consideration that have been shown to the new employee in the personnel department and in the lecture room and on his way to the work floor should be continued in the department to which he is assigned. The average operating executive is working under pressure. There is a temptation for him, unconsciously and without the slightest intent, to greet the new employee hastily. It would probably surprise the foreman himself as well as other executives to learn that, in the case of a certain new employee going to work on a conveyor assembly line, the only two words spoken in his presence by the immediate foreman during the first 3 days on the job were the cryptic instructions to another worker, "Show him." The brevity of this contact was such that, upon being forced at the end of 3 days to approach his immediate superior, the new worker did so with misgivings as to the probable result of his second contact. There is no short cut for the solution of this problem; its solution lies partly in executive action on the part of the higher command and partly in the success of the personnel manager in his staff relationships with the operating chiefs. The problem is to maintain a personal contact with the new employee that will tide him over this critical period. In order to achieve this purpose, it is the practice of the well-organized personnel department to keep in touch with the new employee. In this connection, the personnel department should in no way weaken the position of the foreman in the eyes of his employees. The *function of the personnel department is to strengthen the line organization in personnel matters, not to weaken it.* This position requires considered action and tact.

**The sponsor.** In some companies certain employees who have shown an interest in new employees are designated "sponsors" for new employees. In some department stores, for instance, such persons are called "sponsors" and are organized into sponsors' associations to which it is considered an honor to belong. The sponsor goes to the employment section, where he is introduced to the newly hired employee. After showing him around the building, pointing out such conveniences such as cloakrooms, washrooms, and other employee facilities, the sponsor conducts him to the department, where he is introduced to the section manager, his supervisor, and the section trainer. The sponsor tries to make the new employee feel at home in his new surroundings. It is important to choose sponsors with a positive company attitude and a desire to be of service to newcomers. This is an excellent assignment for a person who is being watched as possible supervisory material. If he handles the assignment of a sponsor properly, it is one more confirmation of his desirability for the position of supervisor. It is the usual practice to grant sponsors pay, in addition to their regular wages, for these added duties. The investment here is slight, but the yield in terms of success in bridging this earlier period of pressure, doubt, and depression on the part of the new employee is great.

Aldens, Inc., a mail-order and retail department store with headquarters in Chicago, has developed a manual for its sponsors, listing their duties as follows:

1. To act as a guide from the employment section to the section for which the new employee was hired.
2. To give information concerning:
   2.1 Working hours.
   2.2 Method and time of pay.
   2.3 Washrooms, time clock, and pass periods.
   2.4 History of Aldens.
   2.5 Type of business, particular job of new employee and its place in the organization.
   2.6 Employees' purchases and discounts.
   2.7 Lunch periods and cafeterias.
   2.8 Recreation rooms and library.
   2.9 Hospital and insurance plans.
   2(10) Promotions and training program.
   2(11) Personal phone calls and Lost and Found.
   2(12) Absences and tardiness.
   2(13) Suggestion system.
   2(14) Other Aldens buildings.
   2(15) Employee counselor.
   2(16) Personnel policies manual.
3. To see that new employee is taken to lunch the first day by old employee or sponsor.
4. To keep up to date a usable sponsor's file containing sponsor's manual, sponsor's bulletins, and personnel policies manual.

**Methods used in presenting to the new employee the desired information.** In companies hiring enough new men to justify its use, the lecture method or the conference is effective. Motion pictures[3] are also used, as well as sound slides. Written material is by far the most common medium of giving information to employees. This material may be included in one book,[4] or it may be broken down into several booklets, each covering a single activity such as safety. These booklets may all be given out at one time or preferably at different times as the occasion arises. Trips through the plant are used at times to give the employee a picture of the organization as a whole. In large plants, departmental or divisional trips are often substituted for the plant trip. Some concerns supply all incoming workers with illustrated catalogues specially designed for their use. Another practice that has found favor in well-run organizations is the use of display boards, showcases, and paneled exhibits of the product in both its assembled and disassembled state. Where the products lends itself to such treatment, one of the best devices for acquainting the new employee with the products of the company is the cutaway assembly. Small models or full-sized samples of the finished products are cut apart so that construction, operation of interior portions, and the like, can be seen. Metal machines have been duplicated in glass, celluloid, or other transparent material for such exhibits. The timing factor, the number of new employees being inducted into the organization, the organizational level of the new employees—such as laborers, toolmakers, engineers, salesmen, etc.—and the formulated objective of the company in its induction program largely dictate the method to be used.

Counselors frequently escort the new employee to his department. This provides the counselor an excellent opportunity to get acquainted with the new employee and offers a chance to drop by to see how things are going sometime during the day. When a plant trip is a part of the introductory procedure, the person who conducts the plant tours usually is an excellent individual to take the new employees to their departments. In one large company the foreman comes to the employment office to escort the new employees to his department. He visits with them on their way in and explains many items of general interest.

**Induction program of Thompson Ramo Wooldridge, Inc.** Allan N. Sheahen, personnel manager of the Tapco Division of Thompson Ramo Wooldridge, Inc., outlined their program for inducting the employee into their company as follows: After interviewing, selection,

---

[3] Motorola, Inc., of Chicago uses an induction motion picture for all new employees. The motion picture has the advantage of presenting to all employees the same information that has been carefully prepared. When it is followed by a question and answer period, it still retains the personal touch.

[4] See Fig. A.3, item 19.

physical examination, and placement, the employment department introduces the individual to the job in the following manner:

1. Through the media of the "Employees' Handbook" which contains:
   A. Greetings from J. D. Wright, Chairman of the Board of Thompson Ramo Wooldridge, Inc., as well as pictures of all other officers and executives.
   B. A brief history of Thompson Ramo Wooldridge, Inc., its organization, products and purpose.
   C. The rights and privileges of each individual working at Thompson Ramo Wooldridge's and the Company's policy in its relationship with all employees.
2. Each new employee is shown Thompson Ramo Wooldridge's induction film, "Working Together." The film runs 30 minutes and pictures the activities of Thompson Ramo Wooldridge and the individual's importance in the Company program.

The Employment Department also offers and explains to the individual the Company-sponsored Insurance and Hospitalization Plans, as well as other items of mutual benefit.

Up to this point the new employee has been given a broad view of Thompson Ramo Wooldridge and is now conditioned for his specific function in the total operation.

A member of the Employment Department takes the individual out into the plant to the Timekeeping Department. The Timekeeper explains the time card system and takes the man to the Foreman of the Department in which the individual will work.

The Foreman explains the location of locker rooms, Dispensary, Cafeteria, etc., and discusses the operation to be performed by the new worker.

The Foreman then introduces the individual to the Personnel Manager or Supervisor in his Division. The Personnel Supervisor further discusses Company policies and practices and encourages the individual to see him whether any questions arise.

The process of follow-up on new employees is stressed and the Personnel Supervisor periodically "visits" the employee at his place of work.

The Employment Department in checking job requirements and changes at the scene of operation also "visits" with new employees.

Other offices and departments which might prove of service to the new worker are made known to him and he is encouraged to seek information whenever necessary.

Another procedure of great interest to the new worker is the method of promotion from within through the use of the Thompson Employee Request for Advancement Form.

The Employee Request for Advancement Form shows the past work experience as well as educational background of the individual and is the formal application of the worker for a higher skilled job.

The pool of such applications is given first consideration by the Employment Department when filling requisitions. This system is carefully explained to the new worker by his Personnel Supervisor and Employee Request for Advancement Forms are always available for interested employees.

The system has been in operation for some time and has proved to be of benefit to the workers as well as the company.

**Problems in maintaining the close personal touch.** Large-scale industry has some inherent advantages, but *the maintenance of the personal touch in human relations is not one of them.* Some business concerns flatter themselves that personal contact between major executives and workers is a reality when the concern in fact has expanded beyond the logical point at which it is possible. Growth takes place gradually. Those who are in constant association with an organization during its growth sometimes do not appreciate that it is taking place. Because of this natural failure on the part of management to realize that its organization is growing slowly but steadily, many concerns, in endeavoring to keep in touch with their employees and to know their qualifications and interests, are relying upon rule-of-thumb methods long after such methods have been outgrown. The difficulty of maintaining this personal contact with the workers increases with the size of the organization.

An executive of an occasional company will boast, "Management relies upon the department head and foreman to maintain that personal contact with the workers which previously existed between management and the workers directly." At times, this can be done with propriety. But, in most companies, the department head is quite unusual who is capable of getting out the work, of attending to the technical duties involved in his position, of working under high pressure, and at the same time of giving time and conscious effort to the practice of such personnel policies as are described in this book. He must combine the capacities and interests of a technical expert in his line with those of a technical expert in the field of industrial personnel. This combination is hard to find. Nothing in this chapter should be interpreted as suggesting that the department head and foreman should not assume responsibility for the administration of the personnel in their departments. The satisfaction and effectiveness of their *workers-in-their-work units* depend almost entirely upon the degree of leadership that they inject into their supervision. Where the sponsor system is not feasible because of size or scattered locations, there can be substituted an informal note from the personnel manager to the new employee inviting correspondence or a return visit to the employment department. Some concerns believe it to be good practice to address such communications to the new employees' homes. Another device that has found favor in large organizations seeking to retain a fair degree of personal contact with all new employees is the *appointment card* that is given at the time of employment or is sent to the new employee. This card lists one or more appointment hours when he is expected to present himself for a follow-up contact with the personnel department. Where such interviews or instruction classes are held on company time, the appointment card becomes the foreman's authority for relieving the employee from duty to meet the appointment.

**The follow-up interview.** A follow-up interview may be conducted by any responsible line or staff executive. Its leading characteristic is the fact that it is a planned interview following a previous interview. The purpose of the follow-up interview as a part of an induction program is that of ascertaining the mental status of the worker; if fears are really present, to learn to what extent they are based on imagination rather than on fact, to explain them away in the case of the former, and to help the employee remove their causes in the case of the latter. In some instances, of course, fear is entirely lacking, in which case the problem is nonexistent. In many other cases, conversely, fear is present, and experience shows that in these instances the worker will talk more freely and with less reserve to a representative of the personnel department (provided that the representative is qualified temperamentally for this important task) than he will with a superior whose good opinion he feels he would endanger by admitting such doubts. There is no better technique for removing doubts and fears than talking things over with someone in authority. The mere fact of expressing them gets a burden off the mind of the new employee. When doubts are revealed in the interview, management is then enabled (through action either on the part of the personnel department or on the part of the department head) to offer such reassurances or to make such adjustments as will offset fears and, in consequence, bring the worker to a higher degree of confidence and personal efficiency.

**Testing the effectiveness of the induction procedure.** It is often difficult to measure the effectiveness of any personnel program. Oral or written tests have been used to check the accuracy of the information imparted. True and false and other written tests are not always adapted to the rank and file of workers. They are much more applicable to clerical staffs, engineering groups, salesmen, and others, who usually have a higher educational training. An analysis of later personnel interviews and separation interviews may shed some light on the effectiveness of the induction program. A check on the number of mistakes that are made will provide a fair index of the effectiveness of a particular instruction covering the items involved. A special interview by a noninterested party with some of the recently inducted employees may shed some light on the program, particularly the attitude of the employees toward it.

CHAPTER 19

# Training Employees

**Necessity for training.** Even if there were no new processes or methods requiring the training of old employees, the training requirements of most businesses would be substantial. New employees replacing those persons leaving as a part of normal labor turnover amount to 5 per cent or more during reasonably prosperous periods. Actually labor turnover is in excess of 10 per cent in most industries. Labor turnover arises from normal separations due to death or physical incapacity; through accident, disease, or superannuation, promotion within the organization, and change of occupation. In addition to the normal replacements, with an increasing population, industry has tended to increase in size, thus requiring additional men. Inexperienced men must be given detailed training, not only in the special methods of the individual enterprise, but also in the basic principles of the particular trade or task. Prolonged depression periods increase the need for the training of skilled workers for the obvious reason that there is a tendency for industry to discontinue training programs during a depression, when the supply of labor is in excess of the demand, and for the secondary reason that the unemployed skilled workers tend to lose their skills when out of work over a period of years.

A wise management uses training as a tool of control. Training has been a successful method of reducing accidents, reducing waste, and increasing quality. There is the ever-present need for training men on the job to meet changing techniques or to improve old methods that are woefully inefficient.[1] Jobs have a way of changing. Men must be trained to handle the new jobs and properly to meet the requirements of the new methods. The *dynamic viewpoint* concerning

[1] See Gordon S. Watkins, Paul A. Dodd, Wayne McNaughton, and Paul Prasow, *The Management of Personnel and Labor Relations*, 2d ed., McGraw-Hill Book Company, Inc., New York, 1950, pp. 572-574.

284

personnel problems stresses industrial education and training. Training is an activity intimately associated with all the other personnel or managerial activities. It is an integral part of the whole management program, with all its many activities functionally interrelated. Personnel management is management, and training is a very important phase of the management program.

**On-the-job training.** Figure A.6 shows the training picture of modern business. Eighty-six per cent of the firms participating in the 1957 survey had formal on-the-job training programs. Various methods of training on the job are described below (Fig. 19.1).

**The vestibule school.** The vestibule school gets its name from its location near the regular workplace, often in a vestibule, but not actually a part of regular production. The vestibule school is economical only when there is a substantial number of employees to be trained. It has marked advantages over training on the regular work floor: (1) more efficient use can be made of the instructor's time and skills in that he has his students more conveniently located and under closer supervision; (2) regular production is less impeded by learners who cannot hold up their end of the work; (3) the general atmosphere is more favorable to learning in that there is not so much confusion to the beginner unfamiliar with machine production; (4) since production is of secondary importance, emphasis can be laid upon the phases of the work in which the learner is weakest without disrupting production; (5) usually instructors more highly skilled in the art of teaching are used, and more effective use of their time can be made; (6) the vestibule school is well adapted to training regularly employed workers for promotion. The last use of the vestibule school is usually made at times other than during the normal shift of the regular worker. For instance, a second-shift trucker may learn metal finishing for about a half day on the day shift, or a day-shift worker may attend the vestibule school during the evening. The disadvantages of the vestibule school are claimed to be as follows: (1) With the passage of time there is a tendency for the instruction and equipment of the vestibule school to lag behind the actual situation in the shop. (2) The emphasis in the vestibule school tends to be upon successful completion of a task, with too little attention to the time element involved, a condition that is definitely unrealistic. (3) A retraining period is required on transferring the employee to the shop in order to orient him to production speeds and operating conditions; this period frequently is a discouraging one in the absence of the sympathetic instructor and results in a heavy turnover among men on whom the company has already spent considerable money.

Labor turnover is especially high among new employees before they have actually learned their jobs and have been accustomed to the work. The vestibule school, where the training of such workers is centralized, systematized, and supervised by expert teachers, is one of the best methods available to management for meeting the problem. Such a school not only helps to make the employment of short-term workers on semiskilled jobs profitable but also aids in increasing the average length of service of the newly employed worker. This means

FIG. 19.1. Cutaway of model door is used by young draftsman to help develop contours. It takes several men and many drawings just to design and lay out one door. While college training in engineering is valuable, a great majority of the jobs in the body design and drafting department are filled by men who took mathematics (through descriptive geometry) and drafting in high school or night school. The rest they learned on the job. (*Courtesy, Fisher Body Division, General Motors Corporation.*)

a reduction in the labor turnover rate for such workers, caused by quickening the process of bringing the worker to standard production efficiency, thus ensuring normal earnings in a shorter time than would otherwise be the case, and avoiding the discouragement resulting from the more prolonged period of less than normal earnings. The vestibule school is best suited to an industry having a relatively constant need for a large number of new men to do one of a few different kinds of jobs. It has found wide acceptance during critical emergencies such as wars.

**Training apprentices.** The training of apprentices has been recognized by Federal and state laws. Its history antedates United States history and may be traced back to the ancient guilds. In 1936 a Committee on Apprenticeship Training was established in the Department of Labor. Minimum standards have been established in keeping with the needs of each particular industry. The length of time required for this training varies with different trades. The Federal Committee on Apprenticeship Training recommends that a signed agreement be executed for each apprentice. A large number of industrial concerns have used various forms of apprentice agreements. The form suggested by the Federal Committee on Apprenticeship Training is given in Appendix B. Many of the apprentice training courses could be shortened by careful selection of the trainees, effective instruction, and careful supervision. Instead of forcing each apprentice to spend the customary 4 years on the program, it would be more logical to let each man progress according to his individual capacity. Some persons with superior abilities can easily finish in 2 or 3 years an apprentice course that would require 4 or even 5 years for slower individuals. Any sound training program starts with the present abilities of the trainees and progresses according to the demonstrated abilities of the learners rather than forcing all of them into a fixed pattern. It is doubtful that the new impetus to apprentice training will do much to shorten this training period. Custom is a powerful stabilizer. Most of the men in charge of apprentice training have themselves served the traditional training period and are not particularly interested in shortening it. Unions also frequently object to shortening the apprentice training period.

Until the instructors in the apprenticeship programs are better trained in the art of instruction and are more highly motivated to instruct the apprentices, there will continue to be much waste in the programs. Of course the real waste is of the learner's time. In some cases the employer may profit by prolonging the period during which the learner is kept in training. Actually most of the excessive training time merely arises from following custom. A special supervisor of apprentices who is not responsible to the line supervisors but who calls on each apprentice daily will tend to eliminate some of the abuses. Many of the executives of some of the older concerns have come up through the organization through the apprenticeship route. The Allis-Chalmers Manufacturing Company of Milwaukee has an excellent apprenticeship program. Other well-organized and widely known programs are to be found in the following plants: Ford Motor Company, Chrysler Motor Corporation, Carnegie-Illinois Steel Corporation, General Electric Company, the Western Electric Company.

**Some special methods of instructing on the job.** *Training by an experienced worker* has the advantage of placing the learner in the situation in which he will remain. Hence, there is no transition period after he learns. In employing this method, care should be taken to ensure three things: (1) that the experienced worker is a *good teacher;* (2) that the experienced worker has an *effective incentive* and *sufficient time* for carrying out his teaching duties; (3) that the experienced worker is provided with an *accurate account of the training needs of the worker he is to teach.*

Instructing the employee by the supervisor is the same as instruction by the skilled or experienced worker, except that the instructing is done on the job by the worker's immediate supervisor. It is necessary that the factors outlined in the preceding paragraph as essential be carefully observed if good results are to be achieved.

A *specially trained instructor* increases the effectiveness of the training on the job. Of course the supervisor may have special training in instructing, but he has so many other duties that he seldom can give the time to instructing that a special instructor can. The special instructor is chosen primarily because of *his ability to teach.* This is something entirely apart from trade skill and trade knowledge. It is generally recognized that the skilled worker may not be equally skilled in teaching and doing. The special instructor is chosen secondarily because of his special skill in the work for which he is training others. It should not be inferred that the instructor need not be skilled in the manual arts that he teaches. By all means he should be able to perform the tasks with accuracy at a normal speed, but it is not necessary for him to be the outstanding performer. Many instructors are not so well trained in the techniques and principles of instruction as they should be. It has often been found desirable to give instructors special training in how to instruct. The Training within Industry (TWI) program sponsored by the War Manpower Commission during World War II was especially valuable for instructors and others who train industrial workers.

**The understudy system of instructing.** This system may also be called the "helper system." The understudy program presumes that a worker will learn by helping another worker to do his job. This method places the worker on a given task with the definite purpose of his serving as an understudy to the man doing the work. The understudy is taught by the man actually working on the job, to whom he is an understudy. This is a good system when the person understudied is himself a good workman, provided that he will take an interest in training his helper rather than in using him to lighten his own burdens.

**The flying squadron.** The "utility squad" is another name used for a special group of workers who are given wide experience on many jobs and who are used to fill vacancies arising from absentees. The flying-squadron program has been closely associated with the training of minor supervisors and college men. This phase of training will be discussed in the following chapter. The presence of a body of men in the organization who are capable of stepping into many vacancies eliminates the necessity of carrying excess men in each department. It results in an actual saving in the number of workers carried on the force. These men receive training usually from another worker when they are first placed in a department. Men chosen for this department are usually selected from those who have shown considerable adaptability (other than when placed there for training to become supervisors). Men on the utility squad are often used as instructors of others when needed. At times there may be no call for these men, in which event they are often placed in a new job just to learn it in case they later may be called upon to fill a gap in production.

**Company schools.** Company schools are usually organized to provide special courses to meet some emergency or to meet the needs of some particular group of workers. Such training courses are usually designed to fit the employee for larger responsibilities either in his present position or in different work. Mention of a few of many courses will indicate their scope: shop mathematics courses for mechanical workers, stenographic courses for typists who wish to become stenographers, salesmanship courses for prospective or present salesmen, management courses for foremen and department heads, special courses for adjusters, and many courses of general cultural interest to employees such as public speaking, dressmaking, etc. A few companies have developed such courses, both formal and special, to a point where the list rivals the crowded curriculums of our foremost colleges. The work is organized and placed in the hands of a corps of instructors, who conduct their classes in classrooms and in laboratories provided with apparatus and equipment. Some of the instructors

Fig. 19.2. Supervisor congratulates winner of scholarship award at General Motors Institute of Technology, while general supervisor of process engineering (right) and the administrative chairman of the Institute's program look on. The winner of the award was a participant in the Institute's spare-time training program. (*Courtesy, General Motors Truck & Coach Division.*)

devote all their time to instruction, and others are regular employees who teach one or two classes. Company schools differ from the vestibule schools in that they are not primarily concerned with job training. They may include job training, but they always include activities beyond that normally thought of as belonging to the vestibule school.

The educational activities of some of the company schools seem at times to constitute a real industrial university. Some of these schools are of college grade and grant degrees, such as the General Motors Institute of Technology at Flint, Mich. (Fig. 19.2). Other well-known company schools are sponsored by such companies as the Western Electric Company, the Chrysler Corporation, the General Electric Company, and the American Telephone and Telegraph Company. The Woodward Governor Company of Rockford, Ill., brings together engineers from manufacturers who use its equipment and conducts a Governor School once a year. These schools may be financed and controlled by the company, by the employees, or by both jointly. Regardless of the formal organization, it is highly desirable to tie the employees into the program in an intimate manner over and above the mere receiving of instruction.

**Instructing in safety.** A safety program cannot be separated from the personnel program as a whole. Safety is as important and should receive as much careful attention as any other distinctly personnel activity. The actual safety-department location may not be under the personnel director, but he must be interested in any activity that so vitally affects the workers. It is customary to have a variety of committees working on safety from different angles, under the leadership of a trained safety director.

**Retraining.** The retraining program in industry is merely one phase of the important industrial training program. It has one peculiar feature in that it largely concerns employees old in terms of service, not, as a rule, new employees. The training process never ceases in a dynamic industry that promotes from within, takes care of its employees whose jobs no longer exist, or provides new jobs for its old or handicapped workers.[2] The necessity to retrain old employees may arise from several different conditions, namely:

1. Some employees are engaged in a confined phase of a particular task and lose their all-round skills in their particular trade. Retraining is often necessary to keep active their all-round skills as a reserve in case of need.

2. During prolonged layoff periods arising from depression conditions, employees on certain highly skilled jobs may have to be given retraining when they are called back to work.

3. Technological changes may abolish the job on which an employee is working, and the company desires to retrain the employee rather than discharge him.

4. An employee, because of illness, accident, or incapacity due to age, no longer can carry on his share of the task that he performed when in normal health and strength.

5. Depressions or cyclical variations in production create conditions where, in part, employment stabilization may be achieved by having a versatile work force capable of performing more than one job.

The depression period of the thirties added to retraining problems. Unemployment taxes with merit rating provisions have also provided an added incentive for desiring to retrain employees whose jobs have run out, rather than to hire new men already trained, thus losing the favored merit rating. Not only is the retraining program promoted by sound economic motives, since it pays to keep older employees whose loyalties have been proved, but it is also supported by social ap-

---

[2] See National Industrial Conference Board, Inc., "Training White Collar Employees," "Time Schedules in Job Training," "Employee Education," *Studies in Personnel Policy* 36, 55, 119, New York, 1941, 1943, 1951.

proval, especially with respect to the older, crippled, or physically incapacitated employees.

**Economic education.** Some companies have been interested in giving their employees an understanding of our economic system. Their motives have been at least twofold: (1) to give employees an understanding of the nature of our economic system in the hope that they would seek to preserve a free economy and resist the lure of socialism or even communism, and (2) to give the employees an understanding of cost-price relationships in the hope that such an understanding would cause employees to strive to increase production, thus to increase earnings without inflation. Most management men subscribe to the objectives, but some of them question the propriety of industry's trying to train their employees in economic matters. They fear their efforts will be interpreted as propaganda and thus result in reactions the opposite of those intended. Other managers believe firmly in the intelligence and integrity of their workers. They believe that the facts when clearly presented will speak for themselves and that the fear of being accused of propagandizing is merely what the state Socialists and Communists want. They have more faith in their employees and our economic system than a fear of being misunderstood.

Economic education for the rank and file of employees is not an inexpensive effort if undertaken on a scale that may give promise of positive results. Relatively few companies have undertaken it. Some companies have tried to get across to their employees the importance of costs through special employee annual reports so written as to be understood by people not trained in accounting. Some companies have also reported economic matters in their employee papers and made available to their employees economic information through their information racks. Possibly the best method is to train the supervisors in economic matters and let them train their workers. Certainly it would be futile to try to spread economic understanding among workers before being certain that the supervisors were trained.[3]

One of the most carefully prepared and widely used programs in employee economic education is HOBSO (How Our Business System Operates), originally developed by Du Pont. It has been made available to other companies through the National Association of Manufacturers and other sources.

[3] See National Industrial Conference Board, Inc., "Employee Education," *Studies in Personnel Policy* 119, New York, 1951; also American Management Association, *The Education of Employees: A Status Report*, by Douglas Williams and Stanley Peterfreund, New York, 1954.

**Methods used in the educational efforts.** The previous discussions give a bird's-eye view of many of the efforts in business to discharge the educational responsibilities. The remainder of this chapter will be devoted to educational aids and methods. Some of these, such as the bulletin board, the employees' paper, and the company libraries, are indirect aids in the educational process.

**How to teach.** Merely knowing how to do a thing does not guarantee good teaching. Of course knowing the methods of instruction, alone, is not enough to make a good instructor. *Technical proficiency is a must in teaching*, but this alone does not ensure good teaching. Teaching is an art that does not come as a natural gift to most people, but it can be learned. The essence of the training program sponsored by the TWI Division of the War Manpower Commission during World War II as set forth on its Job Instruction Card may be summarized as follows:

*The Job Instruction Card*

The outline of the job instruction program, as it appears on a pocket card, is made up of "How to Get Ready to Instruct":

HAVE A TIME TABLE—

How much skill you expect him to have, by what date.

BREAK DOWN THE JOB—

List important steps.
Pick out the key points. (Safety is always a key point.)

HAVE EVERYTHING READY—

The right equipment, materials, and supplies.

HAVE THE WORKPLACE PROPERLY ARRANGED—

Just as the worker will be expected to keep it.

The four steps of "How to Instruct":

Step 1. PREPARE THE WORKER.

Put him at ease.
State the job and find out what he already knows about it.
Get him interested in learning the job.
Place in correct position.

Step 2. PRESENT THE OPERATION.

Tell, show, and illustrate one IMPORTANT STEP at a time.
Stress each KEY POINT.
Instruct clearly, completely, and patiently, but no more than he can master.

Step 3. TRY OUT PERFORMANCE.

Have him do the job—correct errors.
Have him explain each KEY POINT to you as he does the job again.
Make sure he understands.
Continue until YOU know HE knows.

Step 4. FOLLOW UP.

Put him on his own. Designate to whom he goes for help.
Check frequently. Encourage questions.
Taper off extra coaching and close follow-up.
*If the worker hasn't learned, the instructor hasn't taught.*

It would be an error to think that anyone could memorize this card and thus become a proficient instructor. The TWI course lasted for 10 hr., during which time these principles were carefully developed and illustrated. Essentially the same steps used by TWI for training manual workers may be used for any kind of training. In summary they are as follows:

1. The instructor should convey to the learner an attitude of patience, painstaking effort, and good will. Such an attitude tends to become reciprocal and begets confidence.
2. The instructor should have clearly in mind a definite objective for the individual lesson or conference, or else there will be much wasted time and effort.
3. The instructor should carefully analyze the particular subject or task into its instructional factors.
   3.1 These factors should be arranged in their logical sequence for teaching purposes.
   3.2 Having determined the logical sequence of the steps to be presented, the instructor should develop a plan of presentation for each step in order to ensure effective results. The skill of a conference leader is measured by his ability to direct the conference along carefully planned lines.
4. The actual teaching should be carried on with the major objective in mind and in keeping with the organized plan. The lecture may be used for imparting information, but the conference is more productive of constructive thinking on subjects concerning which the group has had experience or about which it has previously studied.
5. In teaching one of the skills such as operating a machine, the following steps should be followed after the instructor has made adequate preparation:
   5.1 *Explain* to the worker the nature of the work, hazards to be avoided, value of the equipment and product, the use of any special tools, specifications, gauges, etc.
   5.2 *Demonstrate* the work with the learner in the position, as nearly as possible, that he himself will be in when he performs the same task. The first demonstration may well be at the normal production speed. The second demonstration should be performed slowly enough for the worker to see each step in the operation in detail and the relationship of each

operation to its succeeding operation. The "why" of each operation should be explained as well as the "how."

5.3 After the learner has had ample opportunity to familiarize himself with the details required, he should be allowed to make his initial *trial* under the direct guidance and supervision of the instructor. (Scientifically, the desired skill and speed will be acquired more quickly if the learner, from the beginning, completes the entire operation at standard production speed. From a practical standpoint, this is seldom feasible where the value of the equipment or material is high, since the scrap and breakage under such a procedure are excessive.)

5.4 *Correction* by the instructor should accompany the initial trials as well as later ones. This should be carried out by suggestion and demonstration.

5.5 *Follow-up* is essential, not only during the early part of instruction but also as the learner progresses, in order to avoid the formation of bad work habits. The one best known method is the one that should be taught and adhered to until a better method is devised, when the new method becomes the one taught.

**The use of lectures and conferences as an instructional device.** A lecture supported by visual aids is an effective method of giving information to groups. Lectures for departmental groups covering operations in the department, the interrelations of those operations, and the relation between the work of a given department and the work of other departments and divisions have been found of much value in bringing about a better *esprit de corps* and in solving production problems requiring a high degree of cooperativeness between groups of workers. Lectures for occupational groups, divisional groups, etc., are of value in increasing the effectiveness of the work done by the groups involved. The success of the lecture method depends upon the relevancy and intrinsic interest of the topics presented and upon the ability of the speaker to convey his ideas. The lecture method is frequently conducted as a group conference with ample opportunity for questions and answers. Outlines of pertinent material covered may be distributed following the lecture. Some have increased the success of lecture and conference meetings by arranging for a luncheon or dinner either in the company restaurant on in a hotel. In some cases the group is broken up into small groups of five or six people for a short period during which the group formulates a question that it wishes to ask the speaker. During the next half of the meeting these groups ask their questions, and the speaker strives to answer them. Such a technique encourages participation. More intensive participation and thinking on the part of the participants are encouraged by the conference method than by the lecture. The number of persons involved in a conference should not exceed 20 or 30, whereas hundreds may listen to a lecture.

President Irl Martin of the Woodward Governor Company, Rockford, Ill., holds group meetings with all his employees from time to time on subjects of general interest. At times special committees of employees will report to the entire work force. President Joseph Sunnen, of Sunnen Products, St. Louis, likewise holds group meetings of his employees. Both companies frequently have outside speakers who discuss general economic subjects of timely interest.

**The employees' paper as a device for instructing.** Naturally there are limits to the use of the employees' paper for instructional purposes. It is not suited for instructing in many phases of technical requirements nor for skills. On the other hand economic information may readily be included in the employees' paper. Naturally, instruction through the company paper has to be extensive rather than intensive. To be effective the articles have to be written in the language of workpeople. Technical operations have to be treated in a popular manner. Pictures are particularly effective. The paper provides an excellent medium for explaining a new company policy. However, the company paper should never be relied upon as the sole device for explaining company policies. The foreman is the real leader of his department. He is the person who should take the initiative in explaining policies. The article in the paper can well aid him in his task.

**Use of the bulletin board in imparting information.** It is not unusual for a labor law to require the employer to post certain notices with respect to the law on the bulletin board or in some other conspicuous place. These are seldom read save when some person has a complaint to file regarding their violation. Perhaps the desired purpose is accomplished when they are read only when needed. The bulletin board serves the excellent purpose of creating interest in safety when attractive pictures are displayed properly and changed often. Bulletin boards should be changed often and not be too full at any one time. It requires real ingenuity to get the most out of them.[4] Company announcements or even certain policies may be posted on the bulletin board. Such items might well have a footnote, "See your foreman for further explanation."

**Use of sound slides and motion pictures.** One large Chicago manufacturer uses a sound motion picture to explain a great deal of the information given new employees during their induction period. Whether or not this method is to be preferred to the personal explanation of a real personnel man may be an open question. The fact does remain that such a device ensures that each person gets the exact

---

[4] See National Industrial Conference Board, Inc., "Bulletin Boards," *Studies in Personnel Policy* 138, New York, 1953.

information intended to be given. Motion pictures provide a method of giving uniform instruction, thus multiplying the efforts of a good instructor. Some things can be done with the motion picture that are difficult to accomplish in any other manner. It must be remembered, however, that the motion picture can seldom take the learner beyond the introductory stage. In the same category with the motion picture are sound-slide pictures, a device that synchronizes slides with a record on which the desired message has been recorded. This equipment is somewhat less expensive than the motion picture and serves essentially the same purpose. One of the largest banks in Chicago has made extensive use of this method of instructing its employees in the proper use of the telephone.

Currently available equipment for making nonprofessional motion pictures with sound track has greatly extended the use of motion pictures in instruction. Instead of assembling salesmen from all sections of the country at one large convention, the sales manager of a company may prepare an educational talk concerning the product or whatever the subject may be. This may then be distributed, in the form of a talking picture, to all the various sales districts over the country. All the district salesmen are gathered at a meeting at some convenient point in their respective local districts, and the information is given to the entire sales force of an organization simultaneously, without their leaving their various districts. Motion pictures have a wide range of use. Pictures can be used advantageously in teaching a worker many complicated mechanical processes that could scarcely be conveyed in any other way. "Slow-motion" pictures reproducing action at a fraction of its real speed are especially enlightening for some processes. The cartoon technique makes it possible to portray graphically operations, such as the "insides" of an internal-combustion engine, that cannot readily be reproduced photographically. Extensive use of this invaluable educational training aid has not been made because of the lack of suitable films and the high costs. The various training techniques require constructive imagination and careful follow-up. They are not self-perpetuating. As a matter of fact, any attempt to use a given procedure or device too long is the greatest weakness of these techniques. For instance, great expense may be incurred in developing a training film covering a given process. Processes frequently change rapidly with new developments. In a short time the film is likely to be out of date. Often the training department uses a film that is no longer representative of current operations.

**Company libraries and reading rooms.** As this paragraph is being written a request has just arrived from the librarian of a well-known company seeking information regarding a master's thesis on the organization of the industrial engineering department. The educational value of a company library is limited only by the constructive imagination of the librarian, the willingness of employees to use the service, and available funds. Many of these company libraries are limited in use to office personnel, supervisory personnel, and technical employees. Even where the libraries are not restricted in use, however, these groups are the ones that use them the most. The company libraries are often linked with public libraries, so that a wide assortment of books is made available, changes being made as rapidly as the circulation of given books ceases. There is often a provision whereby a worker can apply for a book in the morning, and the book can be secured from the public library during the day if it happens that it is not in the company library. Reports from company libraries are reassuring, not only from the point of view of the surprisingly large number of employees who use the library facilities, but also from the point of view of the large number of technical books withdrawn for study. The general library may develop a special division to render specialized service of a technical or business nature, or the company may establish a special library of this nature. With the widespread growth of public libraries, it would seem logical that private company libraries would become increasingly of the special type designed to render a special technical service. Such a library may render valuable service to the technical division of the industry and employees interested in technical and business matters. Librarians of special libraries have a professional association of their own, the Special Libraries Association, with headquarters in New York.

Rest rooms, clubrooms, or reading rooms for workers afford an excellent opportunity for placing educational material in the hands of the workers. It is obvious that much care must be exercised in the selection of material which will be truly educational and at the same time attractive enough to compete on its own merits. Most reading rooms contain only magazines and newspapers. Their educational value is very limited. These rooms are excellent places to locate reading racks that may include some educational material.

**Using the facilities and services of universities and colleges.** Extensive program in vocational education are being carried on in practically all cities or towns of any size and in state-supported colleges and universities. These are financed in part by funds provided under the Smith-Hughes Act of 1917, the George-Ellsey Act of 1934, and the George-Deen Act of 1936. In many communities, the business interests are closely cooperating with the schools. The public schools frequently provide the instruction required in the apprentice training programs, the students being released from the shop to attend the classes at certain times during the week. Shop practice and business subjects are being taught with increasing efficiency in vocational classes in public schools. Part-time programs are being worked out in some cases. These have been more successful in colleges than in high schools. Progressive schools and colleges are realizing the importance of preparing students more adequately for industrial activity. The cooperative plan of education in operation at the University of Cincinnati, at Antioch College, Drexel Institute, Massachusetts Institute of Technology, General Motors Institute of Technology, Georgia School of Technology, Northwestern University Technological Institute, and some 16 other colleges and universities is an outstanding example of educational endeavors in this connection. Under the cooperative plan, students alternate between periods of academic work in college and periods of work in various jobs in industrial concerns. In this way, the academic and industrial work is related in an attempt to give the student a well-balanced education, including adequate theoretical as well as practical preparation for any industrial pursuit he may elect to follow. There is always the problem of correlating the work experience with academic training. This is by no means a simple task. Students frequently complain in their senior year that the work experience is valuable in teaching them to work with others but that it does not tie in with their academic work to an appreciable degree.

University extension programs provide instruction, under university control, to be given to students unable to attend regular courses of instruction. These plans have great possibilities from an industrial viewpoint if industry will but expend the effort to inform the educators of industrial conditions so that they in turn can direct their students how to become more effective workers. This sort of cooperation and coordination should result in enriched apprenticeship training methods, for the schools can emphasize those things which will enable the apprentice and future skilled worker to become a better citizen, and industry can supply him with the training that will enable him to become a more effective worker. Some concerns make a practice of encouraging promising employees to take courses in various sorts of schools. They offer, as an incentive, part payment of the tuition beforehand, or, through the educational refund plan, they pay part tuition after the employee has successfully completed an approved course of study in an accredited school. Some organizations do likewise for employees taking correspondence courses.

**Evening schools.** New York, Chicago, Detroit, Cleveland, and St. Louis and many others have large evening divisions of their universities and colleges. Some of these evening divisions have registrations in excess of 10,000 adult students. Literally hundreds of smaller communities have creditable evening divisions in their junior colleges. Several evening schools provide graduate study leading to a master's degree. Some schools give complete courses both for the undergraduate and the graduate in law, pharmacy, liberal arts, business administration, and engineering. Others give courses in parts of these fields. Encouragement to take advantage of such opportunities can be given to those workers who would really benefit from such supplementary instruction. Care should be taken, of course, to prevent the lamentable waste of time and money by those workers whose ambitions lead them to persist in night school work and correspondence courses yet who are taking courses that are demonstrably beyond their abilities and capacity to learn. On the other hand, personnel administration has an equally strong obligation to instill in the worker of unusual ability the desire and ambition to fit himself for positions of greater skill or responsibility by attendance at a well-conducted night school. There are men operating machines who have the native capacities to do doctoral work if they would apply themselves.

Many a promising young man in business finds that his liberal arts or engineering training did not equip him for some of his responsibilities in management. These deficiencies in human relations, organization, accounting, budgeting, and similar areas, may be made up in many evening courses in colleges. In addition to the work done at the college level many technical high schools have evening classes in shop mathematics, blueprint reading, shop practices, and many other technical subjects. Other evening high schools provide training in practically every phase of secretarial science.

**Correspondence courses.** Correspondence courses provide excellent educational opportunities to persons who have the "staying qualities" to finish the courses. The Minnesota Employment Stabilization Institute found in its study that only 6 per cent of the persons starting correspondence courses finished them. Companies that have many plants or branches or salesmen far from the home office have organized correspondence courses for their own employees, writing special materials adapted to their own use. Both Swift and Company and Armour and Company have such courses. The incentive to complete correspondence courses initiated and given by the company is greater than when there is no follow-up by the employer.

Correspondence courses are provided by some private institutions that are engaged in this work on a strictly business basis. Some of these courses are of a high order. Certain recognized universities and colleges also offer correspondence courses with or without college credit. Naturally, correspondence courses designed by outside agencies are not so specifically pointed toward company needs as those written by a given company for its own use. Ambitious employees, either at the supervisory level or workers at the bench, may take many college courses that lead to graduation or help meet business requirements. English, mathematics, business law, accounting, statistics, industrial management, personnel management, marketing, retailing, and many other courses are available through correspondence. Most of these courses use the same texts and other material that the regular full-time students cover.

CHAPTER 20

# Training Executives and Supervisors

**Determining training needs.** Training is an individual matter so far as the person trained is concerned. Some of the needs of trainees may be of such a nature that they readily may be met in groups. To discover the training needs of a given company, a complete survey of the present status of each supervisor is required. This might well be a managerial audit. Such an audit reveals vacancies to be filled according to an estimated time schedule. A check of available replacements for persons listed for retirement (assuming that there is a policy for retiring at a given age) provides an indication of training needs for certain individuals. This audit may indicate certain areas that are common to large numbers of supervisors. During the survey each supervisor should have a personal training requirement developed. A summary of these individual training needs reveals the total company training requirements.[1] The tools for setting up the training program might be expressed as follows:

*Organization chart + individual appraisals and indicated needs*
*= specific training for present personnel + selection and training*
*of replacements.*

Figure 20.1 represents pages from the United States Rubber Company's management appraisal form. From these forms a replacement training table for each executive in the program is constructed. Also from these charts an organization replacement table is constructed. The use of aids of this type requires courageous appraisals

---

[1] See Roger M. Bellows, M. Francis Estep, and Charles Scholl, Jr., "A Tool for Analyzing Training Needs: The Training Evaluation Check List," *Personnel*, March, 1953, pp. 412–417; L. David Kork, "How to Determine Supervisory Training Needs," *Personnel*, January, 1956, pp. 335–352.

and organizational planning. It will be observed that page 5 of the appraisal form (Fig. 20.1, page 306) is not to be shown to or discussed with the employee. The reason for this is self-evident.

**Evolution of training procedures.** The older training programs consisted largely of the *absorption process,* or the understudy system. Business was carried on in its traditional form. The learning of the accepted traditions and customs within a given enterprise constituted a large part of the training, even as it continues to be important today. Many of the leaders in business had grown with the expansion of their enterprises, learning as the business expanded. Their sons or successors were denied the privilege of watching the enterprise grow from a humble beginning and of securing the intimate knowledge and understanding that come from close association with every detail of the business. This situation demanded a new technique. A more careful use of the understudy system for the top executives was the result. For the minor executives at first there was little change from the old apprentice system and the feeling that a man who knew how to do a job himself knew how to direct others in doing the same thing. Many of the older foremen knew only the techniques of the line officer, who commanded and discharged if his orders were not carried out. They were experts in technical processes and equipment but deficient in the ability to handle men under the changing social order. Most of the early foreman training programs were largely devoted to the problems of handling men from the standpoint of company policies. The training by absorption may suffice for a small organization, but it almost never results in a succeeding generation of executives who are superior to the current ones, for the understudies tend to absorb the bad as well as the good features of their sponsors. A carefully organized and planned training program, or training by *intention,* tends to raise the general level of the supervisory and executive personnel, since this program emphasizes the best characteristics of the various leaders and provides checks to avoid the less desirable features.[2] In reality there are three phases to the training program for executives and supervisors: (1) foreman training; (2) training for middle management; (3) top management training.

**Differences in the needs of foremen, middle managers, and top managers.** A careful job analysis of the responsibilities of foremen, middle managers, and top managers reveals that their jobs are markedly different. From the very nature of the different jobs that

[2] See National Industrial Conference Board, Inc., *Studies in Personnel Policy* 15, 18, 36, 66, 77, 107, 124, 140, 160 and 161, New York, 1939, 1940, 1941, 1944, 1946, 1950, 1952, 1953, 1957, for a series of excellent studies in this field.

**NOTE:** *When reviewing the performance of an individual, be sure to evaluate this in terms of the duties which you have outlined to him, covering the normal requirements and objectives of his assignment. Wherever possible, give specific examples.*

**A. RESULTS** - Looking at him in his present position, what results has he obtained in terms of:

QUANTITY OF WORK - To what extent does he accomplish more or less than would be normally expected?

QUALITY OF WORK - To what extent does he do a higher quality job than would be normally expected?

**B. METHODS** - To what extent has he demonstrated an ability to:

ORGANIZE HIS WORK - How well does he organize his work for maximum efficiency?

PLANNING - How well does he plan ahead and anticipate changes?

GET ALONG WITH OTHERS - To what extent is he tactful, diplomatic and cooperative with others?

In his dealings with Superiors?

Individuals at his own level?

INSTRUCT OTHERS - How well do others learn from him?

**C. KNOWLEDGE OF THE JOB**

JOB FUNCTION - To what extent does he have a thorough knowledge of his job?

RELATIONSHIPS - To what extent does he know the relationship of his job to other jobs in his department?

FIG. 20.1. Page 2 of management appraisal form. Page 1 of the form gives the statement of policy, detailed instructions, personal data, the name of the person doing the rating, and the person checking the rating. Page 5 gives outstanding abilities, areas needing improvement, evaluation of the individual, and training plans. (*Courtesy, United States Rubber Company.*)

**D. PERSONAL QUALITIES**

Indicate the degree to which he has demonstrated the following personal qualities by placing a check (X) in the most appropriate block on the scale.

|  | HIGh | | | | | | | | LOW |
|---|---|---|---|---|---|---|---|---|---|
| **DEPENDABILITY** Can you always count on him? | | | | | | | | | |
| **JUDGMENT** Are his conclusions sound? | | | | | | | | | |
| **DECISIVENESS** Does he act without hesitation? | | | | | | | | | |
| **POISE** Is he at ease in all situations? | | | | | | | | | |
| **INITIATIVE** Is he a "self-starter"? | | | | | | | | | |
| **ATTITUDE** Is his outlook constructive and optimistic? | | | | | | | | | |
| **INTEGRITY** Is he sincere and honest in his dealings? | | | | | | | | | |
| **ENTHUSIASM** Is he eager and willing? | | | | | | | | | |
| **LEADERSHIP** Does he inspire and motivate others to action? | | | | | | | | | |
| **EXPRESSION** Can he express himself clearly and understandably to an individual or group? | | | | | | | | | |
| **ACCEPTANCE** What impression does he make and how do people react toward him? | | | | | | | | | |

**E. OVER-ALL VALUE**

Considering both present performance and capacity for development, how valuable is this person to you and to the company when compared with others of the same experience and job classification?

_____

_____

Is he well suited to the type of work he is now doing? Yes____No____If not, what do you recommend?

_____

_____

_____

_____

Fig. 20.1. (*Continued*)

these three levels of executives perform it should be apparent that training programs designed for foremen do not satisfy the needs for the other two groups. This does not mean that these two higher groups do not profit from participation in the foreman training program. They get better acquainted with the lower levels of supervision and make a contribution to the training of this group. Nevertheless, the program does not meet the real needs of middle management or top manage-

**CAPACITY FOR ADVANCEMENT**
(Confidential, not to be discussed with nor presented to, the employee)

I.   Check in the boxes, provided below, what capacity this man has for advancement to a position of greater responsibility. Considering the factors of age and health, over-all ability, as well as the results of the appraisal.

POTENTIALITY FOR ADVANCEMENT - possesses capacity to assume greater responsibility.

1. ☐   Can be considered immediately promotable to a position in the next level of responsibility.

2. ☐   Can be considered capable of assuming greater responsibility after training.

DOUBTFUL CAPACITY FOR ADVANCEMENT

3. ☐   Performing satisfactorily on this job and well suited to it but probably more suited to this work or similar responsibility than to a position of greater responsibility.

4. ☐   Inadequate performance. Performance in present assignment is below standard and/or lacks ability to meet standards of performance for such assignment.

Action recommended:_____

_____

II.   Give reasons for above recommendations, pointing out those qualities in the man influencing your opinion:_____

_____

_____

III.   A.   If this man has potentiality for advancement, what, in your opinion, is the next step ahead for this individual?____

_____

     B.   Does this man have further potential beyond the next step?_____If yes, in what management activity?

_____

IV.   Is there any condition of a business, personal or other nature, which would limit this man's flexibility for advancement or relocation? Explain:_____

_____

_____

Is the above condition temporary or permanent?_____

V.   Comments:_____

_____

_____

_____

_____

_____

_____

FIG. 20.1. (*Continued*)

ment.[3] From a training standpoint middle managers are the forgotten men of industry; yet their needs are great. They usually are given the same training as foremen in spite of the fact that their responsibilities and executive requirements are markedly different. To direct the efforts of foremen is definitely a different problem from directing the

[3] Titles for foremen differ widely in various companies. In one large company the title foreman applies to the lowest level of supervision. In another large

efforts of a work group. Middle management has to get things done through others. Middle management has to exercise controls through reports, budgets, and plans. The training of middle management should arise from an analysis of the tasks these men have to perform. The program should definitely be pitched on a high intellectual and content level and should include:

1. Principles of organization on a seminar basis.
2. Executive leadership of foremen and department heads.
3. Budgeting (how to build the budget and operate it).
4. Planning and control.
5. Forecasting.
6. Executive counseling.
7. Plant expansion and location.
8. Product design.
9. Market research.
10. Corporation finance.

To the foregoing might readily be added a rotating internship for certain middle management men who are current prospects for being promoted to top management. In a company having many plants a planned program for giving middle management men operating experience in the various plants has merit. It would be immeasurably more logical to combine the training of middle management and top management men than to combine foreman and middle management training. A program for top management similar to the one suggested above for middle management would be beneficial. Naturally it should be pitched to the level of the top management group. If the senior operating head of top management has a genuine interest in strengthening his group, much of this training can be built around and can become a part of actual operations.

**What do supervisory and executive training programs strive to do?** The primary objectives of executive training include the following: (1) to provide adequate leaders; (2) to increase the efficiency of

---

company the section chief is the lowest supervisor. In this company the names are section chief, assistant foreman, foreman, general foreman. Other companies use such titles as lead man or assistant jobmaster for the supervisor at the work level. A foreman in some companies may have more men under him than the factory superintendent in another company. Middle management comprises that great group of key executives below the senior executives but above the level of first-line supervisors. They are the majors and colonels of industry. They include division superintendents, chief industrial engineers, some personnel directors, office managers, some heads of accounting divisions, the plant engineer, some chief engineers, and similar persons. The exact status of certain positions listed above depends upon the particular organizational philosophies. For instance, some personnel directors and chief engineers are vice-presidents. In such cases these men are considered members of top management.

performance of current executives; (3) to serve as a means of control in operations; (4) to develop a unity of purpose and improve morale. A more detailed summary of these objectives is given below:

1. To develop a supply of supervisors and executives to meet the requirements of the expanding enterprise, to replace persons who leave for various reasons or who are promoted within the business. Those who leave may include the voluntary quits and discharges, the deaths, retirements, or withdrawals due to health or accident.

   1.1 It should be a truism, but it is a fact often overlooked, that the requirements of an executive training program should be carefully developed from an analysis of the respective positions, a comparison of the capacities of the present personnel with the requirements placed on them. This analysis should result in the formulation of a personnel budget. All too many training programs are inaugurated merely because an executive thinks it would be a good idea.

2. To upgrade the present supervisors and executives and thus help them perform their present tasks more effectively.

3. To serve as a means of control in current operations through:

   3.1 Giving information regarding current problems. It is presumed that men of good will do what is required when they know what the requirements are.

   3.2 Coordination of effort. Given the job to be done, with a knowledge of the timing, coordination naturally follows.

   3.3 Developing cooperation through an acquaintanceship with the personalities of others. The conference is an excellent place to get acquainted.

   3.4 Securing information regarding the operation of policies and procedures. The conference is a good way to get a collective opinion on present or proposed policies.

   3.5 Bringing supervisory grievances to the attention of top management. One large company has a suggestion box for the exclusive use of the supervisors and executives who attend conferences. These suggestions do not have to be signed, although most of them are. The director of training follows through any grievance, even to the president if it is necessary to get a final answer.

4. To develop morale and a feeling of belonging to management. The giving of information and the getting of advice promote morale. The association of top management with lower supervisors (even though only at the annual training banquet) stimulates the lower executives. It may serve as an outlet for supervisory grievances, and it provides a large-scale opportunity for consultive supervision.

As a training program progresses, it should be modified from time to time to meet changing conditions. When this is done, it is advisable to incorporate this modification in the statement of the objectives. It should be frankly admitted that this is seldom the practice; however, this failure in practice is no argument against the desirability of the procedure. To check an innovation carefully enough to incorporate it into the statement of the objectives of the executive training program requires the careful evaluation of the change and at times will serve to reject a program that looks good on the surface but that does not stand up under careful scrutiny. Thus mistakes and unnecessary waste may be avoided. When properly handled, executive training may provide a meeting ground where the participants apply constructive group thought to the solution of problems and thus not only learn of the company policies but also participate in the formulation of policies that pertain to the internal direction of the enterprise.

**Responsibility for executive and supervisory training.** Each executive of whatever level has the responsibility for training his subordinates. This statement is sound in theory, but in practice some otherwise successful leaders simply have not the inclination or ability to be effective trainers. In this event, the man above the ineffective trainer has a dual responsibility. Of course, in most large enterprises the line officers have the assistance of staff men whose specialty is training. To the extent that the line officer can be encouraged or aided to do a good job of training, the more easily will the program be accepted and the better the results. The size of the organization, the objectives behind the training program, the over-all organizational philosophy, and, to a limited extent, the interests of the major executives determine the place of the training program in the organization.

It is common practice in large enterprises to have a functional officer, usually a staff member of the personnel department, assigned the duties of supervising and coordinating the policies of the executive training program. This is true even though the actual training may be carried on by the regular line supervisors.[4] In some organizations, the actual training is carried on by staff members of the training department with the aid and guidance of the line supervisors. It is unusual in a large organization to find a major executive who has the time, training, and inclination to initiate and carry on the details of an executive training program.

In some enterprises where there is a staff department charged with the organization function the responsibility for training supervisors and executives is located in this special department along with job evaluation and wage administration. There is nothing wrong with this structure, but it really splits the personnel function without any special advantage. Of one thing there can be little doubt: to be successful the director of training should be a man of real leadership

---

[4] See National Industrial Conference Board, Inc., "Training Solutions of Company Problems," *Studies in Personnel Policy* 15, New York, 1939, pp. 44–58, for the discussion of a training program conducted by the regular supervisory staff.

standing. It is because of the prestige factor, in part, that major line executives (when they have the time and ability) make excellent leaders of executive training conferences. A second advantage of tying the responsible executives closely to the training program is the value they personally receive from their participation. Where the operating officials accept the executive training program as an integral part of the operations and use it not only for imparting training information but also as a medium of control, the separate staff will retain vitality and be accepted by the trainees in the same light as the direct supervisors. *This balanced relationship is a delicate one that can be realized in the long run only if it is a vital part of the clearly defined training objectives.* It requires painstaking effort on the part of the training staff, for it is so easy to use the old material and not to vitalize the program with current practice.

**Selection, an important phase of executive development.** Great care should be exercised in starting men up the executive ladder to see that a substantial number of them have the native ability to keep on going. Naturally this does not mean that every foreman has to be a potential superintendent. Recently the top management of a large branch plant in surveying its executive status awakened to find that several key positions would have to be filled within a period of 3 years. The manager frantically appealed to the central office to help him get some men from the outside. He reluctantly agreed to have a careful check of the men within his plant to see whether or not any of them could be trained for the vacancies. He was surprised when he found that he had more men than vacancies in every case save one requiring a highly trained technical man. In spite of this illustration there has been a tremendous waste in trying to train men for increased executive responsibilities who simply did not have the mental capacity or the emotional stability required for new positions.

Some students of the problem of providing adequate leadership for business advocate selecting men while they are young, training them as rapidly as possible for positions of responsibility, and placing them in these positions while they are still young.[5] This is the so-called elite selection process. Others believe in starting a substantial number of qualified young men, giving them an intensive training program such as 1 year, placing them in responsible supervisory positions of lower rank, and advancing them on a basis of merit when compared with all other persons available. Certainly this second method has

---

[5] See American Management Association, *Management Education for Itself and Its Employees*, Part I, Lyndall F. Urwick, "Management Education in American Business," New York, 1954, p. 15.

merit in terms of our democratic concepts. It will work if someone seriously makes it his responsibility not to let these able young men be overlooked in the routines of operations.

In selecting men to be moved along, a substantial number of them should possess high mental acuity, emotional stability, and technical competence. Mental acuity is reasonably easy to measure. Some tests may be helpful in testing for emotional balance, but this is one area in which a great deal of further research is still needed. Careful observation of the individual on the job provides the best-known method of appraising his mental health. Technical competence can be strengthened by training if it is not already possessed. Of course this statement presumes that the prospective candidate has adequate mental ability and aptitude. Men possessing the required capacities may come from among college recruits or outstandingly capable men who have never been to college. Special assistance may have to be given this latter group in the form of guided reading, correspondence courses, or night classes. The important item in training executives and supervisors is not whence they came but whether or not they have the native capacities and interests to profit from the training. Care in selecting the trainees markedly influences the results of the training.

Training programs designed for executives are not new even though most of them from a statistical standpoint are of recent origin.[6] Some excellent work was started in the 1920's, largely laid aside during the 1930's but revived during the 1940's. The literature is full of case histories of successful executive training programs. General Foods, Standard Oil of New Jersey, Johnson and Johnson, Ford Motor, International Harvester, and various divisions in General Motors have done outstanding work in this field. The approaches in these companies differ widely. All of them are experimenting. The task is big and will not be settled for a long time, if ever. A few companies have used outside management consultants to conduct their executive training programs. Some college professors do this kind of work on a part-time basis. Such a program may be desirable in a small company that cannot afford the expense of having a high-caliber training program. Some large companies use consultants in an advisory capacity in their executive training programs. The outside aid will be most effective

---

[6] See American Management Association, *Management Education for Itself and Its Employees,* Part I, Lyndal Urwick, "Management Education in Business," 1954, Part II, Joseph M. Trickett, "A Survey of Management Development," 1954, Robert G. Simpson, Part III, "Case Studies in Management Development," 1954, and Douglas Williams Associates, Part IV, "The Education of Employees: A Status Report," 1954, for a comprehensive study of the development of executive training programs and the status as of the date of the survey.

when it is closely tied in with a steering committee of top executives. Such a committee serves as a training medium for the members of the steering committee and ties the program closely to company policies and needs.

**Training the new supervisor.** The new supervisor, regardless of where he comes from, needs training in the requirements of his new assignment. The exact amount of training needed depends in part upon his past experience. He may come from one of the following situations:

1. From without the organization with work experience but no supervisory experience, thus needing training in the technique of supervision as well as orientation in company procedures, customs, and policies.
2. From without the organization with previous supervisory experience, thus needing orientation in company procedures, customs, and policies.
3. From within the organization, thus having a background of understanding of company policies.
4. From without the company with no work experience, such as direct from college, thus requiring training in the operating business process, supervisory techniques, and orientation in company procedures, customs, and policies.

A few relatively large companies give men with work experience a 2 weeks' intensive training period in supervisory techniques and policies. This is an excellent procedure with new supervisors. Men who have had no work experience should be given this experience through either observing or actual operating. A man from the outside with previous supervisory experience may be broken into company policies and customs through a rotating internship, special assignments, understudy period, or many of the other techniques to be described below.

**Training on the job (possibly as an understudy).** When the executive is thoroughly committed to the need for developing his subordinates and is qualified and willing to give time to the detailed consultation required, such a program has real value. The subordinate may have any title or assignment. An understudy may be assistant to _____, special assistant to _____, or any of the regular supervisory or executive positions, depending upon his special assignment. He may be assigned as an understudy solely for training, or he may be assigned as a staffman or line assistant to a busy executive who really needs his help. The understudy may have regular duties for which he is solely responsible; for instance, a man may be the general foreman and still be in training as an understudy to the superintendent. In this case, the general foreman will usually assume the duties of the superintendent in case the superintendent is absent. The understudy system does not tend to upgrade the organization, since it is unusual for the understudy to rise above his mentor in performance unless he is a superior person. The understudy system does offer one advantage. It provides a specific incentive for the understudy. This incentive will be strong or weak in proportion to the reasonable likelihood that the understudy will be called upon to fill his superior's position in the not too distant future. To be effective, the understudy system requires absolute honesty on the part of management. Training on the job may also be carried on as a matter of regular operational procedures without any emphasis upon the understudy factor. If each executive is charged with developing his subordinates and takes this assignment seriously, on-the-job counseling provides an excellent training procedure. One aspect of on-the-job counseling and training is known as *consultive supervision. Consultive supervision is a process or technique of management whereby the supervised not only are consulted before action in which they are interested is taken but are urged to contribute constructive thought to the solution.* H. H. Carey listed the advantages and disadvantages of consultive supervision as follows:[7]

1. Advantages.
    1.1     Employees feel that they are working *with* and *not* for the supervisor.
    1.2     The supervisor gets the benefit of the individual's experience and training.
    1.3     It gives employees a chance to sound off.
    1.4     It develops the individual's initiative and self reliance.
    1.5     It increases the individual's confidence in management.
    1.6     It builds up the individual's self-respect.
    1.7     It builds up the individual's confidence in the supervisor and increases his willingness to cooperate.
    1.8     The supervisor can get to know the employee better and to understand his attitude and feelings.
    1.9     It makes the individual feel more responsible for his job and not merely a cog in a machine.
    1(10)   It keeps the individual on his toes.
    1(11)   It improves employee-company relations, since the employee feels that the supervisor and the company are interested in him as an individual.
    1(12)   In making work assignments the supervisor can more easily make sure that the individual understands the job.
    1(13)   It broadens the employee.
    1(14)   It tends to improve performance.
    1(15)   It develops straight thinking.
2. Disadvantages.
    2.1     The supervisor may lose face with a certain type of employee.

[7] See American Management Association, *Personnel,* Vol. 18, No. 5, March, 1942, pp. 283–284.

2.2    The system may overdevelop the self-esteem of some employees.

2.3    It takes too much time (the supervisor's and the individual's).

2.4    It may give the employee the idea the supervisor doesn't know his job—can't make up his mind.

2.5    The employee may think the supervisor is trying to shift responsibility.

2.6    It will destroy morale if employee's ideas or point of view are asked for and then ignored or if insufficient credit is given to them.

**Rotating assignments as a device for training supervisors and executives.** A planned program of transferring certain executives to various operating or staff assignments is an excellent device for giving them broad experience and training. The actual performance on these rotated assignments may be strictly as if the executive were to stay on the job permanently or it may be on a basis similar to an internship. Each method has advantages. The internship approach may be more appropriate if the individual is going to be on the job a relatively short time. If it is a rotating internship, the actual productivity of the executive is not the primary objective. Although the work performed frequently contributes to production, it is primarily for training purposes. For instance, while the department or division head is absent on vacation or for any other reason, the intern may operate in his place. The internship is usually a part of a scheduled program to give a wide background and operating experience. It frequently includes experience beyond that of the division in which the intern expects to work. It may readily include written reports of experiences as well as of operating principles and techniques and an organized reading program covering the various phases of the work. To be most effective, the intern should attend all committee and other meetings that are held. In some of the larger industries, the trainees live in dormitories, have special clubs or junior engineering organizations, and are essentially graduate students of manufacturing or commerce. The entire program should be under the guidance of a strong coordinator who has executive prestige. When properly conceived and administered, the internship is one of the best methods of training either the prospective foreman or higher executives. The executive having an intern assigned to him should look upon his training in the same light as the doctor whose professional code requires him to train the intern. When this approach becomes general, supervision will achieve the status of a profession.

**The flying squadron, or "utility squad."** The flying squadron, or "utility squad," approach to training supervisors is usually for persons preparing for their first supervisory assignments. The varied experience gained by workers on the flying squadron is usually supplemented by systematic classroom instruction at stated hours during the week. Such supplementary instruction may deal with technical information, history of the particular industry and the particular company, principles of economics, business administration, and industrial management. This training agency has proved very useful, as shown by the number of industrial organizations, offices, banks, and department stores utilizing this method of training. Concerns select a group of college graduates or promising men of experience from within the organization to form a training group. These graduates are routed from one department to another, so that they cover all the most important elements of the business. In addition, the members of the training group attend regular classes and lectures, where they are given a comprehensive knowledge of the plant, its raw materials, products, policies, and purposes, as well as instruction concerning the broad problems of management and administration. The electrical industry has for a long time been one of the leaders in the development of extensive educational programs for graduate students, leading to executive, technical, and research positions. Goodyear Tire and Rubber Company, the United States Rubber Company, and many other companies have used the flying squadron as one means of executive training.

**Correspondence courses.** The armed services have made extensive use of correspondence courses in the training of reserve officers. Some companies, such as the meat packers, have a large number of branch houses scattered throughout the country. Both Swift and Company and Armour and Company have used correspondence courses with success in their training programs. The record of completion of the traditional correspondence course purchased from a commercial organization is low. Correspondence courses developed by companies to meet their specific needs have met with much higher success in the completion than the commercial correspondence courses.[8] Group instruction is to be preferred when the number being trained justifies the expense. However, training programs have to be adjusted to meet the needs of particular situations. Regular correspondence courses provided by outside agencies are seldom specific enough to be of great service to supervisors of a particular company, although they can readily cover broad principles and procedures. It would be possible to tie in such courses with specific cases, but the authors know of no such development.

[8] See Peter C. Krist and Charles J. Prange, "Training Supervisors by Mail: The Railway Express Program," *Personnel*, Vol. 34, No. 2, September-October, 1957, pp. 32–37.

**Universities and colleges.** Evening programs in certain urban universities and colleges provide almost any kind of course that executives may desire. These programs include courses in industrial management, personnel management, time and motion study, cost accounting, budgeting, and many other subjects related to the executive's problems. Technical subjects such as chemistry, physics, and engineering are valuable aids to the executive and may be studied in many evening classes. These courses, by the very nature of the circumstances, do not fit the specific needs of a particular company but deal with general principles and typical cases. When a particular company has enough students to make a class, the course can frequently be pointed more specifically toward the requirements of the company. With the increased use of the case method of instruction, real situations are approached in the classroom. These courses are supplementary to the executive training program and are not designed to take the place of an effective training program within the business enterprise itself. Individual enterprises that are too small to employ a trained supervisor of executive training find the colleges particularly helpful. Some of the state-supported colleges and universities have specialists who conduct extension courses in communities not easily accessible to the colleges. These specialists are supported in part by Federal aid. College-level courses are valuable to supervisors and executives with a good educational background or to others with an interest in education. Some Chicago executives have completed full 4-year college courses in evening school. In some instances, the firm pays all or part of the tuition expenses of the students taking these courses (see Fig. A.6, item 6). In many cases, the personnel department gives advice as to the particular courses that are of value to the student in improving his efficiency in his present position or in providing for promotion. In some of the larger schools, a complete 4-year engineering or commerce course may be taken in evening classes.

A substantial number of universities conduct formal programs for executives. These programs range all the way from the formal 1-year program at Massachusetts Institute of Technology through the Harvard 13-week program to some programs of 2 weeks. Other programs are part time, running for 1 year or more. Most of these programs are of a high level and are limited to persons holding executive positions. The subject matter covered nearly always includes human relations, organization, some accounting or budgeting, some finance and forecasting, marketing, and a rather broad course that might be called social responsibilities of business. It is truly inspirational to see a group of executives drawn from many different fields of business attack some of the knotty problems presented by the cases studied. Many of these programs limit the number of persons that may be enrolled at one time in their programs. They desire wide participation so that viewpoints of many different companies may be presented. A few of the universities other than the ones already mentioned giving these programs are Columbia, Cornell, Illinois, Michigan, Ohio State, Indiana, Northwestern, Wisconsin, University of California, Los Angeles, University of Texas, North Carolina, Pittsburgh, and many others. Just what the future of these programs may be is difficult to predict. Most of them pay their own way, thus not being a drain on the regular university funds. Tuition and expenses range all the way from $450 for the shorter courses to $3,000 for one of the longer courses.[9] In time of depressed business these courses may encounter difficulty in securing enough students to keep going. If these courses can be judged by the answers of participants, most of them seem to be meeting a need.

**Company schools.** General Electric has a comprehensive program for executives rivaling in coverage the programs offered by universities. They have a separate faculty, college buildings, and all the requirements of a high-grade educational program. International Harvester, General Motors, Chrysler, Western Electric, and General Electric have regularly organized schools, a part of whose functions is the training of executives, especially on the lower levels. Some schools hold state charters. The General Electric and Chrysler schools are essentially graduate schools for young college graduates. These young men spend a part of their time in shopwork and attend classes after work, or, as in the case of the General Motors Institute of Technology, they work in the respective plants a certain number of weeks and attend school a certain number of weeks. The students are usually divided into two groups, one group working in the plants while the other is attending school. Although teaching the technical aspects of manufacturing, these schools usually lay more emphasis on the managerial problems than the regular engineering or commerce schools do.

**Coverage of the supervisory training programs conducted by industry.** Most of the in-service programs are designed for operating supervisors. Often they are given some choice of subjects that they think to be important to them in their work. It is very common to find the following topics included in the in-service training programs. These are listed without regard to any particular sequence.

[9] See National Industrial Conference Board, Inc., "Executive Development Courses in Universities," *Studies in Personnel Policy* 160, New York, rev., 1957.

1. The supervisor's place in the organization.
2. The supervisor's responsibilities.
3. The supervisor's analysis of his job.
4. The supervisor's responsibility for training his men.
5. Principles and practices of instructing on the job.
6. Techniques of influencing men.
7. The supervisor and the National Labor-Management Relations Act.
8. The supervisor and the Fair Labor Standards Act.
9. The supervisor as an interpreter of company labor relations policies.
10. The supervisor's relationship to the suggestion system.
11. The supervisor's relationship to safety.
12. The supervisor's responsibilities in wage and salary administration.
13. The supervisor's relationship to the time and motion study department.
14. Time and motion analysis (sometimes a complete course is given in this subject).
15. The supervisor's responsibility for the budget.
16. The supervisor's relationship to cost control.
17. Cost records and cost accounting.
18. Direct labor costs.
19. Indirect labor costs.
20. Direct material costs.
21. Indirect material costs.
22. The supervisor's responsibility for quality.
23. The function of the inspection department.
24. Production planning and control.
25. Absenteeism and tardiness.
26. The grievance procedure.
27. Morale and discipline.

These topics by no means exhaust the field covered by various executive training programs. One company spent an entire year studying various angles of department management, a second year on outlines of industrial economics, a third year on the history and development of industrial processes, and a fourth year on industrial management. The question as to whether or not printed material should be used in training programs is ever a live one. Practically all the professional agencies engaged in this work make use of printed material. Some companies prepare their own text material, which is developed to meet their own particular needs. The use of printed matter has the advantage of avoiding the omission or misinterpretation of policies and items covered and also serves as a manual for later reference. Whether or not formal printed matter is distributed prior to the executive training conferences, it is highly desirable to make minutes of these conferences and distribute them to the persons attending the conferences. The use of texts promotes uniformity of interpretation of a given topic and tends to aid in the retention of the conclusions.

**Basic decisions in supervisory and executive training programs.** Of course the first decision is whether or not to have a formal training program. A careful audit of supervisory personnel nearly always indicates the need for a training program in companies of 300 or more employees. On the assumption that an organized training program is felt to be needed the following questions need to be answered: (1) Shall the training be held on company time or the employees' time, and how often shall the conferences be held? (2) Shall men of different executive levels be included in the same training conference? (3) How many men shall be included in one group conference? (4) How can the effectiveness of the training program be measured? (5) How can the cost of the training program be computed?

To hold the training conferences on company time where operating conditions permit is nearly a standard practice. Such a practice gives added emphasis to the training and does not appear to be a frill tacked on to see if it works. In some of the smaller organizations, it is always possible to hold these conferences during working hours. In case the conferences are held after work or on Saturday mornings in the event of a 5-day week, the problem of overtime pay arises for those employees who come under the Fair Labor Standards Act and who have worked more than the allowed time per day or week. All these questions have to be settled in terms of the basic policies of the company and in keeping with statutory regulations. Some conferences are held once a month. This seems to be too infrequent. Weekly conferences are more systematic and tend to get and hold the interest of the executives more readily. Conferences are frequently suspended during the week between Christmas and New Year's Day, as well as during the warm summer months, when vacations are being taken. A few companies take middle management and senior executives to some resort for a 3- to 5-day training conference, thus to get entirely away from the work situation and devote all their efforts to the consideration of the problems to be discussed.

Mixing of supervisory and executive personnel of various levels is a continuing question with advocates and critics. An argument against the mixing of men of different levels is the fear that the minor executives will hesitate to express themselves freely in the presence of their superiors. The other side to this question is the fact that some executives hesitate to compete with many of their subordinates in fields not directly related to their specialties. Each of these views has merit; however, the extent to which either one of them is controlling depends largely upon the open-mindedness of the executives. In one case the plant manager, drawing $25,000 per year, sat alongside one of his inspectors whose salary was $4,500. The plant manager was an excellent man even though he had only an eighth-grade formal training, whereas the particular inspector was a college graduate. Both men entered freely into the discussions with mutual benefit. The plant manager sat in on each of the six conferences held weekly in his plant and frequently expressed the opinion that it was time well spent, since it gave him an excellent opportunity to be known by his men and to know them. Other organizations have striven to group their men according to executive levels and found such an arrangement satisfactory. Still other organizations have gone so far as to group men not only according to executive levels but according to related divisions of work. It is not the formal organization of the training program but the effectiveness of the leadership that counts in the long run.

The size of the training conference depends in part on the skill of the conference leader, the physical facilities, and the philosophy of management. The method used in the training group largely determines the size. For lectures, motion pictures, and to a limited extent demonstrations, the group may vary from 10 to hundreds. For the conference, it is desirable to have 10 to 20 and under special conditions as many as 30. The conference group should not be so large that each member is unable to participate freely in the discussions.

The case method of group instructing in executive conferences has grown in popularity over the years. In the hands of a skilled leader it is an excellent device for adult training. Practically every known method of training that can be applied to the training of supervisors or executives is used. The conference technique is the most popular where executives are being trained in groups. Relatively few of the so-called conference procedures are used in the pure form. Most frequently the conference technique is combined with the lecture, demonstration, or even the question type of discussion. In other words the method is modified to fit the situation. The method itself is not so important as the acceptance by the participants. Frequently a group will request a modification of a procedure that is being used.

There are so many intangibles that it is extremely difficult to measure the results of supervisory and executive training.[10] If an audit of executive personnel shows that there is an adequate supply of trained persons for all executive and supervisory needs, at least one phase of

[10] See American Management Association, "The Research Approach to Training" *Personnel Series* 117, by William McGee, for a challenge to training directors; see also a more recent article by the same author, "Are We Using What We Know about Training-Learning Theory and Training?" *Personnel Psychology,* Spring, 1958, pp. 1–12.

the objective of training has been met. The status of the executive group before and after the training gives some clue to its effectiveness. The number of labor grievances before and after the program has been well under way is a partial measure. Employee morale as measured by one of the many techniques is another measure. Suggestions for improvements of processes and procedures may offer another index. Performance as measured by the attainment of budgetary standards is another measure. None of these indexes is conclusive in itself; yet each will shed some light upon the effectiveness of the program.

A few of the measurable costs of executive training may be determined by computing the total cost of the time of the men spent in training conferences. Add to this the cost of the time of the supervisor and others actively engaged in the training program, and the salary costs may be determined. The costs of mimeographing minutes and text materials and the cost of the room or buildings used for training purposes are readily determined. It is well to compute the costs of the training program from time to time, not so much for the purpose of eliminating the activity, but primarily as a check against the effectiveness of the program. As with industrial research, the question is often not whether a given enterprise can afford the costs but whether it can afford not to have such a program.

CHAPTER 21

# Employee Representation and Collective Bargaining

**Employee representation.** The need for employee representation is seldom felt in the small company, where the face-to-face contacts with top management are a reality. When the enterprise is large, however, the lines of communication are complicated, sometimes obstructed, and indirect. The larger the enterprise, the more difficult it becomes to maintain personal contacts. Misunderstandings lead to industrial disputes that result in great social and economic waste. Employee-representation plans are designed to bring the employer and his men closer together for the benefit of both. To the extent that this is accomplished, such a program *actually pays*. It should be frankly admitted that ulterior motives may be behind some such plans on the part of either the employer or the employees. It is possible for the employer and his employees mutually to agree to an action that is not for the public good. It is important to realize that a poor plan operated with intelligent sincerity has better chances of success than a good plan in which sincerity and right intentions are lacking. "Employee representation" as used in this chapter includes the committee form of representation, the industrial-democracy type of representation, the company union, the independent nonaffiliated union as well as the union affiliated with one of the federations such as the AFL or the CIO, multiple management, or any other method of representing the collective will of the employees.

**Background of the representation movement.** Formal unionism appeared in the United States during the early 1800's. The less formal types of employee representation were developments of the latter part of the nineteenth century in the United States. Works (Whitley) councils appeared in England during the early part of the twentieth century. These councils enjoyed a phenomenal growth during World War I, when the organized trade unions did not seem capable of meeting the rapidly changing conditions. In the United States, the Filene Cooperative Association of 1898 had certain characteristics of an employee-representation plan. In 1904, the American Rolling Mill Company formulated its plan for employee representation. In 1911, the highly publicized Hart, Schaffner and Marx plan of employee-employer representation was inaugurated. The Philadelphia Rapid Transit Company started its program in 1910. The International Harvester Company's plan was approved by its employees by a secret ballot in 1919. Not all these well-known plans were alike. Some of them, like the Hart, Schaffner and Marx plan, provided machinery for collective effort between the employer on the one hand and an organized trade union on the other. In the case of the International Harvester Company, the program was organized entirely within the framework of the corporation and was between the company and its employees without the intermediary of an outside organization. Each plan strove to bring about a mutual understanding and respect between the management and the workers.

During World War I the Federal government created a number of organizations whose major functions were to facilitate cooperation between management and workers. With patriotic fervor, management and men learned to cooperate in a way that neither was accustomed to prior to this time. A few of the commissions or boards that were thus created were the National War Labor Board, the U.S. Railroad Administration, and the Emergency Fleet Corporation. The program of employee-employer cooperation grew during World War I, but even greater growth took place during the years immediately following the war. Independent unionism, which according to our definition may be included in employee representation, reached a peak in 1920 and declined until the 1930's. Paralleling the growth of independent unionism was the growth of representation plans confined to the employer and his workers. World War I had given *scientific management* its golden opportunity. Scientific management as one of its *primary fundamentals of organization* has *due regard for the personal equation.*[1] Both men and management had learned from their war experiences that cooperation pays.

**Works councils.** Works councils have been supplanted by other forms of representation today. They have only a historical interest in this chapter. The fundamentals of the works-council plan provided for representatives of employees and representatives of the employer to sit as a committee to consider items of interest primarily of a person-

[1] See Richard Lansburgh and William R. Spriegel, *Industrial Management,* John Wiley & Sons, Inc., New York, 1955, p. 4.6.

nel nature. In the case of large organizations, there were departmental or divisional councils to handle items of interest to these divisions and plant councils to handle items of plant-wide interest. Companies having more than one plant occasionally had a joint company council to represent the joint company-wide interest of employees and management. Since the basic concept behind the works council was cooperation, most of the items of interest to employees were confined either to their division or to their plant and did not in general extend to plants located at a distance from their home plants. In the case of voting, the works council quite generally had the representatives of management and the representatives of the workers vote separately, but in the same room as a part of the committee. A majority of each group would decide the vote of that group. Usually, the works council was composed of an equal number of representatives from both management and workers.

**Industrial-democracy type of employee representation.** In the industrial-democracy type of employee representation, there usually was a lower house, or *house of representatives,* made up of delegates selected by the workers, an upper house, or *senate,* composed of supervisors such as foremen, and the *cabinet,* composed of representatives of the top management. A proposal usually could originate in either house and after being approved by both houses was submitted to the cabinet for final approval or veto. The cabinet could refer the proposal back to both houses with recommended changes. Since the representatives of workers and management did not meet together, the industrial-democracy type had the disadvantage of lacking the personal contacts that frequently were more productive of mutual understanding than the representation itself. This form of representation has disappeared from industry.

**The company union.** The National Industrial Recovery Act (NIRA) of 1933 encouraged employees to select their own representatives to bargain with management. Section 7(a) of this act gave all efforts toward employee representation a boost. In many cases management gave encouragement to the organization of a union of its own employees in an independent union. The term *company union* has now quite generally come to mean an independent union of the workers, whose membership is limited to workers of a particular company. With the Supreme Court's approval of the National Labor Relations Act of 1937, company unions have definitely taken the form of employees' organizations established for and by the employees without company aid or dominance. A company union is a form of employee representation, but many forms of employee representation are not company unions. Several of the large oil companies have company unions. One of the authors has arbitrated a labor case for one of these unions. It presented its case with as much care and force as the unions of the federations in whose cases he has participated. Independent company unions that meet the requirements of the National Labor-Management Relations Act have made a creditable showing.[2] When viewed from an impartial standpoint, it would seem that there is no special reason why the independent company union should not continue to develop side by side with the so-called outside, or independent, unions. The independent union does not, as a rule, have the highly professional leadership that the AFL-CIO can provide in times of stress.

**The basis of successful employee-employer relationships through a formalized program.** Any plan that evolves from a feeling of need for a formal structure to represent the employees to management has the essential ingredients of success from the employee's standpoint. In other words, if most of the employees really want representation, they are likely to give to the organization established, the loyalty that is needed to make it a success. Such an organization will usually grow and facilitate industrial peace if dealt with intelligently by the employer. An organization forced upon a group of employees either by the employer or by an outside agency is not likely to command the loyalty of its membership or fill a real need in their lives. Enlightened cooperation and leadership are just as essential on the part of management in dealing with an independent union as in the case of no representation plan whatever. Employers frequently complain about the type of labor leader with whom they must deal. As a matter of practical fact, they usually get the type of labor leadership that they themselves help train. If the employer's attitude is one of antagonism, he will usually be faced with a belligerent labor leader, since this will be the only type who can compete with him. (This statement will not be true if the group or leaders are communistic.) On the other hand, if the employer recognizes the right of his employees to be represented by men of their own choice, he will usually find that the employees select intelligent leaders. Of course a given employer may be caught in a vicious circle. This fact has been well illustrated by the hearings of the McClelland Committee revealing labor racketeering. The foregoing does not mean that the employer must take the demands of

[2] See John Collins, "Independent Unions—Three Years After," *Personnel*, May, 1940, pp. 189–190.

labor organizers lying down.[3] He should have a sound economic and social philosophy and stand squarely upon it, having due regard for the rights of others. Suspicion on the part of either the employer or the representatives of the employees tends to breed suspicion in the other. Trust and respect tend to command trust and respect. There is no one formula for industrial peace, but whatever formula is used must have as its basis sincerity and a desire to seek an equitable solution.

**Trade agreements.** The sentiment of the people in the United States is by no means uniform in relation to the social desirability of trade agreements on such a large scale as that in the coal industry and more recently in the steel industry. Collective bargaining on such a large scale definitely places the public at a disadvantage when the union decides to exercise its monopolistic power to shut practically all the mines or steel mills down at once. Of course, management could also decide to shut the operations down at once, but they never have done it and are unlikely ever to do so. The public simply would not stand for such a thing. This same public has become alarmed at the excesses of big unions, but it hesitates to take the necessary action to prevent them. It is not an easy matter to prevent the paralyzing effect of such large-scale strikes as that in coal and steel without hampering the effectiveness of unions in other situations that are less critical. Besides management is by no means uniformly opposed to multiemployer bargaining. Within limits certain employers believe firmly in multiemployer bargaining. As yet no device has been brought forward that would protect the interests of workers, management, and the public. Trade agreements can seldom be consummated unless employers as a group are banded together in a strong association and the employees of the particular industry are well organized. City-wide agreements are more common than regional ones. These are particularly prevalent in the building trades and related industries. Trade agreements as a rule cover every phase of industrial relations, such as wages, working hours and overtime, working conditions, seniority rights, vacations, procedures to be followed in the adjustment of grievances or in interpreting the agreement, etc.

Unless the agreement covers a substantial portion of the industry involved, the trade agreement is in substance little, if any, more effective than individual agreements with the respective employers. Trade agreements tend to stabilize those phases of an industry which

[3] See A. A. Imberman, "Labor Leaders and Society," *Harvard Business Review*, Vol. 28, No. 1, January, 1950, pp. 52–60; also Harold Stevens, "How Unions Are Run," *Personnel Journal*, Vol. 12, No. 8, January, 1950, pp. 279–284.

pertain to labor relations. Minimum standards are desirable in labor relations just as in processes and materials. An individual employer is not prohibited by the trade agreement from having standards for his employees that are more advantageous to his employees than those specified by the agreement. The standards established by the trade agreement tend to be the established practice, and there is little incentive to go beyond them, particularly if the employer is a party to the agreement. Trade agreements in the United States usually are on a regional or city-wide basis. The anthracite coal industry is covered by one trade agreement. Bituminous mining was for years covered by regional trade agreements; however, collective bargaining has for many years been conducted on a nationwide basis. The Full-fashioned Hosiery Manufacturers of America, Inc., and the American Federation of Hosiery Workers have negotiated trade agreements covering a major portion of the northern section of the Atlantic coast. The trade agreement is especially advantageous from the union viewpoint and to a lesser degree from the employer's viewpoint when there are a large number of employers involved. The total number of employees covered is not particularly important. If all the workers in the needle trades are covered by a trade agreement in a given city, they may be fewer in number than the workers covered by one contract signed by one of the large automobile or steel corporations. In the needle trades, as an illustration, there may be hundreds of small enterprises, which create a real administrative problem if individual agreements are to be negotiated. In the case of the automobile or steel industries, individual agreements do not present such a serious administrative problem.

Even though employers have long had their trade associations, few of them are empowered to sign trade agreements for their members. It is not unusual for a separate association to be formed for the specific purpose when it is agreed among employers that they will enter into collective trade agreements. The traditional employers' association is a rather loose organization with relatively few powers.

**Vocabulary used in collective bargaining.** Some of the terms used in collective bargaining have been defined by statute.

 ## COLLECTIVE BARGAINING

Collective bargaining as defined by Title I, Section 101, Subsection 6(*d*) of the National Labor Relations Act:

. . . is the performance of the mutual obligation of the employer and the representative of the employees to meet at reasonable times and confer in good faith with respect to wages, hours, and other terms and conditions of employment, or the negotiation of an agreement, or any question arising thereunder, and the execution of a written contract incorporating any agreement reached if requested by either party, but such obligation does not compel either party to agree to a proposal or require the making of a concession: . . .

This definition includes the adjusting of grievances arising under a contract. The essence of collective bargaining as here defined is the exercise of good faith in striving to reach a solution to the problems under consideration. There are at least three different situations in which collective bargaining may take place, namely, (1) when the union is first recognized and negotiates for the first time; (2) when an old contract is about to expire, has expired, or it is desired to amend it when it still has a substantial time to run; and (3) when it is necessary to adjust grievances or to resolve disagreements concerning the interpretation of a contract. In negotiating a contract the company should be represented by an executive clothed with authority to act within broad areas of managerial discretion, including the right to sign a contract. This, of course, does not mean that he cannot consult his associates or superiors on matters of basic policy. He should be a man of executive rank. From an organizational standpoint the president or an executive vice-president would be the desirable company representative provided that he had the time and the necessary background and temperament for the bargaining table. As a matter of practical necessity in the large multiplant companies, it is impossible for men of either of these ranks to handle such matters if separate contracts are negotiated. This is true even though they may have to pass on the basic policies involved. In such cases a representative of top management, such as the director of industrial relations or a specialist in labor relations either in the industrial relations department or answering to a vice-president, may do the negotiating.

*Union security* refers to the status of the union in relation to whether or not all employees must belong to a union to get a job, must join the union within a specified time after being hired as a condition of continued employment, must retain this membership in the union if they are members at the date of signing the contract or must continue their membership (if they join after the signing of the contract) for the life of the contract, or may join or not join or withdraw from the union at will. The "checkoff" of union dues by the employer is sometimes included in the concept of union security.

The *closed shop* refers to the union relationship in which the employer agrees not to hire anyone who is not a member of the recognized union. Some unions do not like the use of the term *closed shop* but prefer *union shop*. There is a real difference between the two. In the case of the closed shop the union must first accept the applicant, or else he cannot be hired. In such cases the worker is dependent upon the union for the opportunity to get the job. In the case of a union shop the employer may hire whomsoever he desires, but the new employee is required to join the union within a given period of time, such as 30, 60, or 90 days. Prior to the Taft-Hartley Act the union could refuse to accept the worker, in which event the employer would have to discharge him. The union seldom ever exercised this right, but it was usually alert to see that he did join within the appointed time. The union did occasionally expel a man from the union as a matter of union discipline, in which event the employer was required to discharge the employee. Under the Taft-Hartley Act the employer in a union shop is not required to discharge a man who tries to join the union and is rejected or who is expelled from the union for any reason other than for a failure to pay the regular dues and assessments to which all other members are subject. Under the 1951 revision of the Taft-Hartley Act a union shop may be established through negotiations between the management and union without the prior election required by the original act. The closed shop is prohibited by the Taft-Hartley Act.

*Open shop* refers to the situation where the union is recognized as the spokesman for its members but not for all employees unless it has been so certified by the National Labor Relations Board. (It should be remembered that management may recognize a union without NLRB certification.) *Open shop* may also apply to a company where the union represents all the employees but management may hire anyone it wants to hire and the new employee is not compelled to join the union, neither is a union member compelled to remain a member. A *preferential shop* is a union-management agreement wherein management stipulates that preference will be given to union members in hiring new employees. In some cases the newly hired non-union man is required to join the union within a specified period. A *preferential shop* may exist without the compulsory feature but it seldom does.

The *maintenance-of-membership* clause came into popular use under the orders of the National War Labor Board during World War II. In substance the maintenance-of-membership provision requires any employee who was a member of the union at the time of the signing of a contract or who became a member of the union during the life of the contract to remain a member of the union in good standing as long as the contract continues in force. The NWLB included in most of its cases after it got under way an "escape clause," which permitted an employee to withdraw from the union in case he desired to do so within a specified period, such as 15 days, after the signing of the contract or some other date similar to or near the date of the contract. It is interesting to note that relatively few employees exercised the right to withdraw. The *agency shop,* or *dues shop,* is one in which all the employees must either join the union or pay dues to the union to represent them even though they may not be required to join the union. The argument advanced for this type of shop in case an individual does not want to join the union is that since he gets the benefits secured by the union he should pay his proportionate share of the costs. This type of shop is rare. A probationary period before having to pay dues could be served just as is usually true in the case of the union shop. The *checkoff* in a union contract provides that the employer will deduct from the employee's pay check the union dues and pay them to the union. This, of course, relieves the union of the necessity of collecting dues. Under the Taft-Hartley Act the checkoff is illegal unless the individual worker authorizes it. His authorization cannot last beyond the period of 1 year, but it may be renewed for each 12-month period.

**The collective bargaining procedure.** The actual negotiating of a contract is or should be merely a friendly discussion between businessmen who are honestly trying to work out a solution to a mutual problem. Management should proceed on this basis even though some union representatives may not. Management should check its proposals and agreements against sound principles yet should not become petty. When an agreement has been reached, great care should be exercised to reduce the exact intent to writing. It is so easy to agree upon one thing and to have an entirely different situation presented later, with the claim that it is covered by the contract. In negotiating the first contract the union representative should be treated as an equal even though his actions may have been obnoxious during the organizing campaign. The union nearly always makes more demands than it expects to have granted. Management should make counterproposals and tell why it rejects the union demands. In the case of the negotiating of a new contract to replace an old one, management should come to the bargaining table thoroughly prepared with such items as:

1. Recommendations of the foremen as to certain clauses that have been a source of trouble.
2. Statistical data on grievances and their sources as far as the contract is concerned.
3. Rates in the company and community.
4. A clear understanding of job evaluation as used in the company.

Management should be represented by an executive trained in the legal requirements of collective bargaining and skilled in the bargaining process itself. The representative should:

1. Possess an open mind in relation to union-management relationships.
2. Accept the principle of collective bargaining as laid down by the Labor-Management Relations Act and court decisions.
3. Understand group psychology, particularly as it applies to the union leaders with whom he is dealing.
4. Be absolutely honest personally and act as if he expected others to be likewise.
5. Not seek temporary advantage.
6. Say "no" when the facts of a situation require it and "yes" when it is in order. In dealing with certain union negotiatiors who are inclined to "horse-trade," management may have to hold back on certain approvals it would like to make in order to meet the peculiarities of such an individual. Such a situation is unfortunate, but nevertheless at times it occurs.
7. Possess the ability to appraise a situation, to sense that a meeting of minds is imminent, and to reduce this to writing in clear, unmistakable language.
8. Be thoroughly informed regarding the law and court decisions under the law.

**Contract provisions.** The union management contract is the most important document that sets forth the responsibilities and rights of the management, union, and employees. In some situations where the union and management recognize their responsibilities for the success of the enterprise the union contract might be thought of as the bill of rights of management-employee relationships. Great care should be exercised in reducing the exact terms of the agreement to writing. When a dispute is submitted to an arbitrator, he can resolve it only in terms of what the contract says, not what may have been intended but not included in the contract. It is not necessary to resort to stilted legal terminology to include the exact terms of an agreement in the contract. It is common practice for the contract to be headed by the names of the company and the union, respectively. This is frequently followed by a statement covering *recognition*, detailing the employees covered by the contract. This section often includes a statement in which the company agrees not to interfere with, restrain, or coerce employees because of their membership or lawful activities in the union, and the union agrees not to coerce or intimidate employees in their right to work or in respect to union activity or membership. Under the Taft-Hartley Act either of these activities would be an unfair labor practice. At times contracts may include definitions of terms used. Under the statement of recognition in recent years there has usually appeared a statement that the union is recognized as the sole bargaining agency of the employees covered.

After the preliminaries the contract usually covers the details of the agreement, including such items as:

1. Wages—system used for payment, escalator clauses, shift differentials, "call-in pay," pay for waiting time, deductions for poor work, and pay for an employee temporarily transferred.

2. Hours of work—starting and finishing, meals and rest periods, cleanup time, and similar activities.

3. Overtime—equal distribution of, seasonal tolerances if agreed to under the Fair Labor Standards Act, meals when working over a certain length of time, etc.

4. Vacations—basis for granting, time allowed, and pay for same.

5. Time studies and standards of output.

6. Provisions for pay for Sundays and holidays.

7. Leaves—for union officers, sick, maternity, to attend school, and for other reasonable purposes.

8. Seniority and merit rating.

9. Layoffs and recalls.

10. Promotion, demotion, transfer, and discharge.

11. Grievance procedures.

12. Arbitration.

13. Strikes and lockouts.

14. Safety and health.

15. Profit sharing or any other financial arrangement such as pensions and insurance.

**Adjusting grievances.** Different unions and companies establish different procedures for handling grievances. Sound personnel management avoids amending a union contract through the grievance procedure. In some cases the grievance procedure is used only to cover items that are included in the contract. In the main it is desirable to have the employee first try to adjust the grievance with his immediate superior with or without the assistance of a representative of the union. This first contact may be informal. In case the problem is not settled on an informal basis, it should be reduced to writing and submitted to the immediate supervisor for his answer. If the written answer is not satisfactory and the union thinks that the employee's case merits being pressed, it is usually taken to a next higher line officer, such as the division superintendent. At each stage in the procedure usually there is set forth a time limit within which answers must be given in writing. Should the division superintendent's answer be the same as the foreman's, the next step in the procedure may be to one of the following:

1. The general superintendent.

2. The director of industrial relations.

3. The factory manager.

4. The president.

In case the union does not agree with the decision given by the last step in the grievance procedure, the final step may be to go to arbitration or, in the case of some large companies, to an impartial permanent referee whose decision is final and binding on both parties.

**Arbitration.** Arbitration is the process of submitting a disagreement or grievance to a third person or to a committee for a decision. In case a committee is used, the two parties usually name a representative to the committee. The two representatives frequently name the third member of the committee, who is supposed to be impartial. The National Arbitration Association has a list of approved arbitrators for practically every part of the United States. The arbitration process is not confined to labor matters. It may be used in settling the disagreement over the interpretation of any type of commercial dispute. Nations and states have used arbitration in resolving disagreements. The third party or committee hears the claims of each party, tries to determine the facts, and renders a decision that is binding on both parties. It is not a sound managerial procedure to arbitrate most items unless they definitely come under the terms of the contract. For instance, assume that there is a prolonged disagreement over some basic issue in negotiating a contract, such as a union shop: to submit this to arbitration merely means that collective bargaining has been abandoned in favor of a third party. On the other hand, assume that the contract provides that promotion shall be on the basis of merit, with seniority controlling when merit is the same. Unless the contract specifically states that management is to be the sole judge of merit through its organized merit rating system, there may arise a grievance claiming that the wrong man has been given the promotion. Such a case may logically be referred to an impartial referee, umpire, or arbitrator. Frequently, the contract provision setting up the arbitration procedure specifies the types of items that are *arbitrable*, usually stating that they are confined to interpretations of cases arising under the terms of the contract. In actually submitting a case to arbitration, unless this is a part of a continuing program of using an impartial referee, both the union and management should agree in detail just what is the issue that is submitted. This is a safeguard against an arbitrator's going far afield in his decision to write in his personal managerial philosophy, which is not the question at issue.

There may be an exception to the recommendation above about not submitting any part of a contract to arbitration in the case of a prolonged strike in a critical industry like steel, coal, or transportation. It may, at times, be economically and socially desirable to submit certain items, like work rules involving feather bedding, to arbitration.

It is well to have arbitration as a final step in case of a failure to agree in the grievance procedure in spite of the problems involved. The contract should specify exactly how the arbitrator is to be selected. Frequently management names one arbitrator, the union names one, and the two select the third one. This process tends to protect the interests of both parties. Naturally the expense of a three-man arbitration panel is greater than that of a one-man arbitrator.

Some arbitrators think that their decisions should strive to please both parties to a dispute rather than being based on the facts of the case as measured against the written contract (when there is one). Compromise has a place in conciliation, but conciliation is quite a different matter from arbitration. In the case of conciliation the third party is trying to find a common ground on which the two can agree. It is not a judicial process. Arbitration is a judicial process even though the formal rules of evidence may not be used.

**Collective bargaining and the personnel division.** Opinions differ among management men regarding the role to be played by the personnel department in collective bargaining. In some instances, personnel managers take an active part in negotiating labor agreements. In a few cases, these personnel men actually negotiate the agreements. Other personnel men are of the opinion that a personnel director should not participate in the negotiating of a union agreement; that operating management is largely responsible for carrying out the details of a union agreement and so they should be solely responsible for the details, with the personnel director rendering advice as to principles but not taking an active part in the actual agreement; that the personnel manager's responsibility is to aid in the carrying out of the signed agreement along with his other personnel responsibilities but that his effectiveness in this relationship is impaired if biased by being a party to the agreement itself. It is highly probable that the organizational philosophy of the particular enterprise will largely determine the exact role to be played by the director of personnel in collective bargaining.

In large multiplant companies someone other than the top executive, of necessity, has to negotiate union agreements. In such cases a special representative performs this task. His organizational assignment may be in the industrial relations or personnel administration department, or it may be directly under a top management operating executive. If it is in the personnel department, it usually is a separate function not directly related to the other personnel functions. The department handling union relationships as a unit in the personnel division is often called the *labor relations department* or the *industrial relations department.* An extreme viewpoint held by a few employers is that there is no place for a personnel director or a personnel department in union-management cooperation. One large Chicago manufacturer says that the union looks after all matters that commonly come under the jurisdiction of the personnel division. This company does not even have an employment officer. When a department needs a man, the department head makes out a requisition that is signed by the plant superintendent. The requisition is either mailed or telephoned to the union or given to the shop steward. The union provides the man, and the payroll department makes out all employment records.

CHAPTER 22

# The Labor Movement

**Early efforts at union organization.** The first local craft union in the United States was organized by the Philadelphia shoemakers in 1792. It disbanded in less than a year.[1] During the 1790's carpenters, printers, shoemakers, coopers, and tailors in their respective crafts banded together to exert group pressure to attain their objectives. These early efforts were local in character and did not exert a very strong influence, but they did lay a groundwork or pattern for more successful activities later. The New York Society of Journeymen's Shipwrights was incorporated in 1803. Out of the carpenters' strike in Philadelphia in 1827 for a 10-hr. day there grew a Central City Union. This organization tried its hand at politics but did not secure an appreciable following. The General Trades' Union of the City of New York was founded about 1833. Some 21 groups attended its first annual convention. This group struggled along for a few years and disappeared. Printers formed their National Typographical Union in 1852. A national convention had previously been held in 1850. This union became an international union in 1869. The Journeymen Stonecutters' Union of North America (1853), the National Trade Association of Hatfinishers (1854), and the Iron Molders' Union of North America (1859) were other unions that emerged prior to the Civil War.

**The labor movement after the Civil War.** Rapid cost-of-living increases tend to cause workers to seek collective action for higher wages. During all our major conflicts prices have risen rapidly. These high prices have continued for a time following each war. (This statement is true even though there was a prolonged depression period beginning a few years after the Civil War.) Some of the early union movements were tinged with a strong flavor of socialism. The National

---

[1] See U.S. Department of Labor, "Brief History of the American Labor Movement," *Bulletin* 1000, 1957, pp. 65–85, for a listing of important dates and events in the labor movement.

Labor Union (1866) sponsored many cooperative societies of skilled workers in which they owned and operated their own plants. These did not successfully compete with existing establishments. In addition to the interest in the cooperative movement, the National Labor Union promoted the 8-hr. day, advocated the exclusion of Chinese laborers, and sought the establishment of a department or bureau of labor in Washington. The influence of the National Labor Union had practically ceased by 1872. The Noble Order of the Knights of Labor was organized in 1871. This union sought to serve its members through cooperative efforts in both production and selling. In the early days, the Noble Order of the Knights of Labor was primarily a secret organization; later the secret phase was largely abandoned. At one time (1886) there were somewhat more than 700,000 members. The group sponsored strikes and was active in political affairs, although the public attitude was not sympathetic to a union's mixing in politics. The Noble Order of the Knights of Labor declined rapidly with the rise of the craft unions, particularly under the leadership of the American Federation of Labor (AFL).

The Industrial Workers of the World (IWW) evolved with the decline of the Noble Order of the Knights of Labor and the rise of the AFL. The Socialist Trade and Labor Alliance came into existence in 1895 and was supported by the Socialist Labor party. The Western Labor Union (1898) emerged from the Socialist Trade and Labor Alliance. This gave way to the American Labor Union (1902). In 1905 the IWW took up the left-of-center movement and openly advocated the principle of direct action to gain its ends, as well as political action. Its approach and philosophy were known as *revolutionary syndicalism*. The IWW was composed of many elements. Some of its members were by no means extremists but persons who advocated industrial unionism in opposition to the craft union. Others were extreme Socialists who strove to develop a deep-seated class consciousness. Many of the leaders of the IWW placed their ideology above the national war effort of World War I. (This was duplicated in World War II by the Communists.) It is interesting to note that some of the people who had frequented the halls of the IWW became the militant organizers of the 1930's and promoted such radical activities as the sit-down strike. This does not mean that the union upswing of the 1930's was merely a revival of the IWW. It merely refers to a continuing left-wing movement, small though it is, which has beset the best efforts of the genuine friends of labor.

**A shift in labor's emphasis.** The extreme radical activities of a few unions led to legislation in the Taft-Hartley Act (discussed in detail in Chap. 32) to require unions seeking the protection of the act to file certain reports with the Federal government and to establish standards for their officers that they should not have been members of the Communist party nor have served a prison term for the previous 5 years. This provision in the act is not directed at any law-abiding labor leader. It is designed to give the workers the facts regarding persons who offer themselves as their leaders. A genuine Communist would gladly swear to a lie if it would promote his cause, but he hesitates to do so when the Federal report is involved for fear of the results, as Browder and others learned to their regret. The labor movement is by no means a single movement. Aside from certain radical left-wingers and the great mass of "middle-of-the-roaders" and conservatives, there are strong camps, the AFL-CIO, as well as the railway brotherhoods, several large unaffiliated unions, the United Mine Workers and the Teamsters,[2] and hundreds of independent unions, some of which represent large companies.

**The American Federation of Labor (AFL).** The AFL has been the staunch advocate of craft unions.[3] The craft union provides economic strength as well as social values that are frequently as important as the economic ones. Since the skilled workers were usually better paid than the less skilled, they seldom were interested in political reforms that led to state ownership of the means of production. Another thing that bothers the craftsman even today is the fact that he practically loses his influence in the councils of the industrial union, since he is so outnumbered by the unskilled or semiskilled workers. There are

---

[2] Some of these large unions have been in and out of one or more of the large federations. Some persons lament the fact that there is not a single labor movement in the United States, and others see in multiunionism a healthy sign of experimentation and growth. There is no question but that the factional fights have resulted in both a social and an economic loss to society. On the other hand, both the AFL and the CIO before their merger, as well as the other groups, have made contributions to the union movement. Certainly the railway brotherhoods have been as stalwart advocates of collective bargaining and some of the other commonly supported union objectives as the large federations.

[3] The terms *craft unions* and *industrial unions* are used so freely in the newspapers that it may seem unnecessary to define them. The craft union is a union composed of members of one skill, such as carpenters, painters, brickmasons, tool- and diemakers, and machinists. The term trade union is frequently used interchangeably with craft union and at other times to indicate a group of craft unions such as the Painters and Decorators Union. It is not unusual to hear the term trade union used to refer to any union. This is probably a misuse of the term when referring to industrial unions. An industrial union is a union that includes all or most of the workers of a given company or industry. For instance, if the salespeople, delivery people, maintenance workers, and possibly office clerks in a department store were organized into one union, it would be known as an industrial, or vertical, union. The same would be true if all the employees in any manufacturing plant or utility belonged to one union.

some skilled workers outside the fold of the AFL, notably the railway brotherhoods. Nevertheless the AFL has been and continues to be the home of most of the craft unions. The AFL has had some industrial unions, such as the United Mine Workers, which has been in and out of the ranks of the AFL at least twice.[4] Samuel Gompers, the father of the AFL, was a delegate from the Cigar Makers Union of New York City to the convention in Pittsburgh in November, 1881. At this meeting the Federation of Trades and Labor Unions of the United States was formed. This group called another conference in Columbus in December, 1886. From this convention emerged the AFL, with Samuel Gompers as its first president. From the beginning the AFL was an international union, including Canada within its jurisdiction. The AFL was a relatively loose federation of national unions. It does have certain unions that answer directly to the officers of the federation. The Federation of Government Employees was one of the most important of these unions.[5] As a whole the AFL had a long and distinguished record. Along with other groups and persons, it supported many improvements in social, economic, and government relationships. Gompers believed firmly in keeping his union out of party politics. He was definitely an economic unionist, not one who turned to political parties for preferment. He would support either a Democrat or a Republican if he thought that the candidate would work for the interests of organized labor. His philosophy was "Reward your friends, and punish your enemies." One of the most difficult problems faced by the AFL has been the conflicting claims of different unions for the workers in a given occupation. This is commonly known as a "jurisdictional dispute." The new AFL-CIO federation has a committee striving to resolve jurisdictional disputes between industrial unions and craft unions. The AFL group is still working on this difficult problem.

**The Congress of Industrial Organizations (CIO).** The CIO (Committee for Industrial Organization) was formed by a group of eight union leaders in Washington, D.C., in November, 1935. This meeting was largely an outgrowth of a disagreement in the 1935 AFL convention, in which certain aggressive leaders contended that the AFL was not taking full advantage of the opportunities provided in the NIRA of 1933. The objective of the original committee was not to form a competing federation but to organize the mass-production in-

[4] John L. Lewis took his mineworkers out of the AFL for a second time in December, 1947.

[5] We are using the past tense in referring to the AFL as a separate entity because of the recent AFL-CIO merger. In spite of the merger many persons and union members of AFL unions still think of the AFL as a going entity.

dustries into industrial unions within the fold of the AFL. The executive council of the AFL recommended that the CIO be dissolved on the basis that its efforts represented a move in the direction of dual unionism and was contrary to the decision made at the preceding annual convention of the AFL at Atlantic City. The members of the CIO ignored the request and promoted a vigorous organizing campaign. Accordingly the executive council of the AFL suspended the members of the CIO in September, 1936. The AFL then inaugurated an active organizing campaign in the mass-production industries not as yet organized, as well as in many instances ones already organized by the CIO. It was commonplace for both the CIO and the AFL to be on the same ballot in an election sponsored by the NLRB. General Motors, Chrysler, and Ford, as well as U.S. Steel, eventually signed contracts with the CIO. These large corporations, plus the large membership in the original unions that comprised the CIO, gave the new organization great confidence in itself and seemed to guarantee its future. The frictions were not solely the result of different ideologies with respect to the directions in which the union movement should go. They were in part the inevitable result of the clashes between strong personalities striving for leadership. John L. Lewis was one of the moving spirits in the original CIO. Later he withdrew from the CIO and played a lone hand for a season. Finally he rejoined the ranks of the AFL. Again in 1947 he left the fold of the AFL.

The CIO made phenomenal strides from its inception until its constitutional convention in Pittsburgh in November, 1938. There were some 42 unions active under the general leadership of the then CIO. At this convention the name of the organization was changed to the Congress of Industrial Organizations. The CIO was a militant organizing group. By the nature of most of its unions there have been fewer jurisdictional strikes than in the AFL. This, of course, did not prohibit one CIO union from trying to raid the ranks of another industrial or craft union. The CIO almost from the beginning has taken an active part in matters political. The election of 1952 certainly did not show the power of both the AFL and the CIO to deliver a labor vote. Union strength in 1958 was weak; its influence in 1960 may have been greater than in 1952 or 1958. Many workers have deeply resented levies made by their union for the support of a particular candidate. One hears very little criticism from the workers themselves regarding the restrictions the Taft-Hartley Act placed on the spending of union or company funds in national elections. The CIO achieved phenomenal success in growth during the first 15 years of its existence. By 1952 the cutting edge of the new federation began to get dull. The AFL had accepted the concept of industrial unions when it was advantageous, while still promoting craft unions for their skilled trades. Its membership had far outstripped that of the CIO. The crusading spirit of the CIO had become less dominant after its early successes in skimming off the cream of the large industrial potential. The death of Phil Murray, president of the CIO, and William Green, president of the AFL, within 2 weeks of each other removed two of the strong personalities that stood in the way of uniting the AFL and the CIO. John L. Lewis had withdrawn from both the AFL and the CIO.

**The merger of AFL and CIO.** The internal situations of both the CIO and the AFL had markedly changed from those prevailing in 1935 when the CIO came into existence. Phil Murray and William Green were no longer present to carry on their personal opposition to the other's leadership. The ambitions of Walter Reuther and John L. Lewis were still strong, but each had received many honors at the hands of organized labor, and their rivalries took on a more subtle approach than their aggressive organizing programs of 1935. Since the AFL was willing to organize industrial unions, this no longer was a force holding the two groups apart. Philip Murray was succeeded by Walter Reuther as president of the CIO, and George Meany followed William Green to the presidency of the AFL. The leadership of Meany and Reuther was not solidly supported by some of the other heads of large unions in the respective federations. Dave Beck, president of the powerful Teamsters Union, the largest union in AFL, gave the impression of being friendly with David McDonald, the president of the Steelworkers, a powerful CIO union. The able John L. Lewis seemed to be eager to form a third federation built around the Teamsters, Steelworkers, and Miners. Should the CIO have lost the Steelworkers, it would have been a relatively insignificant federation. Such a possibility created a favorable atmosphere in the CIO for a merger that might be strong enough to hold the major groups together. The same fears of possible loss of the Teamsters caused many AFL leaders to look with favor on a merger of the AFL and the CIO.[6]

A no-raiding agreement was worked out by representatives of the AFL and CIO prior to their conventions in 1954. Their respective conventions ratified this no-raiding agreement, which became effective Jan. 1, 1955. This agreement laid the groundwork for the merger. A final plan for the merger was worked out Feb. 5, 1955 which was

---

[6] See Neil W. Chamberlain, *Labor*, McGraw-Hill Book Company, Inc., New York, 1958, pp. 54–61, for an excellent discussion of the merger, its background, and possible gains for labor and the problems posed for the unions and the public.

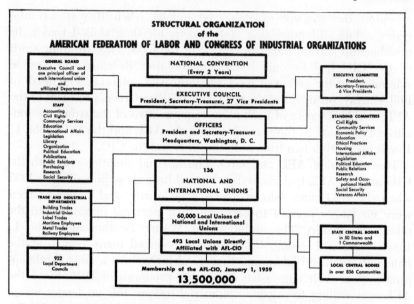

Fig. 22.1. Structural organization of the AFL and the CIO.

ratified by the last conventions of the separate organizations, Dec. 1 and 2, 1955. The merger became effective Dec. 5, 1955.

It should be remembered that the AFL-CIO is not a union but a federation of unions. It has a few unions that answer to the federation directly rather than through a national or international union. Most of these are known as *federal unions*. Figure 22.1 shows the organization structure. The final laws or power rests with the convention held every 2 years. The president is elected by the *convention*. Reporting to the president is the executive committee, composed of the president, secretary-treasurer, and six vice-presidents, who are elected by the convention from the membership of the *executive council*. The executive committee meets every 2 months. Below the executive committee is the executive council, composed of the president, secretary-treasurer, and 27 vice-presidents named by the convention. The executive council is the governing body between conventions. The federal unions and a substantial number of important committees report to the executive council. The general board, composed of the executive council and all national and international presidents and department heads, reports to the executive council and meets at least once a year. The six departments, building and construction, metal trades, union label, maritime, railway, and the department of industrial organizations, report to the general board. These departments are almost *subfederations* within the AFL-CIO federation. The international unions and national unions report to the convention, as do the state federations councils as well as the city centrals. The local unions (save the few that belong to the federal unions) report to their national or international organizations.

**The railway brotherhoods and other independent unions.** The railway brotherhoods constitute the best-known group of independent unions. Their respective names are the Order of Railway Conductors of America, the Brotherhood of Locomotive Engineers, and the Brotherhood of Railroad Trainmen. The Brotherhood of Locomotive Firemen and Engineers joined the AFL-CIO in 1956 after an unaffiliated history of 83 years. The three independents plus the Locomotive Firemen and Engineers are also popularly known as the Big Four. The Big Four dominate the railroad labor field. They have sponsored legislation regarding safety, length of the workday, retirement, and most phases of the work with which they are vitally concerned. For years they have worked in harmony with each other; yet in the early days there were jurisdictional disputes.

There are a number of other large independent unions of various sizes, from an independent for a large plant of 16,000 to a small plant of 150 employees. An independent union may be confined to a single employer or to many employers. It is usually considered independent when it is not affiliated with the AFL or the CIO. An independent union confined to a single employer is often called a *company union* or a *company independent union.* The Directory of National and International Labor Unions in the United States, 1957, lists three national federations of independent unions, two state councils, and two regional councils.[7] The three national federations are Confederated Unions of America, with headquarters in Baton Rouge, La., Engineers and Scientists of America, Washington, D.C., and the National Independent Union Council, Washington, D.C. Independent unions have the same protection under the Labor-Management Relations Act of 1947 as the affiliated unions.

**Union objectives or goals.** Over the years there have appeared three main groups of unions so far as general characteristics are concerned, namely, the *economic union,* the union interested in *social and economic uplift,* and the *revolutionary union.* The economic, or *business,* union has as its major objective the improvement of working conditions and earnings of its members. Unfortunately from a total social standpoint most of the unions' efforts have been to try to get a larger

[7] See U.S. Department of Labor, Bureau of Labor Statistics, *Bulletin* 1222, November, 1957, p. 28.

slice of the pie for their members rather than to strive also to increase the size of the pie. Unions will not be living up to their social opportunities unless they seriously turn their efforts to increasing the total goods to be distributed as well as to increasing the share that their members receive. Restriction of production is definitely antisocial and detrimental to society as a whole. One can understand the urge of workers to stretch their jobs in times of slack employment, but restriction of production is hard to understand when people are begging for homes to shelter their loved ones. "Feather bedding," or restriction of output, is not a serious problem in most work groups. Its most glaring examples have been in certain aspects of railroading, music, and the building trades. *Union leaders, business leaders,* and the *citizenry* at large should strive to get every man in every walk of life to recognize that *we cannot have more by producing less.*

The *uplift unions* such as the Knights of Labor stressed social, intellectual, and moral gains. As a group, uplift unionists strive to build up a strong class consciousness. The economic unionist does this to a small degree, but the traditional American worker resents the concept that he must remain a worker and can never rise to the employer class. The *revolutionary* unionist is best illustrated by the IWW group. Numerically they have never played a very important role. The revolutionary groups in recent years have been boring from within some of the traditional unions without revealing their true colors. Some of the CIO unions have been dominated by this group. During recent years the CIO has striven to drive the uplift group out of the control of any of its unions. It has been largely successful but not entirely. The revolutionary unionist is usually a follower of the Marxist line. He is well disciplined and knows all the tricks of propaganda and outstaying the other fellow. The average worker wants to get home to his family, and so he leaves his union hall at a reasonable hour. The revolutionary is willing to talk for hours on the European situation or any other pet subject so that he and his kind will be left when the others leave in disgust, thus to be able to retain control of a union. Workers could easily eliminate the influence of this group in practically any union if they would only become aware of their tactics and act accordingly. The number of radicals is small, but frequently they are entrenched in key positions. In a few cases the rank-and-file workers have voted to retain their radical leaders after their union has been suspended from one of the federations that was trying to clean house.

**The future of unions.** Modern unions have a greater influence on congressional legislation than their numbers and vote-delivering power justify. In spite of the public disapproval of union racketeering revealed by the McClellan Committee it seems reasonable to predict that unions will be an economic, social, and political power for a long time. Unions no longer can claim that they need special privileges because of their weakness in representing the downtrodden workers. Large unions like the Steelworkers, the United Mine Workers, and the United Automobile Workers are giants. They have the power to shut down entire industries that exert a profound influence upon the total economy. With the highest wages of any large group of workers in the world, one of these unions has only recently paralyzed the entire steel industry. Some method is needed to protect the public interest from the unbridled power of these giant unions. It is not a simple matter for the government to protect the public from union excesses and not get into the unacceptable position of setting wages, prices, and profits. Some of our socialistic-minded citizenry would like nothing better than to get the government into a form of state socialism without the name. It is safe to say that most union leaders do not want government dominance. Certainly business leaders do not want government control of prices, wages, and profits. It is to be hoped responsible union leaders and business leaders can find a way to industrial peace without exploiting the public by ever-rising prices.

Some students of the subject seem to think that inflation is inevitable and that this is to be preferred to the strong measures needed to prevent the inflation. These same persons think that full employment is impossible without inflation. Of course prolonged deficit financing by government also contributes to the inflationary pressures. There is no question that the modern union movement has strong political overtones as well as economic interests. Federal legislation helped to build the union strength to its present height. The Taft-Hartley Act of 1957 and its modification in 1959 were designed to protect the public interests. These two laws are not strong enough to protect the public from union power as exerted in crippling strikes. An enlightened union membership and leadership have in their hands the greatest power for good ever concentrated in the hands of one group. It is to be hoped that it will be used for the public good rather than for the interest of a small percentage of the entire public.

CHAPTER 23

# Influences Other than the Monetary Wage

**Work defined.** Work is the expenditure of human energy for direct remuneration or pay. Work is to a considerable extent the expenditure of energy that would not be expended were it not for the reward. Closely related to this is the concept that work itself is somewhat distasteful, that it is not desired as an end in itself. Much of the world's work is distasteful in a limited degree; yet this should not lead to the conclusion that all work or even most work is unpleasant. It is largely a matter of time and degree. Many people thoroughly enjoy the feeling that comes from the expenditure of energy just so long as the time devoted to this is not excessive. The term "excessive" does not imply that it need be harmful. Workers, either mental or physical, usually have private interests and hobbies to which they desire to devote considerable time. This statement is particularly true for young or even middle-aged persons. It is not so true of older persons nearing retirement or who have recently retired. To them work has become a "way of life," a process of giving meaning to life. It is a symbol of usefulness. When the regular work of younger and middle-aged workers leaves time and energy to follow private interests, the work is usually not considered excessive.

Play is different from work in that play is essentially the end in itself, whereas work is a means to an end. The incentive to play is the pleasure itself derived from the playing of the game or whatever it may be. The incentive to play may be social approval rather than the pleasure of the game itself. Many a tired professional man or businessman has played bridge because his social group considered it the "thing to do." The student who in a very real sense strives to prepare for a career is working. If he is studying merely for the pleasure of the learning process, his endeavors would be classed as

346

play and not work. However, if the student labors at his task with the expectation of deriving some reward, either material or non-material, he is working. The apprentice usually is paid for his work in part; yet many would gladly pay for the privilege of learning if they could afford to do so and could not learn their trade any other way. Only recently medical students in Chicago had to pay a substantial amount for the privilege of working under the supervision of a maternity hospital. They delivered babies, at times under extremely difficult conditions, in the homes of needy persons, often working very long hours. It was a part of their training not materially different from the work experience of the apprentice. *The incentive that motivates most people to work is some form of reward either in the present or in the reasonably near future.* This reward may be received in the form of some service, aesthetic value, or material.

**Satisfactions derived from work.** Business is both an economic institution and a social institution. Workers strive not only to maintain their economic and social status but, as a rule, to improve this status. This urge serves as a strong incentive to performance. Frequently, workers oppose the replacement of hand skill by a machine even though there is no reduction in wage for the individuals concerned. This opposition often arises from fear of losing social status by becoming machine tenders rather than skilled artisans. As man develops his culture and economic status, his wants increase in both magnitude and number. He may not want more food, but he does desire a greater variety. As his culture expands, custom frequently decrees that he have different dress for different occasions. From the early stages of cultural development, the individual acquires status in the group. A man without an approved status is an outcast and frequently is the open prey of any other person who has status.[1] Z. Clark Dickinson has classified the incentives to work as follows: "(1) desire for livelihood and fear of want; (2) desire for approval of master and fear of punishment; (3) desire for praise and fear of being despised; (4) impulse to activity or joy in work and dislike of inactivity; (5) the moral command and fear of conscience."[2]

Most people work because they have to work in order to eat and to enjoy the many comforts that they want. This is a fair statement; yet there are many other factors that determine why people do certain kinds of work, work in certain communities, and work for certain

[1] See William R. Spriegel and Ernest C. Davies, *Principles of Business Organization and Operation,* 2d ed., Prentice-Hall, Inc., Englewood Cliffs, N.J., 1960, Chap. 3, "A Business Culture."

[2] Z. Clark Dickinson, *Compensating Industrial Effort,* The Ronald Press Company, New York, 1937, p. 9, summarizing the classification of Adolph Wagner.

companies or persons. Many persons find employment in a particular company largely through chance. In spite of the factor of chance, there are many considerations that influence the satisfactions that people derive from their work. Some people work because they think that it is the ethical thing to do; they believe not only that the "laborer is worthy of his hire" but that one who is able to work has a moral responsibility to do so. This belief arises in part from custom among our people; yet it is also influenced by the Puritan spirit that contributed greatly to establishing the custom. Other people derive pleasure from a feeling of doing something that contributes to the total well-being of society. The work process is satisfying to them provided that the work itself is not distasteful. In this country it is the socially accepted thing for men to engage in some form of productive employment. Actually, those who do not work are looked upon as social parasites. In other words, it is the accepted thing in America, for men in particular, to engage in some form of productivity.

Certain types of work are held in higher esteem than others. The "white-collar" worker is usually thought to be higher than the man who works with his hands. In recent years, this separation of workers into manual and white-collar workers has lost some of its social appeal. In the case of women, the social status of the factory worker is still lower than that of her sister who works in an office or clerks in a store, even though the factory worker often earns more money. Within groups of workers, there are also certain occupations or trades that carry with them special social approval. The railroad engineer, airplane pilot, toolmaker, and patternmaker are aristocrats among workers. The bricklayer considers himself to be economically and socially superior to his helper. The professions definitely lead in social approval and give to the members of the respective professions social status. The successful businessman also occupies an enviable social position when his personal habits are in keeping with his business standing. Within business itself there is a hierarchy of jobs or positions that serves as a carrier of social values. To be privileged to occupy one of the jobs that carries with it social standing is a strong incentive for most people. Many a man has refused to accept a job lower in the hierarchy of jobs, preferring to be unemployed for a time rather than to work beneath his skill.

**Incentives.** If a given wage is as high as the prevailing wage in the community, it may, with proper checks to see that quantity and quality are up to standard, serve as the only incentive necessary to motivate workers. Even under the foregoing conditions, the wage is not the sole incentive. For many people, industry not only provides a means of earning a livelihood; it is a vital part of life itself. In many respects, it is a way of life. The more satisfactory the industrial relationships become, the stronger are the nonfinancial incentives. *Positive incentives are those agreeable factors associated with a work situation that prompt a worker to strive to achieve or excel the standards or objectives set for him.* (In some instances, he may participate in the establishment of these standards.) *Negative incentives are those disagreeable factors in a work situation to avoid which the worker strives to meet the standards required.* Positive incentives include the wage, expected promotion, continuity of employment, preference in case of layoff, approval of the supervisor, fellow workmen, and the community; competition with others and with the worker's own previous record; and the worker's own sense of fair play and honesty in relation to rendering a just service for the total consideration given him by his employer, associates, and the community. Negative incentives include fear of layoff, discharge, reduction of wage, disapproval of employer and fellow workmen, and the sting of the worker's conscience for not having lived up to his expected possibilities.

The primary interest in this chapter is in those positive and negative incentives not included as a part of the regular wage. Group pride as manifested in increased production when two gangs are competing with each other is an illustration of the nonfinancial incentive. The increased production may carry with it increased compensation, but when the production is increased as a result of group competition, it is highly probable that the strongest motivating force is not financial. Competition may serve as a stimulus for desired goals other than mere increased production, such as accident reduction, waste elimination, improved quality, suggestions for improvements, etc. The desire for approbation is a strong incentive for most people. The approval of the supervisors and executives also exerts a strong influence upon the average employee. This is especially true when these supervisors and executives are respected by their men. It is worthy of note that most supervisors of average ability are respected by their subordinates unless they have done something to destroy this respect. As a rule, men like to look up to their leaders. The sensibilities of the group are offended when its members feel that their leaders have "let them down."

**Desire for security.** The memory of the prolonged depression of the thirties still lurks in the minds of most workers forty years old or older. Their children also have been influenced by the talk of the period of the "dole." The desire for security occupies a prominent place in the minds of our people. There is a difference, however, between reasonable security and security in anything like the absolute sense. The worker's interest in the security of his job is greatly magnified during periods of depression when jobs are hard to get. During normal business activity, job security to him is basically the *knowledge that he can get another job* if he loses his current one. World War II's experience demonstrated clearly that *many men are not so interested in the security of a given job as they are in the feeling of confidence that they are secure in the opportunity to get another job if they so desire.* In general, the age of the worker and his family ties and responsibilities greatly influence his desire for security in a given job. Employers whose experience spans both the twenties and the period since 1940 know full well that *security of opportunity,* not security in a given job, is the primary concern of the American worker. The fact still remains that many persons do establish social and personal attachments to a given company and work group. These attachments are the strongest forces keeping many workers on their jobs. Men may give more thought to job security in the future than they have in the past. This is probably to be expected as a result of our coming of age nationally. The unusual emphasis in recent years upon seniority as a method of holding onto the job is in part a manifestation of the desire for security by the persons possessing seniority.

Seniority in and of itself can scarcely be called an incentive for anything other than sticking to the job. The highest type of security incentive is probably that which arises out of a feeling that opportunity and job security will go to those whose performance merits promotion and continuity of employment. A feeling on the part of workers that loyal and meritorious service will be recognized provides a strong incentive to positive action. Nothing will destroy this confidence quicker than nepotism, internal politics, or any type of special favoritism. Management can well inaugurate a program of promotion and tenure on the basis of merit.

Of course there are other interests of employees than the mere desire for job security and good wages. These include a desire to be recognized as an individual and to be given credit for performance; the desire for promotion; the desire to participate in a socially approved endeavor (the worker likes to be able to point with pride to the company's products); and the desire to be wanted—to feel that he belongs. Most of these desires can be satisfied through the efforts of line management. The role of the personnel function is to advise line supervisors in these areas and to assist them, but not to take over their responsibilities.

**The working environment as an incentive to produce and remain on the job.** The working environment is made up of the material environment and the intangible influences. Equipment, sanitation, heat, light, ventilation, production control, standardized materials and operations, group spirit, factionalism, rest periods, night and day shifts, shift rotations—in fact the entire relationship of the worker and his work directly influences his reaction to his job and is a part of his working conditions. The regard in which a worker is held by his associates is a very important phase of his working conditions. Harmonious relationships between workers and their supervisors provide a strong incentive to workers, to desire both to work within a given organization and to work effectively for that organization. Industrial unrest is both a cause and an effect in relation to working conditions. Unsatisfactory physical environment, hours of work, shifts, etc., may promote industrial unrest. On the other hand, unsatisfactory personal relationships will produce unsatisfactory working conditions in spite of a satisfactory physical environment. As between physical environment and unsatisfactory personal relationships, the physical environment is less important.

The personnel function seeks to establish satisfying relationships in both the physical environment and the morale segments of the environment. The personnel activities are staff or advisory in nature and possibly less effective in the area of the physical environment than in the nontangible one. Anything that will increase the employee's "will to work" or cause him to stay on the job, in contrast to excess absenteeism or quitting, is a legitimate interest of the personnel department.

**Special privileges.** One of the greatest popular fallacies is the statement that all men want to be treated alike. If there is anything that they do not want, it is to be treated just like everyone else. Of course they want to be treated as favorably as others in their own group or as members of groups lower in the economic and social hierarchy. Certain employees are frequently exempt from the practice of having to punch time cards. These employees are usually ones who have achieved special recognition in the organization in that they have responsible positions, have a record for long service, or have been rewarded for some special purpose. Frequently, there are two or more classifications for payroll purposes, such as factory, office, and executive. Often additional prestige is attached to being on the office or executive payroll. The mere transfer of an employee to one of the preferred groups frequently is more desired by the employee than a change in his income. These special classes of employees are at times entitled to wear a special company button that enables its wearer to go from department to department or to enter the plant without a special pass. There is an almost universal desire for status within the group. Special groups of employees have additional privileges such as vacations or longer vacations in case the vacation program applies to all employees. The recent trend to give all workers a vacation has in part removed the special privilege that office employees formerly held. Even at present it is not unusual for factory workers to get 1 week's vacation and office employees 2 weeks' vacation. Other organizations attach much significance to seniority in such matters as layoff, recall, profit sharing, vacations, sick leave, and, to a limited degree, promotion. Where seniority is considered, it makes a special appeal to the employee's desire for security, in addition to the other desired prerogatives. Seniority frequently gives preferred status and a feeling of belonging.

One company, the Clevite Corporation of Cleveland, Ohio, has a policy of recognizing length of service by giving a $1,000 company-paid life insurance policy to employees who complete 5 years of service, a $100 cash award to employees who complete 10 years of service, and a $1,000 cash award to employees who complete 25 years of service. All employees with 10 years' or more service are members of the Cleveland Graphite Bronze Old Guard, which is a social organization that has picnics, banquets, etc. *True Bearings*, the employees' magazine, features the presentation of awards and the activities of the Old Guard. Membership in the Old Guard is highly prized. In 1950 somewhat more than one-third of the employees belonged to the Old Guard.

**Some suggestion programs have been promoted largely through an appeal to nonfinancial incentives.**[3] Such programs call for notation on the employee's employment record of all suggestions made and the resulting savings from these suggestions. In addition to noting on the employee's record all suggestions made, due publicity is usually given to the employee in the company paper. This publicity and official recognition make use of the individualistic appeal to the employee. When group approval for suggestions is the sole reward, its success depends largely on the fact that the morale of the group is high and there is no serious restriction of production.

[3] See Davies, *op. cit.*, p. 393.

**The influence of group on personal satisfaction.** The worker belongs to many groups: the family, the union, his bowling team, the parent-teachers' association, and others. Some of these groups may have conflicting interests. At times the fishing group may run counter to the family and church group when fishing is on Sunday morning. A union group may call a strike at a time when family responsibilities would dictate that the worker does not want to strike. The worker is forced at times to make difficult choices. There may be a lack of harmony between the individual and his group, between groups within an organization, and between the leaders and the group as a whole or certain members of the group. These situations tend to minimize both group and individual satisfactions.

In every organization, there are the service objectives of the organization to be harmonized with the personal objectives of the individual workers. It must be recognized that in the short run these two objectives do not always coincide. The problem of integrating the interests between the company's service objectives and the individual's personal objectives is a vital one for creating a positive incentive to bridge temporarily diverging interests.[4] This can be achieved only by a recognition that personal objectives of the employees within the organization can be realized by the continuing success of the company in its service objectives. *This integrating of interests results from a frank effort on the part of management to take the workers into its confidence during smooth sailing and prosperity so that mutual respect will bridge the gap during times of stress and strain.* When workers understand the need for sacrifices, they usually are willing to make them. Morale may even be on a higher plane than at any other time when individuals identify their individual interests with those of the organization to overcome organizational difficulties. This is manifest when utilities' service crews are making great personal sacrifices to keep the service open during periods of storms and floods. The big factor is to convey to the working force honestly and frankly the need for the sacrifice. Men like to identify their interests with those of the organization when they can see the reason for so doing.

**Nonfinancial incentives for executives and supervisors.** There has been so much emphasis on employee relations during recent years that some persons (reformers in particular) tend to forget that supervisors and executives are also employees with sentiments as strong as the manual workers'. When these leaders' sentiments and desires are not

---

[4] See Ralph C. Davis, *The Fundamentals of Top Management,* Harper & Brothers, New York, 1951, pp. 544–547.

being largely satisfied, the best efforts of the leaders will not be forth-coming. Of one thing we can be certain: the influence of our leaders has much to do with the level of our production and standard of living.

The incentives that cause men to accept executive responsibilities may be broadly classified in three categories: (1) prestige and power; (2) material and financial gain; (3) the satisfaction of doing some-thing constructive, or attainment.[5] Prestige is to the executive the same thing as status. It is an entirely laudable desire to want recognition, standing, and prestige. There is serious question about the desirability of seeking power unless it is sought as a means of achieving a socially desirable goal. Men who crave power for power's sake are usually not the ones who should have it.

Top executives have lost ground in comparison with manual workers since 1939 in terms of the purchasing power left to them after paying taxes. This loss of relative purchasing power has hit top executives at the time that the demands upon the top executive have been increas-ing. With Federal taxes taking 50 to 80 per cent of many top execu-tives' salaries, incentives other than salaries became increasingly important. Pension and stock-purchase plans have been used instead of increases in salaries in some cases.

A great incentive for some executives is the feeling that they are helping others achieve their goals. They take great pride in developing their subordinates and seeing them grow. Managers still respond to the desire to be in a position to do something truly worthwhile. This is particularly true of men who have built up their own businesses and want to leave a worthwhile, going concern to posterity. It is also true of men directing large corporations as employees, but possibly to a lesser degree than the owner-managers. This last statement would not apply to men who have to work to live: if they have to work, certainly they want the feeling of doing something worthwhile, just as do all other normal people in our land. It refers merely to those who are in a position to retire from the active management of their concerns and are quite willing to let others assume the responsibilities and grief. These same men often work at activities in which they are interested but which do not require so much of their energies.

**Summary.** "Man does not live by bread alone" is as true today as it was when it was written into the sacred literature nearly 2,000 years ago. Man is as much a social creature as he is an economic person. Often the demands of his social existence are stronger, relatively, than

[5] See Lawrence A. Appley, "Changing Incentives for Executives," *Management News*, May 24, 1949.

his economic needs. This is especially true in the economy of the United States. During recent years we have tended to act as if man's social and emotional needs would be taken care of if his economic needs were satisfied.[6] Nothing could be further from the truth. Man's reaction to his economic and social environment is a complex mixture of social forces and economic demands, with the emotional and senti-mental flavor being clearly recognized by the impartial observer. The management that recognizes these inherent reactions of employees will get a larger return for its monetary expenditures.

[6] See F. J. Roethlisberger, *Management and Morale*, Harvard University Press, Cambridge, 1941, pp. 49–53, for a fascinating description of primitive man's reaction to social demands in contrast to his economic needs.

## CHAPTER 24

# *Stabilization of Wages or Employment*

**Background.** The first annual wage plan in the United States was inaugurated by the Columbia Conserve Company in 1917. The Procter and Gamble Company started its guaranteed employment plan in 1923. There has been substantial interest in stabilizing employment or income since the early 1930's. Among the plans that were started during the 1930's which have received wide publicity are those of the George A. Hormel & Company of Austin, Minn., the Nunn-Bush Shoe Company of Milwaukee, Wis., and McCormick and Company of Baltimore, Md.

The original Fair Labor Standards Act of 1938 made provision for exempting the employer who guaranteed his employees 2,080 hr. per year from the penalty of time and one-half for overtime. This was the first Federal legislation offering an incentive to an employer to provide steady work for his employees. In the early days of discussing the guaranteed work program organized labor was suspicious; however, during World War II the Steel Workers tried to get the War Labor Board to order a guaranteed employment program.[1] From this time forward, big unions have been pressing for some form of guarantee as to employment or income. Of course many minor contracts were negotiated between unions and employers under the provisions of the Fair Labor Standards Act. The strong play made by the big industrial unions in 1956–1957 brought a watered-down edition of income stabilization. In fact, this move so far has merely strengthened unemployment compensation. The fact remains that unions are talking in a big way about guaranteed employment or income. Most of the earlier programs were intiated by management. The initiative has now been passed to the unions, at least in the asking stage.

[1] See Edwin E. Witte, "Steadying the Worker's Income," *Harvard Business Review*, Vol. 24, No. 13, Spring 1946, pp. 306–325, for an interesting account of the development during this period.

Most businessmen are keenly sensitive to the problems faced by their employees who are unemployed. In spite of this fact, business faces some very serious problems when it assumes the responsibility of guaranteeing either wages or employment. As yet, many companies are not in a position to make such guarantees. Many managers recognize the desirability of stabilizing employment but as yet have not found a means of doing it.

**Causes of unemployment.** The purchaser largely determines whether or not the employer may give his workers steady employment. The buyer is influenced in his buying habits largely by the changing seasons. There are also the cultural and technological factors, the cyclical factors, and to a lesser degree the personal instability or incapacity of certain workers.

Only a relatively few employers are in a position, by the very nature of the industry, to stabilize employment. The number who may stabilize income is somewhat greater. The ability of an employer to stabilize income is largely dependent upon his successful forecasting of his annual production and the willingness of his employees collectively to enter into agreements to work at times longer than their pay would indicate and to be paid at other times more than their work would call for. In consumers' goods where the cyclical and seasonal fluctuations are slight, it is easier to stabilize actual employment. In most producers' goods and in certain consumers' goods where the unit price is relatively high and the size of the product prohibits mass storage for several months, actual stabilization of employment is difficult. In such industries, some form of stabilization of income is more practical. In industries in which the labor cost in relation to the total cost of the product is relatively low and the product is not too large to produce for stock, regularization of employment is feasible when funds are available to carry the inventory and the style element is not a serious factor. Many employers do not have available funds to carry the necessary inventories to produce for stock on an annual basis, to provide income-drawing accounts, or to stabilize the income by paying an even salary, spread over the year (unless the program is started at a time when production is greater than the wage being paid, in which event either the employees or the employer would provide the funds for carrying the program, depending upon the exact point in the fluctuations at which the program is started). Employees will seldom object to being paid on an annual basis, provided that the process starts at a time when the pay will be greater than what they are currently receiving. They will not be so ready to agree to working longer hours at the time of starting such a program and receiving less pay than the hours call for; neither are they so willing to waive by collective agreement the overtime charge. The fact remains that this type of contract has been written. Successful solution of this problem requires cooperation between the employer and his employees. An even wage or a relatively stable one is socially desirable even though the total annual wage may not be greater than under the violent-seasonal-fluctuation basis.

**Seasonality.** While the severest unemployment arises from cyclical movements, the seasonal fluctuations cause much of the annual dislocations. Climatic conditions limit the growing season largely to the spring and summer; hence, the great bulk of the processing of fruits, vegetables, and, to a less marked degree, meat is confined to a 3- to 6-month period. Changing temperatures necessitate different protective covering for man; hence, the clothing manufacturer has definite seasonal demands. Purchases of coal used for household purposes increase during the winter season. Climatic conditions definitely restrict or handicap building construction, the building of highways and bridges, and water transportation, which in turn restricts the activities of industries dependent upon water transportation, such as the ore mines of the Lake Superior region, etc. The whole social structure is influenced by seasonal changes. During the hot summer months, retail sales drop off. People are not particularly concerned with buying new things but are trying to keep cool. Of course, the manufacturer of electric fans and refrigerators has his peak demand in the spring and summer; on the other hand, he has little demand during the winter.

**Technological unemployment.** Unfortunately, technological or scientific progress may throw some workers out of work. If two ears of corn can be made to grow where only one grew before, the number of people required to grow the needed corn is reduced. Duco took the place of varnish on automobiles and greatly reduced the production time and men required. The flat-built tire replaced the core-built tire for passenger cars and doubled the output per worker. No one as yet can predict what some of the synthetic fibers may do to the growing of wool and cotton. The mechanical cotton picker has already shown signs of replacing the hand cotton picker in some areas. It is conceivable that atomic energy when once harnessed may throw producers of other sources of energy out of work. Technological progress benefits society as a whole but may cause a hardship on certain persons employed in industries using the older methods.

**Cultural and other causes of unemployment.** Most cultural changes that influence employment take place gradually. However, changes related to style, particularly to women's styles, may be rather sudden. For instance, the length of women's skirts may be shortened 4 or 5 in. in 1 year. Taken collectively, this may reduce tremendously the quantity of cloth required for their dresses. On the other hand, the shortening of skirts will tend to increase the number of stockings required. Again, the shift to anklets occurring at the same time as the shortening of skirts reduces *in toto* the fabric required. The reverse of the foregoing situation is also true. Witness the increase of material used for women's dresses in the fall of 1947. This change increased the demand for cloth and somewhat reduced the demand for silk and rayon used in stockings. Cultural changes and technological developments will continue unless we approach a static social state in which there is practically no social progress.

**Worker incapacity.** Even during the super-boom days following World War II and the Korean conflict more than 1,500,000 workers were unemployed. Many of these were only temporarily unemployed for reasons discussed above, such as seasonality and technological change. On the other hand many were not working because of ill-health, accidents, and temperamental or emotional conditions. The persons suffering from temperamental and emotional disturbances may have been employed intermittently during the year, but being the so-called problem employees, their coming and going, or labor turnover, is high. Persons of this type are often hired in the case of an acute labor shortage but are usually the first to be let out during a layoff and have real difficulty in finding employment during periods of work shortage. Such individuals are not static. Some of them show up at times when they have had a long, successful work record behind them. They may have developed minor complexes that will disappear if properly handled. A mental illness is just as bad as, if not worse than, a tangible physical disease but frequently responds to treatment. The person physically handicapped, either congenitally or as the result of disease or accident, is often one of the unemployed. Two Federal statutes recognize this problem: the Fair Labor Standards Act makes provision for waiving the minimum-wage requirements, and the Social Security Act makes available additional funds for vocational training or rehabilitation of the physically handicapped. On the other hand, the unemployment-insurance law tends to cause employers to hesitate to employ such persons when there is any likelihood of their not succeeding.

**Management.** Management may fail to recognize the possibilities in employment stabilization and to take effective action to place the needed remedies into use. Management cannot change the seasons

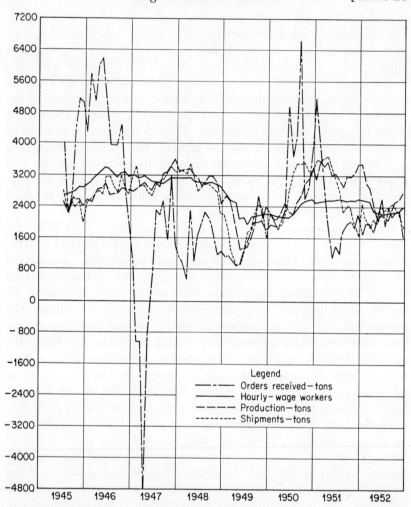

FIG. 24.1. An attempt to stabilize employment in the face of violent fluctuations of orders.

or do very much about the cases of personal instability; yet it can plan its activities to mitigate the fluctuations arising from seasonal changes and to a considerable degree can influence the fluctuations arising from technological changes.

**Facts—the basis for planning employment stabilization.** Research precedes planning. Research provides the facts from which a plan may evolve. Some companies have available the data required for an analysis needed for a plan of stabilization; others have not. These companies would need to establish procedures for securing the information. The success of Procter and Gamble in leveling its production schedules resulted from a careful analysis of its sales for a number of years. A number of companies have succeeded in giving their employees steady employment even when there was no guarantee of such results. After all, the goal is steady employment, not a contract to give steady employment that cannot be kept. The facts of a sales program may demonstrate that a guarantee of annual employment or income is not feasible; yet current performance may be improved.

Figures 24.1 and 24.2 portray the experience of a well-known employer who found postwar conditions so unpredictable that he could not guarantee employment, but success was achieved in minimizing the fluctuations.

Naturally in collecting the facts as to the possibility for stabilizing production an employer would examine the success of others in his industry or other industries. Each of the following methods has been used with varying results by some companies:

1. Increasing selling efficiency.
2. Securing advance orders.
3. Developing new markets.
4. Careful planning of production schedules.
5. Careful timing of changes.
6. Diversification of product.

**Increasing selling effort and efficiency.** Increased sales effort is the most natural area to investigate when sales are down. If workers are to be kept busy during the season when their product is not generally being used, it is necessary that the product be stored by someone. In some cases, this is done by the manufacturer. In others, it must be done by either the dealer or the consumer. The consumer is not going to purchase a product in the off season unless it can be demonstrated to him that it is to his advantage to do so. This advantage may be

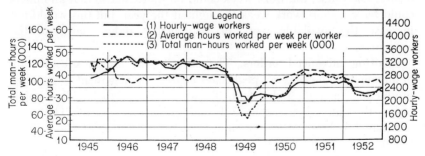

Fig. 24.2. An attempt to stabilize employment. See Fig. 24.1 for orders received.

conveyed to him through intensive advertising campaigns and through price differentials. A provident householder will buy coal in the summer if the saving is sufficiently great to cause him to invest his money in advance of need. The saving has to be truly worthwhile, or it will not motivate him to action. In order to reduce the price during the slack season to offer a real inducement to the buyer, not only can the operator in the case of the coal mine afford to reduce his unit profit, but the workers may well consider a lower unit wage for the same period. Such a cooperative program between an individual operator and his men may offer a means of stabilizing employment. It should be noted in this connection that this solution does not stabilize employment in the industry as a whole; at least it does not in the short run, for the coal sales made to the householders in the summer will not be made in the winter. Of course, there may be certain types of business where the total sales volume can be increased by effective selling. Such is not the case in the heavy industries, mining, many household appliances, and similar items.

Even though efficient selling may not substantially increase the total goods of a certain type purchased during the year, such a program would in the long run be socially desirable; whereas in the short run it might cause some hardship on some members of the industry, it would improve the status of the more efficient operators and of the men who initiated the program. For instance, if a given operator could run a full schedule during the normally slack period as well as during the period of peak requirements, he would take business from other operators, thus increasing their unemployment even during busy periods. Should all operators stabilize production and retain their relative quotas of the available business, those miners who were lucky enough to be retained would have steady work but others would be permanently unemployed unless they could find work in another industry. Of course, the work week could be shortened so that all miners could have a short work week throughout the year, but this would not increase the available work or appreciably reduce costs to the consumers.

**Securing advanced orders.** The securing of orders substantially in advance of the season's peak sales enables management to stabilize production to a limited extent. These orders are to be filled on or before the date when customer demand begins to increase. The product may be shipped in September to a Florida dealer, who will be billed for payment in December or January, when the tourist trade causes the demand to increase. The same situation may hold for Alabama, with shipping in October or November and billing for payment in February or March. The same program is followed as the season progresses, making shipments to states farther north. Automobile tires offer opportunities for this type of advanced selling. Under this program, the dealer provides the storage, and the manufacturer finances the inventory. For nonstyle products where the unit value of the product is not excessive, this program offers opportunity for employment stabilization. Automobiles cannot be handled in this manner very satisfactorily for two reasons: (1) the product is so large that it creates a real storage problem for the dealer; (2) the unit value is so great that the capital investment is excessive.

**Developing new markets.** Developing new markets not now served by a company creates very keen competition unless it is for a new use for his product. If it means merely selling in an area now being serviced by someone else, it will mean tough selling. Such sales involve additional costs in shipment. New markets in the same general climatic area seldom improve the stability of production; however, new markets in South America, Australia, and South Africa are opposite to ours as to seasons and provide excellent outlets for our products that have a seasonal demand. From a production standpoint, these markets south of the equator are not exactly opposite ours in relation to time, but nearly so. Factually, from the standpoint of manufacturing, they are opposite ours, less 1 month, which time is required for shipments and distribution when they reach the country to which they are shipped. Even in our own country, our Southern states, particularly the ones along the Gulf, are outlets in January and February for many products that are sold along the Great Lakes in June and July. This is especially true of items such as clothing and building materials. A manufacturer who cultivates these regional markets to supplement his normal area of distribution may do much to stabilize his employment.

**Efficient scheduling and stabilization of employment.** The development of a reasonably accurate annual sales budget is a prerequisite to success in stabilizing employment through production control. This method *in toto* or in a modified form has been successfully used by many companies. It requires careful forecasting and accurate inventory control, or the program may prove very expensive. Stabilization through careful production control may be realized through three general methods: (1) producing the estimated annual requirements on an annual basis, distributing the total somewhat equally by months, storing the excess over demand during the slack season, and shipping from stock largely during the rush season (this method is commonly referred to as production for stock); (2) careful production scheduling in keeping with demand, but increasing or decreasing the number of days in the work week or the number of hours in the workday, or both; (3) careful production control of monthly requirements so as to avoid sudden rush orders even though the production may not be leveled as in case 1. Naturally, planned production control (case 3) is presumed in the first or second method named above; however, for those companies which do not have careful production control, this method offers an improvement. Production for stock on a large scale is limited to articles that are not subject to violent style changes, to articles of not too great bulk, and to companies with sufficient capital or credit to finance the accumulated inventories.

Overtime pay for work in excess of 40 hr. in a work week serves as a brake on using the fluctuating work week as a means of stabilizing employment. The Fair Labor Standards Act provides a means of suspending this weekly overtime requirement when the employer and representatives of his workers have an agreement that is sanctioned by the administrator of the Wage and Hour Division. This provision of the act has not been extensively used. One drawback is the fact that the employer is forced to pay time and a half overtime to all covered employees who work a total of more than 2,080 hr. per year. Should the work week be reduced to less than 30 hr., the older employees are almost certain to complain, except during prolonged depression periods. The older employees have seniority rights and would not lose their jobs by reducing the force; hence, they are prone to complain of the reduced work week if it drops much below 30 hr. Spreading the work is satisfactory for short periods but raises serious problems for long periods. Union leaders tend to favor spreading the work, partly on a humanitarian basis and partly for the sake of union solidarity and dues collecting.

**Proper timing of technological changes.** There is little that a manufacturer can do to change the whimsical choices of persons buying a style product, other than to be on the alert to detect trends and to adjust his program accordingly. Advertising may direct the style movements to a limited extent. The employer who is fortunate enough to lead in research may materially influence trends and thus be in a position to bring his employees a higher degree of employment stability than his less fortunate competitors. At best the problem is a difficult one, to which no one satisfactory solution has been found. The automobile manufacturers have moved back the date of announcing their new models to the early fall, thus throwing the shutdown period to a time that causes the least distress as well as increasing the sale of cars during the fall and winter months. One manufacturer, who also has a leveling wage program, has announced, "As a protection against wiping out the savings account in case of unusual prolonged slack periods, we will withhold for certain lengths of time from the market, new products which we have developed, and they will be released only to stimulate sales during the slack periods."

**Diversification of product.** Diversification may help an individual firm stabilize its work force, but it can do little to stabilize employment for a nation. If Company *A* increases its total production in order to keep its men steadily employed by producing a part of the expected output of Company *B*, the result is less employment for the workers of Company *B*. This increased efficiency on the part of Company *A* may force Company *B*, in order to stay in business, to make a part of Company *A*'s major product or merely to be content with a reduced volume of business. In the long run, society will profit by increased productive efficiency; yet, in the short run, total unemployment may be increased by reducing partial unemployment. Combinations such as furnaces and iceboxes or refrigerators, radios and electric refrigerators, automobile parts and oil burners, etc., have been successfully used, but there simply are not enough of such combinations to solve the problem. The introduction of these supplementary lines creates a management problem that is not always readily solved. Often the men are available, but the equipment is not suitable for manufacturing both products. The marketing channel for one is often different from that of the other. This method presents an attractive solution when the various factors can be harmonized.

**Stabilizing wages or income.** The major distress features of unemployment may be lessened by reducing the unemployment or by providing some means of giving employees pay for more than they earn during slack periods or layoffs. The funds approach may be the providing of a drawing account to be repaid later out of work or the accumulating of a fund while working full time to be used when the employees have reduced employment. Both the employer and employees may contribute to this fund, or it may come solely from what otherwise would be paid the workers. Several companies have used the guaranteed-employment basis, guaranteeing full or partial employment, notably the Visking Corporation, Procter and Gamble Company, Swift and Company, McCormick and Company, and the Upjohn Company. Swift and Company began experimenting with employment stabilization in 1911, guaranteeing 75 per cent of the work week, which was then 60 hr. Unless a company is reasonably certain of its program, it may be better not to guarantee employment until the feasibility of the program has been established. This does not mean that all phases of the program other than the guarantee should not be put into effect. Public utilities and certain other individual employers give regular employment without the guarantee. The Nunn-Bush Shoe Company does not guarantee full-time employment. Nunn-Bush guarantees 52 pay checks per year.

The Procter and Gamble plan that began in 1923 is still in use, with modifications to meet changing conditions. At first this plan applied only to the soap activities. The guarantee was extended July 1, 1947, to the drug-products factory and Jan. 1, 1952, to the Macon and Portsmouth factories (edible products only). The essential characteristics of the plan in effect since 1946 are as follows:

1. The following provisions constitute the plan known as "The Procter & Gamble Guarantee of Regular Employment," and will apply at such factories of The Procter & Gamble Company and The Procter and Gamble Manufacturing Company, as have been duly notified in writing of their inclusion in said plan by order of the Board of Directors of The Procter & Gamble Company.
2. This plan supersedes all former plans for guarantee of regular employment and will become effective September 10, 1946, and thereafter will be the only plan in effect, until terminated, modified, or withdrawn as hereinafter provided.
3. To the employees located at such factories as above stated, whose pay is computed on an hourly rate, and who have had at least twenty-four (24) consecutive months of employment immediately preceding the application of this plan to their employment, the undersigned Company hereby guarantees regular employment for not less than forty-eight (48) weeks (or its time equivalent) in each calendar year less only time by reason of holiday closings, vacation with pay, disability due to sickness or injury, voluntary absence, or

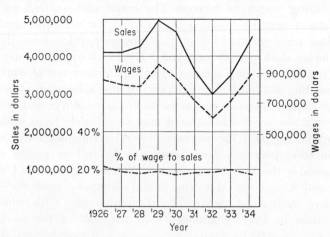

FIG. 24.3. Relationship of sales to production wages in Nunn-Bush Company. (*Source: The Nunn-Bush Share the Production Plan, Nunn-Bush Shoe Company,* 1946.)

due to fires, floods, strikes, or other emergency whether like the foregoing or not, and subject to the following provisions:

a. Regular employment shall be understood to mean employment for not less than the hour week established from time to time by the Company as the standard hour week at each of its factories.

b. When an employee first comes under this guarantee after January 1 of any calendar year, the Company guarantees to him under the terms and provisions outlined herein that he shall not be unemployed in excess of four (4) weeks (or its time equivalent), plus time lost for reasons herein stated, during the remainder of the calendar year.

c. The Company reserves the right under the guarantee to transfer any employee to work other than that at which he is regularly employed, and to compensate him for the same in accordance with the wage rate which prevails for the work to which he has been transferred.

d. Upon authorization from the Board of Directors and without changing the established hour week, the hours of work for employees coming within the terms of this guarantee may be limited to 75% of the established hour week less time lost for reasons stated above, whenever in the opinion of the Board of Directors such action seems justified.

e. Any individual hired to replace an employee leaving for military service or training, or for other services made necessary by a national emergency, shall be considered a temporary employee and he shall be so informed at the time of his employment. The Company will not consider such an employee within this guarantee. If at a later date subsequent to his employment conditions should warrant it, within the sole discretion of the Company, he may be informed that he is then eligible for this guarantee in accordance with the terms of this plan.

f. The right to discharge any employee at any time is reserved to the Company employing such employee.

4. This guarantee of employment has been established because the Company believes it to be sound business practice and a desirable protection for its employees. It is the intent of the Company to maintain it, but the Company must and does reserve the unqualified right, to be exercised at its sole discretion, to withdraw this guarantee at any of its factories, or to terminate or to modify this guarantee at any time.

The Nunn-Bush Shoe Company of Milwaukee has had a successful stabilization program for a number of years. This company, prior to the beginning of its operating year, estimates the number of working hours per year that the plant will operate. Each employee's annual salary is initially determined by multiplying the hourly rate by the budgeted hours it is planned to work the plant. The yearly salary is divided by 52 to get the employee's weekly salary.[2] At the beginning of each year, a group salary fund is established. "This fund is the agreed upon percentage of the wholesale value of the estimated vol-

[2] See "Annual Wage and Guaranteed Employment Plans," *Monthly Labor Review,* July, 1938, pp. 52–59; see also "Guaranteed Wages," pp. 317–337; in this same report the Nunn-Bush plan is described, pp. 338–350.

ume of business." The 1950 labor contract (still in effect in 1958) called for a "Flexible Percentage of Added Value Plans" according to the following schedule:

|  | *Labor receives per cent of added wholesale value of* |
| *Cost of raw material* | *shoes packed* |
| --- | --- |
| 43 per cent or under............ | 36 per cent |
| 43.0 to 45 per cent............. | 36⅓ per cent |
| 45.01 to 47 per cent............ | 36⅔ per cent |
| 47.01 per cent or over.......... | 37 per cent |

From this fund weekly payrolls are taken. If as the year progresses the total weekly salaries exceed the proportionate amount set aside and it becomes apparent that the fund will not be in balance at the end of the year, the weekly payments are reduced. In 1943 it was "agreed that each worker should carry a personal reserve which would be created by using the period end-balances instead of paying them out in cash until the reserve stood at a figure which each associate contracted to keep. This reserve may be used for vacations and for illness, subsequent period balances being used to replenish the re-

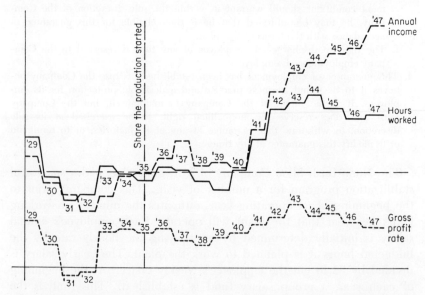

Fig. 24.4. Graph showing the trend of the annual income of a skilled worker together with the number of hours worked each year, 6½ years before the plan and the 12 years since. The gross profit rate of the company is also shown. (*Source: The Nunn-Bush Share the Production Plan, Nunn-Bush Shoe Company, 1948.*)

*Table 24.1. Statement of Associate's Share of Nunn-Bush Production*

For month of _____ September 1958 _____

Clk. No. _____ Name _____

Overtime premium pay _____ } Hours worked _____ Yearly differential $ _____

Your total earnings for month $ _____ Hourly earning $ _____ (excluding overtime premium pay)

Your earnings for previous 12 months (including gifts, bonus, & compensation for other than shoemaking work) $ _____

| | | | |
|---|---|---|---|
| Pairs produced for month _____ 54,630 _____ Average price per pair $ 13.10 | | | |
| Value of production | $ | 712,582.99 | |
| Less cost of raw material | $ | 288,097.30 | |
| Added value | $ | 424,485.69 | 36.50% total earnings $ 154,937.28 |
| Additional credits { Group share of upper leather saving | 2,094.17 | | |
| Additional overtime credit | 41.39 | } | $ 2,346.90 |
| Miscellaneous | 211.34 | | |
| Total earnings for period | | | $ 157,284.18 |
| Deduct hourly wages paid Class HA, HB, C, and D Workers | | | $ 16,307.94 |
| Balance earned by associates | | | $ 140,976.24 |
| Total drawings of associates (excluding overtime premium pay) | | | $ 101,752.16 |
| Excess of earnings over drawings | | | $ 39,224.08 |

*Your Individual Earnings, Drawings, and Reserve Fund*

Your reserve as of _____ 8/31/58 _____ $ _____

Cash paid you with last statement _____ 10/10/58 _____ $ _____

Balance reserve as of _____ 8/31/58 _____ $ _____ Interest

Your share of earnings (excluding overtime premium pay) _____ $ _____

Deduct drawings for sick leave, holiday, or vacation _____ $ _____

Deduct earned drawings (excludes overtime premium pay) _____ $ _____

Excess of earnings over drawings _____ $ _____

Your total reserve _____ 9/30/58 _____ $ _____

Reserve you contracted to keep (25% of yearly differential) _____ 9/30/58 _____ $ _____

Balance _____ 20% _____ of balance withheld to build reserve

**To** figure your earnings for month, multiply the "balance earned by share production workers" by the amount of your earned drawings (excluding overtime premium pay), and then divide this amount by "Total drawings for Share Production Associates."

369

serve as necessary. The most important use to which the reserve may be put is to maintain the level of drawings if, for some temporary cause, earnings do not cover drawings."[3]

Any surplus remaining in the fund above the personal reserve is distributed to the employees at the end of the year. Figure 24.3 shows the relationship of wages to sales in the Nunn-Bush Shoe Company. Figure 24.4 shows the trend of annual income of a skilled worker, the hours worked, and the gross profit rate of the Nunn-Bush Company by years from 1929 to 1948. Table 24.1 gives a form used by the Nunn-Bush Company in computing the employees' share of the Nunn-Bush production in the Nunn-Bush Share the Production Plan.

The George A. Hormel & Company has what might be called a budgeted work plan. They budget the work of each department for the year and allocate the number of men required for it on the basis of a 40-hr. week with vacations and sick leave allowed. If at the end of the year a department has produced less than its budgeted volume, the members of the department individually and collectively are "indebted to the company for producing that much work at the first opportunity." If the production is in excess of the budget, bonuses are paid the employees on the basis of what it would have cost if extra employees had been added to perform on the departmental basis, it being optional with the employees of a department as to whether or not they come under the plan.

## UNEMPLOYMENT COMPENSATION

**Unemployment Federal legislation.** In the order of their passage the Federal government has passed three acts: (1) the Social Security Act of 1935, (2) the Fair Labor Standards Act of 1938, and (3) the Employment Act of 1946. The Federal Social Security Act provides that funds will be allocated to the several states to cover the administration of the state unemployment-compensation acts largely on the following considerations: (1) the state's population; (2) the number of persons covered by the state law and the cost of administering the law; (3) such other factors as the Board finds relevant. The regulations laid down by the Board are designed to secure efficiency, to eliminate political preference in the selection of personnel and in the administering of the act, and to secure the carrying out of the objectives of the act. The Fair Labor Standards Act strives to spread em-

---

[3] *The Nunn-Bush Share the Production Plan* issued by the Nunn-Bush Company, Milwaukee, 1946, revised March, 1948, and still in effect as we go to press.

ployment by imposing a penalty for working more than a 40-hr. week in the form of one and one-half pay for all time over 40 hr. in 1 week. Provision is made for waiving the time and one-half pay in the case of certain contractual agreements between the employer and employees for a guaranteed work period. The Employment Act of 1946 sets up a committee to study general business conditions and trends and to make recommendations for action that will tend to give full employment.

**State unemployment acts.** All the state unemployment acts must comply with standards established by the Social Security Act and the Social Security Board in order to receive funds collected by the Federal government that are supposed to pay the cost of administering the state acts. To meet these standards, the state acts have much in common. The Federal act covers employers of eight or more employees. The state acts at least meet the Federal requirements, but many of them cover employers of fewer than eight employees. The Federal tax is 3 per cent, with a provision of rebating to the states 90 per cent of this amount. All the states require a contribution of 2.7 per cent, with the exception of a very few states, where the contributions may be slightly higher according to a fixed schedule when the funds in the account fall below 1 per cent of payroll. A few items of general interest are discussed below.

**Types of funds.** The *pooled fund* is the one most commonly used. It is merely the keeping of all the money in one fund from which all unemployment payments are made. A pooled fund may or may not be used in connection with merit rating of the individual employer.

**Merit Rating.** Merit rating refers to the fact that the employer's contribution may be reduced under certain conditions of having had a low rate of persons leaving his company, thereby having built up a substantial credit. The requirements of the merit rating programs vary in the different states.

**Coverage.** Coverage refers (1) to the type of industry covered by unemployment compensation and (2) to the number of people an employer must have to come under the law. In general, the state laws exempt the same type of work as specified in Section 1607 (*a*) of the Internal Revenue Code as amended Aug. 10, 1939, namely:

1. Agricultural labor.
2. Domestic service in private home or local college club, fraternity, or sorority.
3. Casual labor not in the course of the employer's trade or business.
4. Members of the crew or officers of a vessel on navigable waters in the United States.

5. Children under the age of twenty-one in the employ of their parents or any individual in the service of his son, daughter, or spouse.

6. Employees of the United States Government or of the several states of political subdivisions thereof.

7. Employees of charitable, religious, educational, or scientific organizations.

8. Certain other special groups such as newsboys, employees of foreign governments, medical interns, etc.

**Employee contributions.** Two states have employee contributions. In Alabama the employee contributions vary from 0.1 per cent to 1 per cent depending upon the rate assigned to the employer under the experience-rating plan. The average rate for the past few years

| States | Workers, no dependents | Weeks |
|---|---|---|
| Alaska, New York | $45 | × 26 |
| Wyoming | $43 | × 26 |
| California, Connecticut, Delaware, Idaho, Oregon | $40 | × 26 |
| Utah | $39 | × 26 |
| Wisconsin[1] | $38 | × 26 ½ |
| Minnesota | $38 | × 26 |
| Nevada | $37.50 | × 26 |
| Pennsylvania | $35 | × 30 |
| Louisiana | $35 | × 28 |
| Arizona, Colorado, Maryland, Massachusetts, New Jersey, Washington | $35 | × 26 |
| Kentucky | $34 | × 26 |
| Kansas | $34 | × 20 |
| Maine, Missouri, Ohio | $33 | × 26 |
| Indiana | $33 | × 20 |
| North Carolina, New Hampshire, Illinois | $32 | × 26 |
| Montana | $32 | × 22 |
| Nebraska | $32 | × 20 |
| District of Columbia, Michigan, Mississippi[2], Rhode Island | $30 | × 26 |
| Iowa, New Mexico, West Virginia | $30 | × 24 |
| Tennessee | $30 | × 22 |
| Georgia | $30 | × 20 |
| Florida | $30 | × 16 |
| Oklahoma, Vermont | $28 | × 26 |
| Texas | $28 | × 24 |
| Alabama, South Dakota | $28 | × 20 |
| Virginia | $28 | × 18 |
| South Carolina | $26 | × 22 |
| North Dakota | $26 | × 20 |
| Arkansas | $26 | × 18 |
| Hawaii | $35 | × 20 |

[1]Maximum increased to $42 but will return to $38 on 7/18/59, unless 1959 Legislature provides otherwise

[2]Maximum subject to possible reduction by a one-way escalator at 55% of wages

Fig. 24.5. Maximum weekly benefits and duration. (*Adapted from National Industrial Conference Board, Inc., "Road Maps of Industry," Studies in Personnel 1162, New York, 1959.*)

has been 0.3 per cent. In California the act provides that "the rate of contributions required for a worker shall not in any year exceed 50 per cent of the general rate required of employers."

**Employer contributions.** The maximum rate in most of the states is 2.7 per cent of the payroll up to $3,000 for each employee. The minimum rate ranges all the way from 0 to 1.3 per cent of the same payroll. The specific percentage cost of payroll for an individual employer depends upon his particular merit rating and the individual state law.

**Benefits and waiting period.** The most common minimum benefit is $5 per week. The various states have minimum benefits that range all the way from $4 to $10. The maximum weekly benefits run from $25 to $45, with $30 being the most common amount (see Fig. 24.5). The maximum duration for drawing unemployment compensation is 26½ weeks. The 26-week maximum is the most common period. The lowest maximum period for any state is 16 weeks.

The common waiting period is 1 week, with longer periods for those who have been discharged for a cause for which they were responsible and which they could have reasonably avoided or for those who have quit their jobs. In most cases, men on a strike may not participate, and in others the waiting period is longer. In all states, the number of payments to which an employee is entitled is dependent upon his previous work experience or record during the period from which his payments are drawn.

In some states the unemployment benefits vary somewhat with the number of dependents. For instance, one state has a maximum of $26 for a man with a nonworking wife and no children and $40 for a claimant with a nonworking wife and four children.

Partial unemployment benefits may be drawn by employees in several states. For instance, if an employee earning $30 a week regularly was reduced to $8 a week in a state with a $16 maximum benefit, the employee could draw $8 partial unemployment benefit, provided, of course, he would have been entitled to the $16 benefit had he been totally unemployed. In some states, the employee gets the difference between his actual earnings and his maximum total benefit plus $1 or $2. In Illinois, for instance, in the case above, the employee would have received $8 + $2, or $10, partial unemployment benefit. In all cases, recipients of unemployment benefits must be registered at the public employment office and be available for work to draw benefits. The refusal of a recipient to accept an appropriate job will cancel his benefits.

**Summary.** Unemployment compensation as practiced in most states has undoubtedly mitigated the suffering of persons thrown out of work. It is exceedingly difficult to say that a particular unemployment compensation is adequate for all time. For instance, a $30 limit for 1961 is not so great as a $16 limit was in 1939, when viewed from the standpoint of the purchasing power of the dollar. On the other hand, when the amount is too high, it serves to cause people to refuse to take jobs that may be in another community even though accessible by bus or other ordinary means of transportation.

## CHAPTER 25

# Wage and Salary Administration

**The control function in wage administration.** In the absence of some agency to look at the entire wage picture, inequalities creep in regardless of a clear-cut policy statement. Policies are not self-implementing. Large enterprises have located the function of wage and salary administration in various places, (1) under the personnel division, (2) under the industrial engineering department, (3) under the organization department,[1] (4) under the treasurer or comptroller, and (5) under a top executive. In each of these cases there is a department that concentrates on the details. These locations of this function in the organizational structure have been arrived at through the struggle of the forces that are usually present in organizational evolution, namely, (1) custom, drifting, and temporary expediency, (2) the desire of every specialist to report as high in the organization as possible, preferably to top management, and (3) a scientific attempt to group related activities to take advantage of specialization and to recognize the basic principles of organization, particularly the span of executive control.

Expediency leads to all kinds of abnormalities and unnatural combinations depending upon the personal whims of certain strong personalities or ownership preferences. The desire of specialists to report to top management arises from two sources: the feeling that their tasks will not receive the support needed unless sponsored by someone high in the councils of management; the personal feeling of possessing a derived status from the officer to whom the specialist reports. The first of these is understandable and laudable, but it is based upon a false premise in many cases, since top management is interested in having a needed function performed properly whether it is appended

[1] See Paul E. Holden, Lounsbury S. Fish, and Hubert L. Smith, *Top-management Organization and Control*, McGraw-Hill Book Company, Inc., New York, 1951, pp. 49–51, 91–103.

to an organizational level three steps down the ladder or is reporting direct to the president or an executive vice-president. In other words, when top management knows sound organizational principles, it desires a balanced structure of such nature that each function is properly performed and contributes to the effectiveness of the entire enterprise. The second cause merely manifests an almost universal struggle for status. It is too bad when this struggle is permitted to decrease efficiency in an organization. Its greatest weakness is the tendency to overload executives with too many persons to supervise, which results in little supervision being given. This of course is a violation of the span of executive control. An illustration of an extreme attempt to report to top management is the case of a large Middle Western plant whose home office is in New York. For more than 10 years the wage and salary department reported to New York and not to the local plant manager. Recently, however, the department was transferred to the local plant manager and now receives only staff advice from New York.

In some cases rate setting and standards for productivity are functions of the time-study department, which is a division of manufacturing. The setting of time values for an operation is an engineering function and may appropriately be in the time-study department. The pricing of the operation performed is an economic function for which engineers are not especially well trained. If the pricing of a job falls within an established pattern already arrived at by the industrial relations department, the pricing of this job may readily be done by the motion- and time-study department that sets the time values. It is a good idea to have the job rating section and the wage administration section separate, although they may both be in any of the departments or divisions listed above. To keep them separate tends to cause each to stand on its own feet and not lean on the other. For instance, if a particular classification of labor is scarce, the rating should not be changed to give it a higher wage and thereby attract the needed employees. It may be necessary to pay them more money, but this should be done on an economic basis—not on the basis of rating higher merely to justify an abnormal wage situation. The actual department that controls wages should have access to detailed job descriptions and job ratings. Job descriptions and ratings are supposed to be based upon factual data without regard to the prices paid for the jobs. The particular wage level may arise from collective bargaining. While employee cooperation may establish the ratings of jobs, it should be directed toward the finding of facts—not toward collective bargaining as the term is commonly used.

**Who determines the wage level?** Actually, the wage level of a given company is not solely under the control of management. Outside forces may be controlling. In spite of these outside factors, top management must approve a wage structure whether it arises from collective bargaining or from following a policy of paying rates consistent with community levels. The actual operating within a given rate level is a detail that need not and should not command top management's attention, with the possible exception of the salaries of executives above a given level. The details of keeping rate structures in line, giving justice both to workers and to the company, can readily be handled by a section of any of the divisions or departments listed above. The authors' preference would be to have this section in the personnel division or in the organization department. The related activities of these groups promote the efficiencies of specialization. Such a location of the wage administration section does not overload top management.

**Wage and salary committees.** The greatest advantage of a *wage and salary* committee is the greater acceptance of a wage decision that is handed down by a committee, rather than one person. No one who is a careful student of groups would argue that a committee is better able to collect statistical data than a specialist. Few people would argue that a committee is a better administrative agency than a qualified executive. If the committee is used for advice and other agencies do those things which the committee does ineffectively, the combination has merit. Frequently, there are several wage committees: the top administrative committee for the entire company; the factory wage committee; and the salary and office wage committee. In such a situation the top administrative committee sets the pattern and passes on executive salaries. The two other committees operate on a more detailed basis for the two major classifications of employees. When a company has many plants, there may be a home-office committee for the office and salary group, a factory committee, and at times the top administrative committee. These act largely as advisory agencies to similar committees in the various plants. On all salary committees a technical expert gives many points of view on wage administrative policies. The functions of the wage and salary committee are:

1. To approve in a broad, policy-determining manner the system of job description and job evaluation.
2. To approve, and in the case of the top-management wage policies, to formulate policies for the administration of the wage program.
3. To recommend changes in the salary or wage level.
4. To pass on specific raises for executives above a specified limit.

5. To review wage programs between departments. The data for the review should be provided by the wage administration section.

6. To check all activities of the salary administration group against the company policies.

**Principles of wage administration.** Wage administration, in the face of temporary pressure, should be guided by basic considerations rather than by expediency. Some of these basic principles of wage administration may be summarized as follows:

1. Job descriptions and ratings should be periodically checked to keep them up to date.

2. Wage policies should be carefully developed, having in mind the interests of (a) management as the representative of the owners, (b) the employees, (c) the consumers, and (d) the local community.

3. Wage policies should be clearly expressed in writing to ensure uniformity and stability.

4. It is management's responsibility to see to it that each employee knows what the wage policy is.

5. Wage decisions should be checked against carefully formulated policies.

Pressure is constantly being exerted from below by executives, supervisors, and employees. Unrestrained or uncontrolled, this pressure would serve to boost the wage expenditure of the company above the funds available for the payroll. It would also result in glaring injustices, for the rewards that belong properly to the efficient workers would be granted instead to those who could "press" the hardest. The aggressive department head may possess in an unusual degree that commendable loyalty to his people that prompts him to take a belligerent stand with reference to salary increases. The well-balanced organization will not be materially influenced by belligerency of this kind. The salary committee or salary administrator almost inevitably will yield more often to the department head who is aggressive in the defense of his recommendations than to the department head who defends his with less ardor. Where a departmental budget system is used, it serves to offset, at least in part, this constant pressure from below. On this basis, if a given department threatens to exceed the budget allowed it, the department head is immediately thrown on the defensive and compelled to explain the reasons for the threatened departmental deficit. Furthermore, he is likely to feel that the economical administration of his department will give him credit in the eyes of his superiors. This feeling in itself is not unwholesome, provided that the word "economical" is interpreted in its true sense as implying *the ratio between expense and departmental output*, rather than having to do solely with expense. An investment in increased salaries, granted wisely, is frequently the best remedy for a department that is running at a loss. The salary committee, by virtue of its central position and available records, can readily serve as a much-needed brake upon the supervisor whose wage scales are definitely higher than is justified by sound company practice and as a spur to the supervisor who is constitutionally opposed to paying a higher rate than is required. Sound practice in wage administration calls for raising wages which are too low as well as curtailing those which are too high. Effective wage and salary administration recognizes the need for a direct tie-up between performance and reward. In this balance between the individual's value to his company and the reward he receives from his company lies *economic justice* and a *powerful incentive* to all members of the organization to excel in their work. In the great majority of companies, there are serious inconsistencies in the wage scale that are often far more apparent to the employees in the ranks than to the department heads and officers. These inequities are usually brought out by a thoroughgoing job-evaluation program when carried to the place of being tied in with the wage scale. Job evaluation is essential to any sound wage-administration program.

When job-evaluation programs are properly kept up to date and merit rating is effective, many of the wage problems will be handled in due course. However, where an employee is being paid on a piece-rate basis and his performance is higher than the limits set, his particular earnings may be higher than the normal maximum. Action must be taken at times in a partial or complete change in the entire wage structure of a plant or industry. Such general reductions or increases are usually due to general economic conditions that have brought about a change in what is commonly called "real wages."

The expression *real wages* has to do with the purchasing power of the dollar. It is plain that if a dollar will purchase two sacks of flour when formerly it purchased only one, real wages are twice as high as before. Conversely, when the cost of living rises to the point where the dollar will again purchase only one sack of flour, real wages have been cut in half. At times, therefore, it is necessary to make readjustments in the wage scale. When this occurs, and the jobs are properly rated and classified, they will still retain the same relative position to each other. In the case of raising the wage level, it may be on a percentage basis or merely by adding a flat amount to the base rate for each classification. The method of lowering the wage scale may be the same as that for raising it. The percentage basis will raise the higher rates in the absolute more than the lower rates. This may or may not be desirable, depending somewhat upon the prevailing wage in the community. The percentage basis is more likely to be used, at least in a modified form, in lowering rates than is a flat cut. This gives the lower rates a smaller reduction than the higher ones. This is a logical procedure, but it is equally logical to raise wages on a percentage basis.

Some companies pay for *services rendered* without regard to *length of service* and reward service by special considerations such as vacation privileges, insurance policies, profit-sharing allotments, special sick-leave allowances, etc. This practice is not uncommon where the basis of payment is the piece rate. Salaried employees, hourly rated employees, and others paid on a time basis are frequently paid, to some extent at least, with service as a factor even though it may not be controlling. Within limits, sound arguments can be presented both for and against the *consideration of length of service* in rate determination. Where service is considered, it is usually wise to count service for a limited period such as 5 or 10 years rather than to add a flat percentage or rate for each year. It is doubtful that a man with 10 years' service should be paid more for doing the same job than a man with 5 years' service.

**Making wage adjustments.** The primary responsibility for recommending wage changes rests upon the employee's immediate supervisor. A special form, upon which the department head gives the name and clock number of the employee, the occupation to which he is assigned, his present salary and the salary it is recommended to be allowed, the employee's rating (when individual employee rating is used), and the department head's reasons for the recommendation, is used for rate changes (Fig. 25.1). This "increase blank" is sent to the personnel department for consideration.

In the personnel department, the qualification card for the individual is withdrawn from the file, together with the occupational description for his position, showing the facts bearing on the situation. Then the personnel manager or the head of the wage administration unit reaches his own decision as to whether the recommendation is justified. At this time the periodic ratings assume great importance. The personnel manager is concerned with the employee's standing in each of the qualities provided for in the rating scale. He is also concerned with the degree of improvement or lack of improvement shown by the employee in these qualities during recent months. Similarly, the personnel manager has reference to the personnel control chart. He visualizes the effect the proposed increase would have upon the other employees in the same group and in allied work throughout the organization. Of course, the main issue is *how well the employee does his job*. If the personnel manager agrees with the recommendation and the raise comes within approved limits, he approves it and sends his approval to the payroll department with a copy to all interested parties. If it is a raise that requires approval of the wage committee, he sends it to this committee with his recommendation for approval. If his judgment does not agree with the recommendation of the department head, he arranges a conference with that executive at the earliest possible moment and points out the grounds on which his disagreement seems to rest. If they reach an agreement, their joint recommendation is made to the salary committee.

If it is impossible for the personnel manager to establish an agreement with the department head, the personnel manager submits the department head's recommendation to the salary committee and presents with it a memorandum on the subject. The salary committee ordinarily meets periodically and takes up the recommendations that

REQUEST FOR SALARY INCREASE*

Date_____

Name of employee_____Date employed_____

Job title_____Department_____

Present salary_____per_____Salary range: From_____To_____

Last increase_____Date_____

Proposed increase_____Proposed effective date_____

Current merit rating: Score_____Date_____

Previous merit rating: Score_____Date_____

Reason for proposed increase_____

_____

Submitted by_____

Supervisor

Approved_____Approved_____

Personnel manager                        Department head

ACTION TAKEN

☐ Rejected     Reason_____

Next review date

☐ Accepted     Amount_____Effective date_____

Secretary, salary committee

Date_____

Notification dates

Department head_____

Personnel department_____

Payroll department_____

* Adapted by permission from Booz, Allen & Hamilton, Management Consultants, Chicago, Ill.

FIG. 25.1.

have been received since the last meeting. Where there is no difference of opinion between the department head and the personnel
manager, the committee ordinarily takes action accordingly, except,
of course, where discussion may disclose some unseen factor that
seems to reverse the combined judgment of these two executives.
Where the recommendation is unanimous, the salary committee is
governed largely by the facts provided by the personnel control chart.
If the employee's rate is below the median line for the occupation,
the committee will have little hesitancy in granting the increase. If,
on the other hand, it is above the median line, the committee may demand evidence of merit on the part of the employee.

Some companies make it a practice to review the salary or wage of
each employee at stated intervals such as every 6 months or once a
year. Where employees are rated at regular intervals, these salary reviews frequently (for convenience) coincide with the time of rating.
The mere fact that an employee is considered for a raise at a specific
time does not guarantee that he will receive one at that time, nor does
it preclude his receiving a raise at any time other than when he is being considered as a matter of routine. It is merely a procedure for
guaranteeing that employees will be given systematic consideration
and not be overlooked. Periodic reviews of the wage status of employees have much to commend them.

**Discussing wage matters with the employee.** It should be remembered that wages can go down as well as up. If an employee has been
given a merit raise and later falls down in his output, it is logical to
reduce his rate to correspond with his productivity. (It must be admitted that this reduction is frequently not made because of the
reluctance of the supervisor to do so.) In general, wages for the past
20 years have gone only one way—upward. The supervisor should explain all rate changes to the employee. If it is a reduction in rate, the
employee should be told what he needs to do to have it again raised.
If it is a raise, the supervisor has a golden opportunity to congratulate
the employee, thank him for his part in the success of the department,
and tell him that his salary is to be increased "from now on" to a given
amount. This is intelligent, constructive personnel work that recognizes the elementary desire we all have for a personal acknowledg-
ment of our work. This principle is applicable whether the employee
be the office boy, the clerk, the machine operator, the advertising
manager, the production superintendent, or the chief engineer.

If management's policy is to reward employees on productivity and
merit and it really makes good on such a policy, there will be no need
for a request for a raise by the employee. The worker who waits for

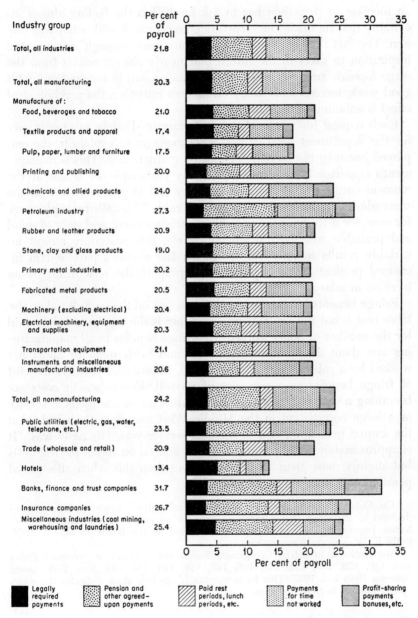

| Industry group | Per cent of payroll | Graphic scale 0–35 |
|---|---|---|
| Total, all industries | 21.8 | |
| Total, all manufacturing | 20.3 | |
| Manufacture of: | | |
| Food, beverages and tobacco | 21.0 | |
| Textile products and apparel | 17.4 | |
| Pulp, paper, lumber and furniture | 17.5 | |
| Printing and publishing | 20.0 | |
| Chemicals and allied products | 24.0 | |
| Petroleum industry | 27.3 | |
| Rubber and leather products | 20.9 | |
| Stone, clay and glass products | 19.0 | |
| Primary metal industries | 20.2 | |
| Fabricated metal products | 20.5 | |
| Machinery (excluding electrical) | 20.4 | |
| Electrical machinery, equipment and supplies | 20.3 | |
| Transportation equipment | 21.1 | |
| Instruments and miscellaneous manufacturing industries | 20.6 | |
| Total, all nonmanufacturing | 24.2 | |
| Public utilities (electric, gas, water, telephone, etc.) | 23.5 | |
| Trade (wholesale and retail) | 20.9 | |
| Hotels | 13.4 | |
| Banks, finance and trust companies | 31.7 | |
| Insurance companies | 26.7 | |
| Miscellaneous industries (coal mining, warehousing and laundries) | 25.4 | |

Per cent of payroll

Legend: Legally required payments; Pension and other agreed-upon payments; Paid rest periods, lunch periods, etc.; Payments for time not worked; Profit-sharing payments bonuses, etc.

FIG. 25.2. Fringe payments as per cent of payroll by industry groups, 1,020 companies, 1957. (*Source: Chamber of Commerce of the U.S., Fringe Benefits 1957, p. 12.*)

383

an increase in pay, then has to ask for it, has the feeling almost inevitably that he made the company come through with what was due him. The fact that "he made the company come through" removes the inspiration to excel in the future that nearly always results from the wage increase properly handled. If management, in recognition of his good work, increases his salary on its own initiative, the psychological effect is unfailingly stimulating.[2]

Each request for a raise that is not warranted offers an opportunity for the department head or personnel manager to explain to the employee *just why* the increase cannot be granted *now*. This is management's opportunity to explain just why the employee is not at the moment entitled to an increase in salary and to point out how in the succeeding months he can qualify for a raise. This calls for diplomacy, for care, for a study of the individual's temperament and state of mind and probable reactions. When well done, this procedure almost invariably results in renewed energy on the worker's part and in increased productiveness that later can properly be recognized by an increase in salary.

**Fringe benefits.**[3] When an employee is put on the payroll today, the labor cost is not the contract price; neither is the employee solely paid for the number of hours worked. His fringe benefits in all manufacturing are about 22 per cent of payroll, and he is paid for hours not worked by a substantial vacation period. Figure 25.2 portrays the cost of fringe benefits as a per cent of payroll. Fringe-benefit costs are becoming a real cost to business. The director of the medical service of a large corporation in the Middle West was recently asked what the annual per capita cost of medical service was. His reply was, "It is approximately $9.50 per capita when figured on direct payroll costs but slightly more than 20 per cent more than this when all costs of pensions and other costs are included."

[2] On Oct. 11, 1948, the Supreme Court refused to review a lower court's decision to the effect that a merit increase for an employee was subject to collective bargaining. This principle was reaffirmed by the Board on May 3, 1951, in the E. W. Scripps Company case.

[3] See National Industrial Conference Board, Inc., *Studies in Personnel Policy* 100, 116, 128, 130, 133, 141, 146, 147, 148, 149, 151, 154, New York, issued between 1948 and 1957. This large number of studies, alone indicates the widespread interest in fringe benefits.

## CHAPTER 26

# Financial Aids to Employees

**Financial aids defined.** A financial aid to an employee is *any tangible benefit other than monetary wages that an employee receives from his employer or in part through his employer's efforts or contributions.* Financial aids include decreased expense, or other advantage that can be measured in terms of money, savings and investment programs, educational opportunities, medical and dental service, hospitalization programs, recreational facilities, building and loan associations, company stores, company loans to needy employees, health, life, and accident insurance other than that required by statute, dismissal wages, company pension plans, etc. Our interest is in voluntary financial aids not prescribed by state or Federal law. Financial aid to employees would include unemployment compensation, workmen's compensation for accidents or sickness, and pensions *over and above those required by law.*

**Attitudes of unions and management toward financial aids.** Practically every financial aid has been initiated by some employer. The same aid has been resisted by some other employer when sought by his organized employees. There is no agreement among all employers as to all financial aids. The same diversity of opinion is found among the attitudes of unions. Unions have at times given up some "fringe benefits" or aids in return for a flat wage increase. Other unions have asked for the same benefits given up by a sister union. Both management and the unions recognize that a given service or financial aid may give employees an income-tax advantage as of a given time. These same groups also know that fringe benefits to employees do not reduce the expenditures of government; that money not paid in taxes by virtue of a given fringe benefit for one group of employees must be made up by someone else or even by the same employees in the form of another form of taxation such as the sales tax. Few people would deny the fact that the tax angle influences companies' contributions to pension plans and to some insurance plans.

**Why do employers give financial aids to their employees?** Ignoring the tax angle, it is fair to say that employers are motivated by both economic and humanitarian reasons. If the financial aid is the result of collective bargaining, the reason is rooted heavily on an economic base with some humanitarian impulses thrown in. To some degree such activities as those listed above, actually, in the minds of their sponsors, pay for themselves in increased production, reduced labor turnover, improved morale with its attendant effect upon efficiency, favorable public opinion that often forestalls burdensome regulation and taxes, or reduced hidden costs. There is nothing inherently contradictory between long-run good business, as interpreted in its broadest economic and sociological sense, and enlightened self-interest. Viewed from the humanitarian standpoint (managers are neither more nor less humanitarian than other individuals of similar educational and social background), management likes to do for its corporate employees the same things that it would do for persons working for the management representatives as individuals. For instance, there is a normal impulse to keep aged workers long after they have ceased to be efficient. Where there is no formal pension plan, humanitarian and economic motives often prompt special informal pension allowances. The company store selling company-made products arises out of a desire to make these products available at special discounts to the men who help make them. It arises out of a feeling of community of interests.

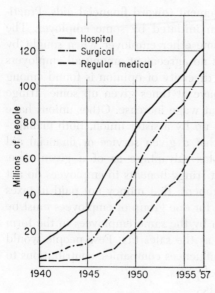

Fig. 26.1. Growth of hospital, surgical, and regular medical expense protection. (*Source: 12th Annual Survey—The Extent of Voluntary Health Insurance Coverage in the United States, as of December 31, 1957— Prepared by the Health Insurance Council, August, 1958.*)

*Table* 26.1   *Group Life Insurance in Force in the United States*\*
(000 *Omitted*)

| Year | No. of master policies | No. of certificates | Amount |
|------|------|------|------|
| 1920 | 6   | 1,600  | $  1,570,000 |
| 1925 | 12  | 3,200  | 4,247,000 |
| 1930 | 19  | 5,800  | 9,801,000 |
| 1935 | 18  | 6,400  | 10,208,000 |
| 1940 | 23  | 8,800  | 14,938,000 |
| 1945 | 31  | 11,500 | 22,172,000 |
| 1950 | 56  | 19,288 | 47,793,000 |
| 1955 | 89  | 31,640 | 101,300,000 |
| 1956 | 106 | 34,918 | 117,324,000 |
| 1957 | 120 | 37,378 | 133,794,000 |

\* Source: *1958 Life Insurance Fact Book*, Institute of Life Insurance, New York, p. 27.

**Group insurance.** Figure A.5, item 2, shows that group life insurance is provided by 96 per cent of the participating companies. This is undoubtedly a higher percentage than for industry as a whole, but it is a reasonably representative picture for most companies of 250 or more employees. Table 26.1 also shows the growth of group life insurance. Item 3 of Fig. A.5 shows that 90 per cent of the participating companies have accident insurance. Item 5 of this same figure shows that group health insurance is purchased by 89 per cent of the companies. Group hospital insurance has grown at a fabulous rate during the past 15 years (see Fig. 26.1). Group accidental death and dismemberment insurance is also of more recent origin. This type of insurance is nearly always sold only in combination with group life or group accident and health insurance. Group insurance enables employees to purchase protection usually at a lower cost than they could individually purchase the same protection.[1] It is usually written under a master policy that is issued to the employer by the insurance company.[2] The contract with the company usually provides that a specified proportion of the employees must participate before the insurance becomes effective. Some professional associations such as the American Society of Mechanical Engineers (ASME), some small

[1] See National Industrial Conference Board, Inc., *Studies in Personnel Policy* 9, 10, 11, 16, 17, 112, and 143, New York, 1939, 1951, 1954, for extensive surveys in this general field.

[2] Each employee participating in the group insurance is issued a certificate setting forth his rights.

business groups, and other business groups may secure many of the benefits of group insurance for their members. Group insurance introduces the economies of wholesale buying into the insurance field. It may be classified into four main types, namely:

1. Group life insurance.
2. Group health, hospitalization, and accident insurance.
3. Group accidental death and dismemberment insurance.
4. Group pensions and annuities.

Group insurance may be under any one of three plans, namely, (1) noncontributory, where the company pays all costs; (2) contributory, where the employees and the company share the cost on some predetermined basis; and (3) where the employee pays the entire cost. Nearly always the company pays the cost of handling the plan and in many cases pays a portion of the premium. In practically all the plans, the company reserves the right to discontinue the plan. Being a form of term insurance, group life insurance policies have no cash surrender value. The employees are not required to take a physical examination. On leaving the employ of the company, the employee usually may convert his policy into an individual policy without examination at a premium consistent with his age at the time of conversion. Occupational accidents are usually covered by workmen's compensation laws and are not included as a rule under group accident and health insurance as discussed in this chapter. The average plan calls for continuing disability payments for 13 weeks.[3] The amount of the benefit payments either may be a flat rate for all employees or may be graded according to classes. Malingering has not presented a serious problem save in isolated cases. There is an increasing tendency to extend the privileges of hospitalization to the members of the employee's family. Health insurance is receiving increased attention in government circles. There are many advocates of compulsory health insurance under government control. Others are violently opposed to the government's entering this field.

**Mutual benefit associations.** Figure A.5 shows that the mutual benefit association has decreased while the credit union has increased in popularity. The mutual benefit association is still found in about one out of five companies. There are at least three different types of mutual benefit organizations, namely, those entirely controlled by the employer, those entirely controlled by the employees, and those controlled jointly by the employer and the employees. Even in those associations entirely controlled by the employees, the employer often

---

[3] National Industrial Conference Board, Inc., "Company Group Insurance Plans," *Studies in Personnel Policy* 112, New York, 1951, p. 36.

aids either by direct contributions in money or by indirect contributions such as free clerical help and office space, deduction of dues from payroll, and advice from the personnel department. Sound personnel practice suggests cooperative employee-employer operation in so far as possible. Membership may be either voluntary or compulsory. Voluntary membership is usually to be preferred; however, where there is collective bargaining, compulsory membership arising out of the bargaining contract may be reasonably expected to cause less dissatisfaction than would otherwise be the case. Eligibility varies widely. Some groups have no limitations other than a preliminary waiting period; others bar both the very young and older workers above a given age.[4] An initiation fee may or may not be required; in any event, it is usually small. Membership is usually forfeited when the employee leaves the firm. Dues may be uniform, ranging from 50 cents to $1.50 per month for each employee, or they may be graduated according to classes of employees and their respective earnings. Benefit payments correspond in general to the monthly dues and benefit-payment experience. There is often a waiting period of 1 week or more before benefit payments are made. When the incapacitated employee has been absent from work for the required period, the benefit payment may be made from the time he was first absent or it may not include the waiting period. Benefit periods may extend from a relatively short period to as long as 1 year, 10, 13, 16, and 26 weeks being popular periods.

The death benefits of mutual benefit associations tend to be relatively low in terms of today's costs. The fact, however, is offset substantially by the increase in group life insurance coverage, which provides a part of the funds for burials. Also, persons covered by Social Security are entitled to $250 burial allowance if the family representative applies for it. Mutual benefit associations are among the oldest employee cooperatives in this country. Mutual benefit associations in the early days arose largely out of employees' efforts, supported by the employer. In recent years, the employer has often taken the lead in initiating the program, working through the employees and the personnel department. Mutual benefit associations have occasionally extended their activities to include social, recreational, educational, medical, and other fields. Employee-representation plans have often grown out of the mutual benefit association.

**Medical assistance.** The first-aid station and the doctor's office are generally accepted institutions in modern businesses employing 400 or

[4] See National Industrial Conference Board, Inc., "Mutual Benefit Associations," *Studies in Personnel Policy* 9, New York, 1938, p. 8.

more persons (see Fig. A.3, items 2, 7, and 8). Physical examinations are usually given prior to employment and may be given before a transfer or at periodic intervals for employees who may be subject to occupational diseases.[5] This service is usually free to the employees. A few industrial companies extend their medical facilities to the members of the employees' families; however, this practice encounters opposition from the local doctors. In some cases, medical aid is given through a group arrangement with the local medical association or a group of doctors or hospital. Dental aid is much less common than medical assistance. A few companies have dentists who extract teeth and make necessary fillings. Frequently the actual costs of materials used are charged the employees. A few companies and several employers' associations maintain hospitals for the care of major injuries and, occasionally, of employees who are sick. Group hospitalization for employees and their families has increased in popularity during recent years. The employers may or may not contribute to this program; in any event, they make payroll deductions for the employees to pay wholly or in part for this service. Another practice has grown up in recent years of requiring key executives to take a thorough physical examination annually.

**Company loans to employees.** The National Industrial Conference Board, Inc., *Studies in Personnel Policy* 145, 1954, page 40, shows that 27 per cent of the companies in the survey make direct loans to their employees. These loans are not made through credit unions or similar groups. The authors' own study (1957) also shows 27 per cent of the responding companies make loans to their employees (see Fig. A.3, item 13). This study shows a decrease in this practice from 40 per cent in 1940 to 27 per cent in 1957. The basis of loans is nearly always *need,* but the amount available to any employee may be influenced by the employee's length of service and rate of pay. This type of loan, however, is seldom governed by any rigid rule, each case being determined on its own merits. Many of the personal loans carry no interest, which may be either due to the desire of the company to help the employee or because the company charter does not permit the lending of money at interest. Informal company loans to certain employees have been made for centuries.[6] They will undoubtedly continue to be made for a long time by certain employers.

[5] See National Industrial Conference Board, Inc., "Medical and Health Programs in Industry," "Company Medical and Health Programs," and "Cooperative Medical Plans: A New Solution for Small Industries," *Studies in Personnel Policy* 17, 96, 134, New York, 1939, 1948, 1953, on this subject.

[6] Metropolitan Life Insurance Company Policyholders' Service Bureau, *Company Loans to Employees,* New York, n.d., p. 1.

*Table* 26.2   *Selected Statistics Representing Growth of Federal Credit Unions for Period* 1941–1957*

| Year | Number chartered | Number canceled | Number operating | Shares | | Loans outstanding | | Members | |
|---|---|---|---|---|---|---|---|---|---|
| | | | | Thousands | % increase | Thousands | % increase | Thousands | % increase |
| 1941 | 583 | 89 | 4,228 | 97,209 | ... | 69,485 | .... | 1,409 | |
| 1942 | 187 | 89 | 4,145 | 109,822 | 13 | 43,053 | −38 | 1,357 | −4 |
| 1943 | 108 | 321 | 3,938 | 117,339 | 7 | 35,376 | −18 | 1,312 | −3 |
| 1944 | 69 | 285 | 3,815 | 133,677 | 14 | 34,438 | 3 | 1,306 | −0.5 |
| 1945 | 96 | 185 | 3,757 | 140,614 | 5 | 35,155 | 2 | 1,217 | −8 |
| 1946 | 157 | 151 | 3,761 | 159,718 | 14 | 56,800 | 62 | 1,302 | 7 |
| 1947 | 207 | 159 | 3,845 | 192,410 | 21 | 91,372 | 61 | 1,446 | 11 |
| 1948 | 341 | 130 | 4,058 | 235,008 | 22 | 137,642 | 51 | 1,628 | 13 |
| 1949 | 523 | 101 | 4,495 | 285,001 | 21 | 186,218 | 35 | 1,820 | 12 |
| 1950 | 565 | 83 | 4,984 | 361,925 | 27 | 263,735 | 42 | 2,127 | 17 |
| 1951 | 533 | 75 | 5,398 | 457,402 | 26 | 299,756 | 14 | 2,464 | 16 |
| 1952 | 692 | 115 | 5,925 | 597,374 | 31 | 415,062 | 38 | 2,853 | 16 |
| 1953 | 825 | 132 | 6,578 | 767,571 | 28 | 573,974 | 38 | 3,255 | 14 |
| 1954 | 852 | 122 | 7,227 | 931,408 | 21 | 681,970 | 19 | 3,599 | 11 |
| 1955 | 777 | 188 | 7,806 | 1,135,165 | 22 | 863,042 | 27 | 4,032 | 12 |
| 1956 | 741 | 182 | 8,350 | 1,366,258 | 20 | 1,049,189 | 22 | 4,502 | 12 |
| 1957 | 662 | 194 | 8,735 | 1,589,191 | 16 | 1,257,319 | 20 | 4,898 | 9 |

*Note:* Since credit unions are removed from the operating list when they commence liquidation (well before the charter is canceled), the number operating will not necessarily reconcile with the number of charters granted and the charters canceled.

Total assets increased from $106,052,400 in 1941 to $1,788,768,332 in 1957.

* Source of data: Bureau of Federal Credit Unions, U.S. Department of Health, Education and Welfare, Social Security Administration, 1957 *Report of Operations, Federal Credit Unions*, pp. 2, 3.

**The credit union.** The workers' bank or the credit union has grown in popularity while the mutual benefit associations and direct loans to employees have decreased (see Fig. A.5, item 6). Table 26.2 likewise pictures the phenomenal growth of credit unions.

The first credit union was established in the United States in 1901. Massachusetts passed a law in 1909 legalizing the credit union and provided a working model for other states to follow. The movement grew slowly. During the twenties, rapid progress was made under the impetus provided by the late Boston merchant, Filene, and his associates in the Credit Union National Bureau. The Seventy-third Congress (1933) authorized the organization of Federal credit unions and established a bureau in the Farm Credit Administration to supervise them and encourage their promotion. Credit unions may be organized under either the respective state laws or the Federal law. During periods of great prosperity, workers do not need to borrow very much; hence almost the only outlet for the credit union's funds at such times is government bonds, which pay a very low rate of interest.

The record of a few credit unions leaves a good deal to be desired. A few personnel directors have questioned management's giving encouragement to institutions of this nature unless they are closely supervised by management's representatives. When management encourages employees to save through their credit unions and an occasional embezzlement is encountered, some managers have had a feeling of partial responsibility even though the credit unions are entirely independent institutions. It may be that closer inspection is called for by the chartering agency.

The credit union provides an excellent savings and investment institution for employees with money to invest and an excellent place, for employees needing money, to borrow. Rates of interest charged employees vary from 5 to 12 per cent. Dividends paid the members on deposits vary from 0 to 10 per cent, with the prevailing rate at present (1959) being 3 to 5 per cent. Since the members of the credit union know each other and the costs of operation are low, the losses on loans are relatively insignificant, the safety of the principal is high, and the return on deposits is above what the depositors could ordinarily get in the banks.

**Pension plans.** Figure A.5, item 4, shows the growth of pensions since 1930. Since all of Chap. 34 is devoted to Social Security and Pension Plans, our interest here is merely to point out the importance of pensions as a financial aid to employees. The Chamber of Commerce of the United States[7] reports that payroll costs for pensions are 7.4 per cent of payroll. Figure 26.2 from the same publication shows the phenomenal growth of fringe benefits, including pensions, since 1947.[8]

**Educational assistance.** Training in *company schools* is provided by 21 per cent of the companies in the authors' 1957 survey (see Fig. A.6, item 4). This particular item has not changed markedly since 1930.

---

[7] *Fringe Benefits* 1957, p. 31.

[8] See National Industrial Conference Board, Inc., "Pension Plans and Their Administration," *Studies in Personnel Policies* 199, New York, 1955, for a comprehensive study of pensions.

Item 6 of the same chart shows a marked increase in the number of companies that pay part of the expenses of employees in furthering their education. Some companies pay all or part of the tuition only for courses that give some promise of increasing the employee's efficiency on his present job or one for which he is preparing. This qualification is often interpreted rather liberally. Other companies pay a part or all of the tuition for employees taking courses of any

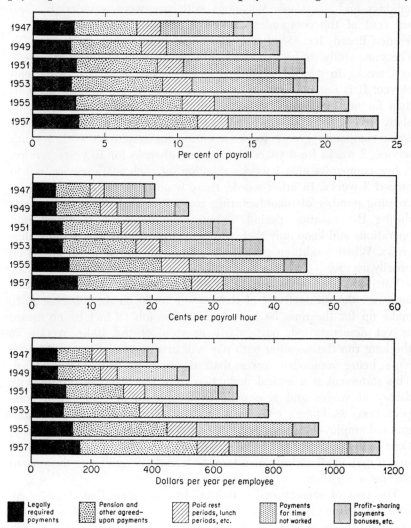

Fig. 26.2. Comparison of 1947, 1949, 1951, 1953, 1955, and 1957 fringe payments for 102 identical companies. (*Source: Chamber of Commerce of the U.S., Fringe Benefits 1957.*)

general nature in approved schools. Tuition aid is, in nearly all cases, predicated on the satisfactory completion of the course.

**Vacations with pay.** Figure A.4, item 17, shows that vacation plans for workers are nearly universal. Figure 26.2 portrays the increase in pension costs for the companies from 1947 to 1957 as a per cent of payroll. The Chamber of Commerce study[9] shows that 7.3 per cent of payroll goes for payment of time not worked, which includes holidays and vacations. Vacations with pay were reported by 99.5 per cent of the companies studied in the National Industrial Conference Board, Inc., *Studies in Personnel Policies* 145, 1954, page 31. The same study shows that the length of vacations varies from 1 week to 4 weeks, in general, according to the length of service of the employee. It is not unusual for office employees to get longer vacations than factory employees. Other plans treat all employees alike. Some plans have a flat vacation allowance for employees of longer service. Some companies give 1 week's vacation for employees with 1 year's service, 2 weeks for 5 years' service, and 3 weeks for 10 years' service. A few companies give 1 week's vacation for each year's service, not to exceed 3 weeks. In other words, there is no uniform program. An increasing number of manufacturing companies shut down their plants during the vacation period. Others shut down all manufacturing operations and keep only their shipping departments and maintenance crews. When conditions permit the shutdown, economies of operation usually accrue.

Vacations are a substantial cost of production. Unless the vacation increases the productivity of the worker while on the job enough to make up for the time he is away from the job (a fact by no means as yet demonstrated, particularly in view of the 40-hr. week), in the long run the vacation with pay will in all probability result in the pay's being somewhat lower than it otherwise would have been. This statement is a logical deduction from the marginal-productivity theory of wages and is equally applicable to unemployment compensation, workmen's compensation, and certain other financial aids granted employees. In spite of this fact, it is highly probable that vacations with pay will tend to increase rather than decrease. In the long run, it may in effect become a form of forced saving during the year to pay for a vacation.

**The cost of recreational activities.** In companies that strongly encourage employee recreational activities, the corporation usually provides a recreational director in the personnel department who aids the employees in organizing their recreational activities. The major

[9] *Op. cit.,* p. 31.

part of the expenses are defrayed through admission charges to dances, basketball games, bowling contests, etc. In large cities, the regular facilities of the city are often used; yet certain large corporations have built club facilities, athletic fields, etc. In the smaller communities, the company frequently has to take the initiative in providing facilities. Company programs for employees' recreation are in general more important in companies located in small towns or rural communities; however, they have been eminently successful in some of the large cities such as Chicago, Detroit, and Akron.[10] The Hawthorne Works of the Western Electric Company of Chicago has an elaborate program, financed largely by the employees themselves but supported in part by the company through the provision of buildings and grounds. The G.M.C. Truck and Coach Division of General Motors Corporation has a similar program. Goodyear Tire and Rubber Company is another company that has fostered a successful recreational program.

**Severance pay.** The popularity of the dismissal wage (Fig. A.4, item 14) has decreased since 1940. In view of the prolonged period of prosperity this decline is understandable. The theory behind dismissal payments is that the money is to be used to aid the employee while he is seeking new employment and becoming adjusted to his new employment. Payments are made both in a lump sum and on a weekly or monthly basis, with occasional combinations of both bases. Those who oppose the lump-sum payments do so on the theory that the employee is likely to spend his money recklessly and thus defeat the major objective of the plan. Dismissal compensation was primarily a product of the depression of 1930–1935; however, the Delaware and Hudson Railroad paid a dismissal wage in 1922, Hart, Schaffner and Marx paid a dismissal wage to some of its cutters in 1926, and the United States Rubber Company paid a dismissal wage in 1929. Many European countries have recognized the dismissal wage by statute. Several Latin-American countries likewise have laws requiring dismissal compensation according to a specific schedule. A few companies have plans whereby they pay employees laid off through no fault of their own an allowance for the "waiting period" required by the state unemployment law. This program may or may not be classified as a dismissal-wage plan, but it is closely related to it, and the amount paid is frequently determined by the employee's length of service.

[10] See National Industrial Conference Board, Inc., "Employee Recreation Activities," *Studies in Personnel Policy* 106, New York, 1949, for an interesting discussion of the entire subject.

Some union contracts provide for severance pay. Such plans usually are on a graduated basis, increasing with the length of service. In addition to the graduated type of severance pay there are other plans that give a uniform payment of 1 or 2 weeks' wages on being discharged.[11] There is no great uniformity in the payments of dismissal compensation under the graduated-compensation type. Each company usually sets up a schedule in keeping with its interpretation of the needs of the employees and local conditions. Where the age of the employee is considered, this schedule may become quite complicated. For instance, an employee of 10 years' service who is thirty years old may receive a 3 months' dismissal allowance, whereas an employee of the same service but fifty years of age may receive twice that amount. Such differentials are predicated on the theory that it will take the older employee longer to find employment and make the necessary adjustments. Dismissal payments are nearly always made only in case the employee is released at the instigation of management and usually because there is no employment available to the worker.

**The company store.** The company store as a separate department specializing in selling goods to employees is decreasing in popularity (see Fig. A.3, item 15). This same chart shows a much larger per cent of companies who aid their employees in purchasing personal supplies related to their work, also in purchasing company products through special stores, special discounts, etc. Organizations of employees, such as the mutual benefit association, have frequently owned and operated company stores. In such cases, profits go to some worthy employee activity. In many other cases, the stores are operated by the company. When prices to the workers are substantially lower than prices of the same products purchased on the outside, it really matters little who owns the stores; however, if prices are comparable with prices on the outside, employee participation is highly desirable for the good-will effect. Company stores, although making a definite appeal to employees, have almost universally encountered local dealer opposition. Dealers argue that they are entitled to the normal business that would come from the company employees. This dealer opposition has contributed considerably to the decline in company stores. Dealers oppose the sale of company products as well as other products.

A number of companies aid their employees in the purchase of items without maintaining a store. Often the company sells only its

---

[11] See National Industrial Conference Board, Inc., "Dismissal Compensation," *Studies in Personnel Policy* 1, New York, 1937, p. 5. See also *Studies in Personnel Policy* 50, 1943, and 145, 1954, p. 41.

own products, merely receiving orders in the morning, having some department such as stores fill the orders during the day, and permitting the employees to pick up their purchases at the close of work. Other companies do not maintain a regular store but sell employees such items as paint, fertilizer, and many items handled by the buildings and grounds or maintenance department. Many other companies give a part or all of their employees access to purchases through their purchasing department, thus making available to their employees, in part at least, the savings of large-scale purchases.[12] This type of aid to employees is of considerable value in the purchase of items for the home. It would seem that, under normal business conditions, convenience items related to the employees' comfort at work and the company's own products are about all that have any special claim upon the company store. Dealers as a rule are opposed even to these items being sold by companies engaged in other activities.

**Company cafeterias or other food services.** The company cafeteria frequently runs at a substantial loss aside from the cost of the space used and the facilities. In spite of the cost problem of running employees' lunchrooms, they continue to be popular and have not appreciably changed percentagewise since 1940 (see Fig. A.3, item 3). There is no uniform rule for the operation and cost of this service.[13] The company usually provides the equipment and space either on a free basis or at a nominal charge. Many cafeterias are operated by specialists in this work as outside contractors. Frequently the food cost to the employee is actual direct cost plus a fixed fee such as 5 per cent. In case of a profit above the agreed amount, it is often divided between the contractor and some employee fund such as the mutual benefit society.

**Additional financial aids to employees.** Various activities resulting in financial savings to employees have been tried by companies from time to time. Some companies have at times fostered building and loan associations to promote thrift and to aid their employees in acquiring homes. Some companies have directly participated in housing programs for their employees, to the employees' financial advantage. Another practice calls for the payment of a fixed sum or for a given number of hours to employees who report for work and find that there is no work available, "call-in pay." Certain annual

[12] Some state laws forbid this practice.
[13] See National Industrial Conference Board, Inc., "Company Food Services," *Studies in Personnel Policy* 104, New York, 1950. See also "Personnel Practices in Factory and Office," *Studies in Personnel Policy* 145, 1954, p. 49.

wage guarantees have characteristics in part related to financial aids. Limited legal aid is granted employees by certain firms. This program seldom calls for appearance in court by the employee. Many of these aids are relatively insignificant when compared with the total wage cost and therefore may not, even in the long run, influence the normal wage. The situation, however, is quite different in the case of such items as workmen's compensation insurance, unemployment insurance, pensions, vacations with pay, etc. *In toto*, these items become a real cost that cannot reasonably be expected to be borne solely out of profits. Since most of them do not increase the workers' productivity, it is reasonable to assume that they will generally be paid out of what would otherwise be in the long run a part of the wages paid directly to the workers. This is not necessarily a criticism of these programs.

**Summary.** The total cost of fringe benefits has been going up for a number of years. In 1957 it was 22.6 per cent of payroll according to the Chamber of Commerce of the United States. There is nothing inherently wrong with these indirect costs just so long as it is realized that these are costs of production that must be recovered in the price of the goods sold. The ever-upward spiral of wage costs not accompanied by a corresponding increase in production is inflationary. It means cheaper dollars and higher costs to everyone.

CHAPTER 27

# *Wage-payment Plans*

**Wages and productivity.** There is a tendency for persons who are not familiar with the cold facts of economic life or those persons who shrink from the rigid discipline of facing the facts to think of wages as coming from a pool unrelated to production. During the last half of 1958 as we emerged from the recession some union leaders seemed to be disturbed that production had increased faster than employment. Many of them seemed to imply that this was a social tragedy instead of both social and economic progress. For several years prior to this event wage increases had been greater than productivity in spite of the billions of dollars that had been spent on improved tools, equipment, and facilities.

The paying of higher wages *not* justified by increased production definitely added to inflation.[1] Inflation is a cancerous growth on our economy that reduces the purchasing power of the savings and pensions of widows and the aged. In the final analysis real wages are directly related to the productivity of the persons to whom wages are paid. Workers who have access to electrical energy and fine tools and equipment are fortunate indeed in comparison with their less favored brothers who work as hard or harder and nearly always longer yet must use animal or human energy and hand tools. Of course the costs of providing the tools and electrical energy must be recovered in the price of the goods sold. In spite of this fact the wages to workers have increased immeasurably more and faster than the return to the persons providing the capital.

In a very real sense productivity and real wages are reciprocal in an economy of free enterprise. High real wages can be paid only when the productivity per worker is high. The fluctuating pool from which wages are paid, if the analogy is permissible, is supplied solely

[1] See Murray Shields, "Wage Cost Inflation: Our Most Important Problem," American Management Association, *Personnel Series* 172, 1957, pp. 73–76.

399

from the productivity of the persons involved. If their productivity is high by virtue of sincere effort, modern tools and equipment, and efficient management, the real wages will be high. The relative division of the productivity between the owners of capital and the workers will depend substantially upon the relative supply of capital and labor. If capital is scarce as it is in many of the less highly developed countries, the price paid for capital will be higher than that paid in other countries such as the United States. For instance, São Paulo, Brazil, is a more modern city in many ways than Chicago, but capital is relatively scarce. It does not possess enough electric generating equipment to enable it to run all the machinery in the city at one time. Certain high-electrical-consuming equipment has to be run at times when other demands are light. Relative real wages in São Paulo are lower and payments to capital higher than in Chicago. In spite of the higher rates being paid for capital in São Paulo it has been unable to attract all of the capital needed.

**Misconceptions about wages.** Frederick W. Taylor read his famous *A Piece Rate System* before the Society of Mechanical Engineers in 1895. He was disappointed because the public took up the form of his system but ignored the scientific preparation for its installation. In the early days the restriction of production under the piece-rate systems had not fully developed. Management's errors caused this practice to emerge very rapidly. The early systems were not based on scientifically determined time standards.

Modern industry faces a different situation. While today's standards of what workers may reasonably be expected to do without injury to themselves still leave much to be desired, they are, nevertheless, better understood than when incentive systems were first being introduced. A few unions have excellent industrial engineering departments. Management has likewise more carefully studied worker productivity. The choice of a particular wage plan today depends upon the local situation, custom among the workers, the accuracy of standards, and worker and management preference. With a given set of standards, practically any of the wage systems to be described later could be used and would pay the same desired rate when the worker reaches standard. Of course, it would be unscientific to pay a straight day rate as high as an incentive rate without regard to production on the day rate.

**A satisfactory wage.** Standardized conditions including motion and time study, quality specifications, written standard-practice instructions, inspecting, training, and the like, should precede the installation of any sound wage plan. When management is convinced of the merits of a plan, it should seek the workers' cooperation and see that the interests of all parties are fairly considered. The interested parties are the consumers, the general public in the immediate community, the owners of capital, management, and the workers. The consumers are interested in securing a product at a reasonable price. The public is interested in the standard of living of the workers. Capital is entitled to a fair reward for its contribution, and the workers should be rewarded for their output. The actual selection of a certain plan, or combination of plans, for a given department, plant, or industry should be preceded by an estimate of the probable effect of a number of plans under consideration. The two things always to be kept in mind are the effect of the plan upon the relationships between the parties involved in the wage agreement and the quantity and the quality of the work paid for.

Two elements enter into the determination of wage payments: first, the requirements of a day's work, *i.e.*, the definition of the quantity and quality of work each worker is to render and likewise the condition, materials, and equipment the employer is to supply; second, the price to be paid for the work done. The most obvious factors to be considered in wage-payment plans are workers' capacity and age, material costs, education necessary, length of service, hazards, promotional possibilities, cost of living, standard of living, the prevailing wage in the community, stability of employment, demand for the product, and profits of the business. Any system that would include the following characteristics would embrace the ideals of practically all the better known wage-payment plans:

1. The wage should be related to the individual's productivity, with differentials for various factors such as skill, versatility, class of work, working conditions, etc.
2. The wage plan should be easily understood by the employees.
3. The wage plan's administration and standards should not promote friction with workers who are not on an incentive system.
4. The wage program should be easily related to the budget and cost control system.
5. The wage system should facilitate the comparison of the efficiencies of the various departments.
6. The wage plan should make adequate provision for learners.
7. It is desirable that the wage program should not involve excessive clerical detail.

Any plan, regardless of how perfectly it is worked out, will fail to stimulate workers to the maximum output unless it is intelligently operated. The first question that naturally confronts an organization earnestly desiring to solve its wage-payment problem is "What constitutes a fair or a just wage?" A fair day's wage is one thing in one organization and an entirely different thing in another. A wage may be fair in one community and unfair in another, or it may be just today and unjust tomorrow. To define a fair day's wage absolutely once and for all is as yet a goal unaccomplished. Dickinson says, "Most of us agree in principle that a fair *wage* is simply the full competitive rate which the work will bring in the market and time where it is offered."[2] To this concept we might add that a fair wage usually results from a consideration of all the available factors in relation to the work in question and an agreement between the parties involved.

Wage plans may be classified into two groups, (1) those based on measured time and (2) those based on output or productivity.[3] Payment on the basis of time is the oldest form of payment used in modern industry and possibly the oldest form used in free enterprise.[4] In the final analysis, time payment does not ignore output, for the high producer usually is paid a higher wage than the low producer. Time payments do emphasize the time element, and care must be exercised, or the worker will tend to consider time as the major factor. Care must also be given to reward the high producer on the time basis, or he will be underpaid on a comparative basis with the low producer. Since the high producer is seldom rewarded in most time-payment systems in proportion to his production, the tendency is for the capable worker not to produce up to capacity.

Since the ordinary time basis of wage payment seldom rewards the efficient producers in proportion to their output, it is not unusual to find them leaders in the union movement, which appears to them to be their only hope for raising their wages. In view of this situation, it is natural that unions in general favor payment on a time basis rather than on the basis of output. It is necessary to point out one factor often overlooked in discussing payment on the basis of output, namely, that time is a factor in the original determination of payment for output even though the output may be the base when once the standard

---

[2] See Z. Clark Dickinson, *Compensating Industrial Effort,* The Ronald Press Company, New York, 1937, p. 65.

[3] A possible exception to this generalization is to be found in the special method of paying certain foundry labor, notably puddlers, in the Amalgamated Association of Iron, Steel, and Tin Workers. In this group, the wages are at times computed periodically on the basis of the *selling price* of the product; nevertheless, it is still a payment for measured production with a fluctuating base. The Eagle-Picher Mining & Smelting Company of Miami, Okla., had such a clause in their contract, which was signed July 1, 1949. It was abandoned in 1953 when prices of lead decreased rapidly and there was no longer a correlation between the cost of living and the price of lead.

[4] See Fig. A.4 for a graph showing the use of the various wage plans.

is established. In other words, in the original setting of output rates, the time required per unit largely determines the rate per unit.

Wage theorists by no means agree on the division of the earnings arising from above-standard production. Various philosophies and assumptions underlie different wage systems. One school of engineers holds that *excess direct earnings* above a set standard *should be shared* in various ratios between the *production workers* and the owners, *but that the workers should receive more than straight piece rate by virtue of the fact that the owners automatically participate in the profits of the excess by having the overhead expenses reduced.* Still another group of industrial engineers holds that the *direct excess should be distributed between the production workers,* on the one hand, *and the nonproduction workers and managers,* on the other, *leaving to the owners all the profits that such greater production automatically* brings about through reduced overhead expense.

**Straight time payments not based on carefully established standards.** The essential feature of the time-rate plan is that the returns are constant, while production may fluctuate. During peak periods, the worker receives no more per unit of time worked than in slack periods, and penalties or rewards are not immediate, as is the case in piece-rate or bonus plans. Although the time-rate plan offers no immediate or direct remuneration as a reward for excellence, the constancy of returns in itself is a reward and, in many cases, a fine incentive for inducing a worker to exert reasonable efforts and create the finest work of which he is capable; however, "Time is for use: it is not for sale." The time-rate plan presupposes a variable amount of work done, and there is usually a more or less arbitrary minimum amount of output below which correction is called for and a continuing maximum above which an increase is in order. Nevertheless, the straight time rate considers the workers' *time* primarily without immediate penalties or rewards.

The payment of wages on a time basis has the advantage of simplifying payroll procedures, is easily understood by workers, but *makes labor-cost predetermination difficult.* Payment on the time basis is especially advantageous (1) where the work is unstandardized; (2) where the *volume of work is largely beyond the worker's control;* (3) where *quality is especially important;* (4) where the *volume* of a particular work *is highly diversified and of short duration;* and (5) where the *work requires considerable ingenuity and planning* as in maintenance and millwright work.[5]

---

[5] Millwright and maintenance work can be placed on incentive wage payment, but it is frequently not thus placed.

**Symbols used in the wage formulas.** In this chapter certain symbols are used in the wage formula. These are:

$S$ = standard or allowed time for completing a particular operation or task. To illustrate, if a particular operation should be completed in 6 min. and a given operator completes 12 pieces in 1 hr., his $S$ is equal to 1.2 hr., even though his actual time is only 1 hr.

$T$ = actual time worked.

$R$ = rate per hour or piece as the case may be.

$N$ = number of pieces produced.

$P$ = premium percentage.

$E$ = employee's earnings.

**The Halsey premium wage plan.** The Halsey premium plan guarantees a day rate. The time allowed for completing the task is set from records of *previous performance* rather than by time and motion studies,[6] which were later introduced by Frederick W. Taylor. The amount of time saved multiplied by the hourly rate forms the sum that is shared between the worker and the owners according to the ratio agreed upon, usually one-half to each. The standard length of time for doing a job, not being derived through the use of time and motion study, is usually greater than would be the case under more scientifically measured procedure. The Halsey plan has been used more extensively in Canada and England than in the United States. Under this system, a definite time is determined for a certain task, and any saving of time is divided in various ratios between the employer and the worker. The uneven requirements of various jobs performed by the same worker, with the resulting temptation for the worker to take time from a difficult job and distribute it among others, thus obtaining premiums on other jobs at the expense of one particular job, create some of the shortcomings[7] of the plan, whereas its simplicity and ease of introduction, requiring no drastic change in method or conditions, are its leading merits. It is a good plan to use during a period of transition from a day rate to some incentive system based upon carefully established standards. The formula for computing the employee's earnings is

$$E = RT + p(S - T)R.$$

**The Rowan plan.** The Rowan wage plan originated in Glasgow, Scotland. Like the Halsey plan the standards were based on past experience rather than careful timing. Wages above standard are

[6] Time studies could be used with the Halsey system, but they seldom have been used.

[7] This juggling of time of course cannot be done where careful checks are made on the starting and closing time for each job.

increased by a percentage equal to the percentage that the worker has saved on the standard time allowed for the particular job. The premium is a percentage of the time worked rather than the time saved. The day rate is guaranteed. The Rowan plan is difficult for the employee to understand and involves considerable clerical detail. Labor-cost predetermination is difficult in the case of both the Halsey and the Rowan plan. An analysis of the formula given below shows that the premium of the Rowan plan can never equal the guaranteed day rate, for the fraction $(S - T)/S$ can never equal unity unless $T$ is equal to 0. The Rowan premium is usually larger than the Halsey premium. If the Halsey premium is 50 per cent, the Rowan premium is larger up to 50 per cent of the time saved. The formula is

$$E = RT + \frac{S - T}{S} RT.$$

**Piece rates based on past performance.** Piece rates set on the basis of previous nonstandardized day-work performance may reasonably be expected to increase production by approximately 50 per cent. The day rate may be guaranteed in a piece-rate system, but such a guarantee is not inherently a part of the system. The guaranteed day rate when used is frequently 33⅓ per cent lower than the expected piece-rate earnings. Piece rates are particularly severe on most beginners unless special provision in the form of a flat day rate or some other equalizing factor is used. When not based upon carefully established time standards, there is considerable likelihood that there will be a conscious limitation of output by the workers for fear of rate cutting by the management. This temptation for management to cut rates is greater for piece rates than for either the Halsey or the Rowan plan, since the workers in these premium plans share with management the gains above standard. Piece rates are easily understood by the workers and are simple to compute for payroll purposes, facilitating labor-cost predetermination within reasonable limits. The formula for figuring earnings on a piece-rate basis is

$$E = RN.$$

**Piece rates based on carefully established time standards.** Under present laws, where workers are engaged in interstate commerce, workers, under any system, must be paid at least the $1 minimum wage per hour. This $1 minimum rate is much lower than what most piece workers would consider satisfactory. There are indications that the minimum rate may soon be changed to $1.15 or $1.25. The worker may still bear risks of the failure to achieve his standard through no fault of his own unless he is protected by a guaranteed base pay higher than the minimum set by law. In the absence of a guaranteed base pay, the piece-rate system places a special burden upon management to keep working conditions such that the worker can earn at least the equivalent of a guaranteed day rate under practically all conditions. There is little temptation for management to cut rates under carefully set standards for piece rates. Unit costs are fairly well cared for under piece rates; yet there is not the same urge to make the standard as in some of the premium bonus plans. There is a tendency for workers to take the attitude that they alone are the losers if their production is below standard, forgetting that often overhead costs are as great as the direct labor costs. It is not unusual for some supervisors to be so lacking in their understanding of the fundamentals of costs as to agree with the workers that it is no major concern of anyone other than the worker if the worker does not make standard. Adam Smith was of the opinion that workers "are very apt to overwork themselves" when they are liberally paid by the piece.[8] There is little evidence to support this contention. While workers may restrict production when working under piece rates and standards set by motion and time study, they are not likely to do so.

**Frederick W. Taylor's differential piece rates.** Taylor's entire approach to wages and working conditions that affect wages may be summarized as follows:

1. The task should be clearly defined and carefully circumscribed.
2. Conditions should make it possible for the worker daily to make his task.
3. The worker should receive high pay for achieving task and low pay in case of failure.

Taylor's wage plan called for two piece rates, a high one when the worker equals or exceeds task and a low one when he fails to equal task. If the standard called for 100 pieces per day at 20 cents per piece, the rate in case of failure to make task would be less, such as 19 cents. In such a situation, the worker would earn $20 for making task and only $18.81 in case he fell short of task by one piece. This differential exerted a powerful pull on the worker to push himself constantly to make task. Taylor's task standards were carefully established so that an average man who was properly instructed and consistently followed instructions could make it. There was no guaranteed day rate. (This of course does not prohibit guaranteeing a day rate.) This placed a heavy burden on management to keep conditions standard so that the worker would not be unjustly

[8] *Wealth of Nations*, Book I, Chap. 8.

penalized. This plan was manifestly too severe on the workers unless management consistently did its part. It never received wide use. The formula for computing the worker's earnings was the same as any other piece-rate system but used two rates, namely,

| | | |
|---|---|---|
| Below task, | $E = RN.$ | (1) |
| At or above task, | $E = R'N,$ | (2) |
| in which case | $R'$ was higher than $R$. | |

**The Gantt wage system.** H. L. Gantt, an associate of Frederick W. Taylor, guaranteed a day rate and paid on the basis of standard time instead of the piece. The principle of Gantt's system would permit various percentages for bonus payments; however, he often used 33⅓ per cent. Gantt paid the worker for all he did above task. The worker was stimulated to finish his task within the standard time by the payment of a liberal bonus for successful performance. If he fell below task, he was paid his day rate. Both the Gantt and Taylor systems were relatively simple to compute. Both systems aided in labor-cost predetermination. Both Taylor and Gantt paid a bonus to the foreman. Gantt paid an additional bonus to the foreman if all his men attained their tasks. Gantt's system is equivalent to a high piece rate and exerted a strong pull to get the worker to achieve task. Since the workers were paid largely in terms of standard hours, it was possible to compare the efficiencies of departments by comparing the standard hours of each in relation to the actual hours worked. The formulas for computing a worker's earnings are

| | | |
|---|---|---|
| Below task, | $E = RT.$ | (1) |
| At or above task, | $E = 1\frac{1}{3}RS,$ or | (2) |
| | $E = RS + pRS,$ | |

in case a percentage other than 33⅓ is used.

**The Emerson premium plan.** Harrington Emerson's *Twelve Principles of Efficiency*, published in 1911, exerted a profound influence on the public's interest in scientific management. The Emerson plan paid for the standard time worked plus a bonus for performance above task, with a guaranteed day rate and a sliding scale of bonuses for performance from 66⅔ of standard up to standard. Emerson developed this sliding scale of bonuses empirically. The premium scale ranged from 0 at 66⅔ per cent efficiency to 20 per cent on reaching standard. His program was predicated on the theory that carefully predetermined standards would require an increase of production approximately equivalent to 50 per cent over the old unmeasured-rate performance. With this in mind, using the measured standard as a base, he gave an initial bonus when the worker exceeded the old day-rate performance, which was 66⅔ per cent of the measured standard. This served to spur the worker to increase his efforts to reach standard and was not so discouraging when he fell short of standard performance. The Emerson bonus was computed on the basis of the performance for the pay period and not for a particular day or hour. A few plans currently in use are modifications of the Emerson plan and pay on the basis of daily performance. This aspect of the Emerson plan, in all probability, causes it to exert less pull to equal standard performance at a given time than the Taylor or Gantt systems. It does, however, tend to exert a steady pull to reach standard performance. The Emerson plan is difficult for the worker to understand and involves considerable clerical detail. It is customary daily to post the worker's efficiency or earnings for the previous day's performance. This practice reduces somewhat the criticism that the plan is difficult for the worker to understand. The Emerson system is fairly satisfactory as an aid to labor-cost predetermination. The worker receives full pay for all his standard time above task, but the premium is computed on the *basis of actual time worked rather than standard time*. This is equivalent to a high piece rate even though it is computed on the time basis. The formulas for computing a worker's earnings are as follows:

From 66⅔ per cent of task up to task,

$$E = RT + p(RT). \tag{1}$$

The value of $p$ is taken from a table constructed empirically, a part of which is given in the table on page 409. At or above task,

$$E = RS + 0.20RT. \tag{2}$$

**100 per cent time premium wage plan.** The standard hours for the given production at or above standard provide the basis for payment in the 100 per cent time-premium plan. Below standard the worker is paid for the actual time worked. In many respects, it is the forerunner of *measured day work*. A task time is set for each operation. The rate paid the worker may be based either on the worker himself or on the job on which he is working. It is simpler when the worker has a given rate attached to him regardless of his job; however, this is seldom the case. When the rate attaches to the task, a worker may have more than one rate during the day. In case the rate is attached to the job rather than the worker, each job usually carries a guaranteed base rate. Regardless of whether the rate attaches to the worker or to the job, the actual work performed is expressed in terms of standard hours. The sum of the total standard hours worked on

| Percentage of efficiency | Emerson bonus percentages | | Percentage of bonus |
| --- | --- | --- | --- |
| | Percentage of bonus | Percentage of efficiency | |
| 67.00–71.09 | 0.25 | 89.40– 90.49 | 10 |
| 71.10–73.09 | 0.5 | 90.50– 91.49 | 11 |
| 73.10–75.69 | 1 | 91.50– 92.49 | 12 |
| 75.70–78.29 | 2 | 92.50– 93.49 | 13 |
| 78.30–80.39 | 3 | 93.50– 94.49 | 14 |
| 80.40–82.29 | 4 | 94.50– 95.49 | 15 |
| 82.30–83.89 | 5 | 95.50– 96.49 | 16 |
| 83.90–85.39 | 6 | 96.50– 97.49 | 17 |
| 85.40–86.79 | 7 | 97.50– 98.49 | 18 |
| 86.80–88.09 | 8 | 98.50– 99.49 | 19 |
| 88.10–89.39 | 9 | 99.50–100.00 | 20 |

each job gives the worker's allowed time for the day. The 100 per cent time-premium plan of wage payment has an advantage over straight piecework in that, in the case where the rate attaches to the worker, rate changes may be made by merely changing the worker's base rate without changing a series of piece rates. It simplifies the record-keeping problems in the case of rate changes and also has certain psychological advantages. Under close supervision, labor costs can be predetermined with a fair measure of accuracy. The formulas for computing the worker's earnings are

At or below standard,    $E = RT.$    (1)
Above standard task,    $E = RS.$    (2)

**Measured day rates.** In addition to the rate that attaches to each job, each employee receives special inducements based upon his versatility, quality of work, dependability, quantity of production, and length of service. The exact number of factors used to make up this additional reward may vary with different companies using the system. This system requires careful job evaluation as well as rating of the employee. At the beginning, the employee is usually rated about once a month to establish his additional reward. When the system is generally accepted and firmly established, the worker is usually rated every 3 months, when his rate may remain the same, be lowered, or be raised on the basis of his record. This requires the keeping of accurate records of the worker's attendance, quality of work, productivity, etc., to make possible the evaluation of the relative value of the worker. Measured day rates are similar to 100 per cent time premium when the rate applies to the job. Measured day work lays a special burden upon supervision to keep the worker's production up to standard volume. For mass-production industries using mechanical conveyors that set the pace, this is not so serious a problem as it might seem at first. The clerical work is considerably less than that required for many of the incentive systems; however, the keeping of the necessary records for accurately evaluating the worker's efficiency is practically as great as for straight piecework. Little friction arises as long as the worker's rating is not reduced, but considerable friction may readily arise when a worker's rating is lowered. The system makes possible fairly accurate labor-cost predetermination.[9]

**The Bedaux wage-payment plan.** Under the Bedaux system the amount of work a man will do per minute is known as a standard work minute or standard work unit. Each job is rated in terms of the number of standard work minutes allowed for its performance. The worker is guaranteed the base rate for each job and is paid a bonus for performance above standard. Formerly, this bonus in most installations was somewhat less than the full standard in excess of actual time, most frequently being 75 per cent of the time saved. In most of the present installations, the workers are paid the full time saved. The allowed or standard time for a worker for a given period is determined by dividing by 60 the number of standard work minutes that he has been allotted for the work completed. The system makes possible the comparison of the efficiency of one department with another, since all the work is reduced to a common denominator. The Bedaux system is used extensively in industry today. Labor-cost predetermination is fairly easy by this system. One of the objections raised to this plan is the difficulty experienced by the production workers in checking the pay received against the amount they think is due them. Like any other form of wage payment, it is not of itself an efficiency-creating device but depends upon the workers' reaction to it for its effectiveness. Earnings are computed as follows,

$$E = RT + p(S - T)R \text{ or } RS,$$

when the worker is paid for the full allowed time.

**A comparison of various wage plans.** No one wage system of itself is the sole instrument for developing efficiency, and the value of every plan depends upon its administration. It is possible that a certain wage plan with many seemingly undesirable features tending toward inefficiency may prove to be successful through intelligent administration and to create the necessary incentive in a particular instance.[10]

[9] Charles Walter Lytle, *Wage Incentive Methods,* The Ronald Press Company, New York, 1942, pp. 142–143.

[10] See *ibid.,* for a detailed discussion of practically any wage plan. This book is a classic in its field.

*Table 27.1   Types of Wage-payment Plans in Use*

| | Total firms answering questionnaire | | | | | |
|---|---|---|---|---|---|---|
| | 325 firms, 1947 | | 628 firms, 1952 | | 852 firms, 1957 | |
| | Number | Per cent | Number | Per cent | Number | Per cent |
| 1. Straight time (day rate).............. | 285 | 87.7 | 521 | 83.0 | 685 | 80.4 |
| 2. Straight piece rate (without guaranteed day rate)......................... | 26 | 8.0 | 39 | 6.2 | 45 | 5.3 |
| 3. Group or gang piece rate............. | 63 | 19.3 | 111 | 17.7 | 136 | 16.0 |
| 4. Piece rate (with guaranteed minimum). | 113 | 34.8 | 195 | 31.1 | 192 | 22.5 |
| 5. Task and bonus (Gantt)............. | 20 | 6.2 | 38 | 6.1 | 37 | 4.3 |
| 6. Premium plan (Halsey, Barth, Rowan). | 18 | 5.5 | 44 | 7.0 | 49 | 5.8 |
| 7. Increased-efficiency plan (Emerson).... | 16 | 4.8 | 21 | 3.3 | 37 | 4.3 |
| 8. Group bonus plan (Wennerlund)....... | 26 | 8.0 | 57 | 9.1 | 60 | 7.0 |
| 9. Differential piece rate (Taylor)........ | 6 | 1.8 | 14 | 2.2 | 17 | 2.0 |
| 10. Point premium plan (Bedaux, Haynes). | 28 | 8.6 | 46 | 7.3 | 47 | 5.5 |
| 11. Contract method.................... | 16 | 4.8 | 39 | 6.2 | 52 | 6.1 |
| 12. Sliding scale (selling price of product).. | 2 | 0.6 | 7 | 1.1 | 5 | 0.6 |
| 13. Measured day rate.................. | 19 | 5.9 | 34 | 5.4 | 53 | 6.2 |
| 14. Other plans....................... | 34 | 10.4 | 72 | 11.5 | 106 | 12.4 |

Figure A.4 shows the use of the various wage plans for the years 1930, 1940, 1947, 1952, and 1957. Table 27.1 compares the usage on a percentage basis for the years 1947, 1952, and 1957.

A study of the graph (Fig. 27.1) comparing the wage-payment plans shows that engineers like Parkhurst and Taylor applied one theory to wage payment, whereas Bedaux and Ficker applied another.[11] All the plans that result in a payment of some amount greater than the straight piece rate take into consideration the fact that, when workers exceed the standard set, the owners immediately participate indirectly in the excess through a relative reduction of overhead. It should be plain that factory overhead costs per machine may be cut in half, for example, if the workers in a plant are expected to complete 50 machines in 1 month but produce 100 instead. The owners have paid for the 100 machines only half as much foremen's and executives' salaries and half as much on investment, light, heat, depreciation, and the like. Therefore, owing to such reduction in cost, workers may logically be paid per piece (unit) an amount in excess of the straight piece rate.

[11] See *ibid.*, for a discussion of wage plans mentioned but not discussed in this chapter.

This statement of course ignores the fact that management may have expended considerable additional cost to help the workers produce the 100 machines.

**Group wage plans.** Payment of the group for a given volume of production has certain psychological advantages. To pay persons as a group who can, by their efforts or lack of effort, directly influence the total output of the group is to make it not only desirable to cooperate but profitable to do so. Group payments tend to encourage workers to take the necessary steps of their own volition to eliminate "bottlenecks." They also tend to aid supervisors in keeping potential loafers steadily on the job. The foregoing is predicated on the assumption that the group is small enough so that workers can see the results of their efforts. Groups of 10 to 20 men possess most of the desirable characteristics as far as cooperation and individual incentive are concerned. Some groups have been as large as 600 or more. This may work satisfactorily when speeds are controlled mechanically, but most of the desired characteristics other than payroll or clerical advantages are absent from such large groups. The unofficial leader, present in

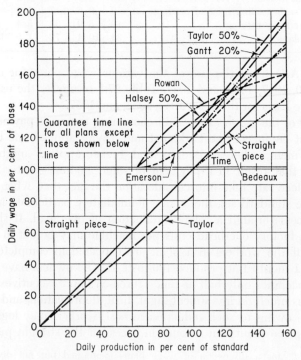

FIG. 27.1. Chart comparing various wage plans. (*Courtesy, Adolph Langsner.*)

nearly all groups, cannot function effectively when the group is much larger than 20. In the case of group piece rate, the group is paid a given amount per piece. The total amount earned by the group is then divided on some predetermined basis among the members of the group. This basis may be a day rate for each worker or any other scheme that may be acceptable to all parties concerned. Most of the other programs may be likewise adjusted to the group. It is highly desirable that the record-keeping department issue daily reports to the group so that the members of the group may know what they have earned. The payment of beginners raises a serious problem in certain cases of group payments. In a large group, a learner may not pull down the earnings of the group materially, but, in small groups, the payment of a beginner out of the group earnings becomes a real problem. Under such conditions, the learner may not share in the group earnings at first but be paid a flat day rate.

**Wages for salespeople.** The problems of selling differ all the way from selling locomotives and mammoth steam shovels to neckties, thread, and ladies' garments. Again the problems of paying salesmen who travel differ widely from paying department-store salespeople.

The wage plan should be adjusted to the needs of the particular situation. These adjustments may include special provision for collections, calls on new prospects, calls on regular customers whether or not sales are made, securing prospects for other departments than the one represented by the salesman, etc. Straight salary has the advantage of permitting the company to transfer the salesman to any part of the store or to any territory, without special detriment to the salesman, thus permitting greater flexibility. Where the incentive system of rewarding salesmen is used, a basic salary or drawing account is customary. A quota is frequently assigned for which a flat salary is paid, with a bonus for sales above this quota. When salesmen are on straight commission with a drawing account, drawings in excess of the commission earned are charged against the salesman's account, to be paid back later out of commissions earned above his drawings. Over long periods of reduced sales such as the depression periods, these excess drawings are frequently written off by the company, particularly for regular salesmen who have been with the firm for some time. The payment of salesmen on a straight commission basis has the same disadvantage as straight piecework for factory workers. This is especially true of the lower-paid salesmen.

**Wages for office employees.** Most clerical workers in factories are paid on an hourly basis. The preferred social status of clerical workers and the resultant relatively excess supply tend to make the wages of clerical workers lower than factory workers of equal ability and responsibility. Factory workers have also as a rule been more highly organized than clerical workers, which may have contributed somewhat to this situation. In the past clerical workers have had certain other advantages, such as vacations with pay, steadier work, etc. This difference as to vacations is no longer so great as formerly; yet even today office workers frequently get a longer vacation than the factory workers in the same plant. Clerical workers in the large offices in factories, stores, and other institutions are usually paid on a salary basis with overtime pay when they come under the Fair Labor Standards Act. Clerical workers have been placed on incentive wage systems in some cases where there were enough of them to justify the expense of establishing the necessary standards and caring for the details involved. Large insurance offices, banks, mail-order houses, and other institutions having a large volume of clerical work have frequently made use of incentive systems for output of clerical workers, particularly typists, file clerks, etc.

**Salaries for executives and supervisors.** Top executive salaries of companies that file reports with the Securities and Exchange Commission are reported. Other executive salaries are not readily available to the public.[12] Relatively few companies[13] have done a constructive job of rating salaried employees. This field is commanding increasing attention in management circles at present. A comparison of government salaries and business salaries for corresponding work may be made in general as follows: (1) salaries for the lower grades of service tend to be higher in government agencies than in industry; (2) salaries in the average or medium levels tend to be somewhat higher in government agencies; (3) salaries in the upper supervisory levels tend to be definitely lower in government service than in corresponding work in business.

Regular foremen or department heads are nearly always paid on a

[12] See National Industrial Conference Board, Inc., *Studies in Personnel Policy* 100, 106, 111, 113, 122, New York, 1949, 1950, 1951. The American Management Association makes periodic surveys of executives' salaries that are available to their company members. These are particularly valuable; see also *Harvard Business Review*, September–October, 1955, p. 121, November–December, 1956, p. 124, September–October, 1957, p. 125, and September–October, 1958, p. 129, for a series of articles by Arch Patton on executive salaries.

[13] The United States Steel Corporation has worked out a plan for inventory and appraisal of executive personnel. See "Executive Compensations Compared with Earnings" and "Compensation of Executive Officers of Steel Companies," *Harvard Business Review*, January, 1936, July, 1937; John C. Baker, *The Compensation of Executive Officers of Retail Companies*, 1928–1935, Harvard University Press, Cambridge, Mass., 1937; see also John C. Baker, *Executive Salaries and Bonus Plans*, McGraw-Hill Book Company, Inc., New York, 1938.

straight salary basis. At times, they receive a bonus based either on profits earned or on the efficiency of their departments. Supervisors above the rank of foremen are almost universally paid on a monthly or yearly basis. The higher their rank, the more frequently they participate in bonus or profit-sharing programs. Some inspectors and assistant foremen are paid on an hourly or day rate and at times are included in the group wage. These supervisors are supposed to represent management; yet the wages paid them, the continuity of their employment, etc., are so often the same or nearly the same as for the regular workers that in fact their attachments and outlook on life are not with the broader management approach but rather with the restricted worker view. The social prestige and economic status of a supervisor definitely influence his effectiveness. This whole field is as yet unsatisfactorily explored and inadequately solved by many managements. A few companies have striven to reward supervisors in such a manner as to ensure that their earnings will be higher than the earnings of the men they supervise. For instance, one well-managed company pays each first-line supervisor 20 per cent more than the average of the five highest-paid men under his direction.

**Escalator clauses.**[14] General Motors Corporation in 1948 introduced the clause agreeing to increase or decrease wages, according to a prearranged schedule, if the consumer's price index of the Bureau of Labor Statistics should rise or fall a given amount. This type of agreement continues in their 1958 contract. This type of clause has not received wide acceptance but is included in a few of the large company agreements (see Fig. A.4). This concept has been used by other companies in the past such as the Philadelphia Rapid Transit Company. Escalator clauses are popular with workers while the cost of living is rising but are not so readily acceptable when the cost of living is declining. The General Motors contract also provided an annual improvement factor of 3 cents per hour. Undoubtedly General Motors can absorb such an improvement factor if the future can be measured by the past. On the other hand many companies and industries could not.

Escalator clauses may be applied either to day rates or to incentive systems. It is easier to apply them to hourly rated jobs, but a factor can be computed that is used as a multiplier for earnings based upon any incentive system.

[14] See National Industrial Conference Board, Inc., "Cost of Living Provisions in Union Contracts," "Escalators and the New BLS Index," *Studies in Personnel Policy* 113, 137, New York, 1951, June, 1953.

## CHAPTER 28

# Profit Sharing and Employee Stock Ownership

**History of profit sharing.** The International Cooperative Congress, Paris, France, in 1889 defined profit sharing as:

. . . an agreement freely entered into, by which the employees receive a share, fixed in advance, of profits. In the discussions of this Cooperative Congress, profits were further defined as being the actual net balance or gain realized by the final operations of the undertaking in relation to which the scheme existed, and the sums paid to the employees out of the profits were directly dependent upon the profits.[1]

This conception further stipulated that an appreciable fraction of employees must be profit sharers—not less than 75%.[2]

*Profit sharing is the payment to employees in cash, stock, or future credits of some amount over and above the normal remuneration that would otherwise be paid to these employees in the given situation.* The payments do not have to be derived from the current period involved but may be taken from an earned surplus from prior periods of operation. This definition does not require an agreement fixing the percentage in advance.

Payments could be made from current profits without any prior agreement, although it is believed that the morale-building effect would be greater if these payments were made in conformity with a well-organized plan. Certain bonus payments made to employees, particularly executives, would be, according to our concept, partly wages and partly a share in profits. For instance, it is not uncommon to pay an executive a base salary sufficient to care for his normal living costs and to pay him a bonus depending in part upon the volume of

---

[1] See "Survey of Experiences in Profit Sharing and Possibilities of Incentive Taxation," *Senate Report* 610, 75th Cong., 1st Sess., p. 53, quoting from the report of the International Cooperative Congress in Paris, France, 1889. This is a comprehensive survey of profit sharing in the United States.

[2] Z. Clark Dickinson, *Compensating Industrial Effort*, The Ronald Press Company, New York, 1937, p. 331.

business or profits. In such cases, it is often expected that a substantial part of the salary will be in the form of a bonus and that the salary would be higher were there no bonus.

Charles Babbage, the English economist, in 1832 wrote regarding product sharing, as follows:[3]

These extraordinary cases, are, perhaps, of more advantage to the owner of the mine than even to the men; for whilst the skill and industry of the workmen are greatly stimulated, the owner himself derives greater advantage from the improvement of the vein. This system is introduced by Mr. Taylor into the lead mines of Flintshire, into those of Skipton in Yorkshire, and into some of the copper mines of Cumberland; and it is desirable that it should become general because no other mode of payment affords to the workmen a measure of success so directly proportionate to the industry, the integrity, and the talent which they exert.

Le Claire, the Parisian house painter, introduced profit sharing in 1842.[4] His success was phenomenal, and his firm continued the essential features of his program until modern times.

It is recorded that the success of the "Le Claire" plan was due to the fact that Le Claire knew his craft and the men who practiced it; he knew their temptations and their difficulties; he knew their weaknesses and their impulses and he constructed his plan in such a way as to govern, control, and protect men against themselves.

. . . John Stuart Mill held up M. Le Claire as an example to employers of labor, and most subsequent writers on political economy, in England and America, have agreed with Mr. Mill. Professor Jevons and Professor Fawcett distinguished themselves by earnest advocacy of industrial partnerships.[5]

Profit sharing in the United States was introduced by Albert Gallatin in his glassworks at New Geneva, Pa., in 1794.[6] Horace Greeley inaugurated a profit-sharing program for the employees of the *New York Tribune*. Pillsbury Flour Mills Company of Minneapolis introduced a profit-sharing plan in 1882. In 1884, the B. & O. Railway Company introduced a "pension relief savings plan." Procter and Gamble Company began its program in 1886.

Gradually other companies adopted profit sharing, prominent among them being the Simplex Wire & Cable Co., of Cambridge, Mass., in 1901; Hibbard, Spencer, Bartlett & Co., of Chicago, in 1902; the R. J. Reynolds Tobacco Co., Winston-Salem, N.C., with 15,000 employees, and the Eastman Kodak Company with some 24,000 employees in 1912; the Edison Electric Illuminating Co. of Boston, in 1913; the California & Hawaiian Sugar Company, of Crockett, Cali-

---

[3] Charles Babbage, Esq., A.M., *On the Economy of Machines and Manufactures,* Charles Knight, London, 1832, pp. 178–179.
[4] See Dickinson, *op. cit.,* pp. 329, 370, 371, 374.
[5] *Senate Report* 610, 75th Cong., 1st Sess., p. 71.
[6] *Ibid.,* pp. 72–77, for the source of material used in this paragraph.

fornia, in 1914; the Cleveland Twist Drill Co., of Cleveland, in 1915. Of the more significant plans inaugurated in later years, we find in 1916 the Sears, Roebuck and Company, of Chicago, having a normal employee group of over 30,000, initiated a plan under which the company pays 5 per cent of its net profits which has prevailed against war period and depressions. Even in 1931 this company paid $1,000,000 into its profit-sharing fund.[7]

**Profits defined.** There is a great deal of fuzzy thinking among large segments of the population about the nature of profits. Persons with a reform complex and others with a "mental set" against constituted authority derived from ownership are prone to look upon profits as something evil to be avoided by righteous men. *Profits through service* (the only basis for a continuing business) is an ethical concept.

We are interested only in profits after expenses (including taxes), for these are the profits which are available for distribution. We are interested in *net profits that would remain after deducting from income all expenses for land, labor, and capital as figured on the basis of the market rate for each.* Net profits as thus conceived would be somewhat different from the accountant's net profit in a case where management deliberately paid a wage higher than the necessary market rate. In such a situation, management would be distributing in the form of wages a portion of the profit. On the assumption that all expenses correspond to the prevailing expenses that would normally be encountered in a given situation, *net profits would equal total income minus the expense of securing the income.* It is the fleeting nature of profits that has caused some representatives of labor to oppose profit sharing. For instance, management may, if it so elects, pay itself a wage considerably higher than the market value of its services and thus by increasing expenses reduce what would otherwise be a profit to a loss. Social reformers who speak derogatorily about profits forget that profits are a by-product of successful operations and that profit sharing cannot be realized unless the profits are first earned. They also forget that even during prosperous years many corporations have deficits rather than profits.

Profits vary in the same company from year to year, vary between different companies in the same industry, and vary between different industries. An entire industry by virtue of its high productivity per man and its favorable competitive situation may not only pay high annual wages to its employees but also be in a position to share its profits with its employees, whereas another industry during the same

---

[7] *Ibid.*, p. 73. At the close of 1959 Sears, Roebuck and Company had 139,967 employees participating in their profit-sharing program. The total amount in the fund was in excess of $1,322,327,797. The fund owned about 26.9 per cent of the Sears stock.

period may be unable to pay a wage anything like so high as the first one and may have no profits whatsoever to share. The individual employees and management may work as hard in the second industry as in the first. Profits do not arise alone from the efforts of an individual or single enterprise in many instances but frequently from economic forces and competitive conditions quite beyond the power of the individual concern to control. This inherent nature of profits has caused many serious students of the subject to conclude that, since profits are a residual after paying the normal costs of doing business and since the owners are the last of the factors of production to be paid, the owners are primary risk bearers and as such should receive the profits, if there be any, as a reward for risk bearing.

Material and equipment do not produce a going enterprise. There must also be employees, from the hired manager to the humblest workmen. In the beginning, the employees bear relatively little risk in comparison with the suppliers of finance; yet, over a period of years, the employees do in a very real sense share in the risks of the enterprise. A salesman who has devoted 20 years of service to a department store is vitally interested in the continuing success of the enterprise and has during his service shared a considerable part of the risks of the institution. In proportion to his ability and capacity, he has often shared even a greater risk than many of its larger stockholders. This statement is not based upon a communistic or socialistic philosophy. It merely recognizes a factual situation. To recognize this relationship and to share in part the profits of industry is one of the soundest methods of perpetuating our capitalistic system.

**Why share profits?** There need be little fear of the destruction of private ownership so long as a majority of the people participate in the fruits of the system and have a feeling of proprietary interest. One objective of profit sharing is to develop in the minds of the participants a feeling of mutuality of interests between the employers and employees. When this feeling becomes a reality, the other objectives will tend to be realized as a by-product.

Z. Clark Dickinson has enumerated the purposes sought by profit sharing as follows:[8]

1. To promote efficiency, when measurement of individual results or close supervision is impossible.
2. To prevent waste.
3. To prevent labor turnover.
4. To promote industrial peace.
5. To promote effective management.

[8] Dickinson, *op. cit.*, p. 334.

6. To ensure the continuance of management.
7. For humanitarian purposes.
8. For the stabilization of employment.

Stabilization of employment, industrial peace, and humanitarian purposes are essentially social in their major emphasis. These factors also directly or indirectly affect the economic status of employees as well as the company. Increased production, elimination of waste, reduction of labor turnover, and the promotion of effective management are all factors that have a direct economic connotation. It is true that these objectives also have broad social implications.

It is not necessary to give employees a substantial control of the operation of the business in order to give them a proprietary interest in the success of the enterprise.

Many persons prefer to provide capital for a business enterprise and to take preferred stock or bonds rather than take active participation in the management. It would be foolish to infer that these persons are not vitally interested in the success of the enterprise. It is very doubtful as to the desire of the rank and file of employees for active participation in the determining of major business policies other than those which directly affect them. It is undoubtedly true that workers like to have a voice in the determination of the hours of work, wages, working conditions, etc., especially in those situations where management's action is less satisfactory than the workers may reasonably expect.

**Employment stability and profit sharing.** Profit sharing provides the employer more flexibility in his cost of labor than the freezing of the "profit share" into the basic wage.[9]

To add the profit to the regular wage would mean the assumption of a relatively fixed cost. If there are no profits, they naturally will not be distributed and that portion of the remuneration given the employees for the previous period is not a cost that has to be recovered in the selling price of the product. Such flexibility in meeting competition, other things being equal, tends to stabilize employment. It is true that a similar condition would result from a reduction of wages; however, anyone familiar with employees' psychology knows that it is a difficult problem to reduce wages. Some may say that, if all industry participated in profit sharing, the advantage claimed above would not be realized by a given manufacturer, since there would be no advantage in comparison with his competitors. This criticism is true only in part, since the industry that had shared profits, having been in a

[9] See National Industrial Conference Board, Inc., "Sharing Profits with Employees," *Studies in Personnel Policy* 162, New York, 1957, p. 13, for an interesting and comprehensive research on the entire profit sharing program.

more advantageous position than the one that had no profits to share, would tend to remain in a more advantageous position unless other factors were introduced that had no relation to the wage costs. It is also highly probable that the economy as a whole would not have such violent cyclical swings if it were capable of adjusting more readily to changing costs.

**Two basic types of profit sharing.** In general there are two basic types of profit-sharing programs, (1) the current-distribution plan, in which the full amount of the employee's profit share is given him at the time of allocation, and (2) the deferred-distribution plan, in which the employee's share of profits is given to him at some future date such as at the end of 5 years, at retirement, disability, death, or termination of employment. Of course there could be a combination of these two methods on practically any basis, such as 30 per cent of the employee's share to be distributed currently and the 70 per cent to be distributed on a deferred basis.[10] The deferred profit-sharing plans may or may not have an employee's participating savings feature. Plans calling for the employee's saving in order to be eligible for his full share in profits may have almost any ratio of allocation of profits in terms of participation. For instance, if the plan be a combination of current payments in cash or stock and a deferred payment, the deferred part may depend entirely upon the employee's participation in the savings plan. The combined current and deferred distribution of profits seems to be gaining in popularity. There is no doubt that such a plan has a stronger pull on the employee, particularly the newer employee, to increase his efforts to add to the profits available for distribution. Since the deferred plan builds up an estate for the employee more rapidly than any form of current distribution, this deferred distribution is likely to be preferred by the longer-service employees. This is particularly true of the middle-aged or older employees.

**Vesting interests in the deferred profit sharing plans.** Practically any legitimate vesting plan would be approved by the Internal Revenue Department. The only barring feature would be an attempt to have the allocated profits return to the company. If an employee leaves before the specified time, his share of the allocated profits may go to the persons remaining in the profit-sharing plan but not back to the company. One company established 5-year classes annually when it allocated profits. At the end of the 5-year period the accumulated amount of the profit share was paid to each employee. During the long depression of the 1930's this company paid to its employees who had been discharged because of the shutdown of plants their full

[10] See National Industrial Conference Board, *ibid.* p. 8.

amount of the maturing classes. On the other hand one large company ties its profit-sharing plan to its retirement program. The company pays the entire cost of the retirement pension. In this company an employee who leaves before the eligible retirement age receives no pension or interest in the allocated profits. His share of allocated profits goes to the persons remaining in the plan.

It is difficult to pass judgment on vesting. Employees like to have an irrevocable interest in any share of profits allocated to them. On the other hand, if one of the objectives of the employer is to reduce labor turnover, it is desirable to vest only when the employee is eligible to retire.

**Unions' attitude toward profit sharing.** Some unions support profit sharing, and in the past other unions opposed it. In 1958 Walter Reuther of the United Auto Workers tried to include a profit-sharing clause in their contract. His program was not a simple one but a complicated one involving economic philosophy. It was rejected by the automobile companies. It is conceivable that unions and management may include a workable profit-sharing plan in future contracts just as they have pension plans. As a matter of fact a carefully planned profit-sharing program may well become a part of a pension plan. Organized labor's former opposition is based essentially on distrust of the motives of management. In part, it may be due to a fear that, if the employees in fact embrace the partnership idea, there will be less class consciousness and possibly less feeling on the part of the workers that they need the protection of the union. Management would be unwise if it originated a profit-sharing program for the purpose of preventing the organization of its employees or to weaken the existing organization of its employees' choice. The Senate Committee reported the opinion of the president of a prominent American labor union as follows:[11]

We are emphatically opposed to any form of so-called profit sharing because it creates the mistaken idea in the minds of employees that such plans make them "partners" in industry and divert their attention from unionism. It seems to become a substitute for collective bargaining. These plans are used to keep salaries and wages at status quo and even lower levels. Such minor returns as employees have received have been unimportant in comparison to increase, dignity, and independence gained through organized unionism.

In the same report, William Green, the late president of the AFL, is quoted as saying:[12]

[11] *Senate Report* 610, 75th Cong., 1st Sess., p. 91.
[12] *Ibid.*, p. 92.

Labor is not opposed to principles involved in profit sharing, but it is opposed to the way in which it has been developed and operated—recognition of real partnership and frank acceptance of the privileges and rights derived therefrom would be the greatest incentive to sustain efficiency in work that industry could devise—if the earnings of the industry would justify an equitable distribution of the profits of industry between investors, management, and employees, let it be done with a full understanding and in full cooperation with the representatives of the workers. The one trouble about profit sharing, as practiced by a number of corporations, is that it has created suspicion and distrust, because the workers know nothing about the basis upon which the profits were distributed . . . there is a great need of frankness and open dealing between the management and the workers today. Let the workers know the truth.

**Profit sharing's relation to wages.** Profit sharing is *that part of the employee's remuneration over and above what he would otherwise receive if he were paid the going rate in the community for the services rendered.* By this definition a man's wage will not be lower because he shares in profits. His share of profits may be in proportion to his wages, since this is a common method of allocating profits. It is not unusual to consider length of service in the total allotment, but, even when this is considered, it is usually tied to the employee's wage as a basis of computation. In the case of ordinary workers, it is highly improbable that the regular wage is materially lower under normal conditions than it would be if profits were not being shared. The situation may be somewhat different in the case of some of the higher executives. Since executives are usually in a better position to influence profits, it may be reasonable to remunerate them in a greater degree through profit sharing than the regular workers. Executives are also as a rule in a better position to bear the risks of not receiving their expected amount in profits, if these expected profits are considered in determining their base salaries. To illustrate, it might well be the policy to pay an executive $18,000 a year as a base salary plus a predetermined share in expected profits. It might be that the board of directors in reality estimated that the executive would ordinarily receive a total remuneration of $30,000 including his share of profits. Such a situation is more logical for an executive than it would be for an ordinary worker to receive anything like such a proportion of his total remuneration in the form of profit sharing. It does not follow that the executive's salary in the illustration above would have been set at $18,000 had there been no profit-sharing program. It would most probably have been considerably higher than that amount.[13]

[13] See National Industrial Conference Board, Inc., *Studies in Personnel Policy* 162, New York, 1951, 1957, for excellent researches on various phases of this subject.

On the other hand in a company whose business followed rather closely the ups and downs of the business cycle there might be some logic in relating the upper 10 per cent of the expected earnings to profit sharing. This would especially be true if the cost of living followed the level of business activity. During the 1957 recession the cost of living did not drop in proportion to the fall in business activity. Unemployment compensation, wage rigidities, and government price maintenance of farmers' products contributed to this failure of the cost of living to be so sensitive to the volume of business as during previous years.

**Some problems in profit sharing.** Profit sharing may result in negative morale as well as positive attitudes. If there are no profits to be distributed and the workers have been expecting them after having received them for a period of years in cash, morale is certain to be lowered. The objective of building up an estate for the worker is achieved more readily by giving him his share of profits in annuities, to which he may or may not contribute in part. When this is done, it probably serves as a weaker incentive to the worker in the beginning of his career than the profit sharing program in which the distribution is in cash; however, the motivating effect of annuities, etc., tends to increase with the passage of time and the accumulation of an estate. The plan of requiring an employee to contribute some of his own earnings to a profit-sharing program should be carefully worked out so that the employee's contribution is safeguarded and earns a reasonable return. A failure to do this may readily defeat the fundamental purpose of profit sharing when depressions cause the employee's contribution to be worth less than he originally invested. In view of the uncertainty of profits and the fact that their sharing involves considerable waiting, if their major objectives are to be achieved, profit sharing seems to offer a stronger incentive to executives and supervisors than to the rank-and-file workers.

The basis for distributing of profits also presents certain problems illustrated by the following questions and comments:

1. Will the shared profits be computed before or after taxes? The profits shared with employees up to 15 per cent of the employee's earnings are a deduction to the company as an expense.

2. Will the profits to be shared be computed after allocating a certain amount to the owners of the company's stock? Some persons argue that a reasonable return should be made to the owners before sharing profits with employees.

2.1 Should this allocation to the owners be in relation to the book value of the stock, to its market value, or on what basis?

2.2 What per cent allocation should be made to owners before sharing profits with employees? Should this per cent be related to general interest rates for risks similar to that borne by the company? One thing is relatively certain: there will be no profit sharing in the absence of satisfactory return to the owners unless it is forced on management by a strong union.

3. Having determined the basis of computing (1) and (2) above, how will the amount of profits to be shared be computed? Will it be on a 50–50 basis between owners and employees, 40 per cent to employees and 60 per cent to owners, or on what basis?

4. Having determined the amount to be distributed to employees as a share in profits, shall it be allocated on the basis of earnings for the period, earnings plus length of service, or what basis to those eligible to participate? No formula may be used, but the allocation may be on the basis of estimated contribution of the employee to earning the profits. In this case the allocating of a disproportionate amount to top executives would probably be questioned by Internal Revenue.

5. Who should participate in the profit-sharing program? Shall it include all regular employees regardless of length of service or only persons with 1, 2, or 5 years of service? The program will have a stronger incentive to produce if it applies to all employees after a reasonably short period of service. If the plan is a deferred type to be paid only at retirement or some reasonably long period such as 5 years, some companies do not include employees under the age of twenty-five or even thirty. Such plans are frequently related to the pension program.

6. If the profit-sharing plan includes a deferred feature, who will operate the fund created? Will it be operated by trustees made up largely by management's representatives, by a bank or trust company, or by what agency? May the funds be invested in the company's own stock on some percentage basis or entirely?

The foregoing questions and comments are illustrative of the decisions to be made in a profit-sharing program. Profit sharing does not take the place of collective bargaining or other personnel procedures. Actually it is the better part of wisdom not to consider profit sharing unless the other phases of personnel management are functioning smoothly.

**Employee stock ownership.** Figure A.5, item 8, shows that stock-purchase plans are receiving renewed attention after the unfortunate experience of the 1930's. Twenty-nine per cent of the companies participating in this survey have a formal stock-ownership program for employees. This impetus to employee ownership is undoubtedly related to the prolonged period of prosperity beginning in 1940 and the inflationary prices of stock. Advocates of stock ownership by employees feel that it promotes thrift, a feeling of ownership or partnership in the company, employee security, and increased efficiency of the employee in that he feels that his efforts are in part for himself. Stock has been made available to employees on various bases, namely, (1) purchase at market price, the company financing the purchase and deducting specified amounts from the employee's pay until the stock is paid for; (2) purchase at a price somewhat lower than market and paid for by the employee the same as above; and (3) an outright gift to the employee as a part of his share in a profit-sharing program. The employee may pay all, part, or none of the market price of the stock depending upon the policy of the company. The particular stock sold the employees may be the regular common stock, preferred stock, or a special stock issued for the purpose. Occasionally, the company may pay the employee a special bonus such as $2 extra for each share of stock he held for a period of 5 years or some agreed period. Most of these purchase programs of the twenties progressed nicely so long as the market value of the stock remained above the purchase price to the employee. When the market price fell below the worker's purchase price, this tended to have a morale-depressing effect rather than a morale-building effect, particularly if the employee had not paid in full for his stock and especially if the market price fell below the amount he still owed on his stock, a situation that arose at times. Of course, if the stock had been given to the employee as a share in profits, the depressing effect was not so great; yet, even in such cases, the employee would frequently ask himself, "How much better off would I have been if I had sold my stock when the price was up?"

The average worker can ill afford to have any appreciable amount of his funds tied up in either common or preferred stocks, owing to the tendency for stocks to fluctuate in price to the extent that they do. This is doubly true when it is recalled that these depressions in stock prices usually come at a time when the employee has reduced earnings or in some cases no earnings at all. The desired security is not present if the employee is forced to sell his stock at a loss when he is laid off. Another fundamental in investment is also violated, namely, diversity in holdings. If both the employee's investments and his wage come from the same "basket," he has usually placed too much of his "hoped-for financial security" in one place. Some companies may be in such a stable financial position that they guarantee the employee's investment, but such companies are rare.

Ownership of stock by executives is much more common than by employees. In order to give major executives a special incentive as well as certain tax advantages, they are frequently given certain favorable stock options. Some companies give the executives their share of profits in stock.[14]

---

[14] See National Industrial Conference Board, Inc., "Executive Stock Ownership Plans," *Studies in Personnel Policy* 120, New York, 1951, for an excellent discussion of this subject; see also National Industrial Conference Board, Inc., "Stock Ownership Plans for Workers," *Studies in Personnel Policy* 132, New York, 1953.

**Summary.** The recommendations of the special committee of the Seventy-sixth Congress[15] may be slightly optimistic in the light of ensuing experience; nevertheless they do present the point of view of many companies actively engaged in profit sharing:

It was first demonstrated that out of a group of 774 companies with and without profit-sharing plans, the companies that had some plan, in which labor shared, achieved superior results in the matter of strikes over companies without plans and over companies that had plans for executives or plans in which labor did not share. By isolating companies that had only one plan, and labor shared in that plan, it was demonstrated that the companies that had profit-percentage plans achieved better results than those companies with other types of plans. It was then demonstrated that companies having plans that created the partnership interest, either alone or in combination with some other plan, had a better record than did those companies having only a plan of the nonpartnership-interest type. It was then demonstrated that various combinations of pension and bonus plans showed no significant changes in the employer-employee relations unless the plan was in combination with some partnership-interest plan. Having demonstrated the superiority of the profit-percentage type of plan it was then shown that there was reason to believe that the profit-percentage plan, wherein the workers' share is saved for the future, achieved the best results of any single type of plan or of any combination of plans. . . .

Among bonus plans, the formal (preannounced and predetermined) showed to a good advantage over the informal bonus plan. This might be expected as the formal bonus plan approaches and has several aspects of the profit-percentage plan where cash is distributed. . . .

The intensive study and analyses, hereinbefore presented, of the employee-relations policies operative in hundreds of businesses and commercial and industrial institutions throughout the United States lead us to certain definite and unalterable conclusions, to wit:

1. A profit-sharing plan, based upon percentage sharing wherein the "partner in interest" consciousness is established, is the most effective of all formulas for creating the capitalistic conception with its approval and allegiance to the profit system.

2. The formula of "percentage sharing" definitely creates the partnership relation which in turn promotes a closer, friendlier, and cooperative attitude on the part of the employee toward his employer.

3. Profit sharing on a percentage basis naturally developed the same selfish desire in the employee for the enjoyment of profits as actuate the employer, hence there is established the "common interests" reflecting itself in increased personal interest for company success and in doing all those things which have an influence upon the making of profits.

4. The "conflict of interest" which centers in the wage question whereby the employee's interest and concern is concentrated in the *one* desire for "higher wages" is unquestionably tempered and modified by the introduction of profit sharing as a "differential" which establishes *two* sources of income, causing the employee to look in two directions for personal financial betterment.

[15] *Senate Report* 610, 75th Cong., 1st Sess., pp. 159–160.

5. There appears to be far greater effectiveness for satisfaction, peace of mind, removal of fear of the future, and in the stimulating of ambition by the system of accumulation of funds for the creation of an estate for old-age security, than by regular distribution of the cash resulting from the sharing.

The late Helen Baker about 1940 summarized her research on employee stock ownership with a statement that is as true today as when it was written:

In weighing the experience with and opinions on employee stock purchase plans, it is apparent that such a plan must be hedged about with many guarantees to give to it the double assurance of security and liquidity that is essential to any sound employee savings plan. Many companies have questioned the wisdom of assuming this responsibility or of their absolute ability to do so. More than a majority of companies giving an opinion do not wish to renew such a plan—especially not for rank-and-file workers. About half of the continuing plans are for the sale of preferred stock, a few are for stock not sold on the market, and six are for offerings to higher-salaried employees only. From a comparison of executives' comments on experience and the stock price ranges, it is evident that management is often inclined to underestimate the possible losses to employees. Although there are a few executives who still feel that employee's stock ownership is valued by the workers and that it is an excellent method of gaining their interest in the company's success, the predominant opinion is that this interest may be gained in other ways and the employee savings encouraged in a much less hazardous program.

CHAPTER 29

# Safety, Health, and Recreation

**The socioeconomic results of accidents.** An accident is both an economic and a human-relations tragedy. The lost wages to the employee present an economic problem to the worker and his family. The lost production and broken equipment are tangible economic costs to the employer. The family's loss in wages creates social and human-relations stresses. The group reactions to the injury of a fellow worker result in depressed morale and tensions that tend to lower production.

Both the employer and his workers have a moral and economic responsibility to work all the time to eliminate the causes of accidents. Of course the reduction of accidents would be a worthwhile objective even if there were no economic factors involved. However, there is no escaping the economic consequences of accidents; hence the additional pressure to exert every effort to make the workplace a safe place. Accident reduction really contributes to cost reduction. One of the outstanding records of accident reduction is that of the steel industry, which intensively undertook an organized safety program before 1920 under the active support of the late Judge Gary.

**Industrial and other accidents in business.** Figure 29.1 shows the death rates per 100,000 workers in various major work areas. It is surprising to many people to learn that farming has a death rate four times that of industry. It is also seldom realized that the businesses engaged in trade are practically as fatal as manufacturing. These facts are understandable when it is recognized that manufacturing has a long record of intensive accident-reduction effort. Working at safety practices does get results. Table 29.1 portrays the results of the safety programs of the well-known General Electric Company. Statistics may be dry, but a casual glance at this record readily reveals the outstanding progress made by General Electric in reducing suffering and the costs of accidents.

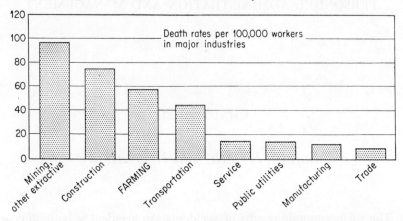

Fig. 29.1. Death rates in farming vs. other industries. Of 13,300 workers killed on the job in all industries in 1958, approximately 3,300 were killed in farm work. Although this was more deaths than occurred in any other major industry, the death rate per 100,000 workers was not as high as in construction and the extractive industries. The death rates for all major industries are charted above. (*Source: Accident Facts, 1959 edition, p. 80.*)

Table 29.1   *General Electric Company's Annual Frequency Rate from*
1917 *to* 1958

| Year | Frequency rate | Year | Frequency rate |
|------|---------------|------|---------------|
| 1917 | 45.20 | 1938 | 4.62 |
| 1918 | 37.40 | 1939 | 4.25 |
| 1919 | 25.20 | 1940 | 4.68 |
| 1920 | 29.80 | 1941 | 6.05 |
| 1921 | 20.85 | 1942 | 6.07 |
| | | | |
| 1922 | 23.20 | 1943 | 6.75 |
| 1923 | 22.65 | 1944 | 7.28 |
| 1924 | 18.40 | 1945 | 6.68 |
| 1925 | 18.33 | 1946 | 5.91 |
| 1926 | 14.50 | 1947 | 6.65 |
| | | | |
| 1927 | 11.20 | 1948 | 5.18 |
| 1928 | 12.50 | 1949 | 4.25 |
| 1929 | 15.34 | 1950 | 3.93 |
| 1930 | 12.06 | 1951 | 3.63 |
| 1931 | 9.30 | 1952 | 3.45 |
| | | | |
| 1932 | 8.55 | 1953 | 3.92 |
| 1933 | 10.12 | 1954 | 3.31 |
| 1934 | 8.53 | 1955 | 2.46 |
| 1935 | 7.99 | 1956 | 2.31 |
| 1936 | 6.60 | 1957 | 2.27 |
| 1937 | 6.53 | 1958 | 2.05 |

Accidents take place not only in large-scale business—relatively the record of small business is worse than of big business.[1] When one recalls the close relationship between owners and supervisors in small business, it would ordinarily be thought that small business would have a more favorable record than large-scale business. If small businesses would give the attenion to safe practices that big business does, their records would undoubtedly be better. Small business does have some advantages, but its safety record to date is not one of them.

The phenomenal reduction in accidents both as to frequency and severity is revealed by Fig. 29.2. The *frequency* refers to the number of disabling accidents per 1,000,000 man-hr. worked. *Severity* refers to the number of *days* lost per 1,000,000 man-hr. worked. Reduction in deaths is portrayed by Fig. 29.3. Unfortunately no one devotes the time and effort under ccntrolled conditions to the reduction of deaths from automobiles.

**Costs of accidents.** Cost data are not all that might be desired, but the information from six states as reported by the National Safety Council, Inc., in the 1959 *Accident Facts* is given in Table 29.2.

**Indirect costs[2] of accidents.** Indirect costs of accidents are estimated to be all the way from two to four times the direct costs.[3] The most widely quoted listing of causes of indirect or hidden costs of accidents is that by H. W. Heinrich as follows:

1. Cost of lost time of injured employee.
2. Cost of time lost by other employees who stop work:
   2.1 Out of curiosity.
   2.2 Out of sympathy.
   2.3 To assist injured employee.
   2.4 For other reasons.
3. Cost of time lost by foremen, supervisors, or other executives as follows:
   3.1 Assisting injured employee.
   3.2 Investigating the cause of the accident.
   3.3 Arranging for the injured employee's production to be continued by some other employee.

[1] See National Safety Council, Inc., *Accident Facts*, 1953, p. 32.

[2] Charles R. Hook, "Industrial Safety, Its Relation to Business of Today," as reported by the National Safety Council, Inc., Silver Jubilee Safety Congress, 1938, p. 21.

[3] See H. W. Heinrich, *Industrial Accident Prevention*, 3d ed., McGraw-Hill Book Company, Inc., New York, 1950, pp. 50–52, for his discussion of the 4 to 1 ratio of indirect costs of accidents. The 4 to 1 ratio was found to be too high by Rollin Head Simonds in his doctor's dissertation, *The Development and Use of a Method for Estimating the Cost to Eight Producers of Their Industrial Accidents*, Northwestern University, 1948. He found the ratio "to be between 1.6 to 1 and 2 to 1, certainly not much over 2 to 1, however, the companies were weighted in the averaging." See also Rollin H. Simonds, "Estimating Industrial Accident Costs," *Harvard Business Review*, January 1951, pp. 107–118.

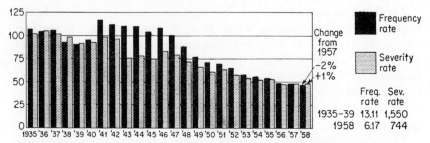

Fig. 29.2. Injury trends since 1935 (1935–1939 = 100). The disabling-injury frequency rate of reporters to the National Safety Council, Inc., decreased 2 per cent in 1958 from 1957 and reached a new low for this measure. The injury severity rate increased 1 per cent. In 1958, the injury frequency rate was 53 per cent lower than the average rate for the five prewar years, 1935–1939, and the injury severity rate was 52 per cent lower. (*Source: Accident Facts, 1959 edition, p. 27.*)

*Table* 29.2    *Source and Cost of Compensable Work Injuries**

| Source of injury | All disabling injuries | | Fatal, perm. total disability | | Perm. partial disability | | Temp. total disability | |
|---|---|---|---|---|---|---|---|---|
| | % of cases | Avg.† cost per case | % of cases | Avg.† cost per case | % of cases | Avg.† cost per case | % of cases | Avg.† cost per case |
| Total.................... | 100.0 | $ 679 | 100.0 | $11,475 | 100.0 | $1,093 | 100.0 | $229 |
| Handling objects, manual... | 24.4 | 568 | 11.2 | 13,080 | 18.8 | 1,094 | 28.7 | 251 |
| Falls..................... | 18.0 | 900 | 16.5 | 11,316 | 16.3 | 1,717 | 19.2 | 271 |
| Same level.............. | 9.5 | 698 | 4.7 | 12,171 | 8.7 | 1,350 | 10.2 | 221 |
| Different level........... | 8.5 | 1,129 | 11.8 | 10,975 | 7.6 | 2,147 | 9.0 | 327 |
| Struck by falling, moving objects.................. | 10.1 | 545 | 6.5 | 10,471 | 13.4 | 724 | 7.8 | 208 |
| Machinery................ | 9.8 | 691 | 3.0 | 14,814 | 15.2 | 937 | 6.1 | 152 |
| Vehicles................. | 7.6 | 990 | 22.3 | 11,017 | 6.6 | 1,549 | 8.0 | 268 |
| Motor................. | 5.6 | 1,066 | 19.0 | 11,105 | 4.9 | 1,630 | 5.8 | 263 |
| Other................. | 2.0 | 780 | 3.3 | 10,506 | 1.7 | 1,311 | 2.2 | 282 |
| Stepping on, striking against objects.................. | 6.6 | 313 | 0.8 | 14,389 | 7.3 | 522 | 6.1 | 101 |
| Hand tools................ | 6.5 | 460 | 1.7 | 15,179 | 7.4 | 738 | 6.0 | 154 |
| Elec., heat, explosives....... | 3.1 | 685 | 8.9 | 10,643 | 2.7 | 999 | 3.3 | 124 |
| Harmful substances........ | 2.6 | 1,059 | 10.4 | 13,951 | 1.7 | 1,318 | 3.1 | 342 |
| Elevators, hoists, conveyors.. | 2.3 | 1,022 | 4.2 | 11,949 | 2.8 | 1,357 | 1.8 | 302 |
| Engines, motors........... | 0.4 | 713 | 0.2 | 6,600 | 0.7 | 902 | 0.3 | 255 |
| Other.................... | 8.6 | 630 | 14.3 | 9,240 | 7.1 | 1,105 | 9.6 | 208 |

* Source: Reports on compensable work injuries from Florida, Illinois, Minnesota, New Jersey, New York, and North Carolina.
† Wage compensation only.

Fɪɢ. 29.3. Deaths and death-rate trends. (*Source: Accident Facts, 1959 edition, p. 23.*)

3.4 Selecting, training, or breaking in a new employee to replace the injured employee.

3.5 Preparing state accident reports or attending hearings before industrial commissioners.

4. Cost of time spent on the case by first-aid attendant and hospital staff when this is not covered by insurance.

5. Cost due to injury to the machine, tools, or other property, or to the spoilage material.

6. Cost due to interference with production, failure to fill orders on time, loss of bonuses, payments of forfeits, and other similar causes.

7. Cost under employee welfare and benefit systems.

8. Cost in continuing the wages of the injured employee in full, after his return—even though the services of the employee (who is not yet fully recovered) may for the time be worth only about half his normal value.

9. Cost due to the loss of profit on the injured employee's productivity and on idle machines.

10. Cost of subsequent injuries that occur in consequence of the excitement or weakened morale owing to the original accident.

11. Overhead cost—the expense of light, heat, rent, and other such items—that continue while the injured employee is a nonproducer.

**Organization of the safety function.** The relative hazard of the work influences the location of the safety function. In a munitions factory the safety director may report to the factory manager. The safety function is an important one in many industries, and the responsible functional officer should report to an important official such as the director of personnel, plant superintendent, or general manager. In the Western Electric Hawthorne Plant, the safety activities were formerly assigned to the public relations department. They are now under the director of industrial relations. In smaller organizations that cannot support a full-time safety director, this function may be delegated to the plant superintendent, employment officer, general foreman, or some other responsible executive.

The primary responsibility for safe operations rests squarely upon the line officers. The director of safety, safety engineer, or any other title that he may use is merely a staff specialist to render aid and special skill to the first-line supervisors. For safety work to be effective, it must be carried to the point of operations where accidents occur. The planning of a safety program can be done in an office, but it must be carried out on the job where people are at work.

The complete organization (see Fig. 29.4) is not feasible in a small plant. The police and fire protection may logically come under the safety department, as shown in the organization chart. However, police and fire protection frequently come under the service division of the plant, along with maintenance, janitor service, internal transportation, etc. The medical department, with its first-aid stations, may come under the safety department; yet it more frequently comes under the personnel department or as a separate department reporting to the general manager. Even though the medical department and the police and fire departments are not directly under the safety department, there must be close cooperation between these departments if each is to discharge its responsibility most effectively.

The functions of the safety department briefly summarized are (1) to focus the attention of management upon the advantages of safe practices and the waste inherent in any deviation from such practices; (2) to develop in the entire working force a wholesome regard for safety in operations and regard for sanitary working conditions; (3) to study the experience of the organization in safety and to devise ways and means of improving unsatisfactory performance; (4) to be ever on the alert for new devices and safeguards to improve conditions, even though for the moment these conditions may seem to be satisfactory in the light of the known techniques.

The safety committee aids in developing safety consciousness and in detecting possible accident hazards (Fig. 29.5). The committee should include foremen and major supervisors, with the ranking executive as chairman and the director of safety as secretary of the committee. This committee should serve as a policy-determining committee with power to pass upon most of the proposals that may come before it. There may also be departmental or divisional employee safety committees, the membership of which is rotated from time to time to get varied viewpoints and to act as an educational medium. The employees' safety committee may well make periodic inspections and recommendations regarding safe practices and procedures. Safety committees will be of little value unless management will take immediate action on their recommendations. If these cannot be put into effect, management should explain the reason at once.

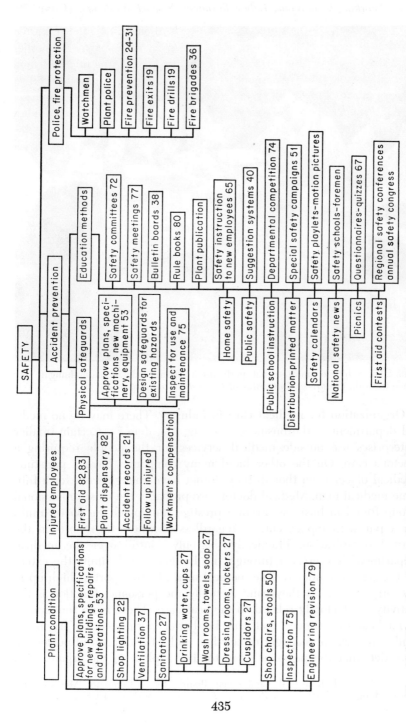

Fig. 29.4. Chart of activities of typical safety department. (*Reproduced by permission of the National Safety Council, Inc., from "Organizing a Complete Industrial Safety Program," Safe Practices Pamphlet* 42, 1939, p. 3.)

435

FIG. 29.5. Safety committee that performs a leading role in maintaining a safe place to work. (*Courtesy, International Harvester Company.*)

**Organization for medical care in industry.** There may be no medical department in the business (see Fig. A.3, item 7). Certain smaller enterprises use outside medical services for the people requiring a doctor's care. On the other hand many companies have a part-time medical officer even though they do not have enough work for a full-time medical man. Medical doctors are probably the most professional group found in business. From a prestige standpoint the doctor ranks on a par with top executives regardless of where he reports in the formal organization. Practically the only control over the medical department is exercised through the budget, which limits the extent of the service rendered. The medical men like to report as high up in the organization as they can.[4] Actually the personnel function is the activity most closely related to medical care. There is no function of a medical department that can be better performed by having it under the general manager rather than under the director of personnel, provided that the personnel director has a place in the organization

[4] See National Industrial Conference Board, Inc., "Company Medical and Health Programs," *Studies in Personnel Policy* 96, New York, 1948, p. 12.

that is commensurate with the natural functions that logically fall under his supervision. The trend in sound organizational procedure is to group like functions under divisional heads and to have these divisional heads report to the general manager rather than to have a large number of unrelated departments report to the general manager.

The medical department may play an important role in reducing accidents by proper examinations of all new employees. This statement should by no means be interpreted to mean that all but the physically perfect should be rejected. Impaired workers properly placed have as good a safety record as normal workers.[5] The important thing is to detect the defects and place the workers on appropriate jobs. Certain accident-prone workers should be sorted in the personnel department and placed on jobs that are suited to their peculiar mental and physical characteristics.[6] Through the organization of a first-aid staff in a company, workmen, including the supervisors, can be given instruction and practice as to how to render first-aid treatment to fellow workers. Many a worker's life has been saved by quick action by his associates in providing skilled first aid. Where the occupations are unusually hazardous, regular classes of workers from each department, meeting periodically for first-aid instruction, are desirable. In less hazardous industries, pamphlets, bulletin-board material, and talks or illustrated lectures may be used to give such information and to impress the workers with the importance of first-aid treatment.

The professional requirements for the industrial doctor are the same as those for the private physician, with added training in the general principles of personnel administration and unemployment and workmen's compensation and a general understanding of the industrial processes as they affect the health of the employees. A large part of the industrial physician's service is in preventive medicine and consultation with employees. Workers frequently reveal things to the physician that are of general concern to the management. Without violating confidence, the industrial physician frequently becomes the medium of solving difficult human-relations problems.

The presence of a first-aid station near the workplace has a tendency to facilitate the employee's having minor injuries treated and thus reduce infections. Approximately 1 out of 12 compensable injuries arise from infections of relatively minor cuts and abrasions. If infection had been avoided, many of these cases would not have been

[5] National Safety Council, Inc., *Accident Facts,* 1947, p. 32.
[6] See Charles A. Drake, "Detecting Accident Prone Workers," *Personnel,* Vol. 18, No. 5, March, 1942, p. 276.

compensable. The physical infection case is a neglected scratch or puncture that, if properly cared for at the time, would not have caused any lost time other than the time out for having the wound treated.[7] Most large companies provide suitable first-aid stations or dressing rooms, equipped to take care of major as well as minor injuries. In some companies, there is a central station or hospital, as well as first-aid equipment distributed at various points throughout the plant for this purpose.

**Employee health.** The maintenance of employee health and the reduction or elimination of accidents is the primary objective of safety and health programs in business. Data regarding occupational diseases are relatively scarce. As yet there is not agreement on the basis of reporting. For instance, is hernia an occupational disease or an accident? Some estimates place the lost time arising from disabling illness as high as 2 per cent and indicate that for every person incapacitated because of illness at least two others were handicapped because of prevalent or chronic diseases to the extent of 10 to 50 per cent of their efficiency.[8] The few studies that have been made public show that lost time due to illness and nonindustrial accidents is in the neighborhood of twelve times as great as the lost time due to industrial accidents.[9] Absenteeism due to industrial or occupational diseases probably does not exceed 3 per cent of the total absenteeism; nevertheless, neglect associated with occupations may be a contributing factor to illness not directly associated with the occupations. The statistical report of the New York State Workmen's Compensation Board, Mar. 20, 1959, for the year 1956, shows that dermatitis was the highest single disease, being approximately 42 per cent of the total. It is highly probable that certain persons are more susceptible to dermatitis than others. Persons who suffer from allergies tend to react more unfavorably to conditions leading to dermatitis. Occupational hernia is the next most prevalent occupational disability, being nearly 13 per cent of the total. This in reality is not a disease but an injury in most cases. Bursitis followed hernia closely in frequency. Tuberculosis represented nearly 5 per cent of the total occupational diseases. There are many other diseases that represent 1 to 2 per cent of the total—such as dust diseases, compressed-air illnesses, and lead poisoning.

[7] National Safety Council, Inc., *Accident Facts*, 1940, p. 26.
[8] National Industrial Conference Board, Inc., "Medical and Health Programs in Industry," *Studies in Personnel Policy* 17, New York, 1939, p. 21; also see W. S. Rankin, "The Economics of Medical Service," *American Journal of Public Health*, April, 1929, p. 360.
[9] National Industrial Conference Board, Inc., *ibid.*

FIG. 29.6. First-aid dispensary. (*Courtesy, Thompson Products, Inc.*)

Medical service is more productive in rendering preventive aid than in curing the patient once he is afflicted. First-aid stations treat minor diseases arising from work such as skin ailments and allergies (Fig. 29.6). Figure A.3, items 2 and 7, shows the prevalence of first-aid stations and medical services. The physical examination for employment is designed to aid in placement. In companies having work that is likely to present a health hazard such as handling lead compounds it is common practice to require periodic physical examinations to catch incipient cases of poisoning. With proper records, these examinations also point out the dangerous spots in the industry and lead directly to suggestions for the safety engineer. Whole departments have been reorganized by virtue of the fact that the medical department discovered certain hazards unrecognized before. In carrying out a health program, every effort to secure the cooperation of the foremen and the rank-and-file workers has to be made. They must understand and sympathize with the program so that they will desire to protect their own health and that of others. It is also necessary to cooperate with the community and health agencies, for the relation between industrial health and the local water or milk supply or sewage systems, for example, is obvious. Figure A.1, item 10, shows the practice of using the physical examination for employment. Management strives to achieve the following results by the giving of physical examinations:

1. The proper placement of those unfitted for one type of work but entirely fitted for another.
2. The maintenance of the health of those who are healthy when employed.
3. The detection and prescription for remediable defects.
4. The elimination of those who are unfitted for the job and the elimination of those with communicable diseases.

Preventive medicine is as important as treating the injured and sick. The medical department can only give instructions and advice about proper diet and food values, but the company can actually provide proper and healthful food for the employees. The development of factory lunchrooms or cafeterias was an outgrowth of the realization on the part of management that properly cooked, healthful, and nourishing food supplied to employees makes for a healthy and, hence, a more efficient working force. The visiting nurse is interested in preventive aspects of health maintenance as well as in assisting the sick and injured. It is difficult to establish a proper attitude on the part of the employees in regard to the visiting nurse. If she finds illness and distress, she can render the most valuable assistance and be of service. If, however, she finds no sickness and discovers that an employee is out for other reasons and so reports, she is immediately looked upon as a truant officer. It is because of the difficulties encountered by visiting nurses that they are not used extensively by industry.

**Educational efforts to promote safety and health.** Education is the most fruitful method of developing a positive attitude toward safe practices and the preservation of health. There is room for group effort as well as individual instruction. Positive attitudes toward safety and sound health practices often are more effectively developed in a group than in individual instruction. However, actual work habits are individually acquired; so individual instruction should not be omitted. To plan an educational program for safety and health maintenance requires an appraisal of the facts of the situation needing to be improved. The facts usually are revealed from a careful analysis of the records. Both the industrial doctor and the safety director may reach large numbers of employees through well-written articles in the employees' paper.

The medical department accumulates valuable records. The frequency of cases from the various departments should be studied from time to time by both the medical department and the safety director.

Table 29.3    *Cause of Accident, Work Injuries in Pennsylvania, 1957\**

| Cause of accidents | Total | Per cent of total |
|---|---|---|
| All accidents.......................................... | 82,444 | 100.0 |
| Unsafe acts: | 73,560 | 89.2 |
| Using defective or unsafe tools or equipment, or using tools and equipment unsafely............................. | 45,071 | 54.7 |
| Unnecessary exposure to danger (principally vehicles, tools, and machines)...................................... | 17,029 | 20.7 |
| Overloading, crowding, poor arrangement................ | 6,686 | 8.1 |
| Failure to use safety devices.......................... | 2,598 | 3.1 |
| Other unsafe acts..................................... | 2,176 | 2.6 |
| No unsafe act......................................... | 4,891 | 5.9 |
| Unclassified—insufficient data......................... | 3,993 | 4.9 |

\* Source: Bureau of Research and Statistics, Department of Labor and Industry, Commonwealth of Pennsylvania, *Summary: Work Injuries in Pennsylvania*, Harrisburg, Pa., 1957, p. 8.

A careful investigation of the cause of each accident of any consequence will often reveal conditions that demand immediate correction. Table 29.3 portrays the causes of accidents.

A proper classification of accidents is required if their analysis is to be productive. Accidents may be classified according to three main groups, namely:

1. Those due to mechanical causes, unguarded machinery, defective equipment, and the like.
2. Those due to physiological causes such as overfatigue and nervous strain.
3. Those due to mental causes, inexperience, carelessness, emotional disturbances, and ignorance.

An analysis of accidents in the three main groups frequently suggests the remedy. The same situation prevails with respect to occupational diseases. All persons are not subject to the same reaction to working conditions. Some individuals are highly sensitive to the presence of certain chemicals, whereas others are seemingly unharmed by the same chemicals. An alert physician frequently can detect these cases of unfavorable reaction to a given situation and recommend a transfer to another job suited to the individual. A careful analysis of the follow-up records in comparison with the initial hiring physical examinations will frequently reveal certain defects that have no special influence upon the worker's efficiency and others that are a danger signal for certain occupations.

There is definitely a relationship between the frequency of accidents and job changes.[10] This job change includes both newly hired employees and old-timers recently transferred to a new job. It is highly important that an old employee transferred to a new job be instructed in safe practices; some hate to ask for advice and are injured because of not being familiar with the new operation.

Most safety and health programs use safety contests, publicity programs, and any other means of developing a safety consciousness on the part of employees (see Fig. 29.7). One danger that must be guarded against in safety contests between departments is the tendency on the part of department heads to pad their records by keeping men on the job doing half a man's work just to avoid having a lost-time accident charged up against the department. Wholesome rivalry between departments with a graphic record of performance posted in a conspicuous place develops a sense of safety awareness in the organization. These sporadic efforts do not take the place of detailed instruction and follow-up on the job, which is a continuing responsibility of the management. Motion pictures of safe practices may be used effectively. Bulletin boards, when kept up to date, provide an excellent medium of safety education. Departmental inspection by committees is also used effectively in developing safe practices and in discovering potential hazards. Safety education begins with a proper introduction of the new employees. Training of the supervisors is an important phase of safety education. Many of these men themselves have risen from the ranks and are not "sold" on safety practices, especially the caring for abrasions, small cuts, and punctures that cause most of the cases of infection. The executive training conferences should have the subject of safety as an item of special consideration from time to time. These conferences should be built around factual analysis of departmental records and not merely be interest-creating meetings.

**Recreation sponsored by the business firm.** The sponsoring of recreational activities among employees is one of the oldest of the organized personnel activities. This statement does not mean that the personnel department solely has been responsible for recreational efforts among employees. A foreman who is interested in baseball may organize a baseball league. Another foreman who likes to bowl may be the moving spirit in sponsoring a bowling league. As these activities grow, the work involved usually becomes so great that the line officer asks for help. The personnel department is the logical place to allocate such activities. Management's interest in sponsoring recreational activities is to improve the health of employees and to en-

[10] See National Safety Council, Inc., *Accident Facts*, 1951, p. 31. November, 1957, p. 28.

Fɪɢ. 29.7. Board publicizing days worked without lost-time accident. (*Courtesy, Fisher Body Division, General Motors Corporation, Hamilton, Ohio, plant.*)

courage a positive morale among the employees. Chapter 16 covers several aspects of morale. One should not overemphasize the morale-building effect of recreation. Recreational activities are only one phase of promoting a high morale. A device found to be most efficient in some cases is the service insignia. These take many forms, ranging from the service stripe, such as the gold arm band worn by uniformed railroad employees, to the bejeweled lapel button showing the number of years of service. Along with the many other avenues of building a positive morale, recreational activities tend to create a satisfying work atmosphere. When properly organized, employee recreational activities serve the purpose of making the employees' social and recreational lives more interesting and complete. These activities also help the new employees to get acquainted and to find outlets for their social or recreational interests.

Organized employee recreational, social, and athletic events are as wide and the types as numerous as the ingenuity of the various executives, personnel managers, employees, and recreation directors can devise. They range all the way from the informal procedure of

Fig. 29.8. Interior of East Lodge, used by Frigidaire employees and their families. On this large tract of land there is another large club house used exclusively by various organized club groups. (*Courtesy, Frigidaire Division, General Motors Corporation.*)

presenting a sack of flour to a newly married employee to the maintenance of recreational buildings, clubhouses, and parks for formal, organized activities (see Fig. 29.8). Others spend a great deal of time and effort in building up athletic teams and in promoting both company and intercompany leagues for baseball, basketball, bowling, and the like. Some concerns concentrate their efforts on the development of minor games and contests, such as pool, horseshoe pitching, and what not. Still others have musical organizations, orchestras, bands, and drum corps, and some firms have extended employee activities to dramatic and literary clubs. On the other hand, some concerns confine activities of this type to one large annual picnic, to which all employees and their families are invited. The size of the community and community facilities often have an influence on the nature and extent of recreational activities. In the smaller communities, it is not unusual for a large corporation to promote more elaborate recreational programs than is customary in larger cities. Nevertheless, some large corporations in our metropolitan areas frequently have comprehensive programs.

**Service activities.** Restaurants, cafeterias, first-aid stations and medical services, recreational and counseling aids, and educational assistance are a part of the service activities of a company. They are designed to increase efficiency and to improve the morale of employees and to develop a feeling of "belonging" to the organization. To the degree that employees are willing to accept, cooperate in, support, and participate in the various service activities, they may be considered as potential aids to good management. Many of these service features are extremely personal and intimate in character; because of this fact, the slightest suggestion of paternalism on the part of management is likely to create indifference or even resentment among the workers. Employees want to feel that they belong to the organization and that they are actively taking part in protecting their own welfare as well as that of their fellow workers. To accomplish this, a most democratic attitude toward service activities is necessary on the part of management. For example, a group of employees will undoubtedly be far more enthusiastic about a tennis court that they have planned and helped to build and pay for than one that the company laid out and merely handed over to them. Similarly, a professional theatrical performance presented to the employees under the auspices of management might be infinitely better than one given by the employees themselves; yet the latter performance usually will be more appreciated and enjoyed.

## WORKMEN'S COMPENSATION REGULATIONS

**Workmen's compensation.** Workmen's compensation as used in this chapter refers to payments to the worker for lost time arising from an injury caused by his employment, not payment for work performed. It may also be paid for the loss of an arm, eye, or any part of the body. In the legal sense, workmen's compensation refers to the awarding of pay to workers (or their heirs) who have been injured, have become ill, or have been killed in some activity directly traceable to their work. The first theory of workmen's compensation, developed in Europe, gave the injured or disabled employee the right to claim damages if he could establish the proper evidence that the accident was due to some personal fault or negligence of the employer. If the employer could plead "contributory negligence," *i.e.*, show that the workman himself or another worker contributed to the accident in any way or that, through the exercising of ordinary care, he could have avoided it, no damages could be claimed. An employer could also disclaim responsibility on the grounds that the employee had knowingly agreed to assume the risk. Still further, the employer could protest workers' claims for damages when injury or accident was caused through the negligence of fellow workers. Relatives of workers killed on the job were not entitled to damages. It was difficult to show that accidents were the fault of the employer. The result was a rapid increase in litigation, with little benefit to the injured workman. As the problem became increasingly serious, particularly in the more hazardous industries, it attracted the attention of European legislators. Early remedial efforts were directed at a change of the burden of proof; *i.e.*, they attempted to make the employer show that the accident had occurred without negligence on his part, rather than requiring the worker to establish the negligence. The next step was to make the employer responsible for accidents due, not to negligence on the part of either, but to the inevitable hazards of the job. Even these concessions did not cover nearly all the accidents and failed to give satisfactory treatment to workers.

The early history of the movement to protect the worker, in part, against industrial hazards was one of opposition from employers. By 1900 many employers began to realize that industrial risks were a charge against society, and legislation favoring *workmen's compensation* began to appear. In most states, the question of negligence is now eliminated, and the right of workers injured or disabled on the job and of relatives of the workers killed to claim damages, irrespective of the cause, is established. There are two general procedures for handling the workmen's compensation funds: (1) the state collects a tax and administers the funds thus collected for the benefit of the injured employees; (2) the employer makes provision for his risks by the purchase of insurance from a recognized insurance company. In either case, the percentage of payments varies for different employments, being higher for those jobs which are more hazardous and should, therefore, bear a relatively higher portion of the costs of industrial accidents. For example, an employer having a punch-press department is exposing employees to a greater hazard than one employing office help only. One important feature of the better type of such plans is that each employer is given a rating, and, even though the concern may be engaged in a hazardous project, the "accident experience" is taken into consideration in setting the amount paid annually into the fund. Hence, there is a financial inducement for every employer to safeguard his workers. Some states permit the employer a choice of contributing to the state fund or providing proper protection through insurance companies.

The current tendency is for compensation boards to interpret the cause for compensation liberally in favor of the injured workmen. It is presumed that industrial accidents are a charge against the industry in which they occur and can best be compensated for, in so far as this is possible, on an insurance basis, spreading the risks to be paid by the employer on the basis of the total persons employed by a particular firm.

In some states, state, municipal, and educational employees are covered by workmen's compensation, and in others they are not. For instance, a college professor working around machinery may be covered, but one of his associates driving to a field trip with his students may not be. It is not infrequent to find driving on the highway more hazardous than working around guarded machinery.

**The current status of workmen's compensation laws.** Workmen's compensation laws are constantly being changed. Each of the 50 states now has a workmen's compensation law. Unions are constantly pressing for liberalization of the laws. These state laws vary in many details such as the extent of coverage required according to the number of employees; special exemptions based on hazards; whether or not an employer or employee may elect to come under the provisions of the act (suits for damages are open to injured employees if they are not covered by the act; in a few states, suits for damages under certain conditions will be entertained even though the employee is covered by the act); the waiting period before the injured employee begins to draw compensation; the amount of compensation and length of period for which it is paid; the amount and method of payment of death benefits; total disability, partial disability, second accidents, etc. Table 29.4 portrays the maximum weekly benefits, the maximum period of payment, for the various states as of November, 1959. This chart can give only a general picture because an individual state may change its law before this book comes off the press. Some states pay a great deal more for deaths and injuries than others. The payment for deaths in some states, *e.g.*, Illinois, varies with the number of dependents and the earnings of the deceased. Death benefits in Illinois (1958) are 9.25 times the average earnings "but not less than $9,000" in any event. Table 29.5 gives a condensed schedule of the death benefits of Illinois. This state has higher benefits than many other states.

**The second-injury clause.** In many states this clause is designed to protect an employer of a handicapped person from bearing the cost of permanent disability or the higher rates in the case of the loss of the second member when the person has already lost one eye, arm, leg, etc. For instance, the loss of both eyes is a permanent disability.

*Table* 29.4   *Workmen's Compensation Benefits for Temporary Total Disability as of November,* 1959

| State | Maximum percentage of wages | Maximum period | Maximum payments per week, dollars |
|---|---|---|---|
| Alabama | 55–65[e] | 300 weeks | $ 31.00 |
| Alaska | 65 | Period of disability | 100.00 |
| Arizona | 65[f] | 433 weeks | 150.00[a] |
| Arkansas | 65 | 450 weeks | 35.00 |
| California | 61¾[g] | 240 weeks | 65.00 |
| Colorado | 66⅔ | Period of disability | 40.25 |
| Connecticut | 60 | Period of disability | [b] |
| Delaware | 66⅔ | Period of disability | 50.00 |
| Dist. of Columbia | 66⅔ | Period of disability | 54.00[h] |
| Florida | 60 | 350 weeks | 42 00 |
| Georgia | 60 | 400 weeks | 30.00 |
| Hawaii | 66⅔ | Period of disability | 75.00 |
| Idaho | 55–65[e] | 400 weeks;[i] thereafter $12 per week ($15 if dependent wife) for period of disability, plus $4–15 for children | 28.00–48.00[e] |
| Illinois | 75–97½[e] | Period of disability | 45.00–51.00[e] |
| Indiana | 60 | 500 weeks | 39.00 |
| Iowa | 66⅔ | 300 weeks | 32.00–44.00[e] |
| Kansas | 60 | 416 weeks | 38.00 |
| Kentucky | 65 | 425 weeks | 32.00 |
| Louisiana | 65 | 300 weeks | 35.00 |
| Maine | 66⅔ | 500 weeks | 39.00 |
| Maryland | 66⅔ | 312 weeks | 40.00 |
| Massachusetts | 66⅔ | Period of disability | [c] |
| Michigan | 66⅔ | 500 weeks | 33.00–57.00[e] |
| Minnesota | 66⅔ | 350 weeks[h] | 45.00 |
| Mississippi | 66⅔ | 450 weeks | 35.00 |
| Missouri | 66⅔ | 400 weeks | 45.00 |
| Montana | 50–66⅔[e] | 300 weeks | 28.00–42.50[e] |
| Nebraska | 66⅔ | 300 weeks;[i] thereafter 45 per cent of wages, maximum $27.50 | 37.00 |
| Nevada | 65–90[e] | 433 weeks | 41.25–57.12[e] |
| New Hampshire | 66⅔ | 341 weeks | 40.00 |
| New Jersey | [j] | 300 weeks | 40.00 |
| New Mexico | 60 | 500 weeks | 38.00 |
| New York | 66⅔ | Period of disability | 45.00 |
| North Carolina | 60 | 400 weeks | 35.00 |
| North Dakota | 80 | Period of disability | 38.00–53.00[e] |
| Ohio | 66⅔ | 520 weeks | 49.00 |
| Oklahoma | 66⅔ | 300 weeks; may be extended to 500 weeks | 35.00 |

*Table* 29.4  *Workmen's Compensation Benefits for Temporary Total Disability as of November,* 1959  (*Continued*)

| State | Maximum percentage of wages | Maximum period | Maximum payments per week, dollars |
|---|---|---|---|
| Oregon............ | 50–75*e* | Period of disability | 32.31–66.92*e* |
| Pennsylvania....... | 66⅔ | Period of disability | 37.50 |
| Puerto Rico........ | 60 | 312 weeks | 25.00 |
| Rhode Island....... | 60 | Period of disability*k* | 32.00 |
| South Carolina..... | 60 | 500 weeks | 35.00 |
| South Dakota...... | 55 | 312 weeks | 35.00 |
| Tennessee......... | 65 | 300 weeks | 34.00 |
| Texas............. | 60 | 401 weeks | 35.00 |
| Utah.............. | 60 | 312 weeks | 37.00–49.50*e* |
| Vermont.......... | 66⅔ | 330 weeks*i* | *d* |
| Virginia........... | 60 | 500 weeks | 33.00 |
| Washington........ | .......... | Period of disability | 28.85–56.77*e* |
| West Virginia...... | 66⅔ | 208 weeks | 35.00 |
| Wisconsin......... | 70 | Period of disability | 54.00 |
| Wyoming.......... | 66⅔ | Period of disability | 33.46–53.08*e* |
| United States: | | | |
| Civil employees... | 66⅔–75*e* | Period of disability | 121.15*h* |
| Longshoremen.... | 66⅔ | Period of disability | 54.00*h* |

*a* Arizona: $150, plus $2.30 for each total dependent.

*b* Connecticut: 55 per cent of state's "average production wage."

*c* Massachusetts: $45, plus $6 for each total dependent.*b*

*d* Vermont: $36, plus $2 for each dependent child under twenty-one.

*e* According to number of dependents. In Idaho, Oregon, Washington, and Wyoming, according to marital status and number of dependents.

*f* Additional benefits for dependents.

*g* The California law provides for 65 per cent of 95 per cent of actual earnings, or 61¾ per cent.

*h* Additional benefits in specific cases, such as rehabilitation, constant attendant, etc.

*i* In case total disability begins after a period of partial disability, the period of partial disability shall be deducted from the specified period for temporary total.

*j* New Jersey: benefits set in accordance with a "wage and compensation schedule."

*k* Rhode Island: after 1,000 weeks, or after $16,000 has been paid, payments to be made from second-injury fund for period of disability.

This being true, an employer would hesitate to hire a worker with only one eye if he could be charged with a permanent disability should the worker lose the remaining eye. A special fund is created from charges for the first injury, out of which the permanently injured employee draws the additional benefits when he becomes permanently disabled through a second injury, such as losing the

*Table 29.5   Death Benefits in Illinois**

| Dependents | Minimum | Maximum |
|---|---|---|
| Wife (no children under 18)............... | $ 9,000 | $12,250 |
| Wife with 1 child under 18................ | 9,950 | 12,750 |
| Wife with 2 children under 18............. | 10,140 | 13,500 |
| Wife with 3 children under 18............. | 10,330 | 14,500 |
| Wife with 4 or more children under 18..... | 10,330 | 15,000 |

* In effect July 21, 1959.

remaining good eye. The employer working the employee when his second injury occurs is charged only with the loss of one eye. A similar situation applies to hernia, which is one of the most common handicaps among male workers. Tens of thousands of workers work for years with properly fitted trusses. Such men could not get employment if their new employer were to be charged for this injury. The Illinois law (Section 8, Subsection 7, d-1), in force July 21, 1959, reads:

(d-1) An injured employee, to be entitled to compensation for hernia, must prove:
1. The hernia was of recent origin;
2. Its appearance was accompanied by pain;
3. That it was immediately preceded by trauma arising out of and in the course of the employment;
4. That the hernia did not exist prior to the accident.

CHAPTER 30

# Working Conditions and Labor Turnover

**Definition and general considerations.** *Working conditions include cleanliness, light, heat, ventilation, physical energy required, length of the work day, irregularity of the work hours such as night shifts or the rotation of shifts, physical hazards, exposure to possible industrial diseases, and similar conditions, also those social, group, and managerial conditions that directly or indirectly influence the worker's happiness, satisfactions, or dissatisfactions at work.*

Individual or group reaction to a given social situation is largely influenced by the mores of the particular group, which are by no means uniform in different sections of our country or within different segments of people within the same local geographical area. An employer who collaborates with a bare majority of his workers in forcing a union shop upon the other 49 per cent of his workers is creating an untenable situation, particularly where unionism has not established itself as a part of the traditions of the people. *The forcing upon a group of a rule of action supported by only a slight majority is fraught with grave social consequences, particularly when the action taken involves deep-seated emotional bias.* The inauguration of a second shift in a plant that works from Monday through Friday with the rotation of shifts may cause unusual dissatisfaction in a community in which there are many people who observe Saturday as their Sabbath, beginning at six o'clock on Friday and running to six o'clock on Saturday. A minority group in a department may be exceedingly unhappy if the two groups are bitterly divided over some subject such as a lodge or religious membership. The same people may get along very satisfactorily if neither is in the majority and the total group is sufficiently large so that the numerical strength and factional differences between the two otherwise opponent groups are relatively unimportant to the larger group.

Even though the worker may not be penalized for the absence of work, slipshod methods of scheduling and production control tend to

451

break down morale. A well-paid, busy group of workers will have few grievances to magnify. On the other hand, a group of workers waiting aimlessly for work can readily manufacture problems even though their pay is relatively satisfactory. The regularity of work for employees reporting for work exerts a profound influence upon them, particularly when they are paid on an output basis or some incentive plan. Of course, a domineering supervisory force directly affects working conditions, even though the physical factors may be satisfactory. The reverse of this is likewise true: a supervisory force that has difficulty in knowing what it wants and where it is going breaks down employee morale. Workers like to work in a congenial group under a supervisor who is technically proficient, who has high standards, and who strives to help his men achieve the expected goals.

**The influence of monotony and fatigue.** The definition of fatigue is not an easy matter. It is usually defined in terms of its influence upon output. *Fatigue is the reduced capacity for work arising from work itself.* Of course an employee might come to work tired in the morning because of having been kept awake all night due to the illness of his child. He might become excessively fatigued before the close of the day. In this situation his fatigue would not be solely from his work at the place of business but largely because of his condition at the time he started. In spite of exceptions that may be noted *fatigue is usually associated with the reduced capacity for work arising from work itself.* In modern industry cumulative fatigue is seldom encountered. Cumulative fatigue is nearly always the result of prolonged overwork or its counterpart, the lack of sufficient rest. The only cure for cumulative fatigue is more rest or diversion in case it may in part be due to monotony.

A feeling of boredom, often interpreted as fatigue, may arise almost solely from monotony. Individual differences are pronounced in the reaction to so-called monotonous jobs. Some persons enjoy repetitive operations requiring little or no initiative. Others are bored by such operations. Mayo and others have studied the effects of work described as monotonous.[1] In general, monotony (1) is increased when the operation requires the worker to be constantly on the alert, yet there is not sufficient care required to keep the mind fully occupied; (2) is not likely to arise in the case of an operation that is

---

[1] See Elton Mayo, *Human Problems of an Industrial Civilization,* The Macmillan Company, New York, 1933; see also H. M. Vernon, *Industrial Fatigue and Efficiency,* Routledge and Kegan Paul, Ltd., London, 1921, for detailed discussion of both monotony and fatigue.

completely automatic so that the individual is free to let his mind wander at will; (3) tends to be decreased in operations requiring a high degree of concentration. *Monotony* and *cumulative fatigue* tend to produce discontent and in the long run may result in or be contributory factors to industrial unrest.

Both monotony and fatigue may be reduced by properly spaced rest periods. The social meaning of rest periods reduces monotony. With improved morale, industrial unrest arising from fatigue or monotony tends to be eliminated. Scientific management is giving increased attention to the elimination of monotony. Rest periods and interrupted operations, such as a worker's leaving her sewing machine to deposit finished parts on a rack and to get a new supply of work, tend to reduce both monotony and fatigue. The imparting of full information on the relationship of a given operation to the finished product often gives meaning to an operation and reduces the monotony of its performance. Open house, during which the families of employees can visit the company and see where the employee works, gives the family something to talk about, thus giving importance to the job. This tends to reduce the monotony of some jobs in the mind of the worker. As indicated earlier, fatigue is not a particularly serious matter in modern industry. Of course persons with bad feet may be very tired at the close of the day when their work requires them to stand all day. In this case the problem is the defective feet rather than the work. This same person would be tired if he merely stood for the 8 hr. and did practically no physical work, as in the case of an inspector or a life guard merely watching to rescue the person in trouble but seldom having to do anything active.

**The influence of hours of work and rotating shifts.** Excessively long hours in a given day and a long work week definitely influence the worker's satisfaction with his job. Actually there is no strong evidence to support the 40-hr. 5-day week against the 5½-day 44-hr. week. Workers like the 5 day week, particularly women. On the other hand workers also like the additional pay they get for the 44-hr. week. In time of national emergency the 48-hr. week will usually give the maximum production. For a short period a 60- or even a 72-hr. week will increase production. After a period of 8 to 12 weeks on these longer shifts, even in time of war, absenteeism tends to be excessive, and the temporary advantages vanish. As a matter of fact the 48-hr. week resulted in excessive absenteeism on Saturdays in many industries employing a large proportion of women. It might be erroneous to ascribe this solely to fatigue. Many of these women had home problems that demanded their attention. In peacetime production it is unusual to work longer than the 48-hr. week, particularly in industries engaged in interstate commerce, since time and a half is usually required for all time in excess of 40 hr.

The rotating of shifts, especially where there is a midnight shift, creates a serious problem for some workers. The rotating of shifts or working on the second or third shift on a permanent basis presents a more formidable problem than working long hours. Local transportation companies have, in general, two peak periods, one when workers are going to work in the morning and the other when they are going home at night. If sufficient men are on the job to handle the peak periods, there are more than are needed during the period from about nine in the morning until three in the afternoon. The result may be that one group works from five in the morning until nine and then is off until the afternoon, when it again works from three until seven. Certain industries may be operated continuously because of the nature of the processes or services, such as blast furnaces, certain food processing, certain chemical processes, and utilities such as the public light and water companies. Other companies may operate two or more shifts because of conditions requiring a volume of production that cannot be turned out on one shift with the available equipment. A company may deliberately elect to operate more than one shift in order to reduce the unit cost of the product by spreading the machinery burden over a larger number of units of product rather than installing enough equipment to care for the production on the day shift alone.

Multiple-shift operations frequently cause unrest. Some departments may be on a two- or three-shift basis, while other departments are on one shift. Construction work and major maintenance work are nearly always on a single-shift basis even in continuous-process industries, with the exception of the emergency maintenance crew. Table 30.1 shows the shift provision in collective agreements by industry groups. There has been a marked increase in the payment of shift differentials over the past 15 years. Table 30.2 shows the types of shift differentials in union contracts. Differentials are paid either as a flat hourly-rate increase or as a percentage of the base rate. Four, five, and six cents are common figures for differentials when paid on a flat cents basis, and 10 per cent is a common basis when figured on a percentage basis (see Table 30.3). Companies working multiple shifts either may hire all new men on the second or third shift as the case may be and promote them to the day shift strictly on a seniority basis or may establish rotating shifts, each group working a certain number of days on each shift and then being rotated according to an

Table 30.1  Shift Provisions in Major Collective-bargaining Agreements, by Industry, 1958*

| Industry | Number studied — Agreements | Number studied — Workers (thousands) | Provision for shift differential — Agreements | Provision for shift differential — Workers (thousands) | No provision for shift differential — Agreements | No provision for shift differential — Workers (thousands) | Prohibition of shift or nightwork — Agreements | Prohibition of shift or nightwork — Workers (thousands) | No provision for shift or nightwork — Agreements | No provision for shift or nightwork — Workers (thousands) |
|---|---|---|---|---|---|---|---|---|---|---|
| All industries | 1,736 | 7,753.0 | 1,317 | 5,895.7 | 106 | 326.7 | 14 | 73.5 | 299 | 1,457.1 |
| Manufacturing | 1,122 | 4,916.9 | 971 | 4,123.4 | 43 | 128.3 | 12 | 70.6 | 96 | 594.7 |
| Ordnance | 10 | 24.0 | 10 | 24.0 | | | | | | |
| Food and kindred products | 109 | 363.9 | 87 | 321.6 | 7 | 14.5 | 1 | 1.2 | 14 | 26.6 |
| Tobacco manufactures | 12 | 33.2 | 7 | 21.8 | 2 | 4.8 | | | 3 | 6.6 |
| Textile-mill products | 45 | 116.7 | 37 | 91.9 | 5 | 19.9 | | | 3 | 5.0 |
| Apparel and other finished textile products | 47 | 473.7 | | | 1 | 1.9 | 11 | 69.4 | 35 | 402.5 |
| Lumber and wood products (except furniture) | 14 | 39.2 | 8 | 25.7 | 1 | 2.6 | | | 5 | 10.9 |
| Furniture and fixtures | 17 | 29.0 | 13 | 19.4 | | | | | 4 | 9.6 |
| Paper and allied products | 55 | 124.9 | 50 | 111.4 | 3 | 7.7 | | | 2 | 5.8 |
| Printing, publishing, and allied industries | 36 | 71.7 | 34 | 68.5 | 1 | 1.2 | | | 1 | 2.0 |
| Chemicals and allied products | 58 | 112.7 | 54 | 106.7 | 4 | 6.1 | | | | |
| Products of petroleum and coal | 24 | 70.7 | 22 | 55.7 | 1 | 4.5 | | | 1 | 10.5 |
| Rubber products | 25 | 131.9 | 21 | 95.5 | 3 | 35.4 | | | 1 | 1.1 |
| Leather and leather products | 22 | 76.9 | 5 | 9.0 | | | | | 17 | 68.0 |
| Stone, clay, and glass products | 34 | 92.1 | 32 | 86.7 | 1 | 1.4 | | | 1 | 4.0 |
| Primary metal industries | 123 | 723.1 | 118 | 714.9 | 4 | 7.2 | | | 1 | 1.0 |
| Fabricated metal products | 64 | 175.6 | 60 | 166.3 | 3 | 7.8 | | | 1 | 1.5 |
| Machinery (except electrical) | 143 | 402.9 | 136 | 383.7 | 6 | 10.1 | | | 1 | 9.1 |
| Electrical machinery | 106 | 461.0 | 102 | 450.3 | 2 | 1.5 | | | 2 | 9.2 |
| Transportation equipment | 144 | 1,314.3 | 141 | 1,290.9 | 1 | 1.8 | | | 2 | 21.6 |
| Instruments and related products | 23 | 55.4 | 23 | 55.4 | | | | | | |
| Miscellaneous manufacturing industries | 11 | 24.5 | 11 | 24.5 | | | | | | |
| Nonmanufacturing | 614 | 2,836.1 | 346 | 1,772.3 | 63 | 198.5 | 2 | 2.9 | 203 | 862.5 |
| Mining, crude petroleum, and natural-gas production | 16 | 261.1 | 15 | 259.8 | | | | | 1 | 1.3 |
| Transportation† | 109 | 553.6 | 30 | 110.9 | 12 | 37.1 | | | 67 | 405.7 |
| Communications | 75 | 591.7 | 70 | 579.3 | | | | | 5 | 12.4 |
| Utilities: electric and gas | 81 | 204.7 | 63 | 154.8 | 13 | 21.1 | | | 5 | 28.8 |
| Wholesale trade | 14 | 28.2 | 8 | 16.9 | 1 | 2.8 | | | 5 | 8.5 |
| Retail trade | 85 | 219.2 | 42 | 116.3 | 7 | 7.3 | | | 36 | 95.7 |
| Hotels and restaurants | 29 | 146.0 | 8 | 54.1 | 7 | 22.6 | | | 14 | 69.3 |
| Services | 54 | 181.0 | 23 | 69.2 | 2 | 5.0 | 1 | 1.5 | 28 | 105.3 |
| Construction | 148 | 645.5 | 85 | 407.4 | 21 | 102.7 | 1 | 1.4 | 41 | 134.1 |
| Miscellaneous nonmanufacturing industries | 3 | 5.2 | 2 | 3.7 | | | | | 1 | 1.5 |

Note: Because of rounding, sums of individual items may not equal totals.
* Source: *Monthly Labor Review*, Vol. 82, No. 3, March, 1959, p. 272.
† Excludes railroads and airlines.

*Table* 30.2   *Types of Shift Differentials in Major Collective-bargaining Agreements,* 1958\*

| Type of shift differential | Second shift, or general nightwork | | Third shift | |
|---|---|---|---|---|
| | Agree-ments | Workers (thou-sands) | Agree-ments | Workers (thou-sands) |
| Total................................ | 1,293 | 5,831.0 | 1,067 | 4,990.4 |
| Money differentials: | | | | |
| Uniform cents addition to first-shift rates | 777 | 2,886.3 | 625 | 2,171.0 |
| Uniform per cent addition to first-shift rates............................ | 239 | 1,443.1 | 140 | 1,141.6 |
| Uniform cents addition for fixed shifts and variations for swing, or rotating, shifts............................ | 22 | 44.8 | 28 | 45.8 |
| Uniform per cent addition for fixed shifts and variations for swing, or rotating, shifts............................ | 4 | 144.5 | 3 | 142.9 |
| No uniform premium specified but higher wage scales for nightwork, with premiums over first-shift rates varying among occupations or by wage ranges. | 47 | 216.9 | 21 | 107.3 |
| Other money differentials†............. | 63 | 294.8 | 25 | 194.2 |
| Time differentials: | | | | |
| Full day's pay for reduced hours of work. | 69 | 365.5 | 66 | 323.8 |
| Time and money differentials: | | | | |
| Full day's pay for reduced hours of work plus uniform cents differential........ | 10 | 30.3 | 69 | 390.2 |
| Full day's pay for reduced hours of work plus uniform per cent differential..... | 12 | 36.9 | 22 | 61.4 |
| Full day's pay for reduced hours of work plus money differential (no uniform premium specified but higher wage scales for nightwork, with premiums over first-shift rates varying among occupations or by wage ranges)....... | 11 | 39.8 | 23 | 72.0 |
| Other time-money differentials‡........ | 39 | 328.4 | 41 | 340.5 |

*Note:* Because of rounding, sums of individual items may not equal totals.

\* "Shift Provisions in Major Union Contracts, 1958," *Monthly Labor Review,* Vol. 82, No. 3, March, 1959, p. 273.

† Includes agreements which provided for a flat-sum payment for work after a certain hour or between certain hours; those granting a certain percentage payment for work after or between certain hours, not to exceed a set dollar amount; those providing a shift differential of either a certain percentage per hour or cents per hour, whichever sum was greater; and those providing for varying differentials depending upon starting time of shifts.

‡ Includes agreements with time and money differentials, in which either of the differentials, or both, may vary by occupation, ending time of shifts, length of shifts, location of duty station, or combinations of the above.

*Table* 30.3 *Significant Shift-differential Patterns in Major Collective-bargaining Agreements,* 1958\*†

| Shift-differential pattern | | Agreements | Workers (thousands) |
|---|---|---|---|
| Cents per hr. | | | |
| Second shift: | Third shift: | | |
| 4 | 6 | 14 | 257.1 |
| 5 | 8 | 12 | 36.3 |
| 5 | 10 | 69 | 136.3 |
| 6 | 9 | 41 | 119.3 |
| 6 | 12 | 19 | 30.9 |
| 7 | 10 | 24 | 45.6 |
| 7 | 12 | 11 | 19.8 |
| 7½ | 10 | 11 | 18.8 |
| 8 | 10 | 11 | 22.8 |
| 8 | 12 | 75 | 655.9 |
| 8 | 16 | 27 | 70.1 |
| 10 | 10 | 34 | 82.7 |
| 10 | 15 | 48 | 82.9 |
| 12 | 12 | 24 | 91.0 |
| Per cent of regular rate | | | |
| Second shift: | Third shift: | | |
| 5 | 7½ | 10 | 31.5 |
| 5 | 10 | 35 | 627.8 |
| 10 | 10 | 49 | 314.7 |
| 10 | 15 | 13 | 36.6 |
| Total accounted for.......... | | 527 | 2,679.7 |

*Note:* Because of rounding, sums of individual items may not equal totals.

\* "Shift Provisions in Major Union Contracts, 1958," *Monthly Labor Review,* Vol. 82, No. 3, March, 1959, p. 275.

† Includes shift combinations with cent or per cent differentials found in 10 or more agreements.

established schedule. Approximately 10 per cent of the companies having shift differentials in collective bargaining agreements in 1958 had provisions for shift rotation.[2] Some companies follow a pattern of promoting to the day shift on a seniority basis yet reserve the right to assign a person for special reason to the second or third shift regardless of seniority. These exceptional cases arise when the second shift is being built up or in cases of special production requirements. As would be expected, the older employees, whose service would give

[2] "Shift Provisions in Major Union Contracts, 1958," *Monthly Labor Review,* Vol., 82, No. 3, March, 1959, p. 272.

them the day shift, usually prefer the permanent assignment. Many other employees prefer permanent assignments or at least rather long shift assignments.

Rotation on a weekly basis causes discontent among many employees, who claim that they just get adjusted to sleeping days when they have to shift to another time. The author of this chapter has worked under the system of permanent assignments and also under weekly shifts. He prefers a longer assignment, such as 2 months, to either plan. He has heard many individual workers express a similar view; however, he knows of no statistical study involving a large number of employees who have had experience under both plans to verify or refute these observations. Shift rotation is frequently given by employees as a reason for leaving a firm. Opposition to nightwork is often influenced by the tradition in the community. In rural areas unaccustomed to nightwork, there is likely to be keen opposition. In other areas, where nightwork has long been practiced, it is frequently accepted as a matter of routine. Individual differences are pronounced in relation to the ability to adjust to third-shift work. Some persons seem to be able to make the adjustment with little trouble. Others can endure the third shift but have great difficulty in adjusting. The body has an established rhythm for the 24-hr. cycle. During the period of normal rest and sleep blood pressure and pulse rate are lower. Some persons establish a new rhythm when working on the third shift with no difficulty. Others literally have to struggle to keep going.

**Industrial unrest.** Industrial unrest manifests itself in a more or less continuing state of uncertainty, uneasiness, and aimless activity arising out of real or imaginary fears or unsatisfied longings. Industrial unrest is a forerunner of strikes. It contributes to labor turnover. Vague rumors and restrained emotional excitement often accompany early stages of so-called inarticulate social or industrial unrest. These rumors and manifestations of emotional restraints are not confined to the workers themselves but are transmitted to their wives and children. After a time, the entire process of contagion becomes distinctly a group or social phenomenon. Individuals may then come into such a group with a high degree of self-confidence and certainty only to succumb to the group influence in a relatively short time. When the unrest results in open protests and petitioning for requested change, it is out in the open and has become articulate. Its outward manifestations are the parade, strike, boycott, etc. Leadership is a requisite of this phase of unrest. The leadership may be intelligent and make only reasonable demands, or it may be merely opportunistic and demand much with no expectation of getting all that is asked. The articulate stage of industrial unrest is the only phase that most managers know about. This phase is no more important than its predecessor, the inarticulate stage. If inarticulate unrest can be minimized and the individuals and group find satisfaction in their work situations, the more vocal and active stages will seldom arise.

The personnel manager should strive to interpret unrest while it is still inarticulate—in order to avoid the stresses and strains of correction should it become articulate. Management should recognize that social changes are just as inevitable as technological change. Rapid change causes a feeling of insecurity and unrest. Radical change is difficult for the masses to adjust to even though they may have advocated it at the time of its initiation. Gradual change is more in keeping with man's natural temperament. Management must devise techniques that are adequate to cope with industrial unrest before it becomes active. The Hawthorne experiment in counseling, previously described, is one of the modern techniques for achieving this end. Workers like to look up to their supervisors and respond readily to straightforward, scientific treatment. This statement can be made only of the great mass of American workers who are imbued with the traditional American philosophy and not to minority groups whose religion is communism. Such groups are definitely committed to class struggle and will try to interpret decent treatment as a sign of weakness and to magnify the severity of the strong hand when it is used. This latter group of Communists, state Socialists, and radical reformers thrive on strife, strikes, and overt violence. The great mass of union workers do not belong to this group although a small group of their leaders seem to, if their pleading the Fifth Amendment to the Constitution can be interpreted as it looks on the face of it.

**Strikes.** As this is being written, the highest-paid large group of workers in the United States have shut down the entire steel industry because they want still higher wages and have stubbornly resisted any effort to tie increased wages to increased productivity on the part of the workers. In considering strikes and productivity one should always distinguish between increased production arising from the contributions of the workers and increased productivity arising from increased investments of management in improved equipment and technology. Since World War II there has emerged a fashion to the effect that workers must be given substantial increases in wage and fringe benefits annually regardless of their contributions. Table 30.4 shows the major issues involved in work stoppages for 1958. From this table it is evident that wages and fringe benefits are the two outstanding causes of strikes. The public is the real sufferer in many strikes in basic industry such as steel, coal, and petroleum or in the public utilities. Employees on a strike are likely to claim that they are in effect not striking but are victims of a vicious lockout by the employer. They use any device at their command, often with little regard for the true facts, to influence public opinion in their favor. A favorable public opinion is much more prone to grant strikers extra-legal means for enforcing their demands. To infer that striking employees hold the truth lightly and that employers always tell the facts without special coloring would certainly not be true. Modern social controls can easily check upon the employer's claims and often do so. They could also check upon the employees' claims. In the past there has been no particular agency of the government to expose employees' claims. In the case of strikes in industries creating a national emergency the Labor-Management Relations Act, 1947, Section 206, provides for the appointment of a board of inquiry to inquire into the issues involved and to report to the President. This report shall include a "statement of facts" without any recommendation. It is conceivable that this report in the case of such industries may provide the public with adequate information needed to evaluate the truthfulness of the respective claims.

Mass picketing with complete disregard of the rights of others to use the streets is one of the saddest phases of many strikes where management tries to go in and out of its premises. Few people could find fault with a reasonable number of pickets carrying placards publicizing their claim. This is in fact a method of communicating with other workers and may truly be protected under the claim of freedom of speech. Peaceful picketing is permitted in most jurisdictions. However, mass picketing is quite another matter. Anyone who has ever seen employees or the employer try to enter the plant in the face of massed pickets can realize that such picketing is seldom *peaceful*. In view of the attitude of some labor leaders "peaceful picketing" poses a problem in the labor movement that has not been satisfactorily solved. Several of the states have established rules that will tend to reduce violence on the picket line. Individuals and groups should guard jealously any infringements of our civil rights; yet persons who are deliberately taking away the safety of person of others and blocking free egress from or ingress to a plant cannot claim that they are respecting the rights of others.

**Causes of strikes, and when strikes occur.** Union organizing played a leading role in strikes from 1937 to 1941 but decreased in importance after that. The various series of wage demands and miscellaneous working-condition demands have been predominant since

Table 30.4   Major Issues Involved in Work Stoppages, 1958[a]

| Major issues | Stoppages beginning in 1958 | | | | Man-days idle during 1958 (all stoppages) | |
|---|---|---|---|---|---|---|
| | Number | Per cent of total | Workers involved | | | |
| | | | Number | Per cent of total | Number | Per cent of total |
| All issues........................... | 3,694 | 100.0 | 2,060,000 | 100.0 | 23,900,000 | 100.0 |
| Wages, hours, and supplementary benefits... | 1,875 | 50.8 | 1,380,000 | 67.2 | 18,300,000 | 76.7 |
| Wage increase....................... | 1,204 | 32.6 | 979,000 | 47.5 | 11,800,000 | 49.5 |
| Wage decrease...................... | 27 | 0.7 | 6,230 | 0.3 | 77,100 | 0.3 |
| Wage increase, hour decrease........... | 42 | 1.1 | 29,800 | 1.4 | 200,000 | 0.8 |
| Wage increase, pension, and/or health and welfare benefits..................... | 290 | 7.9 | 199,000 | 9.6 | 3,700,000 | 15.5 |
| Pension and/or health and welfare benefits | 21 | 0.6 | 9,150 | 0.4 | 188,000 | 0.8 |
| Other[b]................................ | 291 | 7.9 | 162,000 | 7.9 | 2,330,000 | 9.7 |
| Union organization, wages, hours, and supplementary benefits.................. | 221 | 6.0 | 33,300 | 1.6 | 1,260,000 | 5.3 |
| Recognition, wages, and/or hours........ | 153 | 4.1 | 8,170 | 0.4 | 284,000 | 1.2 |
| Strengthening bargaining position, wages, and/or hours...................... | 25 | 0.7 | 18,400 | 0.9 | 782,000 | 3.3 |
| Union security, wages, and/or hours...... | 43 | 1.2 | 6,790 | 0.3 | 194,000 | 0.8 |
| Discrimination, wages, and/or hours...... | ..... | ..... | .......... | ..... | 1,080[c] | [d] |
| Union organization..................... | 362 | 9.8 | 39,600 | 1.9 | 639,000 | 2.7 |
| Recognition........................ | 252 | 6.8 | 13,300 | 0.6 | 286,000 | 1.2 |
| Strengthening bargaining position........ | 24 | 0.6 | 11,800 | 0.6 | 228,000 | 1.0 |
| Union security...................... | 69 | 1.9 | 11,400 | 0.6 | 98,500 | 0.4 |
| Discrimination...................... | 8 | 0.2 | 290 | [d] | 14,300 | 0.1 |
| Other............................. | 9 | 0.2 | 2,790 | 0.1 | 11,800 | [d] |
| Other working conditions................ | 876 | 23.7 | 558,000 | 27.1 | 3,430,000 | 14.4 |
| Job security....................... | 434 | 11.7 | 254,000 | 12.3 | 1,990,000 | 8.3 |
| Shop conditions and policies........... | 358 | 9.7 | 258,000 | 12.5 | 1,120,000 | 4.7 |
| Work load.......................... | 81 | 2.2 | 43,200 | 2.1 | 295,000 | 1.2 |
| Other............................. | 3 | 0.1 | 2,840 | 0.1 | 27,300 | 0.1 |
| Interunion or intraunion matters.......... | 321 | 8.7 | 42,100 | 2.0 | 218,000 | 0.9 |
| Sympathy.......................... | 59 | 1.6 | 16,200 | 0.8 | 84,500 | 0.4 |
| Union rivalry[e]....................... | 24 | 0.6 | 1,470 | 0.1 | 20,600 | 0.1 |
| Jurisdiction[f]........................ | 232 | 6.3 | 22,400 | 1.1 | 105,000 | 0.4 |
| Union administration[g]................. | 3 | 0.1 | 1,540 | 0.1 | 6,300 | [d] |
| Other.............................. | 3 | 0.1 | 440 | [d] | 890 | [d] |
| Not reported........................ | 39 | 1.1 | 3,190 | 0.2 | 15,500 | 0.1 |

Note: Because of rounding, sums of individual items may not equal totals.

[a] Source: Monthly Labor Review, Vol. 82, No. 6, June, 1959, p. 639.

[b] Issues such as retroactivity, holidays, vacations, job classification, piece rates, incentive standards, or other related matters unaccompanied by proposals to effect general changes in wage rates are included in this category. Slightly less than a third of the stoppages in this group occurred over piece rates or incentive standards.

[c] Idleness in 1958 resulting from stoppage that began in 1957.

[d] Less than 0.05 per cent.

[e] Includes disputes between unions of different affiliation.

[f] Includes disputes between unions of the same affiliation.

[g] Includes disputes within a union over the administration of union affairs or regulations.

the early forties. Table 30.4 shows that wages and fringe benefits lead all other causes by a very wide margin. Union recognition currently plays an insignificant role in strikes.

There does not seem to be any strong  causal relationship between outside factors and the time unions pick for calling a strike other than the simple one of calling it when the union leaders think that they can by striking win demands that they have been unable to win on merit at the bargaining table. Walter Reuther did not call a strike when his contract with the automobile companies expired in 1958 even though he and other union leaders had traditionally used the slogan, "No contract—no work." Professor Dale Yoder suggested in 1950 that sudden changes in price levels may be more influential in strikes than mere business activity.[3] The war periods witnessed rapid advances both in prices of labor and in cost of living, but the cost of living outran the increase in wages during World War I. Strikes were engaged in to raise wages to keep up with the cost of living. On the other hand, during the 1920's, prices fell off gradually, and business activity and wages remained high. During World War II prices rose rapidly, but the "take home" wages rose even more rapidly. Real wages from 1946 through 1959 have been favorable to workers.

Figure 30.1 portrays the work stoppages, workers involved in strikes, number of man-days lost, and per cent of estimated total working time lost by strikes. This chart follows the usual pattern, increasing in number during the spring months, maintaining a fairly high level during the summer and fall, and then diminishing in number with the advent of winter. This is a perfectly natural situation. Labor leaders will not call a strike ordinarily when business is falling off and the employer is not needing production very badly. Production in general is greatly influenced by the seasons, followed in the main by the frequency of strikes. In interpreting Fig. 30.1 it must be understood that this does not represent the total number of man-days lost from strikes. It represents only the number of days lost by the companies directly involved in the strikes and does not consider the tens of thousands of man-days lost by other companies which use the products of the company involved in the strikes. For instance, the coal strikes of 1945 and 1946 idled the steel mills, which in turn caused lost time in thousands of other companies that use steel. Likewise the steel strikes of 1959 idled thousands of coal miners, railroad workers, and others providing services or supplies to the steel mills and others using

[3] See Dale Yoder, *Manpower Economics and Labor Problems,* 3d ed., Mc-Graw-Hill Book Company, Inc., New York, 1950, p. 99.

steel in their process. Actually basic industries like steel have a public responsibility in very much the same sense as a public utility. A strike in steel is not merely a strike against the employer. It is a strike against the public. Strike tactics leave much to be desired from a social standpoint. Regardless of who wins a strike, the community usually loses, since the same end could ordinarily have been attained by peaceful means. Workers are rightfully jealous of their right to strike; yet the future of both management and labor is not on the picket line but around the counsel table solving mutual problems. The Labor-Management Relations Act recognizes the national interest in strikes and establishes machinery to strive to reduce them by getting the disputants to make use of the Conciliation Service when they cannot agree among themselves through the orderly procedure of collective bargaining. If the highest-paid workers in the United States insist on striking against the company and the public for still higher wages, the people in their sovereign right may readily pass special legislation to take care of similar industries with a vital public interest. Workers and their leaders have a right to seek improved conditions for themselves, but they also have responsibilities to the consumers of their products and their communities. Higher wages without increased production are definitely inflationary. Inflation hurts almost everyone but falls with special severity on the aged, widows and orphans, white-

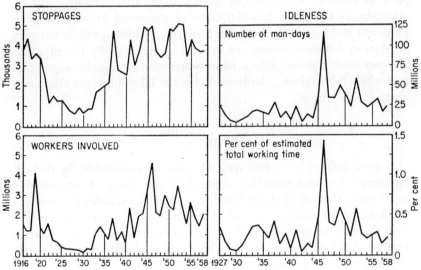

Fɪɢ. 30.1. Trends in work stoppages. (*Source: Monthly Labor Review, Vol. 82, No. 6, June, 1959.*)

collar workers, professional employees, and all persons on fixed incomes.

**Labor turnover.** *Labor turnover is the shifting of a work force into and out of a company.* Net labor turnover is probably the most commonly used measure of turnover. It is defined as the number of repacements per 100 workers in the average working force. Expressed in terms of a formula,

$$\text{Net labor turnover} = \frac{\text{total replacements}}{\text{average working force}} \times 100 \quad \text{or} \quad T = \frac{100R}{W}.$$

The *net labor turnover rate* is identical with the *accession rate* or *separation rate*, whichever is smaller. During periods of expansion in business, the separation rate and net labor turnover rate tend to be equal. During periods of business contraction, the net labor turnover rate corresponds to the rate of accession. During a period of normal business, when the working force is remaining stationary as to totals, the accession rate, separation rate, and net labor turnover rate are all the same. Most people in referring to labor turnover have reference to the ratio of separation to the total working force, usually the average for the period in question. This measure is fairly accurate for most purposes. The separation rate was the rate used by the Bureau of Labor Statistics as the labor turnover rate in its reports prior to 1929. As a measure of labor stability that is controllable by attention to the basic considerations of personnel (other than employment stabilization), the labor turnover separation rate is not very satisfactory because seasonal or cyclical layoffs magnify the situation. The net labor turnover rate is more representative than the separation rate when taken alone. The formula for the labor turnover rate based upon separations is

$$T = \frac{\text{total separations}}{\text{average working force}} \times 100 \quad \text{or} \quad \frac{100S}{W}.$$

A more refined labor turnover rate may be established by deducting from the base used for computing the cases of unavoidable separation. The adjusted net labor turnover rate excludes persons who are leaving for reasons beyond the control of management, such as those leaving because of death, marriage in the case of some women, prolonged illness, drafting into the armed forces, etc. Thus the adjusted *net labor turnover* rate would be

$$T = \frac{100(R - U)}{W}.$$

In this formula, *U* stands for the unavoidable separations, and the other letters are the same as have been used in the other formulas.[4]

The Bureau of Labor Statistics in the Department of Labor publishes monthly data concerning:

1. Number of separations during the period.
   1.1 Number of quits.
   1.2 Number of discharges.
   1.3 Number of layoffs.
   1.4 Miscellaneous separations, including military.
2. Accessions—persons hired.

These data provide detailed information for different industries. Since the Bureau's monthly reports give the detailed rates in terms of the items listed in the outline above for different industries, an employer in any one of these industries or in one similar to one of the specially reported industries may compare his plant's record with the experience of the industry. Although the average of an industry may not be a particularly desirable standard for a well-managed enterprise, it does establish a norm below which the progressive enterprise may constantly strive to keep its performance. In practice labor turnover rates are usually, for operating purposes, published monthly. A statement giving a labor turnover rate would normally be interpreted as the annual rate unless otherwise specified. The *Survey of Current Business* gives the monthly rates, as does the *Monthly Labor Review*. Because of the variation in the number of workdays in the various months, it is not logical to compare one month with another unless it has been adjusted for the difference in the number of days. Each month may be converted to an *equivalent annual rate* by multiplying the actual monthly turnover rate by a factor equivalent to 365 divided by the number of days in the given month.[5]

**Labor turnover costs.**[6] Labor turnover costs range all the way from $50 to $500 or more. It is actually difficult to get an accurate labor turnover cost. In states with a rating provision for unemployment taxes the labor turnover cost may push a given employer up to 2 per cent of payroll when turnover is high. Management loses the services of a man whose skill in his work has been developed at considerable expense. This necessitates the breaking in of a new man and the cost

---

[4] Either of the labor turnover rates may be expressed as decimal or whole number and decimal, as the case may be, without establishing it on the basis of 100 employees, if it is so desired.

[5] This factor is 11.77 for 31 days; 12.17 for 30 days; 12.62 for 29 days; and 13.04 for 1 month with 28 days.

[6] A survey by the Merchants and Manufacturers Association of Los Angeles in 1959 gives the average cost per separate as $480.82.

of giving him the necessary training to bring him to the same degree of efficiency as the man he replaces. During this period of training, loss, scrap, and waste, both in material and in time, are necessarily far greater than would have been the case had the worker carried on. With the new and untrained man on the job, production is necessarily lessened, not only in the work itself, but in all other occupations that in a routing sense are dependent upon it. Departmental production as a whole is lessened as a result of the disorganizing effect of the exchange upon the other persons in the department. The cost of labor turnover per employee varies with the type of work done by each employee. The office cost of hiring, record adjustment, physical examination, etc., will approximate $10 and in some cases will be much higher. Each person who leaves his job unnecessarily creates an economic loss that society as a whole must stand.

**The importance of labor turnover.** Management is interested in labor turnover, not only from the point of view of the cost of replacing the men who leave, but also from the point of view of the cost of lessened interest and effectiveness throughout the organization. Any study of the causes of labor turnover that leads to constructive action is an attack upon both instability and malingering on the part of those who remain. By the practice of sound personnel policies certain isolated concerns have been successful in reducing their labor turnover to a remarkable degree. These exceptional cases cannot be considered in determining a normal or an average turnover rate. As a matter of fact, what might be a normal rate for a given company this year might have been extremely low last year and may in fact be unwarrantably high a year hence. In most companies there is a nucleus of old-timers supported by others of shorter service but nevertheless inclined to stay put. These relatively stable employees comprise, in most instances, by far the greater part of the total number employed. The others, the unstable ones, however, normally stay such a short period of time in their positions that each is responsible for as many as three or four separations a year. Labor turnover is highest among new employees. This fact emphasizes the importance of proper selection, induction, and training. If an employee can be kept on the job long enough to get accustomed to his work and to earn the going rate for his job, he is likely to remain for a considerable period. If he can be carried beyond the first 3 months, the prospects are good; if he can be held for 6 months, they are much better; and if he can be held for 1 year, he tends to belong. The excess cost of labor turnover is a challenge to the research interest of the personnel man. One of the signs of unrest that frequently leads to labor turnover is excess absenteeism. Departments with high absenteeism rates tend to be the ones with high labor turnover. Greater care in selection, induction, training, and building group spirit or morale reduces absenteeism and labor turnover. Supervisors who inspire employees with confidence so that they will talk over their problems with them and who find time to talk with their men tend to have low absenteeism and labor turnover. A feeling of "group belonging" or "oneness" also tends to hold the employees.[7]

[7] See Floyd Mann and John E. Sparling, "Changing Absence Rates," *Personnel*, Vol. 32, No. 5, March, 1956, pp. 392–408; Robert D. Melcher, "Getting the Facts on Employee Resignations," *Personnel*, Vol. 31, No. 6, May, 1955, pp. 504–514; Irwin W. Krantz, "Controlling Quick Turnover," *Personnel*, Vol. 31, No. 6, May, 1955, pp. 514–520; Frederick J. Gaudet, "What Top Management Doesn't Know about Turnover," *Personnel*, Vol. 34, No. 5, March–April, 1958, 54–59; Louis Cassels and Raymond L. Randall, "Analysis of Worker Turnover Pays Off," *Nation's Business*, January, 1958, pp. 34–35, 70–72.

# CHAPTER 31

## Workers Requiring Special Consideration

**The older worker.** When is an employee too old to work? An impartial observer would think that the answer would be that *an employee is too old to work when his mental or physical condition, because of the passage of time, has deteriorated to the extent that he no longer can meet the requirements of the job.* One man might, under this standard, be too old to work at a given job at fifty, and another man might be successfully performing the same job at sixty-five. Of course such a definition of being "too old" requires hard decisions by some people who prefer to avoid these decisions by letting the calendar make it for them. A substantial number of companies, government agencies, universities, and other institutions have decreed that a man is too old to work for them when he has passed some arbitrary age such as sixty-five. In recent years this "cutoff age" has been pushing up somewhat to sixty-eight or in a few cases seventy. Some employers admit quite frankly that some of their employees at sixty-five are just as good as they were at sixty but argue that they have to have some method of deciding when to let a man go and that they think that the use of the calendar age is the best one they know of. This is equivalent to saying that in this one personnel relationship they prefer to treat all employees on a group basis rather than on a personal basis according to the facts of the individual situation. To them, in this one area, *personnel management is not personal.*

In considering the problems of our senior citizens there are two major points of view, namely, (1) the problem of the employer to find suitable jobs for his workers who have grown old in his service and who can no longer efficiently carry on their work in their accustomed occupations and (2) the problem of the older worker who finds himself out of employment and is faced with opposition to reemployment because of his age. Both these problems are social and economic in their implications. The first one is primarily an economic one for the employer who considers he has social and humanitarian responsibilities. Many employers minimize their problem by forcing their employees to retire before the factor of age creates many problems. Of course some employees may become victims of the aging process before the company's forced retirement age. The second problem is basically social in its larger aspects, but it is fundamentally economic for the aged employee.

Even during the critical manpower shortage of the Korean conflict and the boom period following it, large numbers of "help wanted" advertisements specified age groupings under forty-five. While admitting that generalization is hazardous even when supported by considerable statistical evidence, it would seem that workers are classified as old when they have passed the middle forties or at the maximum age of fifty. Workers past these ages may have no difficulty whatsoever holding down jobs; yet there is a tendency for them to encounter difficulty in finding new jobs if they lose their jobs at this age. During the depression years of the thirties the largest single unemployed group was composed of persons between the ages of twenty and twenty-four. The next largest group of male workers out of employment was made up of persons between sixty and sixty-four. This is understandable from the standpoint of the younger group because they had come of age at a time when job opportunities were scarce. The older men had often been laid off owing to a decline in work and could not get a new job. Many of the men between fifty and sixty had been able to hold their jobs because of seniority, but these same men would have found it difficult to get new jobs had they lost their old ones.

**Causes of discrimination against the older worker.** It would be unrealistic to say that the reasons for not wanting to hire the older worker are based solely on prejudice. Some employers have certain personnel policies that may be, at least in part, interfered with when an older worker is hired. In general the reasons given for not wanting to hire older workers are:

1. The announced policy of promoting all employees from within the organization.
2. Lack of flexibility of older workers.
3. Higher mortality rate of older workers.
4. The normal retirement age of sixty-five or at times even sixty.
5. Added costs of pension plans where these are in use.

No one could deny the fact that the hiring of a skilled older worker may bar an apprentice who has almost finished his training from the opportunity for which he has been working. The same may be true in the case of office workers and executives; however, this is often offered as an excuse and may not be significant in the failure to hire the older workers. Some companies still discriminate against the older worker even when they have no present employees who would be displaced by the older worker. The question of flexibility is one of individual differences rather than calendar years. Some men at thirty are more set in their attitudes and ways than others at fifty. *The older employee with a wider experience may even be more flexible than the younger one.*[1] Mortality rates for older workers may be higher than for younger ones; *yet the accident rate of older workers compares favorably with that of the younger ones.* With the advent of social security pensions, the fear of having to pension workers is largely removed. Most private pension plans pay only in proportion to length of service. Social security pensions should remove any "guilt feeling" of not providing the older worker an adequate pension unless he has worked long enough to earn it. In connection with the inflexibility criticism of older workers, both the workers themselves and management have responsibilities. From the management standpoint, there is the responsibility to offer opportunity to the worker to learn to do new tasks from time to time and thus to avoid becoming a narrow specialist incapable of adjusting to new situations. This usually can be accomplished by transferring men from time to time to new jobs. From the worker's point of view, he must be willing to undergo some inconvenience, possibly the acceptance of a slightly lower rate for a time, in order to learn new tasks when opportunity presents itself. The worker must also consciously strive to maintain an interest in changing conditions. It is natural that the older worker should be somewhat depressed when faced with mounting responsibilities and unemployment; yet this very outlook on life and the defeatist complex are two of his most serious handicaps. It is generally recognized that all older workers do not thus face the future, but, just to the extent that they do, they handicap not only themselves but other middle-aged workers who are looking for employment.

Executives and office workers find it just as difficult to get jobs after passing forty as do manual workers. Men who had had successful careers in managerial capacities found it very difficult to get started again during the depression, even though they were capable and willing to work in positions lower than the ones formerly held. The same situation frequently prevails during normal periods of business when an executive finds himself out of a job because his establishment is

---

[1] See "Age and Achievement and the Technical Man," *Personnel Psychology,* Vol. 13, No. 3, Autumn, 1960, pp. 245–260, for a challenging research on engineers.

closed down or there is an extensive reorganization. In a number of cities in the United States, The Forty Plus Club, Inc., specializes in assisting unemployed executives past forty years of age to secure employment. The Forty Plus Club has rigid standards for persons eligible to use its facilities. Successful Forty Plus Clubs have been established in Boston, New York, Chicago and on the West Coast.

It is not infrequent that the person having the opening into which the older applicant might readily fit is younger than the applicant, which creates at times a mental and social barrier in part founded upon fear of competition and in part grounded on tradition. Governmental units criticize private employers for discriminating against the older worker, and yet their own standards are frequently more severe than the private employer's. Governmental agencies would be well advised to revise their regulations so that employees would be selected solely on the basis of qualifications without regard to an upper age limit. The government retirement system could be adjusted to absorb the portion of the workers' annuities accruing under the Social Security Act, or the entire government retirement program might well be absorbed by the Social Security Board with any adjustments as to the upper brackets that were deemed desirable.

In a study conducted by the New York State Joint Legislative Committee on Problems of the Aging, 1948, when industry was asked "Do older workers produce as much as younger workers?" the answers were as follows:

1. 73 per cent of the firms said "yes."
2. 15 per cent said "no."
3. 7½ per cent said that production varied so much from individual to individual that they could not answer, affirmatively or negatively.
4. 4½ per cent did not answer the question.

In this same study the report on absenteeism was as follows:[1a]

| Absenteeism of elderly compared with younger workers | Nuffield Survey, England (approx.), % | New York State Joint Legislative Committee on Problems of the Aging, % |
|---|---|---|
| Absent more............... | 10 | 7 |
| No difference.............. | 57 | 17 |
| Absent less............... | 33 | 72 |
| No reply.................. | 0 | 4 |

[1a] New York State Joint Legislative Committee on Problems of the Aging, *Birthdays Don't Count,* 1948.

**Social and economic significance of the older worker.** The percentage of our total population whose ages are past forty-five has been gradually increasing (see Fig. 31.1). The 1940 census showed it to be 33.6 per cent; the 1950 census reported 34.7 per cent; and it is estimated that the percentage will reach 39.1 by the early 1960's. By the year 2000 it is estimated that 12.5 per cent of the population will be sixty-five years old or older. Add to this 12.5 per cent the persons between forty and sixty-five and it becomes readily apparent that this group can have tremendous political power. This power can readily lead to legal restrictions that would be burdensome if business is stupid in handling this situation. More than one state has passed laws to restrict an employer's discriminating against an applicant because of race or religion. There is no more logic in discriminating against a worker because of his age than because of his color. The same type of legislation can easily be passed if there is widespread discrimination against workers because of age. Since our working population is definitely growing older, the problem of the older worker in industry will become increasingly a more pressing one. Massachusetts, Connecticut, New York, California, and other states have recognized this problem and made exhaustive studies of the causes, effects, and possible solutions. The dispelling of erroneous ideas is one of the major suggestions for correction. Unless industry meets its obligations to older employees, there is certain to arise a

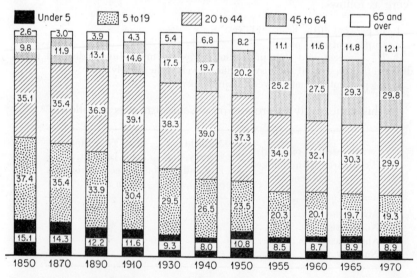

FIG. 31.1. Per cent distribution of total population by age, United States, 1850–1970. (*Source: U.S. Census of Population and Population Estimates P-25.*)

demand for further government regulations to cover this. At least one state has already passed such a law, even though it does not have many teeth in it.[2] It is to be hoped that this problem can be handled satisfactorily without further government interference in labor relations. The only legitimate standard for hiring employees is ability to perform the required work and compatibility with fellow workers.[3]

Technological changes may eliminate the older worker's job. It is the joint responsibility of management and workers to provide training to enable the technologically displaced worker to learn a new occupation. Fortunately, technological unemployment of older workers is not so great as it is often thought to be. Most persons beyond forty-five who lose their jobs do so in the same manner as their fellow workers under forty-five. The prime difference is that all too many employers hesitate to give the man past forty-five the same chance to get a new job that they give his more favored younger brother. For the worker between forty-five and sixty-five the problem of security is one of job opportunities rather than of retirement benefits. *Discrimination against the older woman worker is much greater than against men.* The unemployed woman worker past fifty is in a sad situation in most instances.

**The woman worker.** Legislative restrictions on the kind of work women may do, the number of hours that they may work in a 24-hr. period, and in some cases other limitations create problems for the employer of women. The advocates of special protective legislation are often motivated by a reform complex, and some are frequently not so much interested in the protection of women as they are in removing women from competition with special groups of men. Regardless of the desirability of restrictive legislation covering women workers, the facts of the situation cannot be ignored. The attitudes toward women workers that have resulted in these employment restrictions are not new. Some of them have their roots in the chivalry of the courts of the Middle Ages, when women were supposed to be protected from the realities of life. The concept that the place for the woman is in the home usually carries with it a moral injunction that she should have a home and bear children whether or not she wants

[2] The state of Massachusetts passed *An Act Prohibiting Discrimination against Certain Persons in Employment on Account of Their Age* in 1937. Section 24G of this act provides for the publishing of the name of any employer who, after a hearing, has been found guilty of dismissing from employment or refusal to hire a "person between the ages of forty-five and sixty-five because of his age."
[3] See Industrial Relations Research Association, *The Aged and Society,* New York, 1950. Also New York State Joint Legislative Committee on Problems of the Aging, *Young at Any Age,* 1950.

them or is financially in a position to rear these children according to the standard of living that she wishes for them. It is only one step from this concept to its corollary, that when a woman marries she should be compelled to give up her job.

Large numbers of women who have elected a home career for themselves subscribe to the theory that the place for women is in the home and are, in part through jealousy, delighted to see their working sisters forced to give up their jobs and thus be deprived of the luxuries and comforts that a few of the married workingwomen enjoy.

Some employers have regarded women as cheap labor and not particularly desirable and thus have offered little opposition to discriminatory legislation. Men workers usually recognize that women workers offer them stiff competition, and nothing builds prejudice quicker than what is felt to be unequal competition. Men-dominated unions sometimes bar women from membership; however, in the needle trades and in most industrial unions today, this bar has been removed.

Women played a leading role in rehabilitating war-torn Europe following World War II. Women still do heavy work in Russia and work in the fields in other parts of Europe. Women played an outstanding role in the industrial war effort in the United States, performing tasks formerly thought to be solely within the province of men. In *handicraft production, domestic production,* and *cottage production,* women played an important role as helpers to their men, and, in the case of the weaving and spinning trades, they were masters. Wherever heavy industries calling for men are located, a golden opportunity exists to establish industries providing employment for the wives and daughters of the men thus employed. In such a situation women workers usually can be hired for less than men to do the same job.

The supply of women workers is nearly always in excess of the demand in normal times. It is true that the lack of stability of women workers also tends to depress their wages. By lack of stability it is meant not that women as individuals are less reliable than men in general but that the average working girl is merely marking time until she marries or, if married, she is planning to work only long enough to help her husband buy a home and get started.

Relatively few workingwomen enter the business world with the avowed intention of establishing for themselves lifetime careers. Again, many of the younger women live at home and are not entirely dependent on their earnings; hence they are content to work for less.

Women in general have been less inclined to join unions and add collective strength to their wage bargaining. The tendency of women to be less regular in attendance (this is not always a demonstrable fact, but the general opinion nevertheless prevails) also depresses their wages. The multiplicity of government regulations covering women places an additional employment cost upon the employer of women, thus depressing their wages even in cases where they work on the same jobs with men. (Several states have laws requiring women to be paid on the same basis as men when performing the same work as men.) The generally higher turnover among women also adds an additional cost to the employment of women. Since women in general do not expect to remain in industry, they seldom enter trades requiring long periods of training or apprenticeship, which places women as a group in the unskilled class that nearly always receives low wages. Even when large numbers of them enter occupations requiring a high degree of skill, such as needle trades, these occupations as a rule are already overcrowded and ones for which the skill of the worker is closely related to household skills, for which women have traditionally been trained. No one of these factors is controlling, but, when taken collectively, they exert a profound influence upon the wages of women. The relationship of supply to demand is probably the strongest single factor.

The ratio of women workers to the total work force in manufacturing-industry group is shown in Fig. 31.2. The ratio of women workers to all workers (Fig. 31.3) as well as to all women above the age of fourteen is shown in Table 31.1.

In terms of the mores of workers, jobs that can be done by women rank lower in the job hierarchy than jobs that are preempted by men. They have lower social and economic status as a rule. The increased supply of women willing to work at lower wages than men in the same industry undoubtedly does lower the wages of men doing the same work. The fact that the supply of women workers is more elastic for a given locality than the supply of men also tends to accentuate this situation, particularly during periods of depression, when many women enter the work market because male members of their families have lost their jobs or have reduced earnings. Under such conditions, women workers do tend to reduce the wage ratio in general in the markets they enter. On the other hand, they also tend to increase the total employment and encourage business revival, because the reduced operating costs offer increased opportunity for profitable business operations. Rigidities of labor costs definitely retard

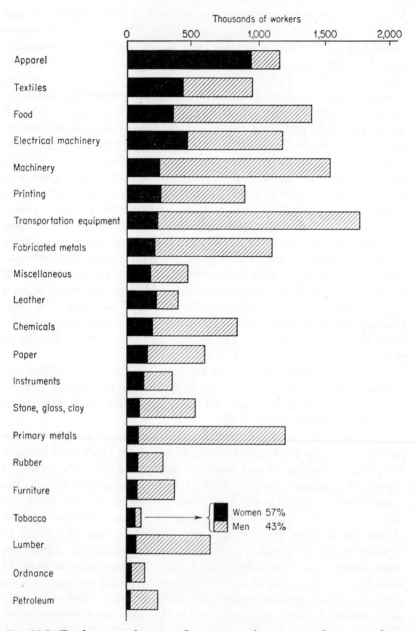

FIG. 31.2. Employment of men and women workers in manufacturing-industry groups. (*Source: "1958 Handbook on Women Workers,"* U.S. Department of Labor, p. 18.)

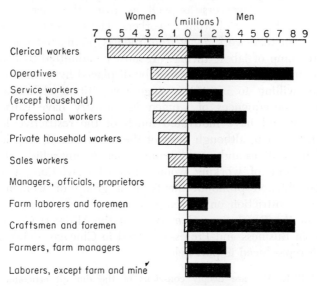

Occupational Groups of Employed Men and Women, 1958

FIG. 31.3. Ratio of women workers to all workers by occupational groups. (*Source: Current Population Reports, P-57 No. 190, U.S. Bureau of the Census.*)

*Table* 31.1   *Women Workers, Aged Fourteen and Over, 1900–1958**

| Year† | Women workers | | |
|---|---|---|---|
| | Number | Per cent of all workers | Per cent of all women |
| 1890 | 3,704,000 | 17 | 18 |
| 1900 | 4,999,000 | 18 | 20 |
| 1910‡ | 7,789,000 | 21 | 25 |
| 1920 | 8,229,000 | 20 | 23 |
| 1930 | 10,396,000 | 22 | 24 |
| 1940§ | 13,840,000 | 25 | 27 |
| 1945 | 19,570,000 | 36 | 37 |
| 1947 | 16,320,000 | 28 | 30 |
| 1950 | 18,063,000 | 29 | 32 |
| 1953 | 19,296,000 | 31 | 33 |
| 1958 | 22,254,000 | 33 | 36 |

* Source: U.S. Department of Labor, Women's Bureau, "*1958 Handbook of Women Workers,*" *Bulletin* 266, 1958.

† Data refer to April, except 1900 (June) and 1920 (January).

‡ Source: U.S. Department of Labor, Women's Bureau, "*Women's Occupations through Seven Decades,*" *Bulletin* 218, 1947.

§ Civilian labor force figures for 1940 (March) adjusted by the Census Bureau to make them comparable with those of later years.

business recovery during depressions. Society gains from the reduced costs of women workers as well as from the increase in total productivity because of women workers. The concept that women in the long run take work away from men is predicated upon the discredited "lump of labor" theory. (It must be admitted that in a given situation in the short run men may be displaced by women unless the men are willing to meet the wage competition of women.) The economic consequences of women in industry have caused much controversy and have motivated much of the restrictive legislation regarding women, although most of the advocates of such legislation claim lofty motives and would readily disclaim any selfish interests.

**The attitude of working women toward restrictions.** One of the most enlightened pronouncements of a group of women workers concerning restriction on the employment of women is found in the *Report of the Resolutions Committee* of the Midwest Conference of Women in Business and Professions held in Chicago, February, 1940, which is reproduced in part below:

PREAMBLE. We are deeply conscious of the difficult economic problems concerning unemployment, women in industry, the maintenance of a decent minimum wage and a proper standard of living, engendered by a conflict of interest between capital and labor, employer and employee; women in competition with men; single women in competition with married women who have other income; married women without additional income in competition with single women with additional income, affecting both men and women in the pursuit of their daily lives.

The Bill of Rights of the Constitution of the United States makes no distinction between the rights of men and women. As women who work, we stand on that premise, and oppose prohibitive and restrictive legislation affecting us.

WHEREAS it is the consensus of opinion of women who work that they no longer need protection so much as they need unrestricted opportunity to advance,

NOW THEREFORE BE IT RESOLVED that legislation of this type, which discriminates against married women, establishes a dangerous precedent and paves the way for further legislation which will eventually eliminate all women from the economic world;

WHEREAS the surveys of the Women's Bureau of the United States Department of Labor and National Industrial Conference Board reveal that it is now the policy of 23% of the reporting companies to dismiss women office employees upon marriage, as compared with about 8% placing the same restriction upon factory workers; followed by insurance firms with 84%, banks with 65%, public utilities, 63%, as compared with 14% of the manufacturing concerns and 11.5% of the mercantile establishments.

NOW THEREFORE BE IT RESOLVED that the social consequences of policies and legislation discriminating against women on account of their marital status would be extremely deleterious and alarming.

. . . and whereas any legislation making it mandatory on the employer to dismiss women upon marriage will greatly increase their difficulty in finding any employment, not to speak of the impossibility of their ever reaching any executive or supervisory positions;

. . . that all such legislation will naturally result in permanently limiting women to the lowest income jobs, leaving no opportunity for advancement into supervisory or executive positions, and should be strenuously opposed.

Management should remove any conditions that might reasonably be the subject of further discriminatory legislation for women, thus to protect both themselves and women workers from the undesirable economic and social consequences of further legislative restrictions. It will behoove women to be on the alert critically to evaluate proposed legislation for their protection regardless of the avowed lofty aims of such legislation and to insist that all such legislation be enlarged to include all workers rather than a special group.

**The physically handicapped.** The physically handicapped may for convenience be divided into three groups: (1) persons born with some physical impairment, (2) persons who are handicapped owing to some injury at work, and (3) persons who are handicapped by some injury or illness not associated with their work. Most employers strive to provide continued employment for persons injured in their service. The other two groups are essentially the same so far as seeking employment or being employed by a company that was in no manner associated with the cause of the impairment.

Practically every large-scale enterprise has jobs that can be performed by persons with some degree of impairment. These persons require some special planning of their workplaces and a little more attention on the part of the supervisor than the regular employees, but the economic and social gains to the community and work group justify the added effort. Blind persons can remove the burrs from castings, can weave, and can perform a number of other tasks if given the opportunity. With properly fitted mechanical tools or hands many a person with one hand can perform satisfactorily many manual tasks. An individual with one or both legs amputated can perform many industrial tasks if he has properly fitted artificial legs. Deaf-mutes, if properly trained in their youth, can do almost any job that does not involve the ability to hear.

Table 31.2 portrays the findings of the Employee Relations Department of the E. I. du Pont de Nemours and Company. This experience has been duplicated by other companies. The outstanding performance in safety, attendance, and job performance can be explained by the high degree of motivation possessed by the handicapped. They appreciate the opportunity to work and are anxious not to forfeit this opportunity by anything that they can control.

Table 31.2 *Safety, Attendance, and Job-performance Ratings, Handicapped Employees, by Job Classification**

| Job classification | Total | Safety record | | | | | | Attendance | | | | | | Job performance | | | | | |
|---|---|---|---|---|---|---|---|---|---|---|---|---|---|---|---|---|---|---|---|
| | | Number | | | Per cent | | | Number | | | Per cent | | | Number | | | Per cent | | |
| | | AA† | A‡ | BA§ | AA | A | BA | AA | A | BA | AA | A | BA | AA | A | BA | AA | A | BA |
| Professional and technical | 163 | 79 | 83 | 1 | 48 | 51 | 1 | 67 | 79 | 17 | 41 | 49 | 10 | 61 | 91 | 11 | 37 | 56 | 7 |
| Supervisory and management | 77 | 45 | 32 | 0 | 58 | 42 | 0 | 32 | 41 | 4 | 42 | 53 | 5 | 26 | 49 | 2 | 34 | 64 | 2 |
| Clerical | 131 | 68 | 61 | 2 | 52 | 47 | 1 | 69 | 50 | 12 | 53 | 38 | 9 | 55 | 64 | 12 | 42 | 49 | 9 |
| Craftsmen | 221 | 78 | 134 | 9 | 35 | 61 | 4 | 81 | 105 | 35 | 37 | 47 | 16 | 61 | 121 | 39 | 27 | 55 | 18 |
| Operators | 258 | 76 | 178 | 4 | 29 | 69 | 2 | 68 | 149 | 41 | 26 | 58 | 16 | 47 | 172 | 39 | 18 | 67 | 15 |
| Service workers | 145 | 46 | 98 | 1 | 32 | 67 | 1 | 41 | 74 | 30 | 28 | 51 | 21 | 19 | 105 | 21 | 13 | 72 | 15 |
| Laborers | 26 | 5 | 20 | 1 | 19 | 77 | 4 | 8 | 16 | 2 | 31 | 61 | 8 | 3 | 15 | 8 | 11 | 58 | 31 |
| Company total | 1,021 | 397 | 606 | 18 | 39 | 59 | 2 | 366 | 514 | 141 | 36 | 50 | 14 | 272 | 617 | 132 | 27 | 60 | 13 |

* Source: The E. I. du Pont de Nemours & Company.
† Above average.
‡ Average.
§ Below average.

480

The Federal and state agencies actively promote the training and placement of the physically handicapped. Figures 31.4 and 31.5 portray a training school sponsored by the Bulova Watch Company for the handicapped and one of their graduates in his work environment. With an increase in automation and electronic controls there should be additional opportunities for handicapped persons with skilled hands and mechanical aptitudes. The wheel-chair patient may readily qualify for this work if the employer only will give him a chance. Some brilliant accountants who were confined to a wheel chair have had difficulty in securing employment. This has been true even when there was a real shortage of accountants. Successful employment of the physically handicapped requires a change in the attitudes of employers as great as or greater than that required in training of the handicapped. Management would be well advised to strive to use the handicapped person on any job that can be adapted to his needs.

**Child labor.** The employment of younger people, even when they meet the legal requirements of age, presents a personnel problem. These young people are the hope of the future; yet the effervescence of youth causes many of their acts to be irresponsible. In view of their fine physical coordination, their accident rates should be low; yet they are not. Child labor should not be a problem for an enlightened employer, for he will not hire workers under the legal age. The Fair Labor Standards Act establishes a minimum age of sixteen for child labor, with the age limit of eighteen for certain occupations declared *hazardous* by the director of the Children's Bureau of the Department of Labor.

Child labor had its roots in various social and economic factors, among which are: (1) poverty of the parents, who need the income of the children to supplement the family earnings, (2) the attitude of certain other parents, who feel that their children should work to aid the family income regardless of the absolute need, (3) the desire of many children to work to earn money and escape a school life that is not particularly suited to their temperaments or capacities, and (4) the attitude of certain employers who are seeking cheap labor. Most of these causes are social in nature and can be removed only by social action, which has already made itself felt in state and Federal legislation.

Public policy relating to the employment of youths differs somewhat with different age groups. It is felt that children under fourteen are too young for employment and that children under sixteen should not be employed during hours when schools are in session. Although employment at sixteen or seventeen is permissible, it is increasingly

FIG. 31.4. Section of training laboratory of Joseph Bulova School of Watchmaking. (*Courtesy, Bulova Watch Company, Inc.*)

recognized that young people who drop out of school before completing high school to go to work are handicapped in their future vocational opportunities.

The employment of youths under eighteen fluctuates substantially with the demand for workers. Between 1940 and 1950 the number of employed children of fourteen and fifteen increased from 290,000 to 916,000; and the number of employed youngsters of sixteen and seventeen rose from 770,000 to 1,553,000. Most of this increase in employment was the result of greatly increased opportunities for part-time work, especially in the service and retail trades. Of the 2,500,000 school-age children and youths employed in 1950, about two-thirds were students working outside of school hours.

The Annual Report of the Labor Force[4] for 1947 showed 2,552,100 persons under seventeen working. Of these, 940,000 were fourteen and fifteen years of age. With proper supervision and under suitable working conditions, some employment combined with school may not be injurious to young people's development and may indeed con-

[4] Current Population Reports, Series P50, No. 85, June, 1958, Bureau of the Census.

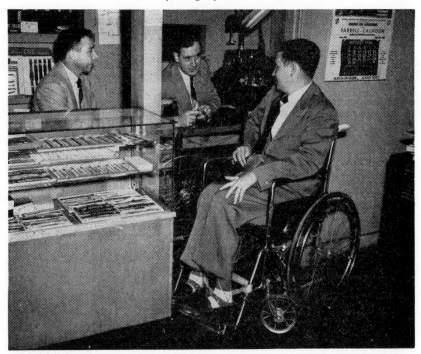

Fig. 31.5. Picture of Jewel Box, Memphis, Tenn., run by three partners, all para-plegics. (*Courtesy, Bulova Watch Company, Inc.*)

tribute to their growth. Supervised school and work programs offer many children some work experience which has educational value and better prepares the child for later vocational competence.

Child labor is regulated by the Federal Fair Labor Standards Act as well as by state laws. The Fair Labor Standards Act covers only children employed in interstate or foreign commerce, in the production of goods for interstate or foreign commerce, or in industries whose products move in such commerce. The child-labor provisions of the act establish a minimum age of sixteen for most employment and eighteen for certain occupations declared hazardous by the Secretary of Labor. As amended in 1949, the act also sets a minimum age of sixteen for agricultural employment during school hours in the district where the minor is living while he is employed.

Every state has a child-labor law applying to minors under sixteen years of age. Some apply also to minors of sixteen and seventeen. While these laws vary considerably in the standards or conditions they establish, most of them set a specific minimum age for general employment, a higher minimum age for employment in hazardous occupations, limit the weekly hours of work, prohibit nightwork, and require that the employer obtain an employment certificate for each minor in his employ.

The requiring of work permits for young people protects the employer from unwittingly hiring boys and girls under illegal conditions. Practically all the states require employment certificates as a condition of employment for children under sixteen, and over half require employment or age certificates for minors sixteen and seventeen years of age. Alertness is required on the part of the employer, or a youngster under sixteen who is large for his age may use the work permit of an older brother who is entitled to a permit.

**The child-labor amendment to the Constitution.** The proposal was submitted by Congress to the states, June 2, 1924. The proposal read:

Section 1, The Congress shall have power to limit, regulate, and prohibit the labor of persons under 18 years of age.

Section 2, The power of the several States is unimpaired by this article, except that the operation of State laws shall be suspended to the extent necessary to give effect to legislation enacted by Congress.

As we go to press, the proposed amendment has not received the required three-fourths of the states' approval. The Supreme Court ruled on July 5, 1939, that if no definite time limit is specified on a proposed amendment (as was the case with respect to the child-labor amendment), Congress alone has the power to determine how long a proposal to amend the Constitution is subject to ratification.[5] Since the Supreme Court's upholding of the Fair Labor Standards Act, the proposed amendment is no longer needed.

[5] *Coleman v. Miller*, 59 Sup. Ct. 972. See *Monthly Labor Review*, July, 1939, p. 142.

CHAPTER 32

# Labor-Management Relations Act and
# State Labor-relations Acts

**Early legislation on the rights of organized labor.** The three acts, the Norris–La Guardia Act, the Railway Labor Act, and the National Labor Relations Act, represent the basic attempts of the Federal government to guarantee the right of collective bargaining by law. The Norris–La Guardia Act of 1932 sets forth the right of the workers to bargain collectively "free from the interference, restraint or coercion of employers of labor or their agents in the designation of such representatives or in self-organization or in other concerted activities ·for the purpose of collective bargaining or other mutual aid or protection. . . ." Section 7(*a*) of the National Industrial Recovery Act (1933) stated:

Employees shall have the right to organize and bargain collectively through representatives of their own choosing, and shall be free from the interference, restraint or coercion of employers, or their agents, in the designation of such representatives or in self-organization, or in other concerted activities for the purpose of collective bargaining or other mutual aid and protection.

No employee, and no one seeking employment, shall be required as a condition of employment to join any "company union" or to refrain from joining, organizing, or assisting a labor organization of his own choosing.

After a series of boards appointed by the President by executive order, Congress by Joint Resolution 44 authorized a three-man labor board in 1934, which continued to function until May 27, 1935, when the NIRA was declared unconstitutional. This three-man board appointed regional boards and developed a body of procedures and principles that were expanded later by the National Labor Relations Board, authorized by the National Labor Relations Act of July 5, 1935. The Railway Labor Act (1935) did for the railway and air-transport

485

industries essentially what the National Labor Relations Act did for other industries engaged in interstate commerce.

**The National Labor Relations Act (Wagner Act) of 1935 as amended.** The National Labor Relations Act has been amended a number of times. The most important amendments were in 1947, when the Taft-Hartley Act changed the name to the Labor-Management Relations Act, and in 1959, by the Labor-Management Reporting and Disclosure Act.

The 1947 Taft-Hartley Amendment is divided into five main divisions, namely,

1. Section 1. Short title and declaration of policy.
2. Sections 101–104. Title I, *Amendment of National Labor Relations Act.* This division of the act includes the modifications of the original National Labor Relations Act. It adds unfair labor practices for labor organizations, modifies the structure of the National Labor Relations Board, establishes a General Counsel, independent of the Board, who has control over investigations and prosecutions, and modifies certain other practices and procedures that had grown up under the original act.
3. Sections 201–205. Title II, Conciliation of Labor Disputes in Industries Affecting Commerce; National Emergencies. This division establishes the conciliation service as an independent agency and prescribes procedures to be followed in the case of labor disputes that "imperil the national health or safety" and in national emergencies.
4. Sections 301–305. Title III. This division covers five different items:
   4.1 Suits by and against labor organizations—Section 301.
   4.2 Restrictions on payments to employee representatives—Section 302.
   4.3 Boycotts and other unlawful combinations—Section 303.
   4.4 Restrictions on political contributions of either unions or corporations—Section 304.
   4.5 Strikes by government employees—Section 305.
5. Sections 501–503. Title V. This division defines certain basic terms, clearly sets forth that an individual shall not be required "to render labor or service without his consent," and provides a separability clause, which preserves the act in case any individual clause may be held unconstitutional.

**The Labor-Management Reporting and Disclosure Act of 1959 has eight main divisions:**

1. Sections 1, 2, and 3, which give the title, declaration of findings, purpose, policy, and definitions.
2. Sections 101–105, Title I, Bill of Rights of Members of Labor Organizations.
3. Sections 201–210, Title II, Reporting by Labor Organizations, Officers and Employees of Labor Organizations, and Employers.
4. Sections 301–306, Title III—Trusteeships.
5. Sections 401–404, Title IV—Elections.
6. Sections 501–505. Title V—Safeguards for Labor Organizations.
7. Sections 601–611, Title VI—Miscellaneous Provisions.
8. Sections 701–707, Title VII—Amendments to the Labor-Management Relations Act, 1947, as Amended.

## TITLE I, TAFT-HARTLEY (1947)

### Statement of policy

Industrial strife which interferes with the normal flow of commerce and with the full production of articles and commodities for commerce, can be avoided or substantially minimized if employers, employees, and labor organizations each recognize under law one another's legitimate rights in their relations with each other, and above all recognize under law that neither party has any right in its relations with any other to engage in acts or practices which jeopardize the public health, safety, or interest.

It is the purpose and policy of this Act, in order to promote the full flow of commerce, to prescribe the legitimate rights of both employees and employers in their relations affecting commerce, to provide orderly and peaceful procedures for preventing the interference by either with the legitimate rights of the other, to protect the rights of individual employees in their relations with labor organizations whose activities affect commerce, to define and prescribe practices on the part of labor and management which affect commerce and are inimical to the general welfare, and to protect the rights of the public in connection with labor disputes affecting commerce.

The inequality of bargaining power between employees who do not possess full freedom of association or actual liberty of contract, and employers who are organized in the corporate or other forms of ownership association substantially burdens and affects the flow of commerce, and tends to aggravate recurrent business depressions, by depressing wage rates and the purchasing power of wage earners in industry and by preventing the stabilization of competitive wage rates and working conditions within and between industries.

Experience has proved that protection by law of the right of employees to organize and bargain collectively safeguards commerce from injury, impairment, or interruption, and promotes the flow of commerce by removing certain recognized sources of industrial strife and unrest, by encouraging practices fundamental to the friendly adjustment of industrial disputes arising out of differences as to wages, hours, or other working conditions, and by restoring equality of bargaining power between employers and employees.

Experience has further demonstrated that certain practices by some labor organizations, their officers, and members have the intent or the necessary effect of burdening or obstructing commerce by preventing the free flow of goods in such commerce through strikes and other forms of industrial unrest or through concerted activities which impair the interest of the public in the free flow of such commerce. The elimination of such practices is a necessary condition to the assurance of the rights herein guaranteed.

It is hereby declared to be the policy of the United States to eliminate the causes of certain substantial obstructions to the free flow of commerce and to mitigate and eliminate these obstructions when they have occurred by encouraging the practice and procedure of collective bargaining and by protecting the exercise by workers of full freedom of association, self-organization, and designation of representatives of their own choosing, for the purpose of negotiating the terms and conditions of their employment or other mutual aid or protection.

The statement of "Findings, Purposes and Policy" of the 1959 amendments recognizes that "breach of trust, corruption, disregard of the rights of individual employees, and other failures to observe high standards of responsibility and ethical conduct" have crept into union-employer relationships and require further legislation. This statement supports the objective of the original legislation.

Both statements of the 1947 and 1959 amendments recognize that both the union and the employer may place a burden upon the free flow of commerce. The statement of public policy is clearly behind the "practice and procedure" of collective bargaining.

**The National Labor Relations Board.** The act of 1947 increased the membership of the Board from three to five. The term of office of each member after the initial appointment of the members is 5 years, with a salary of $20,000 per year. A member is eligible for reappointment. He

. . . shall not engage in any other business, vocation or employment. . . . The Board shall appoint an executive secretary, and such other employees as it may from time to time find necessary for the proper performance of its duties. The Board may not employ any attorneys for the purpose of reviewing transcripts of hearings or preparing drafts of opinions except that any attorney employed for assignment as a legal assistant to any Board member may for such Board member review such transcripts and prepare such drafts. No trial examiner's report shall be reviewed, either before or after its publication, by any person other than a member of the Board or his legal assistant, and no trial examiner shall advise or consult with the Board with respect to exceptions taken to his findings, rulings, or recommendations. Nothing in this Act shall be construed to authorize the Board to appoint individuals for the purpose of conciliation or mediation, or for economic analysis.

The Board's activities are strictly of a judicial nature.

*The General Counsel.* The administrative and legal activities of the Board are carried on under the direction of the General Counsel of the Board. He exercises "general supervision over all attorneys employed by the Board (other than trial examiners and legal assistants to Board members) and over the officers and employees in the regional offices." He has "final authority, on behalf of the Board, in respect of the investigation of charges and issuance of complaints under Section 10, and in respect of the prosecution of such complaints before the Board, and . . . such other duties as the Board may prescribe or as may be provided by law." The General Counsel is appointed for a term of 4 years with an annual salary of $20,000.

**Definitions.** The first 10 of the following terms are defined in Section 101, Subsection 2, of the 1947 amendments:

1. *Section 2:* (1) The term "person" includes one or more individuals, labor organizations, partnerships, associations, corporations, legal representatives, trustees, trustees in bankruptcy, or receivers.

2. *Section* 2: (2) The term "employer" includes any person acting as an agent of an employer, directly or indirectly, but shall not include the United States or any wholly owned Government corporation, or any Federal Reserve Bank, or any State or political subdivision thereof, or any corporation or association operating a hospital, if no part of the net earnings inures to the benefit of any private shareholder or individual, or any person subject to the Railway Labor Act, as amended from time to time, or any labor organization (other than when acting as an employer), or anyone acting in the capacity of officer or agent of such labor organization.

3. *Section* 2: (3) The term "employees" shall include any employee, and shall not be limited to the employees of a particular employer, unless the Act explicitly states otherwise, and shall include any individual whose work has ceased as a consequence of, or in connection with, any current labor dispute or because of any unfair labor practice, and who has not obtained any other regular and substantially equivalent employment, but shall not include any individual employed as an agricultural laborer, or in the domestic service of any family or person at his home, or any individual employed by his parent or spouse, or any individual having the status of an independent contractor, or any individual employed as a supervisor, or any individual employed by an employer subject to the Railway Labor Act, as amended from time to time, or by any other person who is not an employer as herein defined.

4. *Section* 2: (4) The term "representatives" includes any individual or labor organization.

5. *Section* 2: (5) The term "labor organization" means any organization of any kind, or any agency or employee representation committee or plan, in which employees participate and which exists for the purpose, in whole or in part, of dealing with employers concerning grievances, labor disputes, wages, rates of pay, hours of employment or conditions of work.

6. *Section* 2: (9) The term "labor dispute" includes any controversy concerning terms, tenure or conditions of employment, or concerning the association or representation of persons in negotiating, fixing, maintaining, changing, or seeking to arrange terms or conditions of employment, regardless of whether the disputants stand in the proximate relation of employer and employee.

7. *Section* 2: (11) The term "supervisor" means any individual having authority, in the interest of the employer, to hire, transfer, suspend, lay off, recall, promote, discharge, assign, reward, or discipline other employees, or responsibility to direct them, or to adjust their grievances, or effectively to recommend such action, if in connection with the foregoing the exercise of such authority is not of a merely routine or clerical nature, but requires the use of independent judgment.

8. *Section* 2: (12) The term "professional employee" means—

(*a*) any employee engaged in work (i) predominately intellectual and varied in character as opposed to routine mental, manual, mechanical, or physical work; (ii) involving the consistent exercise of discretion and judgment in its performance; (iii) of such a character that the output produced or the result accomplished cannot be standardized in relation to a given period of time; (iv) requiring knowledge of an advanced type in a field of science or learning customarily acquired by a prolonged course of specialized intellectual instruction and study in an institution of higher learning or a hospital, as distinguished from a general academic education or from an apprenticeship or from training in the performance of routine mental, manual, or physical processes; or (*b*) any employee, who (i) has completed the courses of specialized intellectual instruction and study described in clause (iv) of paragraph (*a*), and (ii) is performing related work under the supervision of a professional person to qualify himself to become a professional employee as defined in paragraph (*a*).

9. *Section* 2: (13) In determining whether any person is acting as an "agent" of another person so as to make such person responsible for his acts, the question of whether the specific acts performed were actually authorized or subsequently ratified shall not be controlling.

10. *Section* 8: (*d*) Collective bargaining "is the performance of the mutual obligation of the employer and the representative of the employees to meet at reasonable times and confer in good faith with respect to wages, hours, and other terms and conditions of employment, or the negotiation of an agreement, or any question arising thereunder, and the execution of a written contract incorporating any agreement reached if requested by either party, but such obligation does not compel either party to agree to a proposal or require the making of a concession."

11. *Section* 501: (1) The term "industry affecting commerce" means any industry or activity in commerce or in which a labor dispute would burden or obstruct commerce or tend to burden or obstruct commerce or the free flow of commerce.

12. *Section* 502: Nothing in this Act shall be construed to require an individual employee to render labor or service without his consent, nor shall anything in this Act be construed to make the quitting of his labor by an individual employee an illegal act; nor shall any court issue any process to compel the performance by an individual employee of such labor or service, without his consent; nor shall the quitting of labor by an employee or employees in good faith because of abnormally dangerous conditions for work at the place of employment of such employee or employees be deemed a strike under this Act.

Again in the 1959 Labor-Management Reporting and Disclosure Act the following definitions were made:

Sec. 3. For the purposes of titles I, II, III, IV, V (except section 505), and VI of this Act—

(*a*) "Commerce" means trade, traffic, commerce, transportation, transmission, or communication among the several States or between any State and any place outside thereof.

(*b*) "State" includes any State of the United States, the District of Columbia, Puerto Rico, the Virgin Islands, American Samoa, Guam, Wake Island, the Canal Zone, and Outer Continental Shelf lands defined in the Outer Continental Shelf Lands Act (43 U.S.C. 1331–1343).

(*c*) "Industry affecting commerce" means any activity, business, or industry in commerce or in which a labor dispute would hinder or obstruct commerce or the free flow of commerce and includes any activity or industry "affecting commerce" within the meaning of the Labor Management Relations Act, 1947, as amended, or the Railway Labor Act, as amended.

(*d*) "Person" includes one or more individuals, labor organizations, partnerships, associations, corporations, legal representatives, mutual companies, joint-stock companies, trusts, unincorporated organizations, trustees, trustees in bankruptcy, or receivers.

(*e*) "Employer" means any employer or any group or association of employers engaged in an industry affecting commerce (1) which is, with respect to employees engaged in an industry affecting commerce, an employer within the meaning of any law of the United States relating to the employment of any employees or (2) which may deal with any labor organization concerning grievances, labor disputes, wages, rates of pay, hours of employment, or conditions of work, and includes any person acting directly or indirectly as an employer or as an agent of an employer in relation to an employee but does not include the United States or any corporation wholly owned by the Government of the United States or any State or political subdivision thereof.

(*f*) "Employee" means any individual employed by an employer, and includes any individual whose work has ceased as a consequence of, or in connection with, any current labor dispute or because of any unfair labor practice or because of exclusion or expulsion from a labor organization in any manner or for any reason inconsistent with the requirements of this Act.

(*g*) "Labor dispute" includes any controversy concerning terms, tenure, or conditions of employment, or concerning the association or representation of persons in negotiating, fixing, maintaining, changing, or seeking to arrange terms or conditions of employment, regardless of whether the disputants stand in the proximate relation of employer and employee.

(*h*) "Trusteeship" means any receivership, trusteeship, or other method of supervision or control whereby a labor organization suspends the autonomy otherwise available to a subordinate body under its constitution or bylaws.

(*i*) "Labor organization" means a labor organization engaged in an industry affecting commerce and includes any organization of any kind, any agency, or employee representation committee, group, association, or plan so engaged in which employees participate and which exists for the purpose, in whole or in part of dealing with employers concerning grievances, labor disputes, wages, rates of pay, hours, or other terms or conditions of employment, and any conference, general committee, joint or system board, or joint council so engaged which is subordinate to a national or international labor organization, other than a State or local central body.

(*j*) A labor organization shall be deemed to be engaged in an industry affecting commerce if it—

(1) is the certified representative of employees under the provisions of the National Labor Relations Act, as amended, or the Railway Labor Act as amended; or

(2) although not certified, is a national or international labor organization or a local labor organization recognized or acting as the representative of employees of an employer or employers engaged in an industry affecting commerce; or

(3) has chartered a local labor organization or subsidiary body which is representing or actively seeking to represent employees of employers within the meaning of paragraph (1) or (2); or

(4) has been chartered by a labor organization representing or actively seeking to represent employees within the meaning of paragraph (1) or (2) as the local or subordinate body through which such employees may enjoy membership or become affiliated with such labor organization; or

(5) is a conference, general committee, joint or system board, or joint

council, subordinate to a national or international labor organization, which includes a labor organization engaged in an industry affecting commerce within the meaning of any of the preceding paragraphs of this subsection, other than a State or local central body.

(*k*) "Secret ballot" means the expression by ballot, voting machine, or otherwise, but in no event by proxy, of a choice with respect to any election or vote taken upon any matter, which is cast in such a manner that the person expressing such choice cannot be identified with the choice expressed.

(*l*) "Trust in which a labor organization is interested" means a trust or other fund or organization (1) which was created or established by a labor organization, or one or more of the trustees or one or more members of the governing body of which is selected or appointed by a labor organization, and (2) a primary purpose of which is to provide benefits for the members of such labor organization or their beneficiaries.

(*m*) "Labor relations consultant" means any person who, for compensation, advises or represents an employer, employer organization, or labor organization concerning employee organizing, concerted activities, or collective bargaining activities.

(*n*) "Officer" means any constitutional officer, any person authorized to perform the functions of president, vice president, secretary, treasurer, or other executive functions of a labor organization, and any member of its executive board or similar governing body.

(*o*) "Member" or "member in good standing," when used in reference to a labor organization, includes any person who has fulfilled the requirements for membership in such organization, and who neither has voluntarily withdrawn from membership nor has been expelled or suspended from membership after appropriate proceedings consistent with lawful provisions of the constitution and bylaws of such organization.

(*p*) "Secretary" means the Secretary of Labor.

(*q*) "Officer, agent, shop steward, or other representative," when used with respect to a labor organization, includes elected officials and key administrative personnel, whether elected or appointed (such as business agents, heads of departments or major units, and organizers who exercise substantial independent authority), but does not include salaried nonsupervisory professional staff, stenographic, and service personnel.

(*r*) "District court of the United States" means a United States district court and a United States court of any place subject to the jurisdiction of the United States.

**Unfair labor practices.** In the original Wagner Act of 1935 only the employer was liable for *unfair labor practices*. Under the Taft-Hartley amendments both the employer and the labor organizations may be guilty of unfair labor practices. In substance, the unfair labor practices of an employer are as follows [Section 101, Subsection 8(*a*) 1–5]:

1. Employers must not interfere with their employees in the exercise of their right to self-organization, to form or to join labor organizations, and to bargain collectively through representatives of their own choosing.

2. Employers must not dominate or interfere with the formation or administration of any labor organization or contribute financial aid to the support of such labor organization.

3. Employers must not encourage or discourage membership in any labor organization by discriminating in hiring, discharge, or in any other condition of employment. This does not forbid a union shop when the union-shop agreement is entered into through an agreement between the duly authorized representatives of the employer and the employees. (Prior to the amendment of 1951 the union shop could not be granted unless in an election supervised by the National Labor Relations Board a majority of all the eligible employees had voted in favor of it. The amendment removed the requirement of the election.)

4. Employers must not in any way discriminate against employees who file charges against the company under the Act or who give testimony before the Board under the Act.

5. Employers must not refuse to bargain collectively with duly accredited representatives of their employees.

6. An employer may not terminate an existing contract with a labor organization, without first serving on the labor organization a 60 days' notice prior to its termination date, offering to meet and confer with the labor organization for the purpose of negotiating a new contract containing the proposed modifications, notifying the Federal Mediation Service within 30 days of the existence of a dispute. In case the dispute is in a state or territory having a mediation or conciliation service, notice also has to be served on the state or territorial service at the same time that the notice is served on the Federal Mediation Service.

In connection with unfair labor practices of an employer, Section 101, Subsection 8(*c*), says:

The expressing of any views, argument, or opinion, or the dissemination thereof, whether in written, printed, graphic, or visual form, shall not constitute or be evidence of an unfair labor practice under any of the provisions of this Act, if such expression contains no threat of reprisal or force or promise of benefit.

A labor organization may be guilty of unfair labor practices as follows [Section 101, Subsection 8(*b*) (1–6)]:

1. A labor organization shall not restrain or coerce employees in the exercise of their rights to organize and belong to a union of their choice or to refrain from belonging to a union except to the extent that the right not to belong to a union may be modified by a contract with an employer for a union shop as described above under item 3 for unfair labor practices for an employer.

1.1 The labor organization is not restricted in its right to prescribe its own rules with respect to the acquisition or retention of membership in the union. On the other hand in the case of a duly authorized union shop, "no employer shall justify any discrimination against an employee for nonmembership in a labor organization (A) if he has reasonable grounds for believing that such membership was not available to the employee on the same terms and conditions generally applicable to other members, or (B) if he has reasonable grounds for believing that membership was denied or terminated for reasons other than the failure of the employee to tender the periodic dues and the initiation fees uniformly required as a condition of acquiring or retaining membership" [Section 101, Subsection 8(*a*)(3)].

1.2 The labor organization not only may not restrain or coerce employees in relation to the selection of their representatives, neither can it restrain or coerce "an employer in the selection of his representatives for the purpose of collective bargaining or adjustment of grievances."

2. A labor organization may not "cause or attempt to cause an employer to discriminate" against an applicant for employment or an employee because of membership or nonmembership in a union, subject, of course, to the terms of a union-shop agreement duly entered into according to the Act. (See item 3 above, under Unfair Labor Practices, and 1.1 above, regarding unfair labor practices of labor organizations.) A labor organization may refuse to accept a member who does not meet its standards or dismiss one for cause, but the employer may not discriminate against such an employee if he has paid or offered to pay all regular dues and initiation fees. An employer may dismiss an employee for cause but the cause cannot be the loss of union membership for any reason other than a failure to pay dues or initiation fees. The union may deny membership to a Communist. An employer in his own right may discharge the same man for being a Communist but not because the union has denied him membership for being a Communist. The reverse is also true. An employer may discharge a Communist to whom a union gives membership. In this case, as in the other one, the sole basis for discharge would be Communist affiliation, not union membership.

3. A union that is the duly designated or selected agent for employees may not refuse to bargain collectively with the employer for the employees represented. By definition [101, Subsection 8(*d*)] collective bargaining includes "the execution of a written contract incorporating any agreement reached if requested by either party." Therefore, a refusal to sign a contract covering an agreement reached through collective bargaining is an unfair labor practice for either an employer or a labor organization refusing to sign.

4. A labor organization may not engage in a jurisdictional strike, boycott another employer's goods, or force an employer to cease doing business with another employer.

5. A labor union may not charge fees, "as a condition precedent to becoming a member of such organization . . . in an amount which the Board finds excessive or discriminatory under all circumstances."

6. A labor organization may not "cause or attempt to cause an employer to pay or deliver or agree to pay or deliver any money or other thing of value, in the nature of an exaction, for services which are not performed or not to be performed."

## THE 1959 LABOR-MANAGEMENT REPORTING AND DISCLOSURE ACT OF 1959

**Title I—Bill of Rights of Members of Labor Organizations.** The investigations of the McClellan Committee revealed a substantial amount of the denial of union members' rights. Congress sought to guarantee to the individual and group members the rights that independent men may reasonably expect as industrial citizens. These are primarily set forth in Sections 101 to 105. The entire act in substance is designed to supplement the basic rights of the members of the unions. Sections 101 to 105 of Title I in substance include the following:

1. *Section* 101 (*a*)(1). "Every member of a labor organization shall have equal rights and privileges . . . to nominate candidates, to vote in elections or referendums of the labor organization, to attend membership meetings, and to participate in the deliberations and voting upon the business of such meetings, subject to reasonable rules and regulations in such organization's constitution and bylaws."

2. "Every member of any labor organization shall have the right to meet and assemble freely with other members; and to express any views, arguments, or opinions; and to express at meetings of the labor organization his views, upon candidates in an election of the labor organization or upon any business properly before the meeting, subject to the organization's established and reasonable rules pertaining to the conduct of meetings: *Provided,* That nothing herein shall be construed to impair the right of a labor organization to adopt and enforce reasonable rules as to the responsibility of every member toward the organization as an institution and to his refraining from conduct that would interfere with its performance of its legal or contractual obligations." It will be interesting to see how this last proviso will be interpreted. For instance, may a member exercise his political right to oppose a stand taken by his union on a proposed law such as the "right to work" being voted on in his state. In California during 1958 a large national union expelled some members who supported the "right to work" proposal that was opposed by the union.

3. *Dues.* This section spells out in considerable detail the rights of the members to be protected in relation to the dues and initiation fees charged by his union.

4. *Right to Sue or Appear as a Witness.* This section protects the member in his right to sue the union or its officers, to appear as a witness in any judicial, administrative proceeding, or to petition any legislature or to communicate with any legislator provided, "That any such member may be required to exhaust reasonable hearing procedures (but not to exceed a four-month lapse of time) within such organization, before instituting legal or administrative proceedings against such organizations or any officer thereof: *And provide further,* That no interested employer or employer association shall directly or indirectly finance, encourage, or participate in, except as a party, any such action, proceeding, appearance, or petition."

5. *Protection against Improper Discipline.* "No member of any labor organization may be fined, suspended, expelled, or otherwise disciplined except for nonpayment of dues by such organization or by any officer thereof unless such member has been (A) served with written specific charges; (B) given a reasonable time to prepare his defense; (C) afforded a full and fair hearing.

(b) "Any provision of the constitution and bylaws of any labor organization which is inconsistent with the provisions of this section shall be of no force or effect."

All the above items are taken from Section 101(*a*)(1). In some instances they are direct quotations and in others they are briefed to save space.

Section 102 protects the civil rights of the union member. Any person whose rights secured by the provisions of this title have been infringed by any violation of this title may bring a civil action in a district court of the United States for such relief (including injunctions) as may be appropriate.

Section 103 makes it clear that the *bill of rights* in the act does not repeal or limit the rights and remedies of any member of a labor organization possessed at the time of the enactment of the act but is an extension of the "existing rights."

Section 104 requires a local labor organization to forward a copy of each collective-bargaining agreement made by the local labor organization to any employee who requests such a copy and whose rights are directly affected by the agreement; also a labor organization other than the local organization is required to forward a copy of an agreement to each constituent unit which has members directly affected by the agreement; and the local labor organization is required to make the agreement available for inspection to any employee whose rights are affected by the agreement.

Section 105 requires every labor organization "to inform its members concerning the provisions of this Act."

**Title II—Reporting by labor organizations, their employees, and by employers.** Section 201 requires detailed reporting by each labor organization on such things as name, address, and title of each officer; initiation fee or fees required from a new or transferred member and fees for work permits, and regular dues, fees, or other periodic payments required to remain a member of the union. This section further requires the reporting of detailed standards for practically every phase of the union's operation, selection and qualifications of officers, how often the officers are elected, and supporting documents covering these operations and the constitutions and bylaws authorizing the action. A few of the other things required to be reported are: report of the receipt and disbursement of all money and an audit of same; qualification of and restriction of membership; discipline or removal of officers or agents for breaches of trust; fines imposed, and expulsion or discipline of members and provisions made for notice, hearings, judgment on the evidence, and appeal procedures; authorization for bargaining demands and for strikes, and ratification of bargaining terms; and the issuance of work permits.

Section 201(*b*) requires the labor organization to file an annual report with the Secretary of Labor, setting forth in detail all financial transactions, salaries, loans in excess of an aggregate of $250 per year, and other information as the Secretary may prescribe. Salary and reports on expenses are for employees receiving $10,000 a year or more. All loans made by the union to an employer must also be reported.

This section [201($b$)] requires the union officers to make the foregoing information available to its members. It further requires the labor organization to permit a member, for cause, to examine the books and accounts from which the report is compiled. The member may go to court to secure the information if it is denied him. In such an action the court may, in its discretion, allow reasonable attorney's fees to the member bringing the action. This section of the act repeals Section 9($f$), ($g$), and ($h$) regarding reporting and the no-Communist oath.

Section 202 requires all officers and employees (other than those performing clerical and custodial services) to file an annual report of all transactions with an employer or labor relations consultant whose employees the union represents or is actively seeking to represent. This report covers practically anything that might directly or indirectly be used as a bribe of the union representative. The same report includes the transactions of the unions representative's wife or minor child. The union employee is not required to report income received as a part of his regular employment with the company or transactions in securities or bonds sold on a regular exchange that is regulated by statute.

Section 203 requires of the employer or management consultant reports that are in substance the counterpart of the reports required of union employees. The objective is to expose any action of the employer or labor relations consultant that might be construed as interfering with genuine collective bargaining or the rights of an employee or employees in connection with collective bargaining. This reporting does not apply to regular employees of the company in their legal representation of the employer with the union or to persons representing the employer before any court, administrative agency, or tribunal of arbitration or to the employer's representative agreeing to engage or engaging in collective bargaining with respect to wages, hours, or other conditions or terms of employment.

Section 204 specifically excludes the reporting of the relationship of a duly recognized attorney and his client.

Section 205 authorizes the Secretary to do research on the reports made under this title and to make them available for inspection by interested parties under conditions prescribed by the Secretary. Copies of these reports are made available on the payment of a charge of the cost of the service. This same information is made available to appropriate state agencies without charge.

Section 206 requires all persons filing reports under this title to maintain records that can be checked to verify the accuracy of the reports filed.

Section 208 authorizes the Secretary to prescribe the rules and regulations that are appropriate for ensuring the accurate reporting required. He may authorize a simplified report for small employers or unions for whom the more complete report would be a burden.

Section 209 provides a fine of not more than $10,000 or imprisonment for not more than 1 year or both for willful violation of this title. Each individual who signs the report or is required to file a report is personally responsible for his acts as a representative of the union or employer, or for himself.

**Title III—Trusteeships.** This title is designed to establish proper rules and regulations under which parent union bodies may appoint trustees for subordinate bodies. It prescribes in detail procedures for handling the funds of the union, the conditions under which the union membership may be represented at union conventions, methods of ensuring democratic elections in the subordinate labor organization under a trusteeship, and a limitation on the length of the trusteeship of 18 months unless the court for good reasons authorizes its continuance for a period deemed appropriate.

This section is designed to protect the rights of individual unions and union members from exploitation by certain unscrupulous union officers. Penalties are provided for violations and injunctive relief is authorized.

**Title IV—Elections.** Sections 401 to 404 are designed to ensure democracy and an orderly procedure in electing officers of local, national, and international unions and their intermediate bodies such as committees, system boards, joint boards, or joint councils. By Section 401(d), officers are required to be elected not less often than: (1) national and international unions every 5 years, (2) local unions every 3 years, (3) intermediate bodies such as committees and councils every 4 years. Each member in good standing is eligible to run for office, subject of course to reasonable qualifications uniformly imposed. Each qualified candidate shall have access to the membership roster. Any mailings and notices sent out by the union office shall be open to all candidates on equal terms. Union funds shall not be used to promote the candidacy of any person. If followed, the details governing the conduct of elections will guarantee to all members of the union equal opportunity to be heard and to nominate and to run for union office.

Adequate provision is made to enable a member or group of members to secure compliance with the legitimately prescribed election regulations. They must first exhaust the remedies provided in the constitution and bylaws of the union. If the available remedies have been invoked without obtaining a final decision within 3 calendar months after their invocation, a member may appeal to the Secretary alleging the violation of any provision of Section 401. If the investigation of the Secretary reveals probable cause of a violation that has not been corrected, he will bring a civil action against the labor organization to set aside the invalid election, if any, and to vote upon the removal of the officers under the supervision of the Secretary. If the court finds the evidence to sustain the charge, the court will order an election conducted under the supervision of the Secretary. The law strives to protect the member or members in the discharge of their voting rights, including open advocacy of candidates other than the current officers, and to protect them from "penalty, discipline or improper interference or reprisal of any kind by such organization or any members thereof." It is to be hoped that the provisions of this title will work. If the higher echelons charged with administering the union constitution and bylaws want it to work, it will achieve its objectives. Violence, strong-arm squads, and irregular techniques were not legal before the passage of this act. Local authorities simply have not protected individuals against the organized coercion of entrenched power. This act places the strong arm of the Federal government on the side of democracy in union elections.

**Title V—Safeguards for labor organizations. Fiduciary responsibility.** Sections 501 to 505 seek to guarantee that all money received by the union through dues, assessments, or any other legal channel shall be protected and used only for the benefit of the legitimate objectives of the union; to prohibit the employer or a consultant from paying or giving goods or services of value to a union official or representative union group to influence their actions in a manner contrary to the best interests of the union or collective bargaining. The union is prohibited from loaning an officer of the union money in excess of $2,000; neither shall the "union or the employer directly pay the fine of any officer or employee convicted of any willful violation of this Act" [Section 503($b$)]. The union officers or employees handling money are required to be bonded by an approved agency for an amount not less than 10 per cent of the money handled but not in an amount in excess of $500,000. A union whose property and annual receipts do not exceed $5,000 is exempt from the bonding requirement.

Sec. 504($a$) No person who is or has been a member of the Communist Party or who has been convicted of, or served any part of a prison term resulting from his conviction of, robbery, bribery, extortion, embezzlement, grand larceny, burglary, arson, violation of narcotics laws, murder, rape, assault with intent to kill, assault which inflicts grievous bodily injury, or a violation of title II or III of this Act, or conspiracy to commit any such crimes, shall serve—

(1) as an officer, director, trustee, member of any executive board or similar governing body, business agent, manager, organizer, or other employee (other than as an employee performing exclusively clerical or custodial duties) of any labor organization, or

(2) as a labor relations consultant to a person engaged in an industry or activity affecting commerce, or as an officer, director, agent, or employee (other than as an employee performing exclusively clerical or custodial duties) of any group or association of employers dealing with any labor organization,

during or for five years after the termination of his membership in the Communist Party, or for five years after such conviction or after the end of such imprisonment, unless prior to the end of such five-year period, in the case of a person so convicted or imprisoned, (A) his citizenship rights, having been revoked as a result of such conviction, have been fully restored, or (B) the Board of Parole of the United States Department of Justice determines that such person's service in any capacity referred to in clause (1) or (2) would not be contrary to the purposes of this Act. . . .

**Title VI—Miscellaneous provisions.** This title authorizes the Secretary to inspect records needed for the proper discharge of his responsibilities. Extortionate picketing is forbidden. This title specifically states that legal rights of unions and employers are not impaired unless specifically so stated. This act does not impair the right of the states to pass laws covering crimes that were within their rights prior to the passage of the act. Persons are specifically forbidden to use violence or threats of violence to coerce or restrain individuals from exercising rights to which they are entitled under this act.

**Title VII—Amendments to the Labor-Management Relations Act, 1947, as amended.** Section 201(*c*)(1) states that

the Board, in its discretion, may, by rule of decision or by published rules adopted pursuant to the Administrative Procedure Act, decline to assert jurisdiction over any labor dispute involving any class or category of employers, where, in the opinion of the Board, the effect of such labor dispute on commerce is not sufficiently substantial to warrant the exercise of its jurisdiction: *Provided,* That the Board shall not decline to assert jurisdiction over any labor dispute over which it would assert jurisdiction under the standards prevailing upon August 1, 1959.

(2) Nothing in this Act shall be deemed to prevent or bar any agency or the courts of any State or Territory (including the Commonwealth of Puerto Rico, Guam, and the Virgin Islands), from assuming and asserting jurisdiction over labor disputes over which the Board declines, pursuant to paragraph (1) of this subsection, to assert jurisdiction.

Section 9(*c*)(3) of the act as amended in 1947 is amended to restore the right of an economic striker to vote within 1 year of the beginning of the strike: "Employees engaged in an economic strike who are not entitled to reinstatement shall be eligible to vote under such regulations as the Board shall find are *consistent with the purposes and provisions* of this Act in any election conducted within *twelve months after the commencement of the strike."*

*Boycotts and recognition picketing* are specifically restricted by adding to Section 8(*b*)(4) of the 1947 amended act as follows:

(4)(i) to engage in, or to induce or encourage any individual employed by any person engaged in commerce or in an industry affecting commerce to engage in, a strike or a refusal in the course of his employment to use, manufacture, process, transport, or otherwise handle or work on any goods, articles, materials, or commodities or to perform any services; or (ii) to threaten, coerce, or restrain any person engaged in commerce or in an industry affecting commerce, where in either case an object thereof is—

(A) forcing or requiring any employer or self-employed person to join any labor or employer organization or to enter into any agreement which is prohibited by Section 8(*e*);

(B) forcing or requiring any person to cease using, selling, handling, transporting, or otherwise dealing in the products of any other producer, processor, or manufacturer, or to cease doing business with any other person, or forcing or requiring any other employer to recognize or bargain with a labor organization as the representative of his employees unless such labor organization has been certified as the representative of such employees under the provisions of section 9: *Provided*, That nothing contained in this clause (B) shall be construed to make unlawful, where not otherwise unlawful, any primary strike or primary picketing;

(C) forcing or requiring any employer to recognize or bargain with a particular labor organization as the representative of his employees if another labor organization has been certified as the representative of such employees under the provisions of Section 9;

(D) forcing or requiring any employer to assign particular work to employees in a particular labor organization or in a particular trade, craft, or class rather than to employees in another labor organization or in another trade, craft, or class, unless such employer is failing to conform to an order or certification of the Board determining the bargaining representative for employees performing such work:

*Provided*, That nothing contained in this subsection (*b*) shall be construed to make unlawful a refusal by any person to enter upon the premises of any employer (other than his own employer), if the employees of such employer are engaged in a strike ratified or approved by a representative of such employees whom such employer is required to recognize under this Act: *Provided further*, That for the purposes of this paragraph (4) only, nothing contained in such paragraph shall be construed to prohibit publicity, other than picketing, for the purpose of truthfully advising the public, including consumers and members of a labor organization, that a product or products are produced by an employer with whom the labor organization has a primary dispute and are distributed by another employer, as long as such publicity does not have an effect of inducing any individual employed by any person other than the primary employer in the course of his employment to refuse to pick up, deliver, or transport any goods, or not to perform any services, at the establishment of the employer engaged in such distribution;

Hot-cargo contracts were declared void with certain reservations in the construction and clothing industries, by adding the following to Section 8 of the 1947 National Labor Relations Act as amended:

(7) to picket or cause to be picketed, or threaten to picket or cause to be picketed, any employer where an object thereof is forcing or requiring an employer to recognize or bargain with a labor organization as the representative of his employees, or forcing or requiring the employees of an employer to accept or select such labor organization as their collective bargaining representative, unless such labor organization is currently certified as the representative of such employees:

(A) where the employer has lawfully recognized in accordance with this Act any other labor organization and a question concerning representation may not appropriately be raised under Section 9(c) of this Act,

(B) where within the preceding twelve months a valid election under section 9(c) of this Act has been conducted, or

(C) where such picketing has been conducted without a petition under section 9(c) being filed within a reasonable period of time not to exceed thirty days from the commencement of such picketing: *Provided,* That when such a petition has been filed the Board shall forthwith, without regard to the provisions of section 9(c)(1) or the absence of a showing of a substantial interest on the part of the labor organization, direct an election in such unit as the Board finds to be appropriate and shall certify the results thereof: *Provided further,* That nothing in this subparagraph (C) shall be construed to prohibit any picketing or other publicity for the purpose of truthfully advising the public (including consumers) that an employer does not employ members of, or have a contract with, a labor organization, unless an effect of such picketing is to induce any individual employed by any other person in the course of his employment, not to pick up, deliver or transport any goods or not to perform any services.

Nothing in this paragraph (7) shall be construed to permit any act which would otherwise be an unfair labor practice under this Section 8(b).

Building and construction industries are granted special consideration in making prehiring contracts by adding Subsection (f) to Section 8 of the 1947 National Labor Relations Act as amended.

(f) It shall not be an unfair labor practice under Subsections (a) and (b) of this section for an employer engaged primarily in the building and construction industry to make an agreement covering employees engaged (or who, upon their employment, will be engaged) in the building and construction industry with a labor organization of which building and construction employees are members (not established, maintained, or assisted by any action defined in Section 8(a) of this Act as an unfair labor practice) because (1) the majority status of such labor organization has not been established under the provisions of section 9 of this Act prior to the making of such agreement, or (2) such agreement requires as a condition of employment, membership in such labor organization after the seventh day following the beginning of such employment or the effective date of the agreement, whichever is later, or (3) such agreement requires the employer to notify such labor organization of opportunities for employment with such employer, or gives such labor organization an opportunity to refer qualified applicants for such employment, or (4) such agreement specifies minimum training or experience qualifications for employment or provides for priority in opportunities for employment based upon length of service with such employer, in the industry or in the particular geographical area: *Provided,* That nothing in this subsection shall set aside the final proviso to section 8(*a*)(3) of this Act: *Provided further,* That any agreement which would be invalid, but for clause (1) of this subsection, shall not be a bar to a petition filed pursuant to Section 9(*c*) or 9(*e*).

The foregoing special privileges of the construction and building industry do not apply to states having "right-to-work laws" that prohibit it.

**Representative elections.** The National Management Labor Relations Board will not interfere with management's bargaining with a union or other agency claiming to represent the employees so long as the arrangement is not challenged in an orderly manner according to the various provisions of the act. Section 101, Subsection 9, reads:

Representatives designated or selected for the purposes of collective bargaining by the majority of the employees in a unit appropriate for such purposes, shall be the exclusive representatives of all the employees in such unit for the purposes of collective bargaining in respect to rates of pay, wages, hours of employment, or other conditions of employment: *Provided,* That any individual employee or a group of employees shall have the right at any time to present grievances to their employer and to have such grievances adjusted, without the intervention of the bargaining representative, as long as the adjustment is not inconsistent with the terms of a collective-bargaining contract or agreement then in effect: *Provided further,* That the bargaining representative has been given opportunity to be present at such adjustment.

The Board shall decide in each case whether, in order to assure to employees the fullest freedom in exercising the rights guaranteed by this Act, the unit appropriate for the purposes of collective bargaining shall be the employer unit, craft unit, plant unit, or subdivision thereof: *Provided,* That the Board shall not (1) decide that any unit is appropriate for such purposes if such unit includes both professional employees and employees who are not professional employees unless a majority of such professional employees vote for inclusion in such unit; or (2) decide that any craft unit is inappropriate for such purposes on the ground that a different unit has been established by a prior Board determination, unless a majority of the employees in the proposed craft unit vote against separate representation or (3) decide that any unit is appropriate for such purposes if it includes, together with other employees, any individual employed as a guard to enforce against employees and other persons rules to protect property of the employer or to protect the safety of persons on the employer's premises; but no labor organization shall be certified as the representative of employees in a bargaining unit of guards if such organization admits to membership, or is affiliated directly or indirectly with an organization which admits to membership, employees other than guards.

The Board may be petitioned to conduct an election to certify the proper bargaining agency by (1) "an employee or group of employees or any individual or labor organization acting in their behalf" or (2) "by an employer, alleging that one or more individuals or labor organizations have presented him a claim to be recognized as the representative as defined in Section 9(a)." The Board investigates petitions that have been properly filed and orders a secret election if the findings of facts show that there is a question of representation involved. By stipulation both parties may waive a hearing by the Board for the purpose of a consent election. Employees on a strike who are not entitled to reinstatement are permitted to vote if they have not been out on a strike for more than 12 months.

No election shall be directed in any bargaining unit or any subdivision within which, in the preceding twelve month period, a valid election shall have been held. In any election where none of the choices on the ballot receives a majority, a run-off shall be conducted, the ballot providing for a selection between the two choices receiving the largest and second largest number of valid votes cast in the election [Section 101, Subsection 9(c)(3)].

While the amendment of 1951 discontinues the requirement for an election to precede a union shop agreement, the deauthorization election is retained. On the petition of 30 per cent or more of the employees in a bargaining unit the Board will conduct an election to determine whether or not the union's authority to enter into a union agreement shall be revoked. For a union to use the facilities of the Board, it must conform to certain requirements, specified in the act as discussed below.

**Union recognition by the Board.** Under the current regulations of the Board jurisdiction will be taken according to the following standards:[1]

1. *Non-Retail:* $50,000 outflow or inflow, direct or indirect.[2]
2. *Office Buildings:* Gross revenue of $100,000 of which $25,000 or more is derived from organizations which meet any of the new standards.

[1] As in effect Oct. 2, 1958.
[2] Direct outflow refers to goods shipped or services furnished by the employer outside the state. Indirect outflow includes sales within the state to users meeting any standard except solely an indirect inflow or indirect outflow standard. Direct inflow refers to goods or services furnished directly to the employer from outside the state in which the employer is located. Indirect inflow refers to the purchase of goods or services which originated outside the employer's state but which he purchased from a seller within the state. Direct and indirect outflow may be combined, and direct and indirect inflow may also be combined, to meet the $50,000 requirement. However, outflow and inflow may *not* be combined.

3. *Retail Concerns:* $500,000 gross volume of business.

4. *Instrumentalities, Links and Channels of Interstate Commerce:* $50,000 from interstate (or linkage) part of enterprise, or from services performed for employers in commerce.

5. *Public Utilities:* $250,000 gross volume, or meet standard 1 (non-retail).

6. *Transit Systems:*[3] $250,000 gross volume.

7. *Newspapers and Communication Systems:* Radio, television, telegraph and telephone: $100,000 gross volume. Newspapers: $200,000 gross volume.

8. *National Defense:* Substantial impact on national defense.

9. *Business in the Territories and District of Columbia:*
   D.C. . . . . . . . . . . . . . . . . . . . . . . . . . . . . . . . . . . . . . . . . . . . . . . . . . . Plenary
   Territories . . . . . . . . . . . . . . . . . . . . . . . . . . . . . . . . . . . . . . . . Standards apply

10. *Associations:* Regarded as single employer.

**Prevention of unfair labor practices.** It should be remembered that both the union and management may be guilty of *unfair labor practices*. The Board or any agent or agency designated by the Board has full power to investigate complaints of unfair labor practices, to issue cease-and-desist orders, and

to take such affirmative action including reinstatement of employees with or without back pay as will effectuate the policies of this Act: *Provided,* That where an order directs reinstatement of an employee, back pay may be required of the employer or labor organization, as the case may be, responsible for the discrimination suffered by him.

The Board has the power to petition any circuit court of appeals of the United States or any district court if the circuit court is not in session to enforce its order. The Board's findings shall be based upon a "preponderance of the testimony." The proceedings of the Board in its hearings

shall, so far as practicable, be conducted in accordance with the rules of evidence applicable in the district courts of the United States under the rules of civil procedure for the district courts of the United States, adopted by the Supreme Court of the United States pursuant to the Act of June 19, 1934 (U.S.C. Title 23, Sections 723-B, 723-C). . . . The findings of the Board with respect to questions of fact if supported by substantial evidence on the record considered as a whole shall be conclusive.

Either party may petition the court to introduce additional evidence, and the court may order additional evidence to be taken before the Board if the party can

show to the satisfaction of the court that such additional evidence is material and that there were reasonable grounds for the failure to adduce such evidence in the hearing before the Board, its member, agent, or agency.

[3] Except taxicabs, as to which the retail ($500,000 gross volume of business) test shall apply.

The great bulk of the work of the Board is performed by its regional offices.

In case the evidence is presented before a member of the Board, or before an examiner or examiners thereof, such member, or such examiner or examiners, as the case may be, shall issue and cause to be served on the parties to the proceeding a proposed report, together with a recommended order, which shall be filed with the Board, and if no exceptions are filed within twenty days after service thereof upon such parties, or within such further period as the Board may authorize, such recommended order shall become the order of the Board and become effective as therein prescribed. . . . No order of the Board shall require the reinstatement of any individual as an employee who has been suspended or discharged, or the payment to him of any back pay, if such individual was suspended or discharged for cause.

The Board will not issue a complaint based upon any unfair labor practice occurring more than 6 months prior to the filing of the charge with the board.

Limitations of Section 101, Subsection 13, of the act as amended states:

Nothing in this Act, except as specifically provided for herein, shall be construed so as either to interfere with or impede or diminish in any way the right to strike, or to affect the limitations or qualifications on that right.

Section 14. (*a*) Nothing herein shall prohibit any individual employed as a supervisor from becoming or remaining a member of a labor organization, but no employer subject to this Act shall be compelled to deem individuals defined herein as supervisors as employees for the purpose of any law, either national or local, relating to collective bargaining.

(*b*) Nothing in this Act shall be construed as authorizing the execution or application of agreements requiring membership in a labor organization as a condition of employment in any State or Territory in which such execution or application is prohibited by State or Territorial law.

The Labor-Management Relations Act does not supplant the Railway Labor Act. It does, however, supersede certain phases of the Norris–La Guardia Act pertaining to injunctions in certain specified cases.

**Conciliation.** Section 202 of the act as amended establishes the Federal Mediation and Conciliation Service as an independent agency to effectuate the policies of the act.

[Section 203(*d*) states] Final adjustment by a method agreed upon by the parties is hereby declared to be the desirable method for settlement of grievance disputes arising over the application or interpretation of an existing collective-bargaining agreement. The Service is directed to make its conciliation and mediation services available in the settlement of such grievance disputes only as a last resort and in exceptional cases.

Under Title II of the act as amended (1947) employers and employees in industries affecting commerce are urged:

1. To exert every possible effort to make and maintain collective bargaining agreements and to give adequate notice of any proposed change in such agreements.

2. To arrange promptly for a conference in case of a dispute over an agreement in case a conference is requested by a party or prospective party thereto.

3. To participate fully and promptly in any meetings sponsored by the service for the purpose of aiding in the settlement of a labor dispute.

**National emergencies.** Section 206 of the act as amended provides:

Whenever in the opinion of the President of the United States, a threatened or actual strike or lockout affecting an entire industry or a substantial part thereof . . . will, if permitted to occur or to continue, imperil the national health or safety, he may appoint a board of inquiry to inquire into the issues involved in the dispute and to make a written report to him within such time as he shall prescribe.

The prolonged steel strike of 1959 demonstrated the need for this type of protection for the public interest or even a stronger regulation. The Steel Workers challenged President Eisenhower's using this provision on constitutional grounds. The Supreme Court sustained the legality of its provisions. The President may direct the Attorney General to seek an injunction to enjoin the strike or lockout or the continuing thereof. If the Court finds (1) that it affects an entire industry or a substantial part thereof engaged in interstate commerce or (2) that it imperils the national health and safety, it may issue the injunction. During the life of the injunction the parties assisted by the Service shall strive to resolve their differences. The President shall recall the Board of Inquiry to report to him, at the end of 60 days from the date of the injunction (unless the dispute has been settled), the status of the controversy. Within the ensuing 15 days the Board shall take a secret ballot of the employees on the last offer made by their employer and certify it to the Attorney General within 5 days. The Attorney General then moves that the Court dissolve the injunction. Where the injunction is dissolved, the President reports to the Congress the situation, with any recommendations he may care to make. Thus the public is protected for 80 days, during which time the facts are developed and made public.

**Suits by and against labor organizations.** Title IV of the 1947 amendments to the act (Section 301) authorizes the filing of a suit against a labor organization as an entity in the courts of the United States. The employer has always been subject to suit, but it has been difficult for him to sue labor organizations. Any money judgment against a labor organization is enforceable only against the organization as an entity and against its assets and not against any individual member or his assets. In suits involving violations of a contract,

in determining whether any person is acting as an "agent" of another person so as to make such other person responsible for his acts, the question of whether the specific acts performed were actually authorized or subsequently ratified shall not be controlling [Section 301(e)].

Section 301(a) specifically authorizes suits against labor organizations for violations of contracts.

**Restrictions on political contributions.** Section 304 of the act as amended in 1947 specifically restricted the expenditure of a union's or corporation's funds to promote the candidacy of any person for the presidency, vice-presidency, or membership in the Senate or House of Representatives.

For the purposes of this section "labor organization" means any organization of any kind, or any agency or employee representation committee or plan, in which employees participate and which exists for the purpose, in whole or in part, of dealing with employers concerning grievances, labor disputes, wages, rates of pay, hours of employment, or conditions of work.

Unions have devised methods of conforming to the law's requirements as to expenditure of union funds by their leaders' setting up separate political action groups financed separately from the regular collective-bargaining union structure. Most certainly union leadership is active in the political field.

**Strikes by government employees.** Section 305 of the act as amended in 1947 declares

It shall be unlawful for any individual employed by the United States or any agency thereof including wholly owned Government corporations to participate in any strike. Any individual employed by the United States or by any such agency who strikes, shall be discharged immediately from his employment, and shall forfeit his civil service status, if any, and shall not be eligible for reemployment for 3 years by the United States or any such agency.

**The status of retailing under the act.** Retail establishments have not been unionized to the extent of industrial establishments; because of this fact, the number of cases of interpretation are not so complete. The Taft-Hartley Act continued most of the provisions of the Wagner Act so far as encouraging collective bargaining is concerned. Under the old National Labor Relations Act the Denver Dry Goods Company was held to be engaged in interstate commerce (1947) within the meaning of the law because:

1. More than 50 per cent of its annual purchases were obtained from out of state.

2. More than 1 per cent of its gross sales were shipped out of state.

Under the current status the Board will take jurisdiction of a labor dispute in retailing with a $500,000 gross volume of business.

**State labor-relations acts.** The 1959 amendments to the National Labor Relations Act as amended gives added status to the respective state laws on labor relations. It reaffirms the state's rights to pass "right-to-work" laws and specifically grants to the states the right to handle cases that the Labor Board has not cared to handle because of the relatively small impact on interstate commerce.

In terms of the procedures used by the states having labor relations laws,[4] there are three general approaches, namely, (1) the administrative type patterned after the NLRA, (2) the quasi-judicial type, and (3) the judicial type using the established judicial system. The administrative type uses an agency that combines the functions of investigation, prosecution, and adjudications. This is the most popular system used by seven jurisdictions.[5] The quasi-judicial system uses an established court as the first step in enforcement. There is no investigation prior to the hearing. The complainants are private litigants and may withdraw complaints.[6] The judicial system follows the regularly established judicial techniques.[7]

The various states have legislated at some time or other on the following subjects: picketing; strikes, especially when public utilities are involved; union security; checkoff; secondary boycotts; jurisdictional disputes; licensing, registration, and reporting; suability; political contributions; welfare funds; and fair-employment practices.

A series of decisions of the United States Supreme Court have made great inroads on the authority of the respective states to regulate labor relations within the state provided that the dispute involves a union whose employer is engaged in interstate commerce.[8] The preemptiveness of Federal labor legislation has definitely weakened the states' rights. The states still have the right to punish violence and fraud, to prescribe certain restrictions on union security clauses, and (under

[4] See Harold A. Katz, "Two Decades of State Labor Legislation," *Labor Law Journal,* Vol. 8, No. 11, November, 1957, pp. 748–749.

[5] These are Connecticut, Massachusetts, New York, Oregon, Rhode Island, Utah, and Puerto Rico.

[6] Hawaii, Pennsylvania, and Washington have the quasi-judicial system.

[7] Kansas, Michigan, and Minnesota follow this procedure.

[8] *Guss v. Utah Labor Relations Board; Meat Cutters v. Fairlawn Meats, Inc.; Building Trades Council v. Garmon,* U.S. Sup. Ct., Mar. 25, 1957; see *Monthly Labor Review,* May, 1957, pp. 603–604.

the Landrum-Griffin Act) to regulate those union activities in business firms whose size or other cause has prompted the Labor Board not to take jurisdiction. The Taft-Hartley Act, Section 8($d$), states that either party to a union contract must notify the other 60 days prior to the termination of the contract if it wants to modify or terminate the contract, and within 30 days of the notification the party desiring the change must notify the Federal Service (Conciliation and Mediation) and the state mediation agency if no agreement has been reached by that time. In December, 1958, there were 45 states and Puerto Rico with some kind of mediation law.[9]

The rapid increase in union welfare and pension funds has led a number of states to prescribe rules and regulations for handling union funds and to require various kinds of reporting.[10] Likewise a substantial number of states have passed laws dealing with discrimination against workers because of race or religion. New York added in 1958 to its fair-employment-practices law a prohibition against discriminating against an individual because of age. Fourteen states have mandatory fair-employment-practices acts,[11] and two states have voluntary laws on the same subject.[12]

Right-to-work laws is one area in which the Federal regulations clearly defer to the states. Nineteen states have general right-to-work laws of general application.[13] A few of the states have written such regulations into their constitutions.

Some states prohibit the picketing of homes or residences. Other states prohibit picketing unless a majority of the employees have voted in favor of a strike. Texas prohibits mass picketing. Georgia forbids the use of force, intimidation, or violence to prevent an individual from quitting or continuing in employment.

An unfortunate aspect of the administration of many of the state laws is the fact that local enforcement officers and at times the state

[9] See "State Mediation Laws and Agencies," *Bulletin* 176, Bureau of Labor Statistics, December, 1958, p. 3. At least 17 states passed mediation laws prior to 1900. The first mediation laws in the United States were passed by New York and Massachusetts in 1886. See *ibid.*, p. 2.

[10] See *Monthly Labor Review*, Vol. 81, No. 8, August, 1958, p. 873. Eleven states had regulations in 1958 dealing with financial reporting.

[11] These states are Alaska, Colorado, Connecticut, Massachusetts, Michigan, Minnesota, New Jersey, New Mexico, New York, Oregon, Pennsylvania, Rhode Island, Washington, and Wisconsin.

[12] See "State and Federal Labor Legislation," *Bulletin* 193, Bureau of Labor Statistics, 1958, p. 2.

[13] See "State Right-to-Work Laws," *Bulletin* 904, Bureau of Labor Statistics, 1959, p. 1. These states are Alabama, Arizona, Arkansas, Florida, Georgia, Indiana, Iowa, Kansas, Mississippi, Nebraska, Nevada, North Carolina, North Dakota, South Carolina, South Dakota, Tennessee, Texas, Utah, and Virginia.

administrative officers are frequently more interested in catering to the votes of organized labor than in protecting innocent citizens against the unlawful acts of certain irresponsible unionists. This statement in no manner is to be interpreted as meaning that all or even a majority of unionists are irresponsible. The truth is that most of them are law-abiding citizens. Until there is a better understanding of cost-price relationships, there will be no enduring labor-management peace regardless of state or national laws. All that the laws can do is to minimize excesses and protect the public interest in some of the more extreme cases.

## CHAPTER 33

# The Fair Labor Standards Act of 1938 as Amended
## (the Wage and Hour Act)

**Arguments for minimum wage and time and one-half overtime legislation.** The Federal Wage and Hour Act grew out of the depression of the thirties. It was a part of the "spread-the-work" philosophy. The spread-the-work, or lump-of-labor, theory applied only to men when the advocates of limiting the work week were trying to include men in 1938. Prior to this time attempts to regulate the length of the work week and setting minimum wages were primarily concerned with women and children. Their arguments were based largely on the need for protecting their health. It was a logical step to go from hours of work to minimum wages to support women according to a standard in keeping with common ideas of respectability. The arguments were then expanded to include health, decency, and public morals. Advocates of minimum wages and maximum hours of labor for women and children seldom argued on the basis of the lump-of-labor theory. Most of the advocates of this legislation recognized that, if the hours were reduced so that the available supply of women and children would be in demand, they would have to be reduced to such a ridiculously low level by comparison that there would be no hope for its passage or, if passed, women and children would be placed at such a disadvantage in seeking employment that the legislation would be a serious handicap. Another argument nearly always advanced is the fact that the long hours complained of were detrimental to the health of the future and present mothers of our race as well as to growing children; thus, the number of hours of work should be restricted under the police powers of the state to protect the health and safety of the people. These arguments were not necessarily in favor of a 40-hr. week but were against the 50-hr. and sometimes longer week. On the basis of health alone, it would be difficult to show that a 40-hr. week was especially to be preferred to a 44-hr. week.

The severe depression created a serious unemployment situation in

1933, when the NIRA codes limited the number of hours of work with the avowed purpose of spreading the work. The same situation prevailed in 1938. Labor unionists and social reformers argued that, since there was only so much work to be had anyway, it was socially desirable and economically sound to limit the hours that any one person could work and thus to spread the work among as many people as possible. The fallacy of this argument was discussed in Chap. 24, Stabilization of Wages or Employment. The most ludicrous of all the arguments was the socioeconomic one that, since employees are after all the largest group in the consuming public, hours must be shortened in order to give the workers time in which to consume the articles or services that they produce. The lump-of-labor theory was absurd for a long-run legislative program although understandable during the early days of the depression of the thirties.

**Early efforts at regulating wages and hours by legislation.** In all probability the first wage and hour legislation in the Americas was enacted in the Virgin Islands. The Labor Act of Jan. 26, 1849, was promulgated by the Governor General of the Danish West Indies. Among other things it established a 5-day week of 40 hr. and a wage scale, revoked overtime agreements where no extra pay was given, and required time and one-half pay for work on Saturday.[1] Congress first passed an act limiting the length of the work day to 8 hr. for laborers and mechanics who were employed directly by the government or by private contractors on public works in 1892. In 1911 a rider to a naval-appropriation bill providing for the construction of and the machinery for battleships and torpedo boats prescribed an 8-hr. day. In 1912, the same principle was extended to require every Federal contract to contain a stipulation that no laborer or mechanic was to be permitted to work more than an 8-hr. day, with certain exceptions. In 1913 the act of 1892 was extended to include all workers engaged in dredging or rock excavation in rivers and harbors of the United States. The Bacon-Davis Act of 1931 provided that every government contract above $5,000 for the construction, alteration, and repair of any public building of the United States was to contain a provision requiring the payment of prevailing community wage rates for similar work as determined by the Secretary of Labor. This act was extended in 1935 to apply to contracts in excess of $2,000. The Walsh-Healy Act of 1936 provided that any agency of the United States contracting for the manufacture or furnishing of materials, supplies, articles, and equipment above $10,000 should stipulate that:

---

[1] See J. Antonio Jarvis, *The Virgin Islands and Their People*, Dorrance & Company, Inc., Philadelphia, 1944, p. 136.

1. All persons employed by the contractor will be paid not less than the prevaling minimum wage for such work in the community as established by the Secretary of Labor [Section (1)*b*].

2. No employee will be permitted to work more than 8 hours in one day or 40 hours in any week unless paid for overtime [Section (1)*c*].

3. Males under sixteen years of age and females under eighteen years of age will not be employed [Section (1)*d*].

4. Convict labor will not be employed [Section (1)*d*].

5. No part of such contract will be performed in any plant or facility or under working conditions which are unsanitary or hazardous or dangerous to health and safety of employees [Section (1)*e*].

The Adamson Act of 1916 provided an 8-hr. day for railroad employees and further provided that wages should not be reduced because of the shortened day, pending the report of a commission created to investigate the situation. The Supreme Court upheld this act in the case of *Wilson v. New* (243 U.S. 322, 1917). In 1914 Congress prescribed a maximum 8-hr. day and a 48-hr. week for women in the District of Columbia. In 1918 an act was passed establishing a minimum-wage board for the District of Columbia empowered to establish minimum wages for women and children at such a rate as to meet the "necessary cost of living" and "to maintain them (women and minors) in good health and to protect their morals." The Supreme Court declared this act unconstitutional in the case of *Adkins v. Children's Hospital* (261 U.S. 525, Apr. 9, 1923). The Motor Carrier Act of 1935 gave the Interstate Commerce Commission power to set maximum hours of work for "common and contract carriers and, if need be found for it, of employees of private carriers as well."[2] The NIRA of 1933 made provision for the establishment of maximum hours and minimum rates of pay. This act was invalidated by the Supreme Court. However, the Supreme Court sustained the minimum-wage law for women of the state of Washington in the case of *West Coast Hotel Company v. Parrish* (300 U.S. 379, Mar. 29, 1937), in substance reversing or modifying its ruling in the *Adkins v. Children's Hospital* case, thus pointing the way to the present Fair Labor Standards Act, which became law June 25, 1938. This act was amended in 1949, raising the minimum wage from 40 cents to 75 cents per hour, and again in 1955 raising the hourly minimum to $1 per hour effective Mar. 1, 1956. Some members of Congress have been advocating raising the minimum to $1.25 or even $1.50 per hour. The act [Section 4(*d*)] requires the Secretary of Labor to render an annual report on

[2] See First Annual Report of the Wage and Hour Division of U.S. Department of Labor, 1939, pp. 1–3, for most of the data presented in this paragraph.

his activities for the preceding year and including such information, data, and recommendations for further legislation in connection with the matters covered by this Act as he may find advisable. Such report shall contain an evaluation and appraisal by the Secretary of the minimum wages established by this Act, together with his recommendations to the Congress. In making such evaluation and appraisal, the Secretary shall take into consideration any changes which may have occurred in the cost of living and in productivity and the level of wages in manufacturing, the ability of employers to absorb wage increases, and such other factors as he may deem pertinent.[3]

From the foregoing it can be seen that Congress in the act itself has asked for information that might justify raising the minimum wage at a later date.

**State minimum-wage laws.** The Supreme Court's invalidation of the minimum-wage law of the District of Columbia in 1923 left considerable doubt as to the constitutionality of the state laws. At the beginning of 1933, the year in which the NIRA was passed, only 9 states, in some of which the laws were inactive, had minimum-wage laws. The National Consumer's League sponsored a standard bill that did not attempt to regulate wages generally but provided for an investigation to be made whenever a substantial number of women and minors were receiving less than a subsistence wage, to "determine whether the wages are fairly and reasonably commensurate with the value of the service or class of service rendered." As of July 1, 1959, there were 32 states, the District of Columbia, and Puerto Rico that had minimum-wage laws. Twenty of these had wage boards that established the minimum rates; 10 had the minimum set by statute, and 4 had a combination of wage boards and statutes. Only 11 of these included men under their legal provisions; all of them included women; and all but 5 included minors, and 4 of these states that did not include minors included girls but not boys.[4]

Some of the states establish their minimum wages on the basis of the cost of living, and others consider wages in relation to their being "fairly and reasonably commensurate with services rendered." There is much to commend the program of establishing minimum wages by a board or commission, particularly when the board is empowered to change the rates with changing economic conditions. The fixing of

[3] Section 2 of the Fair Labor Standards Amendments of 1955; effective Aug. 12, 1955. Section 6 of the Fair Labor Standards Amendments of 1955 provides that the term "Secretary" as used therein means the Secretary of Labor.

[4] Source of this information Supplement (dated July 1, 1959) to State Minimum Wage Laws and Orders, *Womens' Bureau Bulletin* 276, Part I, pp. 20–31, and Part II, 1958. The Supplement of July 1, 1959, covered material found in Part II.

minimum rates by statute creates an inflexible condition that may work real hardships should the general level take a serious drop. Most of the provinces in Canada have flexible rates. From the standpoint of the protection of health and viewed in the light of the tendency to work a shorter day aside from legislation, it would appear that there is more logic to applying maximum-hours legislation to women and minors than to men.

**Provisions of the Fair Labor Standards Act as amended.** The act covers four basic provisions, (1) minimum wages, (2) maximum hours, (3) record keeping, and (4) child labor. The first two divisions have always been under the Wage and Hour Division of the Department of Labor. The child-labor provisions were formerly under the Children's Bureau of the Department of Labor. In July, 1947, the child-labor research program and the age-certificate program under the Fair Labor Standards Act were transferred to the child-labor branch of the Wage and Hour Division. The enforcement of the child-labor provisions of the Fair Labor Standards Act has been merged with the field operation branch of the Wage and Hour Division. Congress stated the underlying intent of the law in Section 2(*a*) to be:

The Congress hereby finds that the existence, in industries engaged in commerce, or in the production of goods for commerce, of labor conditions detrimental to the maintenance of the minimum standard of living necessary for health, efficiency, and general well-being of workers (1) causes commerce and the channels and instrumentalities of commerce to be used to spread and perpetuate such labor conditions among the workers of several states; (2) burdens commerce and the free flow of goods in commerce; (3) constitutes an unfair method of competition in commerce; (4) leads to labor disputes burdening and obstructing commerce and the free flow of goods in commerce.

(*b*) It is hereby declared to be the policy of this Act, through the exercise by Congress of its power to regulate commerce among the several states and with foreign nations, to correct and as rapidly as practicable to eliminate the conditions above referred to in such industries without substantially curtailing employment or earning power.

**Coverage of the Fair Labor Standards Act.** Section 6, with certain exceptions under 1961 amendments, sets a minimum hourly wage of $1.15 for 2 years from the effective date and $1.25 thereafter for employees engaged in "commerce or in the production of goods for commerce." With certain enumerated exceptions Section 7 requires the payment of time and one-half after 40 hr. in any 1 week to employees engaged in commerce or the production of goods for commerce. It seems to be a fair evaluation of the administration of the act to say that the Administrator has construed the coverage of the act as broadly as possible without undue violence to the wording of the act in order to extend its coverage to as large a number of persons as possible. The act applies to pieceworkers, day workers, or salaried workers. The coverage of employees, as far as coming under interstate commerce is concerned, is very broad in the act itself. Section 3(*j*) defines *produced* as follows:

> Produced means produced, manufactured, mined, handled, or in any other manner worked on in any State, and for the purposes of this Act an employee shall be deemed to have been engaged in the production of goods if such employee was employed in producing, manufacturing, mining, handling, transporting, or in any other manner working on such goods, or in any process or occupation closely related and directly essential to the production thereof, in any State.

Just who comes under the act and who does not is not easily determined by a casual reading of the act. The only safe practice for an employer is to get a ruling from the Administrator of the Wage and Hour Division in case of doubt. For instance "window washers" employed by a "local window-cleaning company" who wash the windows of a factory engaged in interstate commerce will not be covered. On the other hand, an outside employer whose employees render a service such as repairing or maintaining the machinery or buildings used by a manufacturer of goods entering into interstate commerce is covered. So are employees of a watchman or guard or patrol or burglar-alarm service protecting the producer's premises. On the other hand, a local architect whose activities include the preparation of plans for the alteration of a local building which is used to produce goods for interstate commerce is not covered.

**Examples of activities not covered.** According to the report of the managers of the Congressional Conference Committee (*House Conference Committee Report* 1453, 81st Cong., 1st Sess.) the following specific activities seem to be exempt:

1. Employees of a materialman quarrying stone (within the same state), quarrying, processing, and transporting the stone to the site of a dike being constructed to protect an oil field from being flooded. (The employees constructing the dike would be covered.)

2. Employees of a local fertilizer plant whose fertilizer is used by the farmers in the same state even though the products of these farms are to be sold interstate.

3. Window cleaners doing business within one state even though many of their customers are engaged in interstate commerce.

4. Employees of a local nursery merely because they happen "to include producers of goods for commerce" among their customers.

5. Employees of an independent local restaurant located in a factory producing goods for interstate commerce.

6. Employees of a local exterminator who does some work for a producer engaged in interstate commerce.

7. A local architect who includes in his work plans for a producer whose products enter into interstate commerce.

8. Employees maintaining and repairing the private homes leased or rented by the producer of goods for commerce to his employees.

9. Employees of a local retailer who sells goods to a producer for interstate commerce provided that these goods are not a part or ingredients of the goods produced for interstate commerce.

*Exemptions.* The amended act (1949) (Section 13) specifically exempts the following classes of persons from both the minimum-wage and hours provisions:

1. Any employee employed in a bona fide executive, administrative, professional, or local retailing capacity, or in the capacity of an outside salesman (as such terms are defined and delimited by regulation of the Administrator) [Section 13($a$)(1)].

2. Any employee employed by any retail or service establishment, more than 50 per cent of which establishment's annual dollar volume of sales of goods or services is made within the state in which the establishment is located, provided such establishments meet the tests set forth in the act [Section 13($a$)2].

3. Employees of establishments engaged in laundering, cleaning, and repairing clothing or fabrics more than 50 per cent of which establishment's annual dollar volume of sales of such services is made within the state, provided further that 75 per cent of such sales on the basis of annual dollar volume is made to customers not engaged in manufacturing, mining, transportation, or communication [Section 13($a$)3]. In other words, 75 per cent of the volume in dollars must be with establishments other than the 4 types specifically named above.

4. Retail establishments recognized under Section 13($a$)2 notwithstanding the fact that such establishment makes or processes at the retail establishment the goods that it sells, provided more than 85 per cent of the annual dollar volume of such sales are made within the state [Section 13($a$)4]. Bakeries come under this heading.

5. Employees actively engaged in fishing and closely related activities (other than canning) such as loading, unloading, preparing for shipment, marketing, freezing, curing, storing [Section 13($a$)5].

6. Employees in agriculture including persons operating irrigation systems not owned or operated for profit [Section 13($a$)6].

7. Learners, apprentices, and handicapped workers to the extent exempted by regulations of the Administrator under Section 14 of the act. This is not an absolute exemption but made to the extent necessary in order to prevent curtailment of opportunities for employment.

8. Employees of a weekly, semiweekly, or daily newspaper having a circulation of less than 4,000 the major part of which circulation is within the county where printed and published or counties contiguous thereto [Section 13($a$)8].

9. Employees of a street, suburban, or interurban electric railway, or local trolley or motor bus carrier [Section 13($a$)9].

10. Individuals employed within the area of production (as defined by the Administrator) engaged in handling, packing, storing, ginning, compressing, pasteurizing, dying, preparing in their raw or natural state, or canning of agricultural or horticultural commodities for market, or in making cheese or butter or other diary products [Section 13($a$)10].

11. Switchboard operators of a public telephone exchange of not more than 750 stations [Section 13(a)11].

12. Employees engaged in operating taxicabs [Section 13(a)12].

13. Employees of a retail or service establishment as defined under [Section 13(a)2] of the act who handle telegrams under an agency or contract with a telegraph company, provided the revenue of such agency does not exceed $500 per month [Section 13(a)13].

14. Seamen [Section 13(a)14].

15. Employees engaged in forestry or lumbering operations provided this number so engaged is not greater than 12 [Section 13(a)15].

16. Newsboys engaged in delivering papers to consumers [Section 13(d)]. (Exempt also from child-labor provisions.)

## The amended act exempts the following groups from time and one-half provisions only:

1. "Employees subject to regulation by the Interstate Commerce Commission as to hours of service under Section 204 of the Motor Carrier Act of 1935" [Section (13)(b)(1)]. These are employees who are engaged as drivers, driver's helpers and loaders and mechanics whose work affects the safety of operation of the trucks. It does not include freight handlers who do not load trucks, dispatchers, supervisors, clerical personnel, or anyone not directly related to actual operations.

2. "Employee or employer subject to Part I of the Interstate Commerce Act" [Section 13(b)(2)]. This applies to railroads and shipping lines that have arrangements with railroads for continuous transporting of passengers or freight, also under certain conditions to pipelines.

3. "Any employee of a carrier by air subject to title II of the Railway Labor Act" [Section 13(b)(3)]. The original law exempted air-line employees both from the wage and hours provisions. The revised act of 1949 exempts these employees only from the hours provisions.

4. "Employee-employer in the canning of any kind of fish, shell fish, or other aquatic forms of animal or vegetable life, or any by-product thereof" [Section 13(b)(5)].

5. "An outside buyer of poultry, eggs, cream, or milk in their raw or natural state" [Section 13(b)(5)].

## The foregoing five items are complete exemptions from overtime payments for the entire year.

6. In addition to the foregoing exemptions specified in the law, the act exempts employees otherwise covered by the law from the overtime provisions provided the employer has entered into an agreement as a result of collective bargaining by representatives of employees certified as bona fide by the National Labor Relations Board under the following conditions [Section 7(b)]:

6.1 A guaranteed work program for 26 consecutive weeks of not more than 1,040 hr. If during this guaranteed period more than 1,040 hr. are worked, the hours in excess of 1,040 must be paid for at the rate of time and one-half [Section 7(b)(1)].

6.2 An agreement that "provides that during a specified period of fifty-two consecutive weeks the employee shall be employed not more than 2240 hours and shall be guaranteed not less than 1840 hours (or not less than 46 weeks at the normal hours worked per week, but not less than 30 hours per week) and not more than 2080 of employment for which he shall receive compensation for all hours guaranteed or worked at rates not less than those applicable under the agreement." The act further provides that all hours worked in excess of the guaranteed number during the 52 consecutive weeks which are also in excess of 40 hr. per week, or 2,080 in such period, shall be paid for at the rate of time and one-half of the regular rate at which he is employed. This provision also applies to 6.1 above.

Items 6.1 and 6.2 are seldom used.

6.3 Section 7(b)(3) provides that, in industries found by the Secretary of Labor to be of a seasonal nature, employees may work for a period or periods of not more than 14 work weeks in the aggregate in any calendar year, may work 12 hr. in 1 day or 56 hr. in any work week provided that overtime of one and one-half times the regular pay is paid for all time in excess of 12 hr. per day or 56 hr. per week.

The excess of 12 hr. in 1 day applies only to an employee who works more than 40 hr. in one week. This applies to 6.1, 6.2, 6.3.

The following instances are exempt from the child-labor provisions but not the time and one-half for overtime or hours: child "actor or performer in motion pictures or theatrical productions or in radio or television productions" or a child "employed in agriculture outside of school hours for the school district, where such employee is living while he is so engaged" [Section 13(c)].

**What is the regular rate?** The famous Mt. Clemens Pottery case completely upset what was generally accepted in business as the regular rate on which overtime was to be paid. The Portal-to-Portal Act of 1947 restored the "rule of reason" to the chaotic condition created by the Supreme Court's decision. Section 7(d) of the revised act of 1949 embodies most of the 1947 Portal-to-Portal Act and the rulings of the Wage and Hour Administrator following the 1947 act. It reads, "As used in this section the 'regular rate' at which an employee is employed shall be deemed to include all remunerations for employment paid to, or on behalf of, the employee, but shall not be deemed to include. . . ." After this definition is listed a series of items that are not to be included as a part of the regular pay. The main items not to be included in the regular rate are:

1. Christmas gifts and other special-occasion gifts.

2. Payments for occasional periods when no work was performed: vacations, holidays, illness allowances, etc.

3. Payments made for services performed but where the amounts and the payment itself are solely at the discretion of the employer and not pursuant to any contract. These are merely payments made by the employer because of his wanting to recognize a service. Profit-sharing grants that meet the requirements of the Administrator and that are paid to the employee without regard to hours of work, production, or efficiency come under this heading. Talent fees (as defined

by the Administrator) paid to performers, including announcers on radio and television programs, are also excluded.

4. Contributions irrevocably made for providing old age, retirement, life, accident, or health insurance or similar benefits for employees are not included in the regular wage.

5. Extra compensation provided by a premium rate for certain hours worked in excess of an employee's normal work day or week, or an 8-hr. day or a 40-hr. week, as the case may be.

6. Extra compensation for work on Saturdays, Sunday, holidays, or regular days of rest, or the sixth or seventh day of the work week where the premium rate is at least one and one-half the rate paid for like work in nonovertime hours.

7. Extra compensation provided by a premium rate paid to the employee, in pursuance of an employment contract or collective-bargaining agreement, for work outside of the hours established in good faith by the contract or agreement as the basic work day (not exceeding 8 hr.) or work week (not exceeding 40 hr.) where this premium rate is not less than time and one half of the regular rate.

*The extra compensation paid under items 5, 6, and 7 above shall be credited toward overtime required by the Fair Labor Standards Act* [Section 7(g)]. Assume that an employee's week started Sunday before Christmas, which fell on Tuesday, and worked in this particular week through Saturday, or 56 hr. If the union contract called for time and one-half for holidays and Sundays and his regular rate was $2 per hour, he would earn $24 for Sunday and Christmas. Under the old rule these premium payments would have been included in determining his rate on which the overtime for the sixth and seventh days' overtime would be figured. Under the revised statute the premium pay for Sunday and Christmas is not included in computing the average rate.

$$\text{Rate} = \frac{\text{wages earned}}{\text{hours worked}}$$

This worker's pay for the week would be 8 times $2 per day $\times$ 7 days worked $+ \left( \dfrac{56 \text{ hr.} - 40 \text{ hr.}}{2} \times \$2 \right) + \$16$, the premium pay for Christmas and Sunday, or $112 + $16 + $16 = $144 [Section 7(g)].

While the items listed above, 1 to 7, are not included in computing the regular rate, there are others that would be included. For instance, shift premium pay is included in computing the regular rate. Premiums paid for hazardous or dirty work are included in the regular rate. This type of computing the regular rate is in keeping with accepted business practice. Regular rate of pay $= \dfrac{\text{wages}}{\text{hours worked}}$.

The Belo contract (sanctioned by the 1949 amendment) permits the stabilization of wages of employees whose work, by its inherent nature, is irregular in duration from week to week. This type of stable wage often appeals to employees, who like to know how much money to count on, and may readily result in a net saving to an employer in his overtime wage payments over a year's time. Persons whose work may require irregular hours might be outside buyers, on-call service men, insurance adjusters, newspaper reporters, and photographers, fire fighters, trouble shooters, and private secretaries to major executives, who may have to work according to the requirements of the executive. Section 7(e) requires that the contract provide for a regular rate of pay of not less than $1 per hour and compensation at not less than one and one-half times such rate for all hours worked in excess of 40 in any work week. The distinguishing feature of this contract is that it guarantees the employee a sum which at these rates would be earned in a stated number of hours even though the employee does not work that number of hours in a week. The number of hours by which the guaranteed weekly wage is calculated must not exceed 60 and must reasonably approximate the length of the average work week. When, in any week, the employee works beyond the stipulated number of hours, in addition to the guaranteed wage he receives compensation at the overtime rate for the hours in excess of those so stipulated. The guarantee must be a weekly guarantee and not a biweekly or monthly guarantee. The law does not require the Administrator's approval of the contract; and while its terms must be definitely agreed upon, it may be oral.

An employer should carefully check the practices of his employees, or he will awaken with a jolt and be required to pay back overtime for as long as 2 years for practices that he never expected (nor his employee) to be overtime. There are many of these traps for the unwary, but one will illustrate possible costs. A secretary stops by the bank on her way to lunch to make a deposit daily for her employer. This practice would cost her employer ½-hr. overtime for every day she made the deposit provided that she worked in excess of 40 hr. in 1 week. To be counted as free time for which the employer does not have to pay, the employee must be free to leave the job. This free time must be complete free time and not on a stand-by basis in case something does arise. The employee *must* not be required to stay near the job but must be free to leave it [*Interpretative Bulletin* 785, Dec. 31, 1958, Section 785.3(d)].

**Computing piece-rate overtime.** Since overtime is computed solely in terms of the time worked (not the number of pieces produced), problems arise in its computation. The simplest method would be to compute the worker's earnings for the week and divide this amount by the number of hours worked. The resultant rate would then be applied to the number of hours worked in excess of 40 on the basis of one and one-half time for each hour above 40. Section 7(*f*) provides:

(1) That an employer may, in advance of the work's being performed, agree with the employee to pay him for the pieces produced during overtime at the rate of one and one half of the bona fide piece rate applicable to the same work during non-overtime hours; (2) that in case of an employee working on two or more kinds of work for which different hourly or piece rates have been established, the overtime pay may be computed at rates not less than one and one-half times such bona fide rates applicable to the same work when performed during non-overtime hours; and (3) that the overtime earnings may be "computed at a rate not less than one and one half the rate established by such agreement or understanding as the basic rate to be used in computing overtime: *Provided,* the rate so established shall be authorized by the Administrator as being substantially equivalent to the average hourly rate earnings of the employee. . . . " In all of the three cases above the resultant earnings cannot be less than one and one half times the minimum rate established by Section 6(*a*)(1).

**Definitions of terms used in the act.** Section 3 of the act has the following definitions:

1. "Person" means an individual, partnership association, corporation, business trust, legal representative, or any organized group or persons [Section 3(*a*)].

2. "Commerce" means trade, commerce, transportation, transmission or communication among the several States or between any State and any place outside thereof[5] [Section 3(*b*)].

3. "Produced" means produced, manufactured, mined, handled, or in any other manner worked on in any State; and for the purposes of this Act an employee shall be deemed to have been engaged in the production of goods if such employee was employed in producing, manufacturing, mining, handling, transporting, or in any other manner working on such goods, or in any closely related process, or occupation directly essential to the production thereof, in any State[6] [Section 3(*j*)].

4. "Hours worked."—In determining for the purposes of Sections 6 and 7, the hours for which an employee is employed, there shall be excluded any time spent in changing clothes or washing at the beginning or end of each workday which was excluded from measured working time during the week involved by the express terms of or by custom or practice under a bona fide collective-bargaining agreement applicable to the particular employee[7] [Section 3(*o*)].

The Administrator is directed in Section 13(*a*)(1) to define and delimit persons employed in a bona fide executive, administrative capacity. He has defined these terms as follows:

[5] As amended by Section 3(*a*) of the Fair Labor Standards Amendments of 1949.

[6] As amended by Section 3(*b*) of the Fair Labor Standards Amendments of 1949.

[7] As amended by Section 3(*d*) of the Fair Labor Standards Amendments of 1949.

1. (Executive) shall mean any employee—(Regulations, Part 541)

    (*a*) whose primary duty consists of the management of the enterprise in which he is employed or of a customarily recognized department or subdivision thereof; *and*

    (*b*) who customarily and regularly directs the work of two or more employees therein; *and*

    (*c*) who has the authority to hire and fire other employees or whose suggestions and recommendations as to the hiring or firing and as to the advancement and promotion or any other change of status of other employees will be given particular weight; *and*

    (*d*) who customarily and regularly exercises discretionary powers; *and*

    (*e*) who does not devote more than 20 per cent of his hours worked in the work-week to activities which are not directly and closely related to the performance of the work described in paragraphs (*a*) through (*d*) of this section:

    *Provided,* that this paragraph (*e*) shall not apply in the case of an employee who is in sole charge of an independent establishment or a physically separated branch establishment, or who owns at least 20 per cent interest in the enterprise in which he is employed; *and*

    (*f*) who is compensated for his services on a salary basis at the rate of not less than $80 per week (or $55 per week if employed in Puerto Rico or the Virgin Islands) exclusive of board, lodging, or other facilities;

    *Provided,* that an employee who is compensated on a salary basis at a rate of not less than $125 per week (exclusive of board, lodging, or other facilities), and whose primary duty consists of the management of the enterprise in which he is employed or of a customarily recognized department or subdivision thereof, and includes the customary and regular direction of the work of two or more other employees therein, shall be deemed to meet all of the requirements of this section.[8]

2. (An employee employed in an administrative capacity) shall mean an employee:

    (*a*) whose primary duty consists of the performance of office or nonmanual field work directly related to management policies or general business operations of his employer or his employer's customers; *and*

    (*b*) who customarily and regularly exercises discretion and independent judgment; *and*

    (*c*) (1) who regularly and directly assists a proprietor, or an employee employed in a bona fide executive or administrative capacity (as such terms are defined in these regulations), or

        (2) who performs under only general supervision work along specialized or technical lines requiring special training, experience, knowledge or

        (3) who executes under only general supervision special assignments and tasks; *and*

    (*d*) who does not devote more than 20 per cent of his hours worked in the work week to activities which are not directly and closely related to the performance of the work described in paragraph (*a*) through (*c*) of this section.[9]

---

[8] "The Definition of Executive," *Explanatory Bulletin Regulations,* Part 541, issued Nov. 18, 1958, and effective Feb. 2, 1959.

[9] *Ibid.,* Section 541.200, p. 9.

(*e*) who is compensated for his services $95 or more ($70 per week in Puerto Rico and the Virgin Islands).

3. An employee employed in a bona fide professional capacity shall mean any employee—

(*a*) whose primary duty consists of the performance of work

(1) requiring knowledge of an advanced type in a field of science or learning customarily acquired by a prolonged course of specialized intellectual instruction and study, as distinguished from a general academic education and from an apprenticeship, and from training in the performance of routine mental, manual, or physical processes, or

(2) original and creative in character in a recognized field of artistic endeavor (as opposed to work which can be produced by a person endowed with general manual or intellectual ability and training), and the result of which depends primarily on the invention, imagination, or talent of the employee; *and*

(*b*) whose work requires the consistent exercise of discretion and judgment in its performance; *and*

(*c*) whose work is predominantly intellectual and varied in character (as opposed to routine mental, manual, mechanical or physical work) and is of such a character that the output produced or the result accomplished cannot be standardized in relation to a given period of time.[10]

(*d*) who does not devote more than 20 percent of the hours worked during the week to activities that are not an essential part of and necessarily incident to the work described by the Secretary of Labor (*a*) through (*c*) on page 3 of Title 29, Part 541 of the Code of Federal Regulations as published November 30, 1958; whose remuneration is $95 or more ($70 in Puerto Rico and the Virgin Islands).

Both administrative and professional exemptions have a provision that an employee who is paid $125 per week is exempt, if his primary duty is administrative or professional [Regulation, Part 541.2 and 541.3].

**Record keeping.** By Section 11(*c*) no particular form of record is required, but accurate records must be kept by the employer for all employees covered by the act so as to show:

1. Name, home address, and birth date if under 19.
2. Occupation.
3. Hours and day when workweek begins.
4. Regular hourly pay rate for any week when overtime is worked.
5. Hours worked each workday and total hours worked each workweek.
6. Total daily or weekly straight-time earnings.
7. Total overtime pay for the workweek.
8. Deductions or additions to wages.
9. Total wages paid each pay period.
10. Date of payment and pay period covered.[11]

[10] *Ibid.*, Section 541.300, p. 16.
[11] [Title 29, Part 516, Subpart A, Code of Federal Regulations issued Aug. 31, 1958. Section 516.2(*a*), 1 to 12.]

**Child labor.** Section 3(1) of the act defines "oppressive child labor" to include all labor of children under the ages of sixteen and eighteen in any occupation that the Secretary of Labor shall find and by order declare to be particularly hazardous or detrimental to a child's health or well-being. The Secretary of Labor may provide for the issuance of certificates to children between the ages of fourteen and sixteen to work in occupations other than manufacturing and mining, provided that the work does not interfere with schooling and is not detrimental to a child's health and well-being. To illustrate the provisions as to hazardous employment for minors between the ages of sixteen and eighteen, the Secretary of Labor has ruled that a motor-vehicle driver and his helper are engaged in a hazardous occupation. In this ruling, a helper is considered anyone other than the driver, whose work requires riding on a motor vehicle in connection with the transportation and delivery of goods. Section 12($a$) forbids the shipment of goods in interstate commerce that have been produced in a plant in or about which "any oppressive child labor has been employed" within 30 days prior to the removal of the goods therefrom.

**Penalties.** A willful violation of the act carries with it a possible fine of not more than $10,000, and on a second conviction the offender may be fined not more than $10,000 and imprisoned for not more than 6 months [Section 16($a$)]. In addition to the fine and imprisonment, the employer is liable to his employees for all unpaid overtime and for all underpayments on the minimum wage and in addition an equal "amount as liquidated damages" [Section 16($b$)]. The Court, in an action to recover wages due, "shall in addition to any judgment awarded to the plaintiff or plaintiffs, allow reasonable attorney's fee to be paid by the defendant, and costs of action." The Secretary of Labor in the 1949 act is authorized to bring suit on behalf of an employee for back wages due under this act when requested to do so by the employee [Section 16($c$)]. The 2-year statute of limitations of the Portal-to-Portal Act of 1947 still prevails.

**Summary.** The passage of the Federal act of 1938 was influenced by the prolonged depression of the 1930's. The basic philosophy behind its advocates was well summarized by the Administrator; in his first report, in setting forth the objectives of the act, he said: "It seeks to protect workers from excessively long hours of work and to create additional opportunities for employment by setting a maximum work week beyond which employers may not work their employees without being restrained by the necessity of paying overtime compensation. It seeks to bring about a wider diffusion of that mass buying power upon which industry itself is dependent." The "wider diffusion of that mass buying power" is definitely a part of the "distributing-the-wealth" program. The "additional-opportunities" reference is the old lump-of-labor theory so thoroughly discredited by the facts of business experience. This law in many cases has undoubtedly raised the wages of the marginal workers in some of the more prosperous industries and to some extent the general level of wages in entire industries in certain localities. The Fair Labor Standards Act or the respective state minimum-wage or maximum-hours laws may have no appreciable effect other than to cause management to substitute machinery for labor if marginal labor will not earn the required wage. These acts may also force management to institute improved methods. The current fixed minimum wage or one 10 per cent higher may work no general hardship so long as the general price level does not fall below the level of the early 1940's. Should it fall materially below this level, the law would certainly result in severe dislocations. As to the logic of specifying 40 hr. instead of 44 for a 5½-day week or 48 for a 6-day week, there does not seem to be any, unless one accepts the principle that there is now and will continue to be only so much work to go around and that this should be spread as far as possible. This certainly was not true from 1940 to 1957. There was occasion to limit the work week during the recession of late 1957–1958. It certainly has not been established that an 8-hr. day and a 5½-day week are detrimental to the health of employees.

Paying time and one half for overtime in time of national emergency such as World War II or the Korean effort certainly added to the cost of the war. It also tended to restrict the total national production, until finally the President ordered the 48-hr. week. It would be wise as a national policy to modify the 40-hr. provision to 44 or 48 hrs. in time of a great national war effort, for certainly there is no need to try to spread work when the nation is crying for production. It hardly seems equitable to pay free workers time and one-half for overtime to manufacture the sinews of war when their brothers are risking their lives and enduring great hardships in using these products with no questions asked. There may be some logic in terms of working hardship to pay overtime in excess of a 44- or possibly a 48-hr. week. In principle at least we would be in a more advantageous position if our national law permitted a board to establish the maximum hours, setting, for instance, the 40-hour limit as the minimum below which the board could not go. The same principle might well apply to the minimum wage provisions. The Canadian laws are largely of this type.

CHAPTER 34

## Social Security and Pension Plans

**Changing attitudes.** In 1930 some companies had pension plans, but they were in the minority. Unions supported the Social Security Act of 1935, but at that time they were not so urgent in demanding company pensions. Unions took a strong stand for pensions in the late forties, when the times seemed particularly favorable. They asked for and got pension programs, assisted in part by the report of the President's Fact Finding Committee in the steel strike of 1949 and in part by the earlier Supreme Court decision upholding the National Labor Relations Board's ruling that pensions were a proper subject of collective bargaining. In earlier years most unions had argued that the employer should pay the employee the full value of the employee's services in his pay envelope and let the employee take care of his own old age. Many or perhaps most employers held to a similar view even though it was not uncommon for individual employers to pension office employees and supervisors on an informal basis. The only flaw in this argument is that the workers did not make provision for their old age. Even where the employee receives the full economic value of his services, he simply cannot or does not make provision for his old age. This failure to provide for old age is by no means confined to the manual worker. The same applies to foremen, supervisors, and executives. The General Motors Corporation inaugurated a program in 1940, following the example of other well-managed corporations, of providing a contributory retirement plan for salaried employees receiving salaries of $250 or more per month. This program has expanded since that date until all employees today are covered by some form of pension.

In the earlier days *hidden pensions* were paid by many employers by placing older employees on jobs on which they were paid more than the value of their services and then pensioned them outright when they could no longer come to work. Of course, these practices have as a rule prevailed only in industries that were in a comparatively satisfactory competitive position; yet some industries that were not paying dividends to the common stockholder have continued the payment of voluntary pensions to some of their older employees. As industries with voluntary nonfunded pension plans matured and a larger proportion of their employees became eligible for pensions, the burden became, in many instances, greater than they could bear and still compete with some of the newer competitors in the industry whose working force was still relatively young. This situation encouraged the formation of funded plans, in some of which the employee participated by making contributions in some ratio to the employer's contribution.

Gradually there emerged another attitude toward the costs of caring for superannuated industrial employees, namely, that the care for the aged industrial worker is a legitimate charge against industry and should be included in production costs in the same sense that depreciation of machinery and equipment is handled. This approach in substance recognized that the employer cannot pay the employee the same wage that he would otherwise pay him were he not providing for him a pension, unless, of course, he was paying him too little in the first place. Trade unions in some cases established their own cooperative programs, to which employers contributed in some instances. Municipalities, utilities, and some states soon followed this approach. Finally, the United States wrote this philosophy, in substance, into the Social Security Act in 1935, as amended several times. Today the pension movement embraces nearly 90 per cent of the companies (see Fig. A.5, item 4).

**Pensions defined.** Private pensions are periodic payments, usually for life, to a beneficiary who has been retired because of age, accident, or illness, or for other causes approved by the company. Public pensions usually are essentially the same as private pensions, related to service. However, the socialistic trends of the Federal government have related certain pensions for veterans to their incomes. It would be more appropriate to call these "grants-in-aid" and not pensions. Pensions should be paid to all persons who have met the service requirements. Poverty or improvidence should not be the basis of a pension. Even the social security annuity is denied to persons who earn in covered employment certain amounts until they reach the age of seventy-two. Formal pension plans usually set forth in advance the requirements as to length of service, age to be attained, etc. Men and women frequently have different retirement ages. Informal pensions are granted at the will of the employer to worthy employees and are financed usually out of current income. They lack some of the desired factors possessed by the more certain types of pension plans. It is true that an enlightened employer who is in a favorable competitive position may do as well for his employees on an informal basis as another one on a well-organized, actuarially sound pension plan. In such a case, there may still be lacking that feeling of certainty and security that accompanies a sound formal program. In some cases, the employer bears all the cost of the pension plan. The contributory pension plans are frequently managed by an outside trust or insurance company. The noncontributory plans formerly were largely handled by the company granting the pension. Many of these plans were not on a sound actuarial basis. The recent trend has been to place the funds with an insurance company, which protects the interest of the employees and gives greater stability to the plan.

It would be difficult to describe a typical pension plan because of the many different approaches to financing them and the great variety available. Most of them are related to length of service. The amount of the pension may be only the amount that the accumulated contributions of the employer or both the employer and the employee will buy. On the other hand the company may vary its contributions so that an employee of 10 or more years of service will get a fixed per cent of his average salary for the past 5- or 10-year period just preceding his retirement multiplied by his number of years of service. In some cases there may be a maximum of 60 per cent of his average earnings. To illustrate, if the per cent per year were 1.5 and the employee had 42 years of service he would be limited to 60 per cent rather than the 61 per cent ($1.5 \times 42$). Private pensions may give the pensioner options similar to those available to the person who purchases an annuity. When this is done (such as making payment to the wife in case the pensioner precedes his wife in death), the pension is reduced on an actuarial basis. There is a tendency for pensions not to include the wife, leaving her care to her payments under Social Security. There also is a tendency to raise the upper limits of pensions for persons whose earnings may justify the higher amounts. There may even be two pension programs, one with the lower limit paid entirely by the company and a second one in which the cost is borne jointly by the company and the participating employees. It is essential that any type of pension be actuarially sound. This has not been true of many of the earlier plans.

**Growth of pension plans.** Table 34.1 portrays the phenomenal growth of insured pension plans since 1940. This table does not include many private pension plans not carried with insurance com-

*Table* 34.1   *Insured Pension Plans in the United States in Force with Life Insurance Companies**

| | Group annuities | Deposit administration plans | Individual policy pension trusts | Other plans | Total |
|---|---|---|---|---|---|
| **1940:** | | | | | |
| Number of plans............ | 770 | 20 | 420 | 320 | 1,530 |
| Number of persons covered.. | 575,000 | 70,000 | 15,000 | 40,000 | 700,000 |
| **1945:** | | | | | |
| Number of plans............ | 1,580 | 20 | 4,360 | 740 | 6,700 |
| Number of persons covered.. | 1,150,000 | 70,000 | 220,000 | 80,000 | 1,520,000 |
| **1949:** | | | | | |
| Number of plans............ | 2,250 | 50 | 7,040 | 1,310 | 10,650 |
| Number of persons covered.. | 1,800,000 | 125,000 | 450,000 | 175,000 | 2,550,000 |
| **1955:†** | | | | | |
| Number of plans............ | 8,760 | 990 | 12,530 | 1,720 | 19,000 |
| Number of persons covered.. | 2,410,000 | 950,000 | 480,000 | 325,000 | 4,165,000 |
| **1957:†** | | | | | |
| Number of plans............ | 4,460 | 1,600 | 15,350 | 2,230 | 23,640 |
| Number of persons covered.. | 2,485,000 | 1,415,000 | 580,000 | 380,000 | 4,860,000 |

* Source: Institute of Life Insurance, *Fact Book*, 1951, p. 30.
† Source: Institute of Life Insurance, *Fact Book*, 1958, p. 37.

panies. When it is recalled that the first record of a pension plan in the United States was that of the American Express Company of 1875, it becomes apparent that pensions have enjoyed tremendous growth. This growth is both an economic and a social phenomenon.

**Types of funded plans.**[1] In the common annuity plan a master contract is issued by the insurance company to the employer, and single-premium annuities are bought each year for all employees in amounts to cover current service credits. A second type is a pension trust administered by a bank or trust company. Under this form the contributions of the employer and employees are paid over to the trustee for investment, and the trustee meets the pension obligation out of the fund as it becomes payable for each employee. Under some pension trusts, the pension obligations are self-insured, and no annuities are bought. Under others, an individual policy is bought to meet the pension liability for each employee. Under a nonfunded plan, the em-

[1] See National Industrial Conference Board, Inc., "Pension Plans and Their Administration," *Studies in Personnel Policy* 149, New York, 1955, p. 43, for a discussion of the prevalence of the various methods of funding.

*Table 34.2   Prevalence of Contributory and Noncontributory Pension Plans under Insured, Trusteed, and Combined Plans*

| Type of funding and employee contributions | No. of companies | Per cent of companies |
|---|---|---|
| Insured plans: | | |
| Contributory...................... | 84 | 67.7 |
| Noncontributory.................. | 29 | 23.4 |
| Contributory and noncontributory..... | 11 | 8.9 |
| Total......................... | 124 | 100.0 |
| Trust fund plans: | | |
| Contributory...................... | 31 | 27.7 |
| Noncontributory.................. | 66 | 58.9 |
| Contributory and noncontributory..... | 15 | 13.4 |
| Total......................... | 112 | 100.0 |
| Two or more plans combined: | | |
| Contributory...................... | 3 | 6.0 |
| Noncontributory.................. | 18 | 36.0 |
| Contributory and noncontributory..... | 29 | 58.0 |
| Total......................... | 50 | 100.0 |

ployer merely expresses an intention to pay pensions in accordance with some announced formula and makes payments for current benefits to those who have retired, but funds are not set aside nor are annuities purchased to assure the future payment of benefits. Table 34.2 shows a distribution of the various types of plans as found in the 1955 survey of the National Industrial Conference Board.

**Vesting.** Vesting in the employee a right in the company's contribution to the pension fund has strong advocates and opponents.[2] The amount contributed by the employee nearly always is his, plus compounded interest. The particular kind of plan determines whether on leaving the company before retirement he gets a refund or merely has an interest payable when he reaches retirement age.

One very large company that has had a pension plan for more than 30 years financed solely by the company does not vest the pension rights in its employees when they leave prior to the time when they are entitled to the pension. This company has strenuously resisted efforts of its union to change this plan. Any money credited in the fund to an employee who leaves automatically becomes the property of the remaining employees. Naturally this reduces the cost to the company to provide the desired pension to employees who remain

[2] Vesting is the term used to signify that the pension rights purchased for an employee belong to him regardless of his later status with the company.

until retirement. Vesting a right increases the cost of a pension plan, particularly when employees with short service are permitted to participate in the pension program. This is true largely because the labor turnover is greater among short-service employees. When eligibility for the pension plan requires 3 to 5 years' service or when vesting applies only after service of 3 to 5 years, the additional cost of vesting rights is greatly reduced.[3] Various schedules of the rights of employees in the company's contribution to a pension plan have been used. In vesting in an employee a right, the plan may consider the length of time he has been covered or the length of service, and frequently the age of the employee at the date of leaving the company. It is the opinion of the authors that vesting is a good personnel practice but that it probably should not begin until after a service of possibly 3 to 5 years. The exact amount vested after an employee is eligible might well be on a sliding scale, but it would seem that it should be substantial.

**Union attitude toward pensions.** In some cases, such as the United Mine Workers, pensions are paid out of the so-called welfare fund. In this type of pension management, the individual employer has little voice in the management of the pension fund. He pays a fixed amount per ton[4] of coal mined into the fund, and the fund is managed by a committee of three as trustees. One trustee represents the union, one the public, and one the operators or owners. This type of pension provision has advantages to the worker in that his pension is not determined by his working for one employer. He still has his pension rights so long as he works in a mine that is covered by the union contract. On the other hand, this particular plan has not built up a funded reserve, which leaves much to be desired.

The AFL-CIO in one large city has been trying to get a pension plan to which employers contribute but which will not tie an employee to a particular company in order to build up his rights in the plan. Such a plan could be worked out in such a manner as to be actuarially sound. It is natural that the employer would prefer to have a plan which is related to his company. He seeks low labor turnover and employee loyalty. The union philosophy on the other hand is to strive for worker loyalty to the union and not to the employer.

Some unions insist on bargaining over the terms of the pension and

[3] See National Industrial Conference Board, Inc., "Pension Plans and Their Administration," *Studies in Personnel Policy* 149, New York, 1955, p. 13, Table 13, for the service and age requirement for eligibility for participation in the pension program, and p. 39 for an interesting discussion of *vesting*.

[4] As we go to press, the operators pay 40 cents per ton of coal mined. The employees do not contribute to the fund.

others do not. In the 1955 survey of the National Industrial Conference Board, Inc., it is reported that only 71 per cent of the companies having a union agreement had negotiated a pension plan with the union.[5] This certainly should not be interpreted as a lack of interest on the part of the union. It may merely represent reasonable satisfaction with the current pension agreement or a more pressing interest in other things than pensions. Pensions are not the outgrowth of union activity. In fact, unions opposed pension plans as a rule for years and have been strong advocates of pensions only since about 1940. However, today it is estimated that some 5,000,000 union workers are covered by pension programs. Some unions have satisfactory arrangements whereby the company pays all the costs; the same unions in another plan may agree to employee contributions in addition to the company's. Some companies have sole control over their pension plans even where they have a union contract. Of course, it is also true that many companies with no union contracts also have pension plans.

**The Social Security Act and pension plans.** In most early pension plans, the social security primary benefit was deducted from the employee's expected pension, in the cases where the company was paying the full cost of the pension. During recent years all kinds of compromises have been worked out. One very large union and management froze the amount deducted as a primary benefit at $85 when the primary benefit was raised to $98.50. Other companies have completely divorced their pension plan from Social Security. (This of course does not mean that they do not look at the social security costs in negotiating or planning a pension program.)

When the Social Security Act was first passed in 1935, a substantial number of its advocates thought that it would replace many private plans. To the contrary, it seems to have increased the public interest in pension plans rather than to have caused it to decrease.[6]

**Why should the employer have a pension plan?** Since pensions of some form are so generally recognized (see Fig. A.5, item 4), persons do not ask the reasons for pensions so frequently as they did in 1930. Without any attempt to rate the relative importance of the following items, they have been listed by various persons as reasons for pensions:[7]

1. Humanitarian, a reward for loyal service.
2. Welfare, to provide for the needy former employees.

[5] See National Industrial Conference Board, Inc., *op. cit.*, p. 35.
[6] *Ibid.*, p. 23.
[7] See National Industrial Conference Board, Inc., "Company Pension Plans and the Social Security Act," 1939; also *Studies in Personnel Policy* 149, New York, 1955, pp. 6–8.

3. Increased efficiency, removal of aged and less competent employees to make room for more efficient employees, and to provide room for advancement of younger employees.

4. Improvements of *esprit de corps,* or morale.

5. Reduction of labor turnover.

6. Orderly retirement of employees, thus eliminating hidden pensions and irregular pension programs.

7. Following the trend; Social Security and others are doing it.

8. Union pressure.

9. Influence of tax structures; both the employer and employee have certain tax concessions.

Certainly a scientific analysis of the advantages accruing to an employer would have difficulty in sustaining all the claimed advantages of a pension system. For instance, the morale effect of a pension system would be difficult to prove. Of course, if most employers had a pension plan and a given employer in the same community did not, his failure to have one might react adversely on the morale of his group. Pensions are like many other good things in life; once possessed, they are taken for granted and are not particularly influential in increasing productivity. This is especially true when the employer finances the entire program.

**Municipal and state pensions.** Some states do not have a pension program for state employees. Most of the early state plans were optional with county or smaller government units. The principle of building up a fund by the agency employing the recipients developed slowly among municipalities as the result of enabling acts passed by the legislatures. Later, state employees enjoying Civil Service status were included in certain states. All the states have "old-age assistance" for their needy aged. This old-age assistance for the needy is a part of the social security program sponsored by the Federal government. The states participate in providing the funds for the pensions as follows: (1) for the first $25 the states pay 20 per cent; (2) from $25 to $55 the states pay 50 per cent; (3) the states pay all the pension above $55. To be eligible for old-age assistance the applicant must be sixty-five years or older. The Federal government pays 80 per cent of the first $15 and 50 per cent of the remaining up to $30 for the first dependent child and a maximum of $21 for each of the other dependent children. Neither the aid for dependent children nor the old-age assistance are a part of an insured program but are solely aid to the needy.

**Pensions under Social Security.** The Social Security Act of 1935 as amended in 1939, 1950, 1952, 1954, 1956, 1958, and 1960, has played a leading role in pensions for persons in covered employment. Pensions under the Social Security Act are not based on need. This is as any pension should be. (There is one qualification of the *right*. Persons under seventy-two may not receive their full family benefits if they earn a certain amount.) Many of the earlier benefits which began on Jan. 1, 1940, and later under the revisions of 1950 and 1958, were out of all proportion to the recipients' contributions to the fund. Either these excess payments to certain aged persons will have to be made up from general taxation, or others will later receive in return less than they pay into the fund. As a matter of fact, both these situations will prevail. As a good illustration of the excess payments to some of the older persons, assume an employee to be sixty-two years of age when he first became eligible under the revised act of 1950, and as amended in 1958. His salary is $5,200 a year, but only $4,200 of this came under the act until Jan. 1, 1959. According to the revised law of 1958, which went into effect in January, 1959, the above person will have a pension of $116 per month as found in the table, which is a part of the law, itself. His average monthly salary (covered by Social Security) is assumed to be $350. A person aged sixty-two who first came under covered employment in Jan. 1, 1955, and earned $350 for each month until January, 1959, would be eligible for the $116 per month pension. This is true because he would be entitled to cast off 5 years from the effective date of the revised 1950 law and not count these 5 years in his average. Should this same man have a wife aged sixty-five, she would be entitled to $58 per month. While some few reap outstanding benefits, this is not a serious defect in the law. In fact, this pension program as a whole is both economically and socially desirable.

**Coverage of the Social Security Act of 1950 as amended to 1960.** Each employer of one or more persons, with a few minor exclusions, is required to pay a payroll tax to provide pensions for his employees when they become eligible. The worker also has a deduction from his pay equal to that paid by the employer. The excluded employment includes students working in a local college club, fraternity, or sorority or employed by the university or college; ministers of the various religions; most charitable organizations and government units; and a person working for a spouse, and a child under the age of twenty-one working for his father or mother. Employees of educational and religious organizations (other than ordained ministers or members of religious orders in the exercise of duties required by such orders) may under certain conditions be eligible to coverage. For these nonprofit charitable, religious, or educational institutions to secure coverage for their employees, the officials of the organization would have to file a certificate with the Bureau of Internal Revenue in which it waives its exemption from the social security tax. Those employees who did not sign to come under the act would not have the tax deducted from their wages, but all new employees who entered the service of the organization would come under it. The religious, charitable, or educational organization that has come under the provisions of the Social Security Act may withdraw from same "upon giving two years' advanced notice in writing, but only if, at the time of the receipt of such notice, the certificate has been in effect for a period of not less than eight years" [Section 204(*l*)(1)]. In case an organization elects to withdraw and does withdraw, the organization may not again seek coverage and be accepted [Section 204(*l*)(3)]. Ministers, Christian Science practitioners, and members of religious orders who have not taken vows of poverty may elect individually, as self-employed persons, to come under the provisions of the act as revised Jan. 1, 1955.

The amendments of 1951 brought many self-employed persons under the act. A number of professional people were excluded under the 1951 amendments, but practically all professional people save the medical doctor are now eligible as self-employed. The medical doctor is eligible for coverage when working for a company that is covered. Some of the self-employed activities include any type of retailing, wholesaling, or manufacturing and individual activities such as writing, appraising property, private teaching, and contracting. A farm worker must either be paid $150 or more in a calendar year for farm work or work at least 20 days during the calendar year for one farmer. Maids and other household workers who are paid at least $50 in a 3-month period come under the Social Security law.

**Eligibility for social security benefits.** Social security pensions are available to two groups of persons, namely, (1) "fully insured" and (2) "currently insured." To become fully insured, a worker must have a minimum of 6 quarters of coverage. Persons attaining retirement age or dying after September 30, 1960, are fully insured if they have 1 quarter of coverage for each 3 quarters elapsing since December 31, 1950. A person whose twenty-first birthday is after December 31, 1950, will be fully covered if he has 1 out of 3 quarters of coverage from the last day of the year in which his twenty-first birthday falls to the first day of the year in which his death occurs, also provided his death occurs after September 30, 1960, the effective date of the 1 out of 3 rule. Coverage earned after 1936 may be used to satisfy the 1 out of 3 rule for anyone.

To be currently insured, an employee must have had at least 6 quarters of coverage during the 13-quarter period ending with the quarter in which he died or became eligible for old-age insurance benefits [Section 214(*b*)].

The rights of the fully insured employee are the maximum under the law. The currently insured employee's beneficiaries are not so completely protected as those of the fully insured. Children of a deceased person get the same benefits regardless of whether the person is fully or currently insured. The wife of a deceased, currently insured employee receives a widow's pension only so long as she has a child (less than eighteen years of age) of the deceased husband under her care. This is true regardless of her age. The widow of a currently insured employee does not receive a widow's pension when she becomes sixty-two years of age. Of course such a widow would receive a pension regardless of her age if she had a child of a currently insured person under eighteen years of age in her care. An employee who has worked at least 5 out of the previous 10 years under Social Security who becomes unable to work may receive the same benefits to which he would be entitled at sixty-five. Application must be made to secure the disabled status and the benefits thereof. The employee must have been disabled 6 months before he is entitled to receive disability benefits. The dependents of the disabled employee are entitled to benefits the same as if he had reached sixty-five.

**Insurance benefits under Social Security.** Each fully insured man is entitled to receive his primary insurance amount as defined in Section 215($a$) as amended in 1958. A fully insured woman has the same rights on reaching the age of sixty-two, but her insurance award is lower if she takes it at sixty-two rather than waiting until she is sixty-five.

**Wife's insurance benefits.** A wife of a man drawing a social security pension is entitled to insurance benefits provided that she (1) is at least sixty-two years of age or (2) has in her care a child entitled to an insurance benefit. To be eligible, the wife must be living with the husband from whose primary benefit her benefit is derived and not be entitled to an old-age benefit, in her own right, of 50 per cent or more of her husband's old-age insurance benefit [Section 202($b$)]. A wife's insurance benefit at age sixty-five is 50 per cent of her husband's old-age insurance benefit. Likewise a wife's benefit is 50 per cent of her husband's primary benefit regardless of her age if she has in her care a child of her husband's who is under eighteen. A wife with no child in her care may secure a reduced benefit at the age of sixty-two.

For the purpose of being eligible to receive old-age insurance benefits, the term "wife" has a special meaning. To qualify as a wife under Social Security, a married woman either must be the mother of her husband's child or be married to him for 1 year immediately preceding the day on which she files an application for a wife's insurance benefit [Section 216(*b*)]. Under this regulation, if a woman aged sixty-two marries a fully insured man aged sixty-five, she is not entitled to apply for a wife's insurance benefits until she has been married for 1 year. In this event, she could not receive old-age insurance benefits until she was sixty-three years old.

**Husband's insurance benefits.** A husband (by the 1951 revision) is entitled to his own primary insurance amount on reaching sixty-five, or he may have a derived benefit from his wife who is both currently and fully covered. The dependent husband's benefit is 50 per cent of his wife's old-age insurance benefit. To be entitled to old-age insurance benefits, the wife would have to be fully insured and at least sixty-two years of age. In other words, the wife of a husband entitled to benefits must be both currently and fully insured [Section 202(*c*)]. Furthemore, the husband must be sixty-five years of age and be receiving at least one-half of his support from his wife at the time she became entitled to old-age insurance benefits. Proof of such dependency must be filed within 2 years after the month in which the wife became entitled to insurance benefits. The husband to be entitled to old-age insurance benefits must either be the father of the wife's child or be married to her for at least 1 year immediately preceding the day on which he files his application for insurance benefits [Section 216(*f*)].

**A child's insurance benefits.** Every child under the age of eighteen and unmarried who is the child of a person entitled to old-age insurance benefits or whose parent died fully or currently insured is entitled to a child's insurance benefit. The child's benefit is 50 per cent of the old-age insurance benefit of the parent if the parent is still alive. In case the parent is dead, the child's insurance benefit is three-fourths of the primary insurance amount of the deceased parent. [Section 202(*d*)(2)].

**Widow's insurance benefits.** The widow of a fully insured deceased man receives the same benefits as the currently insured widow while she has children of the deceased under eighteen under her care; she also has insurance benefits when she reaches the age of sixty-two [Section 202(*e*)]. A widow of a currently insured deceased man receives three-fourths of his primary insurance amount only so long as she has a child of the deceased under eighteen years of age under her care. The child's insurance amount is not changed by the marriage of the child's mother. The marriage of a widow would cancel her insurance benefits derived from her first husband, unless she married a man who was himself drawing social security benefits.

**Widow and former wife's rights.** The widow and divorced wife of a deceased, fully or currently insured individual who has in her care a child entitled to a child's insurance benefit is entitled to a mother's insurance benefit, provided that (1) the widow was living with her husband at the time of his death; (2) the former wife was receiving (pursuant to agreement or a court order) at least one-half of her support from her divorced husband at the time of his death and the child is her son, daughter, or legally adopted child [Section 202(g)]. The divorced wife does not receive old-age insurance benefits when she reaches the age of sixty-two. The widow of a fully insured husband would be entitled to a widow's insurance benefits on reaching sixty-two. In the case of either the widow or the divorced wife, the insurance benefits cease on remarriage unless she marries a man who himself is drawing social security benefits. The remarriage of the mother does not cancel the child's insurance benefits. The widow or divorced wife's insurance benefits are three-fourths of the deceased's primary insurance amount.

**Widower's insurance benefits.** The husband of a woman who died fully and currently insured is entitled to an insurance benefit provided that (1) he has attained retirement age, (2) has not remarried,[8] (3) was living with his wife at the time of her death, and (4) was receiving at least half of his support from his wife at the time of her death and filed proof of such support within 2 years of her death or was receiving at least one-half of his support from his wife, who was fully and currently insured at the time she became entitled to old-age insurance benefits and filed proof of such support within 2 years after the month in which she became so entitled [Section 202(f)]. The widower's insurance benefit is three-fourths of the primary insurance amount of his deceased wife.

**Parent's insurance benefits.** "Parent means the mother or father of an individual, a step-parent of an individual by a marriage contract before such individual attained the age of sixteen, or an adopting parent by whom an individual was adopted before he attained the age of sixteen" [Section 202(h)]. On the death of a fully insured person each of his parents is entitled to a parent's insurance benefits provided that the parent (1) has reached retirement age, (2) was receiving at least one-half of his support from the son or daughter at the time of the child's death, and (3) has not remarried[9] since the death of the child providing the support. The parent's insurance benefits in this case are three-fourths of the deceased child's primary insurance amount.

---

[8] Remarriage does not bar a widower from receiving benefits if the marriage is to a person receiving social security benefits.

[9] Remarriage does not bar a parent from receiving benefits if the marriage is to a person receiving social security benefits.

**Lump sum death benefits.** Lump sum death benefits from $99 to $255 are payable if the deceased died currently or fully insured. The amount of the death benefit is determined by multiplying the deceased insurance amount by 3 with a maximum of $255.

**What must be done to receive any benefits?** None of the benefits under Social Security is paid automatically when the recipient meets all conditions other than the filing of an application. They must be applied for to be received. In the case of a beneficiary's being entitled in his own right to an insurance benefit equal to or larger than the insurance benefit that he would get from his relative, he will be paid his own primary insurance amount. A child may be entitled to a child's insurance benefit from more than one person. For instance, both parents may be entitled to the benefits of $116 provided that they have reached the proper age and have worked in covered employment the required length of time at an average annual salary of $4,200. Parents entitled to the maximum pension at the age of sixty-five would have children in their care under the age of eighteen only in the case of adoption. Normally the child's pension would be derived from its father. The total benefits to a family in the above case, with dependent children and both parents entitled to the maximum benefits, would be:

Father............................................................................$116
Children may get up to but not more than $138* from the father's primary benefit or insurance amount
Father and children.....................................................$254
Mother....................................................................... $116
  Total for family. ......................................................$370

* Maximum amount for family with one earner, $254 — maximum of father, $116 = $138 to be divided among all beneficiaries.

The above computation is based on each parent's being entitled to $116 primary insurance amount, and the maximum family allowance derived from one covered parent with $116 primary insurance amount is $254.

Beneficiaries may lose their benefits in a number of ways, namely: by death, by marriage of a child, parent, widow, mother, or widower; by divorce in the case of a wife or husband. A widow of a currently insured employee loses her benefit whenever the child in her care ceases to be eligible for a child's insurance benefit [Section 203(*b*), (*c*), (*d*)]. Should the person die to whom the beneficiary was married, which marriage cancelled the benefit, the beneficiary may again be entitled to his original benefit on application to the Social Security Administration, provided the death occurred within a year of the date of the marriage. Beneficiaries may have their benefits reduced by the insured's earning more than $1,200 in a year before he has reached the age of 72.

**Maximum and minimum benefits.** The 1958 amendments raised the maximum benefits to an individual as his primary insurance amount to $127 and to his family as benefits from his rights to $254. The $127 primary insurance amount will not be available to anyone until he has worked under the new $4,800 base salary limit for a long enough time so that his average monthly earnings will be $400 per month. The maximum family benefits would accrue where each parent is in his own right, from covered employment, entitled to the maximum primary insurance amount. In this case the maximum amount for the family would be $254 derived from the one parent plus the primary benefit of the second parent. Eventually this could, under the present law, be $254 plus $127, or $381. The minimum amount for the primary benefit under the 1958 law is $33. The maximum family benefits for the worker with a $33 primary insurance amount is $56. Whenever a deduction is made from the computed family insurance benefit because it is more than the maximum allowed, the individual's primary insurance amount is not affected but the derived benefits of his wife and children are proportionately reduced to give the legal amount to which the family is entitled.

**Benefits to veterans.** A veteran of World War II who served between September, 1940, and July, 1947, or a postwar veteran until Dec. 31, 1956, will be deemed to have been paid wages of $160 in each month during any part of which he was in the active military or naval service of the United States. This $160 per month is in addition to any wages he actually received while in service. This provision does not apply if the veteran is entitled to a pension based on his military service payable by any instrumentality of the United States other than the Veteran's Administration. Neither does this provision apply if a larger social security primary insurance amount would be payable without its being applied [Section 217(a)].

**Computing the primary insurance amount.** The primary insurance amount is the base entitlement of the insured employee to benefits. All benefits to his dependents or beneficiaries are derived from the covered employee's primary insurance amount. Under the 1958 amendments the primary insurance amount is found by inspecting the table included in the revision. A fully covered employee who attains retirement age after Dec. 31, 1960, has his primary insurance computed as follows: Five years are cast off and not counted. Naturally these 5 years will be the lowest income years. In most cases these years will have been years following Dec. 31, 1950; but they

need not be for a person whose highest wages were earned prior to
1950. Assume that the person attains retirement age after Dec.
31, 1960, the effective date for computing under the 1960 amendments. Further assume that the individual has become fully covered since Dec. 31, 1950, and retires at age 65 during 1963. The year
a person attains retirement age need not be counted for computing
purposes. This man would have a total of 12 years of possible coverage during this period. Five years are cast off. These 5 years may be
years in which he did not work, had the lowest earnings, or a combination of these. The 12 years (of possible coverage) — 5 (years cast
off) = 7 years to be used to establish the constant divisor to be
divided into the total earnings for covered employment for this 7-year
period to establish his average monthly earnings on which his primary
insurance amount is based. The maximum earnings under covered
employment during this period cannot exceed $4,800 for the period
1959 through 1962, $4,200 for the years 1955 through 1958, and $3,600
for the years 1951 through 1954. It would have been possible for him
to have earned: 4 × $4,800 or $19,200 for his last 4 years, 3 × $4,200
or $12,600 for the previous 3 years, or a total of $31,800 for the 7-year
period. $31,800 ÷ 84 (7 × 12 months in each year) = $378.57, the
average monthly earnings on which his primary insurance amount is
based. An inspection of the table in the law reveals that average
monthly earnings of $378.57 gives a pensioner $122 primary insurance
amount. Under the 1960 amendments this man could continue to work
after attaining the retirement age of 65 and build up higher benefits
provided he earns more than $4,800 in covered employment in each
year worked. Actually this man could work 3 more years at $4,800
each and attain the maximum insurance amount of $127. These addi-
tional years of maximum earnings need not be consecutive since his
base divisor of 84 (8 × 12) has already been established. In the case
of a person's working after having attained retirement age, the later
earnings are used in computing his primary insurance amount when
it is to his advantage to do so. Under the present law the maximum
primary insurance amount that anyone can get is $127 and the maxi-
mum family benefit is $254.

**The social security number.** Each worker is assigned a social security number against which all his earnings, as reported by his employer quarterly, are credited. This social security number follows
the worker throughout his work life and is a vital part of his employment record. The worker should keep his social security account
number card in his own possession, merely giving his employer his
number. The employer is required by the 1939 amendments to the

act to furnish the employee periodic written statements showing the employee's wages and taxes in a form suitable for the employee to keep as a receipt.

**Taxes.** Taxes are paid in equal amounts by the employer and the employee on that part of the employee's earnings that come within the prescribed limits. The base was $3,000 in the original act. This base was raised to $3,600 by the 1950 amendments; to $4,200 by the 1954 amendments; and to $4,800 by the 1958 amendments. The current tax regulations for both the employer and the employee under the 1958 amendments are:

| Calendar year 1960–1962 | 3 per cent |
|---|---|
| Calendar year 1963–1965 | 3½ per cent |
| Calendar year 1966–1968 | 4 per cent |
| Calendar year 1969 and later | 4½ per cent |

In the case of the self-employed person the tax rate to be paid solely by the self-employed person is as follows on his earnings up to $4,800 per year:[10]

For any taxable year beginning after:

| | |
|---|---|
| Dec. 31, 1959, and before Jan. 1, 1963 | 4½ per cent |
| Dec. 31, 1962, and before Jan. 1, 1966 | 5¼ per cent |
| Dec. 31, 1965, and before Jan. 1, 1969 | 6 per cent |
| Dec. 31, 1968 | 6¾ per cent |

Should an employee work for different employers during the same year, each employer would be required to deduct the tax of the employee's earnings up to $4,800. Such a situation makes it possible for a worker to pay a social security tax on more than $4,800 in a year. The worker may recover from the government all taxes paid in 1 year in excess of the regular amount paid on $4,800 by filing an application for a refund or by claiming it as a credit on his income-tax return. While a worker can recover any excess payment he may make, an employer cannot; hence it is important that an employer in a multi-plant operation in a given area keep accurate records of new employees hired. Some of them may have already had social security taxes paid for them by the company during the same year in one of the company's other plants.

**The responsibility of the employer.** The primary responsibility of

[10] Before this book is off the press, the limit for the base taxable salary and the tax rate may be raised. Constant inflation (cheaper dollars and higher prices), which has been going on since 1939, may readily push the limit up to an amount that would have been deemed fantastic at the time of the original passage of the act. Deficit spending by the Federal government and wage raises not matched by increased productivity are two of the strongest inflationary pressures. Of course added benefits also require increased income from which to pay for the added benefits.

the employer is to pay his social security tax and to withhold from the worker's pay his tax and pay this sum to the Federal government. Of course these tax payments must be accompanied by complete and accurate records of the wages paid each employee, in addition to furnishing each employee with periodic statements of his taxable wages. In keeping with current personnel practice to render employees services in financial matters, many employers assist retiring employees in filing their applications for the old-age benefits for themselves and dependents. In the case of the death of a fully or currently insured worker, the employer is in a position to aid the surviving dependents, at a time when it is appreciated, to file claims for benefits. There are hundreds of widows with dependent children in the United States who are not drawing the pensions to which they are entitled solely because they do not know their rights and have not filed a claim for them. Relatively few foremen and many personnel men do not know the rights of these dependents. To inform a widow of her rights is a personnel function that should be carefully followed up. It is often necessary for the employer to provide the employee or his dependents with a record of his earnings for the most recent quarters that have not as yet been reported to the Social Security Board or have not as yet been credited to the employee's account. The personnel department may also be of service in aiding the employees to secure evidence required to support his claims, such as proof of age of himself, his wife, and his children, proof of marriage, etc.

**The Railroad Retirement Act.** The original Railroad Retirement Act of 1934 was declared unconstitutional. The Railroad Retirement Act of 1937 followed the recommendation of representatives of the employees and employers. This act has been amended several times since its passage, usually liberalizing the benefits or lowering the age at which employees are eligible to retire.

Employers subject to the provisions of the Railroad Retirement Act include express companies, sleeping-car companies, and carriers by railroad; companies owned or controlled by the foregoing employers which operate equipment or perform regular services in connection with the transportation of passengers or property by railroad; and the national railway labor organizations, their national and state legislative committees, insurance departments, and local lodges. Under the revised act a woman with 30 years of service may retire at sixty. Men who have had 30 years of service may retire at sixty with a reduced pension over what they would receive at sixty-five. Individuals with 25 years of service who have attained the age of sixty may retire with full benefits if they "have a current connection with the railroad industry" and have a permanent physical or mental disability that makes it impossible to carry on their regular occupation. Individuals may also retire with full benefits whose permanent physical or mental condition is such that they are unable to engage in regular employment (not necessarily in the railroad industry) and who (1) have completed 10 years of service and (2) have reached the age of sixty.

A husband may receive an annuity from his wife's coverage under circumstances similar to those in the Social Security Act. Both the employer and the employee contribute 6¾ per cent of the employee's wages up to $4,800 per year (1959 amendment) through 1962 and 7¼ per cent thereafter.

**Who pays the costs of pensions?** Pension costs such as those in Social Security, which covers practically all businesses, do not place any industry at a cost disadvantage. The ultimate cost is largely borne by the workers indirectly in that their wages will not rise so high as they otherwise would in the long run. Of course, even in the case of a universal fixed pension charge, the industry having a relatively small labor cost with a high equipment cost has an advantage over another industry that makes the same product but uses largely labor instead of equipment. There are relatively few such cases.

In industry in general, it is reasonably accurate to say that in the long run the workers themselves will bear the ultimate cost. Temporarily, the cost of the pension plan may not cause a reduction in the wages paid the workers; in the long run, however, wages will tend not to rise so high as they would rise were it not for the additional cost of pensions, unless of course the pension plan causes an increase in productive efficiency equal to the cost of the plan, a causal relationship that is unlikely to exist. In the case of the Federal plan by statute, the workers bear one-half the taxes collected for the specific purpose. The portion of the tax that is levied against the employer was expected by the lawmakers either to be borne by the employer or to be passed to the consumer in the form of increased prices. In certain industries, where the elasticity of demand for the product will permit, it is possible that a portion or all of the cost may be passed on to the consumer; however, in the long run in most industries, this will not occur, particularly in those industries for whose products there is a substitute product, the cost of which has a relatively lower proportion of labor cost. Since the tax is specifically a payroll tax, there will be the tendency as far as is economically advantageous to substitute machinery for labor, and it will largely fall upon the workers as a group. Of course, in those industries which are so favorably situated competitively that they could have and/or would have paid a pension either direct or hidden in the place of giving a higher than economic wage to aged employees, the employer may absorb a portion or all of the tax; yet, even in such cases, the employer might reasonably have been expected to pay a relatively higher wage were it not for the tax.

The fact that workers in general will bear the cost of the tax does not mean that each worker will share in the cost in proportion to his benefits. The lower wage group of workers receive more in benefits than they pay in, whereas unmarried men and the higher wage group receive relatively less than they contribute. Likewise older workers who came under the new law for the first time will receive benefits greatly in excess of what they contribute.

There is serious doubt regarding the wisdom of penalizing a worker who earns more than $1,200 a year by making him ineligible to receive his full insurance benefits. This is especially true of periods of national emergency when his services are needed. This economically questionable regulation is a hang-over from the depression psychology of 1935, when the original act was passed, and has been perpetuated even during national emergencies when it was highly desirable to have every able person working. Back in 1935 certain reformers were anxious to get as many persons out of the work force as possible in order to make room for others who were unemployed. It is to be hoped that Congress[11] will remove the restriction on an eligible pensioner's receiving his pension because he accepts employment and earns more than $1,200 a year. Pensions that are purchased should be paid as a matter of right, and not used to make people nonproductive who otherwise could contribute their efforts to the needed production of the economy.

In spite of some of the shortcomings of the Social Security Act it is both economically and socially a positive contribution to solving a pressing problem. It is perfectly logical for the persons who benefit by a program to pay for it. In a way, it forces individuals to save for their old age. The program is also beneficial to the self-respecting children of aged persons, who would otherwise be forced to support their parents out of filial affection and respect if not by law. This burden upon children of destitute parents usually falls upon the children at a time when their own families are just growing up and it is most difficult to help their aged parents. The principle of contributory old-aged pensions is thoroughly sound.

[11] Congress liberalized the regulation regarding earnings in the 1960 amendments. They provide that a pensioner who earns more than $1,200 but not more than $1,500 shall have his family benefits reduced by one-half of his earnings above $1,200. Should he earn more than $1,500 in any one year, his family benefits will be reduced dollar for dollar to the extent his earnings exceed $1,500 plus the $150 deducted for the earnings between $1,200 and $1,500.

CHAPTER 35

## The Personnel Audit

**What is an audit?** The most common usage of the term *audit* is associated with accounting. In financial accounting, auditing consists in careful checking and investigating to see that all phases of the accounting for financial matters are being conducted according to established procedures and practices. Auditing is not solely concerned with the handling of money. It also involves proper inventory control, proper payment for goods purchased, and adequate checks to see that goods paid for are actually received. The audit is concerned with payroll practices and whether or not persons carried on the payroll are in fact working at the jobs specified. The auditor would try to discover whether or not purchase discounts were taken and "why" in case they were not. In other words an audit seeks to investigate all practices related to the accounting for materials, labor, or any activity that involves a cost.

The audit is not conducted on the theory that people are dishonest, but it is a sensible precaution to create a climate in the business that will encourage them to remain honest. In such a simple matter as paying employees on an incentive basis for production, management invites dishonesty if it merely takes the worker's count for his production and has no other check on what it is paying for. In some of the most flagrant cases of embezzlement one person was responsible for keeping the records as well as for handling the funds paid in or deposited. These people are often long-service, trusted employees. Practically no modern manager would think of running his business without having his operations checked. In a company large enough to justify the expense, special internal auditors are employed by the company in addition to outside auditors.

**Other audits needed.** The financial, or accounting, audit is taken for granted in business circles. This is as it should be. On the other hand there are many activities in a business that should be evaluated to see whether or not they are contributing to the primary objective as intended. One of the primary items that should be appraised from time to time is the organization structure. Does it facilitate getting the work done in the most economical manner without undue burden on a few persons? Are the necessary functions provided for to keep the company competitive? If product research is important, are the energies of this department being dissipated by putting out "production fires"? Is quality being sacrificed because the inspection department answers to the plant superintendent, who is also responsible for quantity of production?

Naturally in investigating the adequacy of the organization structure the persons occupying the respective positions have to be appraised in terms of competence, age, and replacements available. This phase of the investigation leads directly into a consideration of the personnel audit, which is the subject of this entire chapter. The personnel audit is a part of any management audit but not all of it. A management audit to be complete would include not only the personnel of the executive group but every phase of the organization and capital structure in addition to the structural details of all the various functions of the business.[1]

**Objective of the personnel audit.** The labor audit is an *analysis of all the factors involved in personnel administration,* with a *summarized statement of the findings,* followed by *recommendations* to correct any deviations from the desired standard. This definition presumes that there are clearly defined personnel policies, objectives, and standards. Unfortunately in a substantial number of cases these conditions do not prevail. In such situations management may desire a comprehensive personnel audit to be used as a basis from which to evolve a sound personnel program. A sound personnel program should be developed out of the current situation, not be imported from an outside source with an entirely different background. It is psychologically unsound to begin an appraisal of any business situation with the assumption that the existing practices are wrong; it is equally erroneous to assume that current procedures must be correct or they would not have been used for so long. The scientific approach to an audit is to get the facts, consider the objective to be attained, evaluate the factors present in the light of the objective, formulate a plan to improve the current operations so as more nearly to achieve the desired objective (in case it is not fully being realized), and set a time schedule for implement-

[1] See Jackson Martindell, *The Scientific Appraisal of Management,* Harper & Brothers, New York, 1950, for an intriguing discussion of management appraisal.

ing the suggested changes. This approach is just as applicable to evaluating the personnel program as to any other phase of management.

Relatively few businessmen have clearly defined personnel objectives. It might be well to repeat a definition of personnel administration used earlier in our book. *Personnel administration is that activity in an enterprise which strives to mold human resources into an effective organization, provides opportunity for maximum individual contributions under desirable working conditions, promotes individual development, and encourages mutual confidence and understanding between employees and the employer as well as between employees themselves.* In the field of personnel administration and management many an innovation is undertaken solely because some other company is doing it. In this second company the particular activity may readily have grown out of a specific need expressed by the employees and agreed upon jointly by management and the workers. In the first company there may not be the same situation, or a similar situation is being cared for in a different but equally satisfactory manner. The labor auditor's first assignment is to get the facts as they currently exist. He needs some background for a given practice in order to appraise its effectiveness. In getting the facts on which to build the audit, questions similar to the following should be asked about every personnel function:

1. Why was this practice or procedure inaugurated? Is it still required? What would be the result if it were abolished?
2. What need is sought to be served? Is it achieving the desired end?
3. Is this need being in part achieved by some other method?
4. Is this the best possible procedure in the light of existing circumstances?
5. What changes may improve the efficiency of the particular procedure?
6. Should these changes be effected at once or over a period of time?
7. Is the proposed modification a part of another suggested change, or does it stand alone?
8. What is the proposed time schedule for making the change?

Answers to the questions above and the entire labor audit[2] are designed to give management a true picture of the manpower situation. Naturally any shortcomings would call for recommendations to overcome them.

**Who authorizes the labor audit?** In many cases an alert personnel administrator may seek professional counsel to evaluate his entire personnel program. In this event he would seek top management's ap-

---

[2] Other names used for the labor audit are personnel appraisal, personnel inventory, industrial audit, or manpower survey or audit. See Thomas J. Luck, *Personnel Audit and Appraisal,* McGraw-Hill Book Company, Inc., New York, 1955, for an entire book devoted to this subject.

proval of the expenditure as well as top management's cooperation in the audit. Any complete manpower audit should include top executives. Of course top management may be left out of a strictly personnel appraisal if this is management's desire. Often the desire for the manpower audit arises in the top management group; at times it may emanate from the board of directors. Just as the president or board of directors wants a financial audit, so should the sales manager be interested in an audit of sales, the factory manager be interested in an audit of manufacturing efficiency, and the personnel director want an audit of personnel practices, procedures, and relationships. When labor relations have been particularly bad, the board of directors may ask for an outside consultant's appraisal of the personnel program. It is a human characteristic not to like to be measured; so all too few personnel directors conduct or have others conduct a thorough labor audit, unless they are advocating an expansion in their division and hope to have the audit support their recommendations. The result is that complete labor audits are not commonly made in business save in situations that have become so bad that top management has had them forcibly brought into the open. A regular labor audit competently conducted would point out the defects in their embryonic stages and thus be a valuable aid in preventing their development into critical issues. A personnel audit should not only check results against the personnel budget (where there is one) but should point out areas that need attention even though not provided in the budget. For instance, there may be no provision for supervisory training in the personnel budget, but there may be a visible need for such training.

**How often should a labor audit be made?** It would seem reasonable to have a manpower appraisal once a year. This does not mean that the same detailed analysis would be required every year as that required by the first complete audit. In many instances the second year's audit might merely indicate the changes since the previous audit, with special reference to the progress made in carrying out recommended improvements. Management should desire some form of appraisal of its personnel program at least once a year. This may not be a complete audit but a summarized statement of the operation of the division prepared by the director of personnel. It should point out the objective to be achieved, the degree of attainment of the objective, and plans for the ensuing year. This type of limited audit should precede the preparation of the personnel budget. A complete personnel audit might well be made every 2 to 3 years, provided that during this period the entire program has not been covered by special audits similar to those referred to below. In the case of a large company having many plants the central office might well have an over-all audit annually, possibly not in so great detail as it would be if spaced at longer intervals. There is no definite rule to govern the spacing of audits. It is an excellent idea for a more complete audit to be made annually of some special phase of the personnel program, such as:

1. The status of supervisors and executives (including training, promotional plans, retirements expected, etc.).
2. Employee morale.
3. Labor turnover.
4. Safety, etc.

The timing for the audit should be related to need and the use made of the audits. The stimulus provided to the personnel division by making a thorough audit of some phase of its program is tremendous. It is well worth the cost if for no other reason than the lift that it provides to the entire personnel staff. It also gives the personnel director an excellent medium for interesting top management in the various activities of the personnel division. It is one phase of personnel research that is not difficult to conduct, and it pays dividends in that its results are currently usable.

**Who makes the manpower audit?** In the large enterprise with a number of branches the company may well have one or two persons who constantly make internal management audits, personnel audits, and morale surveys. In smaller enterprises the research unit or a member of the personnel staff that handles research activities may do a substantial amount of the audit. Seldom are these people qualified to do a real audit of the supervisory personnel, at least from middle management on up. This phase of the audit calls for an individual of executive standing. The personnel director or the director of executive training might do it. The director of training should possess real status if he is expected to do a management audit of middle management. There is no question but that it is less expensive to have the audit made by some member of the regular personnel division; however, save in unusual cases, this audit is seldom so complete or impersonal as one made by an outside consultant. Certainly there should be no hesistancy in using an internal auditor in cases where funds are not available to employ the outside professional consultant or in situations where management does not believe in using management consultants. Many authorities in the field believe that there is merit in having the outside consultant.[3] In situa-

---

[3] See Ordway Tead and Henry C. Metcalf, *Personnel Administration,* 3d ed., McGraw-Hill Book Company, Inc., New York, 1933, p. 272. Chapters 20 and 21 in this book are well worth reading.

tions where the present personnel has allowed pronounced defects to develop, it is placing a severe strain on an analyst's objectivity to expect him to be as frank in fixing responsibility and pointing to causes as is desirable. This is especially true when the cause may rest with someone higher in the organization than the auditor. The same situation prevails when things are going smoothly. The superior may readily say that things were never running more smoothly; this may be true, and yet certain influences may be developing that will cause trouble if not detected and corrected in their incipient stages. The professional standing of a management consultant should be carefully investigated. Many states have no regulations governing the licensing of management consultants. An outside consultant has the advantage of bringing to his assignment:

1. A wide background of knowledge of what others are doing in similar situations.
2. A professional attitude toward his work.
3. Objectivity in that he personally will not become a party to recommended changes.

Should a consultant be employed, there are certain conditions that should be kept in mind regarding his work:

1. He cannot work miracles. He can diagnose ills and recommend treatment, but the patient must provide the will to get well.
2. He must receive top management's support.
3. He cannot and should not relieve management of its responsibility for making the decisions. He can recommend, but the acceptance of his recommendations rests with management.

**Conducting the labor audit.** It is usually desirable to start the labor audit as high up in the organization as it is to be made and work down. Such a practice gives prestige to the efforts further down the line. When the auditor is talking with a foreman, he usually has no trouble in getting the desired information when the foreman knows that his division superintendent has already covered the same point from the viewpoint of the divisional unit. A clearly defined objective should be approved by top management before starting the labor audit. The regular line and staff officers should be notified through channels what to expect. An organized plan is essential to a successful labor audit. Every person interviewed need not be questioned on every phase of the audit. The individual should be expected to provide information only on those items which come within his responsibility. Of course, many a valuable lead comes from informal conversation outside the line of responsibility. This is especially true if an attempt is being made to appraise morale.

**The use of an audit check list.** Some persons oppose the use of check lists. When the check list is used as a guide, it may serve a useful purpose. Such a list will avoid gaps that should have been closed. If it is a complete audit, naturally the check list will cover every phase of the personnel function. If the audit covers some special phase of the personnel program—such as wage administration, morale, sources of labor supply—the check list will pertain solely to the item being audited. The list of functions and activities given in Chap. 2 covers most of the items included in a labor audit. In order to conserve space, it is not repeated here. The various headings in this list would be expanded considerably in the check list. Frequently the check-list information desired is in the form of a question. The check list shown below portrays the technique used with success by some companies. One such check list used by a firm having several large branch plants covers 37 pages of 8½- by 11-in. mimeographed paper and provides adequate space for answers and comments. A check list for a department store will include certain specific questions peculiar to the problems of a retail establishment having special peak seasons. For instance, under "Source of labor supply" would be included, "Is a list of former salespeople who will work during rush periods maintained?" and similar specialized questions. It can readily be seen from the following illustration that a check list for a complete labor audit is extensive:

1. Employment.
    1.1 Source of labor supply.
        1.11 What is the status of the labor supply in the community?
        1.12 What sources have been used most frequently during the past 3 months? Year?
        1.13 What method of establishing contact has been most successful? Advertising, government agencies, callers at the gate?
        1.14 Do interviewers and personnel manager know of best areas from which to draw applicants? (Applicable only in large cities.)
        1.15 Have reciprocal relationships been established with any local employers?
        1.16 Are available employees in the company canvassed before hiring outsiders?
        1.17 Is there a transfer-desired roster available from which to select persons desiring the vacant job?
        1.18 What procedure is followed to call in persons whose applications are on file?
        1.19 How is the "applications" file kept up-to-date?
    1.2 Handling applicants.
        1.21 Is adequate waiting space available for applicants?
            1.211 Are rest-room facilities available?
        1.22 Is a preliminary application blank used?

1.23 Is a preliminary interview given all applicants in addition to the regular interview?
1.24 Are applicants kept waiting unreasonably long?
1.25 How are turndowns handled?
1.3 Interviewing.
    1.31 Is the interview conducted in a desirable environment?
    1.32 Is adequate time given to the interview?
    1.33 Does the interview successfully:
        1.331 Get the desired information?
        1.332 Give adequate information?
        1.333 Make a friend?
    1.34 What phase of the interview should be improved?
    1.341 What is being done to improve the interviewing?

**The audit report.** Certain aspects of an audit report may be made available to the employees. A morale survey, a safety survey, and similar special items of wide general interest are illustrations of segments of an audit that may readily be publicized. Other phases of the audit may be appropriate to give only to top management. The report should avoid the journalistic style, be based solely on the findings, be presented in a factual manner that is readily available for future reference, make use of the graphic technique where appropriate, and not be any longer than is necessary. The following tabulation gives the essentials to be included in the report:

1. Table of contents.
2. Summary and conclusions, in which the entire report is summarized for the top executives. This may be the only part of the audit that some of the important executives will read. It should be short, not to exceed five to seven pages.
3. Preface giving a brief statement of the objective.
4. The report proper, in which each major division is covered as a special section. It is desirable to have this so typed that any section may be removed and sent to the persons concerned. Each section should be complete and should contain as many supporting data as are practical without making it too voluminous. Other data should be included in the appendix.
5. Summary. This is more complete than the summary and conclusions at the beginning of the report.
6. Appendix. This includes supporting data that would be too voluminous to appear in the body of the report.

**Use of the manpower appraisal or audit.** The labor audit has value to each level of supervision and the personnel department, but its maximum value is to top management and the personnel director. If possible the auditor should persuade the president to call a meeting of the senior executives, division heads, and possibly the chairman of the board of directors and as many of the members of the board as will come, before which the audit will be explained. It will be well for the auditor to go over the main items with the president prior to the meeting with the major executives as a group. One large company has such a meeting for the consideration of many phases of its activities. In this case the person reporting has slides prepared to show the important phases of the report. The same company makes extensive use of outlines and charts printed in large type and assembled on an easel. The reporting person reads the material on each sheet and turns to the next one. Slides may also be used with the "turnover" chart technique. At times each executive is given a four- to six-page outline digest of the findings to take with him. Such a meeting makes certain that the important executives know the contents of the report. The chief executive may turn the meeting into a conference at which policy is determined and action agreed upon. This meeting provides a wonderful opportunity for the personnel director to call attention to the personnel problems facing the company. In addition to being valuable for presentation to the executives, the labor audit provides excellent material for the personnel division's or the line officer's conferences with its department heads.

**Summary.** The labor audit serves the same general purpose to top management in the area of executive personnel and employee personnel that the financial audit serves in the area of finance. Some companies contend that they do not need an audit since they take care of their problems as they arise. This same company may keep a perpetual inventory record yet take periodic surveys of its inventory. Such an appraisal might readily be considerably shorter than the one suggested in this chapter. It could be made by the respective heads of the various activities and subjected to the critical evaluation of the director of personnel. If these department heads had a comprehensive check list against which to evaluate their divisions, such a report would serve as a stimulus to improve performance. If the director of personnel could get such a report before his key executives, this alone would justify the effort in compiling it. Just as the inventory report has value in planning for the next period's production, so should the labor audit be the basis of planning the personnel activities for the period ahead. The labor audit assists materially in justifying the personnel budget. The labor audit may indicate things that need attention that would not have been known in the absence of the audit. If a morale survey is a part of the labor audit, it may indicate that things are not going well in department A. This should call for some intensive study of this department to locate the cause.

# APPENDIXES

# The Trend of Personnel Management as Measured, 1930, 1940, 1947, 1953 and 1957

The personnel practices reported in the accompanying charts and tables were secured from a survey that has been continued since 1930 according to the following dates: 1940, 1947, 1953, and 1957.[1] The number of companies answering the questionnaires is given below:

|  | Number of companies | Size of companies | Total number of employees |
|---|---|---|---|
| 1930 | 195 | 100–240,000 | 2,391,000 |
| 1940 | 231 | 12–265,000 | 1,795,000 |
| 1947 | 325 | 75–500,000 | 3,000,000 |
| 1953 | 628 | 50–500,000 | 4,900,000 |
| 1957 | 852 | 250–500,000 | 6,444,000 |

These companies participating in the study are personnel-minded as a group. No attempt was made to try to get companies that would give a representative sample of all companies. The authors were interested in getting a wide sampling of well-known companies rather than any statistical sample of all companies. Responses from the companies to whom the five-page questionnaire was sent were very good, representing more than 80 per cent of the companies to whom questionnaires were sent. The bar charts that are included with the tables tend to show the relative interest in the particular items at the different periods.

In each survey essentially the same questions were asked. This permitted the tabulating of the answers on a percentage basis and the comparing of the various surveys, thus showing a trend, if any exists.

Tables A.1 and A.2 show the composition of the responding firms on the basis of their size and their geographic location.

Table A.3 portrays the wide variety of firms participating in the survey and the nature of their activities.

[1] This material is reported in greater detail in *Personnel Practices in Industry*, Personnel Study No. 8, Bureau of Business Research, Univ. of Texas, Austin, 1958.

### Table A.1  Firms Classified by Number of Employees

| Employees | Firms |
|---|---|
| Fewer than 250 | 36 |
| 250–499 | 72 |
| 500–749 | 66 |
| 750–999 | 38 |
| 1,000–1,499 | 102 |
| 1,500–1,999 | 63 |
| 2,000–2,499 | 58 |
| 2,500–2,999 | 42 |
| 3,000–3,999 | 59 |
| 4,000–4,999 | 39 |
| 5,000–7,499 | 65 |
| 7,500–9,999 | 30 |
| 10,000–14,999 | 37 |
| 15,000–19,999 | 31 |
| 20,000–29,999 | 28 |
| 30,000–39,999 | 9 |
| 40,000–49,999 | 6 |
| 50,000–74,999 | 12 |
| Over 75,000 | 13 |
| Not given | 46 |
| Total, all firms | 852 |

### Table A.2  Firms Classified by Geographical Location

| Area | Firms |
|---|---|
| New England | 59 |
| Middle Atlantic | 147 |
| East North Central | 284 |
| West North Central | 63 |
| South Atlantic | 28 |
| East South Central | 68 |
| West South Central | 84 |
| Mountain | 28 |
| Pacific | 91 |
| Total, all firms | 852 |

*Table* A.3   *Firms Classified by Product Manufactured or Service Rendered*

| Manufacturing | |
|---|---|
| *Product* | *Firms* |
| Food and kindred products | 58 |
|   Meat packing and products | 6 |
|   Grain products | 11 |
|   Confectionery, bakery, and dairy products | 19 |
|   Canning and preserving | 17 |
|   Brewing and distilling | 5 |
| Tobacco | 2 |
| Textile-mill products | 17 |
| Apparel and related products | 16 |
| Lumber and products (excluding furniture) | 11 |
| Furniture and fixtures | 12 |
| Paper and allied products | 19 |
| Printing and publishing | 16 |
| Chemical and allied products | 41 |
|   Industrial chemicals | 13 |
|   Drugs and medicines | 8 |
|   Soap and related products | 4 |
|   Paints and varnishes | 7 |
|   Plastics, synthetic fibers, and miscellaneous | 9 |
| Petroleum and coal products | 44 |
| Rubber | 12 |
| Leather and leather products | 10 |
| Stone, clay, and glass | 14 |
| Primary metals | 28 |
| Fabricated metal products | 37 |
|   Cutlery and hardware | 5 |
|   Heating and plumbing equipment | 6 |
|   Structural | 5 |
|   Stampings | 15 |
|   Miscellaneous | 6 |
| Machinery (other than electrical) | 81 |
|   Engines | 3 |
|   Farm machinery and tractors | 9 |
|   Construction and general industrial | 22 |
|   Office machinery and household equipment | 19 |
|   Miscellaneous (parts, gears, valves, etc.) | 28 |
| Electrical machinery and equipment | 54 |
|   Industrial | 26 |
|   Communication (radio, television, etc.) | 14 |
|   Miscellaneous | 14 |
| Transportation equipment | 67 |
|   Motor vehicles | 13 |
|   Motor bodies and parts | 23 |
|   Aircraft | 22 |
|   Aircraft equipment | 9 |

*Table* A.3   *Firms Classified by Product Manufactured or*
*Service Rendered*   (*Continued*)

| Manufacturing | |
|---|---|
| *Product* | *Firms* |
| Instruments and related products........................... | 45 |
| Scientific and measuring................................ | 21 |
| Optical and cameras.................................... | 16 |
| Watches and clocks..................................... | 8 |
| Miscellaneous manufacturing............................. | 41 |
| Jewelry............................................... | 4 |
| Pharmaceuticals (other than drugs)....................... | 17 |
| Office supplies.......................................... | 3 |
| Miscellaneous (not elsewhere classified)..................... | 17 |
| Total manufacturing firms.............................. | 625 |

| Nonmanufacturing | |
|---|---|
| *Service rendered* | *Firms* |
| Financial institutions.................................... | 78 |
| Government agencies..................................... | 6 |
| Public utilities......................................... | 46 |
| Retail stores and mail-order houses....................... | 39 |
| Transportation companies................................ | 39 |
| Road transport........................................ | 10 |
| Railroads............................................. | 8 |
| Air lines.............................................. | 12 |
| Shipping companies.................................... | 9 |
| Telephone, telegraph, and radio communication............. | 6 |
| Miscellaneous nonmanufacturing (not elsewhere classified).... | 13 |
| Total nonmanufacturing firms........................... | 227 |
| Total all firms........................................ | 852 |

**The questionnaire.** "This questionnaire is arranged as a simple check
list on your policies and practices of Personnel Management. It has been
subdivided for statistical purposes into six groupings: Employment and Induction; Health, Safety and Maintenance; Payment to Direct Labor;
Security and Employee Relations; Training and Development; and Research Control. The authors of *Personnel Management* hereby assure all
cooperating concerns that no individual replies will be made available to
others, and only the summarized results will be published."

The questions and the summary of the answers are presented in Tables
A.4 to A.25. It should be pointed out that in all cases the answers do not
balance. In some cases individual items were not answered. In other cases
more than one practice was followed, in which case the total is greater
than the number of companies answering the questionnaires. Figures A.1
to A.8 portray in graphic form the relative percentage of companies using

*Table* A.4  *Employment and Induction*

| | Yes | | No | | No reply | |
|---|---|---|---|---|---|---|
| | No. | % | No. | % | No. | % |
| 1. Do you use an application blank?......... | 848 | 99.6 | 3 | 0.4 | 1 | 0.0 |
|    *a.* Is it filled out by applicant?........... | 802 | 94.2 | 17 | 2.0 | 33 | 3.8 |
|    *b.* Is it filled out by interviewer?......... | 79 | 9.3 | 605 | 71.0 | 168 | 19.7 |
|    *c.* Are both methods in use?.............. | 128 | 15.0 | 572 | 67.2 | 152 | 17.8 |
| 2. Are applicants interviewed for selection?.... | 838 | 98.4 | 8 | 0.9 | 6 | 0.7 |
| 3. Are any applicants hired without an interview?................................. | 37 | 4.3 | 800 | 93.9 | 15 | 1.8 |
| 4. Are any new employees furnished by an outside source?........................ | 516 | 60.6 | 45 | 5.3 | 291 | 34.1 |
| 5. Do you use a qualification card other than a mere roster or payroll record for each employee?............................. | 639 | 75.0 | 182 | 21.4 | 31 | 3.6 |
| 6. Do you require written references?........ | 429 | 50.4 | 398 | 46.7 | 25 | 2.9 |
|    *a.* Do you have a special reference form of your own?.......................... | 590 | 69.3 | 202 | 23.7 | 60 | 7.0 |
| 7. Does your personnel department have full authority to hire rank and file?........... | 476 | 55.9 | 361 | 42.4 | 15 | 1.7 |
| 8. Are new employees given a personal introduction to the department where they are to work by a foreman or member of the personnel department?.................... | 780 | 91.6 | 65 | 7.6 | 7 | 0.8 |
| 9. Do you send a special "put-on" form to the department (with perhaps copies to other departments) for each new employee?..... | 500 | 58.7 | 329 | 38.6 | 23 | 2.7 |
| 10. Do you require physical examinations for selection?............................ | 733 | 86.0 | 103 | 12.1 | 16 | 1.9 |
|    *a.* Are they made on the premises?....... | 440 | 51.6 | 295 | 34.6 | 117 | 13.8 |
|    *b.* Are they made elsewhere?............ | 425 | 49.9 | 233 | 27.4 | 194 | 22.7 |
| 11. Do you use tests for selecting new employees?............................. | 678 | 79.6 | 122 | 14.3 | 52 | 6.1 |
|    *a.* Are they stenographic or clerical tests?.. | 660 | 77.5 | 61 | 7.2 | 131 | 15.3 |
|    *b.* Are they trade tests?................. | 290 | 34.0 | 374 | 43.9 | 188 | 22.1 |
|    *c.* Are they mental (intelligence) tests?.... | 537 | 63.0 | 165 | 19.4 | 150 | 17.6 |
|    *d.* Are they mechanical-aptitude tests?.... | 387 | 45.4 | 293 | 34.4 | 172 | 20.2 |
|    *e.* Are they dexterity tests?.............. | 275 | 32.3 | 385 | 45.2 | 192 | 22.5 |
|    *f.* Are they personality or interest tests?.. | 376 | 44.1 | 297 | 34.9 | 179 | 21.0 |
|    *g.* Are they performance tests?........... | 324 | 38.0 | 337 | 39.6 | 191 | 22.4 |
|    *h.* Any other types?.................... | 108 | 12.7 | 305 | 35.8 | 439 | 51.5 |
| 12. Do you make a general practice of securing applicants through the United States or state employment service?............... | 359 | 42.1 | 316 | 37.1 | 177 | 20.8 |
|    *a.* Do you use this service exclusively?.... | 7 | 0.8 | 640 | 75.1 | 205 | 24.1 |
|    *b.* Do you use this service occasionally?... | 507 | 59.5 | 32 | 3.8 | 313 | 36.7 |
|    *c.* Do you avoid this service?............ | 18 | 2.1 | 605 | 71.0 | 229 | 26.9 |

*Table* A.4   *Employment and Induction* (*Continued*)

|  | Yes | | No | | No reply | |
|---|---|---|---|---|---|---|
|  | No. | % | No. | % | No. | % |
| **13.** Do you make a general practice of securing applicants through schools and colleges?.... | 410 | 48.1 | 215 | 25.2 | 227 | 26.7 |
| *a.* Do you use these sources occasionally?.. | 461 | 54.1 | 58 | 6.8 | 333 | 39.1 |
| *b.* Do you avoid these sources?........... | 5 | 0.6 | 602 | 70.7 | 245 | 28.7 |
| **14.** Do you make a general practice of securing applicants through private (fee) employment agencies?........................ | 300 | 35.2 | 409 | 48.0 | 143 | 16.8 |
| *a.* Do you use these sources occasionally?.. | 469 | 55.1 | 95 | 11.2 | 288 | 33.7 |
| *b.* Do you avoid these agencies?.......... | 66 | 7.7 | 522 | 61.3 | 264 | 31.0 |
| **15.** Do you make a general practice of securing new employees through labor unions?..... | 51 | 6.0 | 759 | 89.1 | 42 | 4.9 |
| *a.* Do you use these sources occasionally?.. | 127 | 14.9 | 382 | 44.8 | 343 | 40.3 |
| *b.* Do you avoid this source?............. | 265 | 31.1 | 236 | 27.7 | 351 | 41.2 |
| **16.** Do you make a general practice of securing applicants through your foreman, employees, friends, and other miscellaneous sources?.............................. | 695 | 81.6 | 118 | 13.8 | 39 | 4.6 |

a particular technique, practice, or other device for all the different years of the four surveys.

**Employment and induction.** Table A.4 and Fig. A.1 portray the picture of current practices in the field of employment and induction. Figure A.1 shows the change in these practices from 1930 to 1957. The authority of the personnel department to hire is shown in Table A.5.

Ninety-one and six-tenths per cent of the firms give new employees personal introductions to their new department, either by a foreman or by a member of the personnel department itself. This practice, a result of the trend toward the human-relations approach, has increased in the time since 1940. The same percentage of companies—92—reported in the 1953 survey

*Table* A.5   *Companies in Which Personnel Department Has Full Hiring Authority, Classified by Size Group*

| Number of employees | Number of companies | Per cent of companies in size group |
|---|---|---|
| Less than 1,000............. | 124 | 58.5 |
| 1,000–4,999................ | 216 | 59.8 |
| Over 5,000................. | 114 | 48.7 |
| Not classified.............. | 22 |  |
| Total.................. | 476 |  |

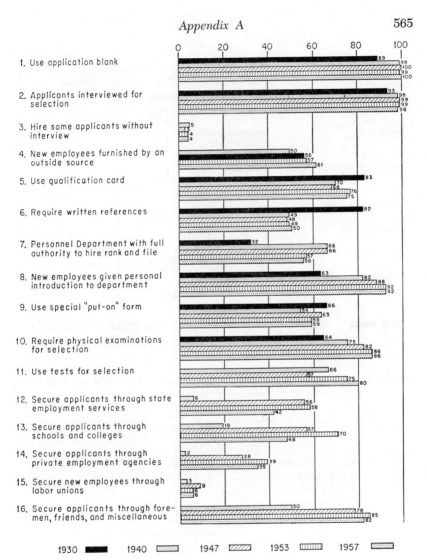

1. Use application blank
2. Applicants interviewed for selection
3. Hire some applicants without interview
4. New employees furnished by an outside source
5. Use qualification card
6. Require written references
7. Personnel Department with full authority to hire rank and file
8. New employees given personal introduction to department
9. Use special "put-on" form
10. Require physical examinations for selection
11. Use tests for selection
12. Secure applicants through state employment services
13. Secure applicants through schools and colleges
14. Secure applicants through private employment agencies
15. Secure new employees through labor unions
16. Secure applicants through foremen, friends, and miscellaneous

1930 ■■■   1940 ☐   1947 ▨   1953 ▥   1957 ▱

FIG. A.1. Employment and Induction.

as in this one that they give special attention to the proper introduction of the new employee. The use of the more impersonal, "put-on" form is a less common element of the introductory process. Approximately 75 per cent of the respondents indicated that they used some form of qualification card for record purposes. Information contained on an application form might rapidly become obsolete if no provision were made for the inclusion of subsequent data.

**Psychological tests.** The current use of psychological tests in hiring is revealed by Tables A.6 and A.7 and Fig. A.2. There has been a marked increase in the use of tests during the past quarter of a century.

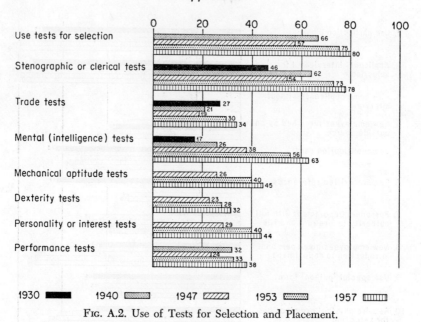

Fɪɢ. A.2. Use of Tests for Selection and Placement.

*Table* A.6  *Companies Using Selection Testing, Classified by Size Group*

| Number of employees | Number of companies | Per cent of companies in size group |
|---|---|---|
| Less than 1,000............. | 135 | 63.7 |
| 1,000–4,999................ | 298 | 82.5 |
| Over 5,000................. | 211 | 90.2 |
| Not classified.............. | 34 | |
| Total................... | 678 | |

### Table A.7  Types of Tests Used

| Tests | Number of companies | Per cent of companies using tests |
|---|---|---|
| Stenographic or clerical tests....... | 660 | 96.1 |
| Trade tests..................... | 290 | 42.2 |
| Mental (intelligence) tests......... | 537 | 78.2 |
| Mechanical-aptitude tests......... | 387 | 56.3 |
| Dexterity tests................... | 275 | 40.0 |
| Personality or interest tests........ | 376 | 54.7 |
| Performance tests................ | 324 | 47.2 |
| Other types...................... | 108 | 15.7 |

The source of new employees is shown in Table A.8. It will be observed that outside sources are of less importance than inside sources.

**Health, safety, and maintenance.** As might be expected, larger firms have a more complete health and safety program than smaller companies (Table A.9). Manufacturing firms have a higher percentage of these programs than other types of businesses (Tables A.9 and A.10).

### Table A.8  Comparative Use of Potential Sources of Applicants*

| Source | Used as general practice | Used occasionally | Avoided |
|---|---|---|---|
| State employment services......... | 42.1 | 59.5 | 2.1 |
| Schools and colleges.............. | 48.1 | 54.1 | 0.6 |
| Private (fee) agencies............. | 35.2 | 55.1 | 7.7 |
| Labor unions..................... | 6.0 | 14.9 | 31.1 |
| Foremen, employees, friends........ | 81.6 | | |

* All figures expressed as percentages of the total number of survey respondents.

*Table* A.9   *Companies Having Free Health Service, Classified by Size Group*

| Number of employees | Number of companies | Per cent of companies in size group |
|---|---|---|
| Less than 1,000............. | 76 | 35.8 |
| 1,000–4,999............... | 145 | 40.2 |
| Over 5,000................ | 94 | 40.2 |
| Not given................ | 17 | |
| Total.................. | 332 | |

*Table* A.10   *Companies Having Free Health Service, Classified by Type*

| Type | Number of companies | Per cent of all companies |
|---|---|---|
| Manufacturing............. | 253 | 40.5 |
| Nonmanufacturing.......... | 79 | 34.8 |
| Total.................. | 332 | |

Figure A.3 gives in graphic form the practices used by various companies from 1930 to 1957 in health and safety.

Table A.11 shows the prevalence of the employee house organ as a tool of communicating with employees. Table A.12 shows the breakdown of the answers for Fig. A.3.

*Table* A.11   *Companies Having House Organs, Classified by Size Group*

| Employees | Companies | Per cent of companies in size group |
|---|---|---|
| Less than 1,000............. | 112 | 52.8 |
| 1,000–4,999............... | 287 | 79.5 |
| Over 5,000................ | 211 | 90.2 |
| Not given................ | 36 | |
| Total.................. | 646 | |

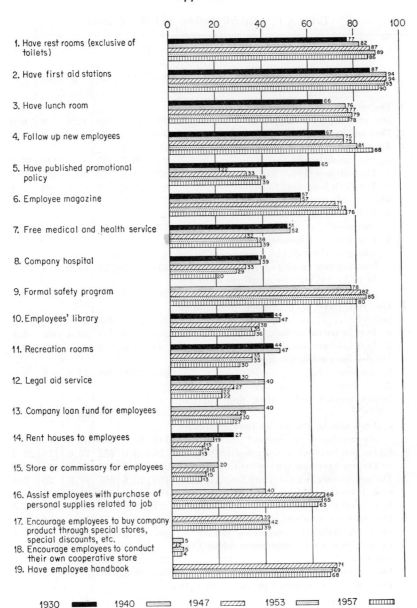

1. Have rest rooms (exclusive of toilets)
2. Have first aid stations
3. Have lunch room
4. Follow up new employees
5. Have published promotional policy
6. Employee magazine
7. Free medical and health service
8. Company hospital
9. Formal safety program
10. Employees' library
11. Recreation rooms
12. Legal aid service
13. Company loan fund for employees
14. Rent houses to employees
15. Store or commissary for employees
16. Assist employees with purchase of personal supplies related to job
17. Encourage employees to buy company product through special stores, special discounts, etc.
18. Encourage employees to conduct their own cooperative store
19. Have employee handbook

1930  ▄▄▄  1940  ▭  1947  ▨  1953  ▭  1957  ▥

Fig. A.3. Employee Health, Safety, and Maintenance.

*Table* A.12  *Health, Safety, and Maintenance*

| | Yes | | No | | No reply | |
|---|---|---|---|---|---|---|
| | No. | % | No. | % | No. | % |
| 1. Do you have one or more rest rooms (exclusive of toilets) for employees?............ | 735 | 86.3 | 109 | 12.8 | 8 | 0.9 |
| 2. Do you have one or more first-aid stations? | 769 | 90.3 | 74 | 8.7 | 9 | 1.0 |
| 3. Do you have a lunchroom?............... | 662 | 77.7 | | | | |
|    *a.* For executives?...................... | 247 | 29.0 | 465 | 54.6 | 140 | 16.4 |
|    *b.* For employees?...................... | 379 | 44.5 | 310 | 36.4 | 163 | 19.1 |
|    *c.* For both together?.................. | 494 | 58.0 | 295 | 34.6 | 63 | 7.4 |
| 4. Do you follow up new employees?........ | 748 | 87.8 | 51 | 6.0 | 53 | 6.2 |
|    *a.* Is it done by the foreman or his representative?.......................... | 713 | 83.7 | 66 | 7.7 | 73 | 8.5 |
|    *b.* Is it done by a sponsor or selected person who goes through the department to see how the new employee is progressing?... | 151 | 17.7 | 527 | 61.9 | 174 | 20.4 |
|    *c.* Is it by calling the employee into the personnel office for periodic interviews?.. | 184 | 21.6 | 502 | 58.9 | 166 | 19.5 |
| 5. Do you have a published promotional policy?............................... | 328 | 38.5 | 486 | 57.0 | 38 | 4.5 |
|    *a.* Is it in narrative form?............... | 288 | 33.8 | 174 | 20.4 | 390 | 45.8 |
|    *b.* Is it in chart form?.................. | 60 | 7.0 | 365 | 42.8 | 427 | 50.2 |
| 6. Do you have a "house organ" or magazine for employees?........................ | 646 | 75.9 | 198 | 23.2 | 8 | 0.9 |
| 7. Are employees given free medical and health service (other than first aid and safety)?............................. | 332 | 39.0 | 501 | 58.8 | 19 | 2.2 |
|    *a.* Does this health service provide also for the families of employees?............. | 116 | 13.6 | 488 | 57.3 | 248 | 29.1 |
|    *b.* Do you have a company dentist?....... | 26 | 3.0 | 652 | 76.6 | 174 | 20.4 |
|    *c.* Do you have one or more visiting nurses? | 203 | 23.8 | 475 | 55.8 | 174 | 20.4 |
| 8. Do you maintain a company hospital?..... | 169 | 19.8 | 663 | 77.8 | 20 | 2.4 |
|    *a.* Is it on the premises?................. | 164 | 19.2 | 212 | 24.9 | 476 | 55.9 |
|    *b.* Is it off the premises?................ | 24 | 2.8 | 289 | 33.9 | 539 | 63.3 |
| 9. Do you have a formal safety program?.... | 681 | 79.9 | 137 | 16.1 | 34 | 4.0 |
| 10. Do you maintain an employees' library?... | 307 | 36.0 | 533 | 62.6 | 12 | 1.4 |
| 11. Do you have a recreation room (other than rest room)?............................ | 252 | 29.6 | 590 | 69.3 | 10 | 1.1 |
| 12. Do you have a legal-aid service?.......... | 186 | 21.8 | 661 | 77.6 | 5 | 0.6 |
| 13. Do you have a company-provided fund for loans to employees?..................... | 226 | 26.5 | 613 | 72.0 | 13 | 1.5 |
| 14. Do you rent houses to employees?........ | 108 | 12.7 | 732 | 85.9 | 12 | 1.4 |
| 15. Do you maintain a store or commissary for employees?............................ | 112 | 13.1 | 726 | 85.2 | 14 | 1.7 |

*Table* A.12   *Health, Safety, and Maintenance*   (*Continued*)

| | Yes | | No | | No reply | |
|---|---|---|---|---|---|---|
| | No. | % | No. | % | No. | % |
| 16. Do you assist your employees with the purchase of personal supplies which are related to the job? | 533 | 62.6 | 302 | 35.4 | 17 | 2.0 |
|    *a.* Is it a general practice? | 317 | 37.2 | 276 | 32.4 | 259 | 30.4 |
|    *b.* Is it done only occasionally? | 231 | 27.1 | 215 | 25.2 | 406 | 47.7 |
| 17. Do you encourage employees to buy your product through special company stores, special discounts, or similar measures? | 333 | 39.1 | 480 | 56.4 | 39 | 4.5 |
| 18. Do you encourage employees to conduct their own "cooperative stores," and the like? | 33 | 3.9 | 791 | 92.9 | 28 | 3.2 |
| 19. Do you have an employee handbook? | 575 | 67.5 | 264 | 31.0 | 13 | 1.5 |
|    *a.* Is it distributed to all employees? | 542 | 63.6 | 94 | 11.0 | 216 | 25.4 |
|    *b.* If not, is it available to all employees? | 156 | 18.3 | 78 | 9.2 | 618 | 72.5 |

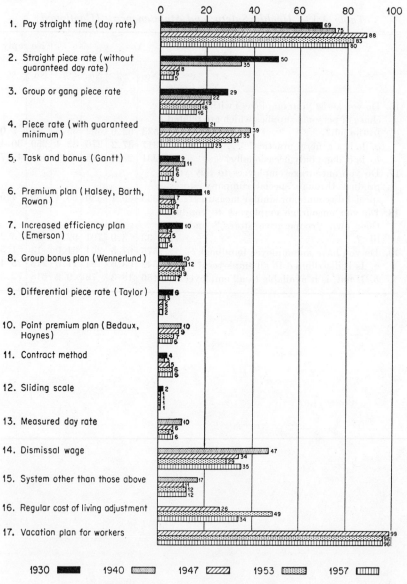

FIG. A.4. Payment to Direct Labor.

**Wage payments.** Table A.13 shows the popularity of the various wage-payment plans, and Table A.14 provides the material charted in Fig. A.4.

**Security and financial aids.** Tables A.15 and A.16 show the efforts of management to stabilize employment. Table A.17 shows the size of companies using some form of *multiple management*. No attempt is made in

### Table A.13   Types of Wage-payment Plans Used

| Plan | Firms | Per cent of all firms |
|---|---|---|
| 1. Straight-time (day rate)............................ | 685 | 80.4 |
| 2. Straight piece rate (without guaranteed day rate)..... | 45 | 5.3 |
| 3. Group or gang piece rate........................... | 136 | 16.0 |
| 4. Piece rate (with guaranteed minimum).... ......... | 192 | 22.5 |
| 5. Task and bonus (Gantt)........................... | 37 | 4.3 |
| 6. Premium plan (Halsey, Barth, Rowan).............. | 49 | 5.8 |
| 7. Increased-efficiency plan.......................... | 37 | 4.3 |
| 8. Group-bonus plan................................ | 60 | 7.0 |
| 9. Differential piece rate (Taylor).................... | 17 | 2.0 |
| 10. Point-premium plan (Bedaux, Haynes).............. | 47 | 5.5 |
| 11. Contract method................................. | 52 | 6.1 |
| 12. Sliding scale (selling price of product).............. | 5 | 0.6 |
| 13. Measured day rate............................... | 53 | 6.2 |
| 14. Other plans..................................... | 106 | 12.4 |

### Table A.14   Payment to Direct Labor

| | Yes | | No | | No reply | |
|---|---|---|---|---|---|---|
| | No. | % | No. | % | No. | % |
| 1. Do you pay straight time (day rate) to direct labor?............................ | 685 | 80.4 | 85 | 10.0 | 82 | 9.6 |
| 2. Straight piece rate (without guaranteed day rate)?................................ | 45 | 5.3 | 636 | 74.7 | 171 | 20.0 |
| 3. Group or gang piece rate?................ | 136 | 16.0 | 548 | 64.3 | 168 | 19.7 |
| 4. Piece rate (with guaranteed minimum)?... | 192 | 22.5 | 508 | 59.6 | 152 | 17.9 |
| 5. Task and bonus rate (similar to Gantt)?... | 37 | 4.3 | 620 | 72.8 | 195 | 22.9 |
| 6. Premium plan (Halsey, Barth, Rowan, etc.)? | 49 | 5.8 | 598 | 70.2 | 205 | 24.0 |
| 7. Increased-efficiency plan (Emerson)?...... | 37 | 4.3 | 616 | 72.3 | 199 | 23.4 |
| 8. Group-bonus plan (Wennerlund)?......... | 60 | 7.0 | 596 | 70.0 | 196 | 23.0 |
| 9. Differential piece rate (Taylor)?.......... | 17 | 2.0 | 623 | 73.1 | 212 | 24.9 |
| 10. Point-premium plan (Bedaux, Haynes, etc.)? | 47 | 5.5 | 603 | 70.8 | 202 | 23.7 |
| 11. Contract method?....................... | 52 | 6.1 | 586 | 68.8 | 214 | 25.1 |
| 12. Sliding scale (selling price of product, etc.)? | 5 | 0.6 | 631 | 74.1 | 216 | 25.3 |
| 13. Measured day rate?..................... | 53 | 6.2 | 572 | 67.2 | 227 | 26.6 |
| 14. Do you pay a dismissal wage to employees permanently discharged through no fault of their own?............................ | 294 | 34.5 | 472 | 55.4 | 86 | 10.1 |
| 15. Any other system than above?............ | 106 | 12.4 | 349 | 41.0 | 397 | 46.6 |
| 16. Do you regularly make adjustments in your wage scale on the basis of cost-of-living changes?............................. | 291 | 34.2 | 509 | 59.7 | 52 | 6.1 |
| 17. Do you have a vacation plan for workers?.. | 817 | 95.9 | 5 | 0.6 | 30 | 3.5 |

this appendix to analyze these data. They are reported in the appropriate section of the text. Figure A.5 and Table A.18 give the details of the practices in business in the area of stabilizing employment and financial aids.

*Table* A.15   *Amount of Minimum Employment Guaranteed*

| Amount guaranteed | Number of companies |
|---|---|
| 52 weeks | 19 |
| 48 weeks | 1 |
| 4 weeks | 1 |
| 1 week | 3 |
| No details | 8 |
| Total | 32 |

*Table* A.16   *Companies Guaranteeing Minimum Employment, Classified by Type*

| | Companies |
|---|---|
| Banking and insurance | 7 |
| Public utilities | 4 |
| Retail stores and mail-order houses | 3 |
| Machinery (except electrical) | 3 |
| Food processing | 2 |
| Steel | 2 |
| Automotive | 2 |
| Chemicals | 2 |
| Rubber | 1 |
| Printing and publishing | 1 |
| Shipping company | 1 |
| Dental laboratory | 1 |
| Hospital | 1 |
| Port authority | 1 |
| Educational institutions | 1 |
| Total | 32 |

*Table* A.17   *Companies Having Multiple Management, Classified by Size Group*

| Employees | Companies | Per cent of companies in size group |
|---|---|---|
| Less than 1,000 | 14 | 6.6 |
| 1,000–4,999 | 10 | 2.8 |
| Over 5,000 | 8 | 3.4 |
| Not given | 1 | |
| Total | 33 | |

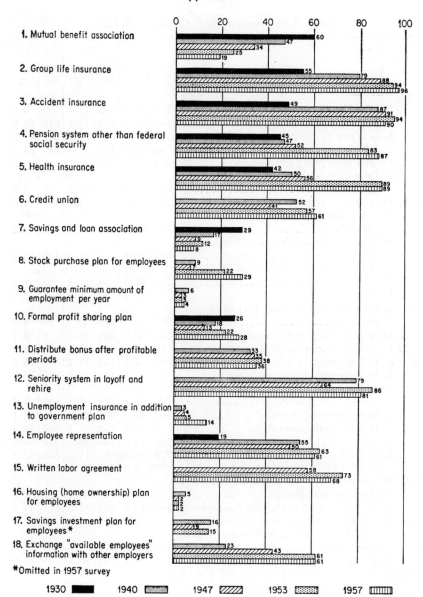

1. Mutual benefit association
2. Group life insurance
3. Accident insurance
4. Pension system other than federal social security
5. Health insurance
6. Credit union
7. Savings and loan association
8. Stock purchase plan for employees
9. Guarantee minimum amount of employment per year
10. Formal profit sharing plan
11. Distribute bonus after profitable periods
12. Seniority system in layoff and rehire
13. Unemployment insurance in addition to government plan
14. Employee representation
15. Written labor agreement
16. Housing (home ownership) plan for employees
17. Savings investment plan for employees*
18. Exchange "available employees" information with other employers

*Omitted in 1957 survey

1930 ■  1940 ▒  1947 ▨  1953 ▨  1957 ▥

FIG. A.5. Security and Employee Relations.

*Table* A.18  *Security and Employee Relations*

|  | Yes | | No | | No reply | |
|---|---|---|---|---|---|---|
|  | No. | % | No. | % | No. | % |
| 1. Do you have a mutual benefit association? | 160 | 18.8 | 662 | 77.7 | 30 | 3.5 |
|    *a.* Is it run by the employees?............ | 106 | 12.4 | 129 | 15.1 | 617 | 72.5 |
|    *b.* Is it run by the management?......... | 11 | 1.3 | 189 | 22.2 | 652 | 76.5 |
|    *c.* Jointly?.......................... | 60 | 7.0 | 152 | 17.8 | 640 | 75.1 |
| 2. Do you have group life insurance?........ | 814 | 95.6 | 32 | 3.7 | 6 | 0.7 |
|    *a.* Do employees pay any part of the premiums?........................... | 571 | 67.0 | 231 | 27.1 | 50 | 5.9 |
| 3. Do you have accident insurance?......... | 769 | 90.3 | 42 | 4.9 | 41 | 4.8 |
|    *a.* Is it a state (workmen's compensation) plan?............................. | 562 | 66.0 | 126 | 14.8 | 164 | 19.2 |
|    *b.* Is it a company plan in addition to the state workmen's compensation?........ | 513 | 60.2 | 209 | 24.5 | 130 | 15.3 |
| 4. Do you have a pension system other than Federal Social Security?.............. .. | 742 | 87.1 | 98 | 11.5 | 12 | 1.4 |
| 5. Do you have health insurance?.......... | 762 | 89.4 | 70 | 8.2 | 20 | 2.4 |
|    *a.* Do employees pay any part of the premium?............................. | 517 | 60.7 | 259 | 30.4 | 76 | 8.9 |
| 6. Do you have a "credit union"?.......... | 516 | 60.6 | 330 | 38.7 | 6 | 0.7 |
| 7. Is there a savings and loan association?.... | 67 | 7.9 | 746 | 87.6 | 39 | 4.5 |
|    *a.* Is it operated by the employees?....... | 47 | 5.5 | 164 | 19.2 | 641 | 75.3 |
|    *b.* Is it operated by the management?..... | 16 | 1.9 | 183 | 21.5 | 653 | 76.6 |
| 8. Do you have a stock-purchase plan for employees?............................. | 246 | 28.9 | 574 | 67.4 | 32 | 3.7 |
|    *a.* Is it for executives only?.............. | 104 | 12.2 | 202 | 23.7 | 546 | 64.1 |
|    *b.* Is it for employees only?............. | 9 | 1.0 | 236 | 27.7 | 607 | 71.3 |
|    *c.* Is it for both?........................ | 138 | 16.2 | 143 | 16.8 | 571 | 67.0 |
|    *d.* Is it for common stock?............... | 223 | 26.2 | 98 | 11.5 | 531 | 62.3 |
|    *e.* Is it for preferred stock?.............. | 29 | 3.4 | 230 | 27.0 | 593 | 69.6 |
| 9. Do you guarantee any minimum amount of employment per year?.................. | 32 | 3.8 | 798 | 63.7 | 22 | 2.5 |
|    *a.* Are you currently studying this problem? | 107 | 12.6 | 362 | 42.5 | 383 | 44.9 |
| 10. Do you have a formal profit-sharing plan?.. | 242 | 28.4 | 586 | 68.8 | 24 | 2.8 |
|    *a.* Is it for executives and major officers only?............................. | 105 | 12.3 | 211 | 24.8 | 536 | 62.9 |
|    *b.* Is it for rank-and-file employees also?... | 142 | 16.7 | 169 | 19.8 | 541 | 63.5 |
| 11. Do you distribute a bonus (other than a direct production bonus and formal profit-sharing plan) after profitable periods?..... | 309 | 36.3 | 521 | 61.2 | 22 | 2.5 |
|    *a.* Is it for executives and major officers only?............................. | 168 | 19.7 | 206 | 24.2 | 478 | 56.1 |
|    *b.* Is it for rank-and-file employees also?... | 155 | 18.2 | 191 | 22.4 | 506 | 59.4 |

*Table* A.18   *Security and Employee Relations*   (*Continued*)

| | Yes | | No | | No reply | |
|---|---|---|---|---|---|---|
| | No. | % | No. | % | No. | % |
| 12. Do you have a seniority system in laying off and rehiring employees?.............. | 691 | 81.1 | 114 | 13.4 | 47 | 5.5 |
|    *a.* Is it a strict (like some railroads) seniority system?....................... | 283 | 33.2 | 347 | 40.7 | 222 | 26.1 |
|    *b.* Is it a "seniority and efficiency" system? | 414 | 48.6 | 189 | 22.2 | 249 | 29.2 |
| 13. Do you have unemployment insurance in addition to the governmental plan?........ | 116 | 13.6 | 718 | 84.3 | 18 | 2.1 |
| 14. Do you have employee representation?.... | 518 | 60.8 | 203 | 23.8 | 131 | 15.4 |
|    *a.* Multiple-management type?........... | 33 | 3.9 | 342 | 40.2 | 477 | 55.9 |
|    *b.* Independent union?................... | 144 | 16.9 | 278 | 32.6 | 430 | 50.5 |
|    *c.* AFL-CIO union?.................... | 521 | 61.2 | 100 | 11.7 | 231 | 27.1 |
| 15. Do you have a written labor agreement?... | 580 | 68.1 | 209 | 24.5 | 63 | 7.4 |
|    *a.* Are your office employees included in your labor contract?.................. | 109 | 12.8 | 524 | 61.5 | 219 | 25.7 |
|    *b.* Do you have an escalator wage clause in your union contract?................. | 145 | 17.0 | 478 | 56.1 | 229 | 26.9 |
| 16. Do you have a housing (home-ownership) plan for rank-and-file employees?......... | 17 | 2.0 | 813 | 95.4 | 22 | 2.6 |
| 18. Do you exchange "available employees" information with other employers?......... | 522 | 61.3 | 310 | 36.4 | 20 | 2.3 |
| 17. Omitted in 1957 survey | | | | | | |

*Table* A.19   155 *Companies Having a Comprehensive Training Program, Classified by Size Group*

| Employees | Companies | Per cent of companies in size group |
|-----------|-----------|-------------------------------------|
| Less than 1,000............. | 15 | 7.1 |
| 1,000–4,999............... | 57 | 15.8 |
| Over 5,000................ | 77 | 32.9 |
| Not given................ | 6 | |
| Total................. | 155 | |

**Training.** The extent of the training function is revealed by Fig. A.6. Tables A.19, A.20, and A.21 show the statistical data for the training function.

*Table* A.20   *Selected Companies Having a Comprehensive Training Program, Classified by Product*

| Product type | Companies | Per cent of companies* |
|--------------|-----------|------------------------|
| Textile-mill products.................. | 5 | 29 |
| Grain products....................... | 5 | 45 |
| Petroleum and coal products........... | 10 | 23 |
| Primary metals...................... | 8 | 28 |
| Construction and general industrial...... | 5 | 23 |
| Industrial machinery (electric)......... | 7 | 27 |
| Aircraft............................ | 11 | 50 |
| Banking and insurance................ | 21 | 27 |
| Public utilities...................... | 11 | 24 |
| Retail stores and mail-order houses...... | 6 | 15 |

* Per cent of companies within the appropriate product grouping.

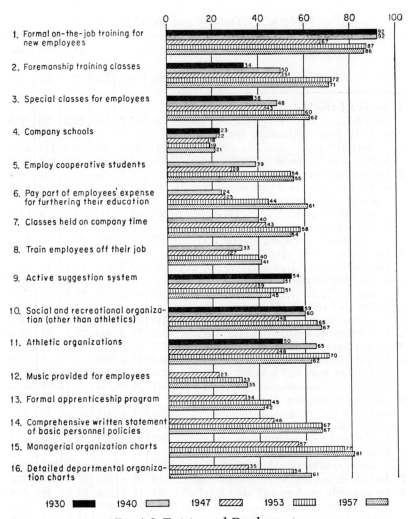

1. Formal on-the-job training for new employees
2. Foremanship training classes
3. Special classes for employees
4. Company schools
5. Employ cooperative students
6. Pay part of employees' expense for furthering their education
7. Classes held on company time
8. Train employees off their job
9. Active suggestion system
10. Social and recreational organization (other than athletics)
11. Athletic organizations
12. Music provided for employees
13. Formal apprenticeship program
14. Comprehensive written statement of basic personnel policies
15. Managerial organization charts
16. Detailed departmental organization charts

1930 ■■■ 1940 ▦ 1947 ▨ 1953 ▥ 1957 ▦

Fig. A.6. Training and Development.

*Table* A.21   *Training and Development*

|  | Yes | | No | | No reply | |
|---|---|---|---|---|---|---|
|  | No. | % | No. | % | No. | % |
| 1. Do you formally train new employees on the job? | 728 | 85.5 | 104 | 12.2 | 20 | 2.3 |
| a. Is it done by foremen and/or fellow workers? | 711 | 83.5 | 27 | 3.2 | 114 | 13.3 |
| b. Is it done by special instructors? | 286 | 33.6 | 326 | 38.3 | 240 | 28.1 |
| 2. Do you have foremanship training classes? | 607 | 71.3 | 193 | 22.6 | 52 | 6.1 |
| a. Do you have special training classes or conferences for executives above the rank of foreman? | 501 | 58.8 | 215 | 25.2 | 136 | 16.0 |
| b. Do you send representatives to university executive training programs? | 485 | 56.9 | 252 | 29.6 | 115 | 13.5 |
| 3. Do you have any special classes for employees? | 532 | 62.4 | 248 | 29.1 | 72 | 8.5 |
| a. Are they classes in safety for the rank and file? | 363 | 42.6 | 255 | 29.9 | 234 | 27.5 |
| b. Are they courses of instruction relating to your products and processes? | 413 | 48.5 | 186 | 21.8 | 253 | 29.7 |
| c. Are they for general education? | 232 | 27.2 | 339 | 39.8 | 281 | 33.0 |
| 4. Do you have company schools? | 177 | 20.8 | 651 | 76.4 | 24 | 2.8 |
| 5. Do you employ cooperative students? | 464 | 54.5 | 357 | 41.9 | 31 | 3.6 |
| a. Are they from high schools? | 235 | 27.6 | 289 | 33.9 | 328 | 38.5 |
| b. Are they from colleges? | 397 | 46.6 | 144 | 16.9 | 311 | 36.5 |
| 6. Do you pay any part of employees' expense outlay for furthering their education? | 521 | 61.2 | 315 | 37.0 | 16 | 1.8 |
| a. Is it paid for night schooling? | 460 | 54.0 | 107 | 12.6 | 285 | 33.4 |
| b. Is it paid for correspondence courses? | 292 | 34.3 | 253 | 29.7 | 307 | 36.0 |
| c. Is it paid for attendance upon public school or other outside classes? | 344 | 40.4 | 207 | 24.3 | 301 | 35.3 |
| 7. Are any classes held on company time? | 458 | 53.8 | 331 | 38.8 | 63 | 7.4 |
| 8. Do you train employees off their jobs? | 352 | 41.3 | 451 | 52.9 | 49 | 5.8 |
| a. Is it done by lectures? | 344 | 40.4 | 102 | 12.0 | 406 | 47.6 |
| b. Is it done by motion pictures? | 306 | 35.9 | 121 | 14.2 | 425 | 49.9 |
| c. Is it done by exhibits? | 276 | 32.4 | 134 | 15.7 | 442 | 51.9 |
| 9. Have you an active suggestion program? | 416 | 44.8 | 415 | 48.7 | 21 | 2.5 |
| 10. Do you have any social and recreational organizations (other than athletic)? | 567 | 66.6 | 272 | 31.9 | 13 | 1.5 |
| a. Are they run jointly by management and the employees? | 270 | 31.7 | 256 | 30.0 | 326 | 38.3 |
| b. Are they run by the employees? | 308 | 36.2 | 148 | 17.4 | 396 | 46.4 |
| c. Are they run by the management? | 32 | 3.8 | 333 | 39.1 | 487 | 57.1 |

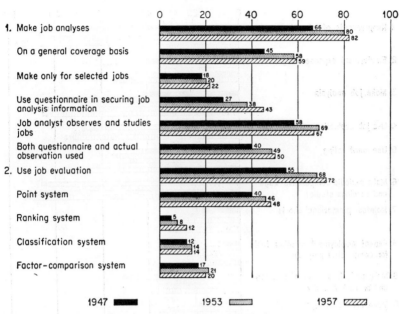

Fɪɢ. A.7. Job Analysis and Evaluation.

the companies which repeat employment or other tests for progression purposes also have a merit rating program.

A method of evaluating the effectiveness of the personnel function, and one which also provides a quantitative assessment, is the analysis of labor turnover. More than 91 per cent of the firms maintain records of this nature, 86 per cent apply them to the whole organization, and 51.8 per cent keep them by departments. In the vast majority of cases, these records are systematically reported to a major executive. A less concrete, but no less interesting, assessment of the effectiveness of a personnel policy is the morale survey. The proportion of companies making morale surveys is still

*Table* A.24   *Use of Job-evaluation Plans**

| Plan | Sole plan used | Point also used | Ranking also used | Classification also used | Factor comparison also used |
|------|------|------|------|------|------|
| Point................. | 111 | ... | 15 | 15 | 32 |
| Ranking.............. | 14 | 15 | ... | 5 | 5 |
| Classification.......... | 13 | 15 | 5 | ... | 6 |
| Factor comparison..... | 29 | 32 | 5 | 6 | |

* Figures indicate the number of companies using the plans listed. Thus, 111 firms use the point system and no other· 15 firms use both point and ranking systems, etc.

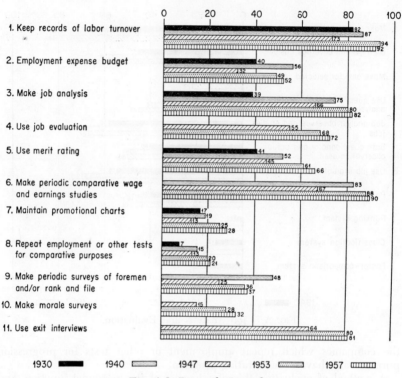

1. Keep records of labor turnover
2. Employment expense budget
3. Make job analysis
4. Use job evaluation
5. Use merit rating
6. Make periodic comparative wage and earnings studies
7. Maintain promotional charts
8. Repeat employment or other tests for comparative purposes
9. Make periodic surveys of foremen and/or rank and file
10. Make morale surveys
11. Use exit interviews

1930 ■   1940 ▭   1947 ▨   1953 ▭   1957 ▥

Fig. A.8. Research Control.

rather low but has increased considerably since 1947 (from 28 to 32.2 per cent). Similar in principle to the morale survey, but in more general use, is the exit interview, given by 81.4 per cent of responding companies.

The growth of fringe benefits is dramatically portrayed by Fig. A.5. Group life insurance is found in well over 90 per cent of the companies. Health insurance is nearly as popular as group life insurance. More than 80 per cent of the companies have pension plans other than Social Security. Some form of employee representation is found in 60 per cent of the companies. This does not mean that all the employees belong to unions but that the company had written labor agreements with some of its employees. Training continues to be a major responsibility of management. Eighty-six per cent of the companies have formal on-the-job training programs for their employees. Foremanship training programs have doubled since 1930 and held their own since 1953. Formal written personnel policies were found in two-thirds of the companies.

*Table* A.25 *Research Control*

| | Yes | | No | | No reply | |
|---|---|---|---|---|---|---|
| | No. | % | No. | % | No. | % |
| 1. Do you keep records of labor turnover?.... | 781 | 91.7 | 65 | 7.6 | 6 | 0.7 |
|    *a.* Are they kept by departments?........ | 441 | 51.8 | 313 | 36.7 | 98 | 11.5 |
|    *b.* Are they kept for the concern as a whole? | 733 | 86.0 | 42 | 4.9 | 77 | 9.1 |
|    *c.* Are they systematically reported to a major executive?.................... | 662 | 77.7 | 114 | 13.4 | 76 | 8.9 |
| 2. Do you keep an employment expense budget?................................ | 445 | 52.2 | 373 | 43.8 | 34 | 4.0 |
| 3. Do you make job analyses?............. | 695 | 81.6 | 138 | 16.2 | 19 | 2.2 |
|    *a.* Are they made on a "general coverage" basis?............................. | 503 | 59.0 | 161 | 18.9 | 188 | 22.1 |
|    *b.* Are they made only for selected jobs?... | 189 | 22.2 | 373 | 43.8 | 290 | 34.0 |
|    *c.* Do you use the questionnaire method of securing job-analysis information?...... | 362 | 42.5 | 282 | 33.1 | 208 | 24.4 |
|    *d.* Does your job analyst observe and study the jobs in preparing the job analysis?.. | 574 | 67.4 | 94 | 11.0 | 184 | 21.6 |
|    *e.* Are both questionnaire and actual observation used in securing job-analysis information?.......................... | 424 | 49.8 | 228 | 26.8 | 200 | 23.4 |
| 4. Do you use a system of job evaluation?.... | 613 | 72.0 | 183 | 21.5 | 56 | 6.5 |
|    *a.* Point system?....................... | 407 | 47.8 | 135 | 15.8 | 310 | 36.4 |
|    *b.* Ranking system?..................... | 98 | 11.5 | 271 | 31.8 | 483 | 56.7 |
|    *c.* Classification system?................. | 122 | 14.3 | 268 | 31.5 | 462 | 54.2 |
|    *d.* Factor-comparison system?........... | 166 | 19.5 | 233 | 27.4 | 453 | 53.1 |
| 5. Do you systematically use merit rating?... | 565 | 66.3 | 269 | 31.6 | 18 | 2.1 |
|    *a.* For executives?..................... | 359 | 42.1 | 260 | 30.5 | 233 | 27.4 |
|    *b.* For rank-and-file employees?.......... | 488 | 57.3 | 147 | 17.2 | 217 | 25.5 |
| 6. Do you make periodic comparative wages and earnings studies?.................... | 763 | 89.6 | 67 | 7.9 | 22 | 2.5 |
| 7. Do you maintain for research purposes any promotional charts?.................... | 234 | 27.5 | 559 | 65.6 | 59 | 6.9 |
| 8. Do you repeat employment or other tests for comparative (progression) purposes?... | 178 | 20.9 | 630 | 74.0 | 44 | 5.1 |
| 9. Do you make periodic surveys covering your foremen and/or rank-and-file employees?........................... | 313 | 36.7 | 502 | 58.9 | 37 | 4.4 |
|    *a.* Do they cover knowledge of product?... | 160 | 18.8 | 199 | 23.4 | 493 | 57.8 |
|    *b.* Do they cover company policies?....... | 246 | 28.9 | 133 | 15.6 | 473 | 55.5 |
|    *c.* Do they cover safety regulations?...... | 225 | 26.4 | 144 | 16.9 | 483 | 56.7 |
| 10. Do you make a periodic labor audit?...... | 320 | 37.6 | 474 | 55.6 | 58 | 6.8 |
| 11. Do you make morale surveys?............ | 274 | 32.2 | 540 | 63.4 | 38 | 4.4 |
| 12. Do you use exit interviews?............. | 693 | 81.4 | 137 | 16.1 | 22 | 2.5 |
| 13. Do you use outside personnel consultants?. | 320 | 37.6 | 510 | 59.9 | 22 | 2.5 |

# APPENDIX B

## An Apprentice Agreement

---

### APPRENTICESHIP AGREEMENT
#### Between Apprentice and Employer

The employer and apprentice whose signatures appear below agree to these terms of apprenticeship:

The employer agrees to employ and train the apprentice in accordance with the terms and conditions

of the .................................................................................., which are made a part of this agreement; or, in
(Name of Apprenticeship Standards)

accordance with the terms and conditions stated on the reverse side of this agreement.

The apprentice agrees to apply himself diligently and faithfully to learning the trade in accordance with this agreement.

Trade ................................................... Term of apprenticeship ...............................
(Hours or Years)

Credit for previous experience ........................................ Term remaining ........................

Date the apprenticeship begins ..............................................................................................

This agreement may be terminated by either party notifying the other or in accordance with the named apprenticeship standards.

---------------------------------------------            ----------------------------------------------
(Signature of Apprentice)                                      (Name of Employer—Company)

---------------------------------------------            ----------------------------------------------
(Address)                                                              (Address)

---------------------------------------------            ----------------------------------------------
(Apprentice's Birth Date)                                     (Signature of Authorized Official)

Approved by ....................................................................................., Joint Apprenticeship Committee.

Date ................................................. by .....................................................................
(Signature of Chairman or Secretary)

Registered by ...........................................................................................................
(Name of Registration Agency)

Date ................................................. by .....................................................................
(Signature of Authorized Official)

586

# Bibliography

## GENERAL

Allen, Louis A.: *Management and Organization,* McGraw-Hill Book Company, Inc., New York, 1958.

Appley, Lawrence A.: *Management in Action: The Art of Getting Things Done through People,* American Management Association, N.Y., 1956.

Barnard, Chester I.: *The Functions of the Executive,* Harvard University Press, Cambridge, Mass., 1940.

————: *Organization and Management,* Harvard University Press, Cambridge, Mass., 1952.

Becker, Esther R.: *Dictionary of Personnel and Industrial Relations,* Philosophical Library, Inc., New York, 1958.

Bethel, Lawrence L., Franklin S. Atwater, George H. E. Smith, and Harvey A. Stackman, Jr.: *Industrial Organization and Management,* 3d ed., McGraw-Hill Book Company, Inc., New York, 1956.

Brown, Alvin: *The Armor of Organization,* Hibbert Printing Company, New York, 1953.

Bunting, J. Whitney (ed.): *Ethics for Modern Business Practice,* Prentice-Hall, Inc., Englewood Cliffs, N.J., 1953.

Bursk, Edward C.: *Business and Religion: A New Depth Dimension in Management,* Harper & Brothers, New York, 1959.

Chase, Stuart, Stanley H. Ruttenberg, Edwin G. Nourse, and William B. Given, Jr.: *The Social Responsibility of Management,* New York University, School of Commerce, Accounts, and Finance, New York, 1950.

Childs, Marquis W., and Douglass Cater: *Ethics in a Business Society,* Harper & Brothers, New York, 1954.

Dale, Ernest: *Planning and Developing the Company Organization Structure,* American Management Association, New York, 1952.

Davis, Ralph C.: *The Fundamentals of Top Management,* Harper & Brothers, New York, 1951.

————: *Industrial Organization and Management,* Harper & Brothers, New York, 1957.

Dimock, Marshall E.: *A Philosophy of Administration,* Harper & Brothers, New York, 1958.

Drucker, Peter F.: *The Practice of Management,* Harper & Brothers, New York, 1954.

Fayol, Henri: *General and Industrial Management,* Pitman Publishing Corporation, New York, 1949.

Gates, James E., and Harold Miller: *Personal Adjustment to Business,* Prentice-Hall, Inc., Englewood Cliffs, N.J., 1958.

George, Claude S., Jr.: *Management in Industry,* Prentice-Hall, Inc., Englewood Cliffs, N.J., 1959.

Holden, Paul E., Lounsbury S. Fish, and Hubert L. Smith: *Top Management Organization and Control,* McGraw-Hill Book Company, Inc., New York, 1951.

Koontz, H. D., and C. J. O'Donnell: *Principles of Management,* 2d ed., McGraw-Hill Book Company, Inc., New York, 1959.

Merrill, Harwood F. (ed.): *The Responsibilities of Business Leadership,* Harvard University Press, Cambridge, Mass., 1948.

Mooney, James D.: *The Principles of Organization,* rev. ed., Harper & Brothers, New York, 1947.

Moore, Franklin G.: *Manufacturing Management,* rev. ed., Richard D. Irwin, Inc., Homewood, Ill., 1958.

Newman, William H.: *Administrative Action: The Techniques of Organization and Management,* Prentice-Hall, Inc., Englewood Cliffs, N.J., 1951.

Niles, Mary Cushing: *The Essence of Management,* Harper & Brothers, New York, 1958.

Petersen, Elmore, and E. Grosvenor Plowman: *Business Organization and Management,* Richard D. Irwin, Inc., Homewood, Ill., 1958.

Pigors, Paul, and Charles A. Myers: *Personnel Administration,* 4th ed., McGraw-Hill Book Company, Inc., New York, 1961.

Rowland, Virgil K.: *Improving Managerial Performance,* Harper & Brothers, New York, 1958.

Schell, Erwin H.: *The Technique of Executive Control,* 8th ed., McGraw-Hill Book Company, Inc., New York, 1957.

Selekman, Benjamin M.: *A Moral Philosophy for Management,* McGraw-Hill Book Company, Inc., New York, 1959.

Seybold, John W.: "How Personal Can a Personnel Policy Be?" *Personnel Journal,* Vol. 37, No. 8, January, 1959, p. 285.

Sheldon, Oliver: *The Philosophy of Management,* Prentice-Hall, Inc., Englewood Cliffs, N.J., 1923.

Spriegel, William R., and Richard H. Landsburgh: *Industrial Management,* 5th ed., John Wiley & Sons, Inc., New York, 1955.

————, and Joseph W. Towle: *Retail Personnel Management,* McGraw-Hill Book Company, Inc., New York, 1951.

Tead, Ordway: *The Art of Administration,* McGraw-Hill Book Company, Inc., New York, 1951.

Terry, George R.: *Principles of Management,* 3d ed., Richard D. Irwin, Inc., Homewood, Ill., 1960.

Urwick, L.: *The Elements of Administration,* Harper & Brothers, New York, 1943.

Urwick, L. (ed.): *The Golden Book of Management,* Newman Neame, Ltd., London, 1956.

Vance, Stanley: *Industrial Administration,* McGraw-Hill Book Company, Inc., New York, 1959.

Watkins, Gordon S., Paul A. Dodd, Wayne L. McNaughton, and

Paul Prasow: *The Management of Personnel and Labor Relations,* 2d ed., McGraw-Hill Book Company, Inc., New York, 1950.
Yoder, Dale: *Personnel Principles and Policies,* Prentice-Hall, Inc., Englewood Cliffs, N.J., 1959.

PART I

The Evolution of the Personnel Function<br>(Organization, Coordination, Policies)

American Management Association, New York:
  *Personnel*
    Vol. 33, No. 2, September, 1956, "Coordination and Control of Executive Functions," by J. H. Healey, pp. 106–117.
    Vol. 36, No. 2, March–April, 1959, "Of Productivity and the Personnel Department," by George S. Odiorne, pp. 51–59.
    Vol. 36, No. 3, May–June, 1959, "Personnel Management in Theory and Practice," by George S. Strother, pp. 63–71.
    Vol. 36, No. 4, July–August, 1959, "Industrial Relations Budgets: Yardsticks for 1959," by Dale Yoder and Roberta J. Nelson, pp. 16–27.
    Vol. 37, No. 1, January–February, 1960, "Company Growth and Personnel Administration," by George S. Odiorne, pp. 32–41.
    Vol. 37, No. 2, March–April, 1960, "Technical Selection: How to Improve Your Batting Average," by John R. Hinrichs, pp. 56–60.
  *Research Report*
    No. 32, 1958, "Management Creeds and Philosophies."
Baker, Helen, and Robert R. France: *Centralization and Decentralization,* Industrial Relations Section, Princeton University, Princeton, N.J., 1954.
Chruden, Herbert J., and Arthur W. Sherman, Jr.: *Personnel Management,* South-Western Publishing Company, Cincinnati, 1959.
Dale, Ernest: *Planning and Developing the Company Organization Structure,* American Management Association, New York, 1952.
National Industrial Conference Board:
  *Studies in Personnel Policy*
    No. 73, 1946, "Organization of Personnel Administration."
    No. 145, 1954, "Personnel Practices in Factory and Office."
    No. 157, April, 1957, "Preparing the Company Organization Manual."
    No. 168, 1958, "Charting the Company Organization Structure."
    No. 169, 1959, "Statements of Personnel Policy."
Stebbins, Kathleen B.: *Personnel Administration in Libraries,* Scarecrow Press, New York, 1958.
Watkins, Gordon S., Paul A. Dodd, Wayne L. McNaughton, and Paul Prasow: *The Management of Personnel and Labor Relations,* 2d ed., McGraw-Hill Book Company, Inc., New York, 1950.
Yoder, Dale: *Personnel Management and Industrial Relations,* 4th ed., Prentice-Hall, Inc., Englewood Cliffs, N.J., 1956.
———, H. G. Henneman, Jr., John G. Turnbull, and C. Harold Stone: *Handbook of Personnel Management and Labor Relations,* McGraw-Hill Book Company, Inc., New York, 1958.

PART II

Personnel Procedures, Tools, and Records (Maintaining the Work Force)
(The Interview, Employment Procedure, Records, Job Evaluation,
Merit Rating, and Transfers and Promotions)

American Management Association, New York:
*Management Report*
No. 16, "Personnel Planning Pays Dividends" (a presentation by
Mead Johnson & Company)
I. The Planning Approach by E. Donald Elliott
II. The Personnel Development Program by Lloyd Pressel
III. The Mead John Institute by Robert W. Barclay
No. 16, "A Job Evaluation Plan for Clerical, Technical, and Supervisory
Positions," by Herbert V. W. Scott.
*Personnel*
Vol. 31, No. 5, March, 1955, "Testing Employees for Promotion and
Transfer," by A. Barry Freiden.
Vol. 35, No. 3, November–December, 1958, "Appraisals: A Valid
Management Selection Tool," By Milton M. Mandell, pp. 63–66.
Vol. 36, No. 3, May–June, 1959, "Forced Choice: Better than Other
Rating Methods?" by Lee W. Cozan, p. 80.
Vol. 36, No. 3, May–June, 1959, "Personnel Records: Along the Road
to Automation," by Paul Duke, pp. 31–40.
Vol. 36, No. 4, July–August, 1959, "How Much Can You Tell from a
Résumé?" by Frederick J. Gaudet and Thomas F. Casey, pp.
62–65.
Vol. 36, No. 5, September–October, 1959, "Lessons of a Technical
Lay-off," by Robert Harman, Jr., and Felix Gardner, pp. 75–77.
Vol. 36, No. 5, September–October, 1959, "The Application Form
Revisited," by Gilmore J. Spencer, pp. 20–30.
Vol. 37, No. 3, May–June, 1960, "What Should Ratings Rate?" by
A. C. Mackinney, pp. 75–78.
Vol. 37, No. 3, May–June, 1960, "A Flexible Approach to Management
Job Evaluation," by Matthew J. Murphy, pp. 36–43.
*Research Report*
No. 9, July, 1946, "Manual of Employment Interviewing."
No. 16, March, 1950, "Handbook of Personnel Forms."
No. 23, 1954, "Company Practices in Employee Transfers and Re-
locations."
No. 24, 1955, "A Company Guide to the Selection of Salesmen."
No. 27, 1956, "Recruiting and Selecting Office Employees."
Becker, Esther R.: *Dictionary of Personnel and Industrial Relations*, Philo-
sophical Library, Inc., New York, 1958.
Bingham, Walter Van Dyke, and Bruce V. Moore: *How to Interview*,
Harper & Brothers, New York, 1959.
Dooher, M. Joseph, and Elizabeth Marting (eds.): *Selection of Management
Personnel*, Vols. I and II, American Management Association, New
York, 1957.
Elrod, John W.: *Origin, Structure, and Philosophy of Job Evaluation*, Ohio
State University, University Microfilms, Ann Arbor, Mich., 1959.

Fear, Richard A.: *The Evaluation Interview,* McGraw-Hill Book Company, Inc., New York, 1958.

Halsey, George D.: *Selecting and Inducting Employees,* Harper & Brothers, New York, 1951.

Jucius, Michael J.: *Personnel Management,* Richard D. Irwin, Inc., Homewood, Ill., 1959.

Kahn, Robert L., and Charles F. Cannell: *The Dynamics of Interviewing,* John Wiley & Sons, Inc., New York, 1957.

Lytle, Charles W.: *Wage Incentive Methods,* The Ronald Press Company, New York, 1942.

National Industrial Conference Board, Inc.:
  *Studies in Personnel Policy*
  No. 117, June, 1951, "Personnel Administration in the Small Company."
  No. 121, October, 1951, "Appraisal of Job Performance."
  No. 122, October, 1951, "Evaluating Managerial Positions."
  No. 131, January, 1952, "Employee Induction."
  No. 144, September, 1954, "Recruiting and Selecting Employees."
  No. 145, November, 1954, "Personnel Practices in Factory and Office."
  No. 152, March, 1956, "Employment of the College Graduate."
  No. 175, 1960, "Forms and Records in Personnel Administration."

Otis, Jay L., and Richard H. Leukart: *Job Evaluation,* Prentice-Hall, Inc., Englewood Cliffs, N.J., 1954.

Patton, John A., and C. A. Littlefield: *Job Evaluation,* Richard D. Irwin, Inc., Homewood, Ill., 1957.

Pigors, Paul, and Charles A. Myers: *Personnel Administration,* 4th ed., McGraw-Hill Book Company, Inc., New York, 1961.

Shartle, Carroll L.: *Occupational Information: Its Development and Application,* Prentice-Hall, Inc., Englewood Cliffs, N.J.

United States Employment Service, Division of Occupational Analysis, *Dictionary of Occupational Titles,* Vol. I, Definitions of Titles, 2d ed., U.S. Government Printing Office, Washington, D.C., 1949.

United States Employment Service, Division of Occupational Analysis, *Dictionary of Occupational Titles,* Vol. II, Occupational Classification and Industry Index, 2d. ed., Government Printing Office, Washington, D.C., 1949.

Yoder, Dale, *Personnel Management and Industrial Relations,* 4th ed., Prentice-Hall, Inc., Englewood Cliffs, N.J., 1956.

——, H. G. Henneman, Jr., John G. Turnbull, and C. Harold Stone, *Handbook of Personnel Management and Labor Relations,* McGraw-Hill Book Company, Inc., New York, 1958.

PART III

The Human Relations and Psychological Approach
(Human Relations, Psychological Tests, and Measuring Morale)

American Management Association, New York:
  *Management Report*
  No. 16, "Is Human Relations Obsolete?" by William V. Machaver.
  No. 16, " 'Bottom-up' Management: A Key to Sound Human Relations," by J. S. Hutchins.

No. 16, "The Democratic and Authoritarian Approaches: A Comparative Survey of Research Findings," by Eugene E. Jennings.

*Personnel*

Vol. 35, No. 3, November–December, 1958, "The Ethics of Personality Testing," by Saul W. Gellerman, pp. 30–35.

Vol. 36, No. 2, March–April, 1959, "What Is Morale?" by Carl E. Gregory, pp. 32–41.

Vol. 36, No. 2, March–April, 1959, "The Dynamics of Organizational Behavior," by Frank J. Jasinski, pp. 60–67.

Vol. 37, No. 3, May–June, 1960, "Changing On-the-job Behavior: How and Where to Start," by Daniel M. Goodacre III, pp. 58–62.

Vol. 37, No. 3, May–June, 1960, "Common Sense about Psychological Tests," by Harold E. Uyker and J. R. Block, pp. 44–50.

Argyris, Chris: *Personality and Organization,* Harper & Brothers, New York, 1957.

————: "Some Problems in Conceptualizing Organizational Climate: A Case Study of a Bank," *Administrative Science Quarterly,* Vol. 2, No. 4, March, 1958, pp. 501–521.

Bellows, Roger M.: *Employment Psychology: The Interview,* Rinehart & Company, Inc., New York, 1954.

Blum, Milton L., and Benjamin Balinsky: *Counseling and Psychology,* Prentice-Hall, Inc., New York, 1951.

Bursk, Edward C. (ed.): *Human Relations for Management,* Harper & Brothers, New York, 1956.

Calhoon, Richard P., E. William Noland, and Arthur M. Whitehill, Jr.: *Cases on Human Relations in Management,* McGraw-Hill Book Company, Inc., New York, 1958.

Cartwright, Dorwin, and Alvin Zander (eds.): *Group Dynamics, Research and Theory,* Row, Peterson & Company, Evanston, Ill., 1953.

Davis, Keith: *Human Relations in Business,* McGraw-Hill Book Company, Inc., New York, 1957.

Dubin, Robert: *Human Relations in Administration: The Sociology of Organization,* Prentice-Hall, Inc., Englewood Cliffs, N.J., 1951.

Finlay, William W., A. Q. Sartain, and Willis M. Tate: *Human Behavior in Industry,* McGraw-Hill Book Company, Inc., New York, 1954.

Ginzberg, Eli, and Ewing W. Reilley: *Effecting Change in Large Organizations,* Columbia University Press, New York, 1957.

Glover, John Desmond, and Ralph M. Hower: *The Administrator: Cases on Human Relations in Business,* 3d ed., Richard D. Irwin, Inc., Homewood, Ill., 1957.

Guetzkow, Harold (ed.): *Groups, Leadership and Men,* Carnegie Press, Pittsburgh, 1951.

Harrell, Thomas Willard: *A Casebook in Industrial and Personnel Psychology,* Rinehart & Company, Inc., New York, 1958.

Hoslett, Schuyler D.: *Human Factors in Management,* Harper & Brothers, New York, 1951.

Katz, Daniel, Nathan Maccoby, and Nancy C. Morse: *Productivity, Supervision and Morale in an Office Situation,* Part I. Institute for Social Research, University of Michigan, Ann Arbor, Mich., 1950.

Laird, Donald A., and Eleanor C. Laird: *Practical Business Psychology*, 1st ed., Gregg Publishing Division, McGraw-Hill Book Company, Inc., New York, 1951.

Landsberger, Henry A.: *Hawthorne Revisited*, Cornell University, Ithaca, N.Y., 1958.

McGregor, Douglas: *The Human Side of Enterprise*, McGraw-Hill Book Company, Inc., New York, 1960.

McLean, Alan A., and Graham C. Taylor: *Mental Health in Industry*, McGraw-Hill Book Company, Inc., New York, 1958.

McMurry, Robert N.: "Mental Illness in Industry," *Harvard Business Review*, Vol. 37, No. 2, March–April, 1959, p. 79.

Maslow, A. H.: *Motivation and Personality*, Harper & Brothers, New York, 1954.

Mayo, Elton: *The Social Problems of an Industrial Civilization*, Division of Research, Graduate School of Business Administration, Harvard University, Boston, 1945.

——: *The Human Problems of an Industrial Civilization*, Division of Research, Graduate School of Business Administration, Harvard University, Boston, 1946.

Menninger, William C., and Harry Levinson: *Human Understanding in Industry*, Science Research Associates, Inc., Chicago, 1956.

Menninger Foundation, Division of Industrial Mental Health, *Toward Understanding Men*, Topeka, 1957.

National Industrial Conference Board, Inc.:
*Studies in Personnel Policy*
No. 166, 1958, "The Alcoholic Worker."

Roethlisberger, F. J.: *Management and Morale*, Harvard University Press, Cambridge, Mass., 1941.

——, and William J. Dickson: *Management and the Worker*, Harvard University Press, Cambridge, Mass., 1950.

Saltonstall, Robert: *Human Relations in Administration*, McGraw-Hill Book Company, Inc., New York, 1959.

Spriegel, William R., and Clark E. Myers: *The Writings of the Gilbreths*, Richard D. Irwin, Inc., Homewood, Ill., 1953.

Tiffin, Joseph: "6 Merit Rating Systems," *Personnel Journal*, Vol. 37, No. 8, January, 1959, p. 288.

Tubbs, David L.: "Morale and the Training Program," *Personnel Journal*, Vol. 37, No. 8, January, 1959, p. 298.

Viteles, Morris S.: *Motivation and Morale in Industry*, W. W. Norton & Company, Inc., New York, 1953.

Walker, Charles R., and Robert H. Guest: *The Man on the Assembly Line*, Harvard University Press, Cambridge, Mass., 1952.

Walker, C. R.: "The Problem of the Repetitive Job," *Harvard Business Review*, Vol. XXVIII, No. 3, May, 1950, pp. 54–58.

Whyte, William Foote: *Money and Motivation: An Analysis of Incentives in Industry*, Harper & Brothers, New York, 1955.

Zaleznik, A., C. R. Christensen, and F. J. Roethlisberger: *The Motivation, Productivity, and Satisfaction of Workers: A Prediction Study*. Harvard University, Division of Research, Graduate School of Business Administration, Boston, 1958.

## PART IV

### Communication, Employee Orientation and Training, and Executive Development

American Management Association, New York:
  *The Development of Executive Talent: A Handbook of Management Development Techniques and Case Studies,* 1952.
  *Effective Communication on the Job,* 1956.
  *Leadership on the Job,* 1957.
  *Personnel*
      Vol. 36, No. 4, July–August, 1959, "Handling Work Assignment and Jurisdictional Disputes," by George R. Koons, pp. 71–77.
      Vol. 36, No. 4, July–August, 1959, "The Crisis in Apprentice Training," by Louis Ruthenburg, pp. 28–33.
      Vol. 36, No. 4, July–August, 1959, "Experience with the Incident Process in Management Training," by Sterling H. Schoen and Wendell L. French, pp. 54–61.
      Vol. 36, No. 4, July–August, 1959, "A Grievance Procedure for Non-unionized Employees," by Reid L. Shaw, pp. 66–70.
      Vol. 36, No. 4, July–August, 1959, "Communicating down the Line: How They Really Get the Word," by Eugene Walton, pp. 78–82.
      Vol. 36, No. 5, September–October, "Methods of Determining Training Needs," by B. B. Jackson and A. C. Mackinney, pp. 60–68.
      Vol. 37, No. 2, March–April, 1960, "The Unsolved Riddle of Executive Success," by Erwin K. Taylor, pp. 8–17.
  *Research Report*
      No. 26, 1955, "Current Practices in the Development of Management Personnel."
      No. 33, 1958, "Defining the Manager's Job."
Argyris, Chris: *Executive Leadership,* Harper & Brothers, New York, 1953.
Bellows, Roger: *Creative Leadership,* Prentice-Hall, Inc., Englewood Cliffs, N.J., 1959.
Bennett, Willard E.: *Manager Selection, Education and Training,* McGraw-Hill Book Company, Inc., New York, 1959.
Black, James M.: *How to Grow in Management,* Prentice-Hall, Inc., Englewood Cliffs, N.J., 1957.
Bower, Marvin: "Nurturing High-talent Manpower," *Harvard Business Review,* Vol. 35, No. 6, November–December, 1957, pp. 66–72.
Bright, James Rieser: "Does Automation Raise Skill Requirements?" *Harvard Business Review,* Vol. 36, No. 4, July–August, 1958.
Christensen, C. Roland: *Management Succession in Small and Growing Enterprises,* Division of Research, Graduate School of Business Administration, Harvard University, Boston, 1953.
Dooher, M. Joseph, and Elizabeth Marting (eds.): *Selection of Management Personnel,* Vols. I and II, American Management Association, New York, 1957.
Gouldner, Alvin W.: *Studies in Leadership,* Harper & Brothers, New York, 1950.
Jucius, Michael J.: *Personnel Management,* Richard D. Irwin, Inc., Homewood, Ill., 1959.

McCormick, Charles P.: *Multiple Management,* Jacobs Press, Clinton, S.C., 1943.

————: *The Power of People,* Harper & Brothers, New York, 1949.

National Association of Manufacturers: "Settling Complaints in the Non-unionized Operation: Information." *Bulletin* 26, New York, 1957.

National Industrial Conference Board, Inc.:
*Management Record*
Vol. XXI, No. 2, "How to Keep a Suggestion Plan Successful," p. 42.
*Studies in Personnel Policy*
No. 125, February, 1952, "Information Racks: A New Communications Medium."
No. 129, December, 1952, "Communicating with Employees."
No. 135, April, 1953, "Suggestion Systems."
No. 136, June, 1953, "Employee Magazines and Newspapers."
No. 138, July, 1953, "Bulletin Boards."
No. 160, 1957, "Executive Development Courses in Universities," rev.
No. 161, June, 1957, "Selecting Company Executives."

Newcomb, Robert, and Marg Sammons: *Speak Up, Management,* Funk & Wagnalls Company, New York, 1951.

Riegel, John W.: *Executive Development: A Survey of Experience in Fifty American Corporations,* University of Michigan Press, Ann Arbor, Mich., 1952.

Rowland, Virgil K.: *Improving Managerial Performance,* Harper & Brothers, New York, 1958.

Roy, Robert H.: *The Administrative Process,* Johns Hopkins Press, Baltimore, 1958.

Shartle, Carroll L.: *Executive Performance and Leadership,* Prentice-Hall, Inc., Englewood Cliffs, N.J., 1956.

Small Business Administration: *Executive Development in Small Business,* Washington, D.C., April, 1955.

Society for Advancement of Management, Reading, Pennsylvania, Chapter: *Suggestion Plan Guide,* 2d in series of Modern Management Treatises, New York, 1957.

Spriegel, William R., Edward Schulz, and William B. Spriegel: *Elements of Supervision,* 2d ed., John Wiley & Sons, Inc., New York, 1957.

Wilcox, William S.: "Reducing Costs by Increasing Employee Suggestions," *Personnel Journal,* Vol. 36, No. 10, pp. 377–380.

Yoder, Dale: *Personnel Management and Industrial Relations,* 4th ed. Prentice-Hall, Inc., Englewood Cliffs, N.J., 1956.

————, H. G. Henneman, Jr., John G. Turnbull, and C. Harold Stone: *Handbook of Personnel Management and Labor Relations,* McGraw-Hill Book Company, Inc., New York, 1958.

## PART V

### The Labor Movement

American Arbitration Association: *Labor Arbitration: Procedures and Techniques,* New York, 1957.

American Management Association, New York:
*Personnel*

Vol. 31, No. 4, January, 1955, "Craft Units in Industrial Plants," by Joseph Krislov, pp. 353–360.

Vol. 32, No. 3, November, 1955, "The Case for the Local Independent Union," pp. 226–233.

Vol. 35, No. 1, July–August, 1958, "Ground Rules of Successful Arbitration," by J. George Piccoli, pp. 77–85.

Vol. 36, No. 5, September–October, 1959, "A Positive Approach to Militant Unionism," by J. P. Burns, pp. 54–59.

Vol. 36, No. 5, September–October, 1959, "Union Philosophy: The Basic Fallacies," by Herbert L. Marx, Jr., pp. 31–37.

Vol. 37, No. 1, January–February, 1960, "The Answer to White-collar Unions," by Reid L. Shaw, pp. 26–31.

Vol. 37, No. 3, May–June, 1960, "The Pros and Cons of Labor Arbitration," by Carl H. Hageman, pp. 27–35.

*Research Report*

No. 12, August, 1948, "Collective Bargaining in the Office."

No. 13, December, 1948, "Survey of Personnel Practices in Unionized Offices."

No. 14, 1949, "Greater Productivity through Labor-Management Co-operation."

No. 17, May, 1951, "Sources of Economic Information for Collective Bargaining."

Bradley, Philip D.: *Involuntary Participation in Unionism*, American Enterprise Association, Inc., Washington, D.C., No. 462 in the series "National Economic Problems."

———: *The Public Stake in Union Power*, University of Virginia Press, Charlottesville, Va., 1959.

Chamberlin, Edward H.: *The Economic Analysis of Labor Union Power*, American Enterprise Association, Inc., Washington, D.C., January, 1958.

———: *Labor Unions and Public Policy*, American Enterprise Association, Inc., Washington, D.C., 1958.

Davey, Harold W., Howard S. Kaltenborn, and Stanley H. Ruttenberg (eds.): *New Dimensions in Collective Bargaining*, Harper & Brothers, New York, 1959.

Golden, Clinton S., and Virginia D. Parker, *Causes of Industrial Peace under Collective Bargaining*, Harper & Brothers, New York, 1955.

National Industrial Conference Board, Inc.:

*Studies in Personnel Policy*

No. 109, September, 1950, "Grievance Procedures in Non-unionized Companies."

No. 155, December, 1956, "Unionization among American Engineers."

No. 172, 1959, "Preparing for Collective Bargaining."

Pound, Roscoe: *Legal Immunities of Labor Unions*, American Enterprise Association, Inc., Washington, D.C., May 1957.

Purcell, Theodore V. S. J.: *The Worker Speaks His Mind on Company and Union*, Harvard University Press, Cambridge, Mass., 1953.

Rayback, Joseph G.: *A History of American Labor*, The Macmillan Company, New York, 1959.

Reynolds, L. G.: *Labor Economics and Labor Relations*, Prentice-Hall, Inc., Englewood Cliffs, N.J., 1959.

Seidman, Joel Isaac: *The Worker Views His Union,* University of Chicago Press, Chicago, Ill., 1958.

Taft, Philip: *The A.F. of L. from the Death of Gompers to the Merger,* Harper & Brothers, New York, 1959.

Taylor, George W., and Frank C. Pierson (eds.), *New Concepts in Wage Determination,* McGraw-Hill Book Company, Inc., New York, 1957.

Yoder, Dale, *Personnel Management and Industrial Relations,* 4th ed., Prentice-Hall, Inc., Englewood Cliffs, N.J., 1956.

——, H. G. Henneman, Jr., John G. Turnbull, and C. Harold Stone: *Handbook of Personnel Management and Labor Relations,* McGraw-Hill Book Company, Inc., New York, 1958.

PART VI

Wage and Salary Administration, Employee
Remuneration, and Other Incentives
(Wages, Stabilization of Employment, and Profit Sharing)

American Management Association, New York.
*Management Report*
No. 16, "Salary Administration at Carborundum: A Case Study," by Stanley H. Robins.
*Personnel*
Vol. 35, No. 2, September–October, 1958, "A Tested Approach to Engineer Salary Administration," by Morton Adelberg, pp. 77–82.
Vol. 36, No. 3, May–June, 1959, "Wages and Productivity," by J. Howell Turner, pp. 8–14.
Vol. 36, No. 4, July–August, 1959, "Must Market Pressure Wreck the Company's Salary Structure?" by Preston P. Le Breton, pp. 34–45.
*Research Report*
No. 8, January, 1946, "Annual Wages and Employment Stabilization Techniques."
No. 29, 1957, "Company Severance Pay Plans, Current Policy and Practice."
No. 31, 1958, "Compensating American Managers Abroad."
*Special Report*
No. 23, 1957, "Controlling Employee Benefit and Pension Costs."

Belcher, David W.: *Wage and Salary Administration,* Prentice-Hall, Inc., Englewood Cliffs, N.J., 1955.

Carroll, Phil: *Better Wage Incentives,* McGraw-Hill Book Company, Inc., New York, 1957.

Christensen, C. Roland: *Management Succession in Small and Growing Enterprises,* Division of Research, Graduate School of Business Administration, Harvard University, Boston, 1953.

Giles, R. Y.: *Credit for the Millions: The Story of Credit Unions,* Harper & Brothers, New York, 1951.

Gilmour, Robert W.: *Industrial Wage and Salary Control,* John Wiley & Sons, Inc., New York, 1956.

Gomberg, William: *A Trade Union Analysis of Time Study,* 2d ed., Prentice-Hall, Inc., Englewood Cliffs, N.J., 1955.

Jucius, Michael J.: *Personnel Management,* Richard D. Irwin, Inc., Homewood, Ill., 1959.

Louden, J. K., and J. Wayne Deegan: *Wage Incentives,* John Wiley & Sons, Inc., New York, 1959.

Lytle, Charles W.: *Wage Incentive Methods,* The Ronald Press Company, New York, 1942.

National Industrial Conference Board, Inc.:

  *Management Record*

    Vol. XIX, No. 1, January, 1957, "Fringe Benefits for Exempt Supervisors," by John O'Brien, pp. 10–13, 23–24.

    Vol. XIX, No. 10, October, 1957, "Productivity and Incentive Pay," by Nicholas L. A. Martucci, pp. 346–349, 376–380.

    Vol. XXI, No. 5, May, 1959, "Severance Pay in Manufacturing," p. 154.

  *Studies in Personnel Policy*

    No. 132, February, 1953, "Stock Ownership Plans for Workers."

    No. 133, 1953, "Employee Savings and Investment Plans."

    No. 137, June, 1953, "Escalators and the New BLS Index."

    No. 141, April, 1954, "Severance Pay Plans."

    No. 151, February, 1956, "Tuition-aid Plans for Employees."

    No. 154, July, 1956, "Company Payment of Employee's Moving Expense."

    No. 156, March, 1957, "Time Off with Pay."

    No. 159, May, 1957, "Trends in Company Group Insurance Programs."

    No. 162, September, 1957, "Sharing Profits with Employees."

    No. 167, 1958, "Clerical Salaries in Eighteen Cities."

    No. 173, 1959, "Compensation of Top Executives."

Pigors, Paul, and Charles A. Myers: *Personnel Administration,* 4th ed., McGraw-Hill Book Company, Inc., New York, 1961.

Riegel, John W.: *Administration of Salaries and Intangible Rewards for Engineers and Scientists,* Bureau of Industrial Relations, University of Michigan, Ann Arbor, Mich., 1958.

Society for Advancement of Management, Reading, Pennsylvania, Chapter: *Suggestion Plan Guide,* 2d in series of Modern Management Treatises, New York, 1957.

Wilcox, William S.: "Reducing Costs by Increasing Employee Suggestions," *Personnel Journal,* Vol. 36, No. 10, pp. 377–380.

## PART VII

Other Operational Problems in Personnel Administration and Management
(Safety, Health, Recreation, Labor Turnover, and
Workers Requiring Special Consideration)

American Management Association, New York:

  *Personnel*

    Vol. 32, No. 6, May, 1956, "Retirement: An Experiment in Group Counseling," by Fred T. Golub, John F. McBride, and Hamilton Stillwell, pp. 544–547.

    Vol. 33, No. 6, May, 1957, "Identifying the Problem Drinker on the Job," by Harrison M. Trice, pp. 527–533.

Vol. 34, No. 6, May–June, 1957, "Supervising Older Clerical Workers," by Waino W. Suojanen, pp. 16–21.

Vol. 35, No. 2, September–October, 1958, "Calculating the Cost of Labor Turnover," by Frederick J. Gaudet.

Vol. 36, No. 1, January–February, 1959, "Can Employers Afford Comprehensive Medical Plans?" by S. Gwyn Dulaney, pp. 52–59.

Vol. 36, No. 2, March–April, 1959, "Employee Relations and the Benefit Plans Disclosure Act," by Robert S. Lane, pp. 78–81.

Vol. 36, No. 5, September–October, 1959, "A Positive Approach to Militant Unionism," by J. P. Burns, pp. 54–59.

Vol. 36, No. 5, September–October, 1959, "Health Insurance Plans: Can Their Costs Be Controlled?" by Robert W. Dvorsky, pp. 69–74.

Vol. 36, No. 6, November–December, 1959, "Shorter Hours and Multiple Shifts," by Clyde E. Dankert, p. 61.

Vol. 36, No. 6, November–December, 1959, "The Crises in Collective Bargaining," by Wayne L. Horvitz, p. 16.

Vol. 36, No. 6, November–December, 1959, "Preserving Management's Rights at the Bargaining Table," by Jules J. Justin, p. 42.

Vol. 37, No. 1, January–February, 1960, "Setting the Workweek: A Vanishing Management Right?" by James L. Centner, pp. 42–47.

Vol. 37, No. 1, January–February, 1960, "Strategy and Tactics at the Bargaining Table," by Thomas G. Downing, pp. 58–63.

Vol. 37, No. 1, January–February, 1960, "The Answer to White-collar Unions," by Reid L. Shaw, pp. 26–31.

Vol. 37, No. 1, January–February, 1960, "Evaluating the Medical Care Program," by Thomas H. Paine and Richard G. Woods, pp. 48–57.

Vol. 37, No. 3, May–June, 1960, "One Way to Reduce Office Turnover," by Edwin A. Fleishman, pp. 63–69.

Vol. 37, No. 3, May–June, 1960, "Does a Liberal Paid-absence Plan Encourage Absenteeism?" by Elmer G. Guilmartin, pp. 70–74.

Vol. 37, No. 3, May–June, 1960, "The Pros and Cons of Labor Arbitration," by Carl H. Hageman, pp. 27–35.

*Research Report*

No. 18, September, 1951, "Organization and Functions of the Safety Department."

Cheit, Earl F.: "Benefit Levels in Workmen's Compensation," *Monthly Labor Review*, Vol. 81, No. 7, July, 1958, p. 723.

DeReamer, Russell: *Modern Safety Practices,* John Wiley & Sons, Inc., New York, 1958.

National Industrial Conference Board, Inc.:

*Studies in Personnel Policy*

No. 119, August, 1951, "Employee Education."

No. 120, September, 1951, "Executive Stock Ownership Plans."

No. 134, February, 1953, "Cooperative Medical Plans: A New Solution for Small Industries."

No. 143, 1954, "Fringe Benefit Packages."

No. 146, January, 1955, "Company Paid Sick Leave and Supplements to Workmen's Compensation."

No. 147, January, 1955, "Company Health Program for Executives."

No. 163, October, 1957, "The Company and the Physically Impaired Worker."

No. 171, 1959, "Company Medical and Health Programs," rev.

Pollak, Otto: *Positive Experiences in Retirement: A Field Study,* Richard D. Irwin, Inc., Homewood, Ill., 1957.

Sherman, Edward L.: "Turnover Cut ⅓ by 7-step Program," *Personnel Journal,* Vol. 37, No. 8, p. 296.

## PART VIII

### Employee Representation and Social Controls

American Management Association, New York:
*Personnel*
Vol. 33, No. 6, May, 1957, "Pension Costs and the Employment of Older Workers," by R. M. Peterson, pp. 563–567.

Chamberlin, Edward H.: *Labor Unions and Public Policy,* American Enterprise Association, Inc., Washington, D.C., 1958.

Davey, Harold W., Howard S. Kaltenborn, and Stanley H. Ruttenberg (eds.): *New Dimensions in Collective Bargaining,* Harper & Brothers, New York, 1959.

Jucius, Michael J.: *Personnel Management,* Richard D. Irwin, Inc., Homewood, Ill., 1959.

Montgomery, Royal et al.: "Collective Bargaining over Profit-sharing: The Automobile Union's Effort to Extend Its Frontier of Control," *Journal of Business,* Vol. XXXI, No. 4, pp. 318–334.

National Industrial Conference Board, Inc.:
*Studies in Personnel Policy*
No. 109, September, 1950, "Grievance Procedures in Non-unionized Companies."
No. 148, May, 1955, "Retirement of Employees: Policies, Procedures, Practices."
No. 149, October, 1955, "Pension Plans and Their Administration."
No. 155, December, 1956, "Unionization among American Engineers."
No. 172, 1959, "Preparing for Collective Bargaining."

Pound, Roscoe: *Legal Immunities of Labor Unions,* American Enterprise Association, Inc., Washington, D.C., May, 1957.

Reynolds, L. G.: *Labor Economics and Labor Relations,* Prentice-Hall, Inc., Englewood Cliffs, N.J., 1959.

Sultan, Paul: *Right-to-work Laws,* Institute of Industrial Relations, University of California, Los Angeles, 1958.

Taylor, George W., and Frank C. Pierson (eds.): *New Concepts in Wage Determination,* McGraw-Hill Book Company, Inc., New York.

Yoder, Dale, and H. G. Henneman, Jr.: *Labor Economics and Industrial Relations,* South-Western Publishing Company, Cincinnati, 1959.

## PART IX

### Measuring Performance

American Management Association, New York:
*Management Report*
No. 16, "Organizing and Auditing Your Employee Compensation Activities," by Eugene S. Horning.

*Personnel*

　　Vol. 32, No. 3, November, 1955, "Quality Control of Personnel Management," by Robert H. Willy, pp. 210–225.

　　Vol. 34, No. 2, September–October, 1957, "Some New Directions in Personnel Appraisal," by Wallace H. Best, pp. 45–50.

　　Vol. 36, No. 3, May–June, 1959, "How to Conduct a Manpower Audit," by D. R. Lester and Marjorie L. Owen, pp. 41–51.

Arensberg, Conrad et al. (eds.): *Research in Industrial Human Relations,* Harper & Brothers, New York, 1957.

Luck, Thomas J.: *Personnel Audit and Appraisal,* McGraw-Hill Book Company, Inc., New York, 1955.

Personnel

Vol. 32, No. 3, November, 1855, "Quality Control of Personnel Management," by Robert H. Willis, pp. 210–235.

Vol. 31, No. 2, September–October, 1957, "Some New Directions in Personnel Appraisal," by William H. Best, pp. 13–50

Vol. 36, No. 3, May–June, 1978, "How to Conduct a Manpower Audit," by D. R. Doyle and Margaret L. Orton, pp. 11–51

Monthly. Conrad et al. (eds.) Research in Industrial Human Relations, Harper & brothers, New York, 1957.

Luck, Thomas J. Personnel Audit and Appraisal, McGraw-Hill Book Company, Inc., New York, 1955.

# Index